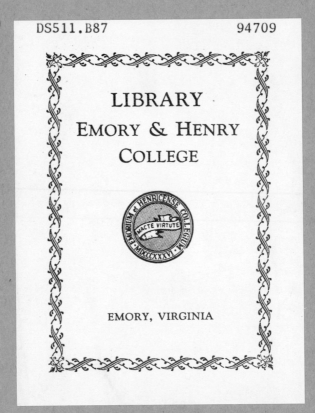

ASIA IN THE MODERN WORLD

CLAUDE A. BUSS

ASIA IN THE

THE MACMILLAN COMPANY, NEW YORK

A History of China,

Japan, South and Southeast Asia

MODERN WORLD

COLLIER-MACMILLAN LIMITED, LONDON

PREFACE

This book is an introduction to the study of Asia. It deals with the half of mankind which dwells in the vast geographic arc which extends from Tokyo to Karachi. It begins with the early civilizations and traditional cultures of Asia and shows the origins of fundamental values in indigenous Asian ways of life. It surveys the long record of contacts between Asians on the one hand and Europeans and Americans on the other. It shows how each affected the other. It represents an effort to place the response to aliens in its proper perspective as an important factor—but only one of many factors—in conditioning the historical development of the peoples and states of Asia. The primary concern of the book is the understanding of the role of Asia in the modern world.

The terms "East" and "West" have been used as little as possible. In an earlier age they were meaningful. Asia was "East" if the journey began in Europe. To voyagers from England or France, anything beyond India was the "Far East" or the "Extreme Orient." In Asia, Europe was "West." Explorers, traders, and missionaries were easily identified as men from the "West." But since the age of discovery, directions have been annihilated. In today's world, there is no East, no West. Everywhere is East, anywhere is West. The Far East of Europe is the Near West of the United States. The great globe is one.

Once the West and the East were strangers, far apart in time and distance, and far removed from each other in intellectual outlook and manner of living. The West knew little about the East and the East knew little about the West. Neither cared because it was reasonably content in its own self-contained and self-sufficient sphere. In the West, the East was thought to be mysterious and inscrutable, wealthy and exotic; in the East, the West was also considered mysterious and inscrutable, wealthy and powerful. Then science gradually obliterated the time-distance, and centuries of contact removed the barriers to mutual understanding.

v

In modern times—that is, any time after the age of European exploration and expansion—contacts between Asians and outsiders represented not the meeting of two worlds, but the meeting of many worlds. Spanish, Portuguese, Dutch, French, and British—and eventually the Russians and Americans—came from the world of the West, but they were far from a common breed. Japanese, Chinese, Indians, and the peoples of Southeast Asia were equally diverse in their representation of the world of the East.

They all had intensive agricultural economies based on rice culture, which demanded a high degree of water control and intensive use of manpower. They had highly organized social structures and they were reasonably well governed. Beyond that they were as distinctive as if they had lived on separate continents. The Chinese were Asians, but fundamentally they were Chinese—in racial origins, cultural concepts, and political and social consciousness. The same uniqueness applied to the other peoples in the area. They developed civilizations which were as individualistic as those which originated in the Mediterranean world of Greece, Rome, Asia Minor, and Egypt.

It was only natural that people from diverse backgrounds—with antagonistic motivations—should clash when they came in contact. Europeans considered themselves superior; the Asians thought they were better. Both had some basis for their feelings; both lacked the understanding which might have avoided the tragedies of conflict and war. The Europeans were the aggressive elements; it was they who crossed the seas and burst open the doors of Asia. It was inevitable that Europeans should win the first round. They were strong in terms of power, and Asians needed time to catch up. As Asians mastered the techniques and weapons of the Europeans, they also learned about such less tangible things as modern science, nationalism, and economic development.

If any major theme appears in the history of Asia in the modern world, it is the theme of rapid change. The characteristic of changelessness—if it ever existed—became a thing of the past. Changeless Asia turned into the fastest changing area in the world. Shocks of humiliation and defeat were required to arouse Asia but, once awakened, it plunged into a revolution which affected every aspect of its life.

The impact of European political ideas shook the theoretic foundations of Asian government and administration. The imposition of a capitalistic, money economy shattered the traditional economic structure of farms, village handicrafts, and the barter system of trade. Europeans brought political stability and economic prosperity to many Asians, but they also inspired Asians to demand the rights and privileges of Europeans for themselves. Under the influence of virulent nationalism, Asians demanded the right to be masters in their own house. They wanted the psychological assurance that they would be accepted as the equals of Europeans. They insisted upon the recognition of the intrinsic values in their own cultural traditions and age-old ways of life. They felt they were entitled to material prosperity and economic security; they demanded more of the better things of life for themselves and their children.

At the end of the nineteenth century, the eyes of Asia's nationalistic-minded leaders turned toward Japan and its spectacular success in modernization. Japan's road to respectable independence was accepted as an ideal and an example. Asia's elite also watched imperial China as it struggled clumsily and unsuccessfully to resist the intrusion of the European powers. In the early twentieth century, the seeds of anti-imperialism began to sprout. They were watered by Woodrow Wilson's doctrine of self-determination and the victory of the "democracies" in World War I.

Asia's nationalists found new inspiration in the success of the revolution in Russia. They derived new support from socialism and communism in their struggle against poverty and their condition of political dependence. The coming of World War II signaled the beginning of the end of the old order. Japan—an Asian power—behaved worse than a European, and it rolled over China. Japan did more than any European nation ever did to crystallize the sentiments of Chinese nationalism. Chinese Communism emerged first as an ally and then as the directing force in Chinese national development. As Japan pushed into Southeast Asia it gave a tremendous boost to local nationalist movements. Japan humiliated and ousted the imperial overlords, and provided the opportunity for young, patriotic leaders to satisfy their deep yearning to be independent.

The philosophy of the Atlantic Charter and the Four Freedoms heralded the new age in Asia. Even in the flush of their victory in Europe, the imperial powers were unable to reestablish their former domains. The United States, Great Britain, France, and the Netherlands retired as gracefully as possible from their previous positions of privilege and responsibility. The transition was not always peaceful, nor was it an unmixed blessing. Inexperienced Asian leaders found it more difficult to discharge the heavy responsibilities of nation-building than it had been to carry the flaming torch of freedom.

These ideas are reflected in the organization of this book, which is designed for the student who is beginning his studies of Asia or who intends to take only one course about Asia in his college career. The six parts of the book are divided according to chronology. Dates cannot be exact but the time periods are clearly distinguishable.

Part I, The Traditional Civilizations of Asia, is descriptive of Asians as they had developed up to the time of arrival of Europeans. Part II, Impact of the West, carries the story through the nineteenth century. Part III, Change, Revolution, and Conflict, covers the period from the beginning of the twentieth century to World War II. Part IV, War in Greater East Asia, is limited to the brief span of years between the Manchurian Incident (1931) and the signature of the Japanese surrender document on board the U.S.S. "Missouri" (1945). Part V, The Shaping of New Asia, describes the transition which occurred within a decade, 1945–1955, when the outlines of New Asia came to be distinguishable. Part VI, The Contemporary Scene, shows the framework, country by country, of major political, economic, social, and diplomatic developments. It provides the background for the interpretation of major contemporary events.

Each part of the book is subdivided into chapters dealing respectively with China, Japan, India, and Southeast Asia. All four areas are examined within each time period. It is hoped that this conceptual pattern of *Asia in the Modern World* will prove interesting and useful to teachers and students.

No argument seems required to put this much of Asia in any college curriculum. A knowledge of Asia is an essential part of a liberal education and is the key to understanding much of this interdependent world. The awareness of what *has* happened in Asia may give some clues to what *is* happening in Asia. If Asians see things differently from Europeans or Americans, it is because they have a different approach to the current scene. They are heirs of a great past, whose good features they intend to preserve. They are in process of selecting and choosing what they wish to adopt from others. They are pouring Western cultural values into the molds of their own lives as they have done with other cultures and civilizations through the ages.

It has taken a long time for Asians on the one hand, and Europeans and Americans on the other, to recognize each other as fellow human beings, subject to identical loves, hates, hopes, and frustrations. There is nothing about Asians that Europeans or Americans cannot understand if they try. There are no achievements made by Europeans or Americans which are beyond the capacities of Asians, if they will work and study. Americans and Europeans have much that they can teach Asians but there is also much that they can learn. Asians have produced rich thoughts about such matters as man's relationship to God; the adjustment of man to nature; the dignity of the individual and the relationship of man to society. The literature, art, and even the science of Western nations are not complete in themselves; and they can only be enriched by contributions from the intellectual treasure houses of the peoples of Asia.

The experiences of forty years of study, teaching, travel, and living in Asia have gone into the preparation of this book. The author was introduced to Asia at the Limitation of Armaments Conference in 1921 and since that date Asia has been his life. He was at various times an American Foreign Service Officer in China, Executive Assistant to the United

States High Commissioner to the Philippine Islands, and an internee of the Japanese. After repatriation to his homeland on board the exchange ship "Gripsholm" he was director of the San Francisco office of the Office of War Information. Then he became an Executive Consultant to the Strategic Bombing Survey of Japan and a Visiting Expert with the Civil and Information Section of the General Headquarters Supreme Commander for the Allied Powers during the occupation of Japan. He taught International Relations at the University of Southern California, initiated seminars in American studies at the University of Tokyo, served as Civilian Director of Studies at the National War College in Washington, and spent two terms as a Fulbright exchange professor at the University of the Philippines. He is currently Professor of History at Stanford University.

The author acknowledges his profound debt to others—scholars, writers of monographs, correspondents, diplomats, officials, and "just ordinary folks"—who have provided the raw materials for many of the ideas which he has made his own. He expresses his deep gratitude to all who have given so generously of their time and thought. He begs indulgence for any mistakes or omissions for which no one but himself is in any way responsible. It is his fondest hope that this book may in some small way bring to others some of the fascination which he has found in the study of Asia and stimulate them to seek further for a deeper understanding of Asia in the modern world.

Claude A. Buss

Stanford University, California

CONTENTS

I

THE TRADITIONAL CIVILIZATIONS OF ASIA

II

IMPACT OF THE WEST

III

CHANGE, REVOLUTION, AND CONFLICT

IV

WAR IN GREATER EAST ASIA

V

THE SHAPING OF NEW ASIA

VI

THE CONTEMPORARY SCENE

MAPS

ASIA IN THE MODERN WORLD

I

THE TRADITIONAL CIVILIZATIONS
OF ASIA

1

China and Its Way of Life

For one half the world, the study of man has centered about the culture and civilization which originated in western Asia and North Africa, flourished in Greece and Rome, and became identified with Europe. For lack of a better term, it has been described as the culture and civilization of the "West." For the other half of the world, the West is peripheral; only the "East" is important. In the East, the foundations of the human story are not to be found in the valleys of the Tigris or the Euphrates— or even the Nile—but rather along the banks of the Yellow and the Wei rivers in China and the Indus in northern India. It is not Greece or Rome, but China and India, which are credited with the finer achievements of the human mind. It is the peoples of Asia, not Europe, who have dis-covered and preserved the best possible ways of life. Asians long thought deeply about the problems of God, nature, and society, and without benefit of contact with Europeans developed concepts and values which were admirably adapted to their environment.

Until the time of Columbus, the West and the East were separated, except for travelers, traders, and conquerors who braved the inhospitable land routes across Central Asia. The quest for gold and glory, coupled with the deep desire to spread the word of the Christian God, drove the men of the West beyond the distant horizons on the sea roads to the Indies. Ships in increasing numbers reached India, the islands of the southern seas, and looked beyond to China and Japan.

The West knew very little about the East, and most of its informa-tion was based on fact and fancy as reported by Marco Polo. Thanks to the imaginative Venetian, the conviction was strong that China was the heart of the East. Therefore knowledge of China was prized by anyone who entertained the slightest hope of garnering for himself a tiny share of the fabled wealth of the Indies. But the breadth of knowledge was limited by the narrowness of its purpose. No one thought of knowledge as the key to mutual understanding. The ignorance of the West was matched by the indifference of the East, with the result that the world was subjected to centuries of conflict which, with more wisdom, might have been golden years of harmony and cooperation.

From the beginning of historical time until the coming of Europeans to Asia, the Chinese grew in consciousness of their greatness. With unmatched pride they called their land the "Middle Kingdom, the center of the universe, the sun around which every satellite revolved." Theirs was an ancient civilization with a glorious past, sufficient unto itself. The Chinese were far more numerous than any other political or cultural group, and they established an empire which comprised a larger territory and persisted without fundamental change for a longer period of time than any other empire the world has ever known.

Whether from north or south, the Chinese had a common way of life, a rich historical heritage and a singular cultural vitality. They developed a complex society which enabled them to cope successfully with the forces of nature. Their theories of politics came from the fertile brains of their own sages and gave them a system of government which they accepted as the perfect expression of their own genius. When modifications were made, these too were the products of Chinese genius. The Chinese possessed an unshakable faith that they were superior to their neighbors and to the Western barbarians who came to their shores. The Chinese superiority complex and the arrogance of the Europeans were like flint and steel; when they clashed they generated the sparks of diplomatic history in modern Asia.

THE LAND AND THE PEOPLE

China proper, exclusive of the pastoral, desert and mountainous border lands, is about half the size of the United States. It extends from Siberia to Indochina and from Central Asia to the Pacific Ocean. Its temperate climate is controlled by seasonal winds. The summer monsoon is hot and moist, bringing abundant rainfall from the south. The winter winds, which blow from the direction of the Siberian plains and the Gobi Desert, are dry and biting cold. Fairly distinct geographic boundaries have limited the extent of China's dominions and given the Chinese a sense of isolation and security. To the north and west are deserts and steppes; to the west and south are the highest mountains and the most inhospitable jungles in the world. China's eastern boundary is the great Pacific. In the nineteenth century, China's coastal cities were journey's end for the navigators from the West, but they were only the beginning

of long journeys by cart over mandarin highways or by junk over the
network of canals to the imperial capital in Peking.

The Chinese landscape is diversified, ranging from the parched
yellow plains of northern China to the lush green ricelands of the south.
China owes much of its prosperity and civilization to three great river
systems: the Yellow, Yangtze, and Pearl. The Yellow, or *Hwang Ho*, is
a river of mud draining the north and discoloring the ocean into which
it flows for fifty miles offshore. It gives life with the rich soil which it

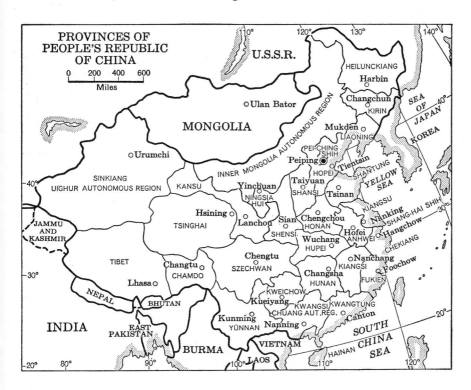

deposits in the alluvial plains. It also spreads sorrow and destruction
with disastrous floods. The Yangtze plunges madly from Tibetan highlands through steep gorges to Hankow and then flows gently for a thousand navigable miles to the sea. Great cities have been built on its banks.
Its valley is the agricultural and commercial heart of China. The Pearl
River is formed by the confluence of three large tributaries which together create the Canton delta. Canton, opposite Hong Kong and two
thousand miles from Peking, is China's historic window to the West.

Any part of China might well be anywhere else in China, although
at least four regions—North, Central, South, and West—possess distinct
geographic characteristics. North China, north of the Tsinling range, con-

tains Hopei, Honan, Shantung, Shansi, Shensi, and Kansu. It is the political center of China. A few Chinese words contain clues to the location of Chinese provinces: *ho* is the word for river and *shan* for mountain. *Pei* (*peh*), *nan*, *tung*, and *si* (*hsi*) are north, south, east, and west respectively. Hopei therefore is river-north, or the province north of the Hwang Ho. Honan is river-south. Shantung is mountain-east and Shansi is mountain-west. Shensi is mountain-pass-west and with its neighboring province Kansu constitutes the corridor from China proper into Central Asia. The Great Wall of North China separates the nomads of inner Asia from the farmers of China, who produce wheat, millet, beans, peanuts, yams, vegetables, and fruit.

Central China—Hupei, Hunan, Anhwei, Kiangsi, and Kiangsu—is the thickly populated valley of the Yangtze. *Hu* means lake and *kiang* means river, the Yangtze in particular. Chungking, Hankow, Kiukiang, Anking, Wuhu, Nanking, Chinkiang, and Shanghai mark the course of the Yangtze to the sea. These cities are markets for wheat, rice, tea, peanuts, eggs, yams, sesamum, rapeseed, wood oil, and ramie. They were formerly the entrepôts through which imported foodstuffs, kerosene, and luxuries and delicacies trickled into interior homes.

South China—Chekiang, Fukien, Kwangtung, and Kwangsi—is the land of rice, tea, mulberry leaves, bamboo, and water buffalo. Torrential rains and a long steamy growing season coax three crops annually out of the fertile soil, but hills and marshes make marketing and transportation difficult. Canton, Swatow, Amoy, Foochow, and Ningpo were the home cities of Chinese who emigrated overseas and the first ports opened to ships from the West.

West China—Szechwan, Yunnan, and Kweichow—is high and wild. The Red Basin of Szechwan, with its natural capital at Chengtu, is the agricultural reservoir of West China. It feeds 100,000,000 people and yields a surplus of silk, ramie, salt, coal, iron, and tin. The mountains of Yunnan look down on the clouds and the canyons are deep. The mighty Yangtze, Mekong, and Salween rivers flow within a lateral distance of a hundred miles, but they are separated from each other by intervening mountains which rise 10,000 feet above the valleys. International travel to Yunnan is possible only over the Burma Road or by the railway from Indochina. Kweichow is among the poorer provinces in China, where it is said: "Three things you will never see: three miles of level road without a hill; three consecutive days of sunshine; or a man with three dollars in his pockets." In the more remote mountain areas primitive tribal groups carry on the way of life which they have known for a thousand years.

China also traditionally includes the island of Taiwan, which the Portuguese called Formosa or "the beautiful." It is about equal to the size of Massachusetts, Rhode Island, and Connecticut combined. It has been described as an unsinkable aircraft carrier lying between Japan and the Philippines, less than a hundred miles off the coast of the Asian mainland. It is about 350 miles west and south of Okinawa, 1,000 miles west of Iwo Jima, 1,500 miles northwest of Guam, and 225 miles north of Luzon. The east coast of Taiwan has comparatively good harbors, but it is cut off from its own interior by steep mountains. The west coast, on the China side, is a gently sloping succession of sand dunes and swamp lands. The Formosa Strait is shallow and dangerous to navigation. Ocean-going vessels cannot come into sight of Taiwan except at a few selected places. The island has only two well-developed harbors: Keelung in the north and Kaohsiung in the southwest. The Tamsui River is navigable for small junks as far as the capital (Taipei) twelve miles inland.

Almost two-thirds of Taiwan is mountainous, with most of the cultivated land along the western coastal plain. The climate is tropical or semitropical, controlled by the monsoons and the warm ocean currents. Agricultural production consists of rice, sugar, vegetables, and fruit. Forests of pine, oak, camphor wood, and bamboo abound. Mineral resources are lacking, but the surrounding seas teem with edible fish. From the standpoint of size, population, and resources, Formosa is tiny compared to the giant mainland of China.

The outlying regions of China—Korea, Manchuria, Mongolia, Turkestan, Tibet, and the ill-defined lands of Southeast Asia—throughout much of their history have been under the domination of China and were frequently ruled by Chinese soldiers and administrators. Kings and khans often occupied a position of vassalage to the emperor of China, exchanging nominal protection for the privilege of sending tribute missions to the court of Peking. Tribute-bearing missions came to China from Japan, Korea, Annam, and Burma, and from such distant places as Nepal, Siam, and Ceylon. The impact of Chinese civilization was also felt in the Philippines and Indonesia.

China's neighbors had distinctive ways of life. Some were nomads or mountain people who were scarcely affected by the superior civilization of China. The hard-riding "barbarians" (as China called them) to the north posed a continuous threat of invasion. Mongols and Manchus conquered China at different periods, but both discovered that "you can conquer a country on horseback, but you cannot rule from horseback." Most of China's dynasties originated on the frontiers of Chinese civilization, but China managed eventually to absorb its conquerors. China was the great ocean which turned into salt all the rivers which flowed into it.

Korea was first and perhaps foremost among China's neighbors, lying to the north and east. Korea borders on Siberia as well as China. The Yalu River, Whitehead Mountains, and the Tumen River separate Korea from Manchuria and the maritime provinces of Russia. The Korean peninsula is

600 miles long and 135 miles wide at its wasp waist. It is the continental bridge to Japan, and in Japanese eyes is the historic dagger pointing to the heart of Japan. It is larger than Minnesota, about the same size as Great Britain, and smaller than Japan. A single pass permits easy communication between China and Korea. Rugged mountains constitute the main difference between North Korea and South Korea; and a rocky mountain backbone divides the eastern half of the peninsula from the west. Mountains, with their forests and minerals, make up three-quarters of Korea's land area. The remaining quarter is arable and produces rice, millet, wheat, beans, and barley. Rice is the staple product and is grown mainly in South Korea. Eighty percent of the population derives its livelihood from rice, but three out of five Korean farmers were tenants as late as 1950.

The people of Korea speak a common language, have their own national dress, and take pride in their native culture. They have ranked with the best of the artists of the Orient in painting, bronzes, and ceramics. For centuries they were students of China and, in turn, the teachers of Japan. They were the active agents in the transfer of Chinese culture, particularly Buddhism, from the continent of Asia to the offshore Japanese islands. Until most recent times, they were under the political sway of China. Their kings were invested by the Chinese emperor; their administrative system was modeled after that of China; and their society was divided into aristocrats and common people, after the fashion of China. Because of internal dissensions and their fiery individualism, Koreans have been referred to as the Irish of the Far East.

Manchuria, next-door neighbor to Korea, is made up of three traditional provinces, Heilungkiang, Kirin, and Liaoning, and is the ancestral home of China's last imperial family (1644–1912). The native people of Manchuria, the Manchus, are distinct from Chinese, but they have been largely absorbed by hordes of recent Chinese immigrants. Although Manchuria is Chinese in culture and speech, it retains a strong sense of regional autonomy. It is of vital strategic importance because of its frontier with Siberia, Korea, and Mongolia. Because of its wealth of agricultural and mineral resources, it has been coveted and partially developed by Russians and Japanese. Moreover, it is the key area in contemporary China's industrialization. With adequate capital and technical skills, Manchuria could support two or three times its present population and could possibly fulfill Japan's earlier dreams of a self-sustaining Asian regional industrial economy.

Mongolia, west of Manchuria, is divided by the Gobi Desert into Inner Mongolia and Outer Mongolia. Until modern times it was a combination of unsurveyed desert and steppes, most noted for Genghis Khan and the Mongol rulers who dominated the heartland of Asia from Peking to Moscow in the thirteenth and fourteenth centuries. Inner Mongolia, including areas known as Jehol, Chahar, Suiyuan, and Ningsia, is a barren table land producing primarily iron and sheep. Outer Mongolia, inclining geographically and politically toward the Soviet Union, is a well-watered rolling country whose landscape resembles Oregon or Pennsylvania. The Mongols are culturally united in spite of their political division. They have a deep-seated age-long scorn of Russia, their ex-vassal. The Mongols ruled China for about a century and they resented the Chinese as the cattleman and the shepherd always resented the farmer, the "revenuer," the petty official and the clever merchant. The Mongolian border was an effective barrier to the expansion of China's agricultural way of life.

Sinkiang, or Chinese Turkestan, lies south and west of Mongolia. It is twice the size of Texas and is like Utah and Nevada in physical appearance. Farmers and merchants have settled near the desert oases, and shepherds wander the lower reaches of the mountain ranges. Most of the inhabitants are Uigurs, Tadjiks, or Kazakhs—being Turkish in appearance and speech and Mohammedan in religion. Less than ten percent of the population is Chinese. Chinese officials served in Sinkiang under protest. They considered the climate atrocious, the food worse, and the way of life completely barbaric. Sinkiang, however, is noteworthy for its textiles, rugs, sheep, horses, and for the finest fruits in China. Its ancient caravan routes were once the silk highway to Europe; now they are avenues between Soviet Asia and greater China.

Tibet, south of Sinkiang, has at most two million people. It covers one million square miles of plateau comparable in height to the peaks of the Colorado Rockies. The plateaus are topped by the most awesome mountains in the world. Tibet is a cold, mysterious Lama-land, which is much more of a barrier than a bridge between India and China. It is the home of nomads and primitive tribesmen, except in the monasteries and patches of agricultural land near Lhasa. Tibet is a region which for centuries has had its own form of government, its own religious and social customs. It is completely isolated even from its nearest neighbors. Eastern Tibet and western China are separated indistinctly by two formidable regions—Tsinghai and Sikang—which have sometimes been designated as separate provinces of China. The tribes which inhabit these regions are among the least civilized in the entire world.

The ill-defined lands of Southeast Asia—described below in some detail—complete the ring around China. The border areas of Indochina and Burma have never been free from the danger of Chinese expansionism, and Thailand (Siam) has been under constant threat from its mighty neighbor to the north. Even the islands of the Philippines and Indonesia have been subject to Chinese political pressure and to the continuing infiltration of Chinese immigrants. China never achieved political mastery of Southeast Asia, but expatriate Chinese came to dominate its economic life.

The resources of China proper always enabled that great empire to provide for its own fundamental needs in food, clothing, and housing. For forty centuries farming was the chief occupation of eighty percent of the people. China was self-sufficient, but its masses lived perilously near the margin of survival. The industrial revolution, which accounted for the prosperity of the Western world, had not even been thought of in China by the time of the arrival of European traders.

Undoubtedly China's greatest resource is its people. The "Chinese people" may be either a political or a racial concept. Politically all citizens of China are Chinese people regardless of race. In this sense Manchurians, Mongols, Turkis of Sinkiang, Tibetans, mountain tribesmen and desert nomads living inside China are included as Chinese people. They already numbered 100,000,000 when the first European colonies were established in America and had reached 410,000,000 when the first war broke out between China and England. There were approximately 700,000,000 Chinese in 1963 and they were expanding at the rate of nearly 15,000,000 per year.

As a racial concept, the "Chinese people" omits China's minorities (about one-sixth of the total population) and includes only the members of the Chinese race. The racial Chinese are a mixture of ethnic stocks, basically Mongoloid, which has been constantly invigorated by the blood of China's neighbors. The "pure" Chinese refer to themselves as the children of Han. The name *Han* refers to their ancestral home in the Han River valley and to the glorious native dynasty which ruled China in the time of Christ.

The people of the Chinese race are often thought of as having common characteristics, but they are as diverse and complex as humanity itself. They have been described as good-humored, shrewd, industrious, and earthy, and possessed of a remarkable sense of individual dignity. But for every Chinese with one array of qualities there is another who is exactly the opposite. Lin Yu-tang has characterized northerners as "hale, hearty, humorous, onion-eating and fun-loving, the raw material from which the characters in Chinese novels of war and adventure are drawn." According to him, southerners are "enterprising, carefree, spendthrift, adventuresome, pugnacious, quick-tempered and progressive, most susceptible to change, reform and revolution." Even his generalities cannot be meaningfully applied to hundreds of millions of Chinese individuals. However, there is nothing unusually mysterious or exotic about the Chinese or nothing particularly inscrutable about the "oriental mind." Chinese are human beings, entirely understandable and subject to the same rational and emotional influences as any other people in the world.

Teeming masses have always chraracterized the Chinese scene. In modern diplomatic history, crowds have always milled around the waterfront of Canton and, later, Shanghai. Crowds jammed the streets or alleys of the smaller Chinese cities, the market places at the country crossroads, or the broad avenues of Peking. The Chinese have packed five thousand to the square mile in the river valleys and along the coastal plains, and have also managed to stay alive in mountains and deserts where the nearest neighbor was a mile away in any direction. The distribution of population for the whole of China ranges from the sparseness of Nevada to a congestion which dwarfs the extreme conditions of Japan. The Chinese have made a living amidst poverty which would have destroyed a less hardy people. In spite of wars, famine, disease, droughts, and floods, they have exhibited throughout their long history an extraordinary flair for survival.

HISTORY

The earliest traces of the Chinese people have been found in the dusty plains of North China. Coping with the treachery of the Yellow River gave the Chinese the strength and the sagacity to conquer the warlike tribes of the north and to spread rather easily over the territories of the weaker peoples who inhabited the Yangtze Valley and southward. China expanded less by military prowess than by the migration of its people and cultural "subversion." Scholars, statesmen, and aristocratic adventurers from the heart of China became the tutors of the less-cultured chieftains of the frontiers.

The story of China usually begins with a mythical Hsia Dynasty, somewhere around 2000 B.C.; but its authenticated foundations go only as far back as the Shang Dynasty, traditionally dated 1766 to 1122 B.C. By that time the Chinese had acquired their written language, a vigorous art, and a political organization of some complexity. They venerated their ancestors, depended upon agriculture for their existence, and used bronze for utensils and weapons.

China was stereotyped before the time of Christ. The age of the Chou rulers was a classical age, 1122–221 B.C. It was an age of kings and feudal lords which gave rise to the professions of soldiery and statesmanship. It was the golden age of Chinese philosophy, which produced China's social and ethical ideals, institutions, and customs. The great philosophers, Confucius and Mencius, were the approximate contemporaries of Socrates, Plato, and Aristotle.

The name China itself comes from the Ch'in Dynasty, 221–207 B.C. The Ch'in emperor, the first unifier of the entire Chinese state between the Great Wall and the Yangtze, destroyed the ancient feudal system and substituted a centralized bureaucratic administration. He ruled China with an iron hand and taxed the people ruthlessly. He caused the burning of the books which he hoped would blot out the memory of the past and enable him to mold the future according to his own totalitarian ideas.

He attained a greatness which no successor could match, so his dynasty disappeared. After the Ch'ins came the Han rulers, 206 B.C.–220 A.D. The new dynasty rejected the practice of tyranny and gradually adopted Confucian ideals as the philosophy of the state. These political ideas dominated China for nearly 2,000 years. The Han leaders extended the empire to South Manchuria, Outer Mongolia, Turkestan, and Indochina. A hundred and forty years before Christ, a Chinese traveler, Chang Ch'ien, who was sent to the western regions to get an alliance against the Hsiung-nu, reached the fringes of the Mediterranean world. In Roman times Chinese silk, hides and skins, furs, rhubarb, and cinnamon moved across the routes of Central Asia in exchange for glass, jade, precious stones, ivory, tortoise shell, wool, and linen.

China's first "New Deal" was attempted by a usurper emperor, Wang Mang, A.D. 8–23. He nationalized and redistributed the land. He monopolized salt, iron, wines, coinage, and mines. He had the state put a floor under prices by purchase of surplus agricultural commodities and generally tried to protect the interest of the farmer against the merchants. Wang moved too fast for his contemporaries and died a sudden and violent death, after which the Han Dynasty was restored. The great Han empire was the universal state of the ancient Asian world, as its contemporary, the Roman Empire, was the universal state of the Western world. And like the Roman Empire, the Han weakened because of barbarian attacks and broke into a congeries of warring kingdoms. During these political dark ages, Buddhism took its place in China alongside the earlier teaching of Confucianism and Taoism.

The old elements of Chinese civilization declined, to re-emerge in the brilliance of the T'ang Dynasty, A.D. 618–906. The T'ang surpassed the glory of the Han; the empire was larger than ever before, more prosperous, and better ruled. People from all parts of Eurasia and adherents of many faiths—Nestorian Christian, Zoroastrian, Manichaean, and Moslem—flocked into the capital city of Ch'ang An, the modern Sian. Persians, Arabs, Jews, and merchants from India came to China by sea and settled in Canton. Chinese goods were sold in the bazaars of Baghdad, Cairo, and Constantinople. China excelled any state in Europe in glamour and general advancement, and sent official envoys to foreign countries.

The cultural brilliance of the T'ang Dynasty belied its military weakness, political division, and economic depression. With the fall of the T'ang empire, China again passed through a period of chaos before its new period of glory in the Sung Dynasty, 960–1279. Under the Sung emperors, who had their seat of government in South China, there was little improvement in the lot of the common people. A reformer, Wang An-shih, 1021–1086, kept China in controversy for an entire century by a second "New Deal" program. His reforms contemplated a state budget, a state monopoly of commerce, cheap state loans to farmers, land redistribution, equitable distribution of land taxes, taxation of all property whether real or movable, abolition of forced labor, compulsory military service to replace the professional army, and the shifting of the emphasis in the civil service examinations from the classics to current problems. Wang's reforms did not take root, but they represented a recurrent Chinese tendency to experiment in statecraft and economics.

Influences from the outside did not penetrate too deeply the fabric of Chinese culture. The items of foreign commerce were handled for the benefit of the very few at the top of the social ladder. Foreigners in China were treated liberally. They were permitted to settle their own disputes and they intermarried with Chinese as they pleased. One Arab rose to high position in the Chinese official hierarchy. Buddhist pilgrims went to India until the middle of the eleventh century, when the roads were tightly closed by the spread of Islam. The Sung period was marked by a renascence in art and education, but it did not bring the physical strength to stand up against the Mongols.

The Mongols looked upon China as the richest part of their vast empire, which extended across the heart of Asia to the borders of Arabia and far into Europe and Russia. The Mongol, or the Yüan Dynasty, 1279–1368, was at the height of its power when visited by Marco Polo. When that Venetian traveler told his fantastic stories in Europe, the Westerners had the same feeling of disbelief and awe about China that Chinese peasants in a later age displayed at the stories of jet planes and atom bombs of the West. The Yüan Dynasty fell before an uprising of exploited tenant farmers against the officials, nobles, and landlords of both Chinese and Mongol stock. After a century of alien rule, the Chinese regained the imperial throne.

The succeeding dynasty, the Ming or "brilliant," 1368–1644, like most of its predecessors, was born of internal chaos and rebellion. It made its power felt as far away as Ceylon. Under the first of the Mings, the empire was elegant, wealthy, and populous, but in time it became sterile and tradition-bound in thought and political administration. It was plagued by depredations of northern border tribesmen, Japanese pirates, the appearance of Europeans by sea, and the rise of the Manchu power in the northeast.

The Manchu, or Ch'ing (pure) Dynasty, was founded in 1644 and it lasted until 1912. The Chinese regarded the Manchus essentially as foreigners and thought of themselves as being under an alien dynasty as they crossed the threshold into modern history. The early years of the Manchus found China at the height of its powers. Two monarchs, K'ang Hsi, who reigned from 1662 to 1722, and Ch'ien Lung, from 1736 to 1796, together gave China over a century of prosperity. K'ang Hsi was the Chinese counterpart of Louis XIV, and Ch'ien Lung was contemporary with the entire life span of George Washington. To the liberals who led the enlightenment in Europe in the eighteenth century, China was a kind of utopia. But at the very moment Europe began its career of growth and expansion, China entered its era of steady decay. At the end of Ch'ien Lung's reign, China was still in outward appearance a powerful and well-ordered country, but within ten years it had begun to degenerate into a miserable state of corruption and misgovernment. However, the antiquity and richness of Chinese history (although unknown and unappreciated) were as much a part of the China which the Europeans originally encountered as the confusion and chaos which met their eyes.

China's Cultural Vitality

An awareness of the place of culture in Chinese life is as essential as a knowledge of their history in the understanding of China's place in the modern world. From their beginnings the Chinese attached great importance to culture and artistic accomplishment. They accepted as a civilized human being, as one of themselves, anyone who understood Chinese ways or behaved in accordance with Chinese standards. They believed that their own classics contained all learning and the essence of all wisdom. They could not conceive of a civilization beyond their own borders and could not imagine anyone who had never heard of Confucius. They held scholars and philosophers in high esteem and looked to these for the enrichment and preservation of their common culture.

The Chinese have been credited with the invention of paper, printing, the compass, and gunpowder. They invented paper in A.D. 105; and in 868 they printed the first recorded book from wooden blocks, a Buddhist sutra which was found in the grottoes of Tunhuang. As late as the eighteenth century, China contained more books than the rest of the world put together. The immense Chinese literary production contained short stories, folk songs, poetry, dramas, novels, and great quantities of translations. One Buddhist monk, Hsüan Tsang, during the T'ang Dynasty, brought back with him from India and translated material twenty-five times as voluminous as the Christian Bible. The Chinese possessed a wealth of dynastic histories, dictionaries, encyclopedias, and collections of every type of work of reference.

Chinese art during 4,000 years expressed itself through an infinite variety of materials and media: jade, bone and ivory, stone, bronze, wood, enamel, lacquer, silk, pottery, porcelain, and calligraphy. The result was intrinsically beautiful and endowed with universal appeal. The Chinese considered the highest art to be a triple masterpiece of calligraphy, poetry, and painting and pointed with most pride to its golden age in the T'ang Dynasty. Ceramics—or chinaware—ranged from the crude pottery remains of earliest times and the funerary figurines of the Han and T'ang dynasties to the fine porcelains of the Sung period. Sculpture was never esteemed by the Chinese as by the Greeks, but the tombs of emperors were often marked by huge figures of men or animals carved in stone. The Chinese landscape was dotted with artistic bridges and picturesque temples. Homes and gardens, with their moon doorways, pavilions, and arches, were symphonies in form and color. The Chinese gave an unmistakable character to fundamental arts and craftsmanship, whether in lacquer, bronze, jade, cloisonné, silks, furniture, or rugs and carpets.

The Chinese created systems of thought which were as rich and varied as their other cultural achievements. The teachings of Confucius (551–479 B.C.) are preserved in the *Analects,* one of China's great books. They have been modified and expanded in historical records and political essays which have survived the ages. Confucius lived in a period of transformation from feudal China to bureaucratic China, when the prevalence of intrigue and local wars tended to destroy the moral values of the past. He wished to preserve those values and to show that in such fundamental virtues as human kindness, benevolence, and a sense of moral obligation lay the foundations of a good society. He believed in the fundamental goodness of man and the necessity of living in harmony with nature. However, he was more than a preserver or transmitter, because he gave expression to new philosophic ideas forever associated with his name.

According to him, the social order was based on five fundamental relationships: son to father, wife to husband, younger to elder brother, friend to friend, and subject to ruler. His disciples taught that these relationships would be ideally fulfilled if everybody from the highest to the lowest would consider the cultivation of personality as his prime obligation. The perfect personality should be cultivated only through learning and would be measured by recognized principles of social conduct. Correct behavior would consist of strict observance of form and ceremony. Violations of the prescribed rules meant loss of face and dignity. Confucius said, "He who knows not the rites has nothing to shape his character."

Just as a hundred flowers bloomed in a garden, a hundred schools of thought developed in ancient China. Some were dissenters within the Confucian tradition. Others objected to fundamental Confucian views on the nature of man, the practice of politics, or the theory of government.

Some groups of philosophers were identified by their founders, such as the followers of Mo Ti, or Mo Tzu, and others were known by their principles, such as the legalists, the eclectics or the dialecticians. The professional diviners, agriculturists, diplomats, and writers all produced their ideological champions, while some distinguished individuals achieved "great name" status in intellectual achievements without benefit of association with any of the well-known schools of thought. The Chinese meditated about and wrote expertly about nearly all the fundamental questions of philosophy which produced the brilliance of ancient Greece.

Chinese philosophy was preoccupied with this-world-ness: man's place in this life, his duties and obligations. "We have not yet learned to know life, how can we know death?" Confucius was more intellectual than religious. He emphasized learning, understanding, and wisdom. "Study widely, inquire minutely, think carefully, analyze clearly and then practice earnestly." China, in contrast to ancient India, seemed relatively unconcerned about gods and immortality. The concept of sin was unknown; evil or crime were looked upon as temporary deflections from the essential harmony of the universe. The simplest religious rites in China sprang from some relationship between man and nature. Ancient China knew no pantheon and no priesthood, and contented itself with homage to abstractions of heaven, earth, mountains or rivers. The closest approach to religion on the part of Confucius was the deference which he paid to the religious ideas of his contemporaries and in the exact rules which he laid down for the worship of ancestors.

Taoism and Buddhism flourished along with Confucianism. The Chinese experienced no difficulty in being Confucian, Taoist, and Buddhist (and later Christian as well) at the same time. Perhaps for precaution or insurance a practical Chinese was likely to invite or hire representatives of all religions to participate in funeral ceremonies for a loved one. Lacking any belief in a jealous god, the Chinese felt no hostility toward a neighbor for his religion or lack of it.

Taoism was a metaphysical system which had its roots in the magic forces of nature and a belief in the *Tao* (the way). Two opposing forces —*yin* and *yang*, representing masculine and feminine, night and day, or light and dark—created *Tao*, or the ideal way of life and it was the whole duty of man to seek harmony with it. Harmony was to be found in nonaction because action provoked conflict and reaction. The chief tenet of the Taoists was "Do nothing and there is nothing which will not be done for you." This was an ideal philosophy for a lazy person or an escapist who sought spiritual refuge in a time of political chaos. Taoism degenerated into a ritual of magic, attracting adherents by promises of rewards and threats of hellish punishment in this world and the next. The Taoists created the kitchen gods, the guardian spirits, and the myths of the Chinese immortals. The Taoist ritual of modern times was in sharp contrast to the original Taoist search for harmony with the essential way of the universe.

Buddhism came from India to China in the second century B.C. and it served a religious need of the Chinese people which had not been satisfied by either Confucianism or Taoism. Buddhism brought with it beautiful art, colorful ceremonies, broad learning and an exquisite sense of inner peace. It was Buddhist belief that all existence is suffering, that the continuation of existence arises from desires and their fulfillment, and that salvation lies in the cessation of personal existence which can be attained only through freedom from desire. No being is limited to a single existence closed by death. All beings are continually reincarnated. Ultimate salvation lies in the elimination of the self, by the Enlightenment, which is a condition preliminary to Nirvana.

One branch of the Buddhists stressed a life of abstention and renunciation as the key to paradise; another stressed good works, faith, and the reciting of the holy Buddhist scriptures. The Chinese preferred the latter and developed the principles of salvation by faith and charity. Buddhist ceremonies at time of death blended very well with Confucian ancestor worship; certain Buddhist figures were transformed into popular Chinese deities. Kuan Yin—the goddess of mercy and the patron saint of Chinese mothers—was the best example. The Buddhist faith in self-discipline and meditation was a welcome philosophy for nonintellectuals who were unable to achieve distinction according to the Confucian prescription. Buddhism had its own church organization, its temples and monasteries and its own priesthood. As it grew in popularity, it became the stronghold of those who protested against the Confucian concept of society. It offered refuge to victims of government disfavor or persecution, and with its ideas of brotherhood and equality it laid an ideological foundation for secret societies.

As a result of the interaction of diverse systems of thought in premodern China—Confucian, Taoist, Buddhist, and their manifold variations—the Chinese were as mature philosophically and as alert intellectually as the Europeans who came to China as visitors, merchants, adventurers, or missionaries. At the same time, Chinese society had evolved into a complex and well-developed organization, proved by a millennium of experience and supported by a wealth of rational ideas.

Social Organization and Economic Life

Chinese society was unique in its organization. It was headed by the imperial family but was thoroughly dominated by the bureaucracy which was recruited from the scholar-gentry class. The bureaucracy of public functionaries was the one percent of the population which owed its prestige and position to its learning and to its success in passing the official examinations in the Chinese classics. There were no feudal lords in imperial China, no military aristocracy, no orders of chivalry to challenge the hierarchy of intellectuals which monopolized the official posts in government service. The bureaucracy was responsible for implementing imperial edicts and managing public affairs. Its authority extended from the highest problems of state to the lowliest quarrels in the village. Over a long period of time the bureaucrats in the state took an active interest in every aspect of life and thought. They ran the army and the administrative system; and they carried out huge schemes of public works including the Great Wall, the Grand Canal, and massive schemes of dikes, canals, and highways. Dynasties rose and fell in China but the bureaucracy remained in effective control of state and society.

The people were divided into rigidly defined classes. The privileged scholar-gentry were at the top of the social scale, owning much of the land and by common consent possessing the knowledge, ability, and moral excellence to serve as the custodians of China's cultural heritage. They were the elite from whom came the philosophers, men of affairs, and the candidates for the official examinations. In theory anyone could take the examinations, but a great deal of money was needed for an education. A young man had to have family backing to pay for tutors in language, calligraphy, history, Confucian ethics, and the practice of government. The scholar-gentry were supposed to be incorruptible and superior men. However, they stooped as low as corruptible human beings anywhere in buying diplomas or titles and in cheating at their jobs after once obtained.

The common people in China lived in a completely different world than the officials. Commoners were divided into peasants, artisans, and merchants. Below these came the soldiers and the mean or lowliest of people.

Eighty percent of China's people were farmers. They supplied the entire population with food. In addition they were subject to forced labor on public works and draft duty in the army. Most peasants owned at least a part of their own land; comparatively few were tenants, in contrast to Japan. Even the landless tenants were not serfs bound to the soil. They were free to buy and sell property and to move from place to place as they pleased. They paid their taxes and rendered their service to a representative of the central government and not to some feudal lord. In an exceptional case, a bright son of a peasant might pass the examinations and rise to the gentry class. In theory it was always possible.

The artisans and merchants lived in villages or towns. They made tools, furniture, vehicles, or luxury products. They were the weavers, carpenters, metalworkers, silversmiths, jade polishers, and ivory carvers. Their lives were regulated by the guilds which laid down the rules for apprentices, journeymen, and masters in a manner similar to that of medieval Europe. The merchants ranged in scope of activity from the street vendor to the large tea and silk merchants. They were also organized into guilds. The successful merchants were always fair game for bribes or payments to bureaucrats; and there was nothing a successful businessman wanted more than a propitious marriage for his daughter or entry into the distinguished ranks of the bureaucracy for his sons.

The military profession was an honorable calling in China; Chinese literature is full of its warrior-heroes. But the poor private soldier was an object of public scorn. He was often an unfortunate social misfit who had run into difficulty with his family or a near delinquent who had his problems with the law. The pay was low, the treatment miserable. It was a fair assumption that a man would not be an ordinary soldier if there were any alternative open to him. The Chinese said, "You do not use good iron to make a nail; nor do you use a good man to make a soldier." Still the soldier was not the absolute bottom of the social ladder. Below him were the mean people—the actors, barbers, prostitutes, and slaves. These were the flotsam and jetsam of humankind.

Every individual or organization in society from the emperor down had a fixed status, with prescribed rights and obligations. The family in its extended form was considered the best of all social organizations and was therefore the basic social unit. The family in this sense included the *lao yeh* or old grandfather, with his wife, their sons and sons' wives, uncles, aunts, cousins, children, and servants. The richer the family, the more extensive the number of relatives under a single roof. The individual was important only as he was a member of the family unit. The family carried out sacrifices to ancestors, took care of the aged and the handicapped, and supplied descendants. It placed a premium upon loyalty and filial piety. In law it was jointly responsible for the failures or crimes of its members. It was the root cause of nepotism, which characterized Chinese political behavior. The Chinese argued that the family worked together to educate its brightest sons; it was their obligation when successful to take care of relatives no matter how distant. To the Chinese it was preferable to pad the payroll with relatives rather than support the unemployed in idleness.

The sexes did not mingle freely in China. Men and women moved in a different realm. It was a man's world. Education was for men only and men were regarded as the head of the house. A man was entitled to a legal wife, a concubine or two, and as many affairs as he could pay for. Women were taken to live in their husband's homes and upper-class women were made to suffer the agonies of foot-binding. Women were given little status politically although the pages of Chinese history are filled with stories of the beauty, will, and achievement of female characters. A woman's place depended much more on her own ingenuity than upon any written rules or regulations. Marriages were arranged by go-betweens or professional matchmakers. The Chinese argued that you fall in love because you are married, rather than vice versa. They also believed that the cold calculations of family councils were more reliable guides to future happiness than eyes blinded by stars. Betrothals were serious and divorces difficult. Since the success of the family system depended upon children, the marriage was deemed successful when the woman produced a son.

The Chinese exhibited through the years an unusual urge to organize into groups. In the cities, it was the guilds. In the countryside, it was a variety of cooperative societies. There were cooperatives for crop-watching, for irrigation, and for marketing and credit. The village, not the individual farmhouse, was the center of rural life. The walled village located on high ground, safe from floods and safest from bandit raids or military attacks, was grouped about a guildhall, an ancestral temple, a magistrate's office, or a seignorial mansion. Near the crossroads at the center could be found the market place or the public grounds for grand festivals or wandering theatrical players. In grim times it might even serve as an execution ground.

Secret societies were important in Chinese community life. A Chinese adult was likely to belong to two or three, with such names as the Yellow Turbans, Long Knives, Elder Brothers Association, Red Spears or White Lilies, or even the Boxers or Righteous Harmony Fists. Secret societies were organized primarily for some religious, business or benevolent purpose, but they usually dipped deeply into politics.

Economic life in China revolved around agriculture. Farmers cultivated every little valley, every slope, and every scrap of marginal terrain. Nearly half of China's land under cultivation was irrigated, about a quarter was terraced. Many of China's agricultural problems stemmed from such natural causes as famines, floods, and droughts; but other problems came from bad political administration, heavy taxes, and inconsiderate human treatment. Life on the Chinese farm changed but little over the span of Chinese history. The farmer consumed most of what he raised, and bartered away only a small part of his product. The prosperity and contentment of the farmer in good times accounted for China's long periods of peace; the wretchedness of the farmers' lot in bad times explained the frequency of peasant revolts and the constant talk of agrarian reform. Politics and economics went hand in hand. The main problem of the government under the Han Dynasty—as well as under the Kuomintang and the Communists—was to keep the farmers well-fed, well-clothed, and reasonably happy. Grinding poverty is the enemy of stable government; discontented spirits prefer rebellion to starvation.

Less than one-quarter of China's population made its living from handicrafts or commerce. No large commercial or industrial enterprises came into being until recent times because of China's lack of resources, dearth of capital, and satisfaction with the economic *status quo.* But it must be noted that the Chinese developed mines for coal, iron, lead, copper, antimony, tungsten, tin, gold, and silver. In the field of transportation they worked wonders with wheelbarrows, carts, and boats. Wherever a boat can go, the Chinese can take it. They built and sailed ocean-going junks sufficiently large for hundreds of people, and they made sampans so light "they could float on a heavy dew." They were by no means too inept to take to the ways of modern industry.

Business in China was carried on by the old-style shop. People lived and worked in the same humble place. One store or one street would deal with one type of commodity. Peking, for example, had its famous Jade Street, Embroidery Street, Lantern Street, and Furniture Street. The workers were poor, but exceedingly skillful. Shops and factories in China made the same things and often by the same methods as those in the West before the advent of power machinery. On the other hand, many products were distinctively and unmistakably Chinese. The individual Chinese was a shrewd merchant, a fierce bargainer, and a genius at making money. He operated on a small margin of profit and took every advantage of the variety of coinage and currency, and weights and measures which existed in China. Still the Chinese were notoriously slow in building enterprises which demanded broad markets or which called for corporate rather than family ownership and operation.

POLITICAL DOCTRINE, STATE AND GOVERNMENT

Chinese sophistication was more evident in the political than in the economic realm. The political ideas and governmental system of China were more than a thousand years old when the Crusades were the newest things in the Western world.

By the eleventh century neo-Confucianism, a synthesis of the ideas of competing Chinese systems of thought, was well entrenched as the cult of official China. The status and activities of the emperor, the bureaucracy, and the scholar-gentry were well defined. Confucian temples were built throughout the empire, and a large part of official duties consisted of religious ceremony. The Chinese placed more emphasis on orthodoxy than on original thought. They believed that Confucius, aided and abetted by succeeding generations of scholar-philosophers, had provided the answers to all problems of the contemporary social and political order, as well as to the moral problems of the universe.

According to the neo-Confucian school, which lasted as long as the Chinese empire itself, heaven symbolized the directing force in the universe. It was by no means synonymous with a personal god—but all life had no alternative except to follow the will of heaven. It was the task of government to bring humanity into harmony with the will of heaven, and the emperor, or the son of heaven, was the chosen intermediary agent.

The emperor was looked upon as the state and the government. The people felt no sense of patriotism toward China—a nation. The dynasty was China, and China, the civilized world. From ancient times the emperor was king and priest, the performer of sacrifices, the symbol of heaven on earth. He was supposed to be the incarnation of moral virtue and was to rule his subjects by education, exhortation, and example—not force. Confucius said: "When the ruler is pious, none among the people will dare to be irreverent; when the ruler loves justice, none among the people will dare to be otherwise; when the ruler loves good faith, none among the people will dare not to keep the faith."

Officials were to be selected from sages and wise men. As "superior men" they were to be examples for the masses. Their credentials were to be found in moral standards rather than in practical or technical training. Mencius, the most famous of Confucius' disciples, contributed to neo-Confucianism his doctrine that the end of government was the welfare of the people. "Heaven sees as the people see, heaven hears as the people hear." He taught that the whole duty of government lay in "sufficient food, sufficient weapons and the confidence of the common people."

It was axiomatic that bad rulers lost their right to rule. When the emperor no longer possessed virtue, he lost the mandate of heaven and the dynasty needed to be replaced. Natural catastrophes, civil wars, disorder, famine, and suffering indicated heaven's discontent and signaled the end of the road for the emperor on the throne. Rebellion against a bad ruler was not the people's right—it was the people's obligation. But if possible it should be accomplished without violence and strife, because the Chinese preferred arbitration and compromise. The worthy scholar was more of a genuine hero than the returning general.

The Confucianists had their dissenters and objectors. One group, the utilitarians, preferred pragmatism to moralism as the standard of official conduct. Another group, the legalists, preached totalitarianism in its crassest form. They argued that the rule of law is the only rule which men respect and that the sole duty of government should be agriculture and fighting. The Taoists were the most vigorous minority. Despising the world, the Taoists said all government was tyranny and argued that the very existence of institutions proved the decline of virtue. "Govern a great state as you would cook a small fish—that is hardly at all." The Taoists were pacifists and taught the folly of war. They deprecated the Confucian emphasis on ceremony and they objected to Confucius' lack of realism.

The Taoists insisted that, contrary to the teachings of Confucius, heaven and earth were not humane, but treated people and things like herbs and beasts. The universe was seen as neither kindly nor righteous but as going its way regardless of human desires or standards of behavior. The reformer was wasting his time because it was useless to cultivate virtue. "Unless you know evil, you cannot recognize the good." The teaching of benevolence and proper conduct was opposed to the *Tao*, which was neither good nor bad. The Taoists pointed out somewhat cynically that when a ruler lives in luxury, his people live in poverty. A ruler is anything but the soul of virtue. Taoists had no faith in the government's brain trust. "The people are difficult to govern because too much learnedness is employed: to govern the state with learnedness is the spoiling of the state; to avoid the use of learnedness in government, that is the happiness of the state." Confucianism was the ideal philosophy for those in power; Taoism was more attractive for the loyal opposition.

The political theory of premodern China was one thing—the government of the state was quite another. In theory the emperor was all-powerful; in practice, he had to rule through an administrative machine which was cumbersome and tradition-bound. The central government under the Manchus consisted of the emperor, his court, and an administrative apparatus which made the fullest use of the Chinese bureaucracy. The machinery of the imperial government consisted of a prime minister, the grand council, grand secretariat and six boards, called civil affairs, revenue, rites, war, punishments, and public works. A censorate, the eyes and ears of the emperor, had the highest duties of advice and criticism. An imperial academy was the final word on all literary controversies or improvements. The army was supposed to be a Manchu monopoly, but its ranks were filled with Chinese conscripts. Chinese generals became more famous than Manchus. There was no elected assembly in Peking and no special board or cabinet office to deal with any foreign affairs except the collection of tribute. Too often the imperial court was a hotbed of sorcerers, astrologers, eunuchs, and concubines.

The provinces were ruled over by a dual administration of a military commander and a viceroy, governor-general, or governor for civil affairs. The subdivisions of a province, called prefects or circuits, were run by officials knows as *taotai* with whom foreigners frequently came in contact. The real government in China was the magistrate of the *hsien*, or local district, the approximate equivalent of an American township. Chinese villages had their own local organizations for purposes of raising the militia or collecting taxes. A village headman was usually selected by a council of family elders but he was very much under the thumb of the magistrate.

The survival of the Chinese system, in spite of the deadening curse of the examination system and the domination of the bureaucratic aristocracy, was a tribute to the sterling worth of the Chinese masses as well as to the intellect and ingenuity of the ruling elite. The Chinese expected the government to collect the taxes and keep the peace, but not to extend relief or interfere in personal affairs. The typical attitude toward government was the Taoist desire to have as little as possible. One of the earliest poems in the Chinese language, reputedly from 2000 B.C. reads:

> From break of day
> Till sunset glow
> I toil.
> I dig my well,
> I plough my field,
> And earn my food
> And drink.
> What care I
> Who rules the land,
> If I
> Am left in peace?

The concept of law in China was entirely different from that in the West. All litigation was discreditable, not only to the plaintiff and the defendant, but to the official in whose court the case was tried. Law was primarily an exhortation or standard of conduct, and it was designed for criminals, bandits, and swindlers. These were not expected to have the status of decent citizens when on trial, so they were subjected to torture, barbarous punishment, and cruel death. The courts were corrupt because influence and money were more effective than evidence. The legal theory of responsibility was thoroughly alien to the common-law concept that no man should be punished for the crime of another. In China, the governor of a province was held responsible for a catastrophe of nature; a family, for the misdeeds of one of its members; an employer, for the crimes of his employees. If the guilty person could not be found, then some other responsible person would have to accept the consequences, whether father, family head, employer, village elder, magistrate, or viceroy.

The standards of official conduct were vastly different between China and the West. Nepotism and corruption were standard practices. Salaries were low and expenses were high. Squeeze seemed natural and unavoidable. If a man spent half a lifetime and a family fortune in obtaining a position, he felt entitled to adequate rewards. Those who handled money automatically kept what they considered to be reasonable deductions. No official received appointment in his native province (too many relatives), and no official would ordinarily stay in the same job more than three years. Local officials were subject to constant investigations by imperial commissioners and were often the subject of secret reports or petitions sent to Peking by their subordinates. It was difficult to persuade Chinese officialdom to accept responsibility or make decisions. Compromises seemed greatly to be desired. If a dispute was not settled locally but was referred to Peking, the official concerned was liable to be reprimanded, dismissed, or punished. Because of this system, China often suffered: a local official would prefer to compromise rather than to take a strong stand against a foreign diplomat, consul, businessman, or missionary.

Each new Chinese dynasty came in with a flourish, swept with a new broom, brought prosperity and then faded away. The wrath of the people was usually the final straw which brought each dynastic cycle to its conclusion. Local bandits, guerrilla soldiers, secret societies and hungry mobs drove out Wang Mang, the T'angs, Mings and the rest. If rebellions failed, their leaders were treated as traitors; when rebellions succeeded, their leaders were enthroned as the new heirs to the mandate of heaven. A change of dynasty was not a profound revolution, it was a change of imperial administration. The scholars and the people flocked to the successful faction and deserted those whose greatest fault was failure.

It was difficult for traditional China to accomplish the transition into the modern world. China cherished its ancient sense of harmony and balance, its grace of living and spiritual poise. China resisted the West the longest and suffered the most. The pressure from outside coincided with the political and cultural crisis within. The age-old Confucian system slowly disintegrated. The accepted dogmas were assailed by Western ideas of rationalism, pragmatism, and materialism. Traditional Chinese complacency was shattered by confusion and doubt. All efforts to adjust the Confucian world to modern conditions, at a Chinese pace and in accord with conservative Chinese ideas, were defeated by the impatience of the diplomats, traders, missionaries, and soldiers from the West.

SUGGESTED READING

Before looking up books on the Suggested Reading list, be sure to consult the General Bibliographic Note at the end of the book. The list of titles in the General Bibliography provides a useful, basic library for students and teachers. (P) indicates a paperbound book.

Creel, H. G., *Chinese Thought from Confucius to Mao Tse-tung* (Chicago, U. of Chicago, 1953).

Fitzgerald, Charles P., *China, A Short Cultural History* (New York, Praeger, 1954).

Fung Yu-lan, *Short History of Chinese Philosophy* (New York, Macmillan, 1960). (P)

Goodrich, L. C., *Syllabus of the History of Chinese Civilization* (rev. ed.) (New York, China Society of America, 1958).

Hightower, James R., *Topics in Chinese Literature: Outlines and Bibliographies* (Cambridge, Harvard U., 1950).

Hughes, E. R., and Hughes, K., *Religion in China* (London, Hutchinson's University Library, 1958).

Lang, Olga, *Chinese Family and Society* (New Haven, Yale U., 1946).

Latourette, Kenneth Scott, *Chinese, Their History and Culture* (fourth ed.) (New York, Macmillan, 1964).

Lin Yutang, *My Country and My People* (New York, Day, 1939).

————, *Wisdom of China and India* (New York, Modern Library, 1942).

MacNair, Harley, (ed.), *China* (Berkeley, U. of California, 1946).

de Riencourt, Amaury, *Soul of China* (New York, Coward-McCann, 1958).

Reischauer, Edwin O., *Ennin's Diary* (New York, Ronald, 1955).

Teggart, Fredrick J., *Rome and China* (Berkeley, U. of California, 1939).

Willetts, William, *Chinese Art* (New York, Braziller, 1958).

Winfield, Gerald, *China: The Land and the People* (New York, Sloane, 1943).

Wittfogel, Karl A., and Feng Chia-sheng, *History of Chinese Society: Liao, 907–1125* (Philadelphia, American Philosophical Society, 1949).

2

Japan and the Japanese

Japan was less known than China when the Black Ships from the United States opened the doors of Japan to the Western world. It was so remote that few travelers had reached its shores; fewer writers had recorded even superficial impressions. Marco Polo wrote that "the people of the great island of Chipango were white, civilized, and well-favored; idolaters dependent on nobody and possessed of endless quantities of gold." Factual knowledge of Japan was not known abroad until comparatively recent times.

In their isolation, the people of Japan developed distinctive characteristics and behavior patterns. They evolved a rich culture and perfected a social organization which enabled them to pursue a way of life of their own design. Japan was by no means primitive when it was abruptly ushered into the company of the modern world. It was a highly organized, complex, and dynamic society. Although plagued by uncertainty resulting from the collapse of its centuries-old political and social order, it was not eager to end its isolation. It was defiant, but fearful. However, once the die was cast, Japan set to work with fanatical zeal to study and to assimilate the ways of the West. Japan quickly outdistanced its Asian neighbors in its struggle for greatness in terms of the Western-power equation.

THE LAND AND THE PEOPLE

Japan consists of nearly four thousand islands lying in a great arc off the east coast of Asia. They would reach from the mouth of the St. Lawrence to Cuba, or from Vancouver to Lower California. They screen the Asian mainland from Vladivostok to Shanghai, running primarily north

27

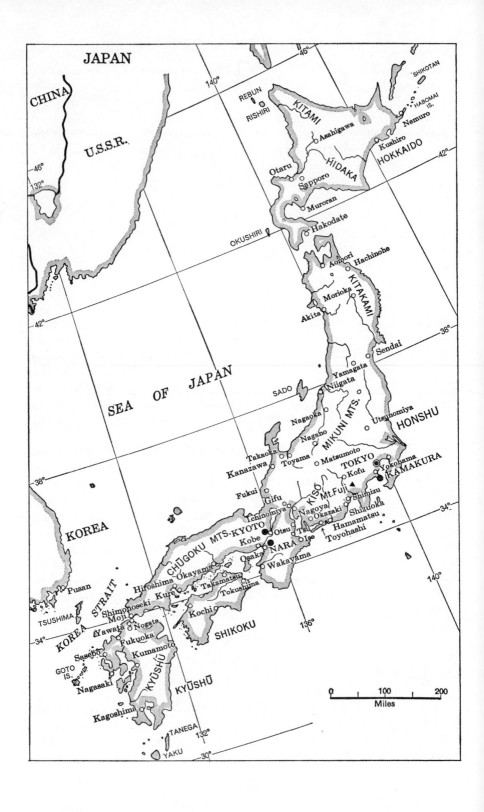

to south but also covering an east-west distance equal to Chicago to San Francisco. The land area of Japan is about the same as Montana or three times as big as Pennsylvania or New York. Japan would fit into the continental United States twenty times over. However, Japan is larger than the British Isles, and it has much the same relationship to Asia that the British Isles have to Europe.

About fifty of the Japanese islands are marked on ordinary maps and a dozen have names which should be remembered. The four main islands are Hokkaido (north sea island) similar to New England in climate and location; Honshu (main island) parallel to Virginia and North Carolina; Shikoku (four provinces) comparable to South Carolina and Kyushu (nine provinces) with a resemblance to Georgia and Florida. At times throughout history Japan has also included the Kurile Islands in the northeast stretching out toward the Aleutians and the large island of Sakhalin or, as the Japanese call it, Karafuto. Japan's sovereignty also extends to the south over Ogasawara or the Bonin Islands and the Ryukyu (Liu Ch'iu) archipelago including Naha Island, commonly known as Okinawa.

Japan is subdivided into forty-six prefectures or provinces which are ordinarily grouped into eight geographic regions. Hokkaido, Shikoku, and Kyushu are considered as single regions. Honshu contains five distinct regions: Tohoku, the north and east, with the city of Sendai as its best known city; Kanto, the eastern edge of the great plain where Tokyo is located; Chubu, or the central section which runs from Niigata and Kanazawa on the west through the beautiful Japanese Alps to Shizuoka and Nagoya on the east; Kinki (also called Kansai) the cradle of Japanese civilization or the western edge of the great plain where Osaka, Kyoto, and Kobe are situated; and Chugoku, in the south and west which has at its one extreme the coldest, most blustery winter weather on the side of the Japan Sea and at the other the calmest, sunniest summers on the side of Hiroshima and the beautiful Inland Sea.

The Japanese islands are uncomfortably close to the continental shoreline. Japan has always been fearful of potential enemies in northeast Asia and at times has chosen to regard Korea, Manchuria, and even North China as its essential lifeline. Hokkaido is only about 150 miles from the coast of Asia, and Sakhalin is a scant ten miles offshore from Siberia. The 125 miles which separate Japan from Korea have been a source of constant worry.

Japan is noted for its picturesque scenery and its temperate climate. Whether in the fishing villages along the coast, in the rice-terraced slopes of northern Honshu, in the snow-covered heights of the Japanese Alps, in the hot springs or the blue lakes of the mountain resorts, among the tiny islets of the Inland Sea, or at the classic Shinto or Buddhist shrines, Japan is a paradise for the color-picture enthusiast. The islands are cut by ribbons of high mountains (Mount Fuji is 12,395 feet high) which are capped in places by active volcanoes which terrorize the country folk with frequent earthquakes. The rivers are short and turbulent. They are excellent for beauty, irrigation, and water power, but practically useless for transportation. They are bountiful in depositing the rich alluvial soil on fertile plains, giving to Japan its best rice lands.

The climate varies from the humid continental to the humid subtropical, with Tokyo remarkably similar to New York or Philadelphia. The summer monsoon blowing in from the southern seas brings heavy rains with frequent typhoons and floods. The winter monsoon from frigid Siberia is offset by the warm *Kuroshio* (Black Current) which flows northward along the west coast of Japan and does for Japan and its climate what the Gulf Stream does for England. The weather in central Japan is seasonal. Summertime is hot and humid; winter is cold, with frost and occasional snows. Springtime is a mass of cherry blossoms and azaleas; autumn is an artist's palette of red, gold, and yellow leaves.

Japan's climate is just right for the cultivation of rice, which is Japan's staple food and traditional measure of value. Without possibility for significant expansion, only fifteen per cent of Japan's land area is arable. It must produce everything: rice, vegetables, mulberry for silkworms, fruits, fibers, and forests. Half of Japan's surface is covered with timber, but the forests must be preserved to prevent erosion. The limited amount of arable land has determined the fragmentary nature of Japan's landholdings and the intensive procedures of Japanese farming. Every available plot of ground seems to be called upon for its contribution to Japan's food requirements. Parks are kept to a minimum if such land could be used for agriculture. Squash vines are used for decoration for even the humblest homes, and castor-bean plants line the narrowest path in the countryside. No group of people work harder under more difficult conditions than the Japanese farmers. A long growing season, ample rainfall, and unstinting application of human effort enable Japan to get from its soil the highest yield of rice in the world, between forty and fifty bushels per acre. Still the farmers are not able to supply all Japan's food needs nor to provide a satisfactory level of living for themselves.

Mineral resources were of little consequence in premodern days, but a glance at Japan's lack of raw materials may help to understand many more recent political and diplomatic attitudes. Japan possesses only coal and copper in appreciable quantities; it is deficient in practically every other requirement of a technological age. The entire annual output of petroleum in Japan is matched in the United States every six hours. Japan's known reserves of iron would not last three months in the United States. Japan must import most of its petroleum, iron, bauxite, zinc, tin, and lead. It must also look abroad for the cotton, wool, and wood plup for its light industries. In spite of these handicaps the Japanese built—and hope to expand—factories turning out steel products, textiles, ships, paper, sugar, machine tools, and the million and one gadgets which earned for Japan the label "Workshop of Asia."

The sea is a major factor in Japan's history. Native waters abound in fish, and Japanese fishermen are among the best in the world. Fish supply the necessary proteins in the national diet, and fishing provides the livelihood for millions of families. Fishing boats manned by Japanese crews ply the seas from Borneo to Alaska. Japanese shipbuilders and sailors have given the nation an excellent navy and merchant marine. Japan has 17,000 miles of coastline, or one mile to every eight square miles of territory. (The United States has 12,877 miles by way of comparison.) Japan has 10,000 miles on the Pacific side, where the bays and harbors are excellent and the winds and currents are gentle. Here are located Tokyo, Yokohama, Nagoya, Kobe, Osaka, and Kyoto. The China side is lashed by the cold currents from the Sea of Okhotsk and the bitter winds from the Asian mainland. Only Kanazawa and Nagasaki have risen to prominence on the western coast. Japan always thinks of itself as having its back on China and facing the United States. The sea has bestowed on the Japanese people a sense of oneness and has afforded them a measure of security. On the other hand, the sea is a highway as well as a moat, and has exposed Japan to a gnawing fear of attack.

The Japanese people are basically Mongoloid, enriched by mixtures of Caucasoid blood from northern Asia and by Malayan and Polynesian strains from the south. Geography has made them a highly homogeneous race, but not more different from the Chinese and the Korean than English are from French or Germans. As in the case of the Chinese, it is dangerous to ascribe specific characteristics to the Japanese. If any generalization is permissible, it may be said that the Japanese are a virile, hardy, and frugal people, possessed with energy and a strong sense of discipline, given to Spartan austerity and intensely proud of their race and nation. They are deeply sensitive, appreciative of the beauties of nature and the minute things in life. They dislike doing wrong things and go to extremes to avoid loss of face. They have matched their skill at copying with a rare inventive and adaptive genius. Although they have different backgrounds and culture values than people rooted elsewhere, they are no more difficult to get to know, to get along with, and to understand than nationals of any other country in the world.

HISTORY

Anthropologists and archaeologists are beginning to unearth factual evidence to add to the references in Chinese chronicles about Japan's early civilization. No paleolithic remains have yet been found, but recently discovered artifacts from neolithic culture show Japan may have been inhabited as early as the third millennium, B.C. Elements of Chinese culture, including use of iron, entered Japan through Korea, then a Chinese colony, as early as the first century, A.D. Japan maintained constant contacts with the continent of Asia after that date and repeatedly invaded southern Korea.

It is probable that Japan at the time of Christ was a land of great clans, descendants of tribes which had migrated from Asia. Clan chieftains were charged primarily with religious functions toward particular deities from which each clan claimed descent. The foremost clan boasted of direct descent from the sun goddess and held court at various spots in the Yamato plain, in the western part of the island of Honshu.

According to the *Kojiki* or "Records of Ancient Matters" and the *Nihongi* or "Chronicles of Japan," compiled respectively in A.D. 712 and 720, the god Izanagi and his goddess Izanami created the sun goddess, who sent her grandson to rule the earth. This grandson, the Emperor Jimmu, bearing the sacred mirror, sword, and jewel as emblems of his divine mission to rule Japan forever, created the state of Yamato on February 11, 660 B.C. (This day, February 11, Kigensetsu, is still one of the great holidays in Japan.) The Japanese myth of creation has inspired innumerable works of art and driven home the idea that the emperor, the land, and the race were themselves divine.

According to the more reliable records dealing with the fifth century and after, rival clans battled for prestige while Japan busily absorbed its continuing importations of Chinese culture. The Soga family came to dominate the chief of the imperial clan, and it championed Buddhism and Chinese learning in general as opposed to its rivals who favored the native way of life. With its sponsorship, frequent missions were sent to China. The greatest of the Soga, Prince Shotoku, was overwhelmed by the brilliance of Chinese culture. As regent in 604, he promulgated a set of injunctions usually known as the Seventeen Articles of the Constitution of Shotoku. He called for the reverence of Buddhism and the adaptation of Confucian ideas of loyalty to the emperor. He attempted to build up a Chinese-style bureaucracy and to lay the moral foundations for national life.

Shotoku's successors continued the uninhibited borrowing of things Chinese. From 645 to 650 the Great Reforms or Taikwa were decreed. These were intended to make Japan more like its dazzling model, T'ang China. The region around the temporary capital of Japan was designated as a central administrative district and the rest of the country was divided into prefectures which were to be ruled by centrally appointed governors. New systems of land tenure, local government, and taxation were introduced, all with the idea of strengthening the central government. While reforms were in full swing, hereditary chieftains of the various clans fought among themselves, not to see who would become emperor but rather to determine who should control him and name his successor. All the chiefs accepted the chief and high priest of the Yamato clan as emperor.

The commonly accepted periods of Japanese history begin with the Nara period, 710–784, when the capital of Japan was fixed at a permanent locality, originally the city of Nara. Actually Nara was created after it was chosen as the capital and it was built after the model of the T'ang capital at Ch'ang An (Sian) which might well have been the most glamorous city in the world at that time. Nara was laid out in checkerboard fashion, with magnificent palaces and residences along its broad avenues. Lands and parks were set aside for great Buddhist temples, which were decorated with artistic masterpieces in painting and sculpture. According to Sir George Sansom, a great scholar of Japanese history, the Nara period was the "blossom time of Japanese civilization, the few bright decades of political ardor, aesthetic awakening and religious exaltation." The power of the Yamato clan expanded throughout central Japan, as the capital city sparkled with its veneer of imperial China. All was new and glittering, but distinctly foreign: Chinese architecture, Chinese costumes, Chinese laws and ordinances, and the very aristocratic Chinese system of writing. Chinese teachers were welcomed, and frequent official embassies were sent to China to study models and precedents. But in the countryside, the peasants continued their dull existence as they looked with awe at the distant city. They grew rice, fed silkworms, paid onerous taxes, served time in the conscript army, and worshiped their native gods.

Nothing shows the antiquity of the Japanese way of life more vividly than the family records of the Fujiwara, whose founder, Kamatari, was associated with the Great Reforms. The Fujiwara family perfected the diarchy or dual system of government: an emperor for prestige and a bureaucracy for power. The emperor should not be bothered by affairs of state or degraded by contacts with common men. His prime responsibility was to guarantee unbroken succession for ages eternal. The Fujiwara made his job easy. Their family furnished all the consorts for the emperor; and as regents or palace dictators they filled the high civil and military posts. They dominated the emperors, who usually passed their lives in the midst of an inane and luxurious court. Fujiwara policy was to act behind the scenes while the emperor enjoyed the ceremony and the dignity of his exalted position.

The next period of Japanese history, the Heian, lasted for four centuries, 784–1185. Because of the intrigue and the weakness of the Nara court, and the growing political menace of the Buddhist temples, the capital of Japan was shifted to nearby Heian-kyo, the modern Kyoto, where it remained until 1868. Kyoto, like Nara, was copied after Sian, and it became one of the world's most beautiful cities. (It was ordered out of bounds and was consequently spared by American bombers in World War II.) While the emperor and his entourage of court nobles dawdled in elegant debauchery, the Fujiwara spent their energies in putting down peasant rebellions, curbing uprisings of Buddhist priests, or fighting against the Ainus, or "hairy barbarians" of northern Japan. Actual power in Japan passed from the central government structure to warrior knights who knew how to handle the swords and crossbows, and who acquired large estates. A provincial military society came into being which was in striking contrast to the effeminacy of the Kyoto aristocracy. This was the beginning of the age of feudalism, vendetta, and local wars, when the loyalty of knights was unreliable, and their services were always obtainable for a price.

When the Kamakura period (1185–1338) was ushered in, the whole country was convulsed by battle, famines, and pestilence. A titanic struggle between two great clans, the Taira and the Minamoto, established beyond question the dominance of the military and gave rise to the system of the shogunate. The successful Minamoto leader, Yoritomo, took for himself the title of Sei-i-tai Shogun, or Barbarian-Subduing-Great-General, and he established his headquarters at Kamakura, near Tokyo, and far from the emperor's capital, which remained in Kyoto. Until 1868, Japan was ruled by successive dynasties of military leaders, nearly all of whom sprang from Minamoto stock. From that time dated the cult of the sword, by which that weapon was invested with mystical qualities which stood for the honor of the Japanese soldier.

Yoritomo called his government the *bakufu* or tent-government. He made his father-in-law Hojo Tokamasa (a Taira) regent, and he did not hesitate to utilize Fujiwara administrators of talent and experience for his constables and stewards. The Japanese governing system during this period was an incredible maze. As Dr. Edwin O. Reischauer has pointed out: "One finds in thirteenth century Japan an emperor who was a mere puppet in the hands of a retired emperor and of a great court family, the Fujiwara, who together controlled a government which was in fact merely a sham government, completely dominated by the private government of the Shogun—who in turn was a puppet in the hands of a Hojo regent."

Under the Hojo regents, foreign affairs were unstable and dangerous. No Japanese mission had been sent to China since 890, but Japanese monks and students had gone to Chinese centers of learning. Japanese pirates roamed the China seas, and adventurers continuously carried out raids on the Korea coast. In 1263 Kublai Khan made Korea his vassal and aspired to the conquest of Japan. Mongol fleets twice reached the shores of Japan but were shipwrecked by the *kamikaze* or "divine winds" which the Japanese believed were sent from heaven.

As the frugal simplicity of the *bakufu* vanished, the shogun became as powerless as the emperor. Wars between the feudal clans multiplied, and their rivalries deepened the schisms between the Hojo regents and their none-too-devoted followers. In the summer of 1333, Kamakura was sacked and burned. The regent and more than two hundred of his loyal retainers committed suicide rather than surrender.

The Ashikaga period (1336–1603) was an interlude of complete anarchy. Old feudal families were wiped out and new ones arose to take their place. The Ashikaga family climbed from obscurity to a position of great power by absorbing the lands and rights of others, including even imperial estates. It established the shogunate in the Muramachi district of Kyoto, close to the imperial palace. No member of the imperial family showed himself capable of mastery or leadership. For nearly a century, there were two claimants to the imperial throne, both residing in or near Kyoto. The imperial institution reached its lowest ebb in 1500 when the body of an ex-emperor remained unburied for six weeks and the enthronement ceremony for his successor was postponed for twenty years because there was no money in the treasury. At the same time, the peasants' lands were trampled over, the crops requisitioned or destroyed, and the taxes increased. The traditions of the military caste were compromised by the great numbers of commoners who took to fighting as the only way to obtain food. The central government exhausted itself in domestic turmoil and had neither the strength nor the sagacity to cope with the Portuguese, Spanish, Dutch, and British who reached Japan.

The stage was set for the introduction of the Tokugawa period (1603–1868) and the three great heroes of Japanese song and story: Oda Nobunaga, Toyotomi Hideyoshi, and Tokugawa Iyeyasu. Of the personality of the first it was said, "If the cuckoo doesn't sing, I'll kill him"; of the second, "If the cuckoo doesn't sing, I'll make him"; and of the third, "If the cuckoo doesn't sing, I'll wait till he does." In 1567 Nobunaga, who came from Nagoya, was invited by the court to restore order in Kyoto. He took command of the capital, becoming dictator of central Japan. He destroyed the power of the great monasteries and took the temple-castle of Osaka after a ten-year siege. An uncompromising individual, he made many personal enemies and was killed by a disgruntled retainer. His successor, Hideyoshi, who was of humble birth but took the name of Toyotomi, a relative of the Fujiwara, was appointed regent in 1584; he succeeded in pacifying most of the country. Political unity was complete, and peace returned after a hundred years of incessant war. Hideyoshi hesitated to demobilize his troops and risked the unsuccessful conquest of Korea. In 1592 he transported 200,000 men to Korea and fought his way to the modern Pyongyang and the extreme northeast frontier along the Tumen River. He slaughtered thousands of Chinese and Koreans and sent their ears and noses back to Japan, where they were buried in the famous ear mound at Kyoto. But he was unable to complete his conquest. In 1598 Hideyoshi died and his expedition collapsed. His son and successor, Hideyori, was defeated at the battle of Sekigahara, October 21, 1600 by Iyeyasu, the chief deputy of Hideyoshi in eastern Japan and the founder of the Tokugawa shogunate.

Japan was entirely refashioned during the Tokugawa period. Iyeyasu's obsession was to build up a political system which would live after his own death. Tokyo became the military, administrative, economic, and cultural center of Japan. The entire country was dominated by a line of shoguns who adopted a strict legal code designed to guarantee domestic peace and perpetuate the shogunate in power. Feudalism did not pass away as in Europe but reached the peak of development. The administrative system became more centralized and autocratic than ever. Power was exercised by the paramount feudal Tokugawa shogun of Tokyo while the emperor continued his sheltered, isolated position in Kyoto. Like their predecessors, the Tokugawa shoguns attempted to freeze society as it was at the moment of their triumph. Economic pressures, spiritual unrest, and internal political rivalry meant that the old system in Japan was ready to explode when Admiral Perry arrived to ignite the fuse.

CULTURE AND CIVILIZATION

The cultural history of Japan is as fascinating as its political history. The Japanese developed a way of life which is as distinctive as the landscape of their picturesque islands. Their homes and social customs have evolved from a thousand years of adaptation to their native environment. The open, airy, structure of houses; the sparing use of materials, chiefly paper and wood; the thick, soft straw mats on the floor; the sliding paper panels instead of walls; the recess for a single display of art objects; the charcoal heating utensils; the peculiar wooden and iron bathtubs; and the exquisite blending of home and garden are unique to Japan. They attest to a cultural vitality which was creative as well as imitative.

The Japanese were never blind imitators. They selected and adapted what they wanted and rejected the rest. They absorbed foreign externals, but they kept their inner selves intact. From the beginning of their history, they were deeply influenced by Chinese civilization. They borrowed Chinese ideographs, but they developed their own system of writing. They borrowed Confucianism, but they modified its ethics and adjusted its political doctrines to their own scheme of things. They accepted

Buddhism, but they remolded its alien characteristics to satisfy their own spiritual needs.

Culture in Japan was the preserve of the aristocracy. This accounts for the meticulous attention to the formal, the ceremonious, the stylistic, and the elegantly expressed in art and learning. The sensuous, effeminate elements in the Japanese cultural tradition reflected the life of the courtiers; the ribald, adventurous stories and pictures were products of ages of feudalism, fighting, lusty living, and quick death. The Japanese noble was a curious combination of the humane, the aesthetic, and the militaristic. The lowliest of the Japanese masses seemed to possess an artistic instinct and an inherent respect for learning.

The Japanese language is difficult but not so impossible as often believed, and it is the surest guide to Japanese psychology and temperament. Japanese is not merely a Chinese dialect. It is a distinct Japanese creation and an integral part of the culture. It has its own rules of grammar and its own script, complicated and enriched by liberal use of Chinese characters. In Japanese words, every syllable is pronounced, without stress on any syllable unless marked with the appropriate accent. In Japanese names, the family name comes first and the given name second. Thus Tōjō Hideki is Mr. Tōjō and Hideki is his first name.

As with China, language and literature are at the core of Japan's culture. The finest example of Japanese prose-writing dates from the eleventh century—Lady Murasaki's *Tale of the Genji*. Through the ages, poetry was the greatest of the literary forms; and its ancient themes were love of beauty and nature. The *Manyô-shû* or *Collection of Myriad Leaves* and the *Kokin-shû* or *Poems Ancient and Modern* were compiled by imperial command and were more than five hundred years old when Columbus discovered America. Poetic ability in ancient times was perhaps more highly prized by the upper classes than any other skill. The composing of poems was an essential feature of court functions, social parties, and romantic adventures. Out of the raw materials of Chinese poetry, the Japanese developed their own exquisite *haiku*, seventeen-syllable poems, and *tanka,* or thirty-one-syllable forms. In time other forms of literature became popular—the sentimental diary, romantic diary, romantic novel, deeply Buddhistic *nô* plays and the more dramatic *kabuki* plays. Poetry, like religion and the arts, was not for specialists and patrons only, but was the common coin of all cultivated men. Even warriors were encouraged to spend half their time in scholarly or artistic pursuits.

Painting was originally the handmaiden of religion and nature, devoted to the lives of Buddha or the saints, and to landscapes, flowers and animals, usually Chinese-style. The ensemble of painting, poetry, and calligraphy was revered in Japan as it was in China. Later it became fashionable to paint political subjects, such as battle scenes or portraits of great warriors. Paintings were more decorative than profound. Japanese fans, gold-leaf screens, and wood-block prints combined manual dexterity and aesthetic sensitivity.

The earliest Japanese efforts at sculpture were crude grave figures in clay and larger hollow figures modeled in dry lacquer. Stone sculpture was rare, perhaps because of the lack of marble and granite. Volcanic rocks were not the best materials for carving. Buddhist statues were made of bronze or wood and at least one piece, the Yumedono Kwannon at Horyuji near Nara, is one of the artistic masterpieces of all time. The Daibutsu or Great Buddha of Kamakura is the largest and the most remarkable example of bronze casting in the world. The most vigorous Japanese sculpture was not evident in human figures or the conventional Buddhas, but in the semihuman guardian-divinities usually seen at the entrance of Buddhist temples.

Although Japanese architecture was heavily indebted to China, there was no mistaking the Japanese quality in the temples at Nara and Kyoto, the gold and silver pavilions in Kyoto and the lavish shrines in Nikko as random examples. Those masterpieces testified to Japan's cultural vitality, but no more so than such commonplace and universal evidences of Japan's creative genius as the *torii* or arches which dot the Japanese landscape, and the native arts of swordmaking, flower arrangement, and the tea ceremony.

The aesthetic sense was as important to Japan as philosophy to China or religion to India. Japan was content to borrow its ideology, or system of thought, from China and only to make those amendments which the Japanese political system required. Because of its isolation and its embarrassing position of apparent inferiority to its overpowering Chinese neighbor, Japan nurtured a fierce pride in its own nationalism. It was touchy about any slur on its own qualities or any lack of recognition of its assumed rights. Because of the prevalence of feudalism and the uninterrupted internal wars, Japan evolved its own peculiar system of *Bushido,* or the way of the warrior. This code for knightly behavior, like chivalry in Europe, was neither so glamorous nor so universally respected as usually implied; but it was accepted as a basis of practical ethics in Japan. Honor, courage, loyalty to chief, self-control, austerity, and generous treatment of a fallen foe were extolled as the greatest of human virtues. The cherry blossom was the ideal symbol of all human life; it was doomed to die at the height of its youth and beauty. The hero in Japanese fiction was the loyal retainer who, in contempt for life, would destroy himself to demonstrate his loyalty to his defeated lord.

In later years, *Bushido* became tied to the emperor system. Loyalty to the feudal chieftain was replaced by loyalty to the emperor. Even in earliest times, clan leaders took pride in their devotion to the emperor, no matter how weak or insignificant he might have been. A sixth-century clan record stated: "By the sea our corpses shall rot in the grass; we will die by the side of our sovereign, we will never look back." Nevertheless, during the civil war between clans, the emperor was neglected. The only loyalty which mattered was that of vassal, as warrior, to his lord. In peacetime, it was difficult to preserve the martial qualities of the men while restraining their energies within the bounds of law and order. Japan's philosophers called upon ancient Confucian teachings of loyalty and propriety and fashioned the code of *Bushido,* which stressed loyalty as a duty and self-sacrifice as a jewel. Death in the service of the state or the emperor was restored in Japanese ethics as the supreme fulfillment of life. Personal feelings were to be disregarded. These ideas were not formalized into precise rules of conduct, but they became dominant themes in historical novels and popular plays. Ordinary Japanese could no more live up to the ideals of *Bushido* than most Christians could live up to the precepts of the Sermon on the Mount. However, they were provided with high standards of conduct, and such standards served to vitalize Japan as it became a modern nation.

The love of beauty and the acceptance of *Bushido* were no more characteristic of Japan than the prevalence of religion in its daily life. Religion was more than ritual worship or church organization; it was the feeling of awe in the presence of the miracles of nature, the exhilaration of the shrine festivals, the serenity of simple faith which does not pretend to understand the great unknown, but feels somehow that all is right between man and his gods. No single religious system prevailed in Japan. Confucianism set the standards of private and public morality, and Shinto provided the outlet for thoughts and feelings about the beauties of nature and the love of country. Buddhism was identified with mysterious metaphysical and spiritual problems. Almost every Japanese was a follower of Shinto and one in two professed faith in the teachings of Buddha. Comparatively few accepted Christianity. Most homes had simple Shinto shrines and elaborately carved Buddhist family altars. Part of the daily domestic routine was to light candles or offer flowers to Shinto deities and to place a small bowl of rice, sweets, or fruits in front of the Lord Buddha. Shinto priests were usually called upon to preside over rites connected with birth, while Buddhists were favored when loved ones died. Everybody liked to celebrate festivals or to make pilgrimages to any shrine or temple, regardless of faith or religious affiliation.

Originally, Shinto was a simple pantheistic worship of the forces of nature. Sacrifices were offered to the *kami,* or spirits, who resided in the sun, moon, mountains, streams, and everywhere. Simple shrines were built in the style of the ancient thatched-roof peasant home. There was no place for worship or a congregation. The ceremony consisted of the worshiper's washing his hands, clapping them together or ringing a bell to attract the attention of the spirits, casting a coin to the *kami*, praying for material blessings, and making a farewell bow. The faith of Shinto was based on appreciation, not fear, and its ceremony was concerned with purity, not sin.

Under later influence from China, Shinto was formalized and institutionalized. The ancestors of the family, the clan and the emperor were added to the list of kami. The central theme of Shinto became, "Thou shalt honor the gods and love thy country, revere the emperor, and obey his will." Thus it became the creed of nationalism and the rallying point for all the disgruntled elements under the Tokugawa Shogunate who looked at the restoration of the emperor as the first step toward national regeneration.

Shintoism was the backbone of Japanese religion, but for a thousand years Buddhism was its flesh and blood. Buddhism brought spiritual comfort and promise of paradise. Buddhism was introduced into Japan early in the sixth century by a Chinese monk from Korea. He brought with him Buddhist images and copies of the Buddhist scriptures. These were not only the teachings of Buddha but the literary treasure house of the wisdom and learning of India and China. From the first, Buddhism stimulated the arts. The Japanese took to copying the Buddhist sutras, built temples for the carved figures of the gods and painted pictures for religious adornment. The priests lived in large monasteries, acquired lands, and became powerful politically as well as spiritually. The common people did not understand the esoteric parts of Buddhism, but they were awed by its art and architecture and intrigued with the idea that they could gain merit, in this life and later, by the performance of good deeds.

Buddhism, like Shinto and Christianity, split into many sects, with such names as True Word, Pure Land, Nichiren, or Zen. Some taught salvation through the gift of the Lord Buddha; others taught that enlightenment came only through introspection, meditation, and self-purification. But all Buddhists had some things in common: indifference to the charms of the world and the search for Nirvana or Buddhist perfection. The advocacy of frugality and the complete mastery of self complemented the code of *Bushido*. Buddhism supplied the emotional outlet and the spiritual stimulus for an entire nation. Buddhism, neo-Confucianism, and Shinto were all deeply imbedded in the soul of Japan when that nation entered the modern stream of world affairs.

SOCIAL AND ECONOMIC LIFE

Japanese society always tended toward rigidity in class structure, with each individual assigned to his proper place. In earliest times, the clans were highly organized, with their chieftains, commoners, and slaves. After the emergence of the emperor system, the members of the imperial family, the court nobles, and the knights formed the upper classes. Commoners included farmers, priests, artisans, and merchants. After centuries of feudalism and the establishment of the shogunate, the emperor and his court kept their unique standing. However, the real power and prestige in Japan's social fabric derived from the shogunate; the daimyo, who were the heads of the leading families and the masters of the great tax-free estates; and the samurai, who were the warrior-administrators in the services of their individual feudal lords.

In contrast to China where the intelligentsia and the scholar-gentry made up the aristocracy, in Japan the military caste enjoyed great distinction. Only the professional warriors were permitted to bear arms. The right to carry two swords and to cut down on the spot anyone who offended or insulted him were the distinguishing marks of the samurai. Far down the social scale, peasants were only peasants and landless tenants were less. Artisans and merchants were looked upon as necessary but unimportant; and the eta or mean people—the beggars, butchers, tanners, and executioners—were treated as though they were outside the human race.

The countryside was the stable and conservative element in Japan's social structure; the rural village was the backbone of its society. As the court weakened, and the shogunate was torn with intrigue and dissension, people in the provinces were obliged to take care of themselves. They depended upon their family, kinfolk, neighbors, and fellow members of labor associations, guilds, and temples for mutual protection. A complicated system called *oyabun kobun* roughly comparable to American bosses and gangsters came into being. Knights or estate managers came to look to their own strength to preserve their lands and position. In exchange for protection, they received the loyalty of landlords, rural leaders in the villages, small landholders, and tenants. The new daimyo or feudal lords outside of Kyoto or Kamakura found their interests much more closely identified with the lesser people in their own region than with the central administration or nobles in the distant court.

The lives of the lesser people revolved around the small family circle, not the elaborate extended family. The traditional household consisted of three generations in direct male line: the husband and wife, unmarried children, eldest son and his wife and children. Members of a family were conscious of their mutual obligations: blood relationship was paramount in getting a job or in receiving help in time of trouble. The family owned the real estate and settled such domestic matters as conflicts over wills, divorce or illegitimate children. The father and the most capable son were the most important members of the household because of their obligations in worshiping the ancestors and providing for the family lineage. Adoption was a common practice. If there was no son in the family, one was adopted. He could have been a cousin, a son-in-law, or a total stranger. The *koseki*, or family record, was the register of vital statistics and was very useful for police supervision. Marriages were arranged by go-betweens, and were based on economic status and social position rather than romantic love. Legal marriage consisted of the formal transfer of a bride's registration from the *koseki* of her father to that of her husband. And the bride went to live in the house of the groom and his mother.

As a matter of fact the position of women in Japan seemed to get worse through the ages. In ancient times women were among the most honored of the gods. They were high priestesses of the clan and frequently empresses. Women were the greatest of Japanese novelists. By the time of the Tokugawa, they were to be "ever on the alert and keep a strict watch over their own conduct." They were to rise early and at night go late to rest, being ever intent on the duties of the household and never weary of weaving, sewing, and spinning. It was better for women "that they should not be educated, because their lot through life must be one of perfect obedience . . . obedience to a father before marriage, to a husband when married and to a son when widowed." Yet it was important "that she should be morally trained, so that she will always be gentle and chaste, never giving way to passion inconvenient to others, nor questioning the authority of her elders." For her no religion was necessary either, because "her husband is her sole heaven and in serving him and his lies her whole duty." Women were to abstain from luxuries, such as tea and tobacco; and husbands were told that if their wives were flighty and liked such vices as visiting temples, they were to be divorced at once.

Feudalism licensed the farmer to live in contented humility most of the time, but it crushed him without scruple when he attempted to assert himself or dared to protest against his assigned role as a plodding beast of burden. High rents and taxes drove thousands from the farms, and prevalent insecurity caused more thousands to surrender their lands to temples or stronger neighbors in exchange for promises of protection. Much of Japan's rural population consisted of landless tenants. Constant worry over paying the family bills gave rise to the common practice of killing the aged or the unwanted girl-babies. Earthquakes, famine, flood, and pestilence kept the farmers perpetually on the verge of desperation.

The ordinary peasant was tied to his paddy and hamlet; to him foreign affairs meant typhoons, floods, earthquakes, or the government. The things which really mattered were the weather, festivals, taxes, land rents, and water rights. Wars, revolutions, and overseas expeditions were only important as they took his sons or emptied his rice bowl. His pleasures were simple, and to the sophisticated city-dwellers farm life seemed drab and onerous. One government official on being sent to the provinces in the last century wrote in his diary: "I have fallen unawares into hell."

Japan would have been doomed to Malthusian stagnation had the economic pressures on the peasants not been relieved by the growth of industry and commerce. Many peasants were spare-time artisans, but Japan produced increasing numbers of full-time highly skilled artisans and handicraftsmen. The ancient records spoke of heredity guilds of sericulturists, construction workers (particularly for temples), yeast brewers, diviners, and highway workers. In due course the Japanese learned to mine gold and silver and to manufacture swords, textiles, sake, armor, and furniture. They were superb in lacquer, ceramics, enamel, bronze, and silk brocades.

The merchants did not rise in the social scale, but they became increasingly active and increasingly wealthy. Under the Ashikaga shogunate, the shogun styled himself "King of Japan" so he could send tribute or trading missions to Ming China. He dispensed licenses to local daimyo and Buddhist temples to take part in the lucrative exchange of Japanese gold, pearls, lumber, fans, and folding screens for Chinese silks, porcelains, books, paintings, and copper coins. In the sixteenth century the eastern seas from Tokyo to Manila and Bangkok were filled with Japanese traders and pirates.

Economic and social life took on a new complexion under the Tokugawa. In perpetuating their power, the shoguns were determined to freeze Japan into an everlasting social mold. Lands were resurveyed. One quarter of the productive land was kept by the Tokugawa themselves, while production and tax quotas, totalitarian-style, were prescribed for the rest. Peasants were tied to their own lands; no change of status or residence was allowed. If a peasant deserted or ran away, his whole village was punished. Strict surveillance over every type of human activity was carried out by *tonari gumi* or neighborhood associations of five to ten families. These omnipresent small groups were combined into ward associations in the cities and into village and town associations in the countryside for purposes of supervision and control.

Tenants and peasants eked out the barest existence, while landowners and villages prospered. The merchants were the favored people; many became fabulously rich. Castle towns became great market places. By 1800 Tokyo had a million people and Osaka half as many. Some merchant families owed their affluence to overseas trade, which the Tokugawa tried to preserve in spite of their fears of the newly arrived European missionaries and traders. In spite of the seclusion policy (which will be discussed later), the shoguns continued to issue licenses to trade with Korea, China, and the South Seas. As many as 10,000 Japanese made their homes in the trading cities of Asia before the shogun issued his famous orders forbidding the construction of ocean-going vessels and the emigration of Japanese subjects.

The merchants did not unite against the government or the nobility as they did in Europe. They reaped profits from government contracts, and they shared the wealth in bribery and corruption. A brisk business flourished in the marriage of wealthy daughters and the sons of nobles. Many of the samurai became merchants and deserted the countryside for the cities. The cities bubbled with life and excitement. The art of the period (which the Japanese called *genroku*)—the flash and color of painting, the popular *kabuki* drama, light and frothy novels, and the preoccupation with *geisha* and the amusement quarters—reflects the glamour and gaudy spirit of the age. Prosperous city people were eager for anything which promised new thrills, higher profits, and perhaps more fredom.

The ferment in the cities was the exception to the Tokugawa way of life. For two hundred and fifty years Japan was ruled by a regime which told the people what religion to support, what clothes to wear, and what foods to serve. Instead of being the lusty, adventurous people who had lived and brawled with abandon in the feudal age, the Japanese became thoroughly regimented and utterly dependent on government authorities to tell them what to do. Spontaneity gave way to discipline and self-control.

The police state forced standards of behavior which are often misinterpreted as Japanese characteristics. Regardless of what the Japanese were like inside, or how they felt, they were constrained to mask their feelings, to be polite and to do the right thing on every occasion. They were taught to laugh, no matter how much they felt like crying. Whether the Japanese committed ceremonial suicide, expressed emotion or looked cold as steel, welcomed the foreigner or fought against him were not matters of mind and heart; they were the dictates of the social code. Law and order were preserved in Japan, but at the price of a strait-jacketed society and outdated feudal structure which were the fruits of the Tokugawa regime.

The Tokugawa Political System

When one considers how little was known of the complicated internal situation in Japan at the time of its opening, it is remarkable that Admiral Perry did as well as he did. In substance, Japan was a "centralized feudalism," as many Japanese scholars call it, a combination of native experience and political importations from China.

The emperor was a mere figurehead living in Kyoto, three hundred miles away from Perry's landing point. The emperor had no power, no responsibilities, and no contacts with strong daimyo. He was expected to devote himself to his religious duties and to the enjoyment of the arts and belles-lettres. He had no personal income from taxes, and he depended upon such money as was allotted to him by the mighty shogunate in Tokyo. He was surrounded by the kuge, or court nobles, who were no longer dictators over anything but matters of style and taste. The most capable of their sons were given jobs in what was left of the ancient bureaucracy or imperial administrative system.

The headquarters of the shogunate was the fortress-castle in Tokyo which subsequently became the imperial palace. The shogun, or the strongest of the feudal lords, made no effort to make himself emperor. He was in theory a generalissimo in the service of the emperor. He was in fact the head of an administrative system which was held together by bonds of family relationships, long ties of friendship and traditions of mutual support. The shogun ruled directly over the central part of Japan containing much of the best agricultural lands and its most important cities. Three cadet branches of the Tokugawa clan were established at three key posts: Mito, Nagoya, and Wakayama. One half of the rest of the country controlled by the shogun was entrusted to *fudai*, or inside lords who gave their loyalty to the Tokugawa before the battle of Sekigahara. These *fudai* were given the best estates near Tokyo and the strategic spots along the highways leading to and from the capital. The rest of the shogun's dominion was placed in the hands of the *tozama*, or outside lords whose loyalty was of a later date. The outside lords—Satsuma, Choshu, Tosa, and Hizen, among others—lived at a greater distance from the capital and consequently were more independent. They were wealthier and, being closer to the shores of China, were more exposed to echoes of ideas from the Western world.

The Tokugawa administrative machine was so efficient that it could operate without a strong personality at the head. The chief policymaking group was a council of state, consisting of four or five elders; and the chief administrative body was a junior council of four to six "junior elders." An extensive bureaucracy handled finance, revenues, and affairs of the temples. Censors and secret police kept the shogun well informed about all classes of society. The chief magistrates in the cities and the shogun's representatives in the countryside were channels of communication between Tokyo and the heads of the local associations.

The law of the land was a kind of peacetime martial law. Laws for the imperial court were meant to prevent intrigue, and laws of the military houses were designed to forestall rebellion. Laws for the people were general admonitions or maxims which could be interpreted according to whim. The whole government was based on paternalism and regimentation.

The shogun took no chances on ambitious or rebellious daimyo. In addition to laying down the laws for their behavior, he bound them to him by repeated loyalty oaths. No daimyo could visit Kyoto. The shogun had to approve all marriages and alliances, and he schemed to keep the daimyo in financial distress. No one but himself could collect tolls or set up check points on public highways. No lesser lord could build a new castle or repair his old one without specific permission. Whenever a daimyo seemed to amass too much wealth, he was given the honor of building a new shrine, improving the roads, or making a contribution to the Tokugawa treasury. Every daimyo had to keep a second and expensive household in Tokyo, where he had to live every other year. When he returned to his own estates, he was obliged to leave his family in the capital city as hostages—thus the constant lookout for women going out and guns going in as weathervanes of rebellion.

Within these limitations, each daimiate was a small world to itself. It made its own laws, levied its own taxes, and maintained its own army. It had its own departments of treasury, justice, census, military affairs, coinage and currency, and public works. A large administrative team was required to take care of the rice storehouse, the arrow and spear arsenal, prisons, theaters, bridges, roads, schools, breakwaters, mills, and the family castle. Technical competence was needed to keep the records in order for the census, tax rolls, paper money and copper coinage, and labor service.

Astute statecraft gave Japan nearly three centuries of precarious peace. But the Tokugawas were not superior men, and they collapsed because of their shortcomings. They were so preoccupied with preserving the old that they were not prepared to cope with the new. They did not open jobs for people outside their own families. The official bureaucracy became notoriously inefficient and corrupt while brilliant rivals entered the priesthood or the army. They could not hold out against new intellectual trends. They relied upon neo-Confucianism, with its doctrines of unquestioned loyalty to the regime and proper relationships between unequals, to provide the theoretic underpinning of the regime. They were unable to satisfy the demands of two rising groups of scholars. One group insisted that Japan should take greater pride in its own national self, should extol Shintoism, and should give its political loyalty to the emperor rather than the shogun. The other called attention to the learning of the West—in medicine, military science, and political power—and urged Japan to discard its isolation. Thanks to their teaching, and in spite of Tokugawa opposition, Japan was spiritually ready to receive the West at the moment of its appearance and was in position to discard its feudal shell in favor of the more efficient political forms of the modern nation-state.

SUGGESTED READING

Anesaki, Masaharu, *Religious Life of the Japanese People* (revised by Hideo Kishimoto) (Tokyo, Kokusai Bunka Shinkokai, 1961). (P)

Beasley, W. G., and Pulleybank, E. G., *Historians of China and Japan* (New York, Oxford, 1961).

Benedict, Ruth, *Crysanthemum and the Sword* (Boston, Houghton, 1946).

Bowers, Faubion, *Japanese Theater* (New York, Hermitage, 1952). (P)

Boxer, Charles R., *Christian Century in Japan* (Berkeley, U. of California, 1951).

Brower, Robert H., and Miner, Earl, *Japanese Court Poetry* (Stanford, Stanford U., 1961).

Henderson, Harold G., *Introduction to Haiku* (Garden City, Doubleday, 1958). (P)

Ienaga, Saburo, *History of Japan* (Tokyo, Japan Travel Bureau, 1959).

Ikku Jippensha, *Hizakurige or Shank's Mare* (trans. by Thomas Stachell) (Rutland, Tuttle, 1960). (P)

Kidder, Jonathan Edward, *Japan Before Buddhism* (volume 10 of *Ancient Peoples and Places*) (London, Thames & Hudson, 1959).

Ono Sokyo, *Shinto, the Kami Way* (Rutland, Tuttle, 1962).

Sansom, Sir George B., *History of Japan to 1334* (Stanford, Stanford U., 1958).

————, *History of Japan from 1334 to 1615* (Stanford, Stanford U., 1960). The third volume, which covers the history of Japan to 1868, was in press in 1963.

Silberman, Bernard S., *Japanese Character and Culture, Selected Readings* (Tucson, U. of Arizona, 1962).

Statler, Oliver, *Japanese Inn* (New York, Random, 1961). (P)

Terry, Charles S., (ed.), *Masterworks of Japanese Art* (Rutland, Tuttle, 1962).

Warner, Langdon, *Enduring Art of Japan* (Cambridge, Harvard U., 1952). (P)

Watts, Alan W., *Way of Zen* (New York, Pantheon, 1957). (P)

3

The Indian Subcontinent

India, with its long history and rich culture, has in large measure shaped the life of its neighbors. It is the largest of the new nations of the world, but it is also the home of an ancient civilization. The influence of India has extended to the north and east to the cultural frontiers of China.

When Europeans first sailed toward the rising sun, the Far East meant the Indies—India and beyond. So far as Europeans were concerned, all the new and strange peoples of south and Southeast Asia were conveniently called Indios or Indians. The Portuguese rounding the Cape of Good Hope before the time of Columbus did not discover India because *Sindhu,* or the country of the river Indus, was already known to the ancient Greeks. In biblical times, Indian products were sought by King Solomon for his temple. Romans squandered their wealth for the spices, luxurious textiles, and jewels of India. The Europeans of the Middle Ages had vague ideas about the wealth of the Indies, but they knew little about India's immensity and complexity. Europeans discovered the new world in their eager search for a passage to India.

On the eve of the arrival of Europeans, India was already a racial and linguistic hodgepodge. It was a land of contrasts between fantastic luxury and wretched poverty, and it was the melting pot of the great religions of Asia. In spite of these diversities, it had achieved a cultural personality and evolved a distinctive way of life. However, it was less fortunate in the political realm. India as a nation or a political unit did not exist. The country was divided into a congeries of rebellious principalities and confederacies. An alien dynasty at Delhi, in spite of its glamour, was without effective power to resist the shrewd traders and lusty adventurers from the Western world.

48

THE LAND AND THE PEOPLE

India, slightly smaller than China and ten times bigger than Japan, forms with Pakistan, Burma, and Ceylon the subcontinent of south Asia. Ceylon is a lush green offshore island separated from the mainland by a shallow strait. Modern Pakistan has no distinct geographic boundary on the Indian side and was part of India until partition in 1947. Burma is cut off from India proper by hills and jungles. It is a transition land which might be treated either as a part of India or of Southeast Asia.

The great peninsula of India, bathed by tropical waters and capped by snowy mountains, is in reality four countries. It extends two thousand miles from Cape Comorin on the south to the Himalayas on the north. Its landscapes vary from the highest peaks in the world to vast river deltas only a few inches above the level of the sea; from the world's dustiest, thirstiest deserts to its most tangled and steaming jungles.

The four distinct regions of India are the roof lands in the north, the river valleys at the foot of the hills, the plateaus of central India, and the coastal plains which fringe the plateau and join together at the southern tip of the peninsula. The mountains are like mountains everywhere— only higher, colder, and more majestic. They form a frontier with China nearly two thousand miles in length. Intrepid merchants and missionaries can cross the passes between China and India, but hostile armies and raiding parties have never been able to muster sufficient strength to advance beyond Tibet or Nepal. Although both India and China are located in Asia, they have had little direct contact with one another through the ages. The subcontinent's northern frontier with Afghanistan is less formidable and is breached by the historic Khyber Pass.

The mountains slope off into foothills and gradually give way to the plains of the Indus River in the northwest and the Ganges and the Brahmaputra in the north and east. The Indus River system, fed by the five streams of the Punjab, is the heart of that part of India which has become modern West Pakistan. It extends from Peshawar and Lahore to Karachi. It waters the parched deserts of Punjab and Sind; and divides Baluchistan on the right bank from Rajasthan (Rajputana) and Gujarat on the left. These names sound strange, but they are to India what the names of the states on the banks of the Mississippi are to the United States. The Indus Valley is the site of the earliest culture of India. In today's world its irrigation dams and canals make the difference between food and starvation for a hundred million peasants.

The Jumna and Ganges rivers, which are to each other as the Missouri and the Mississippi, flow eastward from the Indian continental divide.

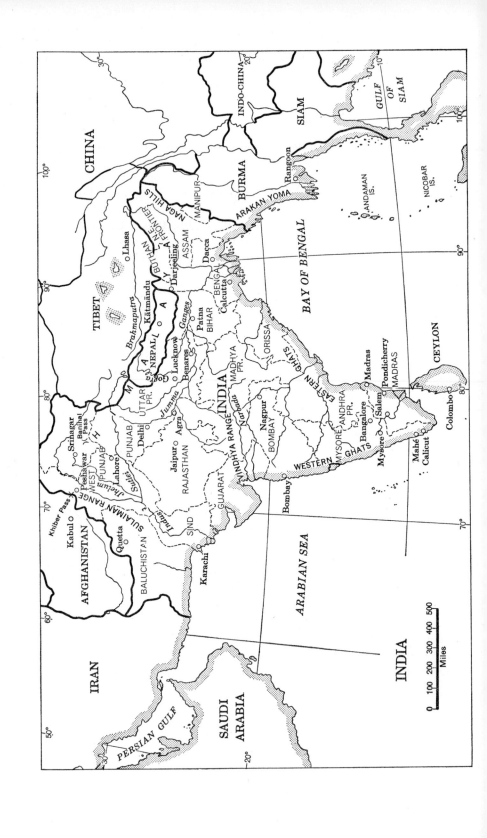

INDIA

Their fertile valleys formed the easy invasion route toward Bengal for raiders who had successfully negotiated the Khyber Pass. The Jumna flows past Delhi and Agra, joins with the Ganges at Allahabad, and continues slowly to the side of Benares and Patna on the way to the sea. The Ganges is the Hindu holy river, and its waters are expected to provide food for one of the most tragically populated areas in the world.

The Deccan plateau, or the clear triangle of central and south India, lies south of the Narbada River. It is separated from the plains of Hindustan (the classic name of the upper Ganges Valley) by burning deserts and the east-west range of the Vindhya Mountains. This tableland averages three thousand feet in elevation and resembles that part of the United States between the Sierras and the Rockies. The soil is poor and the population sparse. The plateau is cut by east or west-flowing rivers and it is separated from the coastal plains by ranges known as the Eastern and Western Ghats.

The strips of land along the seashores are narrow and not easily accessible from the interior. They are fertile and heavily populated. The Coramandel coast on the east was the center of ancient commerce with Malaya and the islands of Farther India; the Malabar coast on the west provided the first havens for mariners who had sailed from Africa.

The climate of India varies from steaming heat and burning winds of the plains and plateaus to the subzero storms and perpetual snows of Mount Everest. It is all a matter of location, season, and altitude. Bangalore, near the equator but high above sea level, is milder than Delhi a thousand miles away. The hill stations are comparatively cool in the daytime and genuinely cold at night. Delhi may be freezing cold in the short winter months and stifling hot (120 degrees) in the long summer. For nine months of the year the sun seems to be a glaring ball of fire which relentlessly consumes all human energy. In the subtropical Deccan, the seasons are marked by the monsoon rains. The oppressive heat of summer is punctuated by torrential downpours. Too much rain brings the terror of floods; but when the monsoon fails, humanity is cursed with drought and famine.

Geography has used a firm hand in shaping the destiny of India. It has determined the agricultural way of life and forced ninety percent of India's people into hundreds of thousands of yellow mud-made villages. It explains the alternation of good harvests and famine years, and why "water" is the ceaseless cry of the land. Living through a calendar year in India makes it clear why the people seem to be slow and deliberate in their movements, why speed and physical drive are alien to India's values, and why meditation in the scarce shade is regarded as one of mankind's most pleasant and rewarding occupations.

Geographical isolation provided India with much—but not complete

—security. The Indians were not in danger from the sea until the arrival of the Portuguese and the British. Indian sailors learned the secret of the monsoons shortly after the time of Christ and were able to make long journeys east or west in search of trade. The Indians were more than able to hold their own with any pirates or marauders. On the land side, it was different. India was never overrun on the northeast by a Chinese army in an expansive mood (until the present decade). But in the northwest, it was devastated by a hundred invasions. The invaders spread easily down the Ganges Valley, established their fortress headquarters in the neighborhood of Delhi or Agra, and subsequently exhausted themselves in trying to expand their conquests southward over inhospitable lands and unwilling people.

These facts contribute to the great diversity of India's people and their languages. The earliest people in India, long before the dawn of history, were apparently forest-dwelling Negroids, ethnically related to the aborigines of Ceylon, Sumatra, and Australia. Still in the prehistoric period, they mixed with Dravidians (dark-skinned, of low stature, with long heads and broad noses) in the northwest; and with Mongoloids (Chinese types) in the area of the present northeast India-China frontier. The first people to enter India in historic times (c. 2000–1000 B.C.) were Aryans from the direction of Persia (light-skinned, tall with aquiline features). The Aryan invaders intermarried with local women and drove the rest of the original inhabitants toward the south. Succeeding invaders repeated the process of stratification and intermixture until more than a half-dozen racial types came to be distinguishable. They range from the almost-black Dravidians in the south to the Aryans in the north who look no darker than some New Yorkers after a winter vacation in Florida.

The languages are as varied as the people. The Dravidians have at least four major dialects (Tamil, Telugu, Kanarese, and Malayalam) each of which is used by tens of millions of people. The basic language family of India is the Aryan, subdivided into Sanskrit, the sacred vehicle of the ancient hymns, and Pali, the language of Buddha. Local Indian groups of people did with Sanskrit what French, Spanish, and Italians did with Latin. With Sanskrit as a base they added local words to produce native languages such as Hindi, Rajasthani, Gujarati, Punjabi, Kashmiri, Marathi, Bengali and a host of others.

One of the most widely spoken languages of India is Hindustani, which many would like to make the national language. It was formed by a linguistic compromise between Hindi, the language of the common people near Delhi, and Urdu, the descendant of the Persian or official language of the court. Hindi and Urdu sound alike, but they are written with different symbols. The former is angular, like Sanskrit, and the latter is curved and flowing, like Arabic. It is necessary to use both styles to communicate with all literate people; just as it is necessary for all-India radio to use some sixteen dialects (plus English) to reach all its listeners.

History

Unlike China, India has no carefully compiled body of historical records. What is known of India's early history has been derived from India's treasure house of literature, accounts of foreign travelers, and recent archaeological discoveries. It is established that man has been in India since the Paleolithic or Old Stone Age. As late as 1921 excavations at Mohenjo-Daro in the province of Sind and Harappa in the Punjab brought to light a civilization which must have been thousands of years in maturing. Dating from about 2500 B.C., it compares favorably with its contemporaries in Mesopotamia, Egypt, Sumeria, and China. Mohenjo-Daro was a large city, with well-planned streets, magnificent temples and brick homes, and ample facilities for public and private baths. No one knows exactly when or how it was reduced to ruins, but there must have been other cities like the one which has been found.

From approximately 2000 to 1000 B.C. the Aryan invasions occurred. Large groups of Aryans—related to Persians, Greeks, and Romans—fought the Dravidians, drove them southward, and established the political capital of Aryan India near Delhi. As Aryans expanded down the Ganges Valley, they established numerous small kingdoms. Aryans fused with Dravidians, absorbed much of their culture, and worked out a common way of life—as is always the case between conqueror and captive.

In the last millennium B.C. India was invaded by Persians, and then by Alexander the Great. That fabulous Greek conquered Persia, then Afghanistan, and finally turned toward India (327–325 B.C.). Some Indians cooperated with him; others fought him. In one battle, the Indian forces included 200 elephants, 150 chariots, 2000 cavalry, and 30,000 infantry. Alexander won spectacular victories but exhausted his own strength in winning. He turned back and died within a year.

After the retreat of the Greeks, the Indians established a dynasty— the Maurya Dynasty—which succeeded in pacifying the scattered kingdoms of the north. A great emperor, Asoka (274–237 B.C.) then attacked the south; and in his campaign it was recorded 10,000 men were slain and 150,000 taken prisoner; many times that number perished of disease and hardship. When Asoka contemplated the figures, he was "filled with remorse." He became a Buddhist and dedicated himself to meditation and good works. He sent missionaries abroad to propagate the Buddhist faith, and in the process he contributed to the spread of Indian civilization. He laid down the principles according to which the empire was to be gov-

erned. His scriptures were engraved on rocks and stone pillars throughout the land. Asoka was a man of great benevolence. Unfortunately goodness meant weakness, and his pacific tendencies brought to an end the only
enduring unity which India was to know for more than a millennium.

From 1 to 1000 A.D. India was exposed to repeated invasions. In the
second century, central Asian nomads called Kushans established a large
border state with its capital at Peshawar, which became a halfway station
for pilgrims and traders westbound to Rome and eastbound to China. In
the fourth century, the Gupta emperors in north India created a dominion which under Chandragupta II (380–413) was described by a famous
Chinese Buddhist visitor, Fa-Hsien, as "peaceful, prosperous and well-
governed." The Huns destroyed the Guptas, and in 606 a ruler named
Harsha brought another half-century of partial unity to north India. Another Chinese traveler, Hsuan-Tsang, in Harsha's day described India as a
land of past greatness but present decay. The pasture land was overrun by
savage beasts, ruined cities were overgrown by wilderness, bandits roamed
the highways, and the Buddhist religion was on the wane. "For five consecutive years the war elephants never quitted their harness nor the soldiers
their armor." And while India deteriorated in strength, its Moslem neighbors became more restive and ambitious.

In the meantime, neither central nor south India knew any more
peace and unity than the north. Various kingdoms—with such names as
Cholas, Pandyas, Pallavas, and Kalingas—rose and fell. They stood up
against attacks from the north, but they could not rise above their own
quarrels and intrigues. The most significant contribution which they made
to the history of India was the development of their own cultural genius.
They dispatched colonists and fleets of traders to Cambodia, Malaya,
Sumatra, and Java.

About the year 1000—998 to be exact—Mahmud of Ghazni, a Turk
and a follower of the Prophet, launched the first of a series of brutal
invasions. In forty years he built an empire which reached from the
frontiers of Mesopotamia to the river Ganges, and from Transoxiana to
the deserts of Rajputana. Under his successors, large numbers of Moslems
entered India peacefully.

About two hundred years later, in 1191, Mohammed of Ghur, an
Afghan leader, raided India. On his death, a Turkish "slave general" in
his army set up the first of a series of Moslem dynasties which ruled in
Delhi, one of the greatest cities in the universe, according to Ibn Batuta,
an Arab traveler who had seen Cairo, Constantinople, and the leading
cities of China. The sultans of Delhi held north India together rather
loosely, spent the usual blood and treasure in trying to pacify rebellious
kingdoms in the south, and succumbed in 1398 to the barbarous attacks
of Timur the Lame—the dreaded Tamerlane of English literature. The

Delhi sultanate was dealt the *coup de grace* by Baber, a Turkish-Mongol chieftain from Ferghana in Turkestan, who had the blood of Genghis Khan and Tamerlane in his veins.

Baber was the founder of the Mogul Dynasty (1526–1858) the succession of rulers under whom the control of India passed to the British. The chronicle of Baber's reign is a succession of battles, as is that of his son, Humayun. His grandson, Akbar, who ruled from 1556 to 1605, was a distinguished emperor. He devoted himself to the unification and pacification of the entire country. He treated the Hindus with consideration and tried to reconcile the conflicting religious views of his subjects. In his own harem he insisted upon a generous distribution of Hindus, Moslems, and Christians.

Akbar's grandson, Shah Jahan (1627–1659) built the Taj Mahal, said to have employed 20,000 workers for fifteen years. Shah Jahan was imprisoned by his own son, Aurangzeb, the last of the great Moguls, who succeeded to the throne through the murder of his brothers. His fanaticism was the last straw in driving Sikhs, Marathas, and Rajputs into open rebellion. Under his reign the empire was reduced to impotence, without the soldiers or the money to preserve internal order or to repel foreign invasions.

The successors to Aurangzeb brought to India nothing but further economic decay and political chaos. Soldiers of Hindu states defeated the forces of the emperor, but could not get together to set up a single succession dynasty. Splintered India was invaded by the Nadir Shah of Persia, who made no effort to annex India. When he returned to Persia, he made off with the Kohinoor diamond and the Peacock throne as part of his booty. Between 1747 and 1769 India suffered no less than ten invasions from Afghanistan. Often Indians in the north collaborated with the invaders rather than risk domination by an Indian family from a neighboring state within India. Thus the real power of the Moguls perished with Aurangzeb in 1707, although his puppet followers were kept on the throne in Delhi for another century and a half. The helplessness of India in the last days of the Moguls provided the British with the opportunity which they needed to expand their trade and consolidate their political power.

CULTURE AND CIVILIZATION

The bare bones of India's history become more attractive when rounded out with fifteen centuries of India's cultural development. The remains of the Harappa culture—which is the term applied to the ruins of Harappa and Mohenjo-Daro—show elements recognizable in contemporary India. These include figurines of gods and men, even in yoga posture; pictures of the sacred pipal tree (under which Buddha is supposed to have preached his first sermon); statues of rams, dogs, and bulls; designs of the swastika; and evidences of the cult of fertility as commonly portrayed by phallic symbols and pregnant mother-goddesses. Harappa writing has not yet been deciphered, but it is clear anyway that Harappa culture was far more advanced than that of its arrogant Aryan destroyers.

Knowledge of the long period of Aryan conquest is derived from their own Vedas or sacred books. The best known of these is the *Rig-Veda* which is probably the earliest book which man possesses. Orthodox Hindus believe it is divinely inspired. It is a compendium of the existing knowledge of the day: hymns to gods; prayers for long life and good cattle; rituals for sacrifice and magnificent nature poetry. It contains elements of mysticism which are the basis of Indian thought and philosophy, life and culture.

From the Vedas, it is known that the Aryans were nomads, organized into tribes, and divided into four castes: Brahmans, or priests; Kshatriyas, or rulers and warriors; Vaisyas, or merchants and traders; and Sudras, or serfs. Each man had his own job to do, and all spoke an archaic form of Sanskrit. They seem to have been a cheerful and intelligent people who were so full of the zest of life that they paid little attention to affairs of the soul. They built no temples, made no idols, but worshiped personified powers of nature with the aid of priests. In the course of time their religious thought became more complicated and their worship more elaborate.

The period from 1000 to 500 b.c. is known as the Epic Age, because of two famous epics which mirror the life of the times and reflect the development of Hinduism. The first epic, the *Mahabharata* is a long poem of human conflict and tribal wars. It contains an episode called the *Bhagavad-Gita,* or the Lord's Song, which is the best-loved gem of Indian literature. The second epic is the *Ramayana* which is a philosophical, spellbinding tale of the adventures of Rama, a god-man and his idealized wife. To this day, songs from the epics are chanted to listening millions wherever Indian culture is a living force.

By the time of the Epic Age, hundreds of years before the Christian era, Hinduism had developed its chief religious characteristics. The old Aryan nature gods had been replaced by a new pantheon: Brahma, the Creator; Vishnu, the Preserver; Siva, the Destroyer; and a host of others with human or animal forms. With new gods came new ideas. The main object of religion was release from the wheel of life. A man might have been an animal in a past existence, a human being in this one, and perhaps a god in the next. Status was the consequence of past actions: every man was given exactly what he deserved. Without hope for improvement in this life, one should fulfill the obligations of the station to which he was born. Rewards would take the shape of better birth next time, and the ultimate reward would be absorption into the absolute.

Hinduism did not become a religion or a church in the Western sense, with an organization, a hierarchy, and a creed. It provided a place for everybody from the most primitive idol worshiper to the most profound philosopher. With its thousands of deities, anyone could worship whom or what he pleased. As will be seen in the next section, Hinduism offered more of a common way of life than a common body of religious precepts. The most that Hindus shared in their intellectual outlook was a fatalism which accepted their lot in life and looked to the Brahmans as the highest caste. In their view "the wise in heart mourned not for those that live, nor those that die . . . as when one layeth his worn out robes away and, taking new ones, sayeth 'these will I wear today,' so putteth by the spirit lightly its garb of flesh, and passeth to inherit a residence afresh." (*Baghavad-Gita*)

Some aspects of Hinduism were not acceptable to Gautama Sakyamuni (563–483 B.C.) who was born into the Kshatriya or warrior caste and who before his death gave to the world the Buddhist religion. He attacked superstition and ceremonial and opposed the Brahmans and the institution of caste. He believed that religion should be a matter of logic and reason with emphasis on ethics rather than metaphysics. He taught that sorrow in the world resulted from desire, and that the way to get rid of sorrow was to obliterate desire. This could be done by right thinking, meditation, and right action. The path of virtue was the path of nonviolence, rest, and peace. As in orthodox Hinduism, birth and rebirth were at the core of Buddhist teaching. It would require more than one life experience to improve one's self sufficiently to merit nirvana, which was the Buddhist term for the ultimate absorption. In India, Hinduism absorbed the philosophy of Buddhism; but outside India, Buddhism grew into one of the world's most influential religious systems.

In the millennium between the end of the Epic Age and the close of the Gupta supremacy (*c.* 500 B.C.–500 A.D.), Indians continued to be preoccupied with philosophy and religion. At the same time they refined their language, expanded their literary output, increased their knowledge of science and industry, and gave classic character to their music, dance, sculpture, painting, and architecture. Their contacts with the Greeks were limited; however, during the period of the greatness of the Kushan state (120–162 A.D.) they created the school of Ghandara art which was Greek in techniques but Indian in spirit. They began to stylize Hindu and Buddhistic art in the same way the Renaissance artists in Europe stylized the faces, figures, and scenes of Christianity.

The Gupta Dynasty, which came to an end in the fifth century, gave

India the golden age of its early civilization. The emperors were Hindus, and patronized a Brahmanical revival. They regularly used Sanskrit for their inscriptions, and they caused the sacred literature, including the *Mahabharata,* to be recast in the form in which it is known today. Their ministers were men of wide culture; their court favorites were dramatists, poets, and writers of fables, fairy tales, and animal stories. Kalidasa, the Shakespeare of India, lived and wrote during the reign of Chandragupta II.

The Gupta period was also the high noon of sculpture and painting. The motif of sculpture was usually religious, but it was often blatantly erotic. Some religious cults believed that the sexual act and organs were symbols of divine creative energy, and their statues left nothing to the imagination. However, the images of Buddha and the stone lions found at Sarnath, outside Benares, are conceded to be the finest examples of Indian sculpture. The most spectacular examples of Gupta painting are the frescoes on the walls and ceilings of the Ajanta caves, near Bombay. The subject matter is anything connected with the Buddhist story; and the paintings are rich representations of religious, domestic, and court life. The grace and vigor of style, and the faces and figures themselves, show a remarkable similarity to cave paintings at Tun-Huang, China, and to frescoes in the Horyuji temple at Nara, Japan—which were done at approximately the same time!

In medicine and mathematics, and in the application of science to industry, Gupta India made outstanding achievements. Its great universities attracted students from all over Asia, including China. Books on medicine discussed obstetrics, diet, hygiene, and infant feeding. Indian doctors were able to perform Caesarean operations, amputate limbs, and remove cataracts from afflicted eyes. Its mathematicians invented the nine-digit "Arabic" system of numerals, utilized the concepts of zero and minus quantities, and used the x symbol to denote unknowns in algebraic equations. Indians were famous for the tempering of iron and steel. They erected an iron pillar twenty-three feet high during this period and it still stands strong, and rust-free, in Delhi. Textile workers turned out the finest quality dyes and fabrics. The English words *cotton, khaki, calico, chintz, muslin,* and *cashmere* are of Indian origin.

In south India, the Tamils and their neighbors shared the cultural glory of the Gupta Dynasty in the north. With the spread of Hinduism and Buddhism, temples and religious art were just as prevalent as in the north. In addition, local peoples developed their own literature, music, and dances. They sent the traders and the Indian colonists who helped Southeast Asians build such monuments as Angkor Wat and Boro Budur. They also dispatched the missionaries who carried the message of Buddha from Ceylon to Burma, Thailand, and the Indochinese peninsula.

With the fall of the Guptas, Indian culture entered a millennium of decline (500–1500). It did not die, but managed to survive throughout the long night of chaos and invasion. Religion degenerated into rituals, philosophy lost its originality, and scholarship developed into scholasticism. Literature became imitative; art and architecture were intricate and ornate rather than beautiful and inspiring. According to Nehru, India seemed to dry up and to lose its creative genius and vitality. "When thought lost its explosiveness and creative power and became a tame attendant on an outworn and meaningless practice, mumbling old phrases and fearful of everything new, then life became stagnant and tied and constrained in a prison of its own making." Cultural decay came along with political helplessness, but revival followed in the train of the Moslem invasions.

The advent of Islam introduced a potent new element into the religious life of India. The religion of one god, Allah, and his prophet, Mohammed and of the sacred book, the Koran, penetrated India for hundreds of years before it became identified with India's conquerors. In the view of the Moslems, Allah was a positive and permanent being, who revealed his will through the Prophet, and before whom all men were equals. Existence on this earth was tremendously important because it was a preparation for an earthly conceived paradise. Therefore life was to be stern, austere, puritanic and strictly regulated by rules covering diet, human association, and compulsory prayer.

After the death of the Prophet in the seventh century, Arab fighters paid less attention to India than to Central Asia, North Africa, and Europe. Subsequently travelers, missionaries, and embassies brought their books and doctrines to India. Islam won some converts but it was not a patient or tolerant religion. When Mahmud of Ghazni invaded India in 998 and Mohammed of Ghur came two centuries later, they made no pretense of tolerance, conversion, or doctrinal synthesis. They destroyed temples, smashed idols, and put thousands of Hindus to the sword. Only as the conqueror remained to become the ruler of India was thought given to religious coexistence. Invaders intermarried with the local populace. Turks and Afghans were absorbed into the cultural stream of India much as the Mongols of Genghis Khan were absorbed into the culture of China.

With the establishment of the Mogul Dynasty (1526), India experienced a cultural reawakening. The glory of the Moguls was not due to the emperors alone. It was the combined achievement of masters and subjects who, though aliens, had profound need of each other. The emperors hired Hindus to administer their affairs, and some Hindus for reasons of their own (tax privileges, favors at court, release from caste obligations, or grants of land) accepted Islam. Trade and industry remained in the hands of Hindus, and Moslem nobles looked to native bankers for grants and loans. Neither group was willing to surrender its cultural identity to the other.

Through the years many cultural traits passed from one group to the other. Moslems and Hindus developed common tastes in music, painting, architecture, and food and clothes. The manners and styles of the Mogul court became the model for both Moslem and Hindu princes throughout the country. Persian was retained as the official language, but Hindi, the Indian vernacular in Delhi, was modified and adopted as a national means of communication. New movements arose which sought liberalization of both faiths with a view to possible reconciliation. A poetic weaver wrote: "God is one, whether we worship him as Allah or as Rama. The Hindu worships him on the eleventh day; the Muhammadan fasts at Ramadan; but God made all the days and all the months. The Hindu god lives at Banaras, the Muhammadan god at Mecca; but He who made the world lives not in a city made by hands. There is one Father of Hindu and Mussulman."

Culture reached new heights in India under the Moguls. The courts were as famous for artists, artisans, and scholars as they were for their luxury and debauchery. Akbar founded an important school of Indo-Persian painting and built the city of Fatehpur Sikri, near Agra, as a monument to his policy of integration. Indo-Islamic architecture, with its bulbous domes, graceful arches, and slender minarets, reached the peak of perfection in the Taj Mahal and the emperor's palace in Delhi. The Moguls rose and disappeared as rulers of India, but they made permanent contributions to its cultural heritage.

The Way of Life

India was already old when the British arrived and in its long history had produced a culture which ranked with the great creations of the human mind. It also gave its people a distinctive way of life. Nehru once wrote, "I think that at almost any time in recorded history an Indian would have felt more or less at home in any part of India, and would have felt as a stranger and an alien in any other country." Like its culture, its way of life was rooted in religion. It owed most to Hinduism, but it was deeply affected by the institutions of successive invaders.

Hinduism was modified by the absorption of Buddhism and the importation of foreign religions (Syrian Christianity, Judaism, or Zoroastrianism) before the arrival of Islam. Every aspect of life, every thought and action, was included in the word *Hinduism*. Anyone might be considered a Hindu who accepted its social code. Hinduism determined a man's status, food, occupation, marriage, and friends with whom he could associate. All this was solidified by the system of castes which John Gunther referred to as "Jim Crowism on a fantastic scale."

The Hindu caste system flourished in full vigor after the Aryan invasions. In was India's answer to the reconciliation of the needs of the individual and society. The individual was relieved of the necessity for competition with his own kind. He was given security within his own group, but was deprived of the opportunity to improve his condition. Society was guaranteed a certain amount of stability which prevented social disorder that might otherwise have resulted from repeated invasions. The whole duty of man was to fulfill the obligations which flowed from his station in life. But the caste system was a strait jacket which doomed India to stagnation. Once a tiller, always a tiller; once a craftsman, always a craftsman. It was the exact opposite of equality: the favored few were confirmed in their privileges and the masses were condemned to perpetual subordination. Each caste looked down on its inferiors; none could look up with the hope of becoming something better some day.

The Aryans themselves were divided into four castes as noted earlier. Classification was determined primarily by occupation, and the boundary lines between the classes was not sharply defined. Gradually class structure became more complicated. New peoples had to be absorbed into special categories within castes, and new types of jobs meant new classifications. Thousands of subcastes evolved, all with their own special rules. At the top were the Brahmans, who were accepted as the arbiters of earthly behavior, the interpreters of the holy writings, honored guests at festivals, and masters of religious ceremonies. At the bottom were the depressed classes or outcasts, one-fifth of the total population, who could not draw water from village wells, enter the temples, or permit their touch, nearness, or even their shadow to pollute the members of any caste above them.

The caste system had two good companions—the joint family and the agricultural village—in shaping the way of life. The typical family consisted of the father, sons, grandsons, and unmarried daughters. The father or eldest son was more like a manager than the head of the house. All members of the family shared jointly in ownership of the property and all income was placed in the family purse. The "joint" feature of the family acted as a curb of ambition. It produced a feeling of security or protectiveness at best, but an attitude of docility at worst. Women were in an unenviable position, although the theoretic position of women was often nullified by female charm or intuition. They were considered as chattels in law and were always subordinate to someone—father, brother, or husband. They were betrothed in childhood and at the mercy of the dowry. Wives had the usual problems with mothers-in-law when they went to live in the husband's family. Children were considered more as the special concern of the entire family than the personal treasure of the mother.

The village was the symbol of India. It was a collection of mud and thatch huts, without chimneys or windows, rarely with tables and chairs, and usually with a dirt floor and only a mat for sleeping. Chickens, geese, goats, and cattle lived as part of the family. Bullocks were precious. They were used to lift the water from the well, pull the ploughs, and thresh the grain. Villagers were the most immobile of people. They were not inclined to protest against their fate. They lived and died where they were born; they seldom traveled more than a day's walk from their homes. The village managed to function no matter how weak the state. The panchayat, or council of elders, settled petty arguments, took care of community needs, and raised the taxes which the government required. Political and military power, as exercised by the rajah, seldom interfered with local customs, as interpreted by the Brahmans. Villagers were expected to look after their own handicapped and hungry people and to procure water for their thirsty fields. Rulers should fight their own battles and find their own solution to political problems which were beyond the horizon and the comprehension of the humble villager.

Nine out of ten people in pre-Mogul India made their living from the soil. They were farmers growing rice, wheat, millet, corn, or pulses, and their lives were entirely determined by a tiny plot of land. Their incomes were sometimes supplemented by livestock and fruit trees. All the nonfarmers together—including artisans, craftsmen, miners, carpenters, actors, and peddlers—made up some ten percent of the population. Cultivators did not necessarily own their land, but they were entitled to a major share of the produce. However, part of the harvest had to be set aside for Brahmans, merchants, and every group in the village which contributed in its own way to community welfare. Land was the key to life and death. No crops, no income; no income, no money for taxes. Without taxes the local rajah and the emperor himself were faced with financial disaster.

It is not surprising that the science of society, more particularly the art of government, was neglected in ancient India. A people which is imbued with a spirit of resignation and a feeling that the material world is only illusion is not likely to indulge in creative political thought. The people felt no sense of responsibility for government and failed to get excited about reform. The ills of this existence would be cured in the next. The Brahmans preferred to contemplate the mysteries of the ages and the universe, rather than address themselves to the problems of their own day and their own country. In China, the superior men ran the government;

in India, they served as ministers and advisers to kings, but they scorned administration.

Continuously after the Aryan invasions, India was divided into kingdoms which were at constant war with each other. Kingship was not sanctified by any theory of divine right, but kings were often treated as past or future gods. Priests and astrologers were the most important figures at the court. The chief function of the king, or rajah, seemed to be to collect the taxes, although he was technically responsible for peace, order, protection against invasion, and the welfare of his subjects. His oath said, "May I be deprived of heaven, of life and of offspring if I oppress you," and the sacred books warned him, "If the king becomes heedless of his subjects, they will fall upon him as vultures upon carrion."

The traditional Hindu way of life was given a new dimension with the infiltration and conquest of the Moslems. The Hindus were exposed to a virile people, a vital new culture, and a radically different code of social relationships. The new emperors, ruling class, military aristocracy, and social elite clung to their habitual manners and were not inclined to be lenient toward the "unbelievers and idolators" whom they had conquered. The Mogul dynasty established its direct rule in Bengal and Assam (modern East Pakistan) and in the northwest frontier region, Baluchistan, West Punjab, and the Sind (modern West Pakistan). It never completed the conquest of central and south India, permitting local Moslem and Hindu princes to remain on their thrones in return for annual payments of tribute and quotas of troops. Throughout India, a substantial number of the people, perhaps one in four, embraced Islam.

The greatest of the Mogul emperors, Akbar, endeavored to come to terms with the Indian scene. He removed the discriminatory pilgrim tax and poll tax against Hindus, and integrated Hindu chiefs into the administration of the country. He realized that his dynasty could not long endure if it remained nothing more than an alien conqueror. He appointed Hindus as nobles and opened to them the highest offices in the empire. He took a Rajput princess as one of his wives. Akbar's successors abandoned his farsighted policies, and in their return to religious bigotry and discrimination they alienated a large portion of the Hindu masses.

When the British arrived in India, they quickly became aware of the complexity of the caste system, the strength of the Indian family unit, and the importance of village life. In these matters, they showed no immediate disposition to alter the *status quo*. On the other hand they encountered political and economic conditions which were to call for more than a century of adjustment.

The Mogul empire was a military state commanded by an emperor whose power was absolute. No priest crowned him, and only Allah and the Prophet were considered his superiors. The court at Agra was more magnificent and luxurious than its contemporary at Versailles. It was described by Sir Thomas Roe, who was in India as the ambassador of James I from 1615 to 1619, in this vein:

> The emperor Jahangir, on his birthday, sat cross-legged upon a throne, all clad in diamonds, pearls and rubies, before him a table of gold, on it about fifty pieces of gold plate. . . . his nobility about him in their best equipage whom he commanded to drink froliquely of several wines standing by in great flagons.

If the emperor was strong, he was a magnificent tyrant or benevolent despot; if weak or disinterested, his administration became ineffective and corrupt. The last Mogul emperor was contemptuously referred to by a British observer as a "king of shreds and patches."

The nobles of the court were primarily of Turk, Afghan, or Persian descent. Every noble or bureaucrat was an officer in the army. Titles were not hereditary, and rank depended upon the number of men and horses in a person's command. Salaries were not regular, but income was derived from land which was assigned for an officer's exploitation. Under the emperor, the government was divided into various departments: imperial household, treasury, military affairs, religious affairs, judiciary, and censorship of public morals. For local administration, the empire was divided into provinces, ruled over by a variety of viceroys, kings, and princes. Some were closely attached to the Mogul court; others were independent. Some rulers were cruel; others were benevolent. Some were wise; others were educated in the harems and came to the throne without knowing a thing about their domains, let alone the world beyond. A state like Hyderabad might have a Moslem ruler while the people were eighty per cent Hindu; or on the contrary, like Kashmir, it might have a Hindu rajah while the majority of the rajah's subjects were Moslems.

A separate hierarchy existed for revenues. Most of the taxes, which together amounted to approximately one-third of the harvest, were sent to the central government, but a small percentage was reserved for local use. During Akbar's reign, taxes were assessed on each annual harvest and paid by the villages. This strengthened the village and weakened the power of the central government in dealing with individuals. In lean years, taxes were reduced. Under Akbar's successors, a system was inaugurated which fixed a lump sum as annual quota from a village regardless of the harvest, and the head man was held responsible for the payment of the quota.

The larger cities had separate governors. Rural districts were under local magistrates who might be humane or beastly. Since administration of local affairs was primarily a matter of finances, justice was honeycombed with bribery. Judicial officials were not independent, but like their administrative counterparts, held office at the pleasure of the emperor. The law meant Islamic law or the personal whim of the Brahman or the rajah. No written codes or bodies of precedent existed. The common people were supposed to be able to appeal to the emperor, but Delhi was far, far away. The political condition of Bengal was described in an official East India Company report as "a government without nerves, a treasury without money and service without subordination, discipline or public spirit."

The emperor and the nobles lived in excessive luxury in fine buildings, very much given to wine and women. A small middle class of merchants and traders devoted themselves to the accumulation of wealth rather than to the service of their wretched fellow men. The cities, with commerce and trade, were generally better off than the countryside, except in years of famine or drought, when millions everywhere suffered and died of hunger or starvation.

In spite of the glory of the Mogul empire, the peasant never seemed to have sufficient food to eat. Most of the time the harvests were good. Since taxes were paid in grain, it was to the interest of the throne to treat the masses with consideration. Government help was extended in irrigation systems and the reclamation of new lands. The people seemed to be reconciled to their lot and well pleased with their gods, nature, and their environment. Agrarian revolts were practically unknown. But then as now India was a poverty-stricken country. The peasant was always in debt and was a prey to otherwise preventible diseases. The journey from birth to burning ghat was often a procession of misery and squalor. For the masses who consoled themselves with religious ritual and the quest for the favor of the gods, life was more grim than gay. With the coming of the British the ancient economic patterns—sometimes consciously and sometimes inadvertently—were rudely shaken out of their ancient grooves.

PRE-BRITISH INDIA

The aim of India's traditional social system was the security and continuance of the group, not the welfare of the individual. The values of its society were goodness, peace, and escape from the wheel of life rather than acquisition of power, wealth, and honor. Obligations, not rights, were important. The social structure became rigid and petrified. It provided no opportunity for an underprivileged class of human beings to climb out of its unhappy condition. India was steeped in its own traditions. The caste system was, in Nehru's words, "wholly reactionary, restrictive and a bar to progress." Indians knew no equality in status, had no concept of political freedom, and were totally unprepared to cope with the social changes which lay ahead.

From an economic point of view, up to the eighteenth century Indian methods of production and commerce could compare favorably with that of the rest of the world. Bills of exchange issued by Indian banks were honored throughout India and Central Asia. India knew all the techniques of trade and shipping and was as advanced as any country before the Industrial Revolution. The tragedy was that India (like China) had known its days of greatness. India was on the way down; Europe was on the way up. The immediate future belonged to the awakening nations, not to those that slumbered and dreamed of their glorious past.

The Mogul empire in its best days was, according to Will Durant, "the best organized and most prosperous then existing in the world." The Moguls gave India a great name, in which Hindus as well as Moslems took pride. They constructed a political framework which might have continued to flourish had Akbar's successors measured up to his standards. But frequent wars weakened the empire, and it was ready to topple when the British arrived.

It does not seem right to divide Indian history into three periods: pre-British, British, and independent India. Most of India's history happened before the British appeared. The British era was comparatively modern and relatively short. It cannot be denied that the British exerted great influence on India—out of all proportion to the duration of their rule. Some was good and some was considered detrimental. But the British came when India was in the midst of chaos and ready for change. The British raj marked the end of the isolation of the subcontinent, helped to open India's own eyes to a new vision of the future, and ushered India into the modern world.

SUGGESTED READING

Boxer, C. R., "Portuguese in India," in H. D. Livermore (ed.), *Portugal and Brazil* (New York, Oxford U., 1953).

Brown, D. Mackenzie, *White Umbrella, Indian Political Thought from Manu to Gandhi* (Berkeley, U. of California, 1953).

Drekmeier, Charles, *Kingship and Community in Early India* (Stanford, Stanford U., 1962).

Foster, Sir William, (ed.), *Embassy of Sir T. Roe in India, 1615–1619* (two vols.) (London, Hakluyt Society, 1899).

Furber, Holden, *John Company at Work* (Cambridge, Harvard, 1948).

Garrat, G. T., (ed.), *Legacy of India* (New York, Oxford, 1937).

Goetz, Hermann, *India, Five Thousand Years of Indian Art* (New York, Crown, 1959).

Griffiths, Sir Percival, *Modern India* (New York, Praeger, 1957).

Hutton, J. H., *Caste in India* (Cambridge, Cambridge U., 1946).

Kabir Humayun, *Indian Heritage* (New York, Harper, 1957).

Life editors, *World's Great Religions* (New York, Time, Inc., 1957).

Macnicol, Nichol, *Hindu Scriptures* (London, Everyman, 1938).

Mascaro, Juan, (trans.), *Bhagavad-Gita* (Baltimore, Penguin, 1962). (P)

Panikkar, K. M., *Survey of Indian History* (London, Meridian, 1948).

Piggott, S., *Prehistoric India* (London, Pelican, 1950).

Radhakhrishnan, Sir Sarvepalli, and Moore, Charles A., (eds.), *Sourcebook of Indian Philosophy* (Princeton, Princeton U., 1957).

Rawlinson, H. G., *Intercourse between India and the Western World* (Cambridge, Cambridge U., 1948).

Tarn, Sir W. W., *Alexander the Great* (two vols.) (Cambridge, Cambridge U., 1948).

Wheeler, Sir R. B. E., *Indus Civilization* (Cambridge, Cambridge U., 1953).

4

Southeast Asia

We have looked at China, Japan, and India, and now we shall examine the area which the Chinese (and Japanese) call the southern regions, which the Indians call Farther India or greater India, and which we know popularly as Southeast Asia. It includes Burma, Thailand (or Siam), the states of the Indochina peninsula (Laos, Cambodia, and Vietnam), and Malaya on the mainland of Asia; and the archipelagoes of Indonesia and the Philippines.

The best way to fix the location and relationship of the states in Southeast Asia is to think of Thailand as the heart of the region. Thailand is surrounded by Burma on the Indian side, Indochina on the east, and the long, skinny Malay Peninsula to the south. Communications routes fan out from Bangkok, the capital of Thailand, as the spokes from the hub of a wheel—west and north toward Rangoon and then, clockwise, north to Chiengmai; northeast to Vientiane and Luang Prabang; east toward Phnom Penh and Saigon, and lastly straight down through Malaya toward Kuala Lumpur and Singapore. In modern days, highways, railways, and international airways give to continental Southeast Asia a basis for regional unity which historically has never matured.

By way of introduction to the geography, history, cultural background, and social structure of the area as it appeared when the first ships and travelers arrived from Europe, it is perhaps appropriate to establish the identity of the states which make up Southeast Asia in our time.

Burma, larger than France, borders on India and China, and except for the Burma Road is practically isolated from the rest of Asia. Its frontier with Thailand has been the scene of constant wars. Burma's neighbor, Thailand—or Siam—is fiercely proud of its political independence and economic prosperity, and feels that it has a good historic claim to borderlands which now belong to Burma, Laos, Cambodia, and Malaya.

The Indochinese Peninsula contains Vietnam, which is sometimes described as a bamboo pole with a sack of rice at either end. The bamboo pole is the narrow mountain backbone and the sacks of rice are the rich rice lands of the Red River and the Mekong. Vietnam was divided in 1954 into the Democratic Republic of Vietnam, under the Communist regime, in the north and the Republic of Vietnam in the south. The Indochina peninsula is also the location of the landlocked kingdom of Laos and the better known kingdom of Cambodia. The long, narrow state of Malaya, which divides the Bay of Bengal and the Indian Ocean from the South China Sea, dates its independent existence only from 1957.

Modern Indonesia is a group of islands that stretches along the equator across the ocean routes from Europe to Asia and from Asia to Australia. It resembles a giant serpent, with its exposed skeleton bent double by heavy weights on its back. The head of this serpent is Sumatra, the trunk is Java, and the vertebrae are Bali, Lombok, Sumbawa, Flores, Timor, and Wetar. The tail is New Guinea or, as the Indonesians call it, Irian. The heavy weights are Borneo, the Celebes, and the Moluccas or Spice Islands. Indonesia covers almost 750,000 square miles of land area and spreads over a distance equal that from San Francisco to Bermuda. Sumatra compares in size with New England and the Middle Atlantic states combined. Borneo is as large as Texas and New Guinea, (Irian) is the size of California.

The Philippine Islands consist of five main parts: Luzon, the Visayan Islands, Mindanoa, Palawan, and the Sulu Archipelago. The two last-named were at one time presumably land bridges to the continent of Asia. On the map the Philippine Islands resemble the head of a donkey: Luzon forms the ears and the forehead, the Visayan Islands the face, Mindanao the mouth, and Palawan and the Sulu Archipelago the upper and lower edges of the neck. The Philippines cover a million square miles of sea and 115,000 square miles of land surface, or about two-thirds the area of Japan. If superimposed on the map of the United States, the islands would reach from the northern boundary of Maine to the middle of Florida.

All these geographic concepts which are meaningful in the world of today must be put aside temporarily in order to appreciate conditions of Southeast Asia as they were in the fifteenth century. At that time there were no modern states—only ethnic groups—to greet the Spanish, Portuguese, Dutch, French, and British who came to convert the "heathen" or to trade and who remained to build their empires.

THE LAND AND THE PEOPLE

The southeast corner of Asia is something like the Balkan Peninsula in Europe. It is backed by high mountains which make communications

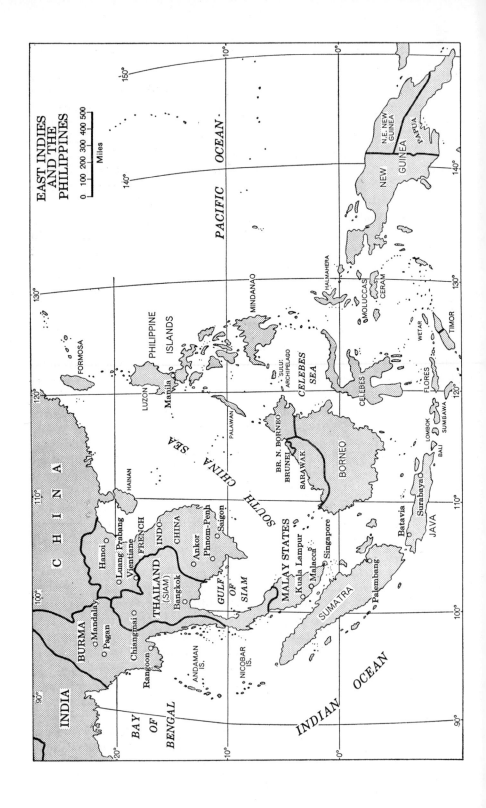

EAST INDIES
AND THE
PHILIPPINES

Miles
0 100 200 300 400 500

difficult over land frontiers. Mountain chains reach down from the great Asian plateaus like fingers from an outstretched hand. It is hazardous to travel parallel to the ranges; it is next to impossible to cross them. Trails are scarce, forests thick, and the jungles treacherous. The highlands are drained by mighty rivers which can be a curse (floods and rapids) or a blessing (irrigation and channels of communication). The Red and the Mekong empty into the ocean in Indochina; the Chao Phraya is often referred to as the "Nile of Thailand"; the Irrawaddy, Sittang, and Salween flow through Burma, and the Brahmaputra skirts the western extremity of Southeast Asia to form a rich delta land in eastern India.

Southeast Asia is inhabited mainly by small, brown-skinned, mongoloid peoples known as Malays or Indonesians who moved into the area in successive waves over a long period of time before the Christian era. They came from north and west China and were driven out of their homes by hunger or by oppressive rulers and warlike neighbors. They moved down the river valleys. Each new wave kept the best land for itself, and the newcomers drove the earlier settlers back from alluvial plains and into the hills. The more primitive tribe survived in relatively small groups from hilltop to hilltop, with the dwellers in the lower levels separating group from group in the hills, or even separating members of the same tribe from each other. The hill people married with their own kind, developed their own language and eked out their meager living from nature. They never learned what the world was like beyond their range of vision.

The more advanced peoples appropriated the valleys of the mighty rivers and the fertile lands of the tributaries. They built cities along the banks and ports for commerce where the rivers joined the sea. They established kingdoms, which were small and often ephemeral, but which in many instances were the seeds of modern states. As in India, the people of Southeast Asia spoke a babel of tongues, but all their dialects stemmed from four main language groups: Tibeto-Burman, Mon-Khmer, Thai-Shan-Annamese (with Chinese affinity), and Malaysian-Polynesian, or Indonesian.

On the mainland, a Tibeto-Burman people originating in Kansu (China) migrated into Burma, set up successive capitals in the neighborhood of Mandalay, and fought continuously for centuries against another group known as the Mons or Talaings, named after Telingana, their supposed ancestral home on the southern coast of India. The Mons, whose capital was in lower Burma, near Rangoon, dominated the lower valleys of the Irrawaddy, the Salween, and the Chao Phraya.

Over the mountains from the Burmans and the Mons lived the Thais— or free people—as they called themselves. The Thais also came from China (south of the Yangtze Valley) and into Southeast Asia over the ancient trail now familiarly known as the Burma Road. The Thais divided themselves into many groups including the Laos and the Shans. Various Thai tribes at one time or another controlled the entire area from Yunnan to Assam.

In addition to Laos, Khmers, and scores of minority groups, with names like Meos, Khas, and Chams, the Indochina peninsula was inhabited principally by Annamites, the ancestors of the people of Vietnam. The Malay Peninsula and Indonesia were the homes of diverse branches of the Indonesian language family whose members evolved into the Malays of Sumatra, Sundanese, Javanese, Balinese, and so forth. The more primitive Malays, like the Bataks of Sumatra and the head-hunting Dyaks of Borneo, retreated into the wilderness to keep themselves safe from the more advanced coastal Malays. The people of the Philippines came from the same racial stock as the people of the islands of Indonesia, with similar variations in appearance, speech, and levels of living.

The diverse immigrants into Southeast Asia came from climates and elevations which were vastly different from the tropical lowlands. Their new homes were hot and in many instances unhealthy. Their salvation was rice agriculture, which was ideally suited to the monsoon climate. Their diet was based on rice, tapioca, coconuts, tropical fruits, chickens, pigs, and fish. These were the things which they prized, not the exotic spices, luxuries, plantation crops, metals, and "strategic materials" which later gave the world hallucinations about the wealth of the Indies.

History

The story of man in Southeast Asia is the oldest in the world. Skeletal remains of human beings have been found on the island of Java which date from the Pleistocene or Great Ice Age which lasted from about 1,000,000 to 8000 B.C. Similar but later types have been uncovered in China, near Peking, and Australia, near Melbourne. After the end of the Pleistocene period, the first migrants into the area were the curly-haired, very dark Australoid-Veddoid people (named after the Vedda tribes of Ceylon) who were the tiny, wooly-haired black Negritos, some of whose descendants still carry on a simple hunting and food-gathering existence in the Andaman Islands, parts of Indonesia, and the Philippines. Then, perhaps about 2500–1500 B.C., from the north came the Indonesian peoples who have just been described. Rice cultivation was known in Indochina, Siam, and Malaya as early as 1500 B.C. and the famous rice terraces of the primitive mountain people near Baguio in the northern Philippines date from approximately the time of Christ.

Southeast Asia enjoyed a brief moment of glory in terms of world history at the beginning of the Christian era. Chinese bronzes were made known to the people of Indochina during the Han Dynasty and at about the same time Malaya and the Indies were taught the use of iron by Indian immigrants. The Roman world provided a market for the luxuries of the East—ivory, ebony, jewels, and spices which grew nowhere else in the world—and Southeast Asia lured traders from Persia, Arabia, India, and China. It was the crossroads of the ancient world. New ports sprang into prominence and the whole area came to life with immigrants who brought new inventions and new customs.

Large numbers of Indians, fleeing from wars at home or seeking trade in the land of gold and barley (Malaya and Java), founded trading settlements along the coasts of Burma, Siam, Malaya, Indochina, Java, and Borneo. These centers grew into kingdoms which practiced Indian religions, used Sanskrit as the sacred language, and adopted Indian ideas of kingship, codes of law, and methods of political administration. Chinese historians give the first glimpse of a Hinduized state, the precursor of modern Cambodia, which was founded in the first century. Legend said that it resulted from the union of an Indian prince and a beautiful lady chieftain of the local tribes. The fate of Funan, and the other leading states which lived and died during a millennium and a half, is shown in the accompanying chart.

For five hundred years Funan was the most important power in Southeast Asia, exercising control over the area which is now Cambodia, South Vietnam, lower Thailand, and north Malaya. It eclipsed the contemporary kingdoms of Champa (central Annam), Kedah, and Langkasuka (Perak) in Malaya and the distant settlements of Java and Borneo. Funan is a Chinese term for the Sanskrit words *kurung* or king and *phnom* or mountain. The "mountain" was a hill—or shrine—in the center of the capital city which was used as a burial place for the king and was looked upon as the abode of the gods. The king was regarded as having supreme earthly power and divine status as "king of the mountains."

An early Chinese account described Funan as a "walled city with elegant palaces" and said the people were "ugly, black, frizzy-haired who went about naked or with only a small piece of cloth tied around the waist." The common people lived in thatched-roof homes built on stilts, as they do today. Their sports were cock-fighting or pig-fighting. The kings and nobles lived in splendor and rode around on elephants, attended by retainers and shaded by parasols. The king must have controlled the trade of the South China Sea and he sent many embassies to the imperial court of China. Funan was conquered in the sixth century by the ancestors of the Khmers, from the region of modern Laos, farther up the Mekong Valley. The first king of the Khmers was Kambudja, for whom the state of Cambodia is named.

CHART TO ILLUSTRATE THE MAIN LINES OF POLITICAL CHANGE IN SOUTHEAST ASIA TO 1500

A.D.	BURMA (PYUS) (MONS)	SIAM	CAMBODIA (KHMERS) (CHAMS)	VIETNAM (VIETNAMESE)	MALAY PENINSULA (PROTO- AND DEUTERO-MALAYS)	SUMATRA	JAVA
100				TONKIN			
200			FUNAN	(UNDER CHINA)	KEDAH / LANGKASUKA		
300				CHAMPA			
400							
500			FUNAN CONQUERED				
600	SOUTHWARD DRIVE		BY KHMERS PRE-ANGKOR KHMER KINGDOM				
700	OF BURMANS					SRIVIJAYA	SAILENDRAS
800	FROME (PYU CAPITAL) CONQUERED / SOUTHWARD DR IVE OF THAIS						
900	PAGAN (BURMAN CAPITAL) FOUNDED PAGAN DYNASTY		ANGKOR KINGDOM			UNION OF SAILENDRAS & SRIVIJAYA	MATARAM
1000				TONKIN GAINS INDEPENDENCE			
1100	THAI ON (MON CAPIT AL) TAKEN		WA RS BET WEEN KHM ERS & CH AMS				KADIRI
1200							
1300	MONGOL INVASION END OF PAGAN DYNASTY	THAI ESTABLISHED IN CHENGMAI	THAI ATTACKS	MONGOL INVASION	TAMERA LINGA	INVASION	SINGHASARI / MAJAPAHIT
1400	PEGU INDEPENDENT KINGDOM	THAI ESTABLISHED IN AYUTHIA	ANGKOR ABANDONED	MING CONQUEST	MALACCA	CONQUEST OF SRIVIJAYA	
1500				VIETNAM GAINS INDEPENDENCE	SIAMESE INVASIONS		END OF MAJAPAHIT

SOURCE: Brian Harrison, South-East Asia, A Short History (second ed.) (New York, St. Martin's, 1963), p. 39. By permission of the author.

As can be reasoned from the chart, the period between 500 and 1000 was marked by the dominance of the Khmer kingdom at Angkor; the southward drive of the Burmans and Thais; and the emergence of Srivijaya in Sumatra. Angkor, near Siem Reap in Cambodia, succeeded to Funan as the supreme Hinduized state in Southeast Asia. The Khmer kings built their royal capital as an image of the world in miniature. The central mountain, dedicated to the Hindu god Siva, was the home of the gods. The wall of rocks, surrounded by the moat, represented the ends of the world encircled by the great oceans. The numerous stone images were dedicated not only to kings but also to gods with whom the kings would be united at death. Both Brahmanism and Buddhism were patronized by the court, but Brahmanism enjoyed special favors because of the close association of the status of the god-king with the cult of Siva. The various temples were mausoleums as well as shrines. Angkor Wat (*wat* means temple), the greatest of the Khmer temples, was the burial place of one of the most famous of the kings and at the same time a sanctuary to the Hindu deity, Vishnu. It was built in the twelfth century and its ruins are among the wonders of the world.

Far to the north and west of Angkor, the Burmans and the Thais made their first entries onto the stage of history during this period. Moving out of China, the Burmans moved slowly across the mountains and established their capital at Pagan, near Mandalay. Less glamorous than Angkor, nonetheless it was the cradle of civilization in upper Burma. The kings of Pagan occupied most of their time and exhausted all their energies in fighting the Mons and the Thais. This period was also the commencement of the great trek of the Thais to the south. When their kingdom of Nanchao, in southwest China, was destroyed, the various branches of their family fanned out through the mountains in search of new homes. Some gravitated toward Indochina and sought a foothold there. Others went far afield and attacked the Burmans on their home front, or nibbled at the fringes of the imposing empire of the Khmers. The main body of the Thais pushed into northern Siam where they were later to found a kingdom of their own.

In the meantime, two Hinduized kingdoms—one in Sumatra and the other in east Java—stirred to new life. The first was Srivijaya, near Palembang, which was in better position than Angkor to derive political and commercial advantage from the trade between India and China. Srivijaya had always enjoyed close trade relations with the Coramandel coast, but it boomed when T'ang China displayed a new interest in the export of its famed bronzes, pottery, and silk. Chinese records and stone inscriptions tell the basic facts about the rise of Srivijaya. A Chinese trade mission was sent to Southeast Asia early in the seventh century and in 670 Srivijaya sent the first of many embassies to China. A Chinese Buddhist pilgrim, I Tsing, spent eleven years in Srivijaya at that time. He reported the presence of a thousand Buddhist priests there and told of the fleets of Persian merchant ships which had arrived from Ceylon. The rulers of Srivijaya were distinguished for their commercial enterprise and their enthusiasm for Buddhism of the elaborate Mahayana school.

The second Hinduized kingdom was that of Sailendra in Java, many sailing days away from Srivijaya. The Sailendra kings responded warmly to the advances of Buddhism, and in the eighth century built the magnificent Buddhist monuments of east Java, including the temples of the Prambanan Valley and the shrine of Boro Budur. The shrine was an immense stupa of nine terraces built on a natural hill, with three miles of circular galleries and hundreds of statues of the Buddha. The sculpture was Indian in inspiration and Buddhist as to subject matter. The bas-reliefs were Javanese and pictured a wonderful panorama of Java's life and customs.

In spite of Buddhist inclinations, the Sailendra kings fought their way to supremacy over rivals at home. They assumed the time-honored Hindu title of "king of the mountains." No pacifists, they. They fought to victory over Angkor and raided the coasts of Annam and Malaya. In 850 the heartiest of their buccaneer-rajahs united his energy with the prestige of Srivijaya and from then until the fall of the Srivijayan empire, the Javanese Sailendras directed its fortunes. The strategy of preservation was to fight when necessary against weaker neighbors, but to avoid conflicts with India, China, and the rising power of the Thais in Siam. At one time when Cholas of India invaded Srivijaya, the Srivijayan forces were out fighting in Java. In its moments of glory, Srivijaya controlled what pan-Malayans would like to see again—a single ruler for practically all the area sandwiched between India and China.

The period from 1000 to 1500 might be called Southeast Asia's age of tragedy. Srivijaya disappeared and left a legacy of piracy and trade monopoly. By the time Marco Polo arrived there (1292) it was less important than neighboring Djambi, the capital of the kingdom of Malayu. The *coup de grace* to Srivijaya came from east Java. While Sumatra suffered, east Java flourished. As a result of civil wars, a political meteor known as the kingdom of Majapahit (which means bitter fruit) flashed briefly in the skies of Southeast Asia. It lasted for more than two centuries (1293–1520), but even this is brief in Asian time. An undistinguished king had a distinguished prime minister—Gaja Mada (1330–1364)—who was the hero of Majapahit. His memory is perpetuated in streets and parks and in modern Indonesia's greatest university. He is remembered—but not revered—for the sharpness of his sword, which made Majapahit the master of the world from the Philippines to the tip of Sumatra. He is the idol of modern Indonesian nationalists because, in the name of the king, he administered justice, protected the lands and crops of the people, and looked after the poor and the humble as well as the rich and the illustrious. While the king "without cares and worries, indulged in all pleasures, since all beautiful maidens in Janggala and Kediri are selected for him, and of those who are captured in foreign countries, the prettiest girls are brought to his harem," his distinguished first minister, Gaja Mada, devoted himself to the welfare of his domain.

After Gaja Mada, Majapahit also faded away. It was regarded as only a "heathen kingdom of a heathen people" by the Portuguese when Albuquerque sent an embassy there after his conquest of Malacca in 1511.

In Indochina between 1000 and 1500 the Khmer kingdom dissipated its brilliance in luxury and conquest. Angkor could not match either Srivijaya or Majapahit in strength or power over its neighbors. While the king disported himself in oriental splendor, "holding audiences enthroned on couches inlaid with aromatic woods and precious stones," or "riding his elephants in dazzling processions," the kingdom sank into decline and ruin. Neither the labor of the slaves nor the limited funds of the royal treasury were adequate to keep up the incessant wars with the Chams to the east and the Thais and the Mons to the west. When Cambodia fell apart, the remnants included the kingdom of the Laos, known as Lan Xang or the Land of a Million Elephants. The prince of Luang Prabang moved his capital to Vientiane where he enshrined a gold statue which he venerated as the guardian deity of his country.

Much of the later destiny of Southeast Asia was shaped by the blustering attitudes of the Mongols after they gained control of China. Mongol envoys tried to frighten Majapahit into surrender, but the Javanese put the envoys to death and defeated the fleet which was dispatched to avenge the crime. The Mongols tried to force the Chams into submission, but as the Mongol power waned the Chams kept their independence and the Chinese lost their Annamite vassal. The Mongols threatened the Thai position in Chiengmai, north Siam, but they only succeeded in driving the Thais into a stronger position farther away from the Chinese menace at Ayuthia, near Bangkok, in the south. The Mongol raiders destroyed the Burman capital at Pagan. From their new base in Ava, near Mandalay, the north Burmans could manage an occasional raid into Siam but they could never muster sufficient strength to annihilate the rival kingdom of the Mons, at Pegu near Rangoon, in lower Burma.

A new force exerted itself during this period in the form of traders, missionaries, and adventurers who gained political power because of their Moslem religion. The founder of Islam had been a member of the trading community at Mecca, so it was natural that expansion should be economic and political as well as religious. As traders moved east and west from Arabia they carried faith with their merchandise. But they could not establish deep roots in Southeast Asia until after the establishment of the Moslem sultanate at Delhi. Chinese records tell of an embassy to the Chinese court in 1281 led by two Moslems from Malayu and two Moslem communities were reported a little later in Sumatra by Marco Polo. Moslem settlements in the Malayan peninsula date from 1386 and the earliest Moslem grave in Java, near Surabaya, has been identified as dating from 1419. By the end of the fifteenth century, some twenty communities in Sumatra, Malaya, and Java had accepted Islam as their religion.

As the Indian merchants—primarily Moslem Gujarati and Bengali—peddled their textiles, they reaped extra dividends in religious converts. The most important ruler to be converted was the rajah of Malacca. He was most eager to woo the Indian trade from his rivals on the Sumatra side of the narrow straits. Malacca was founded in 1403 by a refugee from the fishing village and pirate headquarters at Singapore. Originally Malacca was a typical Hinduized settlement, but after fifty years it became the center of Moslem influence. It grew into one of the most cosmopolitan trading centers in the world. Four-masted junks from China with cargoes of silk, porcelains, damasks, brocades and satins, musk and rhubarb, silver, pearls, and gilded fans exchanged their wares for textiles and opium from India and the spices, incense, saffron, coral, and quicksilver from the Indies. The fame of Malacca spread to Europe, but the bustling city knew no unity or peace. In its struggle for survival it learned the virtue of mixed customs and divided loyalties. It followed alternating policies of diplomacy and war with rising Siam and dying Majapahit. For its own protection it sent embassies and paid tribute-money to China. In deference to China only the sultan of Malacca could wear the imperial yellow color of China and deck himself in Chinese-style hats.

CULTURE AND CIVILIZATION

The early European arrivals in Southeast Asia encountered civilizations which were similar to—yet vastly different from—those of India or China. The peoples of Southeast Asia were not cultural stepchildren of India or China. They gave their own cultural twist to importations and created something entirely unique from the combination of alien ideas and native genius. The art and architecture of Angkor, Pagan, central Java, and the kingdom of Champa were strangely different from mother India. Indonesians (using the word in the general sense of all the early inhabitants of Southeast Asia) who were first exposed to the culture values of India and China were not wild men, but communities with a relatively high civilization of their own.

Before the impact of India, Indonesians cultivated the fields, applied irrigation, and constructed ingenious terraces; domesticated the ox and the buffalo; and knew how to make rudimentary use of metals. They were skilled woodworkers, weavers, and pottery makers. They had canoes made out of hollowed tree trunks and made good use of wind and sails. They were seafarers and understood something of the stars. They lived in wooden houses built on stilts and made clothing from the bark of trees. They were animists who worshiped their ancestors, the spirits of nature, and the gods of the soil. They loved to feast, drink, and dance. Their dances ranged from raucous burlesques on the life and habits of monkeys to solemn ritual dances of the priests. They accorded women a favored place in their families (unlike India) and they clustered their homes in villages. They created and preserved a rich folklore and gradually developed a body of laws and social customs. With all these things in common, they nevertheless developed characteristics as distinctive as the *wayang* or shadow theater; the *gamelan* orchestras and batiks of Java; and the music, dancing, carving and architecture of the Thais.

As Southeast Asia from Burma to Bali received colonists, sailors, refugees, merchants, and missionaries from India, they also absorbed the new religions complete with mythology, philosophy, temples, and statues. They learned the classical Sanskrit language and the art of writing. They enriched their own romantic folk tales with the legends of Hinduism. They were given new knowledge of medicine and mathematics, astronomy and astrology, law and politics, as well as craftsmanship and industrial arts. In an original intercultural exchange program, learned Indian scholars and teachers went to overseas centers to teach, while Burman, Cambodian, or Sumatran students went to Indian universities or temples to study. The centers of Hindu culture in Southeast Asia were hermitages where holy men devoted their lives to study, meditation, and teaching.

Southeast Asians found it to their advantage to take the best of both Hinduism and Buddhism. Buddhist monks were as welcome as Hindu Brahmans. Any single religious site was likely to contain temples as sacred to the one as the other. Pagan was in a valley of Hindu temples, but it was a center of Buddhist culture for two and a half centuries. Angkor, which in 1200 was reported to be "a city of a million people, larger than the Rome of the Caesars" and "more lovely and romantic than anything to be seen in China," was the most brilliant shrine of Hinduism, but was filled with Buddhist statues. In art and architecture the Javanese achieved the union of Hinduism and Buddhism and gave to both their exquisite native touch.

The creeds—if they may be called creeds—of both religions became so mixed together that it was impossible to say precisely what was Hindu and what was Buddhist. The cult of Siva was particularly attractive as local potentates who liked the idea of being assimilated to upper-caste men, with the privilege of building monuments to themselves as gods and kings. They insisted upon "mountains" in the midst of their capitals and they kept Brahmans at their courts as astrologers, soothsayers, and masters of rites and ceremonies. The common people seemed to like Buddhism better, fundamentally because of their resistance to the caste system, their appreciation of equality, and their comfort in the Lord Buddha's religious teaching. Among Burmans and Thais, Buddhism became the mainspring of cultural life. Every village had a temple which served as school, fairgrounds, retreat and home of the yellow-robed priests. Every young man was obliged to spend part of his time as a monk, and the full-time clergy made up a substantial and influential portion of the population.

Southeast Asia was affected differently by China than by India. According to Chinese records, the Han emperors opened a mountain passage through Yunnan, across Burma and thence by the Brahmaputra Valley to the Hellenistic kingdom of Bactria. They also sent seafarers to the populous islands in the south, which sent tribute to China as early as the reign of the Emperor Wu (140–86 B.C.). The usurper emperor, Wang Mang during the time of Christ was supposed to have sent presents to the King of Acheh on the tip of Sumatra and to have asked for a rhinoceros in return. Han pottery with inscriptions dating from 45 B.C. have been found in Borneo, Java, and Sumatra. Artifacts presumably from the same period have been dug up in the Philippines.

It was easy for the Chinese to move down the coast and establish contacts with the Philippines, Java, Sumatra, and ports near the present Malacca on the western shores of the Malay Peninsula. As traders took bronzes and silks, pottery and porcelain to Srivijaya or Majapahit, they also brought the language, philosophy, and way of life of China. Artisans and craftsmen from China established new homes in the southern region, married native girls, and their children went into agriculture, mining, and every phase of economic activity.

Relations between Southeast Asia and China were commercial and diplomatic rather than cultural. The Chinese themselves were importers of religious ideas—primarily Buddhism—and they were indifferent to the promotion of the export of Confucianism. The Chinese assumed that they were superior to local "barbarians" (anyone outside the Chinese culture pattern was considered a barbarian); and they felt that China was the center of the world. As patron and protector, the emperor of China assumed rights of investiture over local kings and demanded tribute from them. On their part the local kings were grateful for his recognition and approval, and they frequently went in person with huge retinues to pay their homage to Nanking or Peking, whichever happened to be the Chinese capital. On their return they brought precious gifts and Chinese who would serve as advisers or teachers of their local craftsmen. The tribute system was an excellent device for commercial and cultural intercourse.

China showed little interest in political control beyond its own borders except in neighboring Tonkin, the home of the Nam Viets. *Nam* is the word for south and Viet or Yueh is a name for the people of South China. For a thousand years beginning with the Han Dynasty, the Chinese exercised power over the Nam Viets—or the Annamites—in Tonkin. (Although the local people called themselves Nam Viets, the Chinese called them Annamites, meaning the people who lived south of An, or the country of peace, as the Chinese euphemistically called themselves.) The inhabitants of Tonkin, the neighbors of China in the northern part of the Indochina peninsula, were thus not subject to the cultural influences of India but to those of China. It was reflected in their language, religion, concepts of government and philosophy. They accepted Chinese cultural influence, but they despised Chinese political domination. At their first opportunity, with the collapse of the Tang Dynasty about the year 1000, they threw off the Chinese yoke, though independence meant civil chaos and constant warfare with the Chinese, Chams, Khmers, Thais, and Laos by whom they were surrounded.

For a brief time under the aggressive Mongols, the Chinese launched attacks on Java and Burma, but the results were disastrous. Again in the fourteenth century, during the reign of the first ambitious Ming emperor, the fleets of Admiral Cheng Ho and his associate Grand Eunuchs roamed the China Seas and the Indian Ocean. The Chinese went to Calicut in India, Ormus on the Persian Gulf, and perhaps as far as the coasts of Africa. Their armadas carried as many as 37,000 troops, forced local sovereigns to accept yellow umbrellas as symbols of their vassalage, and presented rolls of silk, incense, and porcelain in exchange for tribute.

Chinese seapower faded as spectacularly as it arose. When the Mings moved their capital from Nanking to Peking in 1409, they abandoned their interest in trade to Arabs and Indians. In their homeland, they turned to seclusion. Their subjects were forbidden to travel overseas without imperial license, and their coastal ports were closed. Only Canton was permitted to have maritime trade and it was fettered with cumbersome restrictions. The Portuguese did not come in contact with Chinese until they reached Malacca.

Indonesians chose and modified what they wanted from the civilization identified with Islam in the same manner that they had adapted Hinduism and Buddhism in their local environment. Islam in Southeast Asia became a synthetic religion. Fanatic Moslem newcomers were less tolerant than their hosts so they frequently destroyed the temples and monuments of the infidels as they had done in India. But when new mosques were built, Hindu and Buddhistic bas-reliefs were added to the familiar arches, domes, and minarets of central Asia. Traders were effective missionaries, and the exchange of gifts and daughters often made the sword unnecessary. Local rulers sometimes accepted Islam because it symbolized wealth and commercial success. They changed their titles from rajah to sultan but they kept their Indian astrologers and preserved the Brahmanistic rites at court. The common people simply followed the leaders. The new religion meant little more to them than a new name for the gods. It was as easy to adopt Islam as it had been to accept the other religions from India.

The cultural vitality of Islam survived at Malacca. The educated members of the sultan's retinue studied the Koran and read or listened to Moslem historical romances, which were more interesting to an imaginative people than lessons in the difficult Arabic language. The interest in theological speculation was reminiscent of medieval Europe. A sultan offered nine pounds of gold dust and two slave girls to any wise man who could say if those in heaven or hell remain in their respective places forever! The court was not without intellectual interests. Much romance, mysticism, and law, all coming from Mogul India and tinged with Indian ideas, spread from Malacca to the Moluccas. Half the population of Malaya, the islands of Indonesia, and the southern Philippines accepted Moslem ideas of the equality of man and individual salvation. The faith of Islam was on the march, until it was challenged and contained by powerful new beliefs which came out of the West.

THE WAY OF LIFE

When the Portuguese intruded upon the scene, Southeast Asia was not a paradise about to be shattered; it was a region of the world which through a thousand years of leisurely development had evolved a way of life in keeping with the tropics and in tune with its cultural environment. Life had its share of blessings—and of problems. The chronology of rajahs and kings can be pieced together from fragments of the historical record, but the story of the interests and habits of the common people is more difficult to obtain. The masses were much less affected than the local elite by contacts with the outside world.

As the years rolled along, variations increased among the peoples of Southeast Asia. Some primitive tribes remained in the forests and preserved their animistic religions. They practiced ritualistic cannibalism and witchcraft. They listened to medicine men and tattooed their bodies to keep the devils away. At the other extreme, some people prospered because they lived along the paths of commerce. Plural societies came into being where minority groups lived separately yet side by side in a single city or limited geographic area. The masses were uncomplicated farmers and fisherfolk who were poor and patient, opposed to exertion, and interested in the least effort for the most and best food. They slipped from one emotional extreme to another—from love to hate or deep sadness to wild exhilaration. Their lives were short, bittersweet compounds of pleasure and pain. They were pawns to be moved according to the whim of kings, rajahs, or sultans.

The social structure was based on the family unit (often matriarchal) and the village community. Women were theoretically never the equal of men, but the practical position of women belied the theory. They were not held down by the Hindu caste system nor the Moslem purdah. They enjoyed a better status than elsewhere in Asia in matters of marriage, divorce, and property rights; and the say of women in domestic affairs was usually final. The family was a well-knit unit, with its social rights and obligations defined and enforced by the adat, or body of customary law. The village was the responsibility of the head man, whose position was in some places hereditary and in others elective. The village was in charge of its own affairs, with only the responsibility of paying taxes or providing forced labor for the rajah or his representative. Authority was symbolized by the rajah, who was expected to be absolute or despotic except as he was checked by the adat. Rights for the individual were nonexistent. The only security or freedom which the individual knew was that which came from membership in the family, religious, or village group.

On the economic side, land was owned ultimately by the rajah. Much was kept for his own exploitation and sometimes he had a whole army of slaves to work on his own estates. That which was not for his personal account was retained by the village community—not the individual—and a portion was assigned by the community to the individual for his own use. Except for a few capital crops (primarily spices) in the hands of local potentates, agricultural production was on a subsistence basis. Tenancy and rural indebtedness were commonplace. Trade between peasants was a matter of barter, swapping on a basis of subjective desires without any reference to money values. Not even the local rajahs were any match in trade for the sharp Arab, Indian, and Chinese merchants.

Ordinary free men were mostly concerned with their families and the daily demands of their simple level of living. They produced their own staple foods; built their own homes and made their own clothes. All from abundant native resources. For their celebrations they distilled spirits from rice and coconuts. Rice was the staff of life. Even in the river valleys where soil was fertile, the procurement of food was a full-time job. Famines did not curse the land—as they did in India—but torrential rains, tropical weeds, insects, and plagues of locusts were perpetual enemies. Only a few were rich, but no one starved. The economy was geared to self-sufficiency and was entirely "underdeveloped" according to those standards of specialization and large-scale production which were to be required by the world on the threshold of industrialization.

For centuries native peoples took from the earth the gold, silver, tin, iron, coal, copper, and semiprecious stones for their own skilled crafts-men to turn into beautiful ornaments. They had their local industries—"mines, gold-washing, looms, farms, barter, naval construction, raising of poultry and stock, weaving of silk and cotton, distilleries, manufacture of arms, pearl fisheries, the civet industry, the horn and hide industry, etc."—according to the Philippine writer Jose Rizal who was describing his own country before the advent of the Spanish. These things were of tremendous local importance, but of no consequence to foreign ad-venturers in whose eyes the wealth of the Indies meant spices—and later raw materials and markets for their own burgeoning industries.

From a political viewpoint, Southeast Asia in premodern times did not spawn nations nor the idea of nationality as we understand these. Nor did it achieve regional unity. Kingdoms rose and fell, and in their battles they destroyed one another's monuments. They controlled large areas for long periods of time, but they disappeared. They left no suc-cessor kingdoms passionately dedicated to the recapture of real or fancied ancient glories. Sultans became preoccupied with problems of survival or succession. They were frequently involved in petty quarrels or per-sonal fights, usually with neighbors but often with distant foes. South-east Asia was often represented as a land of tropical tranquility; it might also have been pictured as a chain of political volcanoes.

When the Spanish and Portuguese came, Southeast Asia was a patch work of quarreling sultanates and kingdoms. India was in fragments and China was in seclusion. Japan was practically unheard of. The nations of the West were aggressive and adventuresome. They found Burmans di-vided—Ava versus Pegu—and ready to fight the Thais. The ambitious Thais were split—Chiengmai in the north against Ayuthia in the south—and in habitual wars with Burmans and Khmers. Angkor had been swal-lowed by the jungles and like Srivijaya and Majapahit was only a famous name in the minds of the holy men. Sumatra and Java, torn asunder by warring kingdoms, were ready victims for foreign conquest. Vietnam, restless in its uneasy independence, was a battlefield between Hanoi and Hué. The Malay kingdom of Malacca, the symbol of Islam, was a city-state and trading emporium, but it was surrounded by swamps and jungles, and it knew more of piracy and malaria than silver and gold. The Philippine Islands were troubled by nothing worse then feuds and fights between petty chieftains, and they were wide open for the advance of Islam and Christianity. It was easy for the west to prove itself stronger, but that does not mean greater or wiser.

The Crusades had stimulated trade between Europe and Asia. When the Moslems were blocked from Europe, they turned to Asia and obtained a monopoly on the Asian end of the spice trade, which was the most lucrative source of profit in the world. The Moslems collected the spices at Asian ports and in their own ships brought the spices to the Persian Gulf or the Red Sea. From there the spices were forwarded to Alexandria. As Egyption middlemen increased taxes and levies, a steady stream of Moslem merchants followed a new path through Persia to ports on the eastern Mediterranean. The spices were then distributed through Europe, primarily by the merchants of Venice and the other Italian city-states.

Travelers on the highways of Europe spun tall tales about the East, capped by the first appearance of the book of Marco Polo's voyages in 1477. The daring of sea captains and the ingenuity of merchants combined with the imagination of European princes to make the most of the opportunities in the Indies. It was an irony of history that the products of Southeast Asia were to make it possible for Europe to recoil upon Asia. It was perhaps a greater irony that at a later date Europe took to Asia wealth of another kind—the ideas of the French Revolution—which were to inspire Asia to cast out its former masters.

SUGGESTED READING

Beyer, H. O., "Philippine and East Asian Archaeology," *Bulletin of the University of the Philippines,* No. 29, 1948 (Quezon City, 1948).

Briggs, L. P., *The Ancient Khmer Kingdom* (Philadelphia, American Philosophical Society, 1951).

Coedes, G., *Les États Hindourisés d'Indochine et d'Indonesie* (Paris, DeBoccard, 1948).

Cooper-Cole, Fay, *Peoples of Malaysia* (Princeton, Van Nostrand, 1945).

Damrong, Prince, "Siamese History prior to the Founding of Ayuddhya." *Journal of the Siam Society,* xiii, part 2, pp. 1–66 (Bangkok, 1919).

Groslier, Bernard, *The Art of Indo China* (New York, Crown, 1959).

Hall, D. G. E., *Burma* (London, Hutchinson's University Library, 1950).

———, *Historians of South-east Asia* (New York, Oxford, 1961).

———, "Southeast Asia Civilizations," in *Collier's Encyclopedia* (1962, vol. 2, p. 622).

Heine-Geldern, Robert G., *Conceptions of State and Kingship in Southeast Asia* (Ithaca, Cornell U., 1956).

Hinton, Harold, *Chinese Relations with Burma and Vietnam* (New York, Institute of Pacific Relations, 1958).

MacDonald, Malcolm, *Borneo People* (London, Cape, 1956).

———, *Angkor* (New York, Praeger, 1959).

Murdock, George P., (ed.), *Social Structure in Southeast Asia* (Chicago, Quadrangle, 1960).

Vlekke, B. A. M., *Nusantara, a History of the East Indian Archipelago* (Cambridge, Harvard U., 1955).

Wagner, Frits A., *The Art of Indonesia* (New York, Crown, 1955).

Winstedt, Sir Richard, *Malaya and Its History* (second rev. ed.) (London, Hutchinson's University Library, 1951).

Zaide, Gregorio F., *Philippine Political and Cultural History* (two vols.) (Manila, Philippine Education, 1957).

5

Commerce, Christianity, and Colonization

The coming of Europeans marked the end of an era in Asia. The peoples of Asia could no longer live apart from the influences of the rest of the world. Their cultures were to feel the impact of a new religion and the spirit of science. Their social structures were to be shaken and their economies revolutionized by conditions which resulted from the impact of the West. The age of imperialism was about to begin.

The story of the expansion of Europe is quite familiar. Students of European history understand the pushing forces which operated on Portugal and Spain, the Netherlands, and subsequently France and England. The voyages of Columbus and John Cabot; the explorations of Balboa, De Soto, and Coronado; and the settlements in Massachusetts, Virginia, and Florida illustrated the influence of the old world, Europe, on the new, America. But the story had a counterpart—the impact of the old world, Europe, on the older, Asia. The same forces which led the immortal Genoan admiral to America in the service of the sovereign of Spain drove the Portuguese to India and beyond. Columbus landed in the New World in 1492; Vasco da Gama anchored his tiny sailing vessels in Calicut, south India, six years later. The ships of Magellan completed the first trip around the world in 1521.

While Europeans spread over the Americas, they also spread over Asia. While they fought "Indians" in America, they also fought "Indians" in India. While chartered companies reaped substantial profits from the American trade, they also prospered from trade with Asia. Some sailing vessels crossed the North Atlantic to the American colonies; others belonging to the same companies sailed southward—eventually to turn either east or west to the Indies.

British pirates operated in the Spanish Main in the Caribbean; they also chased the Manila galleon in the Pacific. For more than a century

Dutch Protestants fought Portuguese Catholics between Ceylon and Formosa. The British and the Dutch carried on the Wars of a Hundred Years with stakes as diverse as Manhattan in America and the Spice Islands at the opposite extreme of the world. When French fought British, they met in Canada, the Mississippi Valley, Pennsylvania, and India; and when the treaties of peace were signed the mighty powers disposed of Canada, the American colonies, and settlements in Asia as pawns in a global chess game. Many an honored colonial servant left his name in the annals of three continents. After Cornwallis surrendered at Yorktown, he went on to India to carve out a distinguished career.

From the standpoint of Europe, those were the feverish days of ad-venture and excitement, of expanding wealth and increasing power. The young and strong took off for the Indies for the love of God, gold, and glory. The Portuguese established their colonies from Goa to Macao, and the Spanish made their mark for ever on the isles of the Philippines. The Dutch spread the name and fame of their small country from the Cape of Good Hope through Indonesia to the harbor of Nagasaki. The French made settlements in India and converted the Indochina peninsula into their gallery on the Pacific. The British carried their trade, their flag, and their ideas from India to China and created an empire on which the sun never set.

But what about Asia? Asians did not know what was happening in Europe; and they were not to learn until later—much, much later—about the reaction of Americans to European colonialism. As India, Southeast Asia, China, and Japan continued to live and to grow in the time between the first arrival of the Portuguese (1498) and the outbreak of the Opium War (1839), each was to experience and react in its own way to the activities of the Europeans who wanted to make their future in Asia.

INDIA AND ITS FIRST EUROPEANS

The first Europeans received by India were Portuguese. An Indian pilot brought Vasco da Gama safely to the port of Calicut in 1498. The zamorin, or Hindu rajah, treated the Portuguese with friendship and en-gaged in mutually beneficial trade relations. When da Gama disposed of his cargo on his return to Lisbon he netted sixty times the amount of his investment, although a third of his men lost their lives in the enter-prise. During the next ten years, the Portuguese defeated Arabs, Turks, and Egyptians to establish command of the sea route to India. In 1511 they captured Goa. A viceroy of Portugal established his headquarters in Goa and built a city on the coast of India which was reminiscent of his native land. It contained a plaza, or public square, the viceroy's mansion and public office buildings, the fortress, tax headquarters, and the cathedral. From Goa, the Portuguese expanded their empire and enforced their commercial monopoly. All Indian goods had to pass through Portuguese channels and had to be shipped to Europe by way of the Cape of Good Hope. The Persian Gulf and the Red Sea were closed. Goa also became missionary headquarters for the entire Far East. The cross was as familiar as the sword as the symbol of Portugal in India, and the archbishop lived in splendor comparable to that of the viceroy.

Goa and the Portuguese remained on the fringe of Indian life, except for servants and soldiers who took jobs with the Portuguese. The Portuguese profited from the trade monopoly, but so did Indian rajahs and merchants. No Indian navy could challenge the Portuguese, and no native army could stand up against the Portuguese garrison. No Indians registered substantial objections to the little band of Portuguese at Goa. The Portuguese did not have many men to spare for service in the East and made no serious effort to establish colonies in India beyond their fortress capital on the coast. In matters of religion, the Portuguese hated the Moslems more than the Hindus. The Hindus were tolerant; both the Moslems and the Christians were intolerant. Hindus found it to their advantage to side with the Portuguese against the Moslem conquerors. A Portuguese visitor in 1522 to the Hindu kingdom of Vijayanagar described its ruler as "the most feared and perfect king that could possibly be, cheerful of disposition and very merry, he is one that seeks to honor foreigners and receives them kindly." Hindus changed their minds about Portuguese when the latter showed themselves to be as ruthless as Moslems in destroying idols and temples and (through the Inquisition) in trying to control the thoughts of men.

India saw little of the Dutch. Although the Dutch established factories on the Coramandel coast, in Gujarat and Bengal, it was the islands of Indonesia rather than India which received most of the Dutch attention. The Danes and Swedes made slight efforts to develop trading interests in India, and the French established political and commercial footholds which were identified with France for nearly three hundred years. The French were overpowered by the British in India as they were in America, and the tiny settlements which the French retained were little more than monuments to the shattered dreams of a few Frenchmen who would have had France play in India the role which was destined for the British.

India received its first Englishman in the person of Ralph Fitch, who with three companions in 1583 reached the Mogul capital at Agra. As soon as British appetites were whetted for the profits of the India trade, India became a pawn in the world-wide struggle between England and Spain (which had annexed Portugal and succeeded to its empire in 1580). At the time the Spanish armada met disaster in British home waters

(1588), famous sea dogs like Drake and Cavendish hunted down Spanish ships wherever they could be found. With command of the seven seas, the British expanded their commercial interests. They bought cotton, cotton yarn, silk and silk piece goods from India; they sold silver, metals, and cotton broadcloth; and they made money in the carrying trade. After they defeated the Spanish, they made peace with Spain. They concentrated on commercial rivalry with the Dutch, which, after a hundred years of sporadic competition and war, came to a halt with the Dutch paramount in Japan and the East Indies and the British predominant in New Amsterdam (New York) and India.

The British formed a company of "Governors and Merchants of London Trading with the East Indies" in 1600, which was reorganized into the "English East India Company" in 1698. By charter the company was empowered to discover trade, establish factories, build ships, collect customs duties, enlist native militia; build fortresses; send ships of war, men, or ammunition for the security of the fortresses; appoint local governors and councilors; seize interlopers and administer English law and justice. It could coin money and make peace or war with non-Christian nations. To all intents and purposes the company had the blessing of the British government to act in India as a sovereign state. Company officials in Bombay were instructed "to establish such a politic of civil and military power and such a large revenue as may be the foundation of a large, well-grounded sure English dominion in India for all time to come." The company quickly established main factories at three strategic corners of the triangle in India—Madras (1639), Bombay (1661), and Calcutta (1690).

The British felt that war and traffic were incompatible and that a "military-commercial policy had been the beggaring of Portugal and the mistake of the Dutch." Unlike the Portuguese they were not swashbucklers and they were not filled to overflowing with religious zeal. They would have preferred trading to fighting, but the one was impossible without the other. The lives of their merchants and the security of their settlements were at the mercy of Mogul-appointed viceroys and governors. Local sultans and rajahs were constantly in dire economic straits, and they turned to the British for assistance. The company exercised its political prerogatives as a protective response to chronic native wars and the arbitrary actions of the local rulers. Sometimes it was impossible to avoid a fight; other times the company was able to use its influence and its dollars to send "advisers" to neighboring nabobs or to bring about the succession of friendly rulers to local thrones. It was as easy for Indians to get along with the British as it had been to get along with the Portuguese before them. While some Indians harassed the British, others cooperated. No stigma was attached to collaboration, and Indian soldiers manned the regiments which fought under the company's banner.

As the British pushed forward, they solidified their gains by means of treaties. They met the costs of their campaigns primarily by new exactions which were levied on their new Indian subjects. In 1756, to avenge the "Black Hole of Calcutta" where some British prisoners perished during a suffocating night, the company made itself the *de facto* political power of Bengal. It agreed to pay the Mogul emperor a half-million dollars annually in exchange for the right to collect and administer the revenues of Bengal, Bihar, and Orissa. After the loss of the American colonies, the British redoubled their political activities in India against the deteriorating Mogul empire. They marched and fought in the name of protection for their trade. They brought much of India into their sphere of command by wars and intrigue, and by what one British writer called a series of "fortuitous circumstances and lucky flukes." By the middle of the nineteenth century Gurkhas and Sikhs were defeated, and the Maratha confederacy was destroyed. All India except the northwest frontier accepted the British ascendancy and looked to the British for the granting of rights and privileges.

By the India Acts of the British parliament, as early as 1773, the British government took over matters of policy-making for India, but left the detailed matters of trade and administration in the hands of the East India Company. The company appointed a governor-general and council in Calcutta who, under the London directors, carried out the functions of government in India. Subject to the ultimate sanction of parliament, the company officials raised the army and navy and negotiated treaties for the preservation of law and order. They also established an administrative system, created the professional Indian civil service, dispensed justice and collected taxes and revenues. It was their decision to keep the shadow Mogul emperor in his hollow grandeur at Delhi and to pay him the empty homage due his ceremonial position. It was they who permitted the continuation of one-third of India's acreage and one-fifth its people under quasi-independent princely states, which in exchange for the protective wing of the company agreed to accept advisers or residents in their courts. It was they who wanted to disturb the social *status quo* in India as little as possible.

But it was that ultimate responsibility to parliament which prompted the most enlightened of the company's administrators to attack the institutions of slavery, female infanticide, suttee (the burning of Hindu widows on the funeral pyres of their husbands) and *thuggee,* or gangsterism. It was the liberal spirits in England, rather than company officials, who insisted upon the spread of Protestant Christianity, the use of the English language, and the introduction of Western science.

During its period of ascendancy, the company fostered its commercial interests but also discharged its duty "to England and our posterity to propagate the future interest of our nation in India." It was dedicated to the fundamental maxim that security of protection and freedom in person and property with a due regard for the administration of justice must of necessity be stressed in a land under a despotic government. A letter of instructions from London to an officer going to India read: "Never do an act of arbitrary power to hurt anybody. . . . Let your determination be always just, not rigorous, but inclining to the just, merciful side always try the cause, never the party. Don't let passion over-cloud your reason. This will make people respect you whereas one violent sentence or action will sully the reputation of ten good ones."

According to many recent Indian writers, negative aspects of England in India before the middle of the nineteenth century should be stressed. In their view, the British derived disproportionate benefits in their relations with India. When the British arrived, Hindustan had many cities as extensive, populous and rich as the city of London. The British made profits in the exchange of Indian goods and, in protection of their home market, levied heavy duties against the exquisite India imports. Many Indians say that the British merchants were not interested in good government (or any government), but only in dividends and treasure. The company representatives did private business on their own account and were guilty of "corruption, venality, nepotism, violence and greed of money beyond comprehension." In the vassal states, there was a complete divorce between power and responsibility.

Prime Minister Nehru has written that the period of war, conquest, and plunder converted central India and Rajputana and some parts of west and south India into derelict areas full of violence, unhappiness, and misery. Armies marched across India; and in their train came highway robbers, as in the Europe of the Thirty Years' War. Nehru called the areas under British control a "seething delirium of misery" as contrasted to the Maratha's "oasis of gentle security." According to him, it was not the England of Milton or Shakespeare which came to India. It was not the social reformers, but "the conservatives representing the most reactionary class in England." They opposed change in India as they did in England; and when change finally came, it was in spite of them rather than because of them. Nehru called the Indian civil service the world's most tenacious trade union—"in the land of caste the British, more especially the Indian Civil Service was the most rigid and exclusive of all." He argued that although it could be said that the British rescued India from chaos and anarchy, it could also be said that they contributed to the diseases which they cured. In his opinion, maybe India would have found its law and order without the British as it had done many times in its five thousand years of history.

SOUTHEAST ASIA AND THE EUROPEANS

The Indonesian peoples of Southeast Asia were accustomed to strangers and foreigners before the Europeans arrived. Chinese, Japanese, Arabs, and Persians were frequent visitors in waters east of India. Chinese merchants were among the first in Malacca to welcome the Portuguese. Unknown to Asians, a papal bull and a treaty between Spain and Portugal in 1496 divided the unexplored world between those two nations. The Portuguese were allotted what they would find by sailing to the east and the Spanish what they might discover by sailing to the west. The Indies represented the ends of the world where the twain would meet.

Beyond India, the Portuguese advanced to Malacca, the Moslem stronghold which controlled trade with Malaya and Sumatra. Its strategic value was in the monopoly of the pepper trade because "whoever held Malacca had his fingers on the throat of Venice." In 1511 the forces of Albuquerque, who looked upon all mankind as Catholics, heretics, heathens, or Moors, took Malacca. Two hours before dawn, the Portuguese assembled for confession and ablution—then they sacked the city. They rebuilt Malacca after the style of Goa, complete with public square, viceroy's residence, state council chambers, government house, garrison, bishop's house, cathedral, churches and eventually a school for Portuguese and Latin. They demolished mosques and mausoleums and used the stones for donjon towers. From the local population the Portuguese demanded women, civil service employees, troops, artisans, and servants. As in India, the Portuguese confined themselves to their fortress headquarters. They made no attempt to expand their colony. They sent official expeditions to the Spice Islands, China, and Japan and "did the world extend further they would have gone there too."

Portuguese morale was perpetually at rock bottom. Most Portuguese never expected to see their homeland, and their fortress city was under constant attack by Sumatrans, Malayans, and Javanese. Only division among the neighbors enabled the Portuguese to hang on. Religious opportunities were limited. When St. Francis Xavier left Malacca, he shook the dust of the city off his feet forever and ordered the Jesuits to abandon a place so wicked. He wrote that "the knowledge of the Portuguese was restricted to the conjugation of the verb *rapio* in which they showed amazing capacity for inventing new tenses and participles."

Many adventuresome *caballeros* took off without leave and found fabulous jobs as generals and royal advisers to local sultans and kings because of their knowledge of cannons and military affairs. Officials forgot their snobbery and their high calling as Portuguese and went into business for themselves. They squeezed every possible dollar out of the fines, fees, tolls, and licenses of their trade monopoly. Their local population received nothing in return for its taxes; and the only Asians whom the Portuguese seemed to care about were their own Christian children and converts, who were treated to "continual pageantry of feasting, processions, parades, fireworks and ringing of bells." The Portuguese administration was despised for its inefficiency and corruption and hated for its cruelty and greed. The Portuguese fought all the time, but their victories never brought them treaties of friendship or alliance. After more than a hundred years, time ran out for the Portuguese in Malacca. Malacca was taken by the Dutch and their native allies in 1641.

After the formation of the Dutch East India Company in 1602, the Dutch were the most assiduous traders, and the bitter rivals of the Portuguese and the British, in Indonesia. The company was established primarily for trade; but like its British counterpart, it was given parliamentary permission to exercise the powers of government. It offered alliances to local chieftains and protection for their Mohammedan religion in exchange for trade and assistance against the Portuguese. By 1611 the Dutch had secured the spice monopoly of the Moluccas, and in 1619 they founded their trading capital at Batavia.

The company ruled in the Indies for two centuries. It was as supreme and unchallenged in Indonesia as the British company in India. It extended its sway from Sumatra to New Guinea by wars, intervention in civil conflicts, and peaceful agreements. Dutch merchants dealt with sultans and concerned themselves only incidentally with the welfare of the common man. It was firm Dutch policy to preserve local customs intact. The objectives of the company were commercial, not political. Dutch political administration was a matter of "indirect rule." Regents, or important sultans, were the paramount rulers of larger districts; lesser chiefs governed subordinate areas; and headmen ran the villages. They became vassals of the company and were made responsible for the fixed annual deliveries of such agricultural commodities as pepper, cloves, tea, tobacco, coffee, indigo, sugar, and cotton. The Dutch administrative superstructure consisted of a governor-general and the council of state in Batavia, supported by governors in the provinces and residents, assistant local residents, and controllers in the countryside. The Dutch remained in the background as far as possible, but their heavy hands and eagle eyes were responsible for continuing profits.

As profits dropped, the company shifted its emphasis from trade to agricultural development. Chinese were imported for work in the fields or in the factories. As elsewhere, they prospered. They aroused the jealousy of the native Indonesians, and they incurred the hatred of the Dutch.

Their status was always vulnerable and gave rise to frightful massacres. The company was obliged to spend more money on enforcement of its monopoly, and it tried to extend its monopoly to the import of textiles and the export of tin. It was eventually forced into bankruptcy by the wars of which the American Revolution was a part. In 1798 the Dutch government took over the affairs of the Dutch East India Company.

Southeast Asians saw comparatively little of the British until late in the eighteenth century. It might have been better for them had they learned to play the British against the Dutch in their own self-interest. The British operated occasional trading stations throughout Indonesia as early as the Dutch, but they left Indonesia to the Dutch for the sake of concentrating on India. The British did not gain a substantial foothold in that part of the world until they obtained the island of Penang from the sultan of Kedah in 1786. During the Napoleonic Wars they shattered the sea power of the Dutch and took temporary control of all the Dutch possessions in the Indies. They restored the islands to the Dutch by the treaty of peace and established their new position at Singapore which was, at the time of acquisition (1819), an island infested by pirates "of so ruthless a character that not only ships but the very devils of hell hesitate to pass by it." Singapore quickly became the key to the British position in Southeast Asia—the chief port for Chinese junks, Indonesian sailing ships, and British merchantmen from India. As a free port, it symbolized the end of trade restrictions and monopolies and was linked up with the economic and political philosophy of *laissez faire*. In 1824 the political destiny of Southeast Asia was shaped for many years by an Anglo-Dutch treaty which confirmed the British in Malaya and the Dutch in the islands of Indonesia.

While these things look place, the people of the Philippines found their own new world in the coming of the Spanish. The Spanish reached the shores of Asia by sailing west, first around the tip of South America and later directly across the mid-Pacific from their territorial base in Mexico. Unlike the rest of Southeast Asia, the Philippines was saturated by the civilization of its political overlord. The haughty Spanish conquistadores despised trade and manual labor; they came to conquer, to possess, and to rule. In 1519 the Indios—as they were called by the Spaniards—welcomed Magellan with rice, chickens, and fruit; after half a century they greeted his successors with swords and bamboo spears. Spanish arrogance turned hospitality into hostility. In contrast to the Portuguese, the Spanish did not content themselves with isolated fortresses on the coast. They placed their physical stamp on every city and town throughout the islands.

Manila was taken in 1571 and made the colonial capital. It became prosperous due to the receipt of taxes and tribute from the provinces, the commercial activity of the Chinese, and the annual galleon with Acapulco. The officials throttled all commerce except that for their own gain. They used the Chinese in their search of profit, but frequently resorted to persecution and slaughter when they feared the Chinese were becoming too strong or successful. The Spaniards reduced the Indios to tenantry on the tremendous tracts of rice and sugar land which were distributed as rewards to distinguished Spaniards, faithful Filipinos, or friars. Native industries were abandoned or neglected as people were forced to build ships or man the oars as galley slaves. Population decreased as men were taken for costly wars against the Dutch or the British. In the Seven Years' War, when the Spanish were allied with the French, Manila was occupied for two years by the British (1762–1764).

Native culture was despised. The Spaniards deigned to enrich the Philippines with their own blood, language, law, administrative system, and the Catholic Church. Mixed Spanish-Filipino parentage was the hallmark of distinction. Spanish became the language of the native aristocrats as it was the language of the court. Friars came along with the conquistadores. Manila was identified as the religious center of the Spanish as Goa was for the Portuguese. An archbishop was appointed for Manila, who dared to oppose the governor-general and stand up for the rights of his native converts. Hundreds of Spanish priests were imported to staff churches, seminaries, schools, and universities and to take care of the ordinary spiritual desires of the Filipino people. Filipinos often expressed their discontent with the inequities and iniquities of Spanish rule, but they gradually made Spanish culture their own.

Nowhere else in Southeast Asia did native peoples accept or absorb as much of European rule or European civilization. Elsewhere Europe was a thin veneer on the body of Asia. The peoples of Burma, Siam, and Indochina were off the beaten path from Europe to the source of profits in the spice trade; consequently, they received less attention.

Burma, because of its incessant wars and the rumored attractiveness of its life, was a favorite rendezvous for Portuguese adventurers. One of their number, Philip de Brito, ruled over Syriam, near Rangoon, from 1599 until he was captured, tortured, and put to death in 1613 by the king of Toungoo. The British, French, and Dutch set up short-lived factories along the Burma coast; but the climate was hot and the profits were inconsequential. In 1755 an able king, Alaungpaya, launched a series of successful wars against Ayuthia, Chiengmai, Vientiane, and Chinese raiders in the Shans states in the northern part of his own country. He built the new capital, Rangoon (which means the end of strife), and established the kingdom of Burma which fought futilely against the British.

In what was interpreted as an aggressive mood, in 1824 the king of

Burma became involved in border disputes with the British East India Company. War broke out but it was short and uneven. In the treaty of peace in 1826, Burma gave up its claims to territory on the India side of the frontier, ceded Arakan and Tenasserim in lower Burma to the company, and agreed to an exchange of diplomatic representatives. The Burmese would send an ambassador to Calcutta and the company would station a resident in Ava. At that time it seemed as if Burma were about to be absorbed into the pattern of India. The British were on the march through Burma, with Bangkok, Siam, as their ultimate destination.

In the extreme southeast of the continent of Asia, Indochina received occasional political visitors from Malacca and missionaries from Goa or Manila, but it was most involved with the activities of France. French missionaries came to Indochina the same year the Pilgrims landed on Plymouth Rock (1620). The French East India Company sought a base in Indochina at the same time Dutch and British settled their quarrel over New Amsterdam (1664). The peoples of Indochina saw much more of French missionaries than of French traders, because French royalty banked more on the missionaries than the merchants for prestige abroad. France wanted to succeed Spain and Portugal as the protector of all Catholic missionaries, in opposition to the Dutch and British who were more concerned with Protestants.

France suffered reverses in India (which have been noted) and in Siam (which will be noted shortly), and then concentrated its Asian efforts in the Indochinese peninsula. In 1787, on the eve of the French Revolution, the efforts of Pigneau de Behaine, the bishop of Adran, led to the signing of a treaty between the king of Cochin China at Hué and Louis XVI. France received a foothold at Tourane, the offshore island of Poulo Condore, the right to trade and the right to propagate the Catholic religion. In exchange France agreed to help the king regain what he considered to be his rightful position as emperor of Annam. With French help he became the Emperor Gialong in 1801, and dealt favorably with the French during his twenty-year reign. His successors reversed his pro-French policies and began the persecution of French missionaries and Christian natives. French retaliatory action in Indochina was impossible because France was too chaotic at home to support any positive action overseas.

French advances came to a halt in Siam even before the setbacks in Indochina. Rice-rich Siam was more worldly wise than its neighbors and bargained more successfully for European services. The king of Ayuthia had Portuguese advisers the same as the king of Burma. He also had a Portuguese elite corps and a number of Spanish from the Philippines and Japanese in his personal bodyguard. He learned at an early stage the value of using one European against another. In the midst of his troubles with

Portuguese and Dutch (in 1662), he called upon the French for assistance. He was willing to grant trade rights and missionary privileges because he knew of the skill of the missionaries in the construction of forts and the manufacture of cannons. French and Siamese exchanged embassies and in 1685 cemented their good relations by a treaty of friendship and commerce. French individuals rose high in the service of the king, and a former Greek cabin boy on a French ship rose to be the prime minister of Siam. Then in 1688 a revolution broke out. The king was overthrown, the prime minister was put to death, and the French were ousted. As a result of this experience Siam shied away from all foreign contacts for 150 years. A new capital was built at Bangkok, and the present-reigning Chakri dynasty took over the throne in 1782. The Siamese demonstrated their ability to maintain the independence of their country in spite of the menacing position of the British on the Burma side and the French pressures from Indochina.

THE LURE OF CHINA

China was in a different situation than either India or Southeast Asia when merchants and missionaries from Europe came knocking at the doors. Unlike India, China was not on the decline; on the contrary, it was at the dawn of an age of exceptional greatness. The establishment of the Ch'ing or Manchu dynasty in 1644 ushered in a century and a half during which the Chinese court was among the most brilliant in the world. Unlike Southeast Asia, China was powerful and self-confident—convinced that no ruler or people could compare with those of the Middle Kingdom. In 1762 the population of China was 200,000,000 as compared with 18,000,-000 in France and 7,000,000 in England.

China was not inhospitable. It had permitted missionaries and traders within its orders since the days of the Han Dynasty. However, the Ming emperors were skeptical about the Portuguese, whose tales of horror had reached from Malacca to the ears of Peking. In 1517 the Portuguese sent an official mission headed by Thomas Pires to Canton in a pepper-laden ship. The Cantonese liked him and the profits of trade and expedited his visit to Peking. Unfortunately the newly arrived Portuguese sailors continued to act in China as they had acted against the Arabs. They conducted themselves with insolence and looked upon the Chinese, too, as heathens and legitimate prey. Pires was ordered back from Peking to Canton, where he was imprisoned until he died. The Portuguese were denied further access to Chinese ports, where they had been granted trading privileges. In 1557 by means of well-placed bribes they acquired permission for an annual fee to set up a colony on the peninsula of Macao near Canton. Macao was the Portuguese window to China as Goa was to India.

With a primary interest in tea, silk, lacquerware, and porcelains, the Dutch tried desperately to displace the Portuguese. In 1622 they attacked the Portuguese in Macao, but their expedition was defeated. Then they moved up the China coast and established bases in the Pescadores and Formosa. They sent three embassies to Peking in the seventeenth century—seeking a formal political contact with the Manchu court and commercial concessions for their traders.

The first embassy consisted of two ambassadors, four merchants, six servants, a steward, secretary, doctor, two interpreters, a trumpeter, and a drummer. The steward's account of the embassy, which appeared in London in 1669, was the most provocative book about China since Marco Polo. It foreshadowed later accounts of Chinese arrogance and complacency. According to the book, the imperial grand secretary inquired if there really was such a place as Holland. It was his suspicion that the Dutch were sea rovers without a country, living on their ships and landing to plunder. The emperor was neither impressed nor pleased with the Dutch choice of presents—armor, ornamented guns, optical glass, cloves, nutmeg, cinnamon, beads, quilts, and a parrot. He insisted that the Dutch should perform the kowtow before he would receive them. He granted them no special privileges or promises and limited them to the regular channels of trade at Canton.

English ships appeared in China before the end of the Ming Dynasty, but the first ship of the English East India Company did not arrive until 1699. In 1715 the British established a factory at Canton and appointed a merchant consul to look after trade and seamen. In 1742 the first British man-of-war at Canton, the *Centurion* under command of Captain John Anson, captured the Spanish galleon on its run to Acapulco. Relations between the port authorities and the British warship can be surmised from the tone of a British report: "In artifice, falsehood and an attachment to all kinds of lucre, many of the Chinese are difficult to be paralleled by any other people."

After 1757, by decree of the Emperor Ch'ien Lung, Canton was the only Chinese port open to foreign trade. Other nationalities participated in the trade once it was opened up, but the British took the lead. Most of the ships belonged to the East India Company, although English "country-ships" (the name given to ships not belonging to the company) defied the monopoly which was supposed to belong to the company by charter from the crown. French, Swedish, and Danish flags were seen in Canton on occasion. Shortly after 1800 the Russians attempted to open trade by sending the circumnavigator Krusenstern with a shipload of goods into Canton waters, but Russian efforts were stopped by the Chinese. Outside of the British, hardy American sailing vessels from the Atlantic seaboard were the most persistent callers at Canton.

The conditions of trade at the port gave rise to bitter disputes from its inception. Chinese officials treated their own merchants with contempt, but they used their merchants as a smoke screen for their own wealth and power. They considered foreigners engaged in trade as the lowest order of humans who had deserted their homes and abandoned the tombs of their ancestors. In Chinese eyes, Europeans were ignorant of Chinese laws, notoriously turbulent and disrespectful. Barbarous and ferocious, they were of a "piratical nature like the Japanese, with a language which no civilized tongue could master; beards black, brown or even red; eyes not a decent black or brown, but like those of cats, blue and gray." The Chinese were particularly apprehensive about the British because of their prominence, and the spreading fame of their rule in India. It was possible, they thought, that the British might use trade to foment rebellion among the Chinese emperor's own loyal subjects.

The Chinese took the attitude that they had no need of foreign goods, and they assumed that Europeans came to China only in search of China's precious products. Therefore they considered all trade as a favor granted by China, revocable at any time. They levied all the fees and customs they desired, and they subjected traders to Chinese laws and administrative action. The merchants had no legal or treaty rights and no diplomatic protection against arbitrary measures. The Chinese would not accept any limitation on their sovereign powers. They merely said that if the Europeans did not like the Chinese way of doing things, they could always go home.

The Europeans cursed the Chinese as fools, knaves, and cowards, but they could not change the Chinese situation. It was impossible to divide and rule and to establish political dominion as had been done elsewhere in Asia. The profits were so substantial that the foreigners endured their humiliation and swallowed their pride in order to keep the traffic moving. However, they resented the Chinese attitude. They did not like being looked down upon because in their own society they were important people. They wanted recognition of their status and rights, and they made great efforts to get treaty relations with the aloof Chinese empire.

The English East India Company took the lead in seeking negotiations. Six years after the British defeat at Yorktown, a special envoy was nominated to go to Peking, but he died before he reached his destination. In 1792 Lord George Macartney was sent bearing gifts to Peking, but he was "received with the utmost politeness, treated with utmost hospitality, watched with utmost vigilance and dismissed with the utmost civility." Just after the conclusion of the Napoleonic Wars, another mission under

Lord Amherst was dispatched to try to establish official relations with the Chinese court. The British emissary was dismissed without an audience and was told that foreign presents were of no interest or use, and that missions seeking relations with China in accordance with the practice of the Western world were merely a waste of time.

China's experience with foreign missionaries was scarcely less satisfying to the West than the treatment of European traders. Missionaries came to China in the wake of the Protuguese and the Spanish. Jesuits, under the wing of the Portuguese, concentrated in Macao, and Franciscans, from the Philippines, paid occasional visits to cities in China along the coast. In 1582 an Italian Jesuit, Matteo Ricci, a student of mathematics and astronomy, came to Macao. At first he dressed as a Buddhist monk and later as a Confucian scholar. He studied the Chinese language, and after twenty years he was invited to Peking. He brought gifts of clocks, gauges, glass prisms, and books on literature, science, geography, architecture, and mathematics for the emperor. He aided the court astrologers, revised the calendar, and prepared a new map of the world on which he wisely placed China in the center. He instructed the Chinese in the use of the astronomical instruments which the Mongols had brought from India, and he taught Chinese military officials the casting of cannon. He was never permitted to meet the emperor, but before he died he numbered many princes and mandarins among his converts.

Other distinguished Jesuits followed him, one of whom, Adam Schaal, became the chief adviser of the first Manchu emperor. The Jesuits were the transmitters to China of the scientific advancements contributed by the galaxy which included Da Vinci, Copernicus, Galileo, Newton, Boyle, and Descartes. By 1644 missionaries in China had published more than one hundred fifty books on mathematics, natural sciences, physics, philology, astronomy, geography, philosophy, and ethics. The Jesuits were the instruments for transmitting Chinese culture to Europe, where it became extremely popular. In contrast to the merchants, the missionaries sent back to Europe glowing accounts which were largely responsible for the creation of the glamour-myth of China and the Far East.

Missionaries from other orders followed the Jesuits into China. Some of the newer orders objected to compromises which their predecessors had made with Chinese customs, and they precipitated the so-called Rites Controversy, which came to a climax in 1706. The Jesuits tolerated Chinese ancestral rites as civil and commemorative ceremonies; Franciscans and Dominicans felt those rites were idolatrous. The orders differed on the interpretations of Chinese ideographs for such words as heaven, holy, and God. The disputes reached the pope; and the emperor was insulted by the appeal to outside authority. He expelled the missionaries (except those in the service of the court) and forbade Chinese to become Christians. Hundreds of thousands of Chinese had already been converted. The anti-Christian decrees remained on the list of imperial mandates, but they were not rigidly enforced. Like the merchants, foreign missionaries were treated in China only with such tolerance as the court chose to grant them.

At the beginning of the nineteenth century, Catholics expanded their activities largely under the political protection of France. Protestants, with the encouragement of the United States and England, brought new energies (and new problems) to the Chinese mission field. They studied the Chinese language, wrote new dictionaries, and translated the Bible and Protestant hymns into Chinese. They established schools and colleges and placed new emphasis on Western medicine. By example and teaching they exposed the Chinese to Anglo-Saxon political philosophy with its values of liberty, democracy, and the rights of the individual. The Chinese were more deeply moved by these peripheral influences than by the direct impact of the Christian dogma. Canton was not only the port of entry for European goods into China. It was also the headquarters for fervent missionaries who were fanatically eager to spread their own interpretation of the word of God throughout the length and breadth of the Celestial Empire.

In addition to coping with Europeans (and Americans after 1789) who approached them from the sea, the Chinese were obliged to deal with Russian Cossacks, gold prospectors, and fur traders who approached China on the land side. While British ships rode at anchor in Canton, Russians established tiny trading posts in the unmarked border regions which extended from Turkestan to Siberia. An explorer Kharbarov built a fort at the junction of the Amur and Ussuri rivers and in 1651 founded there the city which bears his name. Clashes between Russians and Chinese in the headwaters of the Amur led to China's first war with a European power, and the Chinese got the better of the fighting and the bargaining.

In 1689 Russian and Chinese emissaries signed China's first modern treaty, the Treaty of Nerchinsk. This treaty provided for the cessation of a half-century of border warfare, regulation of trade, and the delineation of the boundary. The Russians were kept out of the Amur Valley, the frontier being fixed at the watershed north of the river. The treaty also provided for the extradition of lawbreakers and for a modified mutual right of extraterritoriality. The document was drawn up in Latin, with the help of the Jesuit advisers to the Chinese delegation.

The Chinese did not treat the Russians with much more consideration than they showed the British at Canton. They were inclined to regard the Russians as nomads, no more than savages in a wild country, and as "rascals who come to hunt, plunder and kill." Nevertheless they permitted a steady stream of Russian commercial caravans and diplomatic missions to visit Peking. While the Chinese kept their back door partly closed to western Europeans in Canton, they opened the front door to Russians in Peking. A Russo-Chinese Treaty of Peking in 1721 allowed the Russians to open a legation in Peking, where might reside four Russian orthodox priests and four youths and two adults who were to study the Chinese language. The Russians did not have the right of access to the emperor, but they might be granted an audience if they came bearing tribute and agreed to perform the kowtow. In 1727 the Treaty of Kiakhta, the border town between Siberia and Mongolia which the Chinese called *Mai-mai-chen* or "buy and sell city," settled frontier problems in the immediate neighborhood and fixed conditions of trade. Every three years camel caravans with traders and diplomatic mail came from St. Petersburg to Peking by way of Siberia, and in 1730 and 1733 the Chinese sent diplomatic missions to the Russian capital. These were the only missions which China established abroad before 1870.

As China grew in strength under the great Manchus, it pushed outward into Mongolia, Dzungaria, and Turkestan. At the same time Russia drove to the south and east. The nomad tribes of Asia and Siberia lost their power as buffer peoples because their bows, arrows, and pony cavalries were helpless against the artillery and weapons of China and Russia. China was obliged to pay more attention to Russians than to the nationals of other European nations, which could reach China only by sea. China and Russia traded overland, and their interests clashed in a vast desert and mountain no man's land which stretched for more than three thousand miles along an undetermined, unmarked frontier. In asserting themselves against the Chinese in northeast Asia, it was inevitable that Russians should also come in conflict with Japan.

JAPAN: THE FARTHEST EAST FROM EUROPE

Russian relations with Japan, before the middle of the nineteenth century, were sporadic, exciting but uncritical. After Russians explored Kamchatka and learned of the Kuriles, they founded Petropavlovsk, discovered Alaska, and visited ports in Japan. Russians came to northern Japan to fish and to hunt, to colonize and to trade. In 1799 the Russo-American Fur Company began its operations throughout the entire northern area, including Japan and Alaska (as far south as San Francisco); and in 1804 the president of the company arrived in Nagasaki in search of a treaty with Japan. He was rebuffed; and in revenge, Russians terrorized the northern Japanese islands. The shogun himself took over defense responsibilities. The Japanese were under isolated pressures from Russian raiding parties in the cold and stormy north during much of the time they were faced with the approach of Europeans who came to Japan from the direction of China. Japan experienced the same perplexities as China in coping with the uninvited advance of the West, but due to its own peculiar circumstances responded in an entirely different way. At the moment of greatest European expansiveness, the Japanese were in transition from internal chaos to a period of national unity. They were on the eve of revolutionary changes which were expedited and remolded by the coming of the West.

In 1542 three Portuguese in a Chinese junk were driven ashore at Tanegashima in the estates of the Lord Satsuma on Kyushu Island. They were welcomed hospitably and their harquebuses aroused excitement. In the midst of civil wars trade in guns was worth a thousand percent in profits. Other Portuguese traders, accompanied by Jesuit priests, arrived in Japan from Macao and Goa. Francis Xavier landed in 1549. At first the missionaries were treated with respect and forbearance, possibly because their religion seemed to be something like Buddhism. Peasants in a living hell-on-earth took to the idea of a paradise hereafter, even if the doctrine of eternal damnation seemed bizarre and unbelievable. The great shogun Nobunaga adopted a friendly attitude toward the Jesuits because he saw in them personal friendship and support against his political rivals, the Buddhist monks.

Nobunaga's successor, Hideyoshi, who was reported to wear a rosary himself, did not disapprove of the religion and the missionaries; but he sensed the political dangers in Christianity. It increased the power of his rivals, who were strengthened by the acquisition of Christian guns. In 1587 he ordered the banishment of the Christians, but he was too busy in Korea to enforce his orders. Then, in 1593, Franciscans from the Philippines entered into what had been the exclusive domain of the Jesuits. One Spanish interloper intimated that the Japanese should treat him carefully or his sovereign would take action. He suggested that "traders and priests were advance guards of expeditions to conquer distant countries." Hideyoshi's reaction was the persecution of Christians and the sterner enforcement of the banishment decrees against his irritating and meddlesome guests.

Hideyoshi's successor, Iyeyasu had seen the Jesuits (Portuguese) agitating to have the Franciscans (Spanish) expelled and both pressing for the exclusion of the Protestants (Dutch). He feared that all types of Christians might combine with his internal enemies, and he was afraid that Europeans might try to do in Japan what the Spanish did in the Philippines, the Portuguese in Macao, and the Dutch in Batavia. By 1600 Japan's total population of 25,000,000 included 300,000 Catholics. Therefore Iyeyasu issued further edicts against the Christians in 1612 and 1613. Churches were demolished, Christian missionaries were expelled, and native converts were tortured and crucified. The orgy culminated in the Shimabara Rebellion (1637) when perhaps as many as 37,000 Christians were put to the sword.

The shoguns wanted no part of the missionaries, but they would have welcomed foreign trade. They appreciated the goods of Europe and the goods of Asia. They welcomed the knowledge which they gained about maps, astronomy, shipbuilding, and metalworking. They seemed to prefer to trade with the Dutch and the English because those two seemed less religiously inclined. They permitted the Dutch to establish a factory at Hirado and the English to do likewise at Edo. But trade and religion seemed inseparable.

The Spanish were ordered out of Japan in 1624; the Portuguese, in 1638. When a Portuguese mission returned to Japan to press for reopening trade, the emissaries were summarily beheaded. The less important members of the mission were dismissed with the warning that should the king of Portugal, nay, the very God of the Christians, presume to enter the dominions of Japan, he would be put to death. After 1636 no foreigners were allowed to come to Japan except Dutch, Chinese, and Koreans—and these under rigorous restrictions. Japanese were not permitted to build ocean-going ships and were warned that if they left the country they would be beheaded on their return. Thus the Japanese habit of friendliness to strangers and their strong sense of hospitable duty, plus their desire for gain, gave way to fear. For more than two hundred years, Japan's only communication with the outside world was through the handful of Dutch who were practically imprisoned on the small island of Deshima in Nagasaki harbor and the Dutch ships which paid an annual visit. No efforts to break down this seclusion policy were successful until Commodore Perry knocked at Japan's doors in 1853.

SUGGESTED READING

Blair, E. H., and Robertson, J. A., *Philippine Islands, 1493–1898* (55 vols.) (Cleveland, A. H. Clark Co., 1903–1909).

Cady, John F., *Roots of French Imperialism in Eastern Asia* (Ithaca, Cornell U., 1954).

Collis, Maurice, *Grand Peregrination* (London, Faber, 1949).

Cortesao, Armando, (trans.), *Suma Oriental of Tomé Pires* (London, Hakluyt Society, 1944).

Cranmer-Byng, J. L., *Embassy to China* (Lord Macartney) (London, Longmans, 1963).

Hahn, Emily, *Raffles of Singapore* (New York, Doubleday, 1946).

Hakluyt, Richard, *The Principal Navigations . . . of the English Nation* (three vols.) (Glasgow, Hakluyt Society, 1903–1905).

Hall, D. G. E., *Europe and Burma* (London, Oxford U., 1945).

Hart, Henry H., *Sea Road to the Indies* (New York, Macmillan, 1950).

Morse, H. B., *Chronicles of the East India Company Trading to China, 1635–1834* (four vols.) (London, Oxford U., 1926–1929).

Phelan, John Leddy, *Hispanization of the Philippines* (Madison, U. of Wisconsin, 1959).

Pigafetta, Antonio, *Magellan's Voyage Around the World* (ed. by James Alexander Robertson; three vols.) (Cleveland, A. H. Clark Co., 1906).

Pritchard, Earl, *Crucial Years of Early Anglo Chinese Relations, 1750–1800* (Pullman, Washington State College, 1936).

Purcell, Victor, *Chinese in Southeast Asia* (London, Oxford U., 1951).

——, *Colonial Period in Southeast Asia* (New York, Institute of Pacific Relations, 1953).

Schurz, William Lytle, *Manila Galleon* (New York, Dutton, 1959). (P)

Snyder, Louis L., *Imperialism Reader* (Princeton, Van Nostrand, 1962).

II

IMPACT OF THE WEST

6

The Opening of China

The meeting of West and East in Canton gave rise to deep misunderstandings which led to war. The emperor of China established a system of commercial restrictions which reflect his contempt for the foreigners and their trade. He was represented by a viceroy or imperial commissioner in Canton who was assisted by a superintendent of customs. The Chinese title for the latter official sounded like *hoppo* to foreign ears, and *hoppo* he was always called. He was responsible for all tariffs, fees, and regulations. He was also in charge of the *Co-hong* or a kind of chamber of commerce which consisted of the officially designated *hongs* or shops with whom the foreigners could trade. Every foreign vessel was secured or assigned to a member of the *Co-hung* who would sell all inbound cargo, provide outbound cargo and make arrangements for the repairs and supplies of the ship while in port. The *Co-hong* was the sole medium of communication between foreign merchants and any Chinese authority. It was the device for maximum extortion from the foreign merchants and the channel for transmitting the stream of wealth to the government. The *hong* merchants were among the world's greatest businessmen, amassing fortunes running into millions of pounds sterling.

Merchants at Canton pressured their own government to ease the "hardships" under which they were conducting their affairs. Their factories (that is, their showrooms, warehouses, business offices, and residence quarters) were confined to an area a quarter of a mile square with a small open space where they might take the air. Their esplanade was "generally so choked up with barbers and fortune-tellers, venders of dogs and cats, quack medicines, and trinkets, with a host of strangers, come to gaze at the foreigners, that it is difficult to move."

The English factories were imposing and luxurious, and the English company was noted for its scale of living and the princely character of its hospitality. But to the merchants of Canton their factories were only a gilded cage. They had to live in the factories during the trading season, from October to March or April, and then retire to their summer homes in Macao.. They could not have their wives "or other foreign women" with them, and they could hire servants only with the approval of the local officials. They could not visit the walled city of Canton and could not ride in sedan chairs on any occasion. They could not row on the river, and only once in a while could they visit the flower gardens on the opposite bank of the river. The accumulated effect of these irksome restrictions was to exhaust the British tempers and to increase the demand for action. They believed the Chinese had no right to operate as they did and that China should open its doors to all traders as an obligation to the civilized world. They were only too eager for a showdown which would force China to mend its ways. When in 1833 the British parliament refused to renew the charter of the East India Company's monopoly of the trade to the East, the position of chief factor of the company at Canton was no longer adequate to represent British interests. Country ships became more numerous than company ships, and national British interests included more of the small traders. The British now wanted a commissioned political and diplomatic representative of the Crown, not merely a commercial official, who would serve as the protector of His Majesty's subjects as well as the overseer of their commercial activities. Such a person could not be treated by the Chinese as a mere chief merchant of the foreign devils.

On December 10, 1833, Lord Napier, a Scottish peer, was commissioned as the first Superintendent of British Trade—all British trade and not just that of the East India Company. He arrived in Macao in July, 1834. He was instructed to use utmost caution and moderation and to convince the Chinese authorities of the sincere desire of the king to cultivate the most friendly relations with the emperor of China. Yet he was ordered to seek a solution for issues which had smoldered for nearly a century.

The British wanted political and diplomatic relations with China after the manner of European states; they wanted the right to deal with Chinese officials on a basis of dignity and equality without the stigma of "dogs" or "devils." They wanted written rules of trade and fixed fees which would free them from the whims of the emperor and his officials. And they wanted permission if possible to sell to all Chinese—not merely members of the *Co-hong*. They wanted the right to enter China at all ports, not just Canton, and to trade and travel throughout the empire.

Bitter experience also convinced the British that they needed the privilege of extraterritoriality, or jurisdiction over their own subjects. The British rejected the Chinese concepts of law and justice. Contracts and property rights were not enforceable against Chinese merchants, and civil rights were not respected for one considered guilty of a crime. There were thousands of sailors in port, all too frequently abusing their liberty, and many were victims of torture or cruel treatment when arrested.

An understanding on the opium traffic was greatly desired. The trade was illegal and repugnant, but it was highly profitable. All countries participated in the trade. Opium was the one commodity which the Chinese craved and it caused the Chinese to spend their own precious specie in international payments. Before opium, silver dollars flowed into China to pay for tea and silk; after opium, the drain was in the other direction. Economic compulsion obliged the emperor to enforce prohibition decrees which had been dormant for over a century. But enforcement was no easy matter. The viceroy, the *hoppo*, and the *Co-hong* enjoined the foreigners to stop the trade; but secretly they connived at the breach of the law for their personal profit. The merchants cursed the Chinese for their duplicity, but they continued the lucrative trade.

The Chinese paid no attention to British complaints. They were not even disturbed when threats of war clouded the horizon. The Chinese believed that the threat of stoppage of trade would bring the British to their senses; and some officials, whose intelligence should have taught them better, scorned the reports of British strength. They could not see why people were dazzled by the name of England just because her vessels were sturdy and her cannons fierce. One Chinese official suggested that British soldiers did not know how to use fists and swords and could not conveniently stretch because their legs were firmly bound with cloth (leggings). The Chinese believed that British power could be controlled by artifice.

On the British side they were fed up with China and the fancy tales about it. They watched China deteriorate after the death of Ch'ien Lung (1796), and they began to talk of war or the use of force. They could see no other means to destroy Chinese arrogance and make it abandon its ancient pretensions of superiority. The British considered China—with all its merits in civilization, resources, courage, and the arts—as an anachronism. They were conscious of their own dynamic power. They had faith that the industrial revolution and their comparative advantage in international trade would provide new sources of profit to replace the iniquitous opium traffic.

The arrival of Lord Napier in the Far East in 1834 ushered in a five-year period of tension which ended in war. He sailed into Canton in a British frigate without waiting for the customary permission from the viceroy. He announced his arrival by letter, instead of a humble petition, and invited thereby the viceroy's displeasure and retaliation. Lord Napier became one of the first to learn how difficult it was to use force on Chinese officials. He was unable to cope with Chinese tactics of delay and procrastination. Exasperation aggravated the torments of his tropical fever and led to his untimely death. He was succeeded by Sir John Francis Davis and then by Captain Charles Elliot, who was the Superintendent of British Trade when a crisis occurred which led to open hostilities.

The Opium War

In 1839, exactly a century before the outbreak of World War II in Europe, a new imperial commissioner, Lin Tsê-hsü, came to Canton "to scrub and wash away the filth of opium." He ordered the foreign merchants to surrender every ounce of opium they owned and to give a bond on penalty of death that they would import no more. Here was a spectacle of a Chinese official honestly attempting to enforce a Chinese law. On order of Captain Elliot, more than 20,000 chests were surrendered, valued at $6,000,000. Before an unbelieving public, 500 Chinese coolies mixed the whole lot with salt, lime, and water, and dumped it into the creek. A disconsolate band of British merchants retired to Macao on May 24, 1839, leaving their factories in the hands of the American merchants.

The problems of conflicting jurisdiction aggravated the crisis. A Chinese was killed at Kowloon in a riot involving American and British sailors. Commissioner Lin accused a British sailor of murder and demanded his surrender. Captain Elliot refused. Commissioner Lin ordered closure of the trade and descended on Macao with a body of toops. The British evacuated to the fifty merchant ships anchored off the barren island of Hong Kong. The British prepared for a long siege and wrote to their agents in Manila to "send up poultry and pigs, also some of your best beer, with some moderately good French claret and some Seltzer water, if it be had with you." Commissioner Lin ordered all the people living at Kowloon and in the neighborhood opposite Hong Kong to stop working for the British and wholly to cut off from the English all supplies. He anchored his fleet of war junks menacingly close to the British merchant fleet.

On November 2, 1839, two small British frigates fought and defeated the entire Chinese naval force. This encounter, the Battle of Chuenpi, did not begin an actual war, as it would have anywhere else in the world. In spite of actual fighting, lawful import trade went on as usual, the season of 1839–1840 being the most advantageous since 1834. The *hong* merchants found ways to get around Commissioner Lin, and the Americans earned substantial and unusual commissions in acting for the discommoded British. The drug business also did exceedingly well. As a matter of fact, the merchants did not register too much protest against Captain Elliot's order to surrender the opium. They were heavily stocked, prices were soft, and His Majesty's superintendent of trade had promised compensation for the stocks destroyed. In the new season the smart traders bought heavily because of increased prices. As often happens, the prohibition enforcement hurt the small man most, because the large opium concerns turned Commissioner Lin's activities to their own advantage.

William Jardine, a parter of Jardine, Matheson and Company, the EWO of the China coast, the largest and most influential trading company in the Far East, had just been elected to the British parliament. He championed the British position before that august body and took his cause to Lord Palmerston, the Foreign Minister. Jardine suggested the British should demand redress for the seizure of British property—the opium—in the form of an official apology, indemnity, and a new treaty. He hinted that a naval demonstration would arouse the Chinese from their slumbers and said that the American traders in Canton supported his belief that a show of force would produce a new treaty basis for the conduct of trade. Most British merchants concurred in Jardine's views.

In February, 1840, after the British ordered to China sixteen vessels of war and transports with 4,000 troops from India, the British government took their case to parliament. Secretary of State for War Thomas MacCaulay argued eloquently that "this most rightful quarrel may be prosecuted to a triumphal close . . . that the name of English valour, but of English mercy, may be established." William Gladstone for the opposition contended that a "war more unjust in its origin, a war more calculated in its progress to cover this country with permanent disgrace, I do not know and I have not read of."

By a majority of nine votes, the parliament passed the motion for punitive action. The British had, as their war aims, payment for the seized opium, a treaty which would accord British nationals and officials treatment consistent with the usages of civilized nations, and the cession of an island where the British would be protected against arbitrary caprice. The war itself was not much of a military contest. A British force of 2,000 men, brought from India in side-wheelers, occupied Canton without opposition. Because of the problems of occupation, they retired voluntarily and moved to the north. They blockaded the Yangtze and Yellow rivers and landed at chosen points up and down the China coast. British troops went through the Manchu spearmen like a "train through a rainstorm." Tiger-skin shields, two-edged swords, and blood-curdling shouts were no match for muskets and cannons. When the British took a city, the local rabble began at once to loot and rob. As soon as the fighting ended, trading, fraternizing, and entertaining began. A British officer described the war in this manner: "At once place we traded, at another we fought; here we extended the right hand of fellowship, while there we crossed our swords in deadly fight . . . there was never a war with so little hardship and so much mercy." Some Chinese shared the British view of mercy: "They (the British) took care of our wounded and distributed rice to the poor." Another Chinese saw the conduct of the British in a different light: "The rebels (British) gave loose to the rapacity, cruelty and wild natures . . . they seized our working cattle, injured our crops, dug out and destroyed the graves of our forefathers and violated our women."

Rather than risk the loss of Peking to the British, the Chinese agreed to surrender. They conducted peace negotiations on board the British ship, *Cornwallis,* anchored in the Yangtze River. On August 29, 1842, after many fine speeches and much consumption of cherry brandy the Chinese and British signed the Treaty of Nanking. It was the end of one era and the beginning of another. Old China was gone. For more than a hundred years the traders from distant lands subjected themselves to rules laid down by the Son of Heaven. During the century ahead, the "barbarians" would dictate the terms on which China would trade and conduct its diplomatic and political relations with the rest of the world.

THE FIRST TREATY SETTLEMENT

The Treaty of Nanking with the British was the first of what the Chinese called "unequal treaties." They were unequal in the sense that all the benefits accrued to the Western nations. China received no reciprocal rights or advantages. For the next century all the Western powers pressed for further treaty rights. It was the practice in China that foreigners would enjoy only the rights and privileges which were specifically granted. This was in contrast to the usual practice in the West, where it was assumed that foreigners enjoyed all rights in a country except those specifically denied. From the Chinese point of view, the most vicious part of the treaty which settled wars or incidents was the "most-favored-nation" clause. By this clause *every* treaty power demanded and received from China every right and privilege originally extended to *any* treaty power. What China granted to one, it automatically granted to all.

The early intercourse between China and the West filled the Chinese with bitterness. They could not appreciate the high value which the foreigners placed upon conditions of trade. They felt that the extraneous political concessions inserted into the treaties in the guise of commercial protection were evidence of Western intentions against China's sovereign rights and political integrity. When the Opium War ended, the emperor Tao Kuang instructed his peace commissioners to make such arrangements with England as would cut off forever all causes of war. The Treaty of Nanking provided:

(1) There shall be peace and friendship between England and China and their respective subjects, who shall enjoy full security and protection within the dominions of the other.

(2) British subjects may reside for the purpose of carrying on their mercantile pursuits at Canton, Amoy, Foochow, Ningpo, and Shanghai, where there shall be a Superintendent of Trade or consular officer to be the medium of communication between the Chinese authorities and the said merchants, and to see that just duties are collected.

(3) The island of Hongkong shall be ceded by China to Great Britain to be possessed in perpetuity.

(4) Indemnities totaling $21,000,000 shall be paid in four annual installments; $6,000,000 for the value of the opium destroyed, $3,000,000 for debts owing by Chinese merchants, and $12,000,000 on account of the expenses of the British military expedition.

(5) The co-hong shall be abolished and the foreign merchants shall trade with whomsoever they please.

(6) Prisoners of war shall be released, amnesty shall be granted to all Chinese who collaborated with the British, and British troops shall be retired when the indemnities are paid.

(7) Communications between British and Chinese officials shall be on the basis of diplomatic equality.

(8) The Emperor of China shall in agreement with the British establish at all open ports a fair and regular tariff, which tariff shall be publicly notified, and when British merchandise shall have once paid the regular tariff at the port, such merchandise may be conveyed by Chinese merchants to any province or city in the interior of the empire of China, on paying a further amount as transit dues which shall not exceed a fixed per cent of the tariff value of such goods.

By a supplementary agreement with England, the Treaty of the Bogue in 1843, the Chinese granted the British "most-favored-nation" treatment, a limited right to travel in the open country surrounding the treaty ports, and extraterritoriality. Other nations sent delegations to China to obtain similar treaty rights for themselves. "The British shook the tree, the others came quickly to help pick up the fruit."

Some Americans had not been sympathetic with the British during the war. In the Congress Caleb Cushing accused the British of base cupidity, violence, and high-handed infractions of all law, human and divine. On the other hand ex-President John Quincy Adams dared to oppose public opinion. Speaking for his New England constituents, he told the House of Representatives that opium was no more the cause of the

Chinese war than the throwing overboard of tea was the cause of the American Revolution. "The cause of the war is the kowtow," he asserted, "the arrogant and insupportable pretensions of China that she will hold commercial intercourse with the rest of mankind not upon terms of equal reciprocity, but upon the insulting and degrading forms of the relationship between lord and vassal."

American merchants on the China coast took advantage of British embarrassments during the hostilities. They diverted British cargoes to their own ships, falsely registered American vessels, and flouted Commissioner Lin's opium decrees. They let it be known by a petition to Congress that they wanted the American government to be as assiduous as any other in taking political and diplomatic measures for the protection of their commerce. They wanted the government to appoint an agent or commissioner with sufficient naval force to guarantee them favored-nation treatment. They did not propose that we should join with the British in fighting for the rights which all foreign merchants desired.

On July 3, 1844, the same Caleb Cushing who had been anti-British in Congress, signed the Treaty of Wanghsia which was the first treaty between the United States and China. The treaty contained the desired most-favored-nation clause, which gave without cost to the Americans every privilege the British had won by fighting. It also provided for theoretical recognition of equality in official intercourse, defined conditions of extraterritoriality, placed upon the Chinese the responsibility for collecting customs duties and controlling opium trade, and made it lawful for officers and citizens of the United States to employ scholars and purchase all manner of books in China. The treaty was subject to renewal or revision at the end of twelve years (1856).

A French diplomatic mission followed on the heels of the Americans. France and China signed the Treaty of Whampoa on October 24, 1844. France too received most-favored-nation treatment but as a special feature in its negotiations assumed the right of looking after the Catholic missions. The French envoy sent a request to the emperor to permit Roman Catholic missionaries to build churches in the treaty ports, to tolerate missionaries, and to take no measures against native converts to Christianity. In a short time, Portuguese, Belgians, Norwegians, and Swedes were given specific assurances of favorable treatment; in fact the ships and merchants of all nations were trading in Canton and the other open ports on exactly the same footing as the British.

BETWEEN WARS: 1845–1856

For the twelve-year period between wars, the Chinese empire was ravaged by rebellions. The survival of the imperial dynasty was at stake.

Defeat in war added loss of prestige to China's recurrent woes of a demoralized bureaucracy, an atrophied social system, and financial bankruptcy. China was swept by the bloodiest rebellion in human history, which was ironically called the *T'ai p'ing* or Great Peace rebellion. It was inspired by a religious fanatic who dreamed that he was the younger brother of Christ and was destined to establish the kingdom of heaven on earth. The rebellion was a curious combination of protest against the ruling dynasty and the establishment of social reform. The rebels were forbidden to smoke opium, drink alcohol, or commit adultery. It was punishable by death if they failed to learn the Lord's Prayer or the Ten Commandments. They cut off their queues (or symbols of inferiority) and enforced a program of land reform. They gained control of more than half of China before they were suppressed. They caused the destruction of hundreds of millions of dollars of property value and brought death to twenty million people.

In the midst of internal turmoil, difficulties increased between Chinese and foreigners. More than ever convinced of its inherent superiority, the court at Peking adopted a sullen attitude of evasion of responsibility. As it bestirred itself to learn a little about the West, it received information from illustrious advisers which seems almost childish. The barbarians were described to his imperial majesty as having dazzling white flesh and lofty noses "their custom is to esteem women and think lightly of men . . . marriages are left to mutual arrangement." Again: "The males mostly wear wool and love to drink wine. The females, when they have not yet married, bind their waists, desiring that they be slender . . . They wear disheveled hair which hangs over their eyebrows, short clothing and layers of skirts." Specifically, the court was told: "The white devils (Spanish and Portuguese) are fond of women; the red devils (Dutch and English) are fond of money; the black devils (Indians and Parsis) are fond of wine." But all barbarians were branded as "inscrutable, inherently cunning and malicious, impatient and without understanding of values, arrogant and anxious to excel. They respect strength and ridicule weakness, military force is the only language they can understand."

The few Chinese on the fringes of the empire who came in contact with foreigners—the compradors, linguists, schroffs, and independent merchants—acted for the most part with indifference or resentment. In some of the new treaty ports, the Chinese made adequate provisions for the residence of foreigners and the conduct of trade. Their arrangements for residence at Shanghai marked the beginning of the system of concessions and settlements as foreign residential districts. The Chinese set aside plots of land, often undesirable and outside the limits of the native city, for exclusive development and autonomous administration by the foreigners. They made ground available on which to build living and business quarters, churches, hospitals, schools, and colleges.

When Shanghai was menaced by T'ai p'ing rebels, the British and the Americans agreed to defend the foreign settlement and, in spite of their quarrels and differences, to protect the interests of the emperor. In July, 1854, they agreed with Chinese officials on the establishment of a foreign inspectorate of the customs which would act for the Chinese government. Thus began a foreign-staffed maritime customs administration which for the greatest part of a century exercised control over all of China's ports. Customs commissioners of all nationalities in the service of China set a high standard of loyalty and incorruptibility and made lasting contributions to China's scholarship and diplomacy.

The officials and populace at Canton continued to be most antagonistic. Their tradition of superiority lingered on. The officials denied the right of residence to foreigners *in* Canton. They interpreted the treaty words "at Canton" to mean "at the factories" and not "in the walled city." They would not hear of direct official intercourse on terms of equality. They attempted to conduct trade on a disguised continuation of the old *Co-hong* system, and they refused to acquiesce in the extraterritorial provisions of the treaties. Some elements in the populace were more inflamed than the officials. Placards appeared which read:

> In the fifth moon of the present year, many Chinese have been slain by foreigners; their bodies have been flung into the river, and buried in the bellies of fishes; but our high authorities have treated these affairs as though they had never heard of them; they have looked upon these foreign devils as though they were gods; they have despised the Chinese as though they had the flesh of dogs; and have not valued the life of men more than the hair which is shorn from the head . . . These rebels, however, regard China with contempt. They have been false and wanton in every respect, the wickedness of their crimes has risen up to the heavens. It is utterly impossible to permit their rapacity and cruelty, and their molestations and injuries to China.

New complications arose which involved government, traders, and missionaries. Protestant missionaries came in large numbers from England and America, but they were slow in making converts. Their message evoked little sympathy from ordinary Chinese and they were sometimes pelted with mud, gravel, or bits of broken pottery. One discouraged missionary wrote home, "I am afraid that nothing short of the Society for the Diffusion of Cannon Balls will give them [the Chinese] the useful knowledge they now require to realize their own helplessness." Most missionaries were not averse to political action which would open the empire for their preaching. It was their philosophy that some good might result from slightly evil means.

The era of clipper ships glamorized the China trade. Clippers set speed records across the Pacific which lasted well into the age of steam. The illegal opium trade flourished. The demand for Chinese labor in California, the West Indies, the Straits, Australia, and South America gave rise to the inhuman coolie traffic. Coolies were kidnaped and huddled together in barracks in Macao until a boatload was procured. The coolies were sometimes months in transit through the tropics in appalling conditions, and the death rate en route reached as high as fifteen percent. In some instances the pay for those who survived amounted to two changes of clothing per year and a wage of ten cents per day. With the settlement of California and the Pacific Coast, the United States developed a new and strictly national outlook on China and the rest of East Asia.

The extraterritorial system tended to work out to the advantage of foreigners, even those who ran afoul of Chinese law. Merchants served as consuls, and they were lenient in passing judgment on their fellow countrymen. In the enforcement of contracts, the Chinese could not expect the favoritism from foreigners which they had previously been accustomed to receive from their own officials.

Foreigners in China were as dissatisfied as the Chinese with their relations. They wanted further privileges and better treatment. They resented the continuation of disrespect and discourtesy. As the authority of the Chinese central government degenerated, the Chinese indulged in repeated attacks against the person of foreigners. Lord Palmerston came to the conclusion:

> The Chinese must learn and be convinced that if they attack our people and our factories, they will be shot and that if they ill-treat innocent Englishmen . . . they will be punished . . . Depend upon it, that the best way to keep any men quiet is to let them see that you are able and determined to repel force by force; and that Chinese are not in the least different, in this respect, from the rest of mankind.

In the meantime, the Russians renewed pressures on the Chinese in the north. Beginning in 1847 Count Muraviev explored and established a strong Russian position in the Amur Basin, although the region had been given to China. He created a Russian government for the Maritime Provinces—that part of Siberia east of the Ussuri River—and moved the Russian naval base from Okhotsk southward to Petropavlovsk. He outmaneuvered the combined French and British fleets in the Far East during the Crimean War and laid the basis for later Russian claims to Sakhalin. He perceived the weakness and indifference of the Chinese and he pressed to advance the borders of Russia to the south. Thus, the war clouds which cast a shadow over China along its seaboard were equally ominous in the area of the land frontier in the north.

WAR—AND THE SECOND TREATY SETTLEMENT

As the earlier treaties approached the termination date, England, the United States, and France sought new treaties. Russia joined with a demand to bring up-to-date treaty relations which were still based on the 1689 Treaty of Nerchinsk. The Chinese resisted. A new emperor came to the throne in 1850 who, although weak and dissolute, was no more well disposed toward the foreigners than his predecessor. It became apparent that nothing short of war would bring the Chinese to terms. The British discovered a convenient excuse for action in 1856 when a Chinese official removed sailors from the lorcha, *Arrow*. At the same time, the French developed a mood for drastic action because of the murder on February 29, 1856, of a French priest, Père Chapdelaine, in Kwangsi Province far beyond the bounds of any treaty port. Although the British were preoccupied in India with the mutiny of the Sepoy regiments, and the French with wars in Europe, they decided upon war in China. They invited the United States and Russia to cooperate, but the invitation was declined.

Hostilities were one-sided. Canton was occupied, the viceroy was taken prisoner, and the city was administered for three years by a puppet government under a committee of the allies. A Franco-British naval expedition to the north blasted its way to Tientsin, only ninety miles from Peking, when the Chinese agreed to peace. American ships took no part in the fighting but came along with the Franco-British allies. The Chinese conducted negotiations with the representatives of all three powers separately but concurrently.

In November 1857, Count Putiatin, the Russian diplomatic envoy, arrived from St. Petersburg at the mouth of the Peiho (North River), near Tientsin, in a paddle-wheel steamer of minute dimensions. On his overland journey across Siberia, he had applied for a visa to enter Peking via Kiakhta. Upon refusal, he passed through Muraviev's territory and learned of Muraviev's plans for Russian expansion. He took ship from Petropavlovsk to join the allied expeditionary force in North China. He found it inadvisable to work his way to Peking alone, so he cast in his diplomatic lot with the allies. He gave it as his opinion the allies should strike terror into the Chinese capital and thus give irresistible force to the arguments of diplomacy. As soon as he found an opportunity to talk with the Chinese alone, he followed a different tactic. He presented a mild front to the Chinese in order to win their friendship and contented himself with a general, most-favored-nation treaty.

The Chinese signed treaties with all four major powers—England,

France, the United States, and Russia—in June 1858. In accordance with the combined terms of these treaties, the powers obtained the right to maintain a minister resident at Peking or to appoint a nonresident minister who could visit Peking at will. He could not be called upon to perform any ceremony which would not be in keeping with the dignity of his position. The term "barbarian" was not to be used in official intercourse. Foreigners were granted the right to travel in the interior for purposes of business or pleasure under passports issued by the foreign consuls and countersigned by local Chinese authorities. Foreign ships were allowed to trade on the Yangtze, and nine new ports, primarily along the Yangtze and in Manchuria, were opened to trade. Missionaries were assured the protection of Chinese authorities. By a subsequent agreement at Shanghai providing for taxes, the opium trade was legalized.

Officials in the Chinese court appreciated their handicap in dealing with the united front of Western nations. They tried to plant seeds of discord and to strengthen their bargaining position against the British and French by treating the Russians and Americans with greater consideration. The treaties with the United States and Russia were ratified with a minimum of chicanery, but the other agreements were not ratified without a renewal of hostilities in 1859 and 1860.

Before the fighting ended, Tientsin was occupied, and the summer palace in Peking was deliberately put to the torch. The Chinese court fled in panic, and the emperor died while in exile in his summer capital. In October, 1860, with enemy troops in Peking, the Chinese agreed to the ratification of the treaties of Tientsin and signed additional Peking conventions. It was specifically recognized that the foreign ministers might reside permanently in Peking. The Chinese consented to additional indemnities to compensate for the costs of the renewed hostilities. They ceded a portion of Kowloon Peninsula, on the Chinese mainland opposite Hong Kong, to the British and opened Tientsin, the near neighbor of Peking, to foreign trade. They agreed to regulations for the coolie trade. The French text of its convention permitted French missionaries to rent and purchase land and to erect buildings in all provinces. As an aftermath to the Peking conventions with the British and the French, the Chinese signed on November 14, 1860, the treaty with the Russians which reaffirmed the Russian advance on the northern frontier.

Strange things occurred in the course of the "war" in China. While fighting disrupted the ancient Chinese tenor of life in the north, trade flourished in the south. Cantonese coolies helped the allies against their own people. The foreign expeditionary force got along famously with the curious Chinese crowds which assembled to look at the strange creatures from the outside world. At the same time the allies fought against the imperial armies in Peking, they assisted the imperial forces against the T'ai p'ing rebels in Shanghai and the Yangtze Valley.

The Russians took advantage of China's helplessness for their own purposes. In May, 1858, Count Muraviev negotiated the Treaty of Aigun (a city in north Manchuria) with local Chinese officials. This treaty established a new international boundary. The Russians advanced, or the Chinese retreated, from the watershed to the north of the Amur to the valley of the Amur itself. The new boundary (the current one) was fixed as along the Amur from its junction with the Argun to the sea. By this treaty, trade was permitted across the border. The Amur, Sungari, and Ussuri rivers were opened to ships of Russia and China. The Maritime Provinces were to be jointly occupied by *both* nations.

The signature of a treaty by a Chinese representative in distant Manchuria was no guarantee of Chinese imperial ratification. The ratification of the Treaty of Aigun and the Treaty of Tientsin was obtained by General Ignatiev who succeeded Count Putiatin as the Russian envoy in Peking. General Ignatiev, in the opinion of the Chinese negotiators, had the "appearance of man but the heart of a beast," but he was a capable diplomat. He knew of allied plans and knew that the allies had no intention of spending a cold winter in Peking. Nonetheless he approached Prince Kung, the Chinese negotiator, and suggested that nothing would stop the allies from occupying Peking except the intervention of a strong power friendly to China. He offered to make an appeal to the allies if the Chinese would offer him a nominal consideration. All he wanted was the rectification of a frontier giving Russia a sterile region "inhabited by robbers and infested by tigers, where no mandarin could make a living, fit only for a penal settlement, with a rugged seacoast where no Chinese sail was ever seen."

The Chinese were taken in. In exchange for a nonexistent favor, they ratified the Russian Treaty of Tientsin, and they signed the Treaty of Peking which superseded the Treaty of Aigun. The Treaty of Peking confirmed the boundary as agreed upon by the Treaty of Aigun. In addition it signed over the Maritime Provinces, not for joint occupation by both China and Russia, but for the exclusive ownership of Russia alone. This was the first of several critical occasions when in desperation China turned to Russia. Prince Kung charted a costly path which was to be followed by Li Hung-chang, Sun Yat-sen, Chiang Kai-shek, and Mao Tse-tung. Russia gave counsel and help but extracted payment in full. In 1860 Russia added six hundred miles to its coastline on the Pacific, drew that much nearer to China and Japan, and founded the naval base and city of Vladivostok, which in Russian means "master of the East."

SUGGESTED READING

Collis, Maurice, *Foreign Mud* (New York, Knopf, 1947).

Downing, Charles Toogood, *The Fan-qui in China, in 1836–37* (three vols.) (London, H. Colburn, 1838).

Dulles, F. R., *Old China Trade* (Boston, Houghton, 1930).

Fairbank, John King, *Trade and Diplomacy on the China Coast* (Cambridge, Harvard U., 1953).

Hail, William J., *Tseng Kuo-fan and the T'ai Ping Rebellion* (New Haven, Yale U., 1927).

Hahn, Emily, *China Only Yesterday* (New York, Doubleday, 1963).

Hughes, E. R., *Invasion of China by the Western World* (London, Black, 1937).

Li Chien-nung, *Political History of China, 1840–1928* (Princeton, Van Nostrand, 1956).

Meadows, T. T., *Chinese and Their Rebellions* (Stanford, Stanford U.; academic reprint of the first edition of 1856).

Morse, H. B., *International Relations of the Chinese Empire* (three vols.) (Shanghai, Kelly & Walsh, 1918).

Oliphant, L., *Narrative of the Earl of Elgin's Mission to China and Japan* (Edinburgh, W. Blackwood & Sons, 1859).

Staunton, Sir George, *Authentic Account of an Embassy from the King of Great Britain to the Emperor of China* (London, G. Nicol, 1797).

Swisher, Earl, *China's Management of the American Barbarians* (New Haven, Yale U., 1951).

Teng Ssu-yu and Fairbank, J. K., *China's Response to the West* (Cambridge, Harvard, 1954).

Waley, Arthur, *Opium War Through Chinese Eyes* (New York, Macmillan, 1958).

7

China's Response to the West

In 1860 the Chinese empire and the traditional Chinese order seemed to be on the verge of collapse. The capital was in ruins and the court in disgrace. The child of the empress dowager, T'ung Chih (1860–1875), succeeded to the throne. The affairs of state were largely in the hands of eunuchs, concubines, and roués masquerading as political advisers. The imperial government appeared to be hopeless and demoralized in the face of foreign invasion and domestic rebellion. Bandits ravaged the interior and pirates infested the coast. The army was discredited and the bureaucracy was honeycombed with corruption. The countryside was more thoroughly devastated than it was by Japanese invaders before World War II.

The T'ung Chih Restoration

China's darkest hours preceded a brighter period known as the T'ung Chih Restoration, which lasted for ten years. Men of outstanding talent joined the government and in their own conservative way endeavored to restore the glories of the traditional Chinese society. They were not impressed by military victories nor interested in western political or philosophical ideas. They wanted peace, recovery of nothing more than the old-style economy, and social harmony based on Confucian principles. Their devotion was to China's cultural greatness and not to its possibilities as a modern nation-state. The only changes which the Restoration leaders desired were those which would contribute to the reinvigoration of ancient institutions.

Within this framework they breathed new life into suffering China. They were responsible for the restoration of law and order. They brought to an end the T'ai p'ing, the Nien Fei (a secret society) and the Moslem rebellions; they suppressed local revolts in practically every province. They made use of foreign assistance from a colorful American general, Frederick Townsend Ward, and from the famous British military adviser Charles George Gordon. They gave China a fairly respectable regime of law in spite of such imperfections as tortures for confession, irregularities in enforcement, and "cruel and unusual" punishments. They reduced the size of the army without adding to civil disturbances by wholesale dismissals. They took timid steps to improve the quality of the armed forces. They encouraged the formation of regional armies (which eventually produced the curse of the war lords), and they increased the militia. They introduced foreign training, built foreign-style arsenals, and acquired a few small ships of war for coastal defense.

In economic matters, the statesmen of the Restoration could not interest themselves in economic development. Industrialization and modernization played no part in the old Confucian order which they wished to restore. Their dreams were of the past, not the future. They worked mightily in rebuilding the devastated areas and they resettled displaced populations. Their prime objective was to rehabilitate agriculture, to increase food supplies, and to provide the major government revenues from the land tax and the payments of grain tribute. They continued to look down on commerce, and wanted to discourage the growth of the class of *nouveau riche* which would flout the ancient way of life. They disliked foreign trade because they believed imports drained away specie and destroyed cottage industries. They felt that the struggle for markets led to war, which they could not hope to win.

They feared the introduction of modern machines, factories, and methods of communication. Such things threatened the end of the old regime. Under protest, they introduced improvements in coal mining and permitted the construction of short rail lines. The first railroad out of Shanghai was bought by Chinese, who tore up the rails and shipped them to Formosa, where they were allowed to rust. They agreed to the construction of telegraph lines connecting Shanghai, Peking, and Tientsin; and they organized the China Merchants Steam Navigation Company which was to become China's official agent in river and coastal shipping. Modest importations of machinery were permitted, and foreign-style banks were created. The Chinese showed quickly that as individual merchants or bankers they were adept at mastering the equipment and techniques of the West. Inside the court there were always some far-sighted men of influence, like Li Hung-chang, who realized that China could not forever remain isolated. They wanted China to move forward, but they were opposed by the powerful advocates of the *status quo*.

During the T'ung Chih Restoration, learning and scholarship flourished. The literati insisted upon history and the classics, but new ideas created new styles in education. Schools for foreign languages were established in Peking, Shanghai, and Canton; and an official translation bureau made European works in science and literature available for Chinese. Technical schools were open, and courses in mathematics, engineering, and astronomy were introduced. Foreign-language newspapers were established in some of the treaty ports, and some Chinese acquired the habit of watching the news from abroad. By the end of the period it was clear that the Chinese played a losing game in trying to insulate themselves against the potent influences from the west. The Christian missionaries and their converts, sailors from foreign ships, merchants and their Chinese compradors, Chinese servants working in homes of foreigners (all of whom were rich by Chinese standards), imports of machinery and foreign goods, foreign-style homes and buildings, letters from abroad, and tales of Chinese travelers contributed to demands for change and modernization which could neither be ignored nor suppressed.

ADAPTATIONS TO THE WEST

For the first ten years after 1860, the Chinese were reasonably successful in their relations with Europeans and Americans. Foreign troops pulled out of China shortly after the signature of the Peking conventions, and foreign pressures were reduced on China's internal affairs. The imperial government determined to make the treaties work, believing that its wisest course lay in limiting the rights of foreigners by the strictest possible interpretation of the treaty provisions. Nothing would be permitted unless the treaty rights were specific and unarguable. Government policy was to avoid any act which might provoke an accusation of bad faith. The Chinese detailed some of their officials to study international law and diplomatic practice, in which they became expert. They set up a Tsung-li Yamen or embryo foreign office which assumed all responsibility for foreign relations. The government realized that China could not treat the powerful outside nations as vassals or inferiors. It must learn the ways of the Western world.

The audience question revealed the lingering antagonisms in the Chinese spirit. The Tientsin treaties gave representatives of foreign powers the right to conduct diplomatic intercourse on a basis of equality. This implied the right of audience, but the empress dowager could not bring herself to permit the barbarians to present themselves to the infant emperor and his court in the imperial palaces. As a matter of form, the diplomats pressed for their prerogatives. The empress dowager succeeded in making the diplomats wait until the sovereign reached his majority, and she granted audiences not in the awe-inspiring throne room but in an ordinary foreign-style house which she built as a reception hall in the midst of her splendid gardens.

The representatives of foreign powers, particularly Anson Burlingame from the United States and Rutherford Alcock from England, developed a policy of cooperation between themselves and China. They showed no disposition for conquest or forcible intervention in China's internal affairs. On the contrary, they exercised forbearance toward China; and they restrained their own overzealous missionaries and merchants. They supported the central government of China in spite of its "rags and rottenness" (Lord Elgin), and recognized the justice of China's aspirations to be treated on a basis of equality and reciprocity. They advocated the peaceful adjustment of disputes between China and the powers, the modernization of China at its own pace, and the steady growth of commercial opportunities for their own citizens. They appreciated the dangers which lurked in the continuing deterioration of China; they hoped that China could become sufficiently strong to preserve its own independence and territorial integrity. With the best of motives, they constantly pointed out to the court the necessity of reforms. Unhappily they were regarded as busybodies and impertinent troublemakers.

After Burlingame resigned as American minister in 1867, he accepted appointment as China's first envoy to the Western world. He made flamboyant speeches in China's behalf, and he used more oratory than reason in presenting China's case. On July 28, 1868, in Washington, he signed with his former chief, Secretary of State William H. Seward, a Sino-American treaty on the basis of equality and reciprocity. This Burlingame treaty provided for American support for China's territorial integrity; Chinese control of their inland trade; appointment of Chinese counsuls in American ports; reciprocal freedom from persecution for religion; encouragement of immigration of Chinese coolies into the United States, but with a prohibition of contract emigration; reciprocal rights of residence and travel; most-favored-nation treatment for Americans in China and for Chinese in the United States (naturalization excluded); access to the schools of either country; and freedom from interference in the development of China.

In many ways the Burlingame mission was a disappointment. The envoy did his clients a disservice in overselling them. The Washington treaty was never ratified. In Europe, Burlingame met with an comparatively cool reception. He extracted from the British a formal declaration that they would not apply unfriendly pressure inconsistent with the independence and safety of China. He got neither a treaty nor a declaration from the French or Germans, and he died from pneumonia in St. Petersburg before he had a chance to reach an understanding with the Russians.

But in a positive sense the Burlingame mission paved the way for the establishment of permanent Chinese legations abroad.

Meanwhile in China, the British representative, Rutherford Alcock, negotiated a convention which was signed on October 23, 1869. This convention provided only for a limited right of most-favored treatment for the British in China; conceded the Chinese right to tax British textiles, imports of opium, and exports of silk; permitted the introduction of steam vessels on an experimental basis on Poyang Lake; opened a few new ports to trade; and gave the British restricted rights of residence and travel in the interior. Largely on the prompting of merchants in China, the British government at home withheld ratification.

The decade of a patient search for understanding between foreign diplomats and Chinese statesmen was brought to an abrupt halt one hot afternoon in 1870 by the so-called Tientsin Massacre. The Chinese could not avoid arguments with missionaries over what the Chinese considered as mysterious and aggravating medical and educational activities. The quest for land and buildings for churches, schools, hospitals, and cemeteries led to innumerable legal arguments. Missionaries were accused of demanding preferential legal treatment for their converts, and indeed they were sometimes duped into acting as covers or protectors for rowdies and hoodlums. Because of their known antagonism to some aspects of Confucianism (including ancestor worship), missionaries were suspected of fomenting rebellion against the dynasty. They were frequently involved in incidents with magistrates, who were the local stalwarts and guardians of the imperial regime.

Rumors circulated in Tientsin to the effect that Chinese children were kidnaped and taken to an orphanage where sisters used the hearts and eyes of children to concoct an elixir of life. On June 21, 1870, a mob attacked the orphanage and the cathedral and burned down the French consulate. Members of the consular staff cut down some of the mob with their swords; in retaliation the consul, two French priests, ten French sisters, and innumerable Chinese Christians were slain and mutilated. In reparation for this Tientsin Massacre the Chinese government was obliged to decapitate the ringleader of the rioters, pay a substantial indemnity to France, and send to Paris a mission of apology.

The problems of missionaries combined with new commercial troubles to aggravate China's relations with the West. The energies released by the industrial revolution, the search for markets, the advent of steam and the opening of the Suez Canal brought China and the West into closer and more competitive relationship. By 1870 foreigners were living in fifteen ports in China—in security and comparative luxury—and often in settlements or concessions which were set apart for their own residence and administration. They collected their own taxes and operated the maritime customs service for the imperial Chinese government. They were entirely separate from the Chinese communities and made little effort to understand Chinese culture or their own environment. The closest many of them ever got to the Chinese language was an affected use of pidgin English. For the most part they were treated with courtesy by the Chinese; they could travel, with the authorization of local Chinese authorities, in the interior with reasonable safety. However, the trading community was eager for expanded opportunities for profit; it exerted constant pressure on its own government to work for more treaty rights and for the opening of all China to commercial exploitation.

In 1876 a young British consular officer, Augustus Margary, was killed in Yunnan while arranging for the survey of an overland trading route to Burma. The murder of this official was seized upon as the occasion for a far-reaching modification in treaty relations between China and England. By virtue of the most-favored-nation clause, new privileges to English traders were extended automatically to others. Every country had a vital interest in the negotiations between China and England which followed the Margary murder. The British demanded and received satisfaction for the death of their official in the form of the Chefoo Convention, which was signed September 13, 1876. In tone and content it was designed to satisfy the British, with slight regard for Chinese interests or sensibilities. By the terms of the Chefoo Convention an indemnity was exacted which included claims of British merchants against the Chinese government, and a letter of apology was sent to Queen Victoria by a special envoy. A British consular official was to be stationed in Yunnan Province and new ports were opened along the Yangtze River. New trade regulations were agreed upon. A code of diplomatic practice was adopted, and new rules were drawn up for the administration of justice in the treaty ports. It was only in a weak country like China that a nation could take advantage of a personal incident in order to gain political concessions for itself and its most-favored-nation colleagues.

INFRINGEMENTS ON CHINESE SOVEREIGNTY

The degeneration of the imperial government was reflected in the spread of internal chaos and in China's inability to cope with the growing ambitions of Western nations in Asia. After 1870 some powers developed new techniques of seeking special rights and privileges in designated areas of China. As a first step, they sought to weaken or destroy China's political control over its vassals and neighbors.

It had been China's policy from time immemorial to surround itself by buffer states to form a protective *cordon sanitaire*. Vassal states administered their own affairs without interference from China, but they recognized the overlordship of China by periodic tribute missions. Each new ruler accepted investiture and received his seal of office from the Chinese emperor. The Liu Ch'iu Islands, Korea, Nepal, Burma, Sikkim, Laos, Sulu, Siam, and Annam came within the category of implied vassalage. On its western frontier the Chinese sought security by control of the nomads who separated China from Russia. In the latter part of the nineteenth century the Chinese saw their boundaries shrink and their ancient prestige evaporate because of aggressive aliens.

The Russians were the first to exert pressures in Central Asia, on the western approaches to China. By the Kulja Convention in 1851, Russians alone obtained rights to trade at Kulja (Ili) and Tarbagatai (Chuguchak). Russians acquired rights to purchase lands for factories, churches, and cemeteries and well-defined rights of extradition and extraterritoriality. Following upon the Treaty of Peking in 1860, adjusting their northern boundaries, Russians and Chinese began the process of delimiting their western frontiers. While the Chinese pursued Moslem rebels into Turkestan, Russia occupied Ili and sought to confirm its control over the strategic pass which ended at that city. A Russo-Chinese treaty signed at Livadia (in the Crimea) in 1879 conceded to Russia substantially what it wanted. The Chinese government refused to ratify the treaty and negotiated a revised treaty at St. Petersburg in 1881. This treaty, renewed every ten years, was the basis of Russo-Chinese relations in Central Asia until the end of the Russian empire. Russia enjoyed the right to maintain consulates in Turkestan and Mongolia. Russians were permitted to buy land; to erect residences, shops, and warehouses; and to trade as far as the Great Wall, without the payment of duties. This treaty structure preserved as much protection as China could hope for and provided a cover for Russia to push its political schemes to the limit of its power in Central Asia.

The French deprived the Chinese of their traditional suzerainty over Annam. The Chinese consistently protested against French pressures on Annam, but they could do no more than protest. In 1883 clashes occurred between French and Chinese troops. In the course of hostilities the French extended their actions to Foochow, Fukien Province, on the mainland. They also occupied points in Formosa and threw a blockade against the island. Peaceful relations were restored by the Treaty of Tientsin, June 9, 1885, which rectified the frontier between China and Indochina in favor of France, surrendered Chinese claims to suzerainty over Annam and established terms for trade between China and French-protected Annam over the land frontiers. The treaty also provided that if China should decide to build any railways in its provinces bordering on Indochina, the French government would give China every facility it might need for the procurement of personnel and materials in France.

Meanwhile the British took away the last Chinese pretensions to suzerainty in Burma and Sikkim and asserted their interest in China's Tibet. In 1886 the British extended their jurisdiction from lower to upper Burma and concluded an understanding with China. British sovereignty in Burma was recognized by the Chinese, and in return the British agreed that Burma might send a tribute mission to Peking every ten years. Also in 1886 China and England signed a convention in Peking in which England agreed not to press unduly for the opening of Tibet. In 1890 China recognized a British protectorate over Sikkim.

Portugal took advantage of French and British negotiations with Peking to press its own claims to sovereignty over Macao and its surrounding waters. On December 1, 1887, China and Portugal made a treaty which formally ceded Macao to Portugal, subject only to the condition that Macao would not be alienated to any other power without agreement with China.

It was the rising new country of Japan which made the most substantial inroads on China's traditional relations with neighboring territories. In 1871 Japan entered into formal treaty relations with China on a basis of equality and reciprocity and began almost immediately to assert its predominant interest in the Liu Ch'iu Islands and Formosa.

Since 1372 the successive princes of the Liu Ch'ius received their investiture regularly from the Chinese emperor, but they paid tribute to Japan as well as to China. In November 1871 a junk filled with Liu Ch'iuans was wrecked on the east coast of Formosa. Fifty-four of sixty-six members of the crew were killed and eaten. Liu Ch'iu turned to Japan—not to China—for help. Japan asked China if it intended to assume responsibility for obtaining justice for the Liu Ch'iuans. China said no. Japan in 1872 invited the king of the Liu Ch'ius to visit Japan, made him a member of the Japanese peerage and constituted the Liu Ch'ius (which the Japanese call the Ryukyus) as a vassal of Japan. The annual tribute from the Liu Ch'ius to China was terminated and the Liu Ch'ius—or Ryukyus—were formally incorporated into the Japanese empire.

In 1874 Japan sent an expedition to Formosa to get satisfaction for the murdered Liu Ch'iu sailors. China retracted while Japan expanded. On October 31, 1874, China and Japan signed a treaty which recognized the Japanese expedition to Formosa as a just and rightful undertaking for the protection of its own subjects. China, as sovereign of Formosa, agreed to pay $750,000—not as an indemnity but as a consolation for bereaved families and as reimbursements for roads and buildings which Japan had constructed in Formosa (Chinese territory) in the course of the expedition. The indemnity was paid within three months, and the Japanese forces evacuated Formosa. This transaction was fateful for China. It advertised to the world that China was unable to fight and was willing to pay.

China was unsuccessful in salvaging any part of its claim to the Liu Ch'ius and lost interest in the effort because of the graver complications of Formosa and Korea. When the Japanese landed in Formosa in 1874, the island was a trading center. But it was also a pirates' lair and a haven for fugitives from justice. It was an integral part of China. Internal conditions were a mixture of maladministration and extortion, neglect and laxity, banditry and intermittent wars between the Chinese and the aborigines. When shipwrecked sailors of any nation were cast ashore in the midst of such anarchy, they were fortunate to escape with their lives. Formosa—or Taiwan as the Chinese preferred to call it—was doubly attractive because of its strategic location. The British cast covetous eyes upon it, so did the French and the Americans. After the events of 1874, the Japanese watched and waited for a propitious moment to make Formosa their own. After the defeat of China in 1895, Japan forced China to give up its legal title to Formosa and the neighboring Pescadores Islands. As expressed at Cairo in 1943, China felt that Formosa was taken away through Japan's "greed and aggression."

LOSS OF KOREA

China's story in Korea was one of perpetual retreat and eventual humiliation. As with its other vassals, China closed its eyes to internal conditions within Korea. It contented itself with the assumption of superiority in foreign relations. Although the nominal overlord of Korea, China was powerless to prevent its conquest by the Mongols in the thirteenth century and to stop the invasions of the Japanese shogun Hideyoshi at the end of the sixteenth. China would scarcely have troubled itself about Korea in the nineteenth century had the powers been willing to let China and Korea alone in their feudalistic vassal-lord relationship.

Jesuit missionaries filtered into Korea from Peking and converted many Koreans to their faith. Converts were persecuted; when France tried to put a stop to the practice, it was told by the king of Korea to take its problems to the emperor of China. When British, French, and Russians tried to open Korea to foreign trade, they too were informed that China was responsible for Korea's foreign relations.

In 1866 Korea was under an infant king and a regency which was violently anti-West and anti-Christian. It was sufficiently strong to repel a French naval expedition, seeking redress for some murdered priests, and to drive off American ships which undertook a survey of Korean coastal waters. All the powers desired treaty relations with Korea, and neither Korea nor China could stave off external pressures forever.

After 1868 Japan, then a newcomer following the footsteps of the West, took the lead in destroying the lord-vassal relationship between China and Korea. In 1875 a Japanese gunboat engaged in marine surveys was fired upon by Korean shore batteries. After quick and forceful retaliation, Japan forced Korea to sign the Treaty of Kanghwa on February 27, 1876. As a consequence of this treaty Korean ports were opened to foreign commerce, Korean independence was recognized by Japan, and the formal connection between Korea and China was ended. To counter the growing Japanese influence in Korea, China adopted a policy of "introducing more poison to kill poison." The Chinese viceroy in Tientsin encouraged Korea to make treaties with the United States (1882), England (1883), Germany (1883), Italy (1884), Russia (1884), and France (1886).

The Korean countryside was a hotbed of antiforeignism; and the court, a nest of jealousy and distrust. The king was a weak individual who vacillated between the demands of his father, the regent, and the will of his wife, the queen. The Chinese resident-general in Korea worked on the king through the father, and the Japanese ambassador exerted his influence through the queen. A riot occurred in 1882, as a result of which both Japanese and Chinese obtained rights to station troops in Seoul, Korea's capital. Chinese-Japanese rivalry led to the brink of war. As a preventive measure the two nations signed the convention of Tientsin in the spring of 1885 which provided that troops of both China and Japan should be withdrawn from Korea within four months, and if troops of either side were to be returned, *advance* notice would be given in writing to the other side. China's problem was to salvage its hegemony in Korea, not to accomplish reforms. China was determined to checkmate Japan, even at the risk of exposing Korea to the new intrigues of Western powers, particularly Russia.

Conflicting forces within Korea lined up for China and the *status quo* on one side, for Japan and modernism on the other. All forms of intrigue swirled about the court—demonstrations, denunciations, palace cabals, assassinations, and revolts. Charge and countercharge were poured into the ears of the puppet king, who was helpless against a civil war which would bring Chinese and Japanese intervention. The crisis came on March 29, 1894, with the murder in Shanghai of Kim Ok-kiun, leader of the progressive groups. His body was returned to Korea, cut to pieces, and placed on ghoulish exhibit throughout the country. In June 1894 the Tonghaks, or members of a reactionary Society for Eastern Learning, confident of success, instigated open rebellion and persuaded the court to call upon the Chinese for assistance. The Chinese sent troops to Korea and notified the Japanese *afterward*. The Japanese immediately sent six times as many soldiers to Korea as the Chinese. The Japanese also sent a new minister to Korea who took an adamant stand for internal reforms which the Chinese were certain to oppose.

Hostilities were inevitable. The whole world believed that the Chinese giant would easily crush the upstart Japan, but Japan's "schoolboy patriotism" overwhelmed the Chinese "undisciplined rabble of tramps." Japan won an unbroken series of victories in Korea, Manchuria, China proper, and on the high seas. On April 17, 1895, China and Japan signed the Treaty of Shimonoseki. The Chinese negotiator was Li Hung-chang, and his adviser was the American John W. Foster (the grandfather of John Foster Dulles). The Japanese negotiators were Count Ito Hirobumi and Viscount Mutsu Munemitsu; and their adviser was also an American, Henry Denison. By this treaty China recognized the independence and autonomy of Korea; gave Japan title to Formosa, the Pescadores Islands, and the Liaotung Peninsula; agreed to an indemnity of 200,000,000 taels; opened four new treaty ports; gave Japan most-favored-nation treatment in China; and promised a new commercial treaty.

The commercial treaty was signed July 21, 1896. At this point, Japan did not act like a downtrodden victim of the West. On the contrary it acted the same as Western powers had acted in pressing unequal treaties upon China. By this commercial treaty it gained many new advantages which the West was delighted to share. Japan obtained the privilege of extraterritoriality in China and the commutation of inland taxation on exports and imports. Japanese were permitted to engage in manufacturing in the open ports, which was the foundation of the system of branch factories in China. By a subsequent agreement of October 1896 the Japanese were guaranteed "national treatment," which was the assurance that Japanese would be assessed the same taxes on their products which Chinese would pay on similar articles locally made. When the Chinese emerged from their bitter encounters with Japan, their country was exposed as being a giant with feet of clay. China was saddled with a huge foreign debt, and it appeared in the picturesque words of John Hay as a "whale, not yet dead," cast upon the shore, awaiting the knives of foreign powers who would cut themselves a slice of steak.

THE SCRAMBLE FOR CONCESSIONS

After the terms of the Sino-Japanese agreements became known, Russia, France, and Germany engineered a triple intervention designed to rob Japan of part of the fruits of victory. His Majesty, the emperor of Russia, supported by the president of France and the Kaiser, found that "the possession of the peninsula of Liaotung, claimed by Japan, would be a constant menace to the capital of China, would at the same time render illusory the independence of Korea, and would henceforth be a perpetual obstacle to the peace of the Far East." Therefore, he "would give a new proof of sincere friendship for the Government of His Majesty the Emperor of Japan by advising him to renounce the definite possession of the peninsula of Liaotung." As a matter of consolation Japan would be awarded a fifteen-percent increase in the indemnities to be extracted from hapless China. The three powers proceeded out of no love for China, but a determination that the newborn power of Japan should not thwart their own schemes in China. During the next five years, China was subjected to a series of agreements granting compensation to Russia, France, and Germany for services rendered. These compensations extracted from China far more than China would have lost to Japan had the three not interceded in China's behalf.

The French took the initiative in wresting thank offerings from the Chinese in the form of economic concessions. The French and Russians —to the exclusion of the Germans—for handsome commissions and substantial interest payments, pressed a loan upon China, secured on the maritime customs, to pay the first installment on the Chinese indemnity to Japan. As further compensation, the French obtained a rectification of the China-Indochina boundary in favor of France, better terms for overland trade between China and Indochina, and a promise that China should apply first of all to French manufacturers and engineers for exploitation of mines in the provinces of Yunnan, Kwangsi, and Kwangtung. China further agreed to the extension of railways and telegraphs from French territory into South China and to the nonalienation of the island of Hainan. Subsequently the French demanded and received a ninety-nine-year lease of Kwangchowwan (a naval base on the southern coast of China near Indochina), a nonalienation agreement covering the Chinese provinces bordering Tonkin, the extension of the Indochina Railway into Yunnan, and the right to designate French advisers to the Chinese post office.

On June 3, 1896, Prince Lobanov Rostovsky for Russia and Li Hung-chang for China signed in Moscow a fifteen-year treaty of alliance, promising to aid one another if either were attacked in China or Korea. Russia was granted the right to build and administer the Chinese Eastern Railway across northern Manchuria as a short cut for the Trans-Siberian Railway and was given special mining rights in south Manchuria. It obtained long-term leases on Port Arthur, which it developed as a naval base, and Dairen, which it developed into a bustling commercial city. Russia also received permission to construct the strategic railway from Harbin on the Chinese Eastern Railway to link up with their newly acquired warm-water ports to the south.

The Germans were given the right to make foreign loans to China to help pay the indemnities and to assist in railway construction. (The power which made the loans would naturally supply rails, sleepers, rolling stock, and technical experts.) Kiaochow Bay was leased to the Germans as a naval base for ninety-nine years; the surrounding territory was declared a neutral zone by the Chinese government; and the whole of the sacred province of Shantung, with its rich mining districts and opportunities for rail, industrial, and commercial development, was designated as a German sphere of interest. German engineers flocked into Shantung much as Russians swarmed into Manchuria. Tsingtao took on the appearance of a German city with its red roofs, churches, clubs, and street signs. Very shortly German shipping lines dumped steel, concrete, and manufactured goods of every kind into the province of Shantung at rates with which other foreign nationals could not hope to compete.

The British could not make up their minds whether to protest against the scramble for concessions or join in the game. Many British began to feel that Japan, not China, was the hope of Asia's future. British reports described China as rotten to the core and every Chinese official, with the exception of one in a thousand, either a "liar, a thief or a tyrant." The British decided to play along. They made loans also on the security of the maritime customs, and extracted from China promises that the inspector general or the customs would be British as long as British trade should be predominant and that China would never cede any territory in the Yangtze Basin to any other power. The British, as "cartographic consolation," leased Weihaiwei for as long as the Russians were to be in Port Arthur and leased (for ninety-nine years) the remainder of the Kowloon peninsula between Deep Bay and Mirs Bay.

Not to be left out in the scramble, the Japanese turned on China and demanded a declaration that China would not alienate Fukien or any part of the China coast to any power. The Italians put in a bid for a leased area, but the Italians were weak and the Chinese refused.

The Americans, made aware of new horizons in Asia by the acquisition of the Philippines, were not disposed to be passive bystanders while the powers carved out chunks of China. They did not wish to participate in the breakup of China, but they sought to safeguard their legitimate interests throughout the entire Chinese empire. They formulated the Open Door policy, which was intended to safeguard the equal opportunity to trade even in those areas in China which the various outside nations had earmarked for themselves. On September 6, 1899, the United States asked each power that in its own leased area or sphere of interest it would not interfere with any treaty port or any vested American interest; that it would apply the Chinese rate of tariff (collected by the Chinese government) on *all* merchandise imported regardless of national origin; and that it would levy no higher harbor dues or railway charges on Americans than on its own nationals. The Americans did not seek to abolish the spheres of interest; they merely wanted to remove the monopoly aspects of the spheres. The American program worked to the benefit of China, but it was opposed by some of the powers—notably Russia—as an international policy.

At the turn of the century, concession hunters joined foreign traders in the quest for quick profits in what they hoped would be the fabulous China market. China, a country nearly the size of Europe, with a densely populated agricultural area generously interspersed with conveniently placed urban centers, looked like an investor's paradise. The plains of north China were flat and cut up by few rivers. Railway construction promised huge and continuing fortunes. Engineers and promoters with well-filled pocketbooks came to Peking. They cultivated the right people: their own diplomats and Chinese officials. They entertained lavishly and they distributed appropriate gifts. They did their best to find out what their rivals were doing, hiding their own successes even from their personal secretaries.

The rivalry between the concession hunters was so intense from the beginning that, in order to make certain of profits for their citizens, Great Britain, France, Germany, Russia (and, in a timid manner, Japan) entered into a series of agreements promising to confine themselves to their specifically designated spheres of interest. These inter-power agreements prevented China from aligning itself with one power as against another or from playing off one power against another. In the meantime, the powers extended their old-time trading privileges. New ports were opened for trade by the Chinese government, and additional inland waters were opened to steam navigation. The international settlement and the French concession at Shanghai were enlarged. Many new concession areas were developed at treaty ports, including Tientsin, Hankow, Newchwang, Amoy, and Foochow. They were like glorified shopping centers conveniently removed at a comfortable distance from the congested Chinese urban areas.

REFORM, REVOLUTION, OR REACTION

In response to these feverish activities on the part of foreigners, Chinese of every description felt the need of counteraction. China could not continue to wallow in helplessness, saying nothing, doing nothing to defend itself against the aggressions from the West. Some Chinese became so angry as "to make their hair stand on end and their eyes stare out of their sockets." Some argued for reform; others, like Sun Yat-sen, advocated a thoroughgoing revolution, and a substantial number of conservatives still felt that China's salvation lay in resistance and reaction.

The emperor's party at court espoused the cause of reform. For a hundred days after June 11, 1898, under the inspiration of K'ang Yu-wei, reform decrees were issued by the dozen. Foreigners and Chinese were left breathless with amazement at the sweeping orders for change. The foreign office was ordered to improve relations abroad; all officials were to learn political science and international law within six months; the legal system was to be reorganized; journalists were to be free to express criticism; a government translation bureau was to be set up for important foreign books; and ministries were proposed for the arts, commerce, and agriculture. All subjects were to be given the right to memorialize the throne, and obsolete and surplus offices were to be removed from the administration. In the field of education a national system was to be established with a national university at Peking. The examination system was to be modernized and revitalized. With regard to commerce, important railway lines were to be completed without further delay, trade was to be assisted and encouraged, and government bureaus were to be inaugurated for railways, mines, commerce, and labor relief. Military reforms called for the foundation of a naval academy, modernization of the army, and the introduction of a conscription system. To cap the climax, the arch-reactionary, the empress dowager was to be imprisoned. The period of the hundred days reform came to a disastrous end when the empress dowager called a halt to the "madness of reform," imprisoned the emperor, and took over the reins of government as imperial regent.

The reaction of the court was reflected in the outrages of the society of the Boxers or the "Righteous Harmony Fists" throughout the provinces. The Boxers capitalized on the growing fear and hatred of foreigners, including missionaries as well as diplomats and businessmen. The conviction grew that every foreigner was at heart a land-grabber, that missionaries were "running dogs of imperialism" and that the Bible was the advance agent of the gunboat. Native Christians were increasingly regarded as traitors. The new railways were particularly objectionable because they reached into the interior where there was gross ignorance and distortion about the West and its intentions. Railways did violence to grave mounds, offended the spirits of ancestors, and threw coolies, porters, and boatmen out of their jobs.

The climax of antiforeignism was reached in the summer of 1900. More than two hundred missionaries were killed, churches were burned, and the capital city of Peking was taken over by the Boxers. Foreigners were besieged at various places in Peking and were subjected to intermittent shelling for more than three months. During the hostilities, the German minister, von Ketteler, and the Japanese Chancellor of Legation, Sugiyama, were killed. An international military expedition of 15,000 troops, in which units of the fifteenth infantry from the Philippines participated, was dispatched to affect the relief of Peking. War was not declared, and force was used only against the Boxers and any Chinese who would oppose the relief expedition in its mission to rescue their fellow countrymen in Peking. While North China felt the impact of invasion, officials in Central and South China kept the peace in their own districts.

Secretary of State John Hay in Washington feared that conditions in China might inspire some ambitious powers to demand outright annexation of parts of Chinese territory (for example, Russia might demand the annexation of Manchuria) as compensation for damages or as a guarantee of future protection for their citizens in China. Therefore he dispatched a second group of circular notes on July 3, 1900, which sought to induce the other powers to subscribe to principles of American policy with regard to China. Secretary Hay wrote:

> The purpose of the President, is . . . to act concurrently with the other powers; first, in opening up communication with Peking and rescuing American officials, missionaries and other Americans who are in danger; secondly, in affording all possible protection everywhere in China to American life and property; thirdly, in guarding and protecting all legitimate American interests; and fourthly, in aiding to prevent a spread of the disorders to the other provinces of the Empire and a recurrence of such disasters. It is of course too early to forecast the means of attaining this last result; but the policy of the Government of the United States is to seek a solution which may bring about permanent safety and peace to China, preserve Chinese territorial and administrative entity, protect all rights guaranteed to friendly powers by treaty and international law, and safeguard for the world the principle of equal and impartial trade with all parts of the Chinese Empire.

The concept of territorial and administrative integrity of China was added to that of equal and impartial trade with all parts of the Chinese empire as an integral part of the Open Door policy. The former was no more acceptable than the latter to some powers as a guide for diplomatic action. It was therefore difficult to restore peace with China, not because China was unwilling, but because the powers could not agree among themselves as to the demands to make. China was in an extremely embarrassing and difficult position. The court was in exile in western China, and Peking was under military occupation. The city had been plundered. Troops of all nationalities were stationed in North China, and legions of Russian soldiers sang their way into Manchuria over the newly built Russian railways. Again it looked as if the Manchu Dynasty was about to topple, but it was given a new lease on life because of difference of opinion among the powers who fashioned the Boxer Protocol of September 7, 1901.

After the terms were agreed upon by the quarreling victors, the protocol was presented to the Chinese for their signature. China was to apologize for the murder of the foreign diplomats and erect a memorial arch to the German minister in Peking, punish officials guilty of anti-foreign excesses, and pay an indemnity of a third of a billion dollars over a period of thirty-nine years. The money was to be divided proportionately among the victors: Russia 29 percent, Germany 20, France 14, Great Britain 11, Japan and the United States each 7. It was apparent who was severe and who lenient. As a security for payments, practically all of China's revenues were mortgaged and placed in the administrative control of foreigners. In accordance with the protocol, the Chinese Tsung-li Yamen was to be reorganized into a modern *Wai-wu pu* or ministry of foreign affairs and the existing treaties of commerce and navigation were to be amended and revised. It was also provided that the Chinese government should reserve a special quarter in the heart of Peking for the *exclusive* use of foreign legations and should recognize the right of all powers to station troops at various points along the railway in order to maintain free communication between the capital and the sea. Never again would foreigners be marooned in Peking, deprived of the possibility of immediate rescue.

This chapter ends on the same note on which it began, in spite of the forty years which intervened between the first and the last paragraphs. The Chinese empire and the traditional Chinese order seemed more than ever to be on the verge of collapse. When the empress dowager with her court returned from Sian to Peking after the signature of the Boxer Protocol, she was no longer able to close her eyes to China's desperate situation. If China was to modernize and to take a place of equality with the other great nations of the world, it would have to emerge from the cocoon of its own past. The court and country would have to cooperate in a massive effort of self-development—perhaps after the model of Japan—if China were to adapt itself gracefully to the tempo of the twentieth century. For the dying Manchu Dynasty, the task was distasteful and the prospect uncertain.

SUGGESTED READING

Danton, George H., *Culture Contacts of the United States and China* (New York, Columbia U., 1931).

Endacott, G. B., *History of Hong Kong* (London, Oxford, 1958).

Fleming, Peter, *Siege at Peking* (New York, Harper, 1959).

Griffin, Eldon, *Clippers and Consuls* (Ann Arbor, Edwards, 1938).

Hsu, Immanuel C. Y., *China's Entrance into the Family of Nations: the Diplomatic Phase, 1858–1880* (Cambridge, Harvard U., 1960).

Hummel, Arthur W. (ed.), *Eminent Chinese of the Ch'ing Period, 1644–1912* (two vols.) (Washington, Government Printing Office, 1943–1944).

Lamb, Alstair, *Britain and Chinese Central Asia* (London, Kegan, 1960).

Langer, William, *Diplomacy of Imperialism* (New York, Knopf, 1951).

Michie, Alexander, *Englishman in China* (two vols.) (Edinburgh, W. Blackwood & Sons, 1900).

Hu Sheng, *Imperialism and Chinese Politics, 1840–1925* (Peking, Foreign Languages Press, 1955).

Pelcovits, Nathan A., *Old China Hands and the Foreign Office* (New York, Institute of Pacific Relations, 1948).

Purcell, Victor, *Boxer Uprising, A Background Study* (Cambridge, Harvard U., 1963).

Steiger, G. Nye, *China and the Occident* (New Haven, Yale U., 1927).

Tan, Chester C., *Boxer Catastrophe* (New York, Columbia U., 1955).

Wright, Mary, *Last Stand of Chinese Conservatism* (Stanford, Stanford U., 1957).

8

The Opening of Japan

As a result of the impact of the West, China lost strength and prestige. By contrast, Japan demonstrated its ability to adapt to its own use the material and mechanical elements of Western civilization. As a result of stubbornness and short-sightedness, China deteriorated to a point where it was beaten in war and thoroughly humiliated by its small island neighbor. As an aftermath of defeat, China saw its independence and territorial integrity placed at the mercy of outside powers.

On the other hand, Japan escaped the ultimate consequences of its own seclusion policy. It resisted the West as long as it could. When the struggle proved to be hopeless, it surrendered as gracefully as possible and proceeded to make an all-out effort to graft whatever seemed of value onto its ancient way of life. Japan suffered losses of sovereignty due to unequal treaties, but it was never in danger of losing either its independence or territorial integrity. In a constant battle of wits with the West, it maintained its dignity and increased its stature. It created a respectable military machine, reshaped its political institutions, gave new direction to economic development and preserved domestic stability while undergoing fundamental modifications in its social order. The Japanese became the first people in Asia to transform themselves into a modern nation-state and to take their place with the great powers of the world.

CHANGES WITHIN JAPAN

On the surface, the structure of Tokugawa Japan in 1850 seemed to have changed very little in the course of its two and a half centuries of existence. The emperor and his court lived in their gilded cage in Kyoto, the *bakufu* or shogunate ruled the country from Edo (Tokyo), the daimyo

142

administered their estates in apparent conformity with the regulations of the shogun, the samurai enjoyed their monopoly in the profession of arms, merchants compounded their fortunes, artisans indulged their tastes and the peasants produced rice. In reality, the feudal state had reached its peak in the Genroku period (1688–1704) and was in process of rapid disintegration. Beneath the surface explosive forces rumbled which were to gather momentum, shatter the bonds of the past and propel Japan into three-quarters of a century of revolution and progress.

Through Japan's long period of seclusion, the restraining regulations of the Tokugawa shogunate could not arrest the process of change within Japan's social structure. Like the imperial court, the *bakufu* lost touch with the people. It was preoccupied with its own ceremonial importance and bound by red tape of its own making. The later shoguns were neither strong generals nor wise statesmen. They became mere figureheads, unable to preserve law and order or to dominate their own system. Important political decisions were made by councilors and implemented by the elaborate and tangled network of bureaucrats. Edo was no more prepared than Kyoto to cope with the rising tide of internal unrest and the appearance of foreign powers at the doors of Japan.

The agricultural foundation of society was shaken by the substitution of money for rice as the basis of the economy. A man's wealth was measured by his accumulation of capital, rather than by the riceland under his control. Manufacturers and merchants prospered more than ever; the feudal lords and their retainers found their prestige outweighed by their debts. Great families like the Mitsui amassed huge fortunes and came to exert strong influence on the government. Small shopkeepers made good profits, and they demanded the freedom which comes with wealth and leisure. The peasants did not share in the rising level of living. Expanding population caused greater agrarian discontent. Rice riots were frequent and violent. Japan approached the place where more than agriculture would be needed to provide jobs for its restless, ambitious people.

The *bakufu* was guilty of administrative blunders. It squeezed every possible dollar out of the land tax and saddled commercial transactions with crippling assessments. Central and local governments operated on chronic deficits. Officials turned to the rich, particularly in the cities, for loans which were never repaid. Laws were not uniformly enforced, and the commoners were without redress for harsh treatment at the hands of the privileged samurai. On the other hand, individual samurai often sympathized with the poor and sided with them in their riots against rich merchants or pompous officials. Japan in 1850 seemed to be on the verge of departing from the traditional peace of the Tokugawa and returning to the earlier feudal law of the sword.

New ideas were as important as economic changes in the creation of modern Japan. It was the policy of the *bakufu* to encourage learning—with the expectation that the study of the Chinese classics would idealize the quality of Confucian loyalty and thus fortify the position of the shogun. However, Japanese scholars came forward with two new ideas—nationalism and imperialism—which rattled the intellectual foundations of the shogunate.

The study of Japanese history showed the recency of the current form of government and revealed the shogun as a usurper of power. The question arose whether the shogun should not step aside and permit the emperor to return to his rightful position as the sovereign of his country. Scholars found greater inspiration in the ancient records of their own country than in the classics of China. They came to accept the theory that the emperor enjoyed the lasting virtues bestowed by his descent from the gods and that Japan was truly the land of the gods. Japanese literature was released from its Chinese shackles. All forms of art were devoted to the expression of the whole gamut of Japanese life and legend. The followers of the Shinto multiplied; the number of Shinto sects grew because of the identity of Shinto as a native religion as contrasted with imported Buddhism or Confucianism. A nationalist scholar captured the prevailing philosophy in his sentiment, "I am a Japanese, the whole country is mine—why should I need a passport to travel from the territory of one feudal lord to another." The feeling arose that perhaps the natural calamities—the earthquakes, floods, famine, and pestilence—might come to an end if Japan would turn back to its ancient ways and put itself under the emperor, who was the paragon of virtue, rather than the shogun, who was after all only a barbarian-subduing-general.

Economic changes and intellectual ferment were effective in Japan during mid-nineteenth century because the whole country was full of restless spirits, dissatisfied with conditions and thirsting for activity. According to the distinguished scholar, Sir George Sansom, "There were nobles who wanted independence and foreign trade . . . samurai who wanted opportunities to use their talents . . . merchants who wanted to break the monopolies of the guilds; scholars who wanted to draw knowledge from new springs; humble peasants and townsmen who wanted just a little freedom from tax and tyranny." As he concluded, "Every force but conservatism was pressing from within at the closed doors: so that when a summons came from without they were flung wide open, and all those imprisoned energies were released."

Japanese Attitudes toward the Opening of Their Country

Although the *bakufu* contemplated no immediate end to the official policy of seclusion, many Japanese argued its pros and cons. In many ways Japan was surprisingly well conditioned for the entry of foreigners. Books from China or books from the Dutch brought much information about the outside world. Science, medicine, anatomy, astronomy, geography, and military affairs were subjects of constant study. Foreign ships—Russian, British, French, and American—appeared from time to time in Japanese waters. The Dutch master of trade at Deshima Island kept his neighbors and even the *bakufu* in distant Edo at least partially informed of current events. The outer lords near Nagasaki were quite aware of the advance of Russia toward Japan, of the desire of the Western nations for trade and missionary activity in Japan, and of China's defeat at the hands of England and France in the Opium War. The annual procession to Edo afforded ample opportunity for discussion of the best policy for Japan to follow in dealing with the West.

The Dutch advised their Japanese friends that it would be wise to open their country for peaceful, foreign intercourse. Some Japanese were inclined to agree, but with reservations. Japan was weak and needed time to perfect coast defenses against the hostile intruder. Young samurai, who had turned their attention to foreign relations, were clearest in their opinions. Honda Toshiaki (1774–1821) was one of the first to advise that Japan should study conditions in Western countries, conserve its natural resources, build ships of its own, broaden the basis of its economy by foreign trade, seek colonies abroad and make fullest use of anything the West might have to offer (including gunpowder and Christianity) in order to strengthen Japan. He would not wait for the lightning to strike in Japan, but he would establish bases in China and Manchuria for defensive purposes against Russia and England.

Takashima Shuhan (1798–1866) took the lead in training, Western-style, two companies of infantry and an artillery battery; but he received little credit for his foresight until after Perry's arrival. Sakuma Shozan (1811–1864) endeavored to arouse the *bakufu* to its military and economic weakness. He thought the whole idea of foreign trade was repugnant and that military force was the only language understood by the West. He was greatly afraid that the British would send their ships to Japan after they finished their business in China. He shared the fears of many that "the mist gathering over China might come down as frost in Japan." Originally he was bitter in his antiforeign sentiments, but he came to believe that friendly relations with the West would be preferable to a war which Japan could not win. While in jail for his opinions he wrote: "When I was twenty, I knew that men were linked together in one province; when I was thirty I knew they were linked together in one nation; when I was forty (1851) I knew they were linked together in one world of five continents." He believed that Japan should become strong internally by a union of the military force of the *bakufu* and the virtue of the throne and that Japan's destiny as a nation should be pursued by a combination of Western science and Eastern morals. He said bluntly that Western science was superior, and Japan had better learn it. Although his ideas provided the inspiration for the founding of Japan's modern army and modern navy, Sakuma was assassinated by a patriot who thought that he was too proforeign.

Yokoi Shonan (1809–1869) was another samurai assassinated for his advocacy of relations with the West. He thought that it was disgraceful to deal with foreign barbarians but that the laws of heaven and earth demanded that Japan should be opened. He foresaw that Japan might become the center of the universe in a way that China had claimed to be in its ancient philosophy. Through its moral force, supported by a powerful navy, Japan might lead the way to universal peace and the brotherhood of man. He took the line that Japan must reform and unify its domestic government, engage in foreign trade, develop its armed strength, and expand in Asia. From the beginning, men of his persuasion were not defensive minded—they never doubted their ultimate place in the sun.

Perhaps the best known of the anti-*bakufu*, westernization group in Japan was the fanatical visionary, Yoshida Torajiro, or Yoshida Shoin (1830–1859). He was an earnest young reformer, obsessed with the idea that the emperor was a divine sovereign of a country with a divine mission. In his view only the restoration of the emperor would wipe away the ills of Japan and bring back the good old days. In his unfettered imagination, the world would be improved if Japan could spread to China, ally with Russia, and capture lands in India, South America, and even Europe. He burned with a desire to travel abroad, and he tried to smuggle himself aboard one of Admiral Perry's ships. He was arrested and allowed to return to his native place, Choshu. As a teacher of politics, he imprinted his views about Japan, the emperor, foreign relations, and the shogun on the minds of Kido, Ito, Yamagata, and others who will appear in the next chapter as leaders of the Restoration. He went back to Edo to try his hand at the assassination of one of the most hated officials of the *bakufu*. He was caught—and beheaded. His sentence read that he was put to death for showing disrespect to high officials "for trying to escape to America; advising the government on coastal defenses while in jail; opposing hereditary succession in office and favoring selection of able men by popular vote; and planning to give his opinion about foreigners to the *bakufu* while in domiciliary confinement." In his last two days in jail he scribbled in prose and verse the "Record of an Uneasy Spirit" which Sir George Sansom called a most pathetic tale of his unsatisfied wishes and his uncompleted plans.

ATTEMPTS TO OPEN JAPAN BEFORE PERRY

Japanese thoughts about opening their country were not produced in a vacuum. An intermittent stream of visitors before Commodore Perry convinced the Japanese that decisions could not be long delayed. It is to be remembered that the Russians were prodding about the northlands and seeking to develop trade when the nineteenth century opened. When the Japanese insisted that they did not need foreign goods and did not want alien ideologies, the Russians became abusive and aggressive. They conducted raids in Sakhalin and the Kuriles, and a famous Russian exploration party ended in a Japanese jail. Russian activity came to a halt in 1813 and was not renewed until 1852. Then, on the persuasion of Count Muraviëv, Tsar Nicholas II sent Admiral Putiatin to the Far East to seek the friendship of Japan in countering the influence of the United States and Great Britain. When Admiral Putiatin arrived in Nagasaki in 1853, Admiral Perry was already on the other side of Japan at anchor in Uraga Bay near Tokyo.

A British frigate forced its way into Nagasaki in 1808 and threatened to bombard shipping in the harbor if it was not given food and supplies. The ship got what it wanted and sailed away. Sir Stamford Raffles pursued his personal war against the Dutch by attacking the factory at Deshima Island, but the British government gave him no support. The British were too preoccupied with fighting in Europe, expanding in India, and opening China to pay attention to Japan. They sent naval vessels to make surveys in the Liu Ch'iu Islands and the coasts of Japan, but they made no concerted national effort to open Japan to trade and commerce.

The Americans were more active. At least twenty-five times before Perry, sailors from both coasts of the United States had set foot in Japanese ports. In 1791 the "Lady Washington" and the "Grace" failed in their efforts to trade furs in Japan. In 1797 the "Eliza," under charter from the Dutch, entered Nagasaki. In 1815 Captain David Porter, the hero of the War of 1812, tried to persuade President Madison to introduce the Japanese people to the world. Edmund Roberts, the first American diplomatic envoy to the East, bore a letter from President Jackson to the Japanese emperor, but he died in Macao in 1832 en route to Japan.

In 1837 C. W. King, an American businessman in Canton organized a goodwill mission to repatriate seven Japanese sailors. He took his wife and three enterprising Protestant missionaries with him to demonstrate the peaceful nature of his endeavors. He was not permitted to land. As a matter of fact he was driven away by cannon fire when it was ascertained that his ship was unarmed. In 1844 Caleb Cushing was authorized to treat with Japan, but he had left China before his instructions reached him. Two years later Commodore Biddle with two ships tried to get to Tokyo, but his policy of considerate treatment was mistaken for weakness. In 1849 Commander Glynn in the "Preble" at Nagasaki succeeded in obtaining the release of some fifteen American seamen who had been months in irons in Japan.

By 1851 the United States was fired by the gold fever in California, the dreams of transcontinental railways and trans-isthmian canals, and the prospects of profits in the markets of Asia. Whalers became more active than ever in the Pacific, and clippers from California replaced the old sailing ships from the Atlantic seaboard on the route to Asia. Furthermore, the age of steam was about to come into its own. Black ships from the Pacific ports of the United States would need the coal and supplies from Japan if they were to make a success of Pacific ocean traffic.

The Japanese were not interested in European or American desires; they were concerned with their own security and welfare. The *bakufu* was loath to admit any necessity for modifying its historic policy of isolation and seclusion. In 1825 it issued a new order called "the no-second-thought decree": if anyone dared to come to Japan, he should be driven away without a second thought. After the defeat of China in the Opium War, Japan relaxed its official attitudes. In 1842 it was decreed that if a foreign ship were to enter Japan, it should be provided with water and supplies—and advised to go away. Under this dispensation, British, French, Dutch, and American ships were treated with comparative courtesy. But it was still the rule of the court that foreigners were not permitted to come to Japan and Japanese were forbidden to travel abroad. Sailors who were shipwrecked or stranded in Japan usually had tales of hardship or cruel treatment to tell if they were sufficiently fortunate to escape with their lives.

JAPAN'S FIRST TREATY SETTLEMENT

The American government decided to use force if necessary to open the doors of Japan. The Dutch at The Hague were notified of the American intention and asked to pass on to the Japanese at Deshima the assurance that the American mission would be a peaceful one. The shogunate received the information in due course and filed it away without action.

Commodore Perry was not a man who could so easily be filed away. He was commander-in-chief, general manager, personnel director, and intelligence officer of the expedition. He drafted his own diplomatic instructions. In Perry's instructions to himself, the Japanese were referred to as "a weak and barbarous people" whose conduct toward shipwrecked sailors had put them among those nations which may justly be conceived as the common enemy of mankind. Perry's objects in going to Japan were to effect some arrangement for the protection of American seamen and property wrecked on those islands; to gain permission for American vessels to enter one or more of their ports for coal, provisions, and water, and permission for the same vessels to enter one or more of their ports for the purpose of disposing of their cargoes by sale or barter. He was to see the emperor in person if possible and deliver a letter of greeting from President Fillmore. He was to explain that the United States was not interested in the spread of any religion and that it was not connected with any government in Europe. He was to seek a treaty of peace and friendship, but to inform the Japanese that if they should be guilty of inhumane treatment to shipwrecked seamen in the future, those responsible would be severely chastised. He was told to "do everything which would impress them with a just sense of the power and greatness of this country and to satisfy them that its past forbearance has been the result, not of timidity, but of a desire to be on friendly terms with them."

On July 8, 1853, Perry's ships steamed directly into Tokyo Bay, deliberately side-stepping Nagasaki and the Dutch. The commodore received the Lords of Izu and Iwami, representing the shogun, notified them of the purpose of his mission, and declared firmly that he would deal only with persons of equal rank with himself. He handed over to the Japanese the president's letter and announced that he would return the next year to receive the Japanese reply.

The *bakufu* was thrown into a state of shock because of the crisis. It could not temporize because of the terrifying ships and the ominous guns—a foreign blockade and Edo would starve. The government was torn between those who blindly insisted upon resistance to the death and those who believed that Japan had no alternative except to bow to the Americans. The difficult choice lay between certain defeat and "giving an inch to gain a mile."

For the first time in over six hundred years of military rule, the shogun asked the opinion of the emperor on an important matter of state and invited the daimyos to express their views. Few were disposed to question the rightness of Japan's ancient policies. Those who advocated a change acted on the basis of expediency. Few cared about such immediate issues as shipwrecked seamen or foreign trade; all were vitally concerned about the ultimate dangers to their divine land. The vast majority would have preferred to remain in seclusion, but they could see the handwriting on the wall. The presence of the Russian fleet in Japanese waters was a potent reminder that others in addition to Americans were interested in the opening of Japan.

On January 16, 1854, Perry arrived back in Tokyo Bay with an impressively reinforced squadron of nine ships. He cast anchor off Kanagawa, a fishing village near Yokohama. After weeks of tragicomic situations—including feasts, lively parties, sumo exhibitions, band concerts, parades, minstrel shows, and exchanges of gifts—on March 31, 1854, the Japanese signed with Perry the Treaty of Kanagawa. This was the first treaty between Japan and a Western power. It was a short treaty, providing for peace and friendship, for the opening of two ports for supplies (Shimoda and Hakodate), for good treatment of shipwrecked seamen, for limited trade under Japanese regulations, for supplies for American ships, and for the most-favored-nation principle. Perry did not worry about the details of the treaty. He wanted to sign a treaty, any treaty, and to get out before the Russian, British, and French squadrons (then engaged in the Crimean War) could sail into Japanese waters and take advantage of the presence of American ships. In August, 1854, Admiral Stirling negotiated a treaty with Japan on behalf of Great Britain; in December Admiral Putiatin signed a Russo-Japanese treaty; and in the next year the Dutch concluded a treaty of friendship with the Japanese.

The most-favored-nation clause made each important treaty provision the common property of the four powers: permission to take on supplies at Shimoda, Hakodate, and Nagasaki; permission to trade through Japanese officials and under their regulations at those three ports; right of residence at Nagasaki; permission to appoint consuls at Shimoda and Hakodate; and a limited extraterritorial jurisdiction. Thus by means of four treaties in 1854 and 1855, Japan brought to an end more than two centuries of living alone. In the midst of great internal confusion, it cast off the cloak of isolation. It embarked on the world's most spectacular exhibition of modernization.

Subsequent Commercial Treaties

The shogun's deputy handed copies of the treaties to the emperor, and in 1855 His Majesty expressed guarded approval and thanked the shogun for his services. It all seemed so regular and uneventful that it obscured the plots, quarrels, and intrigues which revolved about Edo and Kyoto. Most influential Japanese expected that once the treaties were finished, the *bakufu* would go about the business of purchasing guns, building ships, and driving the foreigners out. Instead the *bakufu* practically ignored the complications of the treaties, and entangled itself in the compelling matter of selecting a successor to the childless shogun. The leader of the council of state favored a candidate who would oppose the foreigners but would deal cautiously with them; the lord of Mito proposed a candidate who would be uncompromisingly antiforeign. The former won. With the making of that decision, the *bakufu* turned again to the annoying problems of foreign relations.

On August 21, 1856, an urbane merchant of New York, Townsend Harris, arrived in Shimoda to become the first consul-general of the United States in Japan. He was an "unassuming, upright and sensible" official but he "might have been the devil himself for all the consternation he caused" (Sir George Sansom). The Japanese begged him to go back home, but he was quietly determined to negotiate a new and more detailed treaty. He arrived alone, unknown and unwelcome, and received no instructions for eighteen months. He was housed in Shimoda, a village which became a gathering place for spies and prostitutes "who by their charms might soften the hearts of foreign visitors so that they might be less determined to exact concessions from Japan." Harris was treated with annoyance until the question of the succession to the shogunate was settled, and incidentally until the British and French imposed the Treaties of Tientsin on China. In December 1857 Harris was escorted from Shimoda to Edo in a grand procession of three hundred fifty persons and was ushered into the awesome presence of the shogun himself.

Harris warned Japan about possible dangers from European powers and pointed out that the United States had no territorial ambitions, sought no alliances and had no intention of mingling in the internal affairs of Japan. In response to this sympathetic approach, the *bakufu* did not await imperial instructions but hastened to sign on June 20, 1858, a new treaty with the Americans on board the "Powhatan" in Tokyo Bay. The Harris Treaty provided for diplomatic representation at the capitals of both powers, the opening of new ports where consuls might be stationed, the right of residence at Osaka and Edo, extraterritorial rights for Americans in Japan, the prohibition of the opium trade, freedom of religion, the imposition of customs duties on both imports and exports, most-favored-nation treatment, and possible revision after July 4, 1872. The treaty also provided that the United States would act, if requested, as a friendly mediator in disputes between Japan and any European power; that Japan might acquire ships or weapons in the United States; and that it might hire technical experts in the United States to assist in economic development.

Within three months the Netherlands, Russia, Great Britain, and France concluded treaties on the Harris model; the American treaty remained as the fundamental document in the foreign relations of Japan until 1895. Before the end of the century eighteen nations had concluded treaties with Japan. As was the case with China, Japan was indignant and aggrieved because of its inferior status in treaty relations. For fifty years it was the prime objective in Japan's foreign policy to revise the old treaties or to negotiate new ones on the basis of equality and reciprocity.

The emperor did not want the treaties. He did not like the idea of foreigners living near Edo and the sacred shrines of Ise. However, he was persuaded of Japan's helplessness, and he was assured that in due course the foreigners might be expelled in spite of the treaties. The treaties were therefore ratified by the *bakufu*, but without imperial sanction. Immediately diplomats arrived in Edo, and the most acquisitive of merchants took up residence in the opened port of Yokohama.

Townsend Harris, as the first American minister in Japan, realized that the Japanese had little appreciation of conditions abroad and insisted that the ratifications of his treaty should be exchanged in Washington. He personally made the arrangements for Japan's first diplomatic mission abroad. The Japanese dignitaries arrived in San Francisco in March 1860 and reached Washington in the middle of May, by way of the isthmus of Panama. It is difficult to say whether the Americans were more interested in their strange visitors, or whether the Japanese were more interested in the strange, new land. They visited the White House and the Congress; they stayed in fashionable hotels; they were royally welcomed and lavishly entertained. A subsequent Japanese mission enjoyed a similar reception in Europe and learned at first hand about conditions on the continent. These Japanese diplomatic pioneers became most realistic advocates of modernization, but on their return home they encountered stiff opposition to their ideas and recommendations.

End of the Shogunate

After the conclusion of the treaties, the *bakufu* seemed unable to fix upon a definite policy for the treatment of foreigners. Some officials wanted to carry out the precise terms of the treaties and open the ports immediately. This would satisfy the foreigners and bring badly needed revenues to Japan. Dealing with alien diplomats and erecting coastal defenses was expensive business. Other officials were more equivocal. They would delay opening the ports on any pretext whatever, or they would limit trade to "beef, lacquerware, women or other luxury items which might be required by the foreigners during their stay in port." They hoped that foreigners would go away on their own accord if life were sufficiently unpleasant or unprofitable. The indecision of the government only contributed to the influx of traders, some of whom were admired and others deservedly detested by their Japanese hosts. Yokohama flourished as shops, stores, and offices were built for purposes of foreign trade.

Neither the Japanese people, the court nor the *bakufu* abandoned their antiforeign prejudices. The imperial court sent orders to the Shinto priests at the Grand Shrine of Ise to offer up prayers for the contentment of the mind of the people, the restoration of tranquility to His Majesty's bosom, and the sweeping away of the barbarians. The shogun was regarded as the chief collaborator with foreigners—therefore enemies—although he was only the unfortunate instrument of government who had to do a distasteful job for his country. The regent and leader of the council of state, Ii Naosuke, became the most cordially hated man in Japan; he was assassinated in 1860. Japan did not settle down to peaceful cooperation, but continued to seethe under the surface against its unwelcome alien guests. The first British minister to Japan observed that the Japanese had one object—to expel the barbarians—and that their distrust of foreign powers was indiscriminate. With perfect impartiality they "slay the secretary of the United States Legation and attempt the massacre of the inmates of the British Legation."

During the ten years 1858–1868, a series of crises in foreign relations aggravated a climactic struggle between the emperor and the *bakufu*. It was not a contest between individuals, but it was a clash of institutions. On the side of the imperial institution, two emperors were key figures: the emperor Komei, who reigned from 1846 until his death in 1867, and the great Meiji emperor, who succeeded to the throne as a young man of fifteen in 1867, and ruled until his death in 1912. The emperors were supported by some wise and devoted nobles of the court, clansmen from the western regions of Japan, and wealthy merchant families of the Osaka-Kyoto area. Opposed to them were the three last Tokugawa shoguns, who held office between 1853 and 1868, and a host of their loyal retainers. The struggle ended in the disappearance of the shogunate and the restoration of the emperor.

Some Japanese dreaded the prospect of civil war and sought to effect a peaceful union between the military prestige of the *bakufu* and the imperial symbol of civil authority. As a step in that direction, the shogun married the younger sister of the emperor. Suggestions were made that the emperor should be restored and that government under him should be administered by a feudal council presided over by the Tokugawa. But the schism between the emperor and the shogunate was too deep. The popular slogan throughout the land was "Expel the barbarians, restore the Emperor." As the prestige of the emperor climbed, the daimyo ignored the old ban against visiting Kyoto. Choshu, Satsuma, Tosa, Hizen—clan leaders who hated the Tokugawa—clustered about the emperor. As sentiment for the emperor increased, so did the troubles of the Tokugawa. The shogun himself was an ineffectual character, and his councilors bore the burdens of foreign relations. They were opposed in every maneuver by their own relatives, who were not necessarily disposed to surrender their *bakufu* to the emperor, but who hated the whole business of tampering with time-honored traditions.

Violent antiforeign outbursts on the part of fanatical samurai or ronin (samurai without particular liege-lords) added to Japan's internal crisis. Foreigners were looked upon as the immediate causes of all Japan's economic ills including crop failures and rising prices. It was therefore considered to be highly patriotic to kill a representative of a foreign power or a Japanese official associated with him. In 1859 three Russian naval officers were killed in Yokohama, and in 1860 the Dutch interpreter of the American legation serving under Townsend Harris was put to death as he ventured out at night. In 1861 fourteen *ronin* led by a former samurai of Mito attacked the temporary British legation in Edo and wounded two officials. In September 1862 a British diplomat named Richardson was killed and his three companions were wounded outside Yokohama when they were deemed guilty of a breach of etiquette as the procession of the daimyo of Satsuma passed by. Japan was obliged to pay indemnities for all these outrages, but, unlike China, was not forced to grant new treaty concessions.

It is not difficult to imagine the discomfiture of the *bakufu*, which was caught between the Japanese hatred of the barbarians and the demands of the foreign powers. Because the *bakufu* was unable to afford adequate protection even to the diplomats in Edo and the merchants in Yokohama, it persuaded the British (with the others following suit) to postpone until 1868 the opening of Hyogo (Kobe) and Niigata for trade and the opening of Edo and Osaka for residential purposes. Rumors spread throughout Edo to the effect that all foreigners would be slaughtered. The foreign representatives except Townsend Harris moved temporarily to Yokohama where they would be able to carry on their work in the safety of foreign troops and the guns of foreign ships in the harbor.

Under the influence of his anti-Tokugawa advisers, the emperor took two steps in 1862 which sealed the fate of the shogunate. He ordered a revision of the administrative system, under the terms of which the daimyo would no longer have to spend every other year in Edo nor keep their families as hostages in the shogun's capital. The shogun was obliged to accept a kind of tutor or guardian and to seek the opinion of the daimyo on affairs of state. The emperor also fixed June 25, 1863, as the date on which the expulsion of all foreigners would take place and the ports of Hakodate, Yokohama, and Nagasaki would be closed. The unhappy shogun sent discreet assurances to the foreigners that the emperor's instructions would not be carried out, and he shattered all precedent by paying a personal visit to the emperor in Kyoto.

There was no relaxation of tension in the antiforeign atmosphere in Edo. On February 1, 1863, the newly built British legation was put to the torch by a band of *ronin*. This incident spurred the British to retaliatory action. When they received no satisfaction from the *bakufu* for either the Richardson murder nor the legation fire, they sent their ships directly to Kagoshima in August 1863 to teach the lord of Satsuma the danger of aggravating the British lion. The British sank Satsuma ships and destroyed batteries on the shore before sailing away. The Satsuma reaction was curious. The daimyo saved face in pretending that he had driven the British away, but he recognized the folly of opposing superior arms. He adopted an attitude of friendship toward the British which was heartily reciprocated. He ordered capable young men in his fief to learn about naval affairs from the British. They demonstrated so much skill and aptitude that for fifty years the clan of Satsuma held most of the high positions and dominated the imperial Japanese navy.

Choshu was the next clan to feel the unforgettable power of foreign arms. On June 25, 1863—the date fixed by the emperor for the expulsion of foreigners—the lord of Choshu let it be known that because of the incompetence of the shogunate, he personally would carry out the imperial instructions. He fired on American, French, and Dutch ships which passed through the Straits of Shimonoseki off his domain on the way from Yokohama to Shanghai. The shogun sent envoys to Choshu to plead with the daimyo to stop his rash acts. The daimyo replied that he obeyed the emperor, not the shogun. He put the shogun's envoy to death and seized the ship which brought him. The Americans and the Dutch sent warships from Yokohama to Shimonoseki to punish the daimyo of Choshu. They sank a few of his ships and spiked his cannons, but they did not destroy his defiance. He ordered the closing of the straits for one year, which was a direct violation of treaty provisions.

The four Western powers decided to teach Choshu about the sanctity of treaties. A joint expedition consisting of nine British vessels, four Dutch, three French, and one refugee ship from the American Civil War arrived in Shimonoseki in September 1864. It sank ships in the harbor, bombarded the forts, and sent landing parties ashore. Soundly beaten, the daimyo agreed to open the straits, dismantle his fortifications, and permit vessels to enter Shimonoseki to trade and purchase supplies. Choshu, like Satsuma, learned its lesson—but it concentrated on the army instead of the navy. The daimyo ordered his young retainers to perfect themselves in the military arts of the West, and for the next fifty years the clan of Choshu predominated in the army as Satsuma in the navy.

With the *volte-face* in Satsuma and Choshu, the Japanese mellowed in their attitudes toward the foreigners. Incidents occurred, but they were sporadic. More and more Japanese accepted the idea that their country would gain more from a policy of "open ports" than from one of "expel the foreigners." Western teachers were welcomed more heartily to Japan, and a famous German scientist, Dr. Siebold, was invited to be an adviser to the *bakufu*. Dutch instructors taught Dutch, English, and international law in Nagasaki. Just as eager young Chinese studied foreign subjects in Peking, so young Japanese studied in Nagasaki and Edo. A young Japanese Christian smuggled himself out of Japan on a New England whaling ship, reached America to continue his studies at Amherst College and Andover Theological Seminary, and returned to Japan to found Doshisha University in Kyoto. Many young Japanese discovered ways and means to go to Europe to study naval science, military affairs, political science, and political economy. These activities took place before 1868, while the law was still in effect which prescribed the death penalty for any Japanese sufficiently rash as to go abroad.

During this period foreign affairs were interesting, but they were only the sideshow; the struggle between the emperor and the *bakufu* was the main attraction. When the shogun arrived in Kyoto in 1862, he saw for himself the depth of the intrigues against him. The campaign against the foreigners was a cover for the attack on the *bakufu*. The nobles of the court and the clansmen from the West—Satsuma, Choshu, Tosa, and Hizen—were determined that the Tokugawa must go. After the naval demonstrations at Kagoshima and Shimonoseki, they modified their tactics. They realized that the foreign powers were too strong to be used as pawns in Japan's internal affairs, but they continued to take advantage of conflicting attitudes in foreign relations as clubs to beat the shogunate. In 1864 the feudatory nobles agreed to accept investiture from the emperor, not the shogun; and in the next year they invited civil war by their blatant and somewhat hypocritical opposition to the shogun's forced acceptance of the opening of the port of Hyogo. The samurai warriors of the shogun attacked the combined forces of Satsuma, Choshu, and their allies; but the antiquated swordsmen were no match for the Western-drilled, Western-trained townsmen and peasant folk who were for the first time permitted to engage in the ancient and honorable profession of arms. In August 1866 the shogun Iemochi died in the field. In a face-saving gesture, the emperor ordered that, out of respect for the deceased, the shogun's armies should be recalled to Edo. A stronger personality, Prince Keiki, also of the Tokugawa clan, succeeded to the shogunate; he decided in his own heart that, given an opportune moment, he would petition for imperial permission to surrender his powers to the throne.

In February 1867 the emperor Komei died. The advisers at court became more powerful than ever because of the youth of Meiji. They pressed for the resignation of the shogun, and they planned a military expedition against Edo to defeat him. The shogun was in a receptive frame of mind, except that he was not willing to surrender to the evil counselors with whom his majesty was surrounded. On November 8, 1867, he announced his intention to retire. In a dignified manifesto, he said: "If authority is restored to the Emperor and matters of high policy decided by His Majesty after lengthy deliberation, then by unity in thought and effort the country can hold its own with all nations of the world."

The western clan leaders felt that a spectacular defeat of the shogun in battle would be better for the nation than a peaceful handing over of authority. In Edo, *ronin* in the employ of Satsuma terrorized the populace and set fire to the shogun's palace. The *bakufu* decided it had no alternative but to launch a punitive expedition against the rebellious clan leaders. While the shogun's forces were en route to their defeat at Fushimi, a town near Osaka, the imperial court on January 3, 1868, issued the Restoration Rescript, which abolished the shogunate and the nominal regency.

The last shogun, Prince Keiki, was stripped of his court rank and was displaced as head of the Tokugawa clan. His vassals were ordered out of Edo, and his castle was turned over to the emperor to become the imperial palace. His lands, ships, guns, and armaments were surrendered. He was ordered to live in retirement on the family estates in Mito, and he submitted gracefully to his fate. Hotheads among his followers and retainers continued to fight in desultory fashion, but resistance ended within a year.

In the spring of 1868 the young Meiji emperor announced the Charter Oath of five articles to nobles, daimyo, and officials assembled at the imperial palace in Kyoto. This formed the basis of Japan's centralized state and charted the course of modernization in almost every aspect of life. It provided that deliberative assemblies should be established so that all public matters could be decided by public opinion; the whole nation should be united in carrying out affairs of state; every person should be given the opportunity to pursue a calling of his own choice; absurd customs and practices of the past should be discarded and justice should be based on the laws of heaven and earth; and wisdom and knowledge should be sought all over the world in order to establish firmly the foundations of empire.

The last article spelled the difference between Japan and its neighbors in Asia. It opened the flood gates of Westernization and embarked Japan on the rapid road of progress which is usually known as the Meiji Revolution. The whole era of the Meiji emperor was a long record of growth and development. Technicians from Great Britain, the United

States, France, Germany, and the Netherlands were engaged in wholesale lots to teach pilots, engineers, generals, admirals, financial experts—
in short to train the leaders of New Japan. As many Japanese as possible
were sent to study abroad. Japanese at home discarded the swords, skirts,
and topknots of the old regime. They took to Western clothes and they
asked questions. Unlike the Chinese, who persisted in their attitudes of
disdain, the Japanese set out to learn. They determined to master the
skills, the arts, and the sciences which had contributed to their national
embarrassment.

In the fall of 1868 the name Edo was changed to Tokyo (Eastern
Capital). An astounding group of young leaders from the provinces moved
into Tokyo to take over the reins of government. The emperor himself
emerged from his long seclusion in Kyoto and paid a visit of some weeks
to Tokyo, which in the following year became his residence. A British
historian, Richard Storry, described the emperor's journey in these words:
"As the emperor's palanquin approached the city along the Tokaido (the
eastern road from Kyoto to Tokyo) there was drawn up at a point on the
road, near Yokohama, the regimental band of the British infantry detachment that guarded the foreign settlement; and to the tune of the
'British Grenadiers' the imperial procession passed into the modern age."

SUGGESTED READING

Alcock, Sir Rutherford, *Capital of the Tycoon, a Narrative of a Three Years
    Residence in Japan* (two vols.) (New York, Harper, 1863).
Beasley, William G., *Great Britain and the Opening of Japan, 1834–1858*
    (London, Luzac, 1951).
Boxer, Charles R., *Jan Compagnie in Japan, 1600–1850* (The Hague, Martinus
    Nijhoff, 1950).
Craig, Albert, *Choshu and the Meiji Restoration* (Cambridge, Harvard U.,
    1961).
Foster, John W., *American Diplomacy in the Orient* (Boston, Houghton, 1904).
Gubbins, John H., *Progress of Japan, 1853–1877* (Oxford, Clarendon, 1911).
Harris, Townsend, *Complete Journal of Townsend Harris* (second rev. ed.;
    Mario Cosenza, ed.) (Rutland, Tuttle, 1959).
Jansen, Marius, *Sakamoto Ryoma and the Meiji Restoration* (Princeton, Prince-
    ton U., 1961).
Kuno Yoshisaburo, *Japanese Expansion on the Asian Continent* (two vols.)
    (Berkeley, U. of California, 1937–1940).
Lensen, George A., *Russian Push towards Japan* (Princeton, Princeton U.,
    1959).
Moges, Marquis de, *Recollections of Baron Gros's Embassy to China and Japan*
    (second ed.) (London, R. Griffin & Co., 1861).
Mori, M. G., (ed.), *First Japanese Mission to America* (1860) by Yanagawa

Masokiyo (trans. by Fukuyama Junichi & Roderick H. Jackson) (Kobe, J. L. Thompson & Co., 1937).

Preble, Admiral George Henry, *The Opening of Japan* (Boleslaw Szczesniak, ed.) (Norman, U. of Oklahoma, 1962).

Sheldon, Charles D., *Rise of the Merchant Class in Tokugawa Japan* (Locust Valley, J. J. Augustin, 1958).

Smith, Thomas C., *Agrarian Origins of Modern Japan* (Stanford, Stanford U., 1959).

Walworth, Arthur, *Black Ships off Japan* (New York, Knopf, 1946).

9

Japan: Asia's First Modern Nation

The Restoration touched off Japan's transformation from an ancient civilization into a modern state. In contrast to China where pride drove the leaders deeper into their shell, the Japanese oligarchy struggled with the earnestness of schoolboys to bring their country out of its oriental cocoon. While keeping its identity as Asian, Japan added European and American aspects to its personality. Japanese men and women learned to be as much at ease in Western clothes as in their native kimonos. Japan pioneered the way for other Asian peoples to follow if they would modernize. It set high standards in discipline, hard work, and sense of national purpose; it also succumbed to excesses which others would have no need to repeat. It was the first nation of Asia to obtain the right of equal treatment in the world community regardless of its geographic location.

Japanese culture preserved its classical characteristics, but the Japanese state developed new institutions and encountered new problems. Japan met face to face with the same difficult choices already familiar in the United States and Europe: totalitarianism or a democratic form of government, tyranny or individual liberty, feudalism or industrialization, state socialism or free enterprise, self-sufficiency or partnership in an interdependent world, a strong military machine or second-class status in international relations. Japan was the first nation in Asia consciously and deliberately to remold its way of life to harmonize with the requirements of the world beyond its oceans. Japan, obsessed with the determination to make itself respectable and strong, carried out a revolution in government and society which lasted for half a century. It was not a revolution which boiled up from below. It was carefully planned by an extremely capable and vigorous group of leaders at the top and imposed upon the entire state in the name of the newly exalted emperor.

The Abolition of Feudalism

New Japan assumed immediately a renovated political framework. The shogun disappeared; the emperor became the head of the state. He was catapulted into such eminence that the state itself was considered as an organ of its august sovereign. Modern Japan was born with a degree of centralization which less favored states were never able to achieve. National consciousness was inborn in every Japanese individual. It was the achievement of the Meiji era to turn the sentiment of nationality into political channels which ended in superpatriotism or ultranationalism. The new regime inherited an administrative structure from the Tokugawas which was in good working condition. In contrast to China, comparatively little effort was required for the maintenance of public order.

The affairs of state, which came to be regarded as the wishes of His Majesty the Son of Heaven, passed into the hands of court nobles, distinguished daimyo and a coterie of fewer than a hundred samurai, primarily from the western clans. These men were relatively poor, but they rose to prominence in the struggle against the *bakufu.* They were young and efficient; they had the vision to match their courage. Notable among them were names which became immortal in Japan: Saigo Takamori and Okubo Toshimichi from Satsuma; Kido Koin, Ito Hirobumi and Inouye Kaoru from Choshu; Itagaki Taisuke from Tosa, and Okuma Shigenobu from Hizen. They balanced their emotional fire with good sense as they launched Japan on its daring course of change and innovation.

The bright young men determined that it was necessary to do away completely with the feudal system, although they had grown up under it and they owed to it their own privileged position in society. They persuaded their lords to accept a decree: "There is no soil within the Empire that does not belong to the emperor . . . and no inhabitant who is not a subject of the emperor . . . therefore, we reverently offer up all our feudal possessions . . . so that a uniform rule may prevail throughout the empire . . . Thus the country will be able to rank equally with the other nations of the world." Class distinctions were abolished. In 1869 imperial officials were appointed in every fief, and the land registers were turned over to them. The daimyo were promised half their normal revenues as compensation and were given appointments as imperial governors over their former estates in exchange for surrender of their semiautonomous status. They lost their lands but they acquired government bonds and titles of nobility. By an imperial rescript of August 1871 the clans were disbanded, the fiefs were abolished, and the country was subdivided into ken, or prefectures, roughly comparable to American states. Two years later nobility and samurai were given permission to engage in ordinary occupations or professions.

In the upheaval, the samurai and the peasants suffered the most. Out of Japan's population of more than 30,000,000, well over a million and three-quarters were samurai and their families. The samurai were relieved of their obligations to their lords, but they were also deprived of their support and means of livelihood. They lost their monopoly in the military profession and were robbed of the glory of carrying the traditional two swords. They were no longer entitled to a regular allotment of rice. They were given bonus payments and as ordinary subjects were told that they would have to make their own way in the world. Some rose to distinction in the bureaucracy, and some entered into business; some became teachers, lawyers, or doctors. Many gravitated toward the officer corps in the newly formed national army and navy or became policemen in which case they could continue to wear their swords. But large numbers could not adjust themselves to the "New Deal," and they objected violently to what they considered to be the debasement of their class.

Sporadic revolts occurred, the most serious of which was a rebellion in the stronghold of traditionalism, the island of Kyushu. The Japanese hero, Saigo Takamori, in the service of the lord of Satsuma—and himself a pillar of the Restoration—came to believe that the emperor was a victim of evil advice. Saigo was convinced that Japan should undertake a mighty expedition to Korea. He also believed that Satsuma received less than its just share in the distribution of favors by the new government. He was distressed because the new reforms reduced the samurai to the level of artisans, farmers, and traders. He determined to restore the samurai to their status of honor and to advance the lot of Satsuma in the distribution of government power. For nine months, from January to September 1877, the private samurai army of Satsuma and friendly allies fought savagely against the new conscript "rabble army" from Tokyo. More than a third of the total number of soldiers on both sides were casualties. The rebel army was defeated; Saigo, at his own command, was decapitated by a close friend and faithful follower. This was the last gasp of feudalism. After the defeat of Saigo and the forces of Satsuma, no other champions of reaction dared to oppose the central government's program of progress.

The country folk shared the displeasure of the samurai at the beginning of modernization. Peasants and landlords joined in hundreds of rice riots, fighting side by side with samurai against government officials. The restoration rattled the foundations of rural society. In old Japan, the village was the center of life. A few prosperous peasants who accumulated a little capital to invest in extra land or local industries adopted superior airs and pretended to the sophistication of the city, but most villagers were ordinary farmer or fisher folk. The village took care of its own common matters, mediated disputes, passssed sentence in petty criminal cases, stood responsible as a whole for the misdeeds of any of its members, and enforced the lord's law as its own. The village maintained its own roads and policed its own territory. With a minimum of interference from its distant master and only a few of his official tax-gatherers and rent-collectors to contend with, the village did not have to worry about such things as militarism or the opening of Japan to the West.

Conservative people did not like new things. The idea of reopening Japan to Christianity seemed like subversion of the Shinto gods. The Gregorian calendar was not necessary; the old lunar calendar had been good enough for their ancestors. They did not see any sense in new schools and new subjects. They did not appreciate the glory of serving in the army; they interpreted conscription as a "blood tax." A Western haircut did not look nearly so attractive as long hair piled up in a gorgeous topknot. The craze for new things implied neglect for the old.

The cities and their industries received the attention and the favors; the poor farmers were not helped to rise above their poverty. They felt as though they were cast adrift in being deprived of the protection of their feudal lords. They were given family names, but they feared that the device of family registration might be a prelude to selling their wives, children, or even themselves into bondage.

Rice prices stayed down to benefit the city. The end of feudalism meant that peasants were given lands, complete with titles, to develop or dispose of as they pleased. However, the new lands were subjected to taxes which were unreasonably high. The government taxed the value (not the production) of the land, and the burden was unbearable in lean years. The land tax supplied two-thirds of all revenues which were required to pay operating expenses and to provide capital for industrialization. Before long peasants were head over heels in debt and forced to sell their lands to meet their obligations. Japan's tenant class multiplied. The countryside seethed with unrest. Tenants were dissatisfied with their high rents, low wages, and depressed scale of living. Landlords were unhappy with high taxes, small profits, and the constant struggle to make a reasonable return on their investments.

Ten years were needed to stabilize rural Japan after the Restoration. Many dissatisfied elements took advantage of their new freedom of movement and set out for the cities. Tenants who stayed home lived modestly or miserably, but they at least found security. They kept enough of their crops for a tolerable living after paying the landlord his share of the harvest—which sometimes went as high as sixty percent. As more people deserted the country, a smaller percentage of the total population supplied the food for the entire nation. The price of rice tended to go up, and it was kept within bounds only by government controls. Landless people with agricultural know-how were able to find work on the farms during the busy season, and the rest of the year they were employed as labor in small-scale industries which mushroomed in the villages. Farming became less onerous and more profitable. Laborsaving devices helped immeasurably. Agricultural methods were improved by double and even triple cropping, better seed selection, deeper ploughing, and more widespread use of insecticides. Landlords prospered as tax burdens were shared by commerce and industry. Rural capitalists discovered that their cottage industries could compete successfully with city competition. Discontented samurai, who had constituted a major disturbing element in the countryside, either joined in the trek to the cities or settled into comfortable jobs as village entrepreneurs, estate managers, or independent farmers. Within ten years the government was able to bring peasant uprisings to a halt and to establish an agrarian base for new Japan which was an adequate balance to the urban and industrial sector in the national economy.

WESTERNIZATION AND MODERNIZATION

The abolition of feudalism introduced a nationwide orgy of Westernization and modernization. The mood of the times resembled the earlier borrowing from China and the later copying of the United States. Japan was an eager student, and the world was one vast schoolroom. Two years after Perry's intrusion, the shogunate established a bureau for Western learning, which grew shortly into the University of Tokyo. Japan was introduced to Western classics of humanitarianism and liberalism. After the return of the Iwakura mission, men like Fukuzawa Yukichi—the founder of Keio University—became unabashed advocates of sweeping away old concepts and importing an entirely new culture. Fukuzawa made three extended trips abroad before 1870 and was the best informed Japanese of his day. He wrote an *Outline of Civilization* in "language which a house maid could understand" and an *Encouragement of Learning* which became a best seller. In his many-sided role as publicist, critic, journalist, educator, feminist, businessman, and philosopher, he was the great sage of modernization. He taught that freedom, independence, and equality must be the cornerstone of new Japan, because "all men are equal, without distinction as to high or low, noble or humble." He believed thoroughly in free enterprise. He was vastly more concerned in making Japan a strong and prosperous state than in bettering the lot of the poor.

Due largely to his influence, the law of nations, constitutional law, and political economy became the main subjects of study for those who wished to enter government service. Universities were established which were filled with visiting scholars. Lectures were delivered on law and economy, history and politics, anthropology and sociology, and every branch of the natural sciences. Before the nineteenth century was over, the intellectual and scientific developments of the nation had reached a stage of progress which enabled the leaders to keep informed—if not abreast—of scholarship in the Western world.

Many surface changes occurred in Japan's daily life. None were more conspicuous than the haircut, the style of dress, the Western calendar, and the appearance of a system of writing Japanese characters in Roman letters. The government banned the custom of blackening teeth and shaving eyebrows and in its concern for Western sensibilities prohibited lotteries, mixed wrestling, and the sale of pornographic pictures. In 1876 the oligarchy adopted the system of official holidays, with a half-day Saturday and all day Sunday off. Tentative steps were taken to improve the position of women, which had been degraded by Confucian morality and Buddhist taboos. Women were permitted to enter shrines and temples, given the right to initiate divorce actions, and urged to become more than the docile mistress of hearth and home. Educational opportunities were expanded for women. Charitable organizations, temperance societies, drama and art clubs grew in Japan as they grew in the United States. In Japanese communities one found saloons and beer halls. Lantern slides, talking machines, telephone, and telegraph, moving pictures, horse tramways, newspapers, gas, and electricity came to Japan almost as quickly as to any Western country. Railway stations became prominent landmarks in the cities; Western-style banks, government buildings, stores, and hotels sprang up as rather conspicuous neighbors to shrines, temples, and distinctive Japanese homes and inns.

In 1873 the prohibition of Christianity which had been in effect for two hundred years came to an end. Protestants and Catholics (mostly Protestants) came to Japan in a new wave of missionaries. They preached the gospel, but they also founded schools and colleges. They built churches, hospitals, and orphanages, and they engaged in charitable work among the handicapped and the underprivileged. They met opposition from Buddhists and Shintoists, and also from Japanese empiricists and agnostics. Nothing hurt their cause more than sectarian rivalry; they were all looked upon as non-Japanese—and therefore antinational. Christian missionaries could not subscribe to sentiments of emperor-worship and ultranationalism, and they became associated in the popular mind with liberalism.

While some of the oligarchy surrendered themselves to the task of modernizing Japan in a single generation, others looked after the preservation of traditional values and institutions. They approved of the new branches and flowers on the tree of national culture, but they insisted that the roots should sink ever deeper into the rich soil of ancient Japan. This was seen most clearly in the field of education. A national system of education was accepted as the prime necessity of the modern state. In 1872 the country was organized into eight university districts, subdivided into secondary and elementary school districts, and laws were passed for six years' free, universal, and compulsory primary education. Middle, higher, special, and technical schools—along with universities and colleges— were established to make it possible for Japan to meet the manpower needs of the spectacularly developing state.

The poorest districts offered the same educational opportunities as the richest; the farms and villages were given the same consideration by the government as the metropolitan areas. It took money and effort to build schools and train teachers, but national enterprise and national vision gave Japan the first literate populace in Asia. Subjects in the elementary school included Japanese language and history, arithmetic, geography, gymnastics, and morals. Gymnastics stressed military drill and discipline; morals mean superpatriotism. Hours were long and vacations few. While it was still dark, the uniformed children trudged off to school in the morning and often, after dusk, returned to their homes in the evening with their books strapped to their backs.

Japan was decades ahead of the Germans or the Russians in its use of the educational system for the indoctrination of ultranationalism. From the beginning, a ministry of education in the national government exercised strict control over texts and teachers. Teachers were civil servants in the employ of the state. The broad spirit of Japanese education was contained in the imperial rescript of October 30, 1890.

> Know Ye, Our Subjects:
> Our Imperial Ancestors have founded Our Empire on a basis broad and everlasting, and have deeply and firmly implanted virtue; Our subjects ever united in loyalty and filial piety have from generation to generation illustrated the beauty thereof. This is the glory of the fundamental character of Our Empire, and herein also lies the source of Our education. Ye, Our subjects be filial to your parents, affectionate to your brothers and sisters; as husbands and wives be harmonious, as friends, true; bear yourselves in modesty and moderation; extend your benevolence to all; pursue learning and cultivate arts, and thereby develop intellectual faculties and perfect moral powers; furthermore, advance public good and promote common interest; always respect the Constitution and observe the laws; should emergency arise, offer yourselves courageously to the State; and thus guard and maintain the prosperity of Our Imperial Throne coeval with heaven and earth. So shall ye be not only Our good and faithful subjects but render illustrious the best traditions of your forefathers.

This rescript was displayed in every school together with pictures of the emperor and the empress, and it constituted a kind of shrine. On special occasions it was read with great solemnity while the students stood at awesome attention. This educational spirit was at once the strength and the weakness of the Japanese program of modernization. It was a strength in that it produced strong, capable leaders and an intensely loyal citizenry. It was a weakness in that at the advanced levels it produced scholars who were deprived of the fullest benefits of complete academic freedom. The educational system was as much an instrument of national policy as the army or navy or the growing industrial machine. The schools took their place with the Shinto religion in glorifying the emperor and the state. Constant references to the divinity of the emperor, the land of the gods, and the sacred virtues of the Japanese produced a mystical reverence for Japan's own cultural heritage and a fanatical devotion to the divine mission to spread the blessings of that culture to Japan's less fortunate neighbors.

THE PROCESS OF NATION BUILDING

The old slogan of "Expel the Barbarians—Revere the Emperor" was modernized to become "A Rich Country and a Strong Army." The psychological impact of what happened to China and the awareness of helplessness as contrasted to Russia or the Western powers led Japan to create a new national defense structure. The only troops at the disposal of the central government after the Restoration were those taken over from the fiefs. In 1872 a department of military affairs, with separate organizations for the army and the navy, was organized. The next year a nationally conscripted army was created. Every youth was held liable for seven years of military service—three on active duty, two in the first reserve, and two in the second reserve. European uniforms were adopted; ordnance and materiel were purchased from abroad. Foreign advisers were hired, and the army became Prussian in organization and discipline. The spirit of *Bushido* (the way of the warrior) was intensified and glamorized. The country was divided into six military districts, and Japan developed a standing army of 400,000 trained men.

General Yamagata of Choshu was the directing genius of Japan's new military machine. His faith in the conscripts was more than justified by the showing of the peasant boys against the samurai followers of Saigo in the Satsuma rebellion in 1877. General Yamagata boasted that all Japanese, whether of military class or not, originally sprang from the same blood and when subjected to regular discipline could scarcely fail to make soldiers worthy of the renowned bravery of their ancestors. The spirit of the military was shown in the Emperor Meiji's Imperial Rescript to Soldiers and Sailors issued in January 4, 1882:

> The soldier and the sailor should consider loyalty their essential duty. Who that is born in this land can be wanting in the spirit of grateful service to it? No soldier or sailor, especially, can be considered efficient unless this spirit be strong within him. A soldier or a sailor in whom this spirit is not strong, however skilled in art or proficient in science, is a mere puppet; and a body of soldiers or sailors wanting in loyalty, however well ordered and disciplined it may be, is in an emergency no better than a rabble. Remember that, as the protection of the State and the maintenance of its power depend upon the strength of its arms, the growth or decline of this strength must affect the nation's destiny for good or for evil; therefore neither be led astray by current opinions nor meddle in politics, but with single heart fulfil your essential duty of loyalty, and bear in mind that duty is weightier than a mountain, while death is lighter than a feather. Never by failing in moral principle fall into disgrace and bring dishonour upon your name.

A general staff came into being for the complete separation of the command function from politics and administration. The establishment of a service academy in 1882 instituted a modern system of officer training, and the attention to the military paid off in self-defense and in the two wars, first against China and later against Russia. In 1880 a German military bandmaster took a poem by a young Japanese artillery officer—who became known in history as Field Marshal Oyama Iwao—and set it to music. It was called Kimigayo and was adopted in 1888 as Japan's national anthem.

The navy was considered every bit as important as the army. The Japanese in their island homes needed no reminding of sea power, particularly after the disastrous shelling of Shimonoseki and Kagoshima. Within seven years after Perry's first visit, a Japanese captain and crew took a Japanese warship to San Francisco as an escort to the mission for the exchange of ratifications of the Harris treaty. In 1869 a naval training school was established in Tokyo, with English teachers and instruction in the English language. Within five years Japan had its own naval academy, arsenal, and naval hospital. In 1875 the Japanese built their first war vessel at Yokosuka, but they depended upon foreign purchases for the ships and torpedo boats which they used against the Chinese and the Russians. The navy shared the prestige of the army as the guardian of Japan's national honor and the strong right arm of aggressive foreign policies.

The best of samurai talent seemed to gravitate toward the armed forces; these men rose to power not only in military affairs but also in national politics. The general staff reported to the emperor directly without going through the cabinet, and thus it was immune from the politicians. The army showed contempt for party leaders and democratic processes. It controlled the police and it did not hesitate to use force to sway elections. As liberal forces gained in strength and prestige, the army fought harder to preserve its dominant position. The privy council became the rallying point for the old clan leaders, the court nobles and the military— it was their organization. In May 1900 an ordinance was passed which provided that the war and navy ministers had to be generals or admirals *on active duty*. By this device the military could make or break a cabinet at will. General Yamagata—prince, field marshal, elder statesman, president of the privy council, and undisputed head of the military clique— retired behind the scenes naming his protégés to high office, even the prime ministership. He was secure in the knowledge that the armed forces were an efficient fighting machine and the most commanding voice in the making of political decisions.

As has been seen, the leaders of the Restoration saw the relationship between a "rich country and a strong army." The armed might of a nation depends upon the economic foundation on which it rests. Agriculture received first priority because of the basic need for food and revenue. The government was acutely aware of the dislocations in the countryside due to the new system of landownership and the imposition of the land tax. It was disposed to let the farmers work out their own destiny, but it came through with measures for farm support. It furnished capital for irrigation projects and established agricultural schools and colleges. In 1881 it set up a department of agriculture and commerce within the cabinet. It paid young men to study agriculture abroad. It arranged for importation of high-quality grains, fruit, and vegetables and set standards which enabled Japan to become the world's foremost source of rice, tea, and silk.

Japan's leaders lost no time in developing industry in spite of the shortness of capital. Small amounts were available in loans from wealthy merchants and from daimyo and samurai who had received a windfall in the form of their "bonus" payments. Within a very short time the government created a central banking system, printed paper money, and ordered the exclusive use of the national currency for all business transactions. It sent students overseas to study economic institutions, industrial organization, and production techniques. It used a combination of free enterprise and state socialism to achieve its ends. Young men—whether samurai or of common birth—were encouraged to enter business on their own or to take employment in the new industries or on the railroads. The welfare of the individual was decidedly secondary; Japan's overriding concern was for the strength and greater glory of the state.

Development was slow in its earliest stages because machinery, equipment, and supplies had to be purchased abroad. Teachers and technicians had to be paid for in foreign exchange. A protective tariff was impossible because of the unequal treaties, so the government was obliged to limit its subsidies and encouragement to key activities. In 1872 a railway was built from Tokyo to Yokohama; in 1874 another line was opened from Osaka to Kobe. By 1894 most cities in the tiny empire were linked together in an intricate and efficient network. The British supplied materials, advice, and rolling stock; but foreigners neither controlled nor operated railways in Japan as they were to do in China. Telegraph lines were built and public utilities installed. Arsenals, dockyards, lighthouses, piers, and breakwaters were constructed. Thousands of small businessmen invested in bicycles, printshops, cigar and cigarette factories, steam engines, textile mills, iron foundries, or machine shops. There was limited opportunity for foreign entrepreneurs inside Japan; the Japanese themselves set the pace for their own industrialization.

The pattern of trade began to change. The Japanese wanted to limit their purchases from abroad as strictly as possible, and they ordered their officials to buy home products no matter how crude or inferior. Imports tended to decline as the quality of Japanese goods improved and the variety increased. Japanese bought more raw materials and did their own processing. They manufactured more for export than for their own home market; they preferred to earn exchange rather than to make consumer goods available for their own population. They learned to perform their own services—banking, insurance, warehousing, and shipping—and thus diverted an increasing share of the profits from the foreign merchants who found life so pleasant and rewarding in Tokyo and the settlements in Yokohama and Kobe.

With its affinity for the sea, Japan built, operated, and financed one of the largest merchant marines in the world. The Nippon Yusen Kaisha or Japan Mail, familiarly known as the N.Y.K., inaugurated regular service to Asia, Europe, and America. Other lines carried the Japanese flag to the seven seas. The Bank of Japan, the Yokohama Specie Bank, and other financial institutions were organized to provide the capital and credit for economic expansion. Through government contracts, relatively small fortunes skyrocketed into great empires controlled by one company, usually held by a single family or a small group of financiers. Tightly knit financial cliques known as *zaibatsu* reached out in all directions to manage and acquire the ownership of banks, textile concerns, mines, chemical industries, shipping firms, and a multitude of associated but independently operated companies. The Mitsui Company, largely through astute manipulation of government funds, guided and profited from industrialization. It became one of the financial giants of the world. The Mitsubishi interests, in the hands of the Iwasaki family, assumed leadership in merchant marine, shipbuilding, and a host of economic enterprises. The

Sumitomo companies branched out from copper mining into heavy industries and the manufacture of armaments. The major portion of the new wealth of Japan was concentrated in the hands of a very few zaibatsu who kept close and continuing connections with all political groups and parties.

Because of their common interest in the military budget, the zaibatsu became very close to the oligarchy and the powers behind the throne. It was inevitable that these very rich men should become interested in party leaders and legislators who would have a vote on matters of economic concern. The door was opened to corruption. The zaibatsu shared the contemptuous attitude of the military toward politicians and the democratic process in general. They became convinced that every vote and every politician had his price—it was all a question of how much.

The expansion of Japan's industry and commerce was due to the organizational drive and efficiency of the zaibatsu, based on a labor force that did not expect too much for its work and was thoroughly indoctrinated with the belief that hardship, long hours, and low pay were the essence of patriotic duty. The introduction of the machine age to Japan brought the same complications it produced in the West. Old class alignments disappeared, and new distinctions arose which were based on wealth and achievement. The countryside became primarily concerned with landlords and tenants; the cities, with capital and labor. The country people could appreciate the products of machinery, but they could not hope to accumulate the money to buy any but the simplest gadgets. The workers in the factories, particularly the women, were increasingly at the mercy of the men who owned and operated the mills.

With Japan's lower standard of living, the combination of Japanese skill and Western technology resulted in rapid economic expansion. Increasing population provided an inexhaustible supply of labor. In good times, peasant children gravitated toward the city for jobs; in hard times the unemployed return to the homes of their country cousins. Spokesmen for the underprivileged appeared very quickly on the Japanese horizon. Books on socialism and communism were translated into Japanese. In May 1882 an Oriental Socialist Party was organized, but it was dissolved after three months as a danger to peace and order. Ten years later, an Oriental Liberal Party dedicated to the interests of the working class had an equally brief and precarious career. In 1890 some Japanese temporarily in San Francisco organized an Association for Formation of Labor Unions. When they returned to Japan, they encouraged the formation of unions among the iron workers, railway engineers and firemen, carpenters, masons, cooks, furniture workers, and ricksha men. They made little progress because of the hostility of the police. Then in 1901 Katayama Sen launched the Social Democratic Party with a platform designed to appeal to all tenant, worker, socialist, and liberal elements. Its objectives were extension of the principle of universal brotherhood, disarmament and world peace, abolition of the existing system of class distinctions, public ownership of land and capital, state ownership of systems of transportation and communication, equitable distribution of wealth, equality of political rights, and free education at the expense of the state. It was suppressed by the government on the very day it was founded. It was rather remarkable that in the surge toward industrialization, patriotic Japanese would take interest in social welfare. Their zeal and their frustrations were paralelled in the experience of those who dedicated themselves to political liberalism.

POLITICAL MODERNIZATION

Immediately after the Restoration, the machinery of the new central government in Tokyo showed the influence of Western innovations. Lawmaking and administrative functions were placed in the hands of a council of state presided over by a minister president, or early Japanese version of a premier or prime minister. Embryonic cabinet offices were seen in the various departments: civil affairs, finance, military affairs, justice, foreign affairs, and the imperial household. The members of the council of state were merely advisers to the throne, and they were selected from the influential clans. With the disappearance of Tokugawa absolutism, council members indulged in bitter rivalries which revealed their divergent interests.

The ideas were gradually accepted that minority opinions were not necessarily treasonable and that an opposition could also be loyal. It followed that there should be a legislature or parliament where all shades of opinion could be represented. The government convened periodic conferences of prefectural governors for discussion of public affairs and permitted the calling of prefectural assemblies. In 1878 Itagaki Taisuke of Tosa began a movement which resulted in the establishment of Japan's national diet, or congress. Like all Japanese progressives, he was strongly nationalistic. He believed that Japan would be strongest if public policies were subjected to open debate. He organized a Jiyuto or Liberal Party made up of scholars, writers, medium and small landowners, and all persons who "professed faith in the concepts of liberty and popular rights." According to his teaching, government existed for the people and not vice versa. Only a few sophisticated leaders had any appreciation of such great principles as the dignity of man or the freedom of speech. The majority joined Japan's first political party for reasons of legitimate self-interest, or they were attracted by the dynamic personality of its founder.

In 1881 Okuma Shigenobu of Hizen left the government and organized a second party which took the name of Kaishinto, or Progressive Party. This party acknowledged the same high principles as the Liberal Party, but the two were uncompromising rivals. Each attracted its own supporters, financial and otherwise, and recruited most of its membership from young people in the urban areas. Party loyalty was a fickle thing, with leaders and followers shifting allegiance at will. The parties led a precarious existence because of popular suspicion and police supervision, but the idea of political parties could not be scotched. The government organized its own bureaucrats into the Teiseito, or Imperial Party; these talked like politicians but acted like an official rubber stamp.

With three parties in existence, the throne announced on October 12, 1881, that a national representative assembly would be instituted nine years later. Ito Hirobumi was assigned the task of preparing a constitution and was sent abroad to study the different models. He was so impressed by Bismarck that he even aped the way that the Iron Chancellor smoked his cigar. In anticipation of a constitutional regime, the government distributed about five hundred titles of nobility to men of distinction (including Ito) who might be chosen for the house of peers or house of lords in the forthcoming diet. A cabinet system was established in 1885 with Ito himself as Japan's first prime minister. Three years later a privy council was formed, with Ito vacating the prime ministership to become its president. In the complete secrecy of that post, he put the finishing touches on the draft of his constitution. Japan had no convention or public debate but received its first constitution as the gracious gift of His Majesty the Meiji emperor on February 11, 1889.

The constitution was a short document consisting of a preamble and seven chapters divided into seventy-six articles. According to it, Japan should be reigned over and governed by a line of emperors unbroken by ages eternal. The emperor was the head of the state and the source of sovereignty. He was deemed sacred and inviolable. He was the supreme commander of the army and the navy, with power to make war and peace. He exercised legislative power with the aid of an imperial diet, and he could issue ordinances with the effect of law. The diet was to consist of a house of peers and a house of representatives. The upper house was made up of imperial appointees from among the recently ennobled and the highest taxpayers in the land, and the members held office for life. The lower house was entirely elected, with suffrage rights belonging only to males, twenty-five and over, who paid taxes of one hundred yen per year (about one percent of the population). The diet was given powers of legislation, but no control over the cabinet or the budget. (It met three months per year, only a few hours each day, and could be dissolved at any time by the emperor on the advice of the cabinet.)

The constitution contained a bill of rights which stipulated that all able-bodied men were subject to military service. No subject should be arrested, detained, tried, or punished, unless according to law. No house should be entered or searched without a warrant. Freedom of religious belief was granted within limits not prejudicial to peace and order. Liberty of speech, writing, publication, public meeting, and association should be enjoyed by all—*within the limits of the law.* The qualifying phrases made the guarantees meaningless. Furthermore the recognition of rights should not affect the exercise of the emperor's powers in times of war or during a national emergency. The constitution seemed to provide Japan with a democratic framework; but it made possible the survival of authoritarianism. Along with the constitution were promulgated five special bodies of law equal in authority to the constitution: laws for the conduct of the house of peers, rules for the diet, a law of finance, an election law, and the law of the imperial household.

On July 1, 1890, Japan held its first national election for three hundred members of the house of representatives, who with two hundred fifty appointees were to make up the nation's diet. The election returns were of no importance to the oligarchy which continued to administer the country from its entrenched position in the privy council. Satisfactory election results could always be obtained by sagacious use of bribery, the police, and discreet enforcement of the Peace Preservation Law of 1888 (which permitted the government to take almost any measure it chose to enforce peace and order). Between 1890 and 1900 Japan had a dozen different diets headed by prime ministers—Ito, Kuroda, Yamagata, and Matsukata—who were designated by the Elder Statesmen without reference to party strength. The Elder Statesmen, in authentic Japanese style combined themselves into an informal body called the *genro*, which enjoyed no constitutional status. It evolved into the strongest influence in Japanese politics, advising the emperor in all important matters, particularly the naming of a prime minister. It caused a rescript to be issued which said "the appointment or removal of a minister of state shall be absolutely at the will of the sovereign and no interference whatsoever will be allowed in this matter." Thus a party might win an election, but it still had no right to choose the prime minister as in the British system. In Japan, the cabinet was responsible to the emperor, not to the diet. The locus of effective power was in the handful of men who were close to His Majesty and made decisions in his name.

The introduction of party politics, the institution of a representative assembly, and the planting of seeds of popular democracy constituted a new phase in the never-ending struggle between liberty and authority. The champions of authority continued to steer the ship of state, but the advocates of liberty made their opinions increasingly effective. Okuma of the progressives and Itagaki of the liberals joined forces to form the Kenseito, or Constitutional Party. Their aim was to put an end to rivalries between friend of popular government and to create a single organization to check the power of the clans. Bitter arguments over the military budget and foreign relations marked every section of the diet. Curiously enough, in times of emergency or war the representatives of the people were more uncompromising and chauvinistic than the oligarchy. They were fanatical in advocating overseas expansion and were loudest in demands for satisfaction of the national honor. Yamagata cursed the democratic movement as an "evil poison in the national blood stream," but even he realized that party politics had come to stay. Ito himself, deciding to fight fire with fire, converted the fading Liberal Party into a vital personal political machine officially called the Rikken Seiyukai, or Constitutional Government Friend's Association. Popularly known as the Seiyukai for short, it occupied an important place in Japanese politics for forty years. As the twentieth century opened, the battle line for political power in Japan was clearly drawn. Yamagata, supported by the oligarchy and the military machine, opposed Ito and the proponents of more democratic processes. The two groups differed as to timing and tactics, but they were in complete accord on the necessity of a greater Japan and positive foreign policy. Their politics stopped at the water's edge.

FOREIGN AFFAIRS

As Japan emerged as a modern nation, it developed vigorous foreign policies. Domestic dilemmas were often sidestepped by diverting the nation's energies and attention across the seas. Conversely, Japan from the very beginning of its national existence derived unusual advantage at the diplomatic bargaining tables because its representatives spoke with the voice of one authority backed by the dynamic force of a united people. Japan's rise to a great power was spectacular and unexpected. The quality of its statesmen surpassed the poverty of its resources and compensated for the recency of Japan's entry into the world community.

Japan looked upon its first treaties as a stigma on the national honor, because Japan was not treated as an equal. Its first task was to remove that stigma. Japan hired foreign experts as diplomatic advisers and set up a special office, the Gaimusho, as a department of foreign affairs. After the Restoration, a decree was issued that thence forth the emperor was the supreme authority in international relations and his title, not that of the shogun, would be used in future agreements. In March 1868 foreign diplomats were first received in audience by the emperor, and two years later Japan established its first consulates and diplomatic missions abroad.

As the date for treaty revision approached (July 4, 1872), Japan sent its most powerful political figure, Lord Iwakura, with a mission of forty-eight members, to visit all foreign countries. He was to obtain treaty revision if possible; if not, he was to make a thorough study of foreign law and political institutions, public and private finance, education, and social welfare. His group crossed the United States by rail, and in Europe it was received by the heads of state in practically every country. Lord Iwakura returned to Japan absolutely convinced of the wisdom of falling in line with the international practices of the Western state system. This meant a respectable foreign policy in addition to a strong military establishment.

As a first step toward international equality, Japan insisted on being treated with all the courtesies ordinarily extended to representatives of the sovereign state in the West. Japanese officials refused to remain standing—as had been their custom—during interviews with foreign ministers. In its drive for equal treatment Japan found a sympathizer in Judge John A. Bingham, the American minister in Tokyo from 1873 to 1885. He was impressed with Japan's progress and urged Washington to accede to Japan's overtures for reciprocal treatment. On July 25, 1878, Japan and the United States signed a treaty which conceded to Japan the right to regulate its own tariff schedules and control its coastal trade in exchange for opening new ports and abolishing the export tax. The American treaty was ratified, but was not to go into effect until all the other powers made similar concessions!

In 1882 Count Inouye, the foreign minister, called a conference to see if the other powers might be disposed to make similar concessions. The powers were too closely united to permit Japan to make a substantial dent in their united front. Then a new foreign minister tried new tactics. Instead of negotiating with the powers en masse, he approached them one by one. In 1888 he succeeded in getting a treaty with Mexico which omitted extraterritorial rights, recognized Japan's tariff autonomy, and applied reciprocally the most-favored-nation clause in exchange for opening all of Japan to Mexicans. Mexico was an unimportant country, but the treaty with Mexico was a psychological boon to Japan.

An Anglo-Japanese treaty was signed on July 16, 1894, which took the lead and set the style in Japan's rise to equality with the great powers. This treaty did not provide for tariff autonomy, but it abolished extraterritoriality and consular courts. It contained a mutual most-favored-nation clause and provided for reciprocal rights of travel, residence, navigation, and exercise of religion. It was to become effective in 1889, but only if other powers took similar action. This time there could be little doubt that the others would take similar action because Japan had gained military strength and was about to demonstrate its military superiority in

East Asia. A treaty was signed along these same general lines with the United States in November 1894, and with all the other powers by 1899, when all went into effect at the same time. The few remaining restrictions on Japan's full sovereignty—in matters of tariff control and foreign settlements in Japan's ports—expired in the early years of the twentieth century. After that time no nation had any legal right to interfere in matters of Japan's internal administration or jurisdiction.

Japan's basic concern for its own security demanded the consolidation of the empire, and in the eyes of its statesmen this meant clear title to the Kuriles, Sakhalin, the Bonins, and Ryukyus, and Formosa. In 1875 a Japanese-Russian treaty recognized Sakhalin as Russian and the Kurile Islands as Japanese. In the same year the Bonins, or Ogasawara Islands, were acknowledged as Japanese possessions, and in 1880 they were incorporated for administrative purposes into the Tokyo Metropolitan Prefecture.

The story of the Ryukyus and Formosa has already been told from the standpoint of China's loss; a few details must be added to make clear Japan's gain. At the time of the incident of the shipwrecked Liu Ch'iu (Chinese-style pronunciation) sailors on Formosa, the Japanese authorities invited King Sho Tai to Toyko and made him a member of the Japanese peerage. In October 1872 they formally incorporated the Ryukyus (Japanese-style pronunciation) into the Japanese empire. In successive steps, Japan recognized the people of the Ryukyus as Japanese subjects, assumed all rights to carry on diplomatic negotiations for the Ryukyus, garrisoned imperial troops in the islands, reorganized the internal administrative structure to conform to Japan, and took over the functions of the police and the judiciary. In 1879 the Japanese authorities deprived the king of the Ryukyus of all political rights and gave the name of Okinawa Prefecture to the former quasi-independent island kingdom.

Likewise the events dealing with Formosa should be re-examined to highlight the policy of Japan. In 1874 in connection with its expedition to Formosa, Japan set up an office of Formosan affairs with Okuma as director. For ten years Japan quietly studied the potential of Formosa. It maintained silence as it watched the unsuccessful attempt of France in 1884 to hold Formosa as a guarantee for China's payment of indemnities. Ten years later, when war broke out between Japan and China over Korea, Japan seized the occasion to move into the Pescadores. Within a few months after the Treaty of Shimonoseki legally ceded the Pescadores and Formosa to Japan in 1895, the troops of Japan occupied Formosa. Japan paid no attention to token opposition on the part of China nor to an independent demonstration on the part of some Formosans. On October 10, 1895, General Nogi entered Tainan and set about pacifying guerrillas in the countryside. A civil administration was commissioned the next year, and from that time Formosa too was administered as an integral part of the Japanese empire.

Japan considered the mainland of Asia as scarcely less important than neighboring islands to its own security and welfare. Relations with the rest of the world were looked upon as secondary to its situation in Asia. The principal objective of Japanese diplomacy—whether with China or Russia, or later with Great Britain, the Axis Powers, and the United States —was the establishment of hegemony in its immediate environment. Geography accounted primarily for its interest in Korea, Manchuria, Mongolia, and China. Furthermore, in the midst of the strident nationalism of the late nineteenth century, Japan could see and take warning from what was happening in China. Russia was on the march, so were England and France, and the United States loomed large and menacing on the Pacific horizon. Japan determined to escape the fate of hapless China.

The key to Japan's destiny in Asia was its success in China. Japan was therefore especially gratified by its treaty with China in 1871. True, Japan was not accorded most-favored-nation treatment, on an equal basis with the West in China, but it was officially recognized as an equal by China. This was the final interment of China's presumption of Japanese inferiority. The Japanese foreign minister himself went to China to exchange the ratifications of the treaty and he was the first diplomatic dignitary to be received in audience by the Chinese emperor. In 1876 the Chinese sent to Japan their first diplomatic representatives to be stationed in a foreign country. From that time forward Japan exercised a dual role in China. On some occasions it played upon China's sympathies and posed as fellow-oriental in opposition to the West. At other times it chose to side with the West and to assume an attitude of first among equals in exacting concessions from China.

Japan's first real test of strength with China came in Korea. As has been noted, Japan opened Korea by the Treaty of Kanghwa in 1876. In addition to destroying the old relationship between China and Korea, that treaty established a new relationship between Japan and Korea. It went beyond Japanese recognition of Korean independence and Korean recognition of Japanese equality. It provided for Japanese consular jurisdiction in Korea and for the exchange of ministers and consuls. It stipulated that two ports in addition to Pusan—Jinsen and Gensan—were to be opened to Japan, and that detailed trade regulations would subsequently be agreed upon. Thus at the same time Japan agitated for the absolution of unequal treaties in Japan, it took the lead in clamping similar treaties upon a weaker continental neighbor.

In the riots at Seoul in 1882, some Japanese officials were killed, the Japanese legation was attacked and the Japanese minister was driven to refuge aboard a British ship. In retaliation Japan forced the Koreans to sign the Treaty of Chemulpo on August 30, 1882. This provided for the usual apology and indemnities and was the document which authorized the stationing of Japanese troops (along the Chinese) for guard duty in Seoul. This was a significant step in the solution of Japan's problem in Korea, which was to detach Korea completely from China *as a prelude to its own leadership.*

After the clashes in 1884 it was Ito Hirobumi himself who went to Tientsin to negotiate the convention with Li Hung-chang which provided that troops of both China and Japan should be withdrawn from Korea and that advance notice should be given in writing if either country decided to send troops back to Korea. Until that time Japanese influence did not seem impressive in Korea. The Chinese still dominated the Korean scene. Korea also approached Russia for assistance, and in payment Russia dickered for the lease of Port Lazarev. As a countermove British naval forces occupied Port Hamilton on an island off the southern tip of Korea.

When war clouds lowered in June 1894 after the murder of Kim Ok-kiun, a new Japanese minister arrived in Korea with a program of reforms which Japan insisted should be adopted by the Korean king. The reforms included the eradication of corruption among officials, the establishment of a civil service based on merit, the adoption of changes in the political, military, and fiscal administration, and an improvement in the educational system. He suggested, quite ominously, that it would be difficult to carry out these reforms as long as the Chinese retained their influence in Seoul. There was nothing subtle about the Japanese approach. The Japanese feared internal chaos and the designs of other nations in Korea. Farsighted Japanese began to think about the economic value of Korea as a rice supplier for Japan's burgeoning millions and as an adjunct to its growing industrial and economic machine.

Japan chose to act and to argue later. The Korean government was forced to ask for Japanese assistance in driving the Chinese out of Korea and to sign a treaty of alliance giving freedom of movement and supplies to Japanese troops. Japan refused to withdraw troops prior to the accomplishment of internal reforms and the defeat of China. The course of the war is already known. Japan struck without warning and poured troops into Korea. Japanese also occupied Port Arthur and the Liaotung Peninsula in southern Manchuria and the port of Weihaiwei on the Shantung Peninsula of the China mainland. The Japanese then forced the king of Korea to issue edicts changing the entire governmental system and modernizing, on paper, the economic and social life of Korea almost overnight. Then Japan forced China to sign the Treaty of Shimonoseki which was the next step in Japan's Korea program.

Korea became independent in name only and was never thereafter genuinely independent of Japanese domination. Japanese advisers supervised every branch of the Korean government and Japanese economic interests plunged into the development of Korea's resources. When the headstrong queen turned to Russia for the anti-Japanese support which had previously come from China, she was murdered. The Japanese worked through their old enemy, the Taiwunkun (regent and father of the king), and they made the hapless king their political prisoner. In some mysterious manner the king escaped and took refuge in the Russian legation on February 11, 1896. The pendulum swung against the Japanese, who tried to accomplish reforms too fast and too ruthlessly, with the result that Japan had to contend not only with Korean factions but with a new entry, Russia, in the tag match of Korean politics.

The experience of the triple intervention gave Japan a new slant on international politics. Instead of the respect and awe with which it had regarded the West, it was shocked by the blatant hypocrisy of the Western powers into an attitude of cynicism and distrust. Perhaps this was the turning point in Japan's later career of *Machtpolitik*. Japan could only bow to the will of the three powers which issued the ultimatum to give up the Liaotung Peninsula. The Emperor Meiji told his people that they must "bear the unbearable," which were the exact words used by his grandson in ending World War II in 1945.

After the embarrassment of the triple intervention, Japan was content to work out a temporary arrangement with Russia which would share primacy in Korea. On May 14, 1896, the Russian minister in Seoul, Waeber, and the Japanese representative, Marquis Komura, agreed that Japanese gendarmes should replace military guards for the protection of the telegraph lines between Pusan and Seoul. They further agreed that the small number of Japanese and Russian soldiers on guard duty in Seoul should be withdrawn when peace and order were assured. When Prince Yamagata went to St. Petersburg to attend the coronation of the tsar, he wanted an understanding which would have allotted Manchuria to Russia and Korea to Japan. Failing that, he would have been happy with an understanding which would have given a sphere of influence to Russia in Manchuria and Korea north of the 38th parallel. Japan's sphere would have been limited to Korea south of the 38th parallel. Russia would not listen to these proposals. Then Yamagata worked out an arrangement with the Russian foreign minister Lobanov-Rostovsky for joint economic assistance to Korea. Both powers were to receive equal treatment in matters of economic rights and privileges and both agreed to abstain from participation in the organization and maintenance of Korean police and military forces.

Then it became time for Japan to surrender the initiative to Russia in

Korea. It was the Russians who ignored their agreements. The Russians sent military advisers and instructors to reorganize the Korean army and appointed a Russian director for the Korean arsenal. They converted timber concessions along the Yalu River and their mining concessions along the Tumen River into outright instruments of aggression. They sought control of Korea's customs and financial administration.

However, Russia did not have sufficient talent or resources for all its ambitions in Europe and in Asia, and in Asia it was more vitally concerned in Manchuria than in Korea. Therefore Japan obtained a conciliatory protocol signed on April 25, 1898, by the Japanese foreign minister, Nishi, and the Russian ambassador, Baron Rosen, by which both nations reaffirmed the sovereignty and independence of Korea and agreed to refrain from all direct interference in Korea's internal affairs. Neither would appoint military instructors or financial advisers to Korea without the previous understanding of the other. Russia recognized Japan's peculiar commercial interest in Korea and agreed not to obstruct the development of the commercial and industrial relations between Japan and Korea. This protocol was a straw which indicated the direction of the diplomatic winds: Russia was more active in Manchuria, Japan in Korea. But their conflicts in Northeast Asia were so irreconcilable that they could not be settled by measures short of war.

SUGGESTED READING

Beckmann, George M., *Making of the Meiji Constitution* (Lawrence, U. of Kansas, 1957).

Borton, Hugh, *Japan's Modern Century* (New York, Ronald, 1955).

Centenary Culture Council, (eds.), *Japanese Culture in the Meiji Era* (ten vols.) (Tokyo, Obunsha, 1955–1958).

Fukuzawa, Yukichi, *Autobiography* (trans. by Kiyooka Eiichi; third ed.) (Tokyo, Hokuseido, 1947).

Harrison, John A., *Japan's Northern Frontier* (Gainesville, U. of Florida, 1953).

Hayashi, Count Tadasu, *Secret Memoirs* (A. M. Pooley, ed.) (New York, Nash, 1915).

Ike, Nobutaka, *Beginnings of Political Democracy in Japan* (Baltimore, Johns Hopkins U., 1950).

Ito, Hirobumi, *Commentaries on the Constitution of the Empire of Japan* (trans. by Ito Miyoji) (Tokyo, Igirisu Horitsu Gakko, 1931).

Lockwood, William W., *Economic Development of Japan* (Princeton, Princeton U., 1954).

MacLaren, Walter W., *Political History of Japan during the Meiji Era* (London, Scribners, 1916).

Norman, E. Herbert, *Japan's Emergence as a Modern State* (New York, Institute of Pacific Relations, 1940).

Okuma, Shigenobu, *Fifty Years of New Japan* (two vols.) (London, Smith Elder, 1909).

Satow, Sir Ernest, *Diplomat in Japan* (London, Seeley, 1921).

Smith, Thomas C., *Political Change and Industrial Development in Japan* (Stanford, Stanford U., 1955).

Takeuchi, Tatsuji, *War and Diplomacy in the Japanese Empire* (New York, Doubleday, 1935).

Williams, Harold S., *Tales of the Foreign Settlements in Japan* (Rutland, Tuttle, 1958).

Wilson, Robert A., *Genesis of the Meiji Government in Japan, 1868–1871* (Berkeley, U. of California, 1957).

Yanaga, Chitoshi, *Japan since Perry* (New York, McGraw, 1949).

10

Company and Crown in India

While China submitted to the unequal treaties and Japan struggled to
convert itself into a modern nation, India succumbed to an out-and-out
imperial regime. It is interesting to speculate *why* the three great culture
groups in East and South Asia responded in such different ways to the impact of the West. In the course of their long histories, all three fashioned
ways of life which represented reasonable harmony with their environment. For the most part, they were economically self-sufficient, spiritually
satisfied and artistically expressive. They would have been quite content
if strangers had not come to their shores. They did not understand the
Europeans, and they resented the assertion of superior strength on the
part of the aliens. China's response was to match arrogance with arrogance, Japan's was to clothe itself in the new fashions from overseas, and
India's to hibernate for long years before emerging in its new form of an
independent nation-state.

India was affected only slightly by the first wave of Europeans. The
earliest British traders confined themselves to widely separated factories
in Calcutta, Bombay, and Madras. As the long arm of the company
reached out to surrounding territory, and eventually to most of the subcontinent, the history of India became identified with the history of the
British in India. The English East India Company provided the administrative system for British India and through its residents and advisers
dominated the princely states. The company left its indelible mark on
India's economic development. The welfare of the people of India was
secondary to the steady inflow of profits to the company's shareholders in
London. Social change within the rigid framework of Indian society depended upon the convenience of the trader-conqueror; and the white men
who carried the burden of empire in India by no means reflected the liberal progressive spirit of England in the nineteenth century.

183

The problem of India grew too complex for the company, so the government of India was transferred to the Crown in 1858. Before the transfer, India had been regarded as the fountain of riches—first as a

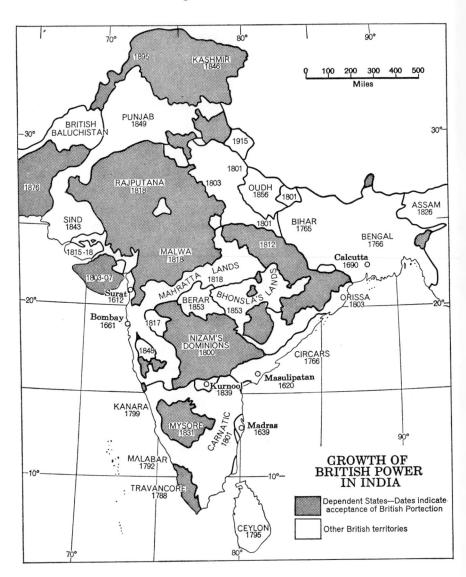

GROWTH OF
BRITISH POWER
IN INDIA

Dependent States—Dates indicate
acceptance of British Portection

Other British territories

source of luxury materials and later as a boundless market for the manu-factured products of British mills. After the transfer, India was not only looked upon as an economic asset; it was hailed as the brightest jewel in the British Crown. To the British, the fate of India was inseparable from their own destiny. India was the focal point in relations with Russia, France, and the rising power of Germany. The route to India was the linchpin of Britain's security. To the Indians, the realization slowly dawned that they were treated as pawns in the imperial game, or as second-class subjects of an alien dynasty. Gradually they saw themselves in a new light. They felt they were entitled to priority in their own country, and they were aroused by the first faint stirrings of nationalism.

In this chapter, we shall look more deeply into the condition of India during its last days under the rule of the company; the events of the great rebellion—or mutiny—which provided the occasion for the transfer of administration from the company to the Crown; the British policies in India during the zenith of imperialism, 1858–1900; and the beginnings of Indian nationalism.

THE RULE OF THE COMPANY

The map shows India in the mid-nineteenth century as a political patchwork and gives a quick review of the major steps in the spread of British power. After the Battle of Plassey on June 23, 1757, the company became the zamindar or landlord south of Calcutta of 880 square miles with enormous rents. Robert Clive and his subordinate officers received a half-million pounds sterling for their personal accounts and revolution was revealed as the best paying activity in the world. The English, both as company and as individual merchants, took advantage of their tax-free privileges and established monopolies which brought immense profits to themselves but no revenues to the state. A group of native landowners protested because "factories of the English gentlemen are many and their agents are placed in all the villages in Bengal; by oppressive means they buy goods at low rates and they oblige the inhabitants and shopkeepers to take them at a high price; they do not pay customs and they are guilty of all manner of seditious and injurious acts." The answer to the Indian protest was a pitched battle at Buxar in October 1764. As a consequence of victory, the company ceased to be a company of merchants engaged in quiet trade. A little body of Englishmen became what one British writer called "the most formidable commercial republic known in the world since the demolition of Carthage." Clive made peace with the Mogul emperor in 1765, and from him received the dewanee (right of civil administration) of Bengal, Bihar, and Orissa. The Emperor gained immense prestige from conferring the right on the company, and in exchange he received a handsome allowance. The genius of Clive was expressed in the system of dual administration which he inaugurated. He maintained the façade of the native forms of government, but behind the scenes he set up machinery by which the company wielded authority. British officials lived and ruled in the manner of oriental potentates, and their fiat was enforced by the company's army.

As soon as the company ran into financial difficulties, it turned to the government for help. In 1773 parliament extended a loan, but it also passed the Regulation Act, which asserted the prior interest of the government, as opposed to the company, in dealing with India. For the first time India was looked upon as a national responsibility instead of a bonanza for shareholders. The governor of Bengal, though a company official, was given royal appointment; and his authority was to extend beyond Bengal to the presidencies of Bombay and Madras. Here was the beginning of the concept of a national administration—of a centralized system to replace the former scattered and free-wheeling local units. English law was introduced into India by the establishment of a supreme court in Calcutta with a chief justice and three associate judges. In London, the directors of the company were ordered to supply parliament with all copies of their correspondence and to submit their accounts for examination.

The English parliament passed a new Regulating Act, usually known as Pitt's India Act, in 1784, which put a complete end to the company's swashbuckling era. The London directors of the company were stripped of all their power, except patronage, and the position of the governor of Bengal was converted into a governor-generalship for all India with unrestricted power and responsibility. The intent of the act was effectively implemented by Lord Cornwallis who, after the surrender at Yorktown, was appointed in 1793 as governor general and commander in chief of the armed forces. He battled against corruption in the civil service, and he reorganized the army, which was in a sorry state. "The contemptible trash of which the army's European force is composed makes me shudder."

His most far-reaching reform was the introduction of the scheme of permanent settlement of lands in Bengal, Bihar, and Benares. The assumption of the Mogul empire was that all land belonged to the state by right of conquest. Land tenure was assigned to court favorites or generals on a temporary basis, and thus a wide variety of relationships came into being. Village proprietors were entitled to the use and production of the land in return for the payment of taxes. The collection of taxes was farmed out to zamindars who paid the assessments and squeezed as much as they could out of the farmers. The aristocratic British officials appreciated the evils of the zamindar system, but they were favorably disposed toward landlords as a class, and they faced the immediate necessity of fixed and dependable revenues.

By the permanent settlement of 1793, Lord Cornwallis vested proprietary rights to the land, not in the occupants, but in the zamindars; not for ten years, but forever. Previously the zamindars enjoyed the lucrative right of collecting taxes; by the permanent settlement they became landlords with titles of ownership. By the stroke of a pen, the hereditary system of land occupancy was destroyed and twenty million small farmers became tenants, bound hand and foot to the tender mercies of a set of exacting rack-renters. In former times, if the zamindar failed to collect the required amount of tax he was reprimanded and flogged —but continued in his job. After the permanent settlement, he either paid or was dispossessed. Moreover, since he was given clear title to the land, he could mortgage, buy, or sell agricultural property as any other property; and the door to speculation in land was opened wide for adventurers and bankers from the big city of Calcutta.

During the Napoleonic Wars, the British in India were extremely sensitive to world politics. The governor-general from 1798 to 1805, the Marquess of Wellesley, the brother of the Duke of Wellington, devoted himself to the expansion of British power. He put an end to war in the kingdom of Mysore, annexed the southern coasts of Kanara, Malabar, and the Carnatic, and negotiated alliances with Hyderabad and Oudh. He defeated the Marathas and entered Delhi, where a blind emperor still occupied a rather decayed state. After Wellesley only Rajputana, Sind, and the Punjab remained outside the Company's net. The British response to this accumulation of grandeur was that Wellesley was recalled, because his operations were over-costly and constituted a "vexatious and painful interruption of tranquillity." The directors were not pleased over territorial greatness; they were distressed because of financial loss.

In 1813 the company lost its trading monopoly and India was thrown open for all British trade. Missionaries were permitted to operate within company territory, and a sum of thirty thousand dollars was set aside annually for the promotion of learning. In an age of nascent liberalism in England the extension of political power in India was regarded with less enthusiasm than the improvement of administrative methods. And the major emphasis was on the maintenance and proliferation of profits. A successful campaign was waged against Nepal, and endemic banditry was suppressed in central India. As a result of a third war against the Marathas, a major portion of the Deccan was annexed to the Bombay presidency. A foreign war was fought and won against Burma (1824–1826), and in the early years of the nineteenth century the great game of England versus Russia was begun in Central Asia.

A great governor-general, Lord William Bentinck, who served from 1828 to 1835, epitomized in India the English spirit of reform. His predecessors were for the most part conservative-minded administrators who patronized Hindu and Moslem festivals, and resisted any temptation to impose English ideas and institutions on Indian society. Their philosophy was to take the country as they found it, without exposing it to the vice of innovation. Lord Bentinck, however, was the exponent of a new age and a new generation. Englishmen at home concerned themselves with such things as the condition of the working classes, the poor laws, a revised penal code, the Political Reform Bill, and the abolition of slavery. Although they agitated for more democracy and improved social welfare for themselves, they were in no position to advocate the blessings of liberty and equality for the people of Inda.

The energetic rising middle class interpreted India in completely new terms. Their economic enthusiasm gave rise to new political and moral attitudes. They looked beyond the Indian market. They hypnotized themselves into a belief that theirs was not only a better economic system but a superior civilization which should be made available to others less fortunate than they. Their philosophy accorded perfectly with the militant Protestant missionaries who hated superstition and idolatry with a passion and felt that their own beloved Christian country should spread the gospel to the "poor, benighted heathen." With faith in reason, liberalism, free trade and the Christian God, they felt they should anglicize the whole structure of Indian society. The crusading spirit was in the air, and the spirit was buoyed up by the unheard-of riches of the industrial era.

Lord Bentinck (in 1829) moved against the phansigars, or thugs who were bound together in gangs by strict religious vows to the goddess Kali and who waylaid travelers and strangled them. It was he who stamped out female infanticide and human sacrifice. He prohibited sati (suttee) or widow-burning in British territories. During his administration, the British took steps in the fields of law and education which left permanent marks on India. In law, the established principle was "uniformity where you can have it; diversity where you must have it; but in all cases certainty." Western courts were set up side by side with those of ancient India. Two grades of Indian judges were created and the process was started which ultimately produced the Indian civil and criminal codes of procedure and the Indian penal code.

In the House of Commons in 1833 Thomas Babington Macaulay called for the "pacific triumph of reason over barbarism; the imperishable empire of our arts and our morals, our literature and our laws." Previous conquerors had been absorbed into the Indian system; it was Macaulay's vision that India should be absorbed into the English tradition. On March 7, 1835, English became the official language of British India, and Western learning became the core of education in India. England would not try to educate everybody, "just those at the top who may be interpreters between us and those whom we govern." A gap would separate the elite and the masses, but England pinned its faith on a "class of persons, Indian in blood and color but English in taste, in opinions, in morals and in intellect."

These decisions were compromises between necessity and virtue, between self-interest and altruism. Macaulay said, "it would be far better for us that the people of India were well governed and independent of us than ill-governed and subject to us; that they were ruled by their own kings, but wearing our broadcloth, and working with our cutlery, than that they were performing their salaams to English collectors and English magistrates, but were too ignorant to value, or too poor to buy, English manufactures." He added, "To trade with civilized men is infinitely more profitable than to govern savages. That would be a doting wisdom . . . which would keep a hundred millions of men from being our customers in order that they might continue to be our slaves."

Macaulay's brother-in-law, Charles Trevelyan, was among those who foresaw independence for India, and "it will come either by revolution or reform." The diffusion of European knowledge and the slow adoption of European institutions would lead eventually to freedom; but that was a preferable alternative to struggle and mutual exasperation. In a pamphlet, *Education in India,* Trevelyan wrote, "The natives will have independence after first learning how to make good use of it, and we shall exchange profitable subjects for still more profitable allies. . . . Trained by us to happiness and independence, and endowed with our learning and political institutions, India will remain the proudest monument of British benevolence; and we shall long continue to reap, in the affectionate attachment of the people, and in a great commercial intercourse with their splendid country, the fruit of that enlightened policy which suggested to us this line of conduct."

In the twenty years, 1836–1856, England was faced with constant wars—in China, Afghanistan, Burma, and within India itself—with the result that emphasis and energy were diverted from programs of internal reform. Rumors and phantoms haunted the British on India's northwest frontier where Russia and England met, not with armies but with diplomatic intrigues. The prime reason for interest in Persia and Afghanistan was to stop the much-feared advance of Russia, and the compelling motive for pacification in the Punjab was the creation of a strong defense area on the India side of the border.

Lord Dalhousie, a former assistant to William Gladstone on the board of trade, was the last but one of the governors-general under the Company. He served from 1848 to 1856. He was obliged to conduct the second Burmese war, and to quell the Sikh uprising in the northwest, but he had no enthusiasm for fighting. His passion was public works. He was the apostle of aggressive Westernization and technical assistance. To him, a "bridge was prized as a ruby and a road was a joy forever." He built irrigation canals, railways, telegraphs, schools, and decent jails. He had faith in steam engines, but not in democracy. His aim was to convert India into a unitary, disciplined, and powerful bastion of empire. He had no patience with Indian princes and threatened to put an end to them all. He invented the "doctrine of lapse" according to which a native state would lapse to British control if the ruler died without natural heirs. He also decreed that in the event of anarchy or misgovernment, a princely state would pass to the British. As a result of these measures Satara, Jhansi, Nagpur, and Oudh were annexed, and all the princes became uneasy. Lord Dalhousie refused to continue pensions to useless Mogul dignitaries, and he abolished honorific Indian titles which implied sovereignty. The dour Scot excelled in doing things, but he fell short in understanding people. He retired with the firm conviction that his successor, Lord Canning, would have nothing to do but to carry on with reforms and construction. Instead Canning reaped the whirlwind.

Last Days of the Company, 1856–1858

From every point of view—political, economic, and social—the situation in India was ready to explode at the end of Lord Dalhousie's administration. Indians were unhappy about the civil service and the army. All posts paying more than five hundred pounds per year were reserved to European members of the company's service. It was not until 1864 that an Indian actually entered the civil service. Indians were permitted to hold only the lower positions in the judiciary, up to the rank of subordinate judge.

The Indian army came into existence as a result of the Anglo-French wars in the eighteenth century. The first regiment of the Madras Europeans had the distinction of having Robert Clive as an officer. Each presidency maintained its independent units, but after 1784 all three (Madras, Bombay, and Calcutta) were subject to the control of the governor-general. In addition to the company's troops, regiments of royal troops were brought out from England in times of crisis; they were kept in India in semipermanent garrison. Indian ranks were trained by Europeans along Western lines, but no Indian could rise to an office higher than a captain. They were strictly a professional body of men, and they were the most efficient native troops in Asia.

The administration of English justice created special problems. In Mogul times, each religious and social community was permitted to follow its own civil laws. The criminal law was Mogul, with a strict Islamic code providing for such harsh punishments as mutilation and impalement. The British made no legal innovations until 1774 when a supreme court was established on English lines. The authority and application of English law was limited to Europeans. Later Lord Cornwallis removed the harsher features of Islamic law until it became more humane than English law. Then the Moslems were removed from the higher ranks of the judiciary, and were replaced by young Englishmen. Civil and criminal courts were taken over by the company, and the English system of district, circuit, and appellate courts was established. The façade was impressive, but the new judges were not familiar with the language or customs of the people for whom they were supposed to dispense justice. The law was Hindu or Moslem, but procedure and interpretation were British. In this lawyer's paradise an enormous body of Indian pleaders, or lawyers, came into being—which added to the confusion and further clogged the flow of justice. In 1840 commissions went to work, and twenty years later they produced a new penal code and procedural codes for both civil and criminal law.

The most frequent clashes between representatives of the government and the people took place at the local level. The center of British rule was the district. Bengal and Bihar were divided into twenty-three districts, Bombay thirteen, Sind three, and Madras twenty. The pyramid of district rule was the collector, and below him were the judge and the magistrate. A code of regulations for district officers was formulated in 1793, and it was the steel framework of the administration of British India. As new territories became British, the district offices were instructed to apply the spirit of the code even if they could not apply the letter. After the annexation of Punjab and Oudh, new district officers, called commissioners, or deputy commissioners, were appointed. Subject only to central authorities above them, they were the fathers and masters of the district. They outranked the local commander of the army, and their wisdom or lack of it accounted for the success or failure of the administration of Calcutta. The governor-general dealt with laws and policies; the district officers dealt with human beings and their problems.

The company was never able to work out a simple set of rules for dealing with the princely states. Originally the governor-general assumed a position of overlord to vassal toward the lesser princes and made treaties with the greater ones. He refrained from interference in their local affairs wherever possible; in the event of trouble he intervened with troops paid for by the prince, but officered by detached members of the company's army. The governor-general rigorously controlled the external relations of the states. He guaranteed protection against invasion or revolution. But personal ambitions were petrified, since no prince could hope for responsibility or status beyond his own domains. Very often the princes turned to vicious or riotous living, and they earned the reputation of being "islands of flame in a dry forest."

India's greatest difficulties were in the economic sphere. The peasants suffered most during the British administration. The company's peace assured an increase in population with a consequent upswing in land values. This worked to the advantage of the landlords because assessments were not changed. Landlords prospered as they bought and sold land in a steadily rising market, and they received more income from ever-mounting rents. While landlords thrived, the peasants sank deeper in debt. Three-fifths of the population consisted of peasants who lived in the ominous shadow of famine. Peasants had to sell produce to get money to pay their rents, and they were at the mercy of the grain merchants and shopkeepers who were the village moneylenders. Illiterate peasant proprietors were overcharged, unmercifully cheated out of their holdings, and forced to join the huge army of landless tenants which made up two-thirds of India's agricultural population. The government constructed irrigation systems and reclaimed waste lands to relieve rural hardships, but public works were not unmitigated blessings. They were costly and they necessitated tax burdens which were unbearable in lean years. Farm families which were able to save their land saw their holdings fragmented into smaller and less economical parcels with each generation, and they found it increasingly difficult to keep the mortgage holder from the door.

The small factory owners, merchants, artisans, and craftsmen were no better off than the peasants. As traders, the company men established the monopoly which deprived India of revenues and returned huge sums to England to finance their own industrial revolution. Even after the monopoly was ended, and India was opened to all British trade, capital shied away from India in favor of Europe or America. The British levied tariffs on Indian goods, and refused to permit India to import machinery. As Indian workers were thrown out of their jobs Lord Bentinck wrote that "the bones of the cotton weavers are bleaching the plains of India." At the same time the British flooded the Indian market with machine-made goods, and they controlled the ships and the banks as well as the trade itself. In the first half of the nineteenth century, India lost the proud supremacy in trade and industry which it had enjoyed for two thousand years. It was gradually transformed into a plantation for the production of raw materials and a dumping ground for the cheap manufactured goods of the West. Exploitation went along with conquest, and India was helpless to stop it. Only the most modest beginnings were made in the development of communications and industry within India itself. Europeans made small investments in textiles, coal mining, iron works, sawmills, and tea plantations. In 1830 a road was built from Bombay to Poona, and steamships were imported for river transportation. In 1839 work was begun on the grand trunk road from Calcutta to Delhi, and ten

years later agreements were signed for India's first railway. By the outbreak of the mutiny some two hundred miles of track had been laid, and
India's first telegraph lines were in operation. Understandably the British
were unenthusiastic about industrial development, and jobs were not
available for India's huge supply of native labor.

Poor Moslems and poor Hindus shared a common fate under the
British, and they tended to draw closer together. Except for their religious
differences, poverty doomed them to a similar fate. At the same time the
social gap widened between the Indians and the British. In the eighteenth
century the English lived in their factories, ate at a common table, and
went out into the country as little as possible. Company officials did not
bring their wives with them; Anglo-Indian children were numerous. The
Indians with whom the Europeans had social contacts were merchants,
or their agents or household servants. Indians and Europeans had little
incentive to understand each other, but neither displayed marked attitudes of superiority. As the company flourished, its officials took on
grandiose airs. In an earlier era, the English sahibs shared common interests with princes or Hindus of high caste. But after Cornwallis, the
company's hierarchy appeared reluctant to indulge in social intercourse
with any Indians on a basis of equality. The English were in the country
but more and more unwilling to come to terms with it.

Indian society was far from static. The spirit of the Indians suffered
by comparison with the buoyant spirit of the British, but British liberals
teamed up with awakening Indian intellectuals to give Indians new confidence in themselves. British orientalists showed keen interest in the
language, literature, and tradition of the Hindus. They made translations of Hindu classics and delved deeply into India's history. They
showed to Hindus the value of their own culture and gave them a sense of
importance in the midst of the flowering of Western science.

The impact of Western rationalism and liberal ideas produced the
reformist activities of India's first modern, Ram Mohan Roy (1772–1833),
who was born into a Brahman family and was at one time an employee of
the East India Company. He was a genius who studied philosophy and
science, and pursued his studies in a dozen languages. He devoted his
energies to the social and religious improvement of his countrymen. His
aim was to produce a synthesis between the new world of the West and
the ancient world of Hinduism. He founded the Brahmo Samaj, or Divine
Society, which would adopt the good ways of the West and abolish the
evil aspects of Hinduism. He was a pioneer of English education and
founded a newspaper. He went to England, the source of authority in
India, to give testimony before the select committee of the House of
Commons which in 1833 considered the renewal of the company's charter.
He showed the way to the reconciliation of political aims which were

Western in direction and inspiration but which were to be pursued in an Eastern environment. He showed that it was possible to agitate for democracy without ceasing to be an Indian, and he was joined in his convictions by many Indian products of the English education system.

After it was decided in 1835 that the content of higher education should be Occidental learning, Indians were given the opportunity to study Western medicine, science, law, and literature. They were exposed to the Bible, Shakespeare, Burke, Macaulay, and John Stuart Mill. They read the best of English poetry and prose and they absorbed dynamic ideas about liberty, equality, and the rights of man. Westernized Indians developed a love of English literature and English schools. They accepted democracy in politics, cricket and hockey in sports, and the tea party as a social institution. Some Indians used their knowledge to follow Ram Mohan in the attempted reconciliation of East and West; others became rebel spirits inspired by Rousseau, Voltaire, or the French Revolution. Some were moderate; others were so foolish as to express their radical ideas by hurling beef bones into Hindu homes. India did not produce a generation which exhausted itself in a frenetic chase after the secrets of the West—as happened in Japan—but it gave birth to the nucleus of a class which, after a traumatic political experience, later assumed leadership toward national independence.

THE GREAT MUTINY

Lord Dalhousie despised public opinion and underrated the strength of Indian tradition. Therefore his successor paid the consequences of misjudgment. When Dalhousie left India, the entire country was in a state of unrest. The princes were unhappy and fearful because of the doctrine of lapse. Landlords were uneasy because of the government's growing interest in the welfare of peasants. The higher castes in the army and outside of it were cynical about equality. The new education stripped the priest of his ancient authority, and Western science debunked the magic of the holy men. British reform measures, although reasonable, were seen as breaks in the fabric of Indian society. It was not difficult to convince the peasants that the British were responsible for their misery. A show of force against the British was timely while many British units were out of India on duty in China or the Crimea.

On three previous occasions, army units had dared to mutiny. In 1806 the British instructed sepoys in Vellore, Madras, to wear special turbans, trim their beards, and give up caste marks. A regiment refused to obey, and the ringleaders in resistance were ordered nine hundred lashes apiece. The sepoys arose and massacred two companies of European troops, only to suffer brutal retaliation. In 1824 a regiment refused to move for action in Burma because it felt that caste would be endangered during the sea voyage. A court martial sentenced hundreds to hard labor and condemned six to death. In 1856 another regiment balked at service in Burma, and its punishment was nothing more than transfer to Dacca in East Bengal.

In 1857 the Enfield rifle was introduced into the army. Before loading the rifle, it was necessary to bite a greased cartridge, which was offensive to both Hindus and Moslems. The rumor spread that biting the grease was a deliberate, militant Christian attack on native religions and subtle effort to force the soldiers to break caste. On May 9, 1857, sepoys at Meerut refused to touch the new cartridges and were given prison sentences. The next day three Indian regiments on the station shot their officers, broke open the jail, and set off on the road to Delhi, forty miles away. No one tried to stop them. Within forty-eight hours Delhi had fallen to sepoys who compelled the old king, Bahadur Shah, to proclaim himself emperor of Hindustan. Uprisings occurred throughout northern India as princes and landlords—Hindu and Moslem—joined with the mutinous army. The rebellion lasted for eighteen months, and it was marked by extreme brutality on both sides. Delhi was retaken by assault on September 14, 1857, and the city was sacked by "troops which were completely disorganized and demoralized by the immense amount of plunder that fell into their hands and the quantity of liquor they managed to discover." Guerilla activity was eventually suppressed by loyal native troops and their British officers.

The suppression of the mutiny did not increase Indian respect for the British nor pave the way for better relations. The Indians added bitter memories to their store of resentment against arrogance on the part of British officials. To the villagers, "British avengers were in the line of marauding Turks and bandits, differing mainly in that their killings were preceded by curious ceremonies called trials; and they were admittedly less concerned with plunder, rapine and torture." Sophisticated Indians—as contrasted with the villagers—realized that they had nothing to hope for from the discredited feudal leaders, and they were convinced that they could not drive out the British by force. The logical conclusion was that India would have to accept the British, no matter how distasteful or repugnant.

The British also learned a lesson from the mutiny. British tempers flared and the press cried for blood: "Oh! that the population of India might have one neck and that all the hemp in India might be twisted into one rope." The tide toward reasonableness turned first in England. It was shown in pamphlets, meetings in Hyde Park, and in the debates in the House of Commons. The British realized that they would have to come to terms with Indian traditions, no matter how much they disliked it. Enlightened opinion was embodied in a new policy, and the major casualty was the company itself.

Parliament passed an "Act for the Better Government of India," and the company turned over the government of India to the Crown. "Let Her Majesty appreciate the gift: let her take the vast country and the teeming millions of India under her direct control; but let her not forget the great corporation from which she has received them, nor the lessons to be learned from its success . . . The Company has the privilege of transferring to the service of Her Majesty such a body of civil and military officers as the world has never seen before."

The queen responded with a proclamation of November 1, 1858, which said, "We desire no extension of our territorial possessions" and denied alike the right and the desire to impose British convictions on India. "Firmly relying on the truth of Christianity," Her Majesty expressed her faith that "with the aid of a beneficient God a new and happy era was to come." The proclamation concluded:

"When by the blessing of Providence, internal tranquillity shall be restored, it is our earnest desire to stimulate the peaceful industry of India, to promote works of public utility and improvement, and to administer the government for the benefit of all our subjects resident therein. In their prosperity will be our strength, in their contentment our security, and in their gratitude our best reward. And may the God of all power grant to us, and to those in authority under us, strength to carry out these our wishes for the good of our people."

India under the Crown

The transfer of sovereignty from company to Crown was a watershed in Indian history. The queen assumed the title of empress of India and the company tycoons became members of an advisory body named the Council of India. Parliament took little interest in Indian affairs, and executive responsibility was lodged in a secretary of state for India. The governor-general in Calcutta became the viceroy or personal representative of the Crown. His legislative council was reorganized to allow for the appointment of two Indian members. The viceroy was assisted by an executive council which evolved into a cabinet of six British officials. The government of India became national in concept and operation, complete with budget, paper currency, income tax, and import tariffs.

Administrative authority in the provinces rested with a governor, subject to provincial legislative councils which were set up after 1861. At the head of the districts remained the commissioners, collectors, and magistrates who exercised all legislative, executive, and judicial powers. The civil service continued as before, except that all positions were put on a competitive basis and Indians were made eligible for the lower ranks. Under the new dispensation, British men brought their families to India with them. The British withdrew from contacts with Indians wherever possible, and more than ever the home, office, and club became the center of their lives. The civil service "in a special ark of its own rode with aggressive impartiality and indifference on the troubled seas of India" (Michael Edwardes).

The Army was reorganized into a field service and security troops. The company forces became the British Indian army. They were organized on a communal basis, with separate regiments for Sikhs, Gurkhas, Pathans, and so forth. They developed high competence and an excellent *esprit de corps*, but they were given no basis for loyalty to an Indian nation. The field service was subject for duty anywhere outside of India, and their expenses were charged to the government of India, not to taxpayers in the United Kingdom. Indians could have commissions from the viceroy, but not from the Crown, and they were limited to clerical positions in the headquarters. Thanks to the army, vendettas and banditry in India came virtually to an end; India knew no real security problems except those on the northwest frontier.

The British cultivated new attitudes toward the princes and sought to win their support. The princes were no longer regarded as flames in a dry forest, but rather as breakwaters in the event of storms. Their right of adoption was recognized (thus assuring the rights of succession), and they were encouraged to interest themselves in matters beyond their own territories. Their boundaries were fixed, and they were guaranteed immunity from interference in internal affairs in all but extreme cases. As a result of the consideration shown to them, they became ardent supporters of the British regime.

The British toned down their administrative procedures to accord with tradition and indigenous customs. They lost their enthusiasm for rapid regeneration of India, and they settled down to what they thought would be a long period of tutelage and trusteeship. They addressed themselves immediately to agricultural problems and passed acts designed to protect the peasants against the landlords and moneylenders. Ownership rights were confirmed for tenants in actual occupancy of land for twelve years and cooperative societies were established to provide badly needed credits at reasonable rates of interest. The government's gospel was "point four," or its public works program. Dams and canals for irrigation were constructed, and the parched provinces of Sind and the Punjab were given wealth and importance. India had two and a half times as much acreage under irrigation as the United States. The government drew up a famine code which promised to make death from starvation a thing of the past.

By 1900 some 25,000 miles of railway track had been laid to complete the largest and best railway system in Asia. Private companies with British capital built and operated the railways in accordance with specifications laid down by the government. The railways were the great catalyzers of the Indian economy because they opened up interior markets and made possible local industries. They brought Indians together from all corners of the subcontinent, and they threw castes together at times in embarrassing intimacy. The public liked the trains, which took thousands cheaply and quickly to religious festivals.

Industrial development was slow because of pressures from British manufacturers. The genius of the Parsi Tata family developed iron and steel industries at Jamshedpur in Bihar. Prosperous Indians teamed up with British firms to revive the cotton goods industry on a mechanical basis, and they opened coal mines. Calcutta thrived on jute mills; plantations in the country made excellent profits on tea, coffee, tobacco, rubber, and cinchona. British technicians (often Scotsmen) emigrated to India, and hundreds of Indian students went to England for industrial training. A few jobs were made available to Indians, but scores of millions of potential workers were given no opportunity to sell their labor. The British government was indifferent toward the formation of a local proletariat and opposed to industrial development which would compete with the mother country. India had no departments of agriculture or industry until after the turn of the twentieth century. What a contrast between India and Japan!

The administration of foreign affairs also showed the difference between the interests of India and those of Britain in India. As the Russians advanced through Tashkent, Bokhara, Samarkand, and Khiva toward India and a warm-water port on the Persian Gulf, London was infinitely more excited than Calcutta. Disraeli, who was impressed by the rattling of sabers and enamored with the fireworks of diplomacy, ordered three Indian armies to cross the frontier in 1878 and take a hand in the internal politics of Afghanistan. His motives were to halt Russia and to gain a better position in dealing with the warring tribes on the northwest frontier of India. The viceroy disliked the maneuver because he saw no reason to spend crores of rupees (hundreds of millions of dollars) on barren mountain ridges or vanishing frontiers. He was not willing to "gamble the fate of India on a random bullet or the dagger of a paradise-seeking Ghazi." The British gained a temporary advantage in Afghanistan but after two years they gave up the adventure, and brought their troops home to India. The third war with Burma (which will be discussed in the next chapter) and the opposition to the German advance toward Baghdad were the results of British imperial diplomacy. India became the center of a vast empire which stretched from the Mediterranean to the Pacific. India was the keystone in an arch which contained Gibraltar, Malta, the Suez, Singapore, North Borneo, Hong Kong, and spheres of interest in China. The route to India became the chief interest of British diplomacy and the British fleet.

The various viceroys had their own ideas about the administration of India. Lord Lytton (1876–1880) felt that it was a mistake to believe that England could hold India by good government, that is, by improving the lot of the *ryot* (peasant), strictly administering justice, and spending immense sums on irrigation. He argued that the peasantry was an inert mass and "if it ever moves at all, it will move not in obedience to its British benefactors but to its native chiefs and princes." He wrote that the only political representatives of native opinion were the *baboos* (Indians with English education) who write "semi-seditious articles in the native press and who represent nothing but the social anomaly of their own position." Therefore he conceived his most urgent task to be "to secure completely and eventually to use the aristocracy."

The outspoken British apologists of imperialism denied that ambition and conquest were crimes. They believed in an uncompromising, straightforward assertion of authority; and in the employment of the instruments of justice and military power to promote the lasting good of India. Their philosophy of government was that efficiency of administration was proof of good government, and that self-government was no substitute for good government. Their best-known ideologue, F. J. Fitzjames Stephen, wrote, "North America would be a hunting ground for savages if the Puritans had not carried guns as well as Bibles," and he compared the *Pax Brittanica* to the universal peace announced at Christ's nativity. Rudyard Kipling was their poet.

Lord Curzon (1899–1905) was the last great viceroy to impose his personal ideas on the administration of India. He knew that no government by a handful of foreigners could ever be popular, and he realized that the Indians "will never be strong and faithful supporters of us." But he felt that the alternative to British dominion was chaos and ruin. He determined to maintain a benevolent regime, which would keep executive power in British hands but give Indians the largest possible share in administration. His policies were not calculated to excite affection, but they won respect and enforced obedience. Of his administration an Indian said, "The sahibs do not understand us or like us but they try to be just, and they do not fear the face of man."

In his way Lord Curzon worked unceasingly and strenuously for the good of India. He put through the Ancient Monuments Preservation Act and appointed a director general of archaeology. He looked after the welfare of the peasants, and he reduced the share of land in the national revenue. He undertook reforms in the army, the police, and the civil service. He was tireless in promoting good relations with the princes. In foreign affairs he dealt cautiously with Afghans and Persians and took a strong stand against the French and Germans as they menaced the approaches to India. He sent a mission under Colonel Younghusband ostensibly to study the situation in Tibet, and he fixed that line of India's frontiers which was to last well into the twentieth century. He made small but steady concessions to the rising Indian nationalists, but he did not understand them nor appreciate the intensity of their emotions. When he divided Bengal into two states—clearly along communal lines, one Hindu and one Moslem—he inflamed all India. Monster mass meetings and protest marches launched the Swadeshi movement, which meant a boycott of Lancashire and an avowal to buy Indian goods. When Lord Curzon left India in 1905, the breach between the British government in India and the Indian nationalists was wide and deep.

Beginnings of Indian Nationalism

By 1905 Indian nationalists were an identifiable group, motivated by a common ideology, and mobilized into a struggling political organization. Leading nationalists came from subordinate but respectable strata of society and were men of good caste. Many had no desire to overthrow the existing social order; they merely wanted to get rid of the British.

The most prominent members of the group were businessmen who were infuriated with British economic policies. They lived in great cities; and most had accumulated wealth, like Chinese compradors, in serving British firms and acting as contact men between the foreign businessmen and native society. They spoke good English, they affected English manners, and they were inclined to like the foreigners with whom they were associated. But they wanted more opportunities for profits for themselves. Their sons and daughters were usually educated in Western colleges and became more fiery nationalistic than their elders. The businessmen were supported by Indians who held subordinate posts in the civil service. They manned the posts, highways, and railways, agricultural and forest services, customs and internal revenue services; and they enjoyed immense prestige because of their connection with the government. However, they were resentful of the discrimination against them, which obtained in spite of the law of 1833 which stipulated that "no Indian shall by reason of his religion, place of birth, descent, color or any of them be disabled from holding any office or employment."

Teachers, lawyers, doctors, and journalists became ardent nationalists. The great poet, Rabindranath Tagore, said he came to the parting of the ways with the English when "I began increasingly to discover how easily those who accepted the highest truths of civilization disowned them with impunity whenever questions of national self-interest were involved." English language and education were the common denominators of all these groups, and they were as hopeful for India's future as they were proud of its past.

They found a sense of nationhood—folk and community—in their own history, and after the mutiny they undertook a new search for the causes of the material supremacy of the West. They found their answers in nationalism and the power of machines. They saw no reason why they could not master the arts and science of the West if they would discard some of their prejudices and pay the price for progress. If they would work hard, they could catch up and possibly surpass those who had the advantage of an earlier start. They did not consider it beneath their dignity to copy the West. They would not borrow at random or grasp for any crumbs which were thrown at them. They would choose what they wanted, and they would accept reforms which seemed reasonable. In the exercise of freedom of choice they found a new source of pride and sense of personal dignity.

There was no doubt about the obligation which the Indian nationalists owed to the British. Teachers and missionaries, as well as lawyers and administrators, brought the ideas of liberty and equality before the law. Forward-looking British in India encouraged Indians in their sentiments of national pride. The voice of Gladstone was heard, saying, "That which is morally wrong cannot be politically right." He declared: "It is our weakness and our calamity that we have not been able to give India the blessings of free institutions." Indian nationalists hated the political double standard for Englishmen at home and England overseas; they determined to lighten the burden of the latter in order to achieve for themselves the blessings of the former. At the outset few thought of independence. Their immediate goals were social emancipation, industrial development, and self-government within the British Empire.

From the beginning, Hindus as distinguished from Moslems or Sikhs, dominated the nationalist movement. Mother India was a political dream, but it was also accepted as a divine reincarnation. Nationalism, in taking on a religious aspect, gave the educated middle class a new feeling of identity with the Hindu masses. Nationalism flourished as it assumed the character of a Hindu Renaissance. In 1875 Swami Saraswati established the Arya Samaj, a fanatical organization devoted to "India for the Hindus." It was the antithesis of the liberal-rational Brahmo Samaj, and it attracted followers by its strident call to Hindus to return to the purity of the Vedas. Swami Vivekananda, who was the first Hindu in modern times to become a world figure, founded in 1897 the Order of Ramakrishna dedicated to the spread of all religions, particularly Hinduism. His message was that the only condition of vigorous national life for India was the conquest of all mankind by Indian thought. The Theosophical Society, led by Mrs. Annie Besant, gained influence throughout the world by its teaching that the revival of the ancient Hindu religion would bring with it a great wave of patriotic life, the beginning of the rebuilding of a nation. The negative and tragic result of the blending of Indian nationalism and the Hindu religion was the progressive alienation of the non-Hindu communities.

No significant progress was made toward political rights for Indians before the formation of the Indian National Congress in 1885. In 1851 an abortive British Indian Association submitted its first proposals for Indian participation in government, and in 1853 positions in the Indian civil service were thrown open to competition. Lord Dalhousie inaugurated the system of legislative and executive councils which was gradually expanded to include Indian members; it was adopted in the provinces as well as in the central government. The Indian Councils Act of the British parliament in 1892 granted the councils the right, not merely to advise, but to discuss the budget and interrogate the government. More unofficial members were added to the councils, but they were not yet chosen by election. However, certain, nongovernmental groups such as local government boards, universities, landholders, and chambers of commerce were permitted to nominate candidates for seats in the councils. The executive councils, in effect quasi-cabinets, gained authority in the provinces very slowly, and did not assume power in the central government until the end of World War II. Large urban areas were gradually given opportunities to share in self-rule.

Concessions of this nature could not eliminate growing Indian anti-British grievances. British planters and businessmen were often more obnoxious than government officials in treating Indians with scorn. Indians disapproved of British use of Indian troops in British battles overseas; and they chafed at every tariff, excise tax or factory regulation which served as a brake on India's economic progress. When Indians read the doctrines of Karl Marx, many were impressed with his analysis of exploitation.

The first sign of effort on the part of Indians to influence the government was in the appearance of a nationalist press. In Bengal, the *Hindoo Patriot,* the *Amrita Bazar Patrika,* and the *Bengalee* became important organs of opinion. In Madras, the *Hindu* and, in Bombay, the *Mahratta* and the *Kesari* (Lion) became sufficiently potent to embarrass the government. Oftentimes the British-owned press was more antigovernment than the vernacular, but the Vernacular Press Act of 1878 was a regulatory measure for native-language papers only. The daily and periodical press appeared as a kind of passport to the new ideas of democracy and political freedom. For the first time in India's history, men from the north, southeast, and west of India felt that they had something in common. Cheap and efficient postal service increased the sense of unity, and the railway helped to bring people together from the furthest points of India.

In the seventies a young Indian, Surendranath Banerjea passed his competitive examinations with a high grade, but he had to resort to the Queen's Bench in London to get his appointment. Shortly afterward he was dismissed from the service on grounds of moral turpitude. In anger because of trumped-up charges, he founded in 1876 the Indian Association of Calcutta. For the first time various races and religions were brought upon the same platform for a common and united purpose—the attainment of political ends. The movement remained constitutional, and it demonstrated the advantages of organized opposition. In 1883 it became the Indian National Conference in Calcutta.

In the same year, a retired English civil servant, A. O. Hume, suggested to the graduates of Calcutta University that they should organize themselves into an association for moral, social, and political revival. The viceroy, Lord Dufferin, supported Hume's efforts. He felt "it would be a public benefit if there existed some responsible organization through which the government might be kept informed regarding the best Indian public opinion." Hume's activities resulted in the first meeting of the Indian National Congress, a political party of seventy dues-paying members, in Bombay in 1885. At the same time the Indian National Conference held its second meeting in Calcutta, and later the two organizations merged. From that moment forward, the word *Congress* in India did not mean a central legislature as in the United States. It referred to the political party which dedicated itself to the fulfillment of India's nationalism.

Essentially the Indian National Congress was a vehicle for moderate opinion, concerned with reforms not freedom. It placed special emphasis on the increase of self-government, spread of education, separation of judicial and executive functions of government officials, and the wider employment of Indians in the higher ranks of the civil service. Its most telling argument was that capital was drained off to England, while India grew poorer. The members of the Congress were mostly middle-class Hindus, especially Brahmans, who represented the new urban elements. They were Anglophile and loyal. Lord Dufferin called them a "microscopic minority," but one of their number, R. C. Mitra, replied: "The educated community represents the brains and conscience of the country and is the legitimate spokesman of the illiterate masses, the

natural custodian of their interests. Those who think must govern those
who toil."

When the Congress was ignored by the government of India, the
former turned to England. It won the approval of John Bright, among
others, and published a propaganda sheet called *India* in London. It
found itself isolated between an indifferent government and a growing
Indian nationalism. It could not move with sufficient grace to keep the
goodwill of the British authorities, nor with sufficient speed to satisfy the
radical demands of its own constituents.

Divisions appeared within the ranks of the nationalists. An extremist wing identified with B. G. Tilak stressed that nationalists should
demand rights; a moderate wing under Gopal Krishna Gokhale preferred
to seek concessions. Tilak coined the phrase *swaraj* or "self-rule" which
he claimed as "our birthright," and he urged independence before reforms. He organized the cult of the elephant-headed god Ganesha, the
remover of obstacles. In festivals, he brought together national sentiment
and religious revival and he built a sense of social solidarity among Hindu
nationalists. He chose the founder of the Maratha empire, Sivaji, as his
hero because "his self-sacrifice, courage and heroic deeds proved that
when the whole nation suffered from misrule, India was not forgotten by
providence." Tilak gave the nationalist movement a much broader base
than neo-Western liberalism could ever supply: the identity of the people of India with the struggle for freedom. In 1896 a government attempt
to enforce plague restrictions in Poona was fomented into a religious war.
Two British officers on special plague duty were murdered, and Tilak
was sentenced to eighteen months in prison for incitement to murder.
This incident took nationalism completely out of the intellectual realm,
and made a term in a British jail the hallmark of a nationalist leadership.

The official British attitude toward the nationalists was neither benevolence nor uncompromising opposition. It sought adjustment. The nationalist appetite grew with the eating, and adjustment became increasingly difficult. Meanwhile, the Moslems took offense at Hindu extremism.
About one-quarter of the membership of the Indian National Congress
was Moslem, but the Moslems began to fear that in the event of self-rule
the larger community (Hindus) would fully override the interest of the
smaller (Moslems). Syed Ahmad Khan, Moslem patriot and nationalist
founded a Mohammedan Anglo-Oriental College at Aligarh which developed the Moslem point of view. Moslem leaders demanded communal
representation and separate electorates (and eventually their own distinct country—Pakistan). After the partition of Bengal the Moslems withdrew from the congress because of their conviction that majority rule
would indeed mean Hindu rule. Hindus claimed that, in opposition to

nationalism, the British began to favor the Moslems and to adopt the sinister policy of divide and rule.

Overseas Indians watched developments within their homeland with more than passing interest. By 1901 more than two and a half million Indians lived in Africa, Ceylon, Burma, Malaya, British Guiana, Mauritius, and Fiji. Most were originally indentured servants and came from the lowest castes. When terms of their contracts expired they remained abroad and took whatever jobs they could find. The discrimination against them by the Boer government was one of the minor causes of the South African war. But in working among his own people in South Africa, M. K. Ghandi first organized passive resistance against authority; and he developed techniques which were to make him a saint in India's struggle for independence.

SUGGESTED READING

Andrews, C. F., and Mookerji, Giriji, *Rise and Growth of the Congress in India* (London, George Allen & Unwin, 1938).

Ballhatchet, Kenneth, *Social Policy and Social Change in Western India, 1817–1830* (London, Oxford U., 1937).

Bhandarkar, D. R., (ed.), *India* (vol. 145 of *Annals* of the American Academy of Political and Social Science, Philadelphia, 1929).

Choudry, K. C., *Diary of an Unknown Indian* (London, 1951).

Coupland, Sir Reginald, *Britain and India, 1600–1941* (London, Oxford U., 1941).

Desai, A. R., *Social Background of Indian Nationalism* (Bombay, Oxford U., 1949).

Dutt, R. C., *Economic History of India under Early British Rule* (second ed.) (London, Kegan Paul, Trench, Trubner, & Co., Ltd., 1906).

Graham, G. F. I., *Sir Syed Ahmad Kahn* (Edinburgh, 1885).

Kincaid, Dennis, *British Social Life in India, 1608–1937* (London, 1939).

Kipling, Rudyard, *Kim* (New York, Doubleday, 1926).

Masani, R. P., *Britain and India* (Bombay, Oxford, 1960).

O'Malley, L. S. S., (ed.), *Modern India and the West* (New York, Oxford, 1941).

Prasad, Rajendra, *Autobiography* (Bombay, 1947).

Roberts, P. E., *History of British India* (third ed.) (London, Oxford, 1952).

Russell, W. H., *My Indian Mutiny Diary* (abridged ed.: edited by M. Edwardes) (London, 1959).

Spear, Percival, *Nabobs* (New York, Oxford U., 1963).

Thompson, E. J., and Garatt, G. T., *Rise and Fulfillment of British Rule in India* (London, Macmillan, 1934).

Thorner, Daniel, and Thorner, Alice, "India and Pakistan," in Ralph Linton, (ed.), *Most of the World* (New York, Columbia U., 1949).

11

The Course of Empire in Southeast Asia

The nineteenth century produced the rape of China, the awakening of Japan, and the establishment of the power of the British Crown in India. It also witnessed the imposition of colonialism in all of Southeast Asia, with the exception of Siam.

The nineteenth century was a vital, exciting era for Europeans and Americans. It witnessed the explosion of industrial capacity and the revolution in technical know-how. It shortened distances by achievements in transportation and bound a shrunken world together in a communications network. It brought all the earth's surface within the range of human exploitation, and destroyed any illusion or hope of isolation as a refuge in international politics. The accomplishments of science expanded the horizons of knowledge; the processes of experiment and inquiry promised to annihilate the obstacles to progress. Social injustice, inequality, poverty, and war remained, but they seemed less important than the promise of the ability to wipe them out. The accumulation of unheard-of wealth provided leisure and opportunity for men to develop their artistic talents. Freedom of the mind accelerated the growth of democracy, and the acceptance of civil responsibilities made possible new grants of civil rights. Confidence and ebullience displaced fear and superstition. The spirit of the Western world was embodied in a single symbol—the Statue of Liberty which was presented by the French to the people of the United States.

Those years were entirely different in Southeast Asia. Specks on the map which previously represented the factories and small footholds of adventurers and merchant companies spread into large areas under the complete political and economic domination of distant imperial powers. People in Southeast Asia were given law, order, and peace such as they had not known for generations. They were also given new prosperity in

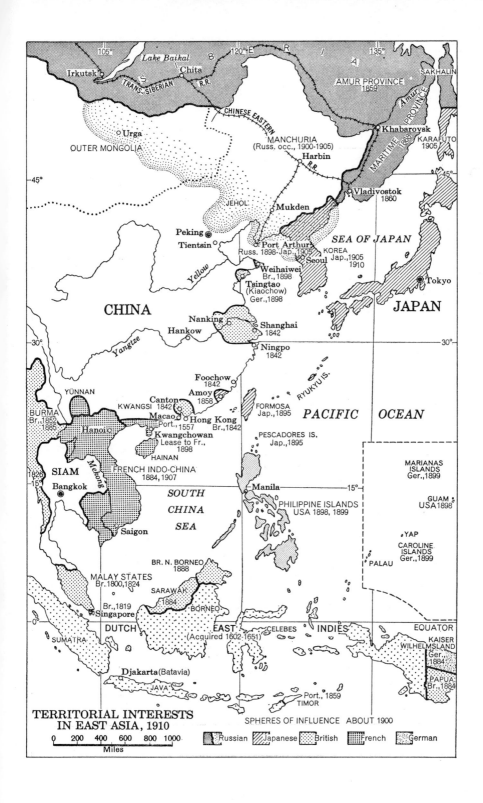

TERRITORIAL INTERESTS
IN EAST ASIA, 1910

0   200 400 600 800 1000
Miles

SPHERES OF INFLUENCE ABOUT 1900

Russian Japanese British French German

	PHILIPPINES	NETHERLANDS INDIES	BURMA	MALAYA	INDOCHINA	SIAM
				1786 Acquisition of Penang	1787 French Foothold	1768 Capital Bangkok
						1782 Chakri Dynasty
1800	1810 Representative in Cortes	1798 Dutch Government in Indies		1819 Singapore		
	1821 Mexican independence	1811 Raffles	1826 First War on British	1824 Treaty with Dutch		1826 British Treaty
		1824 Treaty				1833 U.S. Treaty
		1825 Java Wars			1843 Renewed French Interest	
		1830 Culture System				
	1846 First Newspaper	1848 Transfer to Parliament				1851 King Monkut Modernization
1850	1854 Postal Service	1860 Max Havelaar	1852 Second War on British	1862 Straits Settlements	1859 Saigon Occupied	1855 Treaty with England; Others Followed
			1862 Administrative Reorganization		1862 Cochin China	
					1863 Cambodia	

1875 / 1900						
	1868 Liberal Revolution in Spain 1872 Cavite Revolt	1870 New Policies 1873–1899 Achinese Wars	1867 Treaty of Commerce 1875 Margary Murder in China	1874 Treaty System with Malay States	1867 Cochin China—Western Provinces 1874 Annam Protectorate	1867 Recognized France in Cambodia 1868 King Chulalongkorn
	1880 Cable Service 1887 Rizal's First Novel 1896 Rizal's Execution 1898 Independence		1885 Third War on British 1886 Chinese Recognition of British Annexation of Upper Burma 1895 Made Province of India Boundary Surveys with China	1882 North Borneo 1896 Federated Malay States	1883 } New Annam 1884 } Treaties 1885 Tientsin Treaty 1887 Union of French Indo-china 1893 Laos Claims 1899 Laos Protectorate	1893 Gave up Laos 1896 Independence Guaranteed by France—England
	1901 Insurgency Ended Against U.S.	1901 Ethical Policy				

producing raw materials for insatiable Western machines. However, they were kept immune from the important things which really mattered—the revolutions in individual and group development. They were protected and sheltered from modernization, but they were also deprived of the capacity to cope with social tides which would eventually wash their shores.

Of the European powers in Asia, Portugal lost all but insignificant vestiges of its ancient empire. Spain continued to administer the Philippines, with rising evidences of revolt and with the foreboding fate of losing its possessions to the United States. The Dutch schemed to derive maximum profit from the Indies, and the French struggled to gain a prestigious foothold in faraway Indochina. While the British concentrated on India and dreamed of the vast potential of the China market, they did not overlook Burma, Malaya, and North Borneo. Only Siam managed to preserve the opportunity to develop as an independent nation-state in the Western sense of the concept. The chart shows the nineteenth-century events of Southeast Asia which are most useful in understanding its subsequent history.

This chapter deals with millions of people who until recently were neglected or overlooked. The welfare of the people of Burma was neglected in the course of the Anglo-Burma wars, for example; or the fate of the people of Indochina was overlooked in the French effort to shape Indochina into its balcony on the Pacific. But the thought and spirit of native people are more important than the will and intentions of the alien administrators; and the social fabric and economic welfare weigh more heavily in historical values than political intrigues or even the wars of the imperial decision-makers. The silent resentment of the masses and their leaders against being treated as inferiors or pawns gradually welled up into the spirit of nationalism which became the most potent political force in arousing Asia. Too often Indians were considered only as British customers, Indonesians as Dutch workers, or Vietnamese as potential Frenchmen in language and culture.

The Asian colonial areas themselves were treated as tails on the kites of the European mother countries; benefits from colonial policies which accrued to the Asians were incidental to the welfare of Europeans at home. Such advancements as cables, telegraph lines, steamship services and the opening of the Suez Canal (1869) only made the job of colonial administration more effective. Every country in Southeast Asia lagged far behind Japan, China, and even India in discovering its own psyche and asserting its claim to independence and equality in the modern world.

The Philippines

When Spain colonized the Philippines, the native people lived in *barrios* or villages, under a loose, but fairly crystalized form of government, the prime unit of which was the *barangay,* a group of fifty to one hundred families. Society was composed of three classes—serfs, freemen, and nobles—and distinct rules regulated the lives of the different classes. The Spanish superimposed a royal administration headed by a "governor and captain-general," assisted by an *audiencia* or supreme court, and a treasury official as direct representatives of the crown. Provinces, districts and municipalities were ruled over by inspectors or magistrates (*alcaldes mayores* or *corregidores*). They kept an eye on the tributes and revenues as reported by the *encomenderos* or lords of the feudal manors. They administered the police and the militia and were responsible for roads, bridges, and public works. The Spanish presence in the Philippines in the nineteenth century, including officials, priests, and soldiers, consisted of no more than five thousand persons at any given time.

Filipinos might have wished for more prosperity and more freedom, but they responded warmly to Spanish culture. Until 1821 they were administered through Mexico, a viceroyalty in the Spanish empire, and their links with Spain were by way of Mexico. After the Mexicans obtained their independence, the Filipinos were isolated. They remained so until the advent of the steamship provided fast and direct communication between Manila and Barcelona. They resented the venality and corruption of the Spanish colonial regime, and they often protested locally against the bad behavior of individual officials. Decent treatment by the local hierarchy often depended upon whether a reactionary king sat upon the throne of Spain or whether the mother country itself was in the throes of one of its recurring liberal revolutions.

Spanish economic policy was mercantilist, based on the assumption that the colony existed only for the welfare of Spain. When it was discovered that the Philippines possessed little wealth in spices, the Spanish turned to the possibilities of trade. They conceived the idea of making Manila the emporium of the orient. Teas from Ceylon, teak from Siam, velvets, silks, and brocades from China and spices smuggled in from the Indies were free-lanced into Manila (usually by Chinese) stacked high in the warehouses and loaded on the annual galleon which made the round trip between Manila and Acapulco. Mexican independence put an end to the galleon trade, and the beginning of *laissez faire,* or free enterprise, put an end to the entire system of lucrative government monopolies. Foreign companies entered the Philippines in spite of royal decrees against them. By 1842 a dozen foreign firms operated in Manila, and both the United States and Great Britain maintained consulates there.

Agriculture—rice, hemp, tobacco, sugar, indigo, coffee, coconuts, and hardwoods—formed the basic wealth of the Philippines. Some development took place as Spanish, and to a lesser extent British, put capital into mills and machinery and the government inaugurated a system of crop loans and credit facilities. Distribution and marketing of crops passed into the hands of Chinese who were master merchants, moneylenders, and bankers. Economic progress was substantial although it might have been much greater had the Spanish shown either the ability or the desire to take advantage of the wealth of the natural resources of the Philippines. Roads were laid out, an inter-island system of water transportation was created and harbor facilities were built in various ports. Steamships operated in and out of Manila after 1848, and a postal service was inaugurated in 1854. The Chartered Bank of India and the Hongkong and Shanghai Banking Corporation set up branches in the Philippines, and the predecessor of the Philippine National Bank began operations shortly after 1850. Before the end of the nineteenth century, Manila had a horse-drawn streetcar service, a railway north and south, telegraph, telephones and an international cable. The rich *illustrados* in the Philippines "lived in spacious stone houses, with pianos from Germany, carriages from England, and glassware from old Spain; they patronized music and the arts, read books and newspapers, and sent the most promising of their youth to Europe to complete their education."

Economic improvements brought improvements in social life. The Spanish did not consider the Indios (as they called the Filipinos) their equals; nevertheless, they intermarried, and their children (called Spanish mestizos) became the cream of local society. In 1849 all Filipinos were obliged to adopt Spanish family names. Sir John Bowring, the governor of Hong Kong, on a visit to the Philippines in 1859, wrote: "Generally speaking, I found a kind and generous urbanity prevailing—friendly intercourse where that intercourse had been sought—the lines of demarcation and separation between ranks and classes are less marked and impassable than in most oriental countries. I have seen at the same table, Spaniards, mestizos, and Indios—priests, civilians and soldiers." The Spanish added a rich cultural layer to Filipino civilization. By the end of the Spanish regime, the Philippines had more than two thousand public schools with a total enrollment of more than 200,000. Compared to their neighbors in Southeast Asia, Filipinos enjoyed a high degree of literacy.

Spain tried to prevent the entry and spread of dangerous thoughts, but it was impossible. The first daily newspaper, *La Esperanza*, was established in 1846. The heresies of the French Revolution found their way into the Philippines, often by way of sailors who had time to read and think during the long journey from Europe. Sons of the best families were infected by the virus of liberalism while pursuing their studies in Spain or France. In 1889 another paper, *La Solidaridad,* was founded in Barcelona which throughout its six-year life urged reforms both in religion and government. *La Solidaridad* was an excellent outlet for fervent young writers, prominent among whom was the brilliant Chinese mestizo, the foremost hero of the Philippines, José Rizal y Mercado.

Nationalism sprouted early in the Philippines. The innate Filipino bonds of kinship were strengthened by the language, religion, and centralized political administration provided by Spain. However, protest against domination was as old as domination itself, and a Spanish governor wrote as early as 1765 "they (the Indios) have a universal desire to be free; they are our vassals only because we are strong." Hundreds of isolated revolts began to take on an islands-wide character after the revolution of 1858 in Spain gave Filipinos a taste of liberal reforms. The restoration of royal power in Spain did not put an immediate stop to incessant Filipino demands for recognition of what they believed to be their rights.

On the night of January 20, 1872, about two hundred Filipino soldiers and workers in the Cavite arsenal protested because debatable deductions were taken out of their pay envelopes. The affair was interpreted as a revolt against Spanish rule, fomented by native priests and rebellious leaders. Three Filipino priests—Fathers Burgos, Gomez, and Zamora— were among those put to death for their part in the mutiny; and their martyrdom stirred a deeper dislike, or possibly hatred, of Spanish civil government than had ever existed before. A generation of middle-class intellectuals, headed by such distinguished men as José Rizal, Marcelo del Pilar, the Luna brothers—Antonio and Juan—Mariano Ponce and Graciano Lopez Jaena, voiced their protest against evil practices of the Spanish regime. Some fled to Europe, others to Hong Kong or Singapore where they conducted a publicity crusade usually known as the propaganda movement, which lasted for twenty years. They wanted reforms, not independence, and their aims included equality between Spaniards and Filipinos in the eyes of the law, restoration of Filipino representation in the Spanish Cortes, Filipinization of the clergy, and individual liberties, such as freedom of speech, freedom of the press, and freedom to meet and petition for redress of grievances.

Dr. José Rizal—linguist, poet, sculptor, surgeon, and novelist—was the most brilliant of the propagandists and he published two novels of bitter protest which were entitled *Noli Me Tangere* (translated originally under the title *Social Cancer* and later as *The Lost Eden*) and *El Filibusterismo* (translated as *The Reign of Greed* or *The Subversive*). In the same way in which *Uncle Tom's Cabin* inspired another people in another age, these novels crystallized the anti-Spanish sentiments of the Filipinos and galvanized a long-suffering people into action. Rizal himself was a writer and philosopher, not an organizer. His friends founded *La Liga Filipina* in 1892 dedicated to peaceful reforms. A few days after its establishment, Dr. Rizal was arrested and jailed at Fort Santiago. He was then deported to Dapitan, a lonely Spanish outpost in Mindanao, and with his deportation *La Liga Filipina* died out. The propagandist movement also ceased for lack of funds.

The death of reform was the birth of revolution. On the night of July 7, 1892, when Rizal was banished to Dapitan, Andres Bonifacio and two of his fire-breathing friends founded a new society called the Katipunan or "Supreme Worshipful Association of the Sons of the People." The Katipunan had two aims: to unite Filipinos into one solid nation and to win Philippine independence by means of revolution. Membership was extended throughout the islands, and any person who wished to join was subjected to initiation rites resembling those of Masonry. Secret but unsuccessful efforts were made to win the approval of Rizal and the assistance of Japan, which had "always been friendly to the Filipino people." The Katipunan was discovered by the Spanish authorities on August 19, 1896, and its members fled to the hills. At a mass meeting a week later a thousand Filipinos tore up their cedulas or tax receipts and shouted the "Cry of Balintawak" or "Long Live Independence." The Philippines was in armed revolt and was not deterred by a reign of terror. At dawn on December 30, 1896, Dr. Rizal was executed by a Spanish firing squad on the Luneta, the great public park and parade ground in Manila.

Rizal's death gave the revolutionists new inspiration. For a year they fought in practically every important island of the Philippines. General Aguinaldo became the hero of the masses because of his military successes. Differences between the leaders on the future of the revolution led to the court martial and execution of Bonifacio and contributed to a truce between Spanish and Filipinos. By the truce agreement of December 15, 1897, which is known as the Pact of Biaknobato, general amnesty was extended to insurgents if they would lay down their arms. Money was to be paid to the leaders, who were to go into voluntary exile. Aguinaldo left for Hong Kong on December 27, 1897. He returned to the Philippines on May 19, 1898, as the guest of Admiral Dewey, three weeks after the Battle of Manila Bay. *Before* Spanish sovereignty was surrendered to the United States by the Treaty of Paris on December 10, 1898, Aguinaldo and his compatriots wrote their own ending to the story of Spain in the Philippines. While the Americans waited for re-enforcements to occupy Manila, Aguinaldo established himself as the head of a temporary dictatorship at Cavite. On June 12, 1898, he proclaimed the independence of the Philippines, which was of course not recognized by the United States. A declaration of independence on the American model was signed by ninety-eight persons including one American (Colonel L. M. Johnson of the Artillery), and a Filipino national flag was unfurled. For the first time the Filipino national anthem was played. On June 23, 1898, the dictatorship was replaced by a revolutionary government with Aguinaldo as president. After the occupation of Manila by the Americans on August 13, 1898, and the widening rifts between Americans and Filipinos, the Philippine revolutionary government moved its headquarters to Malolos, Bulacan, outside Manila. On September 29, 1898, the Malolos government ratified the earlier declaration of independence and on November 29 it adopted a constitution for the first Philippine Republic. To patriotic Filipinos, this republic was a fully sovereign government of Filipinos by Filipinos; to the new American rulers of the Philippines, however, the Malolos republic was a regime of bandits. For three years, Americans fought what they called a war to suppress the insurgents. In the Filipino view their "gallant but hopeless struggle" was in reality a war to preserve the independence which they had won from Spain.

The Netherlands East Indies

Throughout the nineteenth century, Dutch colonial attention was concentrated on the island of Java, although the produce of the tropical islands was welcomed by the Dutch wherever they could find it. The Dutch system of indirect rule meant that native chieftains looked after native affairs and European agents concerned themselves in matters affecting the company. The Europeans were enjoined to deal with local officials as elder and younger brothers and to protect the common man against all arbitrary treatment. They were to act more as fathers studying the welfare of their families than rulers governing their subjects. Because so many regents were in the habit of selling or leasing their lands to local Chinese (and thus depriving the company of income) the Dutch prohibited further alienation of native land to foreigners.

These characteristics of Dutch colonial policy disappeared with the Napoleonic Wars. The Netherlands itself was for twenty years a satellite of France, and as such was dragged into wars in the eastern seas. The Dutch lost their commerce, their fleet, and even their possessions. Java was occupied—not because the British wanted the territory but because they wanted the stronghold against the French—and Stamford Raffles was sent by the East India Company from Calcutta as the lieutenant governor of the island. Raffles never doubted the basic iniquity of the Dutch; and he felt that the benighted population of the Dutch colony was entitled to the blessings of English law, economic freedom, and British colonial wisdom. Raffles looked beyond humanitarianism in advocating better treatment for Javanese; he wanted them to prosper so they could become better customers for the cheap goods of British mills.

In 1811 Raffles moved into Java with a new broom. His ideology was that the end of colonial administration should be first the welfare of the native people, secondly the profit of company. He abolished the old Dutch requirements of contingencies and forced deliveries (except in coffee and teak) and put an end to feudal bondage. He introduced the familiar Indian system of taxes based on the value of the land. Assessments were made against the *desas,* or villages, not against individuals, and they amounted to about forty percent of the crop. He operated on the theory that the government was the owner of the land, and the villages were charged for permission to use it. As in India, he tried to give the villages a sense of the proprietorship in the belief that this would generate more economic freedom and at the same time produce more revenue for the government. He substituted British-style direct rule for Dutch-style indirect rule. He sidetracked the regents and sultans and appointed collectors, magistrates, and judges who introduced British procedures, including trial by jury. He sent collectors into the villages to collect assessments directly from village headmen; he had no further use for regents or sultans as go-betweens.

In contrast to the Dutch, he wasted no sentimentality on native customs and institutions. He abolished slavery and made opium-trading a government monopoly. He paid salaries to native officials and forbade them to engage in trade on their own account. He prohibited headmen from hiring out the labor of villagers on any pretext whatever. He was convinced of the superiority of British regulations, and he rushed to make changes which he believed would work for the ultimate good of the masses. In his zeal for commercial reform, he interested himself in cultural matters. His great fault was that his ideas were too expensive and he could not make Java pay. The company disavowed his policies and ordered him home in 1816.

After the defeat of Napoleon, the British decided to rebuild Dutch power in order to keep the Netherlands out of the French orbit. A treaty agreement in 1824 gave the Indies back to the Dutch in exchange for Dutch recognition of British claims on the Malay peninsula. The Dutch were weakened by twenty years of military domination by the French and in no position to resume an effective policy when they returned to their colonies. The king founded a royal trading company and the Java Bank, and his government took the lead in economic development. Governor-General Van den Bosch in 1830 introduced the culture system, according to which the native people would pay in crops and contribute their labor instead of cash payment of taxes. Villages were ordered to set aside one-fifth of their land for the "culture" of export crops, and heads of families were forced to provide the government with sixty-six work days as their annual quota. The government first planted sugar and indigo, then coffee, tea, tobacco, pepper, cinnamon, cotton, and cochineal. Authority was restored to the regents who were responsible for providing the peasant labor for the government plantations or for public works. Contracts were often made with Chinese or Europeans to receive the crops and to process them for export.

The culture system was only one aspect of a comprehensive plan to encourage banking, shipping, and manufacturing as well as commercial agriculture. The whole of Java became one huge estate enterprise. Profits flowed back to the Netherlands, but individual peasants were only driven to harder work by headmen, sultans, chiefs, and regents who were puppets or willing allies of the Dutch administration. As an aftermath of the mid-nineteenth century wave of liberalism in Europe, the Dutch took their Indies out of the hands of the autocratic Crown and made them the responsibility of the cabinet and the more enlightened states-general. Liberal spirits in the Netherlands, particularly a famous playwright, Edward Douwes Decker, who under the pseudonym of *Multa Tuli* wrote a biting novel called *Max Havelaar,* protested against the abuses of the culture system.

Private capitalists for reasons of their own in the Netherlands joined the chorus of condemnation of the government. Private business wanted the profits which had accrued to the government. Together political liberals and the champions of free enterprise put through the Agricultural Law of 1870. The forced culture of crops for export was gradually abandoned, and so was the institution of forced labor. Private planters took over plantations previously operated by the government, but businessmen were less solicitous than the government toward native welfare. The Dutch development of the Indies became a prime example of capitalistic exploitation. On the positive side, Dutch enterprise brought to the Indies higher levels of living by constructing irrigation systems, roads, railways, telegraphs, and an inter-island shipping network.

When the government turned over economic development to private enterprise, its officials became civil servants rather than part-time businessmen. They spent more time looking after the interests of the native workers and often took their side in arguments against Dutch entrepreneur. They enforced the law that native people could not alienate their land. Dutch planters could get long-term leases on waste lands or could negotiate annual leases with villages; but neither Dutch nor Chinese could take land away from the natives by sale, trade, or any legal subterfuge whatever. The Dutch officials treated the villages as something sacred; they studied the adat, or local customary law, and applied it wherever possible.

The Dutch policies accentuated the cleavages in a plural society. In the economic field the growth and operation of foreign-owned enterprises took place apart from the continuing native economic system. Plantations and factories contributed to the export market, but they scarcely affected the native subsistence economy. Chinese, and to a lesser extent the Arabs, flourished under the Dutch. The Chinese varied in class status and wealth from the poor laborers, through middle-class shopkeepers, artisans, craftsmen, and moneylenders, to the wealthiest traders and bankers who operated on an international scale. In the Indies, as elsewhere in Southeast Asia, the Chinese (without any help or even notice from their home government) achieved a somewhat alarming position of economic power. The native population increased from 4,000,000 in 1800 to 28,000,-000 in 1900, thanks to Dutch law, order, and medical services; and it enjoyed an undeniable prosperity. On the other hand, it experienced hardships, even hunger. An Indonesian patriot, Soetan Sjahrir, wrote, "My country lost its freedom—and fell from its ancient proud place to that of a weak, dejected colony."

His observation does not paint a complete picture, but at the very least, the protective attitudes of the Dutch did not prepare Indonesians for the shock of contacts with the dynamic Western world. As a famous British writer, J. S. Furnivall, declared: "The gentle pressure of the Dutch was difficult to reconcile with liberty and law. The Dutch in coddling the Javanese made it difficult for them to stand alone. They were treated as children who never grew up. A villager cannot scratch his head unless a district officer gives him permission and an expert shows him how to do it." The Dutch guaranteed complete freedom of worship, encouraged the use of native languages, and stimulated native arts and crafts. They kept intact the mind and soul of the peoples of Indonesia.

However, the Dutch imperial masters were foreign and therefore subject to opposition no matter how capable or well-intentioned. From 1825 to 1830 they were faced with the Java Wars, occasioned by Dipo Negoro, an aggrieved warrior who was passed over in his claim to the sultanate. For five years he kept parts of Java in turmoil. He was eventually caught and banished to Menado where he died. Expansion of the Dutch administration system from Java to the outer islands was slow and often marked by bitter and bloody fighting. The Dutch completed the conquest of Bali by 1850 and shortly thereafter annexed the "tin" island of Billiton. The Moluccas and Lesser Sundas were scenes of ceaseless and indecisive campaigns against pirates, smugglers, and slave traders. Through two decades, from 1850 to 1870, the Dutch launched pacification expeditions to the Celebes and Borneo (where the British were embarrassingly active). Sumatra was a perpetual battlefield, never completely immune from the risks of an Arab "holy war." It was well into the twentieth century before the Dutch could feel that they had pacified the archipelago and brought the hundreds of self-governing states under their political control. But the sentiment of nationalism was very slow in coming to Indonesia. Before 1900 nothing more than moderate and intellectual protests were heard on the part of Indonesians against the Dutch policies of "unhurried adjustment" to modern needs in education and democratic institutions. A single tragic voice of a beautiful high-born princess, Raden Adjeng Kartini (1879–1904), who was destined to die in childbirth, sounded the call for the emancipation of Indonesian women.

BURMA

Burma attracted the British as the Indies attracted the Dutch. Burma borders on India and controls the western end of mountain passes which lead into southwest China. Burma was off the beaten path to the Spice Islands, but its ports and ship-repair facilities were coveted by both England and France in their wars and diplomatic rivalries. The Burmese people sprang to new life under their aggressive king, Alaungpaya, who defeated his rivals, the Mons, and waged constant wars against his neighbors in Siam and India during his reign, 1753–1760. A son of Alaungpaya who was a "child in his ideas, a tyrant in his principles and a madman in his actions," became the terror of Southeast Asia. He burned Ayuthia, the Siamese capital, in 1767, rolled back invading Chinese armies, and ravaged his neighbors. The ambitions of his successors led to banditry, bankruptcy and, in 1824, war with the English East India Company, the sovereign power in India. In defeating the Burmese, the British employed 40,000 men, of whom 15,000 died of dysentery and fever. A treaty was signed at Yandabo, near Mandalay, on February 24, 1826, which permitted the Burmese to retain their seaports, Rangoon, Martaban, and Bassein, but which ceded to the British the coastal provinces of Arakan and Tenasserim (Lower Burma) and the frontier province of Assam. The Burmese agreed to pay an indemnity and to exchange diplomatic representatives with the English company.

British diplomats—or residents—lost their health and very nearly their minds in dealing with kings who were whimsical, cruel, and even insane. British in Mandalay endured the same kinds of indignities which other British subjects encountered at the same time in Canton. A climax of studied incivility occurred in 1852 when Burmese officialdom kept a British naval mission waiting for hours in a blistering sun. To avenge the insult, a "combustible commodore" destroyed Burmese shipping in the harbor and razed the fortifications on the shore. It was dangerous then to twist the lion's tail. Lord Dalhousie in India felt that "the government of India could never consistently with its own safety permit itself to stand for a single day in an attitude of inferiority towards a native power, and least of all towards the Court of Ava."

England launched a second war against Burma in 1852. The British took Rangoon, occupied Martaban, and proclaimed the annexation of Pegu. The Burmese did not show up to fight because of a rebellion and civil war to choose a new king. The British established *de facto* control in the area and in 1862 amalgamated Arakan, Tenasserim, and Pegu to form the province of British Burma with Rangoon as the capital. Because of Burmese attitudes of distrust and hostility, economic progress was slow-going. The British undertook immediately the cultivation of rice on a commercial scale in the delta lands of the Irrawaddy and sought to develop trade between Lower and Upper Burma. The British were permitted to navigate the full length of the river and to station a British agent in Mandalay. Tariffs were eliminated on river traffic. By a treaty of 1867 —which is reminiscent of the unequal treaties between England and China—the king of Burma agreed with the British to abandon all monopolies except in rubies, petroleum, and timber; to reduce tariffs on imports to five percent; and to recognize the British privilege of extraterritoriality. Burma also told the British they could station an agent at Bhamo and survey the mountain route into China. It was while making plans for the China end of this survey that the British consular official, Augustus Margary, was killed; it was this route which became famous as the Burma Road in World War II.

In 1878 the old king of Burma died without designating which of his forty-eight sons should succeed him. The succession went to Kipling's immortal Thibaw and his domineering queen, Supiyalat. The king was plagued by banditry and rebellions. He needed arms and assistance; but he refused to rely exclusively on the British, who treated him as an ordinary Indian vassal. He even declined to grant audiences to British officials who considered it below their station to take off their shoes in his presence, as was required by Burmese custom. Thibaw tried to play off the French against the British; and the French showed willingness to help Thibaw in exchange for management of the royal monopolies (including the ruby mines) and for concessions for railways, river steamers, banks, and the construction of a highway across Laos into Tonkin. The British sensed Thibaw's game and sent him an ultimatum, ordering him to put all his foreign relations exclusively in British hands. Thibaw replied, "Friendly relations with France, Italy and other states have been, are being and will be maintained."

England declared war on Burma for a third time in 1885. Within two weeks British armies were on the march up the road to Mandalay. Thibaw surrendered, and Upper Burma was added to British India. Thibaw's army retreated into the jungle and fought guerilla action for five years in the same manner as Filipino insurgents later fought against the Americans in the Philippines.

With the completion of political control over Burma, the British imposed the administrative system which they had developed in India. Burma was placed under the direct rule of a chief commissioner located in Rangoon and subject to the government of India. The former king of Burma was displaced, and his ministers and councilors were given honorific jobs as advisers. The British retained the main divisions of the country into provinces, townships, circles (groups of villages), and villages, and they introduced the principles and practices of the Indian civil service. Government on the provincial level was entrusted to European assistant or deputy commissioners who acted as judges, magistrates, and revenue collectors. They were instructed to introduce wherever possible the principles of British liberalism—economic freedom, the rule of law, equality before the law, and the welfare of the governed. At local levels, the Burmese system of hereditary district chiefs and village headmen was preserved, except that local officials became employees of the British, and consequently agents of direct British rule. They were paid fixed salaries and deprived of most of their opportunities to squeeze or oppress the common people.

Economically, the British established internal peace and gave the Burmese better opportunities for prosperity. Upper Burma increased its production of rice, sugar cane, vegetables for oil, corn, cotton, and beans. A small amount of British capital entered Burma to develop the Irrawaddy Flotilla Company, mines, petroleum refineries, and a respectable railway system with main service between Rangoon and Mandalay. The most spectacular economic achievement was the conversion of the hot and steamy mouth of the Irrawaddy into the greatest rice granary in the world. This was not an unmixed blessing from the standpoint of Burma. Under British freedom of enterprise, Indians of the chettyar caste took advantage of easygoing Burmese financial habits to acquire title to most of the ricelands. Cheap Indian labor was imported to compete against the debt-ridden landless Burmese tenants—and these same Indian workers took over the Burmese jobs on the docks and wharves at the waterfront. Indians also proved most successful in becoming doctors, lawyers, engineers, teachers, and subordinate administrators in the civil service. What was left by Indians usually went into the control of the Chinese. As elsewhere in Southeast Asia, the Chinese dominated the arts, crafts, retail stores, rice-milling, and service functions in the national economy. After the British, the Indians, and the Chinese drained off their respective shares of the profits in national prosperity, little remained for the Burmese. And that little was for a favored few and not for the masses.

In contrast to the Dutch in the Indies, the British in Burma did not hesitate to effect changes in life at the rice-roots. Local customs were honored, but not sanctified as they were in Java. Tax procedures were modernized and harsh clauses were removed from the penal code. Burmese justice was forced increasingly into a British mold, and Burmese officials were obliged to live up to British standards. The British did not hesitate to shake some of the pillars of the old order, particularly in the fields of religion and education. In traditional Burma, religious institutions were essential to preserve stability in the midst of political chaos. Buddhism, with its temples, shrines, monasteries, and pagodas, was the center of daily life and social activity. The priests monopolized education and gave Burma a high degree of literacy. Monks occupied a special place in the community, and they were not subject to secular discipline unless they were first unfrocked. But with the coming of the British, law took the place of custom. Monks lost their prestige, and according to J. S. Furnivall, one of the closest students of Burma, they "tended to become an ignorant, disorderly class, preaching sedition and creating unrest." The Buddhists lost their monopoly on education as government schools were created and as Christian mission schools came along with the British administration. By 1900 the government afforded primary education in thousands of schools, and the English language enjoyed the same prestige position in Burma which it enjoyed in India.

Nationalism was perhaps slower in developing in Burma than either in India or the Indies. It was a twentieth-century product. But Burma was far from a hothouse for the preservation of a colorful but outmoded civilization. Its institutions were altered deliberately, and Burma was to a limited extent prepared to cope with the profound revolutionary movements in store. In 1900 it was scarcely aware of the inequities of its international position, but once awakened, it was ready for rapid and drastic action.

MALAYA

The patterns of Burma were repeated in Malaya. The Malay Peninsula consisted of petty states made up of palm-thatched huts built on stilts along the seacoasts or river banks. Three-quarters of the area was covered by forests and impenetrable jungles. There were no roads, public buildings, schools, or courts of law. The states were ruled by sultans or rajahs, often dominated by astrologers, and assisted by territorial and tribal chiefs. Actual administration was usually in the hands of a prime minister and was carried out by chamberlains, chiefs of police, secretaries, treasurers, and port officers. The states had no fixed policies except to collect as many taxes as possible for the splendor of the sultans. No armies were maintained except of swashbucklers and mercenaries, and no money was spent on public works or education. The matrilineal tribal chiefs were responsible for settling land disputes, inheritance problems, debts, and all minor crimes. They exercised police and judicial authority and collected taxes and tribute, keeping an undetermined amount for themselves. The laws which they administered were "tissues of barbarities, inconsistencies and class favoritism."

Until 1867 British interests were confined to the Straits Settlements of Singapore, Malacca, Penang, and Province Wellesley, which were administered by the India office. In that year the Straits Settlements were organized into a crown colony and transferred to the colonial office. At the same time the British began to take official notice of the malignant disorders in the neighboring upcountry states where rival claimants to thrones fought and feuded and Chinese tin miners indulged in incessant tong wars. In 1873 the governor of the Straits Settlements was charged "to rescue, if possible, their fertile and productive countries from the ruin which must befall them if the present disorders continue unchecked."

After 1874 one ruler after another was persuaded to enter into a treaty accepting a British Resident, whose advice *must* be asked and followed in all matters save Malay custom and the Moslem religion. The British in exchange established domestic tranquillity, maintained the sultan in his position, provided him with a steady income, and protected his state against all external dangers. British residents came to the Malay states filled with the same liberalism and the same general administrative ideas which motivated the Indian civil service. They set out to modernize government and to transfer administration from "interested amateurs to disinterested specialists." They conceived their main tasks to be the establishment of security for life and limb; the construction of a system of communications which would weld the isolated districts into a homogeneous state; the protection of civil rights, particularly for Chinese and Indian immigrants; the collection of revenues on a just and equitable basis; and the devotion of public expenditures to the public welfare. Each resident set up a state council, with all legislative and executive authority, which consisted of the resident, the sultan, Chinese merchants, and the leading local chiefs. Reforms, such as the abolition of slavery, cruel punishments and exorbitant and arbitrary taxes, were insisted upon. All revenues were collected, appointments made, and political actions taken, in the name of the sultan. The councils dealt with all matters which might come to the attention of the state: land laws, revenues, punishment of rioters, trespass by buffaloes, elephant-trapping, compulsory vaccination, irrigation, forest conservation, or the construction of railways. The tribal chiefs were made loyal supporters of the British administration by making them government officers and by giving them subsidies and allowances to compensate for their loss of feudal dues and taxes.

In 1896 the four states of Perak, Selangor, Negri Sembilan, and Pahang were joined into the Federated Malay States under the protection of a British resident general at Kuala Lumpur. This federation scheme was a compromise between annexation and abandonment. The sultans retained the prerogatives of sovereignty but received British protection, together with larger incomes and enhanced pomp and ceremony. Without interference from the sultans, the British were enabled to develop uniformity in matters of justice, taxation, and land settlement. Each state in the federation retained its financial autonomy, and each kept its own resident. However, the states gradually lost their power and prestige as the central organization began to think and act on a country-wide scale. The resident general had no executive council; but his staff included a legal adviser, secretary for Chinese affairs, financial commissioner, judicial commissioner, and superintendent of police and public works. The sultans were progressively pushed further into the background, with constantly increasing ceremony and ever-diminishing authority.

Under British law and order, both the Straits Settlements and the Federated Malay States made spectacular economic progress. The Malay peasants and fishermen were given new protection in their traditional activities of farming and fishing. The banner of free trade meant little to Malays, but it accelerated the immigration of Chinese miners and merchants, together with Indian moneylenders, professional leaders, plantation and harbor workers. Singapore grew into one of the ten greatest ports in the world, and a further boom was in store with the demands of the automobile industry for rubber and tin.

Malaya's most baffling social problem stemmed from the tensions inherent in its plural society. Three races lived in comparative harmony, but their differences called for a strong hand at the political controls of the state. The Malays felt that they had an inherent right to the country and that the Chinese and Indians were unwelcome immigrants. The Malays were an easygoing people who lacked business acumen. They enjoyed spending too much, even at the cost of going in debt to Chinese or Indian usurers. They resented the business success of the Chinese, and they despised Chinese social and dietary (pig-eating) habits. Malay Moslems showed no tolerance for Chinese Confucian concepts. Clearly the Malays were no match politically or economically for the Chinese, so the British felt obliged to favor the Malays at the expense of the Chinese. Malays were given the best educational opportunities, and Malays were the only local inhabitants admitted to jobs in the administrative services of the states or the federation. Understandably the Malays were prone to support, and the Chinese to criticize, the British administration.

Privately the Chinese looked upon the Malays with a slight contempt. Their lives were different. Most Chinese came to Malaya to make money and to return home. They had little patience with the lazy Malays, and they frowned upon racial intermarriage. They kept their feelings to themselves because British rule remained reasonably impartial. "While the British held the cow, the Chinese milked it." The Chinese established schools where their children could be educated in the Chinese language and made acquainted with Chinese culture.

The Indians, mostly Tamils from southern India or Singhalese from Ceylon, were less numerous than either Malays or Chinese. They depended more than either of the other two groups on the justice and firmness of the British colonial administration. The Indians were looked down upon as inferiors by both Chinese and Malays, and without British protection they could easily have become a submerged class. In the nineteenth century, Indians came to Malaya usually for a short while, stayed to themselves on the rubber plantations or near the docks, and returned home as soon as they saved some money.

Both the Federated Malay States and the Straits Settlements appeared in 1900 to be exhibits to support Sir Richard Winstedt's contention that "the British Empire is the greatest international good known to mankind." Singapore was prosperous. It was paradoxical that a large amount of the best property had gone to the British or to the "Queen's Chinese," that commerce and industry were largely in the hands of aliens, and that an unbridgeable gap divided the very rich and the indescribably poor. On the surface political conditions appeared tranquil. However, British parks, theaters, courts of law, sporting grounds, clubs, hospitals, and public buildings represented a superstructure which was not firmly welded to the native foundation. Churches, schools, public libraries, and even such organizations as the famed Raffles Institute, dedicated to the "cultivation of languages of Siam, China and the Malay Archipelago and the improvement of moral and intellectual conditions of the inhabitants of those countries," could not prevent the later appearance of the latent force of nationalism.

At this point in the Malay story, attention should be directed toward the activities of the British in Borneo. Steam traffic to the Far East focused attention on the possibility of a port in Borneo as a coaling station between Singapore and Shanghai. The adventurous "White Rajah," James Brooke, was made sovereign of Sarawak in 1841 as a reward for helping the sultan of Brunei put down a local rebellion. He expelled pirates, restored peaceful conditions, and invited Chinese to come to develop his domain. In 1846 Labuan Island was made a British crown colony, and the next year the sultan of Brunei entered into a treaty of friendship giving extraordinary rights to the British in his kingdom. A modest trade in tropical products was developed, and in 1881 the British North Borneo Company was organized. The company obtained sovereign rights over part of the territory of Brunei, and its holdings were shortly converted into a British protectorate. Brunei ceded further territory to Sarawak and British North Borneo and became a mere rump of its former self. In 1906 the sultan agreed to accept a British resident and it was administered like one of the Malay states. The discovery of oil made the cntire North Borneo region extremely desirable to the British in Malaya and to the Dutch in the Indies.

FRENCH INDOCHINA

During the nineteenth century, the French were as active in expanding their power as either the Dutch or the British. But with a marked difference. In France, the affairs of Asia were left to the king and church, while in England and the Netherlands the overseas empire provided the bread and butter for a substantial portion of the population. Indochina was more a matter of prestige than of national prosperity.

In Indochina, France encountered the vestiges of the ancient empire of the Chams, which nursed a precarious independence after more than a millennium under China. In 1802 the King of Annam had assumed the title of emperor of Vietnam, and his dominion was organized into three main divisions. His throne was in central Annam, at Hué; his northern territories of Tonkin were centered around Hanoi; and his southern provinces were called Cochin China, around Saigon. On paper his country appeared as a logically organized, well-run imitation of China. In fact, according to D. G. E. Hall: "The wheels of administration were warped or no longer existed, the cadres of officials were empty, the hierarchy was destroyed, taxes were not being collected, lists of communal property had disappeared, proprietary titles were lost, fields abandoned; roads, bridges and public granaries had not been maintained; work in the mines had ceased. The administration of justice had been interrupted, every province was a prey to pirates; violations of law went unpunished, while even the law itself had become uncertain."

The emperor of Vietnam forgot the obligations of his ancestors to the French and turned against French missionaries and local converts with measures of persecution. He broke up Christian families, burned down Christian villages, branded cheeks with the mark of infidel, and caused the murder of French and Spanish missionaries. After the French recovered from the humiliation and the exhaustion of the Napoleonic Wars, they turned again to East Asia for a place of prestige and political advantage. They considered Basilan Island between Borneo and the Philippines or the Chusan Archipelago off the China coast near Shanghai. The events of Indochina gave the French the reason they needed to concentrate in that area. While the French fleet was occupied primarily in fighting side-by-side with the British in the war against China, sufficient French naval strength became available to occupy Saigon. On June 5, 1862, France obtained from the man who was king of Annam and emperor of Vietnam a treaty which ceded three of his provinces in Cochin China, including Saigon, to France. He also promised that he would never alienate any part of his possessions—north, south or central—to any other power than France. In 1867 the French obtained the remaining provinces of Cochin China; the control of Saigon and the Mekong Delta was theirs.

The French looked upon Saigon primarily as an entryway up the Mekong Valley to China. The first upriver port of consequence is Phnom Penh, Cambodia, so the immediate task was to obtain a political footing there. Cambodia was but a pale shadow of the ancient grandeur of the Khmers, and it was a joint protectorate of Siam and Annam. A new king—King Norodom—won his way to the throne in 1862. In return for French support against his Siamese-backed rival, he agreed to accept French protection. By a treaty which neither Siam nor Annam could prevent, France recognized Cambodian independence from Siam. In return Cambodia admitted French consuls and French trade and agreed to receive a French resident at Phnom Penh who would have the rank of a grand mandarin.

As French expeditions pushed upstream, they quickly discovered that rapids made the Mekong approach to China commercially impossible. Attention shifted to Tonkin—the northern part of the possessions of the king of Annam—where the Red River offered an alternative route to China, by way of Hanoi and Yunnan. Further French designs were halted by the Franco-Prussian War, but as soon as hostilities ended in Europe, the French renewed their efforts against the Annamese sovereign. The hapless king was at the mercy of the French because of the loss of his rich rice basket of Cochin China. A treaty between France and Annam in 1874 reaffirmed French sovereignty over Cochin China, permitted a French resident at Hué, opened Hanoi to trade, gave the French the right to develop the Red River route from Hanoi to Yunnan, promised freedom and protection to Catholic missionaries, and gave extraterritorial rights to French subjects.

Since Annam paid tribute to China, and because the king of

Annam sought hopefully to employ his Chinese connection against France, the Chinese emperor protested against French encroachments. He was in no position to intervene effectively on behalf of his Annamese vassal. Constant skirmishes took place between French and Chinese troops, and the French appetite seemed to grow with the eating. By further treaties in 1883 and 1884 between France and Annam, Annam agreed to become a protectorate of France, to surrender the administrative responsibility for Tonkin to France, and to accept French residents at both Hué and Hanoi. As the French pushed on toward the Chinese border, a war ensued between France and China. The French attacked Keelung in Formosa, occupied the Pescadores, and took over the port of Foochow in Fukien Province. Two war-weary nations concluded the Treaty of Tientsin on June 9, 1885, by which China renounced its rights over Annam and Tonkin, recognized the French protectorate over Annam, and granted the French the right to build a railroad to parallel the Red River Valley. This marked the departure officially of China from the scene in Indochina; the future was in the hands of France and Annam alone. Jules Ferry, "Le Tonkinois," stated the extreme French position: "It is not a question of tomorrow, but of the future of fifty or a hundred years; of that which will be the inheritance of our children, the bread of our workers. It is not a question of conquering China, but it is necessary to be at the portal of this region in order to undertake the pacific conquest of it."

For the next five years, the French encountered guerrilla warfare and were forced to consolidate their position. In 1887 they amalgamated their colony (Cochin China) and their protectorates over Annam, Tonkin and Cambodia into the union of Indochina. Before that date no such thing as Indochina existed except as a geographical expression. A centralized administration was established under a governor-general, but each constituent member of the union retained its essential autonomy. Cochin China was placed under a lieutenant governor who took all responsibility for the direct rule of the colony. A resident general was appointed for Annam and Tonkin with subordinate *"residents particuliers"* for each protectorate. A resident general was continued in Cambodia. The local emperor and his staff were retained for a system of indirect rule in Annam and Tonkin; and the king of Cambodia was relied upon for the façade of government there. The French civil service in Indochina never attained the high standards of the British or the Dutch, so Indochina was largely administered by the "mandarins" or the native elite. As elsewhere in Southeast Asia, the masses had practically no voice in government or in decision-making for their own welfare. In 1899 Laos was made a protectorate of France and placed under a *resident superieur* in the administrative capital of Vientiane.

The French brought substantial economic improvement to Indochina. Saigon and Hanoi were made into attractive cities, with broad avenues and imposing public buildings. The French monopolized shipping, trade, and banking. They were more interested in satisfying the needs of French industry than in promoting the development of their overseas empire. French money was invested in rubber, tea, and coffee and in railways, highways, and mines. Enormous sums were devoted to irrigation and drainage for rice cultivation, but food production lagged behind a rapidly increasing population. Levels of living for the masses remained pathetically low. The Annamese were as helpless in coping with Chinese competition as native inhabitants elsewhere. Chinese bought up lands and acquired a monopoly on the milling and export of rice. They controlled sawmills and sugar refineries; they supplied labor for the plantations, mines, railways, and public services. All the local arts and crafts were in the hands of Chinese. Next to Singapore, the city of Cholon (a suburb of Saigon) became the most flourishing Chinese center in Southeast Asia.

French rule rested lightly on Indochina. The French naturally insisted upon firm control of fiscal matters, defense and foreign affairs, but they kept hands off/local customs so far as compatible with their larger interests. They abolished slavery and such cruel punishments as trampling to death by elephants. They did not interfere with ordinary life in the autonomous villages, and they made no fetish of the general welfare. The ideals of the French Revolution were not applied to Indochina. Schools and institutes were established for the elite. The mandarins became imbued with French culture and enamored with the French language, no matter how much they resented French political domination. Missionaries spread the Catholic faith throughout Indochina, along with its schools, hospitals, and tradition of social service. By the end of the nineteenth century France seemed to inspire as little native opposition as any imperial power in Asia, and it appeared to be most immune to the challenge of nationalism.

SIAM

The Chakri dynasty, which was established in 1782, inherited a century-old policy of isolation, but the barriers disappeared as pressures increased from England and France. Siam had demonstrated its ability to stand up against Burma, Malaya, and warring tribes and kingdoms in Indochina, and it had proved itself a worthy negotiator in preserving its independence from the mighty empire of neighboring China. With the entry of England and France into Southeast Asia, Siam was confronted with a new type of international relations. Treaties were signed with England in 1826 and with the United States in 1833 which granted those nations very limited trading rights.

Only four kings occupied the throne of Siam between 1809 and 1910, and the most distinguished of these were Mongkut (1851–1868) and his famous son Chulalongkorn (1868–1910). Mongkut was a Buddhist monk for twenty-seven years before he became king. During that period he gained a profound knowledge of religion and philosophy, and he became friendly with a few Western missionaries. From them he learned English, French, and Latin and much about the history, politics, and science of Europe and America. He determined to open Siam to Western influence. In 1855, shortly after Perry's ships steamed into the harbor at Yokohama and on the eve of the second war between Great Britain and China, King Mongkut of his own free will concluded a commercial treaty with Sir John Bowring, the representative of England. This treaty gave the British the right to trade freely in all Siamese seaports, to live permanently in Bangkok, to purchase and rent property in and near Bangkok, to travel without molestation in the interior with consular passes, and to trade directly with Siamese individuals without the necessity of middlemen. Like the unequal treaties in China, it contained clauses providing for extraterritoriality, tariff control, and the most-favored-nation treatment. The Bowring treaty served as a model for a dozen treaties which Siam concluded with other nations before the end of the century.

The Siamese kings invited technical experts from abroad to assist them in the administration of their country. The British dominated, but Danes, Italians, French, and even Americans were called upon. At one time as many as eighty-four foreign advisers were on duty in Bangkok. It was the studied Siamese policy to deprive the foreign powers of any excuses for aggressive action, but the French were most difficult to cope with. Their ambitions extended beyond Indochina into Siam. In 1867 the Siamese were obliged to recognize the French protectorate in Cambodia, although Siam managed to keep its position in the provinces of Battambang and Siemreap. In 1893, after a French naval demonstration against Bangkok, Siam surrendered its claims to Laos and acquiesced in the French absorption of that territory into Indochina. But Siam found a new friend and champion in Great Britain. French expansion not only threatened Bangkok—it also challenged the British position in Upper Burma and in Malaya. Both France and Great Britain came to recognize that it would be advantageous to have Siam as a buffer state between them. Therefore they entered into an agreement of January 15, 1896, which defined their mutual spheres of interest in Burma and Indochina and guaranteed the independence of Siam.

Kings Mongkut and Chulalongkorn together accomplished a revolution of modernization in Siam which resembled the Meiji revolution in Japan. They showed conclusively that political control by an outside power might be a useful but was not an essential ingredient in the formula for progress and development. They concentrated their efforts on the welfare of the peasants. The economic life of rural Siam was always bountiful, although it seemed scanty if measured in cold terms of per-capita production or accumulation of wealth. The people had rice—plenty of it—and their diet was enriched by fish, salt, fruits, vege-tables, and spices. They were a race of independent landowners, with a substantial personal stake in the welfare of their own country. They had few worries about shelter and clothes, and they had respectable cottage industries. Their villages were practically self-sufficient eco-nomically, but the forward-looking monarchs determined to bring this idyllic, if primitive, way of life more in line with the rest of the world.

The enlightened kings constructed irrigation canals, built railways and highways and gave Siam a postal service and system of telegraphs. They reduced tax burdens. They stopped the excesses of tax-farming and abolished the practice of forced labor. Mostly they primed the economic pump so that more money would be available to support higher prices for peasant products. They put up Western-style resi-dences, office buildings, and banks. They expanded exports of rice, tin, teak, and rubber and abolished the old royal monopolies on foreign trade. They developed extensive trade and shipping relations with Hong Kong and Singapore and welcomed British investments and ac-tivities in rubber, tin, and teak. They also encouraged Chinese immi-gration, because the Chinese would labor in the mines and do commer-cial work in the city, which was scorned by the agriculturally minded Siamese. No five-year plans were thought of and no steps were taken toward widespread industrialization, but the kings encouraged some of their own children to set up rice mills, saw mills, printing shops, and power stations.

Siam's great kings also accomplished great political and social reforms. They were absolute monarchs but among the best of the benevolent despots. King Mongkut removed the ancient taboo against looking the king in the face, and one of Chulalongkorn's first decrees an-nounced the abolition of the practice of prostration in the royal pres-ence. King Chulalongkorn initiated the custom of driving around the streets in his own carriage and refused to limit himself to the confines of his palace. However, he kept his harem, and he listed thirty-four sons and forty-three daughters as his children.

Due to the impact of the West, the old feudal system was aban-doned. The sanctions of kingship were weakened, although the king lost none of his popular reverence as the head of the Buddhist religion and the defender of the faith. Modernization made no appreciable modification in the place of Buddhism as the center of the arts, culture, and social life of Siam. No other religion, including Christianity, made much headway in the minds and hearts of the Siamese. Western-style education was provided as an adjunct to Buddhist learning, but the decrees were seldom translated into reality. The new Western calendar was officially adopted by the government, but it was neither understood nor followed by the rural masses. The use of the English language was encouraged, but any degree of proficiency was limited to a very small group in Bangkok.

Gradually the concept of government and administration—as apart from the royal household—came into being, but without any concept whatever of responsibility to the people. King and aristocracy belonged to one world; the common people to another. The ancient privileges of nobles and hereditary officials were transferred to a civil service which was staffed and created by the will of the throne. But the idea grew that careers might be open to wealth, for example, or to talent. The national administrative system was completely overhauled. A council of state and a privy council, composed of princes and high officials, were appointed to advise the king on matters of policy. The kingdom was reorganized into circuits, provinces, districts, communes, and villages, according to the model of Burma. Commissioners of the circuits, governors of the provinces, and elected headmen of the villages were given important responsibilities. A new class of government officials began to assume prestige and status. Magistrates received new honor and dignity as the judicial system was modernized and a code of laws was adopted. The army was improved in quality and position, although it was called upon less and less for combat as the entire region was increasingly pacified.

Siam was unique in Southeast Asia as it entered the twentieth century. Its court and royalty were echoes of the past, but it was energized by forward-looking civil servants and modern ideas. It was administered as well as most European dominions in Asia, and it was in full possession of its independence. It contained all the elements of nationhood and was well-advanced in its preparation to cope with problems of political evolution and economic development.

SUGGESTED READING

Agoncillo, Teodoro A., *Malolos* (Quezon City, U. of the Philippines, 1960).
Cady, John F., *History of Modern Burma* (Ithaca, Cornell U., 1958).
Clifford, Sir Hugh, *Bushwacking and Other Asiatic Tales and Memories* (New York, Harper, 1929).

Covarrubias, Miguel, *Island of Bali* (New York, Knopf, 1942).

Gourou, Pierre, *Peasants of the Tonkin Delta* (two vols.) (New Haven, Yale U., 1955).

Kennedy, Raymond, *Ageless Indies* (New York, Day, 1942).

Landon, Margaret, *Anna and the King of Siam* (Garden City, Doubleday, 1944).

Mills, Lennox, *New World of Southeast Asia* (Minneapolis, U. of Minnesota, 1949).

Pe Maung Tin and Luce, Gordon, (trans.), *Glass Palace Chronicles of the Kings of Burma* (London, Oxford U., 1923).

Rizal, José, *Lost Eden* (trans. by Leon Ma. Guerrero) (Bloomington, Indiana U., 1961).

———, *The Subversive* (trans. by Leon Ma. Guerrero) (Bloomington, Indiana U., 1962).

Roberts, Stephen H., *History of French Colonial Policy, 1870–1925* (two vols.) (London, P. S. King & Son. Ltd., 1929).

Shway, Yoe (Sir James Scott), *Burman, His Life and Notions* (London, Macmillan & Co., 1910).

Sudjatmoko, *Approach to Indonesian History* (Ithaca, Cornell U., 1960).

Vella, Walter F., *Siam under Rama III, 1924–1951* (Locust Valley, J. J. Augustin, 1957).

Wolff, Leon, *Little Brown Brother* (Garden City, Doubleday, 1961).

Woodman, Dorothy, *Making of Burma* (London, Cresset, 1962).

III

CHANGE, REVOLUTION, AND CONFLICT

12

The Modernization of China

With the return of the empress dowager and her court from Sian to Peking the curtain rose on the last act of the drama of the Chinese empire. The passing of the Manchu Dynasty marked the end of a way of life and a system of government which had prevailed in China for more than two thousand years. Ancient customs were inadequate for modern times. China would change, but the process would be long and painful. Generations would suffer untold miseries while China in the twentieth century pursued the path of unfinished revolution.

LAST YEARS OF THE EMPIRE

China's humiliation before a handful of foreign troops in the international expeditionary forces of 1900 exposed once and for all the hopelessness of the atrophied, outmoded imperial system. China had failed to measure up in any way to the requirements of a modern state. While the West shot ahead scientifically, economically, and in military power, China wallowed in famine, piracy, brigandage, and incipient rebellion. To the shrewd empress dowager it became clear that China would have to reform (no matter how hateful the idea) or perish. She issued a decree which said: "We should correct our shortcomings by adopting the best methods and systems which obtain in foreign countries, basing our future conduct on a wise recognition of past errors." She was obliged to sponsor policies which she had previously opposed.

As a first step in 1901 she ordered the modernization of the army. A model force was organized in Chihli province and placed under the direct command of a newly established ministry of war. China would have a national army, and its officers would be trained at a "Chinese West Point" built at Paotingfu, not far from Peking. In 1905 she consented to the abolition of the old examination system which had been in existence since the time of Christ. At the same time the central administrative system of the national government was overhauled by eliminating old-style offices and creating new agencies with new functions. The authorities in Peking tried in every way to break down the embarrassing autonomy of the provinces, and they consented to a gradual approach toward a constitutional regime.

The empress dowager was persuaded that Japan's phenomenal progress—particularly its military victory over Russia—was due to its acceptance of Western ways. To her it seemed entirely possible to accept a Western form of government and preserve the throne as the source of all authority. The court would therefore grant a constitution—as the emperor of Japan had done—with primary emphasis on the proposition that "the Ta Ch'ing (Manchu) dynasty shall rule over the Ta Ch'ing Empire forever and ever, and be honored through all the ages." Preliminary steps would include the development of mass education in preparation for popular participation in government, law reform, reorganization of the police, and the introduction of self-government on the local level. It was announced in 1908 that China would have provincial assemblies within a year and a national parliament within nine years.

Immediately after this announcement, the political scene in China changed radically. The emperor and the empress dowager both died in 1908. The infant Hsüan T'ung was named emperor. This was the child who in manhood was known as Henry Pu-yi, who was kidnaped by the Japanese and in 1934 installed as the Emperor Kang Teh of Manchukuo. The father of the child, Prince Ch'un, was appointed as regent. The favorites of the empress dowager, including Yüan Shih-k'ai, were dismissed from Peking, and the newcomers to power were unable to control the swelling currents of reform and revolution. The provincial assemblies met as planned. Although stacked with conservatives, they were surprisingly outspoken. They attacked with vigor the imperial system, the viceroys, and the increasing impingement of the central government on provincial prerogatives. In October 1910 a national assembly was called, seven years ahead of schedule. In no way undaunted or overwhelmed by the imperial presence in Peking, it demanded the introduction of a regular Western-style cabinet system of government at the earliest practicable moment.

China seemed to be moving in the path of stable reform when revolution broke out in the autumn of 1911. The event was not unexpected. For almost a century economic hardship had been the chronic lot of the Chinese peasant. In spite of droughts, famines, floods, war, and disease, population increased steadily. The pressure for food mounted. Living conditions for the average farmer got worse instead of better. His taxes increased, but he received less protection and fewer benefits from the government than ever. Peasant distress habitually led to protest and localized rebellion, and secret forces of opposition to the dynasty slowly gathered strength. Sun Yat-sen organized the *Tung Meng Hui* (the Alliance Society, or the predecessor of the Kuomintang) in 1905 and went around the world collecting money for the cause of revolution. Newspapers in the foreign concessions in China gave Sun an outlet for his ideas; and the new postal service, railway, and telegraph systems made possible a nationwide coordination of rebellious elements. Overseas students (whose numbers were augmented by the scholarships made available by the remission of portions of the Boxer indemnity); graduates of the mission schools, with their emphasis on individualism and knowledge of the West; overseas Chinese; successful businessmen; and often the soldiers of the modernized army joined with Dr. Sun's revolutionary secret society. The Manchus were denounced as the foreign slaves of foreign masters.

Riots, strikes, and starvation accentuated the perennial misery of the Yangtze Valley in the early autumn of 1911. At the same time the argument between central and provincial governments over railway construction reached a crisis. On October 10 (the Double Tenth, or the tenth day of the tenth month), an accidental bomb explosion in a basement in the Russian concession at Hankow revealed the existence of a nest of plotters against the dynasty. Other revolutionary cells incited sporadic uprisings throughout northern and central China. City after city, province after province proclaimed independence from imperial control. The harried prince-regent was obliged to "eat bitterness" and to recall Yüan Shih-k'ai from retirement to take command of the imperial army and navy. The national assembly met again in Peking and "elected" Yüan as premier on November 8, 1911. It renewed its demands for constitutional government and quickly adjourned. It had neither the capacity nor the authority to cope with the rising revolution.

By the end of the year (1911) the revolutionists organized a provisional government at Nanking and on December 28 elected Sun Yat-sen, then in Europe, as provisional president. Neither the Nanking government, nor Yüan Shih-k'ai, representing Peking, had the will, the money, or the military strength to engage in a fight to the finish. They negotiated. On his return to Shanghai, Sun offered to resign as provisional president if Yüan would engineer the abdication of the emperor and accept a Republican form of government. Final terms between north and south were agreed upon on February 12, 1912. The dynasty agreed to abdicate in consideration of a good financial settlement, provision for the upkeep of the imperial tombs, and the continued right of the emperor and his immediate family to live in one of the yellow-tiled palaces in the Forbidden City of Peking. The old dragon flag of China was replaced by the five-barred flag of the Republic, with each bar symbolizing one of China's five equal races —the Chinese, Mongolians, Manchus, Moslems, and Tibetans.

On February 14 the provisional government at Nanking elected Yüan Shih-k'ai president with the hope that he would come south to assume office. Sun Yat-sen wanted a new capital, in the geographic center of China, where the nation could make a new start in building a new life. Yüan wanted to stay in Peking, to carry out the philosophy that any changes in China would be built on the past—the best of which should be preserved and improved. Yüan won, and on March 10, 1912, he was inaugurated in Peking as the first president of the Chinese Republic. On the same day a provisional constitution was promulgated. To symbolize the passing of the old regime, the old lunar calendar was officially abandoned and the new solar calendar adopted. Time thenceforward would be calculated according to the fashion of the West, and 1912 would be known as the year 1 of the Chinese Republic.

FIRST YEARS OF THE REPUBLIC

Yüan Shih-k'ai came to power in China in the same year in which the great exponent of democracy, Woodrow Wilson, was elected to the presidency of the United States. Yüan had nothing of democracy in his personal philosophy, and his country was in no manner prepared for self-government. Yüan distrusted the parliament with which he was saddled, and he engineered its suspension. In August 1912 Sun Yat-sen's *Tung Meng Hui* amalgamated with other revolutionary groups and reorganized itself into an open political party which adopted the name of Kuomintang (Country-People-Party). Because of its adoption of nationalism as its first principle, the Kuomintang became known as the Nationalist Party. In elections to a new parliament in 1913, it obtained a majority of seats. However, it aroused the fear of Yüan Shih-k'ai and was immediately banned as a seditious organization. Since most members of the parliament were also members of the Kuomintang, the parliament passed out of existence. The legislators fled to Central and South China where they kept the flames of revolution burning.

Yüan ruled by means of soldiers and spies. He controlled the military, and he appointed his henchmen to strategic posts in administration. He obtained the money to run his government from foreign powers who believed that a strong man at the helm—no matter how undemocratic—was preferable to the alternatives of national chaos or possible fragmentation of the country. Local warlords emerged to dominate their own areas, and they supported Yüan only to the extent that he respected their interests. They cared nothing for popular welfare; they concerned themselves only with their own power and wealth. They would have doomed China to complete disintegration had it not been for the strength and skill of Yüan Shih-k'ai.

Yüan quietly converted the republic into a veiled dictatorship and plotted to restore the monarchy, with himself as emperor. Resistance to Yüan's scheme was nationwide; frustration hastened his death in 1916. Throughout the period of his presidency, the people of China demonstrated their ability to get along in spite of bad government or no government. Except for the cutting of queues and the prohibition on opium-smoking and foot-binding, the people were scarcely touched by the continuing reforms. The tenor of village life remained undisturbed. The popular attitude was merely that the mandate of heaven had changed hands, and one remote ruler had replaced another. To those who had even a slight amount of political sophistication, Yüan's experience gave a bad impression of "popular government." Votes in the parliament were bought and sold on the open market; bribes or threats of force easily bent the people's representatives to the executive will. The legislature argued endlessly over a constitution, indulged in personal feuds, and sometimes adjourned its sessions with fistfights. No one lamented Yüan's suspension of the parliament, but strong anti-imperial sentiments prevented the restoration of the monarchy.

Yüan Shih-k'ai was succeeded to the presidency by his vice-president, Li Yuan-hung, who owed his position to the fact that he had been a military leader of the central China revolutionists. He would have been pleased to restore the parliamentary regime and to strenthen democratic processes of government. He was thwarted by his own premier, who was a dominant character and pushed the president into oblivion. The issue which made this possible was China's entry into World War I in 1917 on the side of the allies. China shelved democracy at home while it enlisted with those nations which would make the world safe for democracy.

For ten years, from 1917 to 1926, the Republic of China was a country of warlords. No single individual was able to control Peking, let alone the entire country. Peking, as the seat of the central government, was important because it represented the nation. Warlords succeeded to power in Peking, and were in turn driven out of Peking, as in a macabre game of musical chairs. The master of Peking usually remained behind the scenes and placed the city and country in the hands of a puppet president. Foreign diplomats were received and entertained in Peking, and Peking appointed a succession of distinguished diplomats to represent China abroad. In international politics China was sovereign. The foreign powers ignored China's internal anomalies and dealt with the Peking regime as if neither warlords nor revolutionists existed. The central government negotiated for foreign loans and received whatever financial surpluses remained in the national treasury after foreign obligations on indemnities and loans were paid.

Independent struggles for power raged throughout China. The authority of Peking never reached far beyond the city walls, depending entirely upon the armed strength of the man or clique which was in temporary control. Northern, central, and southern China were all subjected to the depredations of warlords. Self-appointed generals recruited the unemployed or juvenile delinquents into their personal armies and used peasants and soldiers as instruments for their own selfish pleasure and power. Self-styled armies were little better than mobs or bandits. They would attack a city or desert an entire area, depending upon the deals which they could conclude. They monopolized the opium traffic and controlled the appointment of local political officials. They collected taxes for as much as twenty years in advance, and they squeezed the merchants or the local chambers of commerce for all that the traffic would bear. When defeated or bought out, generals would abandon their own soldiers, load their belongings and their concubines on trucks or coastal ships and seek havens of safety in the foreign concessions in the port cities or in Hong Kong.

Political anarchy and economic impoverishment went hand in hand. As warlords pillaged, robbed, and murdered, neither landlords nor peasants could look to a government of any kind for protection or relief. Scholars and able civil servants often gave up their government jobs in disgust and disclaimed any responsibility for China's deplorable state of affairs. Bandits flourished throughout the interior. No one could travel safely in many regions after dark. Even a daylight journey was unwise if the corn was sufficiently high to provide hiding places for thieves and highwaymen. Public projects such as dikes and irrigation canals were neglected, and transportation systems were permitted to deteriorate. The most ominous feature of this jungle condition was the association of anarchy and poverty with the newly born republic—itself the crowning importation from the West. Democratic institutions and representative forms of government became disastrously associated with militarism, disorder, insecurity, and poverty.

Some dominant figures emerged from the welter of war and intrigue. Chang Tso-lin, the Old Marshal, established himself as the master of Manchuria; Feng Yu-hsiang, the massive Christian general, gained control in the northwest; and Yen Hsi-shan, the model governor of Shansi, tried to demonstrate that a benevolent rule could be carried out in one province in spite of the misery of his neighbors. In West China the large provinces of Szechwan and Yunnan were isolated from the control or even the influence of Peking. They became the battlefields for old-style militarists. In Shanghai and the Yangtze Valley, warlords rose to power who were best able to accommodate themselves to coexistence with the British and other foreign interests.

South China, as well as the north, suffered from intrigue and civil war. The Kwangtung warlords and the Kwangsi clique battled for control of the Canton area, but there was a new and distinctive factor in their maneuvers and campaigns. The revolutionists, particularly the Kuomintang and the ex-parliamentarians, found refuge in the south. They were not in position to add strength in arms and weapons, but they were full of ideas. The outstanding personality was that of Sun Yat-sen. Gradually he evolved a program which served as a rallying point for Chinese who were concerned with the future of China as a nation.

China's internal political evolution was inextricably interwoven with its foreign relations, which are chronicled in the next chapter. Salient considerations must, however, be noted here. In 1922, Russia, with its political ambitions and communist ideas, re-entered the Chinese political scene. Russians developed contacts with Chang Tso-lin in Manchuria; with the shadow government in Peking; and, most significantly, with Sun Yat-sen in Shanghai and subsequently in Canton. Just as the stage was set for the Kuomintang's rise to national power, the Russians were able to influence its personnel, platform, and philosophy. The Kuomintang was to lead China out of its worst chaos, and Chiang Kai-shek was to succeed Sun Yat-sen as the leader of the party. But both the party and its leadership were associated with the communist camel which gradually occupied the entire Chinese tent.

THE KUOMINTANG AND THE CHINESE COMMUNIST PARTY

When it seemed as if China were about to disappear as a political entity, a new regenerative force was created by Dr. Sun Yat-sen. This remarkable man was born on November 12, 1866, the son of a tenant farmer in South China. He was educated in Hawaii and was graduated as a medical doctor by the University of Hong Kong. He was a Christian, a revolutionary by instinct and inclination, and he liked politics better than medicine. He lived and died for the revolution. He accepted help from anyone, militarist or missionary. When the West failed him, he approved a far-reaching program of cooperation with Russia. He was never distinguished as a practical administrator, but he wielded great influence as a social philosopher, idealist, and propagandist. He tried desperately to induce northern militarists to accept his program, and in 1925 he died of cancer in Peking while striving for national unity. His death and apotheosis were of immense service to his party and country. According to his will, which was regularly read in public with great solemnity, the national revolution must be pursued until China achieved independence and equality. Parks were named after him. His picture was pasted up everywhere, and his mausoleum at Nanking became a national shrine. Chiang Kai-shek's armored train bore Sun Yat-sen's name. Sun's books were accepted as blueprints for reconstruction. Some were vague and moralistic, others were inspiring and farsighted. His *San Min Chu I*, or Three Principles of the People, became the party's manual. The principles were inspired by Lincoln's "government of the people, by the people and for the people" and were translated into Chinese terms as nationalism, democracy, and social welfare. The third term was sufficiently imprecise to leave it to the future to determine whether Sun advocated socialism, a welfare state, or whether he was merely dedicated to an improvement of capitalism. The program of the Kuomintang was easily propagandized by popular slogans. The red color of the new Chinese flag and the blue and white emblem of the party became familiar sights throughout the length and breadth of China.

The fundamentals of Sun's program included a typically Chinese emphasis on the importance of education. All Chinese should be educated to the responsibilities of citizenship, and the most capable citizens should be given training for leadership. Patriotism and respect for law should be considered paramount. China should march steadily onward through three well-defined stages of political development: the end of warlordism and the restoration of law and order, the inauguration of a period of political tutelage during which the party would be in control of government affairs, and the establishment of constitutional government as soon as the people should be ready for it.

While the Kuomintang developed its program, Chinese Communists fashioned their formula for China's future. The first Marxist study groups were organized in 1918 under Professors Li Ta-chao and Ch'en Tu-hsiu at Peking University. The fiery pen of the latter, in a magazine called *New China*, appealed to youth to break down old prejudices, discard old ways, and adopt new ideas in politics, morality, and economic life. He warned that Chinese society would perish if the young in age permitted themselves to be old in spirit, and he called for youth to show unbounded courage "if we are to get rid of corruption and survive." Mao Tse-tung, a young man who worked in the library at the university, was one of those who pondered deeply the words of Professor Ch'en. Students of every persuasion—nationalist, socialist, communist, and independent—

participated in the demonstrations of May 4, 1919, against China's treatment at the Conference of Versailles.

By September 1920, Ch'en Tu-hsiu had moved to Shanghai. With the assistance of agents from Moscow, he assembled leftists of varying shades into a communist cell. Similar cells were organized in Peking, in Hunan, Hupeh, and overseas among the Chinese in Paris and Berlin. In Shanghai the dynamic Professor Ch'en undertook the establishment of trade unions. In 1921 he moved to Canton where he became chief of the board of education. He formed a communist cell in Canton, set up a training school for party workers, and laid plans for a nationwide party platform. In July 1921 the Communist leaders convened the first national party congress at Shanghai with twelve Chinese delegates and an observer from Moscow in attendance. Ch'en was not among those present but he was elected chairman of the central committee. Many of the later leaders of the Chinese People's Republic were among the early figures in the Chinese Communist Party: Mao Tse-tung, Chou En-lai, Chu Teh, and Liu Shao-ch'i.

The Chinese Communist Party dedicated itself to the gradual achievement of a dictatorship of workers and peasants and affiliated itself with the Communist International. It welcomed anyone as a member who would pay dues and accept party discipline. It adopted a program of anti-imperialism, anti-warlordism, labor reform and democratic revolution. It found common ground for a United Front with the Kuomintang since both stood for the immediate objectives of national independence. Communists were permitted to join the Kuomintang, on the understanding that dual membership would not compromise communist ideals or interfere with communistic activities among the peasants, workers, students, soldiers, and overseas Chinese. Together with the Kuomintang, the Chinese Communist Party sent about thirty delegates to the Congress of the Toilers of the Far East in 1922 to become acquainted with Bolshevist views and techniques. Continuous contacts were maintained with Moscow.

From the beginning, the Chinese Communist Party announced its goals as the dictatorship of workers and peasants, the abolition of private property, and the gradual attainment of a communist society. It accepted Lenin's apparatus of democratic centralism and patterned its organization after the Russian model. It subordinated the philosophy of the withering away of the state to the immediate need of creating a bureaucracy, a standing army, and a police apparatus which would pave the way to power. It distinguished sharply between the leaders and the led—the party constituted the leaders, the peasants and the urban proletariat made up the essential followers. It mapped its future in accord with global communist strategy. It was nationalistic, but it was also supranationalistic. It looked beyond China as a nation and planned for a future in which China would be a leading member of an international communist system. China would accomplish its internal revolution; China and Russia together would be the leaders in the world revolution.

The Kuomintang became tinged with Russian influence in its formative years. As a matter of fact, the "old China hands" and a large proportion of foreign diplomats in Peking denounced the Kuomintang as an unwitting accomplice of Russian Bolshevism. A Russian agent, Adolph Joffe, met Dr. Sun in Shanghai in 1922 and worked out an agreement that, although neither communism nor the Soviet system could be considered suitable for China, Russia would send advisers to the Kuomintang, and the Kuomintang would accept members of the new-born Chinese Communist Party as allies. The Kuomintang itself was then reorganized on the lines of the Russian Communist Party, with political commissars, mass propaganda organs, and strict discipline. It gave up all pretense to democracy and worked for a party dictatorship which would govern the country during the period of political tutelage. The great difference between the Kuomintang and the Communist Party was that each sought a dictatorship for its own party. However, the Kuomintang looked to constitutionalism as the ultimate goal of the revolution; the Communists saw only the permanent acceptance of their own political and social system at the end of the road.

Kuomintang-Communist Cooperation (1924–1927)

In 1924 the Kuomintang called its first national congress and committed itself to three great policies: alliance with the Soviet Union, alliance with the Communist Party, and support of workers and peasants. Its manifesto outlined the history and the program of the party. The document called for a new birth of revolutionary ardor and addressed itself not to bourgeois and landlords, but to peasant farmers, city workers, students, youth, and overseas Chinese. In the same year, 1924, the Kuomintang established the Whampoa Military Academy under the superintendence of Chiang Kai-shek, who had recently returned from a study and observation trip to Moscow. Many future generals, both in Kuomintang and Communist armies, were fellow students in military tactics and political doctrine while at Whampoa.

The Chinese Communist Party was committed as clearly as the Kuomintang to coalition and cooperation. The Communists accepted the Kuomintang as "the central dynamic force for the nationalistic revolution and the headquarters for anti-imperialism in China." They were too weak to stand alone. Ch'en Tu-hsiu lamented that "the Communists did the coolie labor for the Kuomintang," but he was reminded by a Russian adviser that "any attempt on the part of the peasants and workers to take an independent course towards political power would have gone down in a sea of blood." A former language-school teacher in Chicago, Michael Borodin, and the German-born General Galen were among the advisers whom the Russians sent in 1924 to help the Chinese in Canton. One of Borodin's secretaries and interpreters was a young Vietnamese named Ho Chi Minh.

The Kuomintang, with the participation of individual communists, succeeded in gaining power and setting up a nationalist government in Canton. Mao Tse-tung's experience illustrates the way the two factions worked together. Mao was at once the head of the peasant department of the central committee of the Chinese Communist Party and a member of the political bureau of the Kuomintang. He was head of the propaganda bureau of the Kuomintang and editor of the Kuomintang's *Political Daily* at the same time he was an outstanding Communist Party worker. Chiang Kai-shek himself exhibited a combination of dexterity and ruthlessness in remaining at the head of the revolutionary movement supported by both young parties. As a matter of expediency, Chiang admitted that "our alliance with the Soviet Union, with the world revolution, is actually an alliance with all revolutionary parties which are fighting in common against world-imperialists to carry through the world revolution." On one occasion he said: "The (Nationalist) revolution cannot rule without Dr. Sun's Three Principles, nor can the revolution neglect Communism. . . . Knowing that we cannot separate the Chinese revolution from the world revolution, why should there be any quarrel amongst us about the Three People's Principles and the Communists?"

The outward appearance of the United Front between Kuomintang and Communists could not obscure bitter subsurface tensions. Chiang never trusted the Communists in spite of his acceptance of their cooperation. Outwardly he endorsed them. For example, at the Third National Labor Conference in Canton, he referred to himself as the younger brother of labor and concluded his speech to the Conference by shouting, "Long Live the Revolution!" On the other hand, he did his best to limit the influence of the Russian advisers and keep the most radical of the Communists out of the top posts in the Kuomintang.

In the summer of 1926, Chiang Kai-shek decided that the time was ripe to launch a military campaign to oust the warlords of northern and central China. Paced by political agitators and propagandists, the Kuomintang armies (with Communists in their ranks) moved gradually toward Changsha, Hankow, and eventually Shanghai. Colorful posters rallied the masses to the banners of the Kuomintang. Some of these posters showed blind mandarins being kicked out of a Chinese house, others showed northern generals caricatured as rats being driven into the Pacific Ocean. Some showed foreign soldiers with ugly faces being turned upon by the peasants. The most effective showed the Chinese people in an open boat on a stormy sea being rowed by a Nationalist crew and guided by the lighthouse of the Kuomintang.

During this period of exhilaration, the Chinese Communist Party increased its membership, developed its techniques in party organization and propaganda, learned about military affairs, and received a first-hand acquaintance with terroristic methods. While the armies won victory after victory on the northward march, the revolution spread in the countryside and in the cities. By 1927 it was reported that 2,500,000 workers had joined labor unions and 12,000,000 farmers had joined peasant unions. These peasant unions, according to their own propaganda, made only two fundamental demands on their members—the immediate establishment of local governments with militia to help them fight lawless bandits and the immediate establishment of cooperative stores and government credit agencies. In a spectacular way Communists fined and paraded opium smokers, burned mah-jongg and gambling paraphernalia, abolished foot-binding, and attacked local superstitions in the area between Canton and Hankow. They initiated public works, made a start at clearing lands, and established unpretentious public schools. Current newspaper accounts described how young organizers went from village to village in northern Kwangtung, playing phonograph records and doing magic tricks to attract audiences, and then launched into their orations for lower rents and tenant unions. Local unions rallied the people against landlords and took the law into their own hands if the magistrate dared to try to halt them. Thousands of peasants took up the cry, "Long Live the Peasantry—Down with the Landlords!" These wild demonstrations constituted the earliest manifestations of "agrarian reform." Landlords abandoned their farms and fled for their lives rather than risk the wrath of howling mobs.

As the joint Kuomintang-Communist revolution veered into radical grooves, the more conservative elements, including Chiang Kai-shek, worried about Communist excesses. They became convinced that China would be better advised to progress with the enlightened support of landlords, merchants, and bourgeoisie (and the democratic Western powers) rather than to surrender itself to communism. More and more Chiang disliked the Russian orientation of his own party, the Kuomintang, and distrusted the Russian advisers.

Incidents involving foreign interests forced the Kuomintang to trim its sails and set its course for the future. When the Nationalists arrived in Hankow in 1926, a mob overran the British concession and forced the residents to flee to the safety of the British ships on the river. When Nationalist armies attacked and captured Nanking in the following spring, they killed various foreign residents. A general massacre was avoided by a barrage from the warships on the Yangtze. When the main Nationalist forces under Chiang Kai-shek took Shanghai, the Kuomintang was forced to make an immediate decision—whether to continue with their Russian advisers or whether to turn to the British and the Americans. On April 12, 1927, Chiang broke with the Communists in Shanghai, putting to death those leaders whom his forces could catch. Chou En-lai was among those who escaped; his sister was among those who were caught. Chiang denounced the former Kuomintang government, which had moved from Canton to Hankow, and formed a new government of Kuomintang conservatives at Nanking. The Hankow faction then split with its Russian advisers (in spite of Stalin's efforts at conciliation), terminated its alliance with the Chinese Communists, and joined Chiang in a unified government under the reunited Kuomintang at Nanking.

The Russian advisers were sent back home. The disillusioned Borodin remarked, "When the next Chinese general comes to Moscow and shouts, 'Hail to the World Revolution,' we had better send at once for the GPU [the secret police]. . . . all that any of them want is rifles." In the Kuomintang purges of the Communists which followed, thousands lost their lives. The Communist party received paralyzing blows which would have destroyed a less resilient people and a less determined movement.

Mao Tse-tung was a victim of the purge in Hankow. Mao disappeared into the rugged border areas between Hunan and Kiangsi, where he organized fellow stragglers into a series of soviets or "councils of delegates of the workers, peasants, soldiers and the city-poor." He joined Chu Teh. They stayed away from the cities and roved about the countryside in the best Chinese tradition of half-bandits, half-outlaws. Soldiers, straggling students and unemployed workers continuously replenished their ranks. As former party leaders were ferreted out of their hiding places in the International Settlement, the French Concession, or the native city of Shanghai, they filtered into the mountain regions to join up with Mao and Chu.

Gradually the Communists transformed their wandering bands into a disciplined army, under the avowed leadership of the party. They progressed from hit-and-run tactics into systematic guerilla warfare. They managed to evade the annihilation campaigns of the Nationalist government; and they established a Soviet republic of their own with the capital at Juichin, deep in the heart of southern Kiangsi. They sought to win the support of the poor peasants by a program of land reform, which meant the extermination of the landlords as a class and the redistribution of their holdings to the poor and the landless. Mao's philosophy was that the "people are the sea, we are the fish; as long as we can swim in that sea, we will survive." They not only survived; they grew stronger. They also kept in constant touch with Communist headquarters in Moscow.

THE NATIONALIST GOVERNMENT UNDER CHIANG KAI-SHEK

In June 1928 the new Kuomintang government under Chiang Kai-shek at Nanking completed the apparent unification of China. The strongest of the warlords, the old marshal of Manchuria, Chang Tso-lin, was driven out of Peking. The party was reorganized and restaffed with conservative-minded students, merchants, industrialists, bankers, landlords, and gentry. Coolies and peasants were neglected. Chiang was placed in charge of the party, the government, and the army. On October 10, 1928 —the anniversary of the Double Tenth founding of the first Chinese Republic—the new government of the Republic of China was proclaimed at Nanking with the blessing of the foreign powers. Its guiding principles were that the party should be supreme over the state, and that the party should guide the nation to constitutional democracy. Political power was lodged in a party pyramid consisting of the national congress, the central executive committee of the congress, and at the apex, the standing committee of the central executive committee.

The government itself consisted of five Yüan or boards, designated as executive, legislative, judicial, examination, and control. The executive Yüan corresponded to a cabinet, and its chief exercised the prerogatives of a prime minister. Above the Yüan, but within the government structure, were two powerful councils known as the council of state and the national defense council. As in the Russian system of government, China was in the grip of an interlocking directorate of generals and politicians, subject to the will of a single individual. The government depended upon the party, and the party, upon the battalions at the command of the man at the helm.

The patterns of government vacillated between the modern ideas to which the Kuomintang was dedicated and the ancient Chinese traditions which were in the marrow of the bones of every Chinese official. Modern conceptions were made to fit into ancient Chinese molds. The spirit of Sun Yat-sen replaced the cult of the emperor, the Western-trained bureaucracy usurped the privileges and prestige of the mandarinate, and the hsien magistrate remained as the sole representative of government to the masses. However, the Kuomintang introduced a new spirit and a new dimension to the process of government. The officials accepted and advertised their responsibilities; they went about their tasks with a discipline and an energy which made Nanking a bubbling, exciting place to live.

Serious limitations crippled the government from its inception. The party was dedicated to training for democracy, but it made no provision for popular elections, not even of local officials. While draft constitutions toyed with ideal democratic methods, political practices in the capital city drifted menacingly toward authoritarianism. Civil rights were not guaranteed. Distinguished Chinese languished in house arrest or disappeared. Officials had no tenure of office. Salaries were ridiculously low; private incomes and public funds were indistinguishable. No political guarantees of any kind could be enforced against the encroachments of the military.

In the light of Chiang's political heritage, his problems were possibly beyond human solution. Division and disunity constituted his immediate challenge. Before the end of a year in office Chiang faced a serious revolt in central China. A coalition of northern warlords forced him to compromise as the price for nominal allegiance of Peiping and Manchuria. (The city of Peking, or *northern capital*, became Peiping, or *northern peace*, with the designation of Nanking as China's capital in 1928.) Rival generals continued their perennial struggles for the dominance of Szechwan without paying any attention to orders or suggestions from Nanking. Independent satraps in the southern provinces of Kwangsi and Kwangtung held undisputed sway over dominions as extensive as those of Chiang himself. Chiang was never a dictator over China. He was obliged to maneuver where he could not command, and to compromise where he could not order. He had to bribe and to bargain beyond the point of his bayonets. When opposing troops were defeated, he could not disband them. He had to incorporate them into his own armies. He followed the ancient Chinese custom of giving a rebel commander a reward, pension, or trip abroad instead of a death sentence, which might have been more appropriate. Chiang's actual authority extended only as far as the limits of his military power, and that was primarily in the lower regions of the Yangtze Valley. Often when Chiang would telegraph commands to a neighboring province, his telegram would be ignored. The telegram itself was often tacked up on a pole or tree and exposed to the mercy of wind and weather.

The chief executive was in constant quarrels with his subordinates within the Kuomintang. At times Hu Han-min, Sun Fo, Wang Ching-wei, or T. V. Soong (Chiang's new brother-in-law) would cooperate with him. At other times they would oppose him, and each other. Some went so far as to set up an independent government at Canton which denied and defied the authority of Chiang. Again, the standard operating procedure was to cajole rather than to eliminate the political opposition.

The greatest obstacle to unity was the civil war with the Communists. Chiang considered the Communists as a disease of the heart, as contrasted with the Japanese whom he diagnosed as a disease of the skin. He tried to annihilate the Communists by expensive military campiagns which baffled his German-trained army and exhausted his resources. He despaired of any truce with the Communists which would ever again bring any hope of peace and cooperation. This was Chiang's attitude in 1931, on the eve of the Japanese invasion.

THE PROGRAM OF MODERNIZATION

Although the Kuomintang was obliged to dissipate a large share of its energies on national unity, it pursued with vigor the twin objectives of complete sovereignty and internal modernization. (The campaign for complete sovereignty is described in the next chapter.) The establishment of the government at Nanking added new impetus to the changes with which China was convulsed, but more importance was attached to the welfare of the state than to the welfare of the individual. Changes —some clearly for the better and some of a more doubtful value—had been brewing for a long time. The Kuomintang made it a primary policy to expedite those changes—but within the limits of the preservation of law and order.

In the economic realm, the government made timid efforts to enforce a laudable legislative program of agricultural reform. Farms were small, farming methods primitive, and conditions of country life difficult and unattractive. Government decrees and laws called for improvement in landlord-tenant relations, rent reduction, more equitable taxes, and guarantees against requisitions. Encouragement was offered for cooperatives for seed improvement, marketing, and credits. Industrial cooperatives were promoted to encourage the added handicraft activities which usually mean the difference between poverty and prosperity on the farms. Schemes were projected for rural drainage, irrigation, flood control, flood prevention, and for the improvement of highways in the rural areas. Technical experts were invited from foreign countries and from the League of Nations. Plans were extensive and utopian; performance was limited or nonexistent. The failure to implement its agricultural program, whether through its own fault or through the compulsion of resisting Japan, was to cost the Kuomintang dearly in its later struggle with the Communists.

Industrialization was a magic formula in China, as elsewhere in Asia. The government was inclined to regard industrialization as a panacea for its economic ills and a rapid transit to national greatness. It expressed hope for a substantial heavy industry, but it could not possibly blind itself to its own weakness. A few light industries—paper, textiles, cigarettes—existed in the cities, thanks primarily to foreign capital. A small beginning was made in the manufacture of steel at the Han-Yeh-P'ing works in Hankow. Manchuria and North China possessed ample resources for an eventual heavy industry, but military conflict was stony ground for industrial seeds. The government endeavored to put its currency on a stable basis and invited foreign capital to invest in joint enterprise. The Kuomintang did its best to improve railway and highway systems, and it pioneered airlines within China and overland to Europe; yet with all its desires and goodwill, it could make no substantial progress in industrialization.

Nor could the Kuomintang do much about foreign trade. The vast numbers of Chinese always enticed prospective exporters to China, but the low purchasing power of the Chinese quickly dissipated dreams of limitless wealth in commerce. The average Chinese bought only twenty-five cents' worth of American goods per year as compared with the average Japanese purchase of three dollars per year, and the average British purchase of twenty-five dollars per year. China handled less one percent of the world's commerce. It sold tea, silk, vegetable oils, agricultural products, metals, minerals, and a smattering of manufactured goods. In return it bought food, raw materials, and some products of Western factories. Few of the articles of foreign commerce affected the daily lives of Chinese in the interior, with the result that it made little difference to Chinese economy whether boycotts, blockades, or embargoes cut China off from the outer world. The China market was valuable to Great Britain and to Japan, and to a lesser extent to the United States; however, sales were limited to China's infinitesimal capacity to pay.

In the cultural realm, the government at Nanking tried to bridge the gap between intellectual Chinese and the common peasants, between the moderns and the old-fashioned Confucianists, between the city dwellers and the "old hundred names" who lived in the villages and on the farms. The educational system was enriched by the application of scientific methods and the introduction of modern subject matter in the arts and sciences. Education—modern style—was considered more than ever essential for entry into public life and position. Unfortunately government jobs offered the only opportunities for employment for college graduates. Mission schools multiplied, so did public schools, and the curriculums of both were geared to bring about changes in the Chinese environment. History lessons stressed the indignities which the foreigners had heaped upon the Chinese and thus added to the fever-pitch of the Chinese revolution. Students came to consider direct political action as important as their studies. Increasing numbers of students were given opportunities to go abroad. Hu Shih and James Yen contributed to a sparkling literary renaissance. Writers dared to use the vernacular as a literary medium, and they launched a mass educational movement with materials written in a thousand basic characters. The press, magazines, radio, mass meetings, and even the moving pictures introduced new facts and ideas to millions who had previously been missed by the stream of modern life.

Telephones, electric lights, railways, and automobiles contributed to the modification of the social structure. The ease and cheapness of moving about, the financial independence of the city workers, and the general uprising of the modern generation against the restrictions of the marriage system brought about substantial modification of the family institution. In spite of the fact that many of the leaders in the Kuomintang, including Chiang Kai-shek himself, were Christians, the religious supports of Chinese society were shaken by the general skepticism rampant throughout the world and by the professional atheism of the Communists.

Beneath the confusion and apparent anarchy, which some thought was the collapse of Chinese civilization, there could be detected the convulsions of a living nation. The Chinese looked to their own philosophers for a new enshrinement of the ancient Confucian virtues of benevolence, sincerity, loyalty, and filial piety which would keep them steady while they were buffeted about by the impact of modernization. The inner struggles were obscured by the outward signs of an entire nation on the move. The gardens of public buildings were converted into playgrounds, always with a makeshift basketball hoop and backboard; temples were used as patriotic museums, with pictures showing foreign gunboats shelling Chinese cities. Boy Scouts and Camp Fire Girls paraded with banners proclaiming "The Revolution Is Not Yet Completed" or urging "Smoke No Opium" or "Plough the Land—Weave Cloth—Read Books." The slogans "Down with Imperialism, Militarism and the Oppressors of the People" and "Execute the Last Will and Testament of Dr. Sun Yat-sen" became national watchwords.

China was unfortunate in encountering its Renaissance, Reformation, Industrial Revolution, French Revolution, and Russian Revolution at one time. In the midst of it all it was engulfed by foreign invasion. In a few years China was to lose to Japan more prestige and territory than the empire previously lost in a hundred years of decay. For China, World War II began at the time of the Manchurian invasion in 1931. Neither the Kuomintang nor any other regime in those circumstances could have guided China's modernization into constructive channels while girding itself to meet the invader from across the Yellow Sea.

SUGGESTED READING

Bland, J. O. P., and Backhouse, Edmund, *Reform Movement in China, 1898–1912* (Stanford, Stanford U., 1931).

Chen, Stephen, and Payne, Robert, *Sun Yat-sen* (New York, Day, 1934).

Chiang Kai-shek, *China's Destiny* (trans. by Wang Chung-hui) (New York, Macmillan, 1947).

Chow Tse-tung, *May Fourth Movement* (Cambridge, Harvard U., 1960).

Hahn, Emily, *Soong Sisters* (Garden City, Doubleday, 1941).

Holcombe, Arthur N., *Spirit of the Chinese Revolution* (New York, Knopf, 1930).

Hu Shih, *Chinese Renaissance* (Chicago, U. of Chicago, 1934).

Hussey, Harry, *Venerable Ancestor* (New York, Doubleday, 1948). (P)

Isaacs, Harold R., *Tragedy of the Chinese Revolution* (second rev. ed.) (Stanford, Stanford U., 1962).

Levenson, Joseph, *Confucian China and its Modern Fate* (Berkeley, U. of California, 1958).

Linebarger, Paul, *China of Chiang Kai-shek* (Boston, World Peace Foundation, 1941).

MacNair, H. F., *China in Revolution* (Chicago, U. of Chicago, 1931).

Powell, Ralph L., *Rise of Chinese Military Power, 1898–1912* (Princeton, Princeton U., 1955).

Reid, J. G., *Manchu Abdication and the Powers* (Berkeley, U. of California, 1935).

Sharmon, Lyon, *Sun Yat-sen, His Life and its Meaning* (New York, Day, 1934).

Sun Yat-sen, *San Min Chu I, Three Principles of the People* (trans. by Frank Price) (Shanghai, Commercial Press, 1929).

Varg, Paul, *Missionaries, Chinese, and Diplomats* (Princeton, Princeton U., 1958).

13

China and the Foreign Powers

While China struggled to improve its internal conditions, it carried on a long and often discouraging campaign to recover the sovereignty which had been lost during the nineteenth century. The unequal treaties had robbed China of some of its possessions and had deprived the central government of the right to develop its own territory as it chose. Because of the treaty system, foreign nations enjoyed unusual privileges of extraterritoriality, tariff control, and stationing of troops in China. The settlements and concessions grew into attractive areas with palatial homes and magnificent offices. Businessmen and missionaries were given unusual protection in the pursuit of their occupations. Foreigners in China were treated exceptionally well, while Chinese abroad were subjected to personal indignities.

These unpleasant facts disturbed the Chinese. At first they were mildly resentful; gradually they became bitter and demonstrative. The feeling of humiliation gave way to cold anger. Political groups, including the Kuomintang and the Communists, whipped the emotions of the masses into a frenzy; and the psychosis of antiforeignism became the dominant characteristic of China's political development. The changes in China's domestic scene, as recorded in the last chapter, took place against the backdrop of foreign affairs about to be described. The chart shows the parallel time relationship between important internal and international events.

Last Years of the Empire

Chinese resentment against foreigners often exploded into isolated incidents against traders, sailors, or missionaries; it was seldom expressed against diplomats or consuls. The fear of foreign governments, with their

	INTERNAL EVENTS	INTERNATIONAL EVENTS	
1900	Boxer Uprising	Boxer Protocol	
		Anti-American Boycott	1905
		Russo-Japanese War	1905
		Treaty of Peking	1905
		Russia-Japanese Agreement	1907
1908	Death of Tzu Hsi		
	Hsuan Tung Emperor		
		Knox Neutralization Proposals	1909
	National Assembly	Russo-Japanese Agreement	1910
1911	Revolution	Four-power Agreement for railway construction	1911
1912	Establishment of Republic	Reorganization Loan	1912
	Yüan Shih-k'ai		
	Birth of Kuomintang		
		Mongolia Agreement	1913
		Tibet: Simla and Delhi Conventions	1914
		World War I	1914
		Twenty-One Demands	1915
1916	Death of Yüan Shih-k'ai		
1917	Era of Warlords	China's Entry into World War I	1917
1919	May 4 Student Movement	Versailles Conference	1919
		Second Consortium	1920
1921	Origin of Chinese Communist Party	Washington Conference	1921
1922	Sun-Joffe Agreement		
1924	Russian Advisers	Russian Treaties	1924
	Kuomintang-Communist Cooperation		
		May 30 Shanghai Incident	1925
1926	Northward March	Christmas Memorandum	1926
1927	Ousting of Russian Advisers	Nanking Incident	1927
		Break in Russian Relations	1927
1928	Establishment of Nationalist government	Recognition of Nationalist government	1928
		Russians in Manchuria	1929
1930		Extraterritoriality Discussion	1930
1931		Japanese Invasion	1931

soldiers and gunboats, acted as a deterrent. The easy victory of the Japanese over China in 1895 shamed the Chinese into a new attitude toward their own helplessness and created an embryonic patriotism which Sir Robert Hart, the great inspector general of the Chinese maritime customs, called "the prelude to a century of change and the keynote of the future history of the Far East." After the Boxer uprising, the tide of anti-imperialism was swelled by new forces. Chinese students in mission schools were urged to rise to the full height of dignity and cast off their sense of inferiority. Superstitious peasants were encouraged to believe that foreign railway trains and telegraph wires were offensive to the gods of wind and water and therefore causes of bad luck. Workers were persuaded that their sweat and tears were exploited to add to the coffers of foreigners' gold. Prosperous merchants and bankers looked with envy upon all the lucrative profits of foreign commerce.

The first manifestation of the newly aroused sense of nationality was the boycott of American trade, adopted by the merchants of China as a means of strengthening the hands of their government in protesting against the immigration legislation of the United States. In 1904 the Americans ended the treaty with China which regulated Chinese immigration and put a stop to the immigration of Chinese labor by means of Congressional law. The Chinese were indignant, but helpless. A boycott against American goods was attempted in most Chinese ports in 1905, but it faded away after a few months because of the strong opposition of all foreign interests in the coastal cities. However, the potential value of the boycott as weapon of nonviolent protest became apparent to young political leaders.

Popular sentiment was reflected in the stiffening attitude on the part of the Chinese government in negotiating for new treaties. After the Boxer Protocol, China was faced with demands for new commercial treaties. More clearly than ever China perceived the rivalries and jealousies among the Western powers, and detected a tiny sense of guilt on their part. At least some felt that China had received a bad deal in the past and was entitled to better treatment. New treaties were made with the British (1902) and with the Americans and Japanese (1903).

The British and American treaties represented new points of view. They continued to lay down conditions to which China was required to conform, but they introduced the idea that these conditions might be alleviated if China would improve its internal situation. Old rules for tariff and trade, and for the protection of the missionaries and their converts, were reaffirmed. New provisions were made for currency and coinage, copyright laws, administration of justice, and working conditions in factories and mines—but it was stipulated that these provisions might be modified if the Chinese would implement satisfactory reforms. Pressures were inserted in the text of treaties to force China to modernize its legal system, adopt a uniform system of weights and measures, and to legalize the importation of foreign opium. The Chinese recognized the value of these objectives, but they resented the procedure which made national goals a matter of international obligation.

The regulation of international traffic in opium gave rise to bitter feelings. The more enlightened elements in China felt that opium-smoking brought nothing but weakness and disgrace to China and its people. Opium came from two sources: domestic poppy and importations of the finished product from British India and Persia. Foreign traders argued that it was futile to stamp out the trade unless domestic sources of opium were also eradicated. The British and the Chinese entered into an agreement in 1906 which provided that importations of opium and local cultivation of the poppy should be progressively reduced to zero within ten years. The agreement could not be enforced, and the Chinese sought to place all the blame for the opium evil on the shoulders of foreigners.

The continuing tendency on the part of the great powers to disregard the rights of China in their international politics poured salt into Chinese wounds. China stood helplessly by while its position was progressively undermined in Manchuria, Mongolia, and Tibet. Russia disregarded China in overrunning Manchuria; Japan did likewise in driving the Russians out. China was the hapless victim of the war between Russia and Japan in 1904–1905. China declared its neutrality, but its soil could not escape the blood bath of actual hostilities. The terms of the Treaty of Portsmouth disposed of China's nominal possessions without China's assent. Japan took away from Russia in 1905 exactly what Russia had stopped Japan from taking from China ten years earlier. By the Treaty of Peking between Japan and China, December 22, 1905, China gave its approval to the terms of the Treaty of Portsmouth as a *fait accompli*. The Chinese-Japanese agreements also opened new ports in Manchuria, agreed to the rebuilding of the strategic railway from Antung on the Korean border to Mukden, and gave permission to a joint stock company to develop forests along the Yalu River. In the unpublished minutes of the conference at Peking which led to the treaty, it was recorded that China should grant no concessions to foreign capital for construction of railways parallel to the South Manchurian Railway, which had just passed from the hands of the Russians to the Japanese.

During the next decade Japan and Russia buried the hatchet and entered into secret agreements delimiting their spheres of interest in Manchuria and Mongolia. China was not consulted and met only resistance when it endeavored to safeguard its basic national interests in those rich areas. On July 30, 1907, Russia and Japan signed a convention promising to respect the principles of the Open Door and engaging to sustain the territorial *status quo*. Japan gave Russia a free hand to develop North Manchuria; Russia did the same for Japan in South Manchuria. Japan recognized the position of Russia in Outer Mongolia, and Russia recognized the political solidarity of Japan and Korea. This was an effective delimitation of spheres of interest which left China out in the cold.

After American efforts to gain a foothold in railway building in Manchuria, and an abortive attempt to internationalize the railways, the Russians and Japanese on July 4, 1910 announced new understandings. The date was significant. On the American holiday, Russia and Japan declared "in the event the special interests of Russia or Japan should come to be threatened, the two nations would agree upon the measures to be taken with a view to common action." In the last years of the Manchu empire, the Chinese had very little to say about the future of either Manchuria or Mongolia.

They were almost as helpless in Tibet. They lacked the power to quell local disturbances. China was helpless in the face of conflicting interests on the part of the Russians in Central Asia and the British in India. As the Russians concentrated in Mongolia to the north, the British expanded their influence in Tibet. In 1904 the British sent Colonel (later Sir) Francis Younghusband into Lhasa, where he negotiated a convention with local lamas which pledged Tibet to pay an indemnity, observe and demarcate the frontier, and open new trading marts. On April 27, 1906, as the suzerain over Tibet, China ratified the agreement between the British and the local Tibetan authorities. In exchange for a British engagement not to interfere in the internal administration of Tibet, China undertook to let no other foreign power intervene in Tibet. In the following year both Russia and Great Britain disavowed aggressive intentions in Tibet and recognized Chinese suzerainty (not sovereignty). Their action was an empty gesture because civil wars within Tibet and the weakness of the Peking government made it impossible to do anything about pacifying Tibet or enforcing its claims to full and complete sovereignty.

The last years of the empire in China were years of financial imperialism. China had no money to build railways or factories or to exploit its mines. Old-style mandarins had no faith in modern financial institutions, such as banks and joint stock companies, and they were hampered by traditional practices of squeeze and nepotism. Consequently China's finances passed entirely into the hands of foreigners; economic development depended upon their will and pleasure. The maritime customs were pledged as security for the Boxer indemnity; provincial revenues were hypothecated; and railway trunk lines were subject to foreign control because they were built with foreign capital.

The principal field for foreign finance lay in railway construction, because railways were the principal means of developing the spheres of interest. Some railways worked out to China's undeniable advantage, but foreign diplomats increasingly used railway politics for selfish purposes. The Russian and Japanese railways in Manchuria, the German lines in Shantung and the French system in Yunnan and Kwangsi provinces illustrated economic ventures which were used for strategic purposes. Railways were constructed, operated, and supervised by agencies of foreign powers, even if the railways were located within Chinese territory. Each nation carried on its financial operations through a single bank or banking syndicate with which China was obliged to deal. When China wanted money for railways or any other development purpose, it was obliged to appeal to these restricted sources.

Americans were well aware of the political overtones of railways in China, and endeavored in a timid way to protect Chinese interests. A group of American bankers obtained a concession to build a railway in South China, which it sold to the Belgians. Mr. E. H. Harriman tried in vain to purchase Russian and Japanese railways in Manchuria in order to fulfill his dream of making the Union Pacific the heart of a round-the-world system. It is only fair to point out that he was more interested in prestige and profits than the welfare of the Chinese. The American Secretary of State, Philander C. Knox, tried to persuade all the powers to neutralize their holdings politically by turning them over to an international syndicate. It was undoubtedly this initiative which prompted Russia and Japan to issue their "hands off" warning on July 4, 1910, which informed the world that those two nations *would take common action* if their interests were threatened. When unable to displace the Russians and the Japanese from their Manchurian stronghold, Willard Straight and other Americans tried to create an American-owned system which would provide competitive service from Peking to the Siberian border.

When the Chinese awakened to the dangers of financial imperialism, they were inclined to reject all offers of large-scale railway construction and to limit themselves to such local activity as they could finance with their own capital. This was the setting for the injection of railway politics into the national revolution. The central authorities at Peking, aware of the possibilities of a transportation network in binding the nation together, and perhaps not averse to well-placed commissions or bribes, favored continuation of the game in spite of its dangers. Local officials chose to support rebellion rather than to be party to a scheme which would be harmful to China and would at the same time weaken their authority vis-à-vis the central government. On the very eve of the revolution, in the spring of 1911, China and the powers announced a scheme which it was hoped would provide the Chinese with money and take the imperialistic features out of economic activities. The United States, England, France, and Germany formed a "consortium" of bankers which would make funds available on an international basis for railway construction and such general purposes as currency reform. Negotiations for loans, which would be as nonpolitical as possible, were underway when the bomb exploded in Hankow.

First Year of the Republic under Yüan Shih-k'ai

The succession of Yüan Shih-k'ai made little difference in the system of China's dealing with the foreign powers. True, the empire was gone; but Yüan was not a socialist, revolutionist, or even a republican. He represented a greater concentration of actual power than the emperor, and he was the type of Chinese ruler whom foreign diplomats found congenial. He accepted the amenities of the treaty system, and he used the approval of the foreign powers as an effective weapon to consolidate his own position. Above all things he stood for law and order. He was accepted by Tsarist Russians, imperial Japanese, and even democratic British and Americans as a god-sent respite from chaos which threatened to be China's fate if the "wild-eyed revolutionists" from Central China were to succeed too quickly. In the form of a "reorganization loan" in 1912, the powers provided the extra money which Yüan needed to run the government.

Peking under Yüan remained as it had been under the Manchu Dynasty. It was the center of pomp and ceremony, and of Chinese art and culture. However, the Forbidden City, the home of the emperor, closed its doors, and the Legation Quarter, the area reserved for foreign diplomats, achieved new brilliance and glamour. Most of the representatives of foreign nations lived like kings, or at least princes, and they concerned themselves but little with the growing pains of China's modernization. They preferred the luxuries of the past to the agonies of the future. Cocktail parties, banquets, the races at Paomachang (a fashionable suburb of Peking), weekends at the resorts in the western hills, and a dilettante interest in China's culture were more attractive pastimes than serious endeavors to probe the minds of students and teachers in Peking's universities. Yüan, his favorites, and Peking high society surrendered themselves to the delusions of their make-believe world. They were happy and gay as long as trouble stayed away from their own door. No need for them to go to the provinces, so long as part of the taxes from the provinces flowed to Peking to keep them in affluence. No need for them to worry about any "wave of the future," for in their own uncritical souls was the satisfactory consolation that they represented the best of all that mattered in this transitory world. China had endured since the beginning of time; the same cultural values which had preserved China would prevail over one more annoying civil disturbance. Such was the psychology of Peking, which was so far removed from the heartbeat of the Chinese masses.

Yüan was obliged at the outset of his administration to look to his outlying regions: Manchuria, Mongolia, and Tibet. In northern Manchuria, the Russians had an area of operations four times as large as southern Manchuria, and the entire area took on the physical appearance of Russian Siberia. On the basis of the clause which gave the Chinese Eastern Railway Company the right to lease lands, the Russians leased the right of way for the railway itself; and in addition they leased lands for schools, hospitals, churches, and industrial enterprises. Municipal areas, including the city of Harbin, were administered by Russian officials. Mines, telegraphs, forests, and river shipping were developed by Russians. By the time of Yüan Shih-k'ai, the Russians had 100,000 immigrants in Manchuria and 30,000 troops there in the guise of railway guards and frontier police. Japan was equally busy in placing its stamp upon southern Manchuria, and Yüan was in no position to register any protest against either Russia or Japan.

In Mongolia, the Russians took advantage of the Mongolian hatred of Chinese traders, officials, and farmers, and supported independence movements. On December 16, 1911—immediately after the Chinese revolution—the religious head of Mongolia, the Hutukhtu, was proclaimed chief of a Mongolian state. He informed Peking that he was going to declare his independence from China as the United States had declared its independence from England. In 1912 Russia sent in arms, increased its consular guards, extended recognition to the new regime, and offered its services as mediator between China and Mongolia. On July 8, 1912, Japan and Russia reached an understanding which recognized eastern Inner Mongolia as a sphere of economic interest for Japan and designated the rest of Mongolia as the preserve of Russia. On November 5, 1913, Russia signed a treaty with China which recognized China's suzerainty over Mongolia but which safeguarded Russia's rights. Then, on June 7, 1915, Russia called a tripartite conference (Russia, China, and Outer Mongolia) at Kiakhta which drew up a treaty that defined the status of Outer Mongolia as it existed at the time of the Russian Revolution. Chinese sovereignty was recognized, but neither China nor Russia was to interfere in the internal affairs of Outer Mongolia. A Chinese dignitary at Urga would bestow the Hutukhtu's title upon him and see that there would be no impairment of China's nominal sovereignty. Outer Mongolia would make no political treaties with foreign powers, and China would consult with Russia on all political and territorial questions involving Outer Mongolia. Russia and China would have limited military detachments in Mongolia; nationals of both countries would pay all internal taxes. Outer Mongolia became in effect a joint protectorate of Russia and China. Imperial Russia made cautious advances into Tannu Tuva and the Barga region on the Manchuria-Mongolia frontier; however, by the time of the death of Yüan Shih-k'ai, Russia's armies were being pummeled in Europe; and the Russian revolution was only months away. The star of Russia in Asia was about to disappear temporarily below the horizon.

In Tibet, Yüan was effectively stymied by the British. Tibet followed the lead of Mongolia in attempting to sever its ties with China upon the outbreak of the Chinese revolution. Yüan was scarcely in position to authorize Chinese troops for Lhasa, but the British minister in Peking informed him that the British government, because of its interest in India, would not consent to Chinese military operations in Tibet. However, the British would agree to the stationing of a Chinese resident in Tibet, with a small military guard or escort. Tibet declared its independence on January 6, 1913, and the British suggested a tri-partite conference (Great Britain, China, and Tibet) in India to discuss the situation. Agreements negotiated at Delhi and Simla in 1914 gave a temporary status to Tibet and partially delimited the frontier between India and Tibet, but the conventions were never ratified. Tibetan affairs faded into the background of British attention during World War I.

The war in Europe, which broke out in 1914, added to Yüan's (and China's) cup of bitterness. Japan, as the ally of Great Britain declared war on Germany and conducted hostilities against the German stronghold in Shantung. Japan took advantage of the wartime situation to disclose its bid for dominance in China, and inferentially in all of East Asia. On January 18, 1915, Japan presented to China the Twenty-One Demands. The demands were delivered to Yüan personally, not to the minister of foreign affairs; and they were printed on the stationery of the Japanese war office which was ominously watermarked with guns and artillery pieces. After long and futile negotiations, China signed, on May 25, 1915, two treaties and thirteen notes which represented the most humiliating of the unequal diplomatic settlements to which China had ever been subjected.

The treaty regarding South Manchuria and eastern Inner Mongolia provided that the leases on Port Arthur and Dairen and the terms of the South Manchurian and the Antung-Mukden Railway agreements should be extended to ninety-nine years; Japanese subjects might reside and travel in South Manchuria, engage in business and manufacturing, and lease land outside the treaty ports for trade or agricultural purposes; the Chinese government should give its permission to any joint Chinese-Japanese enterprises; Japanese subjects be given limited extraterritoriality; China should open to foreign trade and residence suitable places in eastern Inner Mongolia; and the Kirin-Changchun Railway loan agreement should be revised in favor of Japan. By separate notes China conceded that the Japanese should have the right to open new mines, should be given the first chance to supply foreign capital for railway construction, and should supply advisers in South Manchuria if foreigners should be necessary.

The treaty regarding Shantung provided that China should acquiesce in whatever agreement Japan and Germany might reach with regard to the German assets in Shantung, that Japanese capitalists might build the Chefoo-Weihsien Railroad, and that additional places for foreign residence and trade should be opened in the province. China agreed not to alienate any territory within the province or islands along the coast to any foreign power, and Japan indicated its intention of restoring the leased territory of Kiaochow Bay to China under certain conditions.

In a separate exchange of notes, the Chinese gave to Japan the right to participate in the Han-Yeh-P'ing Steel Company, which was the largest industrial enterprise in the Yangtze Valley. In a formal statement regarding Fukien Province, the Chinese government said that it had given no permission to foreign nations to construct on its coast dockyards, coaling stations for military use, or naval bases, and that it had no intention of doing so.

The original Japanese demands called for the employment of Japanese advisers in political, financial, and military affairs; joint Chinese-Japanese organization of the police forces in important places; and the procurement of Chinese arms from Japanese sources. These were successfully resisted by the Chinese and set aside for future consideration.

Shortly after the conclusion of the treaties with Japan, Yüan Shih-k'ai died. As has been noted, his death ushered in a period of endemic civil wars on the domestic scene; it also introduced a new era in international affairs. Peking remained as the center of diplomatic battles, but a new grouping of forces took place. While the European powers fought in World War I Japan rose to uncontested leadership among the foreigners in Peking.

FOREIGN AFFAIRS IN THE PERIOD OF THE WARLORDS

When China entered the war on the side of the Allies in 1917, it took the first significant actions against the privileges of foreign nations in China. It took over the territorial concessions of Germany and Austria, stopped payments on their share of the Boxer indemnity, withdrew their legation and consular guards, closed their post offices, sequestered their public properties and bank accounts, and denounced their treaties, including those which bestowed upon Germany and Austrian nationals the privilege of extraterritoriality. The solid front of the West was broken.

Elated by these diplomatic victories, the government at Peking sent its delegates to the Peace Conference in Paris in a very reflective and hopeful mood. The Chinese were reflective because the West, heretofore the symbol of unity and strength, lay exhausted after four years of fratricidal fighting. Was China wise in trying to follow the example of the West? Why should China strive to build up national strength as the West conceived it, if the ultimate purpose of that strength were suicide or murder? The Chinese were also hopeful because they believed in the slogan "making the world safe for democracy." They hoped that their program for the abolition of foreign privileges in China would be endorsed. The Chinese expected at least a declaration which would serve to establish a new world order upon the foundation of the principles of justice, equality, and respect for the sovereignty of nations.

The Chinese were doomed to disappointment. China received a vast amount of sympathy and publicity and enjoyed the unprecedented experience of sitting at an international diplomatic table as one of the victorious powers. However, considerations of *Realpolitik* dictated the sacrifice of Chinese aspirations upon the altar of Japanese appeasement. Japan, too, was a victor—and Japan demanded the Chinese province of Shantung as the reward of its victory. The wise men of Versailles confirmed Japanese possession of Shantung and refused to vitiate the one-sided Chinese-Japanese treaties which followed the Twenty-One Demands. The Western statesmen lived to regret their decision. They lost the golden opportunity to steer the modernization of China into channels which would have been in conformity with their own expressed ideals. The Chinese were so angry at their shabby treatment that they refused to sign the Treaty of Versailles. They signed the Treaty of Saint Germain-en-Laye with Austria and thus became a member of the League of Nations. China re-established peace with Germany by presidential proclamation on September 15, 1919; it signed a new treaty with Germany on May 20, 1921, based on principles of equality and reciprocity. What an ironical turn of history! China and Germany were enemies during World War I but in mutual exasperation because of the treaty of peace they renewed ties of friendship which became stronger than ever.

When the Chinese delegates returned home from Paris, they expected official censure for their failures. To their utter amazement they were greeted by an outpouring of popular support for the stubbornness which they had displayed. Student demonstrations, strikes, and boycotts, at first in Peking and then throughout the country, protested against the piracy on the part of Japan. Then all the powers came in for denunciation for being accessories to the crime of Shantung. "Anti-imperialism" became a national rallying cry. Those spontaneous expressions of humiliation and hatred in 1919—usually known as the May 4 movement—added incredible fuel to the flames of nationalism and contributed directly to the formation of the Peking cell of the Chinese Communist Party.

The period of the warlords is a drab spot in China's internal record, but it is by contrast a creditable entry in China's diplomatic account. The Chinese government retained the goodwill of the powers. The prospects of economic development gave rise to the formation of a new financial consortium which was prepared to advance new loans. A succession of brilliant representatives abroad argued China's case with dignity and persuasion. Their finest performance was at the Limitation of Armaments Conference in Washington in 1921, when the United States took the lead in calling the interested nations together in order to reduce the tensions which persisted in the postwar world.

At Washington the Chinese program repeated the familiar appeals for the restoration of territorial integrity, political and administrative independence, and the effective application of the Open Door in all parts of China. The Chinese asked the powers to publish and disavow all their claims to special interests, put time limits on existing agreements, and make public declarations that they would refrain from future encroachments. The Chinese wanted specific relief from nonalienation declarations, the fourteen interpower understandings concerning their respective interests in China, and the Sino-Japanese Treaties of 1915. The Chinese also wanted declarations that no treaties in the future would be made concerning China unless China was invited to participate, China's neutrality would be respected in case of war, and future disputes in the Pacific and the Far East should be settled by peaceful methods.

The Chinese program was rejected as a basis for discussion, in favor of a general resolution on China policy introduced by the American delegate, Elihu C. Root. This resolution attempted a precise definition of the vague understandings implied in the Open Door, and it led to the adoption of the Nine-Power Treaty. By this treaty of February 6, 1922, the powers agreed

> to respect the sovereignty, independence, and the territorial and administrative integrity of China; to provide the fullest and most unembarrassed opportunity to China to develop and maintain an effective and stable government; to use their influence for the purpose of effectually establishing and maintaining the principle of equal opportunity for the commerce and industry of all nations throughout the territory of China; and to refrain from taking advantage of conditions in China in order to seek special rights and privileges which would abridge the rights of subjects or citizens of friendly states and from countenancing action inimical to the security of such states.

The contracting powers other than China agreed that they would

> not seek, nor support their nationals in seeking, (a) any arrangement which might purport to establish in favour of their interests

any general superiority of rights with respect to commercial or economic development in any designated region of China; (b) any such monopoly or preference as would deprive the nationals of any other power of the right of undertaking any legitimate trade or industry in China, or of participating with the Chinese Government, or with any local authority, in any category of public enterprise, or which by reason of its scope, duration or geographical extent is calculated to frustrate the practical application of the principle of equal opportunity.

The delegates at the conference used all the legal skill at their command to put an end to the system of spheres of interest, and they went as far as they could to implement China's program. The powers agreed to make public all agreements and contracts involving "any concession, franchise, option, or preference concerning railways, mines, forests, navigation rights, river conservancy, harbor works of public services or for sale of arms or ammunition, or which involve a lien on public revenues and properties." They promised to respect China's position as a neutral in future wars. They agreed finally that "whenever a situation arises which in the opinion of any one of them involves the application of the stipulations of the present treaty, and renders desirable discussion of such application, there shall be full and frank communication between the Powers concerned."

In addition to the Nine-Power Treaty, the Chinese achieved substantial progress in attacking individual items in the treaty system. Foreign postal services were abandoned and foreign jurisdiction over all electrical means of communication, including radio stations, was surrendered. With regard to foreign troops in China, the powers would go no further than to give their assent to "a collective inquiry into the facts and opinions concerning their own intentions and the capacity of the Chinese to assure the protection of the lives and property of foreigners in China." For a long time to come the Chinese were doomed to watch in sullen silence the drills and parades of the well-equipped armies of the foreigners in their irritating, ostentatious displays on Chinese soil.

The Chinese gained marked if only partial success in their efforts to terminate the treaty-tariff, extraterritoriality, leases, and spheres of interest. The powers promised immediate revision of tariff rates without conceding autonomy, and insisted upon the retention of the customs administration. With regard to extraterritoriality, the powers agreed to the appointment of a commission "to inquire into the present practice of extraterritorial jurisdiction in China and into the laws and the judicial system and the methods of judicial administration of China and make recommendations to assist the Chinese in introducing reforms which would warrant the powers in relinquishing extraterritoriality."

China asked for the immediate demilitarization and eventual retrocession of the leaseholds, since leaseholds were no longer needed to preserve the balance of power. Viviani of France agreed to collective restitution. Lord Balfour of England foresaw no objection to the return of Weihaiwei, but pointed out that Kowloon was necessary for the security of Hong Kong. Baron Shidehara of Japan declared Japan had no intention at present of relinquishing the important rights she had lawfully acquired at no small sacrifice. China made no progress at Washington toward the recovery of the residential concessions in the port cities. On February 4, 1922, China and Japan signed a bilateral agreement which provided for the return to China of the Japanese-held former German lease and sphere of interest in Shantung.

By the time of the Washington Conference it had become quite clear that international rivalries in China actually hindered China's economic and political development and produced friction among the powers themselves. Therefore the delegates were disposed to handle the Chinese complaints with sympathy and a large measure of understanding. Individual nations adopted the attitude that they would surrender their privileges just as fast as China could put its own house in order. A Japanese delegate remarked that the powers were disposed to look forward to the future with hope and confidence, but like genteel, retired burglars, they were not willing to relinquish their hold on accumulated swag.

After the conference, the Chinese diplomats returned to the confusion and civil war of their homeland to continue their campaign against the remnants of imperialism. A conference on tariff autonomy and another on the abolition of extraterritoriality met in China to consider ways and means to accord with China's demands. It was no longer a matter of whether China's sovereign prerogatives should be restored, it was rather a problem of *how* to effect the restoration.

Progress could be made only at the pace of the most reactionary and least considerate of China's neighbors rather than by the speed and good intentions of China's friends. For example, tariff autonomy could not be given back to China unless *all* the treaty powers, including Japan, would give their consent. Gradually the extreme antiforeignism of the Nationalists and Communists spread its influence to Peking, and the mild, leaderless foreign office bureaucrats in Peking were inspired to take firmer attitudes toward foreign nations. As successive treaties with Belgium, France, Japan, and Spain came up for revision or renewal, the Chinese followed the technique of dealing with each power separately, without reference to the dean of the diplomatic corps. Unilaterally the Chinese announced the termination of old treaties and the assumption of jurisdiction over the foreigners involved pending the conclusion of new treaties. For the five years between 1922 and 1927 Peking was the locale for an international fencing match, with no blood spilled.

In the meantime, battles raged in the south and the Yangtze Valley. Revolutionists were less inclined than diplomats to limit themselves to polite amenities. Acting in accordance with their Russian advisers, the Nationalists demanded immediate and unconditional cancellation of the treaties, not mere revision. On May 30, 1925, a British police captain fired into a Chinese mob at Shanghai and riots broke out. Trouble spread to Canton. Students, laborers, and merchants took up the cry, "Foreigners have shot down Chinese citizens on Chinese soil." This was the fuel which propelled Chiang Kai-shek's northward march from Canton to Hankow. Antiforeign riots broke out at Chinkiang, Hankow, Kiukiang, and Chungking, and the radical elements among the Nationalists shouted for the return of all concessions, the expulsion of foreign troops, and the immediate abolition of extraterritoriality. Boycotts paralyzed British shipping, and angry mobs jeopardized foreign lives and property throughout China. Kuomintang and Communist exploited popular indignation. They adopted policies of "combatting any country which acts towards China in a spirit of imperialism and exhibiting the most cordial friendship for any country which treats China on a footing of equality." It was precisely in the circumstances which have been described that Russia made its first efforts to gain control of the Chinese Revolution.

RUSSIA AND CHINA (1917–1927)

While warlords were in control of various localities within China, while the Chinese revolution experienced its birth pains, and while the newborn Nationalist leaders sought to lead their country into a position of dignity and equality, Russia emerged from its own revolutionary nadir and tried to regain its influence in East Asia. The Russian government and the Communist International (Comintern) coordinated their procedures. Many White Russians fled the terror of their homeland by taking the long trail across Siberia into Manchuria, and thence to Peking and Shanghai. As soon as the Reds restored order in Leningrad and Moscow, they turned their attention to the east. They put down rebellions in Siberia, and they looked to China as the hope of breaking the quarantine which had been placed on the Bolshevik government.

On July 4, 1918, Grigori Chicherin, people's commissar for foreign affairs in Moscow, informed the Fifth All-Russian Congress of Soviets of a new Russian policy toward China. According to it, Moscow repudiated the encroachments of the tsarist regime in Manchuria, relinquished extraterritoriality in China and Mongolia, withdrew military guards from its consulates in China, and suggested redemption by China of the Chinese Eastern Railway. Nothing happened for a year. In July 1919, after the

Versailles decisions, Lev Karakhan, the assistant commissar for foreign affairs, issued a manifesto which denounced all secret treaties to which Russia was a party and offered to negotiate new treaties with China on the basis of the repudiation of all former Russian privileges in China.

The authorities in Peking failed to respond to the Russian overtures because at that time they were still pro-White and anti-Red in their actions. They cooperated in the blockade of the Bolshevik areas in Manchuria, supported the allied intervention in Siberia, and concluded an arrangement with White Russian elements for continued control of the Chinese Eastern Railway under the White Russian, General Horvath. The Soviet offer, however, made a deep imprint on the students in Peking, who had already been distressed by the callous action of the Western powers at Versailles. Chinese diplomatic and intellectual circles were moved to take a new look at Chinese-Russian relations.

In August 1920, Peking withdrew recognition from the tsarist representatives who had continued to function until that date. The Russian legation was closed, the consulates taken over, the Russian post offices padlocked, and the Russian concessions transferred to Chinese administration. In the following month, the Russian foreign office handed a Chinese mission then in Moscow a second diplomatic declaration which amplified the previous Russian offers. Instead of outright renunciation of former Russian privileges, this new declaration merely proposed a new treaty drawn up with due regard for the needs of Soviet Russia. The improving fortunes of Soviet Russia made the Russians less generous in their overtures.

The Russians sent secret agents to Peking and Shanghai to assist in the organizational work of the Chinese Communist Party; they signed a treaty with Mongolia on November 5, 1921, which encouraged the Mongolians against the Chinese; and they invited both the Kuomintang and the Chinese Communists in January 1922 to send delegates to attend a Congress of the Toilers of the Far East in Moscow. At the same time Peking diplomats in Washington argued China's case against the unequal treaties, unofficial representatives from south and central China in Russia heard Zinoviev warn, "Either you receive your emancipation at the hands of the proletariat, or you are doomed to remain the slaves of an English, American and Japanese camarilla." The Chinese delegation was at least as much impressed by the famine in Russia as by the Communist oratory.

In August 1922 a clever Russian diplomat and publicity agent, Abram (Adolf) Joffe reached Peking. Joffe could not establish a productive rapport with any capricious warlord in the Chinese capital, so he went to Shanghai to discuss Russian-Chinese relations with Sun Yat-sen in the safety of the French concession at Shanghai. Together they worked out the informal understanding which has already been noted. Joffe then moved out of the field of Chinese diplomacy and gave his attention to negotiations with Japan. Other Russians in 1924 encouraged Outer Mongolia to proclaim the first of the people's republics in Asia. Visas for travel to Outer Mongolia could be obtained only in Urga (renamed *Ulan Bator* or Red Hero) or Moscow.

Lev Karakhan, who had drafted the seductive promises to China in 1919 and 1920, followed Joffe to China. On May 31, 1924, he concluded a treaty *with the Peking government* which re-established normal diplomatic relations; extinguished all treaties between China and imperial Russia; and predicated all future intercourse on the basis of equality, reciprocity, and justice. Each party undertook to prohibit subversive activities within its borders and pledged itself not to engage in propaganda against the political and social systems of the other. The Soviet Union recognized Outer Mongolia as an integral part of China and renounced all Russian concessions in China, together with extraterritorial rights and the Russian share of the Boxer indemnity. On the question of the Chinese Eastern Railway, it was stipulated that the road was purely a commercial enterprise. China's sovereignty in the matter was recognized, as well as its right to redeem the railway with Chinese capital within eighty years. A provisional management agreement was drawn up and the categorical statement was made that "the future of the railway was to be determined by the two governments to the exclusion of any third party or parties."

As a kind of insurance, Karakhan negotiated a supplementary agreement with Chang Tso-lin, the Old Marshal of Manchuria, which reaffirmed the principles of the Peking treaty with regard to the Chinese Eastern railway. Chang Tso-lin hated the Russians. He would have driven them out had he been sufficiently strong. He made life as difficult as possible for them in Manchuria, and he accepted an agreement with Karakhan simply because he had no alternative. Tensions between Chinese and Russians there, primarily over railway questions, approached the breaking point, while contemporary differences of opinion between Russians and Chinese aggravated their relationships south of the Great Wall.

In 1924 Russia did not neglect any phase of its China policy. It invited Chinese to Russia—including Chiang Kai-shek. It negotiated agreements with the Peking government and with the warlord of Manchuria. It maintained a close watch over the Communist movement within China. It sent advisers to Sun Yat-sen's Kuomintang, and it supported the Christian general whose troops were driven out of Peking and into northwest China near Russian territory. Soviet tactics looked to the welfare of the Russian state by widening the breach between China and the powers, and to the promotion of world revolution by cooperating with the Kuomintang and the Chinese Communists. While Karakhan, as the Russian representative in Peking, posed as the friend of the legal government of China, other Russians in the south conspired against it. In Peking the salon of Madame Karakhan was the most popular rendezvous of the Chinese elite; in Canton, the Russian advisers worked for the revolutionists who opposed the warlords' regime and the rule of the imperialists in Asia.

After Lenin's death, Stalin and Trotsky differed on China policy. Stalin stressed socialism within a single state; Trotsky stressed the world revolution. Stalin was more cautious, and favored the Kuomintang-Communist *rapprochement* as the ideal tactic to drive the capitalists out of China. Trotsky was more determined. He would smash the Kuomintang-Communist alliance, form Soviets within China, and gamble for all or nothing.

After Sun Yat-sen's death on March 12, 1925, factions within the Kuomintang were plunged into open rivalry for power, and attitude toward the communists was one of the issues. Common resentment on the part of all Chinese revolutionists against the foreigners in Shanghai and Canton after the incidents of May 30 prevented outright civil war. Russian propagandists skillfully utilized Chinese anger to fan the flames of anti-imperialism and to point the finger of blame directly at the British. Early in 1926 Chiang Kai-shek emerged as the most powerful figure within the Kuomintang, and he asserted his personal independence vis-à-vis the Russian advisers. In accordance with Stalin's directions, these advisers pretended not to notice Chiang's dominant position and intensified political work among the troops and peasants. Stalin believed that he could use Chiang and "toss him aside like a squeezed-out lemon" at an appropriate time. Stalin supported the northern expedition but urged caution lest a split should occur prematurely between the Kuomintang and the Communists.

In Hankow, the Kuomintang and the Communists cooperated against the foreigners in the city, although they drifted apart in their internal policies. At this point, the Kuomintang right wing under Chiang Kai-shek and the left wing under Wang Ching-wei came to the parting of the ways. In this dilemma, the Communists looked to Moscow for instructions. Trotsky said: "Fight. Support the peasants against the landlords. Organize Soviets in China." Stalin ruled otherwise. Anything Trotsky proposed at this juncture met with Stalin's opposition. Stalin said that if the peasants fought, they would lose. Therefore the correct Communist line should be to cooperate with the Kuomintang in putting down the peasant revolt. This was not the moment for battle. The Comintern on November 22, 1926, decreed the dual tactic of emphasizing the peasant revolt but of supporting the Kuomintang, many of whose influential members were prosperous landlords! The Indian Communist, M. N. Roy, was sent to China to interpret and to implement these contradictory instructions. This was bitter medicine for the peasants—and some Communist leaders. They had been encouraged to resist, and at the moment of showdown, they were ordered to surrender. In one breath, Stalin had extolled the peasant unions, hailed the agrarian revolution, and supported the confiscation of land. In the next breath, he curbed the peasant revolt and directed the Communists to give in to the Kuomintang. Perhaps Stalin's fight for life and leadership in Moscow accounted for his timidity in China.

In June 1927 he issued new instructions. Chinese Communists were to restrain the peasants and to continue cooperation with the Kuomintang left wing. At the same time and in a contradictory vein, they were to bring new worker and peasant blood into the Kuomintang leadership, to liquidate unreliable generals, to organize a new army with students as commanders, and to punish officers who maintained contacts with Chiang Kai-shek. Stalin's instructions offered no effective guidance to local Communists. It was impossible to cooperate with the Kuomintang left and to work for conditions which would destroy the basis of cooperation.

Roy endeavored to implement Stalin's policies. He believed that the Kuomintang left wing needed the Communists in a possible showdown against Chiang Kai-shek and the right. Mikhail Borodin pointed out the contradictory nature of Stalin's instruction and told Roy that they would lead to an open breach between the Kuomintang left and the Communists. As soon as the local Kuomintang leaders learned of the nature of Roy's mission, they broke with the Communists and, at the end of July 1927, sent Borodin and the other Russian advisers out of the country.

Stalin was no more successful in his government's diplomatic offensive than he had been in his direction of party policies. He had never allayed the suspicions and personal hatreds of Chang Tso-lin. When the wheel of fortune spun the warlord of Manchuria into control of the Peking government in 1926, he took charge of all official relations with the representative of the Soviet government. Chang brought all his anti-Russian sentiments from Mukden to Peking with him. Before he left Manchuria, he made no secret of his opposition to the Russians. He put the Russian manager of the Chinese Eastern Railway in jail and seized a fleet of Russian vessels on the Sungari River. Russian operations in Manchuria were at a practical standstill.

When Chang felt secure in Peking—quite independently of the growing animosity between Chiang Kai-shek and the Russians in central China —he determined to get rid of the Russian diplomats in China's capital city. On April 6, 1927, he authorized a raid on the legally inviolate premises of the Chinese Eastern Railway and the Russo-Asiatic Bank. He seized documents which showed how the Russians in the north abused their privileges of immunity to provide money and directions to the Communists in the south. Chang Tso-lin padlocked the premises belonging to the Russians and broke off relations between China and Russia. When in December 1927 the Russian consulate in Canton became involved in the abortive Communist uprising, the building was closed and the Russians lost their last observation post in China. Thus ended Soviet Russia's first grandiose initiative. Russian stock in China seemed very high in 1924, but within three years it touched bottom. Russians were ousted from Peking, Canton, Hankow, and Shanghai; and they were stalemated in Manchuria.

DIPLOMACY OF THE NANKING GOVERNMENT

With the temporary solution of Russian problems, the new National-ist government was relieved of its major diplomatic headaches. In assum-ing office in Nanking, it was obliged to regain the goodwill of its former friends (the United States and Great Britain) without reducing the in-tensity of the campaign against the unequal treaties or surrendering to the growing demands of Japan. Americans and British did not object to the nationalism and the idealism of the Kuomintang; they objected to its association with Russia and the Communists. The split between China and Russia paved the way for quick restoration of amicable relations.

As early as Christmas, 1926, the British chargé at Peking distrib-uted a memorandum which signaled a new orientation in British policy. It recognized the justice of the Chinese claim for treaty revision and aban-doned the old attitude of rigid insistence on the strict letter of treaty rights. It suggested the possibility of treaty revision *before* the establish-ment of a strong central government. It exhorted the powers not to force foreign control upon an unwilling China and to abandon the idea that foreign tutelage would be required for China's rehabilitation. It presaged a switch of British recognition from the warlord's government in Peking to the Kuomintang government in Nanking. The British hoped by their sympathetic attitude to loosen the ties between the Kuomintang and the Communists and to influence the Kuomintang toward the democratic powers of the West. The British handed back to the Kuomintang the con-cessions at Hankow and Kiukiang, conceded tariff autonomy, and offered to negotiate for the early abolition of extraterritoriality. The British initia-tive met with complete American approval.

Chiang Kai-shek responded cordially to British-American overtures. He did not slacken in his determination to rid China of its unequal treaties, but he substituted orderly processes for mob action and terrorism. He could not stamp out antiforeignism, but he could marshal it as an instrument of diplomatic pressure. He reminded the powers that the fundamental danger to themselves and their property was due to "insistence on conditions which are at once a humiliation and a menace to a nation that has known greatness and is today conscious of renewed strength." He ordered the evacuation of all foreign property occupied by Chinese soldiers, specifically commanded his men not to fire on foreign ships as they plied up and down the Yangtze and not to molest foreign lives nor interfere with missionaries. He promised that he would take steps to terminate unequal treaties and to conclude new treaties through ordinary diplomatic channels.

The Nanking government was recognized by practically all the Western powers in 1928. Within three years China regained its tariff autonomy. A whole succession of international agreements before 1931 returned to China increased portions of the Boxer indemnities; surrendered the administration of residential concessions in Hankow, Kiukiang, Chinkiang, and Amoy; and restored sovereignty over the British leasehold at Weihaiwei. New treaties with Poland, Greece, Turkey, and Egypt conceded to China a status of equality. Old treaties with Belgium, Spain, Portugal, Denmark, and Italy were terminated unilaterally. The sentiment of world peace as fostered by the Kellogg-Briand Pact of Paris in 1928 seemed to be faithfully reflected in the improving atmosphere of China.

The Chinese worked to abolish extraterritoriality. In 1929 the Nanking government sent out notices that the antiquated system should be abandoned since "China now has courts, modern prisons and codes of law." It declared that on and after January 1, 1930, all foreign nationals in the territory of China enjoying extraterritorial privileges should abide by the laws of China. The powers were agreeable to an assumption that extraterritoriality should be abolished in principle, but pointed out that the Chinese were in no practical position to afford protection for either life or property through the courts. Discussions about extraterritoriality lost all interest in the face of foreign invasion.

China was first exposed to the danger of invasion in 1929. The menace came from Russia, not Japan. It may be recalled that when the troops of Chiang Kai-shek moved into Peking in June 1928 to replace Chang Tso-lin, the Old Marshal departed on his special train for his home in Mukden. He never arrived. On the outskirts of Mukden, a Japanese bomb splintered the car in which he was riding and killed him. His son, Chang Hsueh-liang, the Young Marshal, succeeded his father. Chang Hsueh-liang inherited his father's hatred of Russia, but he looked more kindly upon the Kuomintang. Therefore he cast in his lot with Chiang Kai-shek. The Young Marshal accepted a position as the ruler of Manchuria (or the three northeastern provinces), not as an independent warlord but as a subordinate of the central government in distant Nanking. His soldiers were integrated into the national army and the Kuomintang flag flew over his palaces in Mukden.

On May 27, 1929, as agents of the Chinese government, Chang Hsueh-liang's police raided the Russian consulates which had remained open in Harbin, Tsitsihar, Manchouli, and Suifenho. They seized documents and arrested Russian officials. On July 10, the Chinese at Harbin seized the entire telephone and telegraph system of the Chinese Eastern Railway and interned some two hundred Russian workers. Russia's response was prompt and energetic. Russia gave the Chinese three days to release the prisoners and to convene a conference to settle the disputes. When the Chinese sent unsatisfactory replies to the Russian demands, both sides cut off all official and commercial relations. Troops were massed at the border, and until December a state of undeclared war existed. Then Soviet troops under the same General Galens who had been an adviser to Chiang Kai-shek in Canton poured across the border into Chinese territory and disarmed the Chinese forces in Hailar.

The war itself was farcical. Russia unveiled a modern military machine against the impotent comic-opera troops of Chang Hsueh-liang. Russia declined to pay any attention to Secretary Stimson's efforts to outlaw the war method and "expressed amazement that the Government of the United States, which by its own will has no official relations with the Soviet, deems it possible to apply to it with advice and counsel." The Russians and the Chinese achieved a settlement of their differences in the Khabarovsk Protocol of December 22, 1929. They agreed to resume *de facto* relations, pending a definitive diplomatic settlement. The settlement was still pending when the Japanese moved into Manchuria nearly two years later.

In the fall of 1931 the outlook in Nanking was far from gloomy for the solution of such problems as inland navigation, foreign troops, the remaining concessions in the hands of foreign powers and the Legation Quarter in Peiping. China's policies were directed toward securing for China a status of equality and independence in the family of nations—no more, no less. Wang Ching-wei, the prime minister under Chiang Kai-shek, declared that treaties would be revised by friendly discussion and negotiation "conducted on our part with dignity and respect for the principles of law and equity." Chinese resentment was aimed at a system and not at any individuals. Chinese crowds were on occasion aroused to demonstrations which caused inconvenience and suffering, but the Chinese government limited its actions to legitimate protests against treaties which had outlived their usefulness.

The process of adjustment and compromise was halted abruptly by the aggression of Japan. Slogans of "Down with the Unequal Treaties" became strangely meaningless when the treaties themselves could be appealed to as the one forlorn hope against invading armies. "Drive Out the Imperialists," which had been so popular as a slogan in the days of China's cooperation with Russia, was discarded; "Drive Out the Japanese" took its place. Just as China's modernization process halted in its tracks in order to concentrate on the overwhelming task of mobilizing all of China's human, economic, political, and spiritual resources to resist Japan; so anti-foreign sentiments converged on the immediate single objective of opposing Japan's drive for a new order in East Asia. China's national survival was at stake; modernization and freedom would have to wait for successful resistance against an implacable enemy.

SUGGESTED READING

Bau, Ming-chien J., *Open Door Doctrine in Relation to China* (New York, Macmillan, 1923).

Borg, Dorothy, *American Policy and the Chinese Revolution, 1925–1928* (New York, Institute of Pacific Relations, 1947).

Brandt, Conrad, *Stalin's Failure in China, 1924–1927* (Cambridge, Harvard U., 1958).

Dallin, David J., *Rise of Russia in Asia* (New Haven, Yale U., 1949).

Eudin, X. J., and North, Robert, *Soviet Russia and the East, 1920–1927* (Stanford, Stanford U., 1957).

Fifield, Russell H., *Woodrow Wilson and the Far East* (New York, Crowell, 1952).

Hsia, C. L., *Studies in Chinese Diplomatic History* (Shanghai, Commercial Press, 1953).

Levi, Werner, *Modern China's Foreign Policy* (Minneapolis, U. of Minnesota, 1953).

Pollard, Robert, *China's Foreign Relations, 1917–1931* (New York, Macmillan, 1933).

Vevier, Charles, *United States and China, 1906–1913* (New Brunswick, Rutgers U., 1955).

Wilbur, C. Martin, and How, Julie Lien-ying, *Documents on Communism, Nationalism, and Soviet Advisers in China, 1918–1927* (New York, Columbia U., 1926).

Willoughby, Westel W., *Foreign Rights and Interests in China* (Baltimore, Johns Hopkins U., 1927).

Wei, Henry, *China and Soviet Russia* (Princeton, Van Nostrand, 1956).

Whiting, Allen S., *Soviet Policies in China, 1917–1924* (New York, Columbia U., 1954).

Wright, Stanley F., *Hart and the Chinese Customs* (Belfast, Mullan, 1950).

Young, C. W., *International Relations of Manchuria* (Chicago, U. of Chicago, 1929).

14

The Rising Sun: Japan

While China struggled to find the way to international respectability and modernization, Japan experienced its golden period of growth and development. The revolution which began with the Restoration of the Meiji emperor gathered momentum with the passing years. Social and economic changes kept pace with politics. By the end of World War I, Japan seemed to have reached maturity as a nation. Internally it achieved an unprecedented degree of unity and broadened the basis of its physical strength. It energized its policies with an infectious spirit of confidence in its own destiny. Externally it brushed aside or conquered every obstacle to expansion on the Asian continent. Beyond that, it gained universal acceptance as an indispensable diplomatic and military factor in the world-wide game of international politics. It was at least a generation ahead of every other Asian state which would seek full membership in the family of nations.

THE NEW JAPAN

So many changes occurred in the life of Japan, and their influence was so far-reaching, that it was an entirely new country which mourned the death of the Meiji emperor in 1912 as compared with that which celebrated his enthronement in 1868. The soul of the people and the appearance of the land were essentially the same, but social values, manners, and customs were profoundly modified. Japan relaxed its hidebound rules. Hostility to foreigners was replaced by growing acceptance of their gadgets and conveniences. Western clothes became more popular than kimonos; Western furniture was introduced into Japanese homes. Meat, fruits, vegetables, and dairy products were accepted as welcome additions to the standard diet of rice and fish, and dining out became an acceptable pastime. Homes in the country were lighted with kerosene lamps and gradually with electric bulbs.

The school system was called upon to provide Japan with its ever-expanding corps of leaders. The elementary curriculum was broadened to include history, geography, mathematics, science, drawing, singing, gymnastics, sewing for girls and manual training for boys, agriculture, commerce, and the English language. The secondary schools were limited in their facilities, and the universities more so, but they were skillfully tailored to meet Japan's national needs. The liberal arts, humanities, and social sciences were subordinated to the natural sciences and technical subjects, and the fostering of criticism was often sacrificed to the ideal of discipline. Students were obliged to work hard to justify their right to an advanced education. By graduation time they were prepared to raise their level of living, and they were thoroughly indoctrinated with the morals and ethics associated with good Japanese citizenship. Japan trained its own commercial and technical leaders. Its universities were equipped to turn out doctors, lawyers, and engineers who would hold their own with professional people in any country. Whether it was the strict control of the national ministry of education or whether it was something inherent in the Japanese spirit, no country enjoyed a fuller measure of patriotism on the part of its citizens.

The family remained the basic unit of society. Japanese were taught that the emperor was the head of one big Japanese family, and that Japan itself should be thought of as a responsible member of an extended family of states. Respect for parents and elders did not seem to weaken, although Japanese individuals shared a world-wide tendency toward a greater freedom to make one's own decisions. The family was the great haven of security; it was the source of prosperity and happiness. However, industrialization and urbanization struck at the roots of the entrenched family; and young Japanese boys and girls were increasingly inclined to strike out to make their own mark in life. More marriages were made on the basis of individual choice rather than the will of the family, and more women worked actively for the right to follow careers other than as subservient old-style housewives. The seeds of improvement in the status of women which were to blossom during the social upheavals which followed upon both world wars were planted during the Meiji era.

Japan became less rigid in its class alignments. The court and nobility remained above ordinary mortals, but a leveling process took place among the nonnoble classes. Samurai lost their prestige—except in memory—when they transformed themselves to merchants and manufacturers. The outcasts, or etas, moved up slowly in public acceptance. Farm classes were divided into two extremes—landlords and tenants—which brought social discrimination as well as economic antagonism. In the urban areas class distinctions were intensified by the division into capital and labor. Cities like Osaka and Yokohama found themselves with large proletarian populations which were susceptible to socialistic ideas and "dangerous thoughts." The most significant development was the burgeoning of the middle classes. As more people moved from the countryside to the cities and went into business for themselves, they prospered. In Japan, as in Europe and America, the growth of the bourgeoisie laid the foundations for democracy and political liberalism.

The thought life of the Japanese absorbed profound shocks during the Meiji era. Writers look abroad for inspiration, and familiarized themselves with the romanticism of England, the realism of France, the idealism and brooding of Russia, and the freedom of the United States. Japanese literature glowed with the intoxication of national success. The feminism and dilettantism of Tokugawa Japan gave way to a more robust treatment of passions which Japan experienced in dealing with social problems at home and wars overseas. Writers of novels taught the Japanese more of Western ideas and emotions than the schools themselves. Theaters were slow to emerge from the bonds of classicism and to occupy themselves with the themes and practices of the West.

Newspapers and magazines achieved a remarkable place in Japanese society. Every town of importance boasted its own daily, and Tokyo published as many as fifty newspapers at a given time. Papers appeared in English as well as Japanese—and they gave the Japanese reasonably good coverage of news of the world. Periodicals of all kinds made their appearance, including economic, political, religious magazines; scientific, commercial engineering, and shipping journals; literary reviews and trade papers; women's and children's magazines; and comic papers. The Japanese had their equivalent of cheap journalism, devoted to scandal, sex, libelous attacks on individuals, or rabble-rousing. All these publications, as well as translations of Western books, were subject to constant censorship and government supervision. The best of Japanese papers circulated in the millions, and the literate Japanese were addicted to habitual and thorough reading of the daily press.

The native Japanese arts were not substantially improved by the influence of new ideas and techniques. A strong conservative school of Japanese artists flourished which insisted upon the preservation of traditional forms. However, a small group of moderns attempted to glamorize and imitate the masters of the West, and a middle school tried to enrich Japanese traditions with techniques learned in Paris or Rome. Metal work, cloisonné ivory-carving, porcelains, and pottery tended to become decorative and ornate, and only on occasions would workers in damascene, lacquer, embroidery, and weaving excel the excellence of the past. The demands and the possibilities of commerce tended to transform the artist into the artisan; Japanese products which were shipped abroad were prized more for their uniqueness than their esthetic appeal. Japanese architecture maintained its simplicity and harmony with nature. Temples and shrines were virtually unaffected by modernization; but demands for substantial railway station, offices, and public buildings produced steel, concrete, brick, and glass pseudo-Western structures which were new to the Japanese landscape.

The twentieth century brought interesting developments in Japanese religion. The Confucian ethics, morals, family system, ideas of loyalty and filial piety remained an integral part of the Japanese psyche. Shinto, the way of the gods, became a new instrument in the glorification of the state and the emperor. Shinto deities and shrines were classified according to official status, ranging from national shrines like the great shrine at Ise to village shrines dedicated to distinguished patriots. In addition each household had its own shrine for the family ancestors who were treated as *kami* or godlike beings. Most Japanese felt a personal attachment to the nationalistic tenets of Shinto—even if they were not registered as a regular member of some Shinto sect. State Shinto was used to develop devotion to the divine land and the imperial institution by intense indoctrination of the masses in the tales of the divine origin of the land and its rulers. The hold of the cult of Shinto on the minds of the Japanese was unshakable, even though the well-educated and sophisticated rejected the authenticity of the ancient myths.

Millions of Japanese continued to be good Buddhists at the same time that they were believers in the philosophy of Confucius and the faith of Shinto. Buddhist sects were sufficiently varied to admit almost any philosophical system and the Buddhist pantheon was large enough for all the Shinto deities. Buddhism—often considered as pacifistic—made no inroads on the martial spirit of Japan, but continued to exercise its deep influence on the art, literature, and general culture of the country. Its roots lay deep in the past; and its strength lay in its temples, its metaphysical system, and its rituals. The Buddhist priest was related to death rather than to life. Unlike the Christians, the Buddhists did not attempt to develop a moral code nor a far-reaching program of social welfare. Buddhism relied upon spiritual force for its general acceptance.

Christianity made slow progress in Japan. After more than two centuries of interdiction, Roman Catholic and Russian Orthodox priests reentered Japan. Many Protestants from the United States and England joined in the missionary movement. Only a few hundred thousand converts professed Christianity during the reign of the Meiji emperor, but they exerted an intellectual and social influence far beyond their small numbers. Missionaries founded schools, hospitals, and social centers, as well as churches; they attracted many of Japan's outstanding leaders into their fold. Christianity was handicapped because it was regarded as alien, dangerously liberal, and detrimental to the sentiment of blind devotion to the state.

With all their shrines, temples, and churches, the Japanese were inclined to view all religions with respectful skepticism. They seemed more concerned with material than spiritual problems. They looked to the schools rather than to the churches for guidance in their daily lives, and they placed reason on a higher plane than faith in their scale of social values. Love of country was a more universal preoccupation than love of God, and such religious concepts as godliness, righteousness, and purity were made to serve for the making of better political subjects. The twentieth century in Japan, as in Western Europe, brought skepticism and rationalism in its wake and in large measure turned the minds of youth toward scientific and pragmatic matters. Throughout the Meiji period, Japan was in a constant and profound state of social turmoil as it coped with its economic and political problems.

ECONOMIC DEVELOPMENT

Until the end of World War I, the population of Japan did not grow any faster than that of Great Britain. There were more than 30,000,000 Japanese in 1868, some 50,000,000 in 1913. By 1913 only 72 percent of the people lived in small villages in the country, and slightly more than half depended upon agriculture for their living. The trend was away from the farms and toward the cities. Rice production increased, but Japan was obliged to import food. Fewer farmers had to produce more food, and the price of rice tended steadily to mount. Farms were small, tenantry was on the increase. By 1913 nearly half of all arable land was under tenancy, and rents ranged from 50 to 60 percent of the crop.

The constant exodus from the farms provided the cities with an abundant supply of labor and created a psychological bond between the poor people of the country and those of the city. Small factories mushroomed, particularly in textiles, and thousands of girls were always available as workers. Working conditions were usually atrocious. Capital came from within Japan, but foreign investments were welcomed, especially after 1900. Government expenditures skyrocketed because of the costs of military operations, and no profits were forthcoming from politically satisfying overseas adventures. By 1913 nearly 80 percent of Japan's national debt was held by foreigners, mostly banking houses in London or New York.

Almost imperceptibly Japan laid a substantial foundation for industrialization. In 1901 the iron works were established at Yawata, in northern Kyushu, but Japan was handicapped by its lack of good iron ore and coking coal. During World War I Japan was able only to meet one-quarter of its steel requirements from its own resources. Deficiencies in this basic industry go far toward explaining Japan's concern with Manchuria, with its riches in both coal and iron. The paucity of Japan's financial reserves and its limited supplies of raw materials forced Japan to make every economy in its national development, including the heavy concentration of management and ownership in the hands of a very few wealthy and powerful *zaibatsu*. Trade expanded to keep pace with industry. Japan's shipyards learned to build the best of merchantmen as well as battleships, and Japanese vessels carried most of the goods which made up Japan's billion-yen-a-year overseas trade. Japan exported silk, manufactured goods, and cotton yarns—in spite of the fact that it had to purchase almost every raw material that its looms and factories required.

Japan performed most of the invisible services which its businessmen needed—banking, insurance, and shipping—but as a nation it went deeper and deeper into debt. Through such specialized banks as the Bank of Japan for central banking, the Yokohama Specie Bank for foreign trade, the Hypothec Bank for loans for agricultural development, the Bank of Industrial Development, the Oriental Development Company for the exploitation of new lands overseas, and the Bank of Korea, Japan endeavored to make maximum credit available for whichever branch of the economy was in greatest immediate need. The small country seemed to exist on the edge of crisis until World War I flooded it with new orders and converted it from a debtor to a creditor country. Within a few short months, a fabulous war boom changed austerity to prosperity and catapulted Japan into the ranks of the great economic powers of the world. Japan was fortunate in that in the early years of the twentieth century it had created an economic embryo which by the time of World War I was sufficiently matured to produce for profit the materials needed by both sides in their disastrous contest to destroy the wealth and assets of their enemies. Japan traded munitions for gold. It built new factories, enjoyed a wartime El Dorado, and established its consulates and commercial agencies all over the world.

INTERNAL POLITICS (1900–1918)

Japan's political structure preserved its essential authoritarian features as its political processes changed to fit more nearly the patterns of the Western world. The elder statesmen, the bureaucracy, the military, and the *zaibatsu* maintained a firm grasp on political power. They made only such concessions to political parties and democratic tendencies as were needed in the interest of orderly government.

The governing of Japan was a complicated process of balancing rival political groups. The genro or elder statesmen like Yamagata and Ito stayed behind the scenes while their respective protégés, General Katsura Taro and Prince Saionji Kimmochi alternated in the prime minister's position. The genro manipulated the bureaucrats, and the bureaucrats commanded the political parties. Party loyalty was given to individual leaders, not to principles or ideals; the people who sat in the diet were usually little men who interested themselves in the division of political spoils. Elections were controlled easily through police power and bribes. Diets rose and fell on questions of the personal popularity of the prime minister or the condition of the budget. Japan discovered that it was glorious to win victories, but that armies and navies were expensive. Yamagata's group argued that security was Japan's first consideration, and that all military programs were vital for Japan's security. Money had to be found to pay the bills, regardless of the cost. Ito's followers reasoned otherwise. They insisted that provisions for the national security should be kept within ability to pay; security would be meaningless for a bankrupt or debilitated people. Both points of view were reasonable and equally patriotic; they differed in emphasis. Sometimes the one predominated, some times the other—depending largely upon the sense of "clear and present danger." Disputes were bitter, and the issue was never resolved with any finality.

Ito himself was the prime minister in 1900, but he resigned in the face of opposition to the taxes needed to pay the bills for Japan's part in the Boxer uprising. His successor, Katsura, scorned the idea of economy and stressed the necessity of a big navy. His cabinet was weakened because of scandals, but opposition was stilled by patriotic fervor in the Russo-Japanese War. Katsura was driven out of office at the close of the war because of popular dissatisfaction with the peace terms of the Treaty of Portsmouth.

The civilian minded administration of Prince Saionji (1906–1908) had no war fever to sustain it and it could never solve the dilemma of more money for the armed services and cheaper taxes for the public. Katsura returned as prime minister for another three years (1908–1911) to carry out the will of the militarists. The party politicians wrangled among themselves and clouded their good names by scandals and corrupt practices. The party movement received a further setback in the summer of 1910 with the discovery of a socialist plot to assassinate the aging Meiji emperor. On July 30, 1912 the great ruler died and was succeeded by his invalid son, who took the reign name of Taisho or Great Righteousness. The change of emperors caused scarcely a ripple on the surface of national politics. The genro, the bureaucrats, and the military were able to use the Katsura cabinet for their own purposes because the popular opposition was divided and ineffective.

Eventually some party leaders of good intent and honest purpose managed to combine against the government's extravagance and expensiveness. For another brief interlude, they returned Saionji to power (August 30, 1911, to December 5, 1912). He could not prevail against the clamor for larger appropriations for the army and navy, and he was dismissed with his unpopular ideas for a balanced budget. For the last time, Katsura was installed as the head of the government. With all the support of invisible power behind him, he could not stifle the growing public discontent which stemmed from high prices and heavy taxes. It became clear that the voice of the people could not be ignored no matter how inept or imperfect its organ—the political parties. Katsura had to resign on February 11, 1913, although Japan was not ready for a party government.

War clouds hung low in Europe. The responsible statesmen of Japan in their anonymity could not afford to gamble with a policy which would weaken the armed forces at a moment of possible crisis. In the name of the emperor, they called on Admiral Yamamoto Gombei, a fierce partisan of a bigger navy, to form a new cabinet. He lasted until February 26, 1914, when he was discredited by disclosures in Germany that Japanese officers were guilty of accepting bribes in connection with naval contracts. The Japanese diet had no power to conduct investigations into the conduct of Japanese officials abroad, but information leaked out from Germany when a former employee of the Siemens Company was placed on trial for stealing secret state documents.

On April 16, 1914, the eighty-year-old Count Okuma, who had fought consistently against clan subterfuge and political corruption (and who in later life had devoted most of his energies to Waseda University), was brought back as prime minister. He was at the mercy of forces behind the screen. He became enmeshed in a partisan battle to weaken the Seiyukai and assisted in the formation of a new party called the Kenseikai, or Constitutional Association. Its platform stressed economics rather than military chauvinism, and it tended to look after the interests of big business rather than those of bureaucrats and the great landed families. It was Count Okuma who was in office when the Twenty-One Demands were presented to China and when World War I broke out in Europe.

In October 1916 he resigned the premiership and recommended that his foreign minister, Kato Takaakira—who was also head of the Kenseikai —should succeed him. The surviving genro, Matsukata, Yamagata, and Saionji, were outraged that a mere head of government should dare to suggest his own successor. They were jealous of their own prerogative to make and unmake cabinets, and they were rather proud of their record as the architects of new Japan. They felt that the times were too critical to have any but the strongest hand at the helm of the ship of state. They still regarded the diet as nothing more than a troublesome sounding board for noisy opinion, and they had no intention of handing over real power to any group so fickle as a political party. The genro therefore called upon General Count Terauchi Seiki, the governor-general of Korea, to become chief of state; he remained in office until the crisis of the rice riots in 1918.

EXPANSION ON THE CONTINENT OF ASIA

The designation of the early twentieth century as Japan's golden age scarcely follows from internal developments; however, it clearly applies to Japan's record in foreign affairs. Japan's most vital interests lie in Asia. Korea, Manchuria, and the rest of China are of incalculable strategic importance. Japanese statesmen have considered Asia as Great Britain considers Europe and have referred to the continental mainland as "lips to the teeth or a wheel to the axle." In 1904 Japan found itself at war with Russia. The immediate issues were conflicting positions in Manchuria and Korea. Japan attacked Russian ships and then declared war. It defeated the Russian giant on land and sea. It forced Russia to sign the treaty of peace which through the good offices of President Theodore Roosevelt was concluded at Portsmouth, New Hampshire, on September 5, 1905. This was Japan's only major war in carrying out a phenomenal policy of expansion in Asia, an expansion practically completed by the end of World War I. Japan's program covered three separate areas: Korea, Manchuria, and the China mainland.

While Russia struggled to strengthen its position on the fringes of Korea, Japan occupied itself in Seoul, Korea's capital. In 1904—before the outbreak of war with Russia—Japan forced the Korean government to accept Japanese advisers in financial affairs; foreign affairs; and police, judicial, and military matters. The Japanese minister to Korea was authorized to supervise the entire Korean administration. When Japan declared war on Russia, the imperial rescript declared that "the safety of Korea is in danger; the vital interests of our Empire are menaced." During the war, Japanese troops overran Korea and Japan took over the Korean postal and telegraph services. The Japanese compelled the Korean king, whose title had been changed to emperor, to sign a treaty of alliance which guaranteed the national independence and territorial independence of Korea and the safety of the imperial family. Behind this façade, Japan prepared careful plans to convert Korea into a protectorate at an opportune moment. By the Treaty of Portsmouth, Russia agreed to recognize Japan's *paramount* interests in Korea. Russia was effectively removed from the Korean scene.

In November 1905, Japan sent Marquis Ito to Seoul to negotiate a convention which would make Korea a Japanese protectorate. The convention was signed while the imperial palace was under Japanese guard. It gave Japan the control and direction of Korea's foreign relations and provided for the appointment of a Japanese resident-general in Korea. Japan informed the powers that its previous relationship had proved unsatisfactory and that in the future Japan would take and exercise, for reasons closely connected with its own safety and repose, a paramount interest in the political, military, and diplomatic affairs of Korea.

In February 1906 Ito himself became Japan's first resident-general in Korea. He launched a host of Japanization reforms and complained of Korea's insincerity and noncooperation. The Korean emperor was singled out for particular blame, and he was forced to abdicate in favor of his son. A new Japan-Korea agreement was signed on July 24, 1907, which placed the administration of all important state affairs, official appointments and dismissals and the enactment of all laws and ordinances in the hands of the Japanese resident-general. Within a month the Korean army was disbanded. Japan bided its time until August 22, 1910, when by a treaty of annexation it assumed the entire government and administrative responsibility for Korea. As a name and a state, Korea disappeared from the map of Asia. The country was renamed Chosen, and it became a part of Japan.

From a military point of view, Chosen became Japan's headquarters in Asia. Regular divisions of the Japanese army were stationed there, fortresses were built, naval bases established, and railways developed for strategic purposes. The country itself was placed under a Japanese general. Chosen was equipped by the Japanese to play the same role in any northern advance that Formosa was destined to play in the march to the south.

Japan brought law and order to Korea, plus material prosperity, but it paid little attention to the sensibilities of Koreans. The nobility and powerful conservative elements were cajoled into acceptance of Japanese domination. Titles and pensions were distributed liberally. The peasants were ignored or simply mobilized into an all-encompassing program of exploitation. Rice production was steadily increased as a matter of state policy, and the precious Korean grain flowed steadily into Japan. The fish catch in Korean waters was quadrupled, primarily to feed the growing population of Japan. Japan undertook a successful program of reforestation and developed Korea's economic resources. A double standard of wages was maintained, and all important jobs were reserved for Japanese. Koreans were given no political responsibilities or opportunities for economic advancement. Use of the Japanese language was compulsory. Japanese children were provided with adequate schooling, but Korean children were restricted even in the primary grades. All religions except

Shinto and Buddhism were discouraged. Law codes were copied from Japanese patterns with no regard to Korean customs. Japan in Korea was guilty of all the crimes—and benefits—which are usually ascribed to Western imperialism.

Hatred of the Japanese became widespread, but open rebellion was impossible in the police state. Some collaborators resigned themselves to their fate. Hardy Korean anti-Japanese leaders agitated quietly within Korea or migrated to Russia, China, or the United States. Men like Syngman Rhee kept alive the aspirations for a free and independent Korea, but they were thwarted until Japan's defeat in World War II.

Japan was as spectacularly successful in Manchuria as in Korea. By the same Treaty of Portsmouth, Japan succeeded to Russia's position in South Manchuria, or Manchuria south of the Chinese Eastern Railway zone. Russia transferred to Japan—subject to the consent of China—its lease upon Port Arthur, Dairen, and adjacent territory in the Liaotung Peninsula and its interest in the railway from Changchun to Port Arthur, China's consent was obtained by a treaty signed in Peking in December 1905. The agreement of Peking laid the legal foundation for Japan's economic penetration into South Manchuria and North China. More Chinese cities and towns were to be opened for Japanese residence, and the railway between Mukden and the Korean border was to be reconstructed. The Japanese were given the right to have railway guards in South Manchuria as long as the Russians kept theirs in the north. China agreed not to construct any branch railway line in the neighborhood of and parallel to the South Manchurian Railway or any branch line which would be prejudicial to the business of that railway. (Mark this agreement well because it constituted the crux of subsequent arguments between China and Japan in Manchuria.)

Japan organized the South Manchurian Railway Company in August 1906. The Japanese government retained fifty percent ownership in the stock of the company and entrusted to the company the operation of the railway, together with its mines and other appurtenances. Through the years, the South Manchurian Railway Company served Japan in South Manchuria as the Chinese Eastern Railway Company served Russia in the north. As the chief agent for government penetration, it operated railways, mines, hotels, schools, hospitals, shipping lines, research institutes, factories, harbor works, and power plants. It dictated economic and commercial policies and exercised a decisive influence on political decisions not only in Manchuria but within Japan itself.

Japan also organized a government-general for the Kwantung leased area and established garrison headquarters for its newly created Kwantung army. Port Arthur became a strong Japanese naval base. The rest of Manchuria remained under Chinese administrative control, but Chinese officials were sensitive to the opinions and advice of the Japanese. Dairen was reopened as a free port with a Chinese official in charge of collecting the Chinese customs tariff. Japanese settlers came to Manchuria in small —almost insignificant—numbers. The immigrants were primarily concession hunters, developers, smooth operators, and political functionaries, rather than colonists and farmers. It was rather the great influx of *Chinese* farmers into Manchuria which accounted for the expanding production of soya beans, rice, kaoliang, millet, maize, wheat, and barley.

Japanese economic emphasis on Manchuria centered in railways and industrialization. From the Russo-Japanese War to World War I, Japan determined to maintain an exclusive position within South Manchuria and to do so in legal agreement with China. Japan obtained new railway contracts and new concessions for mines, telegraphs, and sawmills. As the Japanese forged ahead, the Chinese offered but feeble resistance. Some genuine cooperation took place; but high-handed or underhanded relationships were more common. Japan did practically as it pleased in developing the rich Manchurian territory. It then began to feel a sentimental attachment to Manchuria—a conviction that the expenditure of much blood and treasure endowed it with a sacred right of proprietorship. Japan conceived of Manchuria as its lifeline. The Japanese became increasingly insistent that China should suppress banditry and afford adequate protection to Japan's accumulated treaty rights.

Japan acquired its most extensive rights in Manchuria as a result of the treaty of May 25, 1915, following the Twenty-One Demands. These rights have already been noted. By the agreements of 1915, Japan had the comfortable feeling that Manchuria—although nominally a part of China —was effectively under Japanese control.

While pursuing its objectives in Korea and Manchuria, Japan also endeavored to entrench itself on the mainland of China. Some Japanese and some Chinese had always believed that Japan and China together should speak as the united voice of the Orient. In spite of Japan's war against China, Sun Yat-sen thought of China and Japan as natural friends, unnatural enemies, and said that, from whatever point of view, China and Japan should cooperate wholeheartedly. He declared the two nations should share common existence or common extinction: "Without Japan there would be no China; without China there would be no Japan." Similarities in language and culture and a complementary economic relationship called for friendship—but Japan preferred to act more toward China as a disagreeable superior than an understanding neighbor.

In the last days of the Manchu empire, the Japanese minister played a Machiavellian game in Peking. Japan's tactics were to cooperate with the Western powers in professing allegiance to the Open Door and the territorial integrity of China. While Japan ostensibly supported the

Manchus, it also gave money and encouragement to Sun Yat-sen and the revolutionists. After the accession of Yüan Shih-k'ai, Japan deserted Sun and advanced loans to Yüan and the warlords to sustain them in their struggles against the nationalists. Because of incidents involving Japanese citizens, Japan was repeatedly tempted to intervene in the course of China's domestic affairs but was restrained by the concerted opposition of the Western powers.

Throughout 1913 and 1914 Japan expressed concern about the leases in Manchuria which were due to expire in 1921. Japan was also worried by China's schemes to enlist diplomatic support against Japan's apparent ambitions in China. The outbreak of World War I gave Japan an unrivaled opportunity to take action. Against the wishes of its own ally, Great Britain, Japan declared war on Germany on August 23, 1914. Japanese troops marched across Chinese territory and seized the German public and private properties, railways and mines, which constituted the German sphere of interest in Shantung. Japan said that it harbored no territorial ambitions in China and would eventually restore to China the German leasehold.

It was at the conclusion of this successful military operation that Japan undertook to settle all its outstanding accounts with China by the Twenty-One Demands. The Japanese minister Hioki warned Yüan that he had better accept these demands or the Japanese would support somebody else for the presidency of China. Yüan published the Japanese terms in the hope that publication would produce unfavorable foreign reaction. Japan accepted no procrastination or vacillation and on May 30, 1915, forced Yüan to sign the treaties which gave Japan almost everything it wanted.

Japanese money kept most of the warlords who succeeded Yüan Shih-k'ai in power. On the pretext of obtaining the most effective cooperation in contributing to the success of the war in Europe, Japan tightened its military control over China. A war participation board was created in Peking which, in exchange for funds, gave Japan access to China's military secrets and practically placed China's military destiny in the hands of the Japanese army and navy. In 1918 China accepted advance payments on Japanese railway loans and in return categorically agreed to acquiesce in the transfer to Japan of Kiaochow and the German rights in Shantung. The fine print on the understanding said that Japan would ultimately restore the leasehold to China and in the meantime would retain and expand the former German economic privileges in the area. Japan felt that it had an airtight case on Shantung—and inferentially a strong foothold in North China—when its delegates boarded their ships at the end of 1918 for the peace conference at Versailles.

JAPAN AS A WORLD POWER

Japan's introduction to world politics, with all their hypocrisy and chicanery, took place at the time of the triple intervention. While nursing its grievances, Japan set about to right the wrongs which had been committed. Japan's immediate objective was to win the support of Great Britain and to deal singly with Russia, France, and Germany in squaring accounts. Treaty relations with the United States were of secondary importance at the turn of the nineteenth century, because neither power rated first-rank in world affairs. After 1900 Japan was no longer exclusively in and of the orient; its decisions and policies were influential in Europe as well as in Asia. In contrast to European powers which subordinated their Asian policies to European requirements, Japan assumed obligations vis-à-vis Europe as they contributed to Japan's welfare and security in Asia. At the outbreak of World War I Japan was a full-fledged member of the combination of powers which opposed Germany and its allies.

In view of Russia's aggressive moves to the Far East in 1901, Japan sought to put an end to its diplomatic isolation. Some Japanese statesmen, notably Marquis Ito and Marquis Inouye, advocated an understanding with Russia. Others, like Viscount Ishii and Count Hayashi, preferred an alliance with Great Britain, with the possible adherence of Germany. On January 30, 1902, Count Hayashi and Lord Lansdowne in London signed Japan's first alliance with a Western power. This had the double effect of strengthening Japan's position in Asia and of expanding its diplomatic horizons to the farthest frontiers of the British empire. For more than two decades, the alliance with Great Britain was the keystone of Japan's international position. The specific terms of the alliance were that the two signatories pledged themselves to uphold the independence and territorial integrity of China and Korea and to observe the Open Door. Japan recognized the *special* interests of England in China, and England recognized those of Japan in China and Korea. If either nation should become involved in war with one power, the other signatory would remain neutral; but if either should become involved in war with two or more powers, its ally was to join in the war.

This alliance served Japan well during the Russo-Japanese War. In preventing France from coming to the aid of its Russian ally, the alliance forestalled a world-wide conflict. After Japan defeated Russia, a new Anglo-Japanese alliance was concluded on August 12, 1905. The scope of the alliance was extended to India. Furthermore each signatory promised to go to the aid of its ally if the latter were attacked by a single power—not two or more as in the earlier edition. Japan and England negotiated a second revision of their fundamental agreement, which was signed in London on July 13, 1911, and which was to remain in force for ten years. The text of the 1911 document was substantially the same as that of 1905 with the exception of a clause which was intended to exclude the United States from the purview of the alliance. The British wanted to protect themselves from an eventuality where they might be drawn into a war against the Americans as a consequence of their commitments to Japan.

While binding itself in alliances with England, Japan astutely mended its diplomatic fences with France. Japan resented the French role in the triple intervention and feared French support for Russian activities in East Asia. However, France and Japan managed to avoid acrimonious disputes. When Japan's ally, England, signed a cordial entente with France in Europe, Japan pursued a similar tactic with reference to Asia. On June 10, 1907, Japan and France signed an agreement and a declaration at Paris agreeing to respect the independence and territorial integrity of China and announcing their special interest in the maintenance of peace and order in the regions of the Chinese empire adjacent to the territories where they had rights of sovereignty, protection, or occupation. Each was to support the other in maintaining peace and security in those regions with a view to maintaining the respective situation and the territorial rights of each on the continent of Asia. Japanese in Indochina and Indochinese subjects and protégés in Japan were to be accorded most-favored-nation treatment. In effect, these agreements amounted to an exchange of Japanese support for the French in Indochina for French support for the Japanese in action they were about to take in Korea.

Japanese diplomacy was most adept in dealing with Russia. The Japanese defeat of Russia exposed the giant with feet of clay; but having convinced itself of Russia's weakness, it proceeded to restore cordial relations with its former enemy. Psychological conditions changed. Confident of its own strength, Japan assumed the initiative. On July 30, 1907, Japan signed two conventions with Russia—the one public and the other secret. The public convention was a routine recognition of the Open Door in China and a mutual promise to sustain and defend the maintenance of the *status quo* in East Asia by all pacific means within their reach. By the secret convention (which was not made public until after the Bolsheviks disclosed the tsarist archives), Japan and Russia divided Manchuria into spheres of influence, the south to Japan and the north to Russia. Japan recognized the special interests of Russia in Outer Mongolia and Russia recognized the relations of political solidarity between Japan and Korea. For three years, the relations between Japan and Russia were remarkably free from friction. They drew even closer because of the financial and railway politics of the United States in Manchuria.

On July 4, 1910, Japan and Russia expanded the scope of their understandings. Japan was no longer worried about Russian encroachments in Japanese preserves; it was concerned primarily with obtaining Russian acquiescence in the further advances of Japan. The two nations declared that in case the *status quo* was menaced, they would communicate with each other for the purpose of agreeing upon effective measures. They were no longer limited to pacific means as they had been three years earlier. Japanese annexation of Korea by treaty took place on August 22, 1910, exactly seven weeks after the Russo-Japanese understandings.

Between 1910 and 1912 Japan sought further agreement with Russia on their respective spheres in Manchuria and Mongolia. Japan's apparent objective was to gain absolute freedom to advance at will in China and to strengthen its Pacific front without fear of a stab in the back from Russia. On July 8, 1912, a new treaty allotted North Manchuria and western Inner Mongolia to Russia for development, and South Manchuria and eastern Inner Mongolia to Japan. Thus the relative role of Japan in Northeast Asia expanded, but Russia was helpless to protest because of its internal problems and its complications in Europe. Japan feared Russia when Russia was strong, but when Russia was weak, Japan used it to bolster its own ambitious program in Asia. Russia was out of the picture by the time that Japan made its Twenty-One Demands on China in 1915.

On July 3, 1916, Japan signed its last alliance with pre-Soviet Russia. At that time Russia was mired in defeat at the hands of the Germans, and Japan feared that the former might drop out of the war. In order to strengthen Russia's faltering morale, Japan sent munitions and supplies to Russia and negotiated diplomatic agreements, as Viscount Ishii explained it, to relieve Russia of anxiety about its possessions in the Far East. The signatories pledged not to be a party to any arrangement or combination against the other and to confer if their territorial rights or special interests were menaced. A secret convention set up a defensive alliance which was to last for five years. To assure that China should not fall under the political domination of any third power hostile to Japan or Russia, the two nations pledged to come to each other's aid should war arise from defense of their respective vital interests in China. To Japan these vital interests in 1916 meant, not the Open Door, but the strengthened quasi-monopolistic position which it had acquired in South Manchuria, eastern Inner Mongolia, and Shantung.

By patient and astute diplomacy, Japan had lined up three of the powers—Great Britain, France, and Russia—behind its program in Asia by the time of World War I. There remained Germany and the United States. Japan acted immediately and unequivocably to settle old scores with Germany. After Great Britain declared war on Germany on August 4, 1914, the British asked for nothing more than limited, local cooperation from the Japanese in destroying German ships in Asian waters. The Japanese were not to be limited or curbed. On August 15, they delivered an ultimatum to the Germans in Shantung demanding the withdrawal or disarming of German ships and the delivery within thirty days of their Kiaochow leasehold to Japan. Germany ignored the ultimatum, and on August 26 Japan declared war on Germany. The Japanese quickly took over all the German holdings in China and they occupied the German islands in the South Seas.

On October 19, 1915, Japan announced its adherence to the Declaration of London, in which the nations fighting against Germany pledged themselves not to make a separate peace and not to offer peace terms without previous consultation among themselves. In a series of secret agreements in February and March 1917, Japan obtained from its allies unqualified support for its demands for permanent legal title to its conquests over Germany in China and to the German islands north of the equator. On April 6, 1917, the United States declared war on Germany and Japan was obliged, hastily and frantically, to make every effort to persuade their new associate to adhere, as others had done, to its fundamental program in Asia.

JAPAN AND THE UNITED STATES

As long as the United States seemed far away and comparatively insignificant in world affairs, Japan paid greater attention to Asia and to Europe. As the strength of the United States mounted, the situation changed. The United States grew into an industrial giant and its trade flowed across the Pacific in increasing quantities. A steady stream of merchant vessels and repeated visits from fighting ships made Japan acutely aware of American naval power. The persistent American interest in equality of commercial opportunity and the territorial integrity of China coupled with the annexation of the Philippines never let Japan forget that the United States was also a factor in Asian affairs. Japan and the United States enjoyed a tradition of good relations which dated from the arrival of Commodore Perry in Tokyo Bay, and until Japan's victory over Russia in 1905 the two nations had no serious quarrels or diplomatic disputes.

Japan's original forward steps on the continent of Asia elicited no protests from the United States. It was interesting for Americans to watch a toddling nation assert its determination to walk like an adult. On repeated occasions, Japan confirmed its adherence to the Open Door. President Theodore Roosevelt never felt any sentimental attachment toward China and he considered Russia as treacherous, shifty, and incompetent. He admired Japan and looked upon Japan as the great balance wheel in Asia. Although Japan was an Asian power and Russia was European, President Roosevelt wanted and worked for a Japanese victory in its war with Russia. However, he took adequate measures to see that a victorious Japan would not threaten the newly acquired American strategic position in the far Pacific. Before the Portsmouth Conference opened, Roosevelt sent his Secretary of War, William Howard Taft, to Tokyo as his personal representative for an exchange of views with the Japanese premier, Count Katsura. On July 29, 1905, the two men affixed their signatures to a memorandum which stated that "Japan had no aggressive designs on the Philippines" and that the United States would approve of Japan's plan to assume control of Korea's foreign affairs. This international log-rolling doomed Korea's existence as an independent nation.

After the Portsmouth Conference, Japan and the United States drifted apart. From 1905 to 1908 crises were continuous. Japanese boycotted American goods in 1905 because they thought President Roosevelt's mediation robbed them of legitimate fruits of victory. The Japanese public was not aware of the inherent weakness of its own forces and believed that its well-earned victories entitled Japan to territorial rewards in Asia and substantial indemnities. President Roosevelt's role as peacemaker looked suspiciously like a revised version of the triple intervention. The Japanese were angry and expressed their feelings in editorials and public anti-American demonstrations.

Subsequent arguments arose over the lack of integration between Caucasians and orientals in the San Francisco schools and the excessive numbers of Japanese immigrants into the United States. Japan was not as meek as China in accepting discrimination against its citizens. Japan did not deny the right of the United States to deal with immigration as a domestic matter, but it wished to avoid a situation where the American Congress might feel obliged to stop the immigration of Japanese labor as it had arbitrarily done with the Chinese. Therefore Japan endeavored to regulate emigration in accordance with the wishes of Americans who were determined to cut down the numbers of incoming Japanese. Legislatures in the western states pressed Congress for absolute Japanese exclusion and anti-Japanese agitation in the United States matched the anti-American displays in Japan.

On October 11, 1906, the San Francisco Board of Education passed a resolution requiring segregation for all Chinese, Japanese, and Korean children in the public schools. Parents were to be protected from having the youthful impressions of their children affected by association with pupils of the Mongolian race. Japanese public opinion at home was inflamed and the ambassador in Washington lodged a formal protest. President Roosevelt was disgusted with "the infernal fools" in California and the "wicked absurdity of segregation." He invited the entire board of education to the White House to persuade its members to rescind segregation in return for a promise to stop the immigration of Japanese labor. In 1907 immigration of Japanese from Hawaii, Canada, and Mexico was stopped by law, and in the next year the details of a "gentleman's agreement" were worked out: Japan agreed to deny passports for laborers other than parents, wives, or children of Japanese residents and settled agriculturists already in the United States. In exchange the United States agreed not to pass exclusion legislation. The fact of the matter was that the gentleman's agreement did not put an end to immigration of Japanese laborers, and Californians continued to seethe.

In the midst of the immigration controversy in 1907, President Roosevelt sent the great, white American fleet on a "good will" cruise around the world. The Navy-minded president called this demonstration of sea power the most important service he ever rendered to peace. Obviously, the Japanese were impressed.

Japan could not be indifferent to American opposition to the former's aggressive policies in Asia, particularly toward China. After 1905 Japan was no longer applauded in the United States as the diplomatic underdog in Asia, but was distrusted as a bully over its weaker neighbor. Japan was in no position to stand up against the United States or to ignore American opinion, so it chose the way of compromise. On May 5, 1908, it signed a five-year arbitration convention with the United States. On November 30, 1908—*after* the immigration crisis and the establishment of Japan's protectorate in Korea—an exchange of notes between Secretary of State Elihu Root and Ambassador Takahira in Washington confirmed a new Japanese-American agreement. The two countries expressed the wish to encourage the free and peaceful development of their commerce on the Pacific Ocean, and pledged themselves to the maintenance of the *status quo* in the "region above-mentioned." They expressed their determination to support by all pacific means at their disposal the independence and integrity of China and the principle of equal opportunity for commerce and industry of all nations in that empire. To the United States this agreement constituted a new engagement on the part of Japan to respect the Open Door and a fresh disavowal of aggression toward the Philippines. In return Japan welcomed the American acceptance of a *status quo* which took cognizance of all of Japan's gains in Manchuria and Korea.

Japan was not halted by President Taft's dollar diplomacy nor his program of financial assistance to China. Nor was Japan inhibited by President Wilson's shift from diplomatic pressure to moral condemnation. When Japan moved into Shantung, China appealed to the United States to guarantee China's neutrality. The American reply was that "it would be quixotic in the extreme to allow the question of China's territorial integrity to entangle the United States in international difficulties." In dealing with the Twenty-One Demands, Secretary Bryan conceded that territorial contiguity created special relations between Japan and South Manchuria, Inner Mongolia, and Shantung Province. However, on November 11, 1915, he notified both Peking and Tokyo that the United States

> cannot recognize any agreement or understanding which has been entered into between the governments of Japan and China, impairing the treaty rights of the United States or its citizens in China, the political or territorial integrity of the Republic of China, or the international policy relative to China commonly known as the Open Door policy.

This was a succinct statement of the American doctrine of nonrecognition.

As soon as the United States entered World War I, Japan sought to derive diplomatic advantage from its new associate. Viscount Ishii came to the United States to obtain American recognition of Japan's *paramount* interests in China. Secretary Lansing was instructed to enter into an agreement on November 2, 1917, which rejected the concept of paramount interests but which accepted the proposition that geographic propinquity creates special relations, consequently the United States "recognizes that Japan has *special* interests in China." In a secret protocol both governments promised not to take advantage of existing conditions to seek special rights and privileges in China which would abridge the rights of citizens or subjects of friendly states. Viscount Ishii also tried, but without success, to get American adherence to the secret arrangements which Japan had made with its allies regarding the disposition of the German territories in the Pacific.

As a wartime measure, Japan and the United States had special relations due to the Siberian intervention. With the collapse of tsarist Russia, the Allies—particularly France—were eager to salvage anything possible from the Russian wreckage. In August 1918 Japanese and American troops were landed at Vladivostok for the purpose of taking control over the Trans-Siberian and Chinese Eastern railways. An inter-Allied expedition was dispatched to aid anti-Bolshevik groups organized in southern Russia, keep military supplies in eastern Siberia out of the hands of the enemy, assist Czechoslovakian prisoners who were trying to escape from Russia, and to intercept any possible German invasion of the Far East. It was tentatively agreed that the United States and Japan should each send 7,000 soldiers to participate in the expedition, but the Japanese felt obliged to re-enforce their army of intervention on a grand scale. Japanese troops occupied strategic points in Siberia as far west as Lake Baikal; they also occupied the maritime provinces and the northern half of Sakhalin Island. The Japanese acted as complete masters in the territories which they took over although they promised they would not interfere in the internal affairs of Russia nor impinge upon its sovereignty. Japan hated and feared the rising power of the Bolsheviks; it dabbled in the civil wars between "Reds" and "Whites" and tried to set up puppet regimes favorable to Japan. These excesses aroused American disapproval, and involved Japan in a political morass which lasted far beyond the conference at Versailles.

SUGGESTED READING

Conroy, Francis Hilary, *Japanese Seizure of Korea* (Philadelphia, U. of Pennsylvania, 1960).

Dennett, Tyler, *Roosevelt and the Russo-Japanese War* (Garden City, Doubleday, 1925).

Dennis, A. L. P., *Anglo-Japanese Alliance* (Berkeley, U. of California, 1923).

Harrington, F. H., *God, Mammon and the Japanese* (Madison, U. of Wisconsin, 1944).

Hulbert, Homer B., *Passing of Korea* (New York, Doubleday, 1906).

Ishii, Kikujiro, *Diplomatic Commentaries* (trans. and edited by William R. Langdon) (Baltimore, Johns Hopkins U., 1936).

Jansen, Marius B., *Japanese and Sun Yat-sen* (Cambridge, Harvard U., 1954).

Kamikawa, Hikomatsu, (ed.), *Japanese-American Diplomatic Relations in the Meiji-Taisho Era* (trans. by Kimura Michiko) (Tokyo, Obunsha, 1958).

Morley, James W., *Japanese Thrust into Siberia, 1918* (New York, Columbia U., 1957).

Nelson, M. Frederick, *Korea and the Old Orders in Eastern Asia* (Baton Rouge, Louisiana State U., 1945).

Price, Ernest B., *Russo-Japanese Treaties of 1907–1916, concerning Manchuria and Mongolia* (Baltimore, Johns Hopkins U., 1933).

Schwantes, Robert, *Japanese and Americans* (New York, Harper, 1955).

Treat, Payson J., *Diplomatic Relations between the United States and Japan* (three vols.) (Stanford, Stanford U., 1932, 1938).

White, John Albert, *Siberian Intervention* (Princeton, Princeton U., 1950).

15

Japan Between World Wars

During World War I, Japanese soldiers gained practically nothing by way of combat experience. German resistance in Shantung was negligible, and the Siberian expedition was more of a training exercise than an advance under fire. Neither Shantung nor Siberia added to the luster of the imperial forces. On the contrary, stories of Japanese chicanery and brutality detracted from the high reputation which the Japanese army had won during the Boxer uprising and the Russo-Japanese War. The navy likewise had no opportunity for great distinction during World War I. Japanese ships kept the Pacific clear of German raiders and provided valuable convoys for supplies moving from Japan to the Mediterranean. The vast sums which the Japanese poured into naval construction brought no spectacular victories at sea. The Japanese public itself was given no immediate acquaintance with the damage and suffering of war. Casualties were light, and whatever fighting there was took place far away from native shores.

The effects of World War I in Japan were not unlike those in the United States. Many Japanese made money—lots of it—and they spent it extravagantly. Japan was the only nation in Asia with an economy sufficiently advanced to fill orders for weapons and munitions. Orders poured in without any consideration for price. Neutral nations turned to Japan for goods which they had previously bought in Europe or the United States. Japanese exports expanded forty percent in bulk and three hundred percent in value. The merchant marine doubled in size and its profits multiplied ten times over. Factory workers increased by seventy percent as countless new stacks poured smoke into Japanese skies. Japanese traders covered China and Southeast Asia; their salesmen penetrated into the farthest corners of Africa and South America. Japan converted a billion-yen foreign debt to a billion-yen foreign credit.

At home the demand for ordinary consumer goods mounted. People had more money to spend, but it became more difficult to find the things they wanted. Hoarding and speculation increased as prices shot upward. The farmers suffered, and so did the poor workers in the cities. They did not share in the prosperity. In August 1918 a number of women in a Toyama fishing village protested against the high price of rice. Riots spread throughout the country and troops were called out to keep order. The Terauchi cabinet resigned, and was succeeded by Hara Takashi, the first commoner in Japan to become premier. He appointed only party people to cabinet posts (with the exception of the army and navy ministers) and he kept his seat in the lower house of the diet. The Hara cabinet seemed to presage the adoption in Japan of European-style parliamentary government.

Hara gave immediate attention to the economic dislocation which was caused by the war. Striking at the heart of distress in the rural areas, he issued a blueprint for agricultural rehabilitation. He decreed measures to increase production, facilitate distribution, and control prices. His immediate objectives were to put more land into production, to encourage more intensive cultivation, and to bring about better farming methods. He ordered the government to provide farmers with educational assistance, cheap credits, and an adequate supply of fertilizer. He concerned himself with the improvement of the economic and social status of tenant farmers and with the welfare of the neglected farm-laborer. He encouraged cooperatives, opened up more public markets, facilitated the transportation of food from farm to city, paid more attention to procedures on commodities exchanges, and controlled prices along every step of the way. It is difficult to see how anyone could have written a better agricultural law, but the best law in Japan was inadequate to cope with rising prices and the maladjustments which occur when demand and supply get out of line.

The Hara government contended with other critical problems. In the war mood of 1918 it was obliged to strengthen the national defense, to subsidize essential industries, and to make large appropriations for costly improvements in transportation and communications systems. It was under intense pressure to pass a bill for universal manhood suffrage. Japan, like other nations, was under the hypnotic influence of making the world safe for democracy. The removal of property qualifications on the right to vote seemed like a reasonable first step in the desired direction. In foreign affairs, the Hara government had to keep Japan on an even keel while soldiers floundered in Siberia and diplomats argued the cause of Japan at the Peace Conference of Versailles.

Japan gained one of its greatest victories in international prestige when it was admitted to the Big Five (the United States, Great Britain,

France, Italy, and Japan) in fixing the terms of peace which were to be submitted to the Germans. The Japanese in Paris were described by a French newspaper as having "features immobile as the sphinx and feelings as enigmatic as the Mona Lisa." In spite of their inscrutability, the Japanese were very precise in their position. As their share of the spoils of victory, the Japanese wanted and expected the German rights in Shantung, title to the former German colonies north of the equator, and a statement in the Covenant of the League of Nations to the effect that every nation should be entitled to equal and just treatment in every respect, making no distinction either in law or in fact on account of race or nationality. The Japanese were not concerned with phases of the peace settlement which were of no direct consequence to their own vital interests.

The Japanese were doomed to bitter disappointment by what they considered as the unfairness of the settlement at Versailles. The only satisfaction they received was in the substantiation of their claims to Shantung. Even there they encountered stiff opposition. The Chinese were bitter and the Americans were resentful. President Wilson felt that Japan had forced his hand—either he had to sacrifice his principles and surrender Shantung to Japan, or Japan would walk out of the conference. The Japanese were not able to get clear title to the ex-German islands in the Pacific in spite of the wartime promises of their allies. Wilson's mood of idealism rejected the concept of imperialism and refused to let islands be transferred as so much chattel from one sovereignty to another. He stood for the principle of self-determination (in spite of Shantung) and for the application of a mandate system to former colonies. Therefore the Pacific islands were not given outright to Japan, but were placed under a mandate, or trusteeship, subject to the supervision of the League of Nations. To the Japanese, mandates seemed like poor substitutes for colonies. The Japanese were also disappointed by their failure to get universal acceptance of the principle of racial equality. The Australian prime minister stated frankly that if "racial equality is recognized in the preamble or any article of the Covenant, I and my people will leave the conference bag and baggage."

The Japanese signed the Treaty of Versailles, including the Covenant of the League of Nations, but they were none too happy about its terms. They were uneasy about commitments to respect and preserve against external aggression the independence and integrity of member states, including China. They disliked the obligation to settle disputes by arbitration, conciliation, or adjudication before resorting to war. They also objected to the article which provided for reconsideration of treaties that had become inapplicable and for the consideration of international conditions which, continuing, might endanger the peace of the world. These inhibitions seemed ominous to a nation which smarted under alleged inequities and wished to prepare itself unilaterally to take steps which it deemed necessary and proper for its own self-preservation regardless of consequences to others.

AFTER WORLD WAR I

As Japan entered the postwar world, the new Japan showed how different it had become during the life-span of the last generation. It was evident that the carefully planned revolution of the Meiji statesmen had outstripped their dreams. They foresaw a strong military and industrial power, but they could not have imagined the extent of democratic political concepts, the broad intellectual life and the liberal social trends which came with the twentieth century. Japan was no longer under the control of a small aristocratic, conservative ruling group. Instead, thousands of bureaucrats, military leaders, businessmen and intellectuals all contended for a voice in the management of public affairs. Strong western influences appeared in Japan's intellectual life and social patterns. It was a new age. The Meiji emperor had passed away in 1912 and his prestige was missed. His successor was mentally incompetent. One by one the old oligarchs disappeared; and after World War I only Matsukata, Yamagata, and Saionji remained of the illustrious genro. The leaders of the new generation grew up after the Restoration. They had never been samurai themselves, and they did not have the pride of bearing nor the singleness of purpose which marked the men of Meiji.

Great commercial interests became increasingly important in Japanese life and politics. The war contributed to the concentration of capital. Five big firms gained control of electric power; two dominated the cotton industry. Five great banks handled one-third of all the deposits in Japan. Of the great *zaibatsu*, Mitsui, Mitsubishi, Sumitomo, and Yasuda represented more than half of the nation's corporate wealth. The Mitsui empire comprised more than a hundred corporations and subsidiaries, with capitalization of over a billion and a half yen. Cartelization took place in mining, iron and steel manufacturing, chemicals, textiles, food, paper, cement, shipping, and even in banking and insurance. The Japanese encouraged huge combinations which could control production, manipulate distribution, and control prices.

Business interests usually opposed the high taxes required for large armies and navies, and they unabashedly distributed bribes and gifts to diet members and party politicians for their sympathy and votes. Businessmen earned the reputation of being antimilitary because they argued that overseas investments and foreign trade brought more glory and profits to the nation than colonial expansion by war and conquest. Their prestige grew with their fortunes, and they took a place with soldiers and sailors as symbols of the new Japan. It was astonishing how Japan pulled away from other Asian nations in economic development. It resembled more a manufacturing country in Western Europe than any of its neighbors in Asia. Its internal problems too seemed more European than Asian.

Material prosperity was intoxicating in its psychological effects, and the influence of the war on Japan's social structure—especially in the cities—was to destroy inhibitions, challenge traditions, and stimulate the urge for modern and exciting things. The Japanese invented the words *mobo* (modern boy) and *moga* (modern girl) to describe what Americans called "Joe College" and the "flapper." Young men took to sloppy clothes, baggy trousers, and slouch hats, while young girls flaunted their short skirts and bobbed their hair. American movies, jazz, and social dancing became immensely popular. Taxi-dance halls, all-girl musical troupes, cafes and beer-joints marked an age when prices did not matter and living was easy. The Japanese called the roaring twenties the era of *eru* (eroticism), *guro* (grotesquerie), and *nansensu* (nonsense).

Daring young couples walked hand in hand on the main streets or sat conspicuously close to one another on public lawns or park benches. College students led the movement for the right to make marriages of love even if against the wishes of the family or the advice of the marriage go-between. Love suicides were spectacular, frequent, and considered glamorous. Athletically inclined Japanese took to tennis, golf, track and field sports, and competitive swimming; with them baseball became a national hysteria. Thousands of popular books were written to cater to restless spirits; the best and worst of Western literature was made readily available in paperback translations. Newsstands mushroomed because business in papers, magazines, and picture books was fantastic. The serious-minded developed a taste for Western music and became as enthusiastic as Americans for a college education.

The peasants looked upon city ways with disapproval; the conservative-minded regarded *mobos* and *mogas* with scorn and hostility. Army and navy officers, rural landowners, the lower middle-class citizens of the smaller towns, and many petty government officials found the changes distasteful and dangerous. They too were educated in the Japanese school system, but they were impressed by the nationalistic and militaristic phases of Japanese indoctrination. They loved the old myths, longed for the good old days, and joined secret societies which were dedicated to the glory of the traditional Japanese nation and the sanctification of the emperor. These groups were out of tune with the times; the moment had not yet arrived for the conservative aspects of national Japanese behavior to assert themselves.

The move toward political democracy was more than skin-deep. A liberal professor of political science at Tokyo Imperial University, Yoshino Sakuzo, organized a *Reimeikai*, or society for the dissemination and popularization of democratic ideas. Students throughout Japan set up societies for the study of the social sciences. Great newspapers like the *Tokyo Asahi* and liberal magazines like *Chuo Koron* published serious and provocative political articles. Japan observed that autocratic nations —Germany, Austria, and Russia—lost the war; and that democratic nations won. The obvious conclusion was that democracy must contain unsuspected elements of strength.

Embryo left-wing movements entered the political scene along with the development of democracy. "Parlor pinks" were popular, and university students flocked to courses on Marxism. Translations of socialist literature sold by the thousands. Teachers, writers, doctors, lawyers, office workers (all underpaid intellectuals) teamed up to form left-wing parties with a variety of names, but none was able to formulate a genuine appeal to the masses. Peasants were interested in their own welfare, but they had no concept of its promotion through direct political action, and they had no comprehension of the language of the city highbrows. The urban proletariat was likewise unaware of its power and was beguiled by its dependence upon the *zaibatsu*. Gradually it awakened, and organized labor unions which were more than mere camouflages for managerial control. Strikes became a part of the political picture in the 1920's. In one demonstration in Kobe, 30,000 strikers at the Kawasaki shipyards paraded through the streets. The Russian revolution caused profound psychological disturbances in Japan's political thinking. Some Japanese worried whether the Japanese imperial system was fundamentally as vulnerable as the tsarist system of Russia; they wondered whether the streets of Tokyo might some day be drenched with the blood of revolution the same as the streets of St. Petersburg. But communism was alien, associated with Japan's ancient enemy Russia, and did not contain the same intellectual appeal as socialism.

By World War I, Japan was irrevocably committed to the procedures of Western-style representative government. The diet and the party system proved to be handy mechanisms for the balancing of political forces. Strong as the militarists and the *zaibatsu* were, they could not rule without the bureaucracy; they needed the façade of democracy to keep in touch with the masses which accepted their leadership. The militarists needed money for their program, and the diet was the place they had to find it. The alliance between the *zaibatsu* and the major political parties was mutually beneficial. The *zaibatsu* served the parties by supplying funds which were necessary for winning elections; the parties served the *zaibatsu* by voting against excessive military appropriations. The major parties were reasonably conservative, and they performed a useful function in choking off leftist movements which might have attracted the votes of tenant farmers and city workers. Not even the Seiyukai, which was increasingly identified with large landowners and consistently supported by the Mitsui and Sumitomo interests, or the Kenseikai (renamed the Minseito or People's Constitutional Party in 1927), which was looked upon as the mouthpiece of the Mitsubishi and the industrial capitalists, ranked high in public esteem. Principles were lacking and corruption was rife. The diet became more and more the meeting place for carefully chosen but normally elected bureaucrats, admirals, generals, and professional politicians who curried the favor and carried out the will of the men of real power who remained behind the scenes. The diet, however, was the key instrument of government. Japan was the first non-occidental land to make full use of a parliamentary system although only a small proportion of its people had any effective means of making their views felt.

Premier Hara was a new-style politician, but he was no knight in shining armor. He was careful to consult closely with the genro and the ranking militarists; and like old-style political figures he kept his body-guard of *soshi*—or bullies—for the rugged in-fighting. Election battles were vicious; scandals were frequent. Criticism of Hara was particularly bitter because he did not fight to put the manhood suffrage law through the diet and because he showed no firmness in handling the delicate situation which resulted from the massacre of several Japanese in the Siberian city of Nikolaevsk in early 1920. He was not equal to the continuing economic crisis which reached the explosion point in 1921. Japan had become dependent on prosperity and it was faced with a great depression. At the heart of the dilemma was the growth in population. The birth rate remained constant; the death rate declined. Life span increased and the population climbed at the rate of a million a year. At a time when new jobs were desperately needed, the end of the war boom brought wholesale layoffs, idle factories, and stagnant commerce. Farmers were forced into bankruptcy and laborers went hungry. Hara used all his ability and the resources of the state to pump life into the suffering economic system, but he was the victim of the world-wide puzzle of the time—what to do when a few rich became richer, and the poverty-stricken masses sank deeper into their own misery.

On November 4, 1921, a week before the opening of the Washington Conference, Hara was assassinated by a railway switchman at the huge central station in Tokyo. He was succeeded as prime minister by his finance minister, Takahashi Korekiyo, who also became the head of the Seiyukai. At the same time the crown prince, Hirohito, was designated as prince regent and took on the burdens of government which had been carried by his invalid father.

THE WASHINGTON CONFERENCE

The Conference on Limitation of Armaments and Pacific and Far Eastern Affairs was called by President Harding in 1921 because not only Japan, but the rest of the world, was in a desperate frame of mind. The "war to end all wars" of 1914–1918 had clearly failed of its high purpose, and national budgets were more heavily laden than ever in an armaments race. Harassed people were nowhere able to pay the taxes which seemed universally in prospect. If the armaments in the mad process of construction were to be called into service anywhere in the world, the Pacific and the Far East seemed to be the place. It therefore appeared statesmanlike to call a conference which would actually bring about a reduction or limitation in armaments, and focus public attention on the critical conflicts of policy centering in Asia. The glaring fault of the conference was the conspicuous absence of Russia and Germany.

The Washington Conference was in many respects an unhappy diplomatic denouement for Japan. The world's sympathy for China was strikingly revealed, and Japan was obliged to give up many of the unequal privileges and special interests which had been patiently acquired during a half-century. Seven treaties were signed; and twelve resolutions were adopted at Washington, in addition to special bilateral agreements which were made between Japan and China about Shantung and between Japan and the United States about an important cable crossing on the island of Yap. The diplomatic settlement achieved at Washington determined the political status of Asia and the Pacific for a decade and regulated the controversies between Japan and the United States until the Japanese invasion of Manchuria in 1931.

The Four-Power Pacific Treaty (signed on February 5, 1922 by the United States, Great Britain, Japan, and France) was an agreement to respect mutual rights in insular possessions and insular dominions in the region of the Pacific and, in case of dispute, to refer the matter to a joint conference for consideration and adjustment. The four powers bound themselves to full and frank communication in order to arrive at an understanding as to the most efficient measures to be taken if the said rights were threatened by the aggressive action of any other power. The same treaty provided for the termination of the Anglo-Japanese alliance. Pressure from the United States and Canada brought to an end the alliance which for twenty years had been the cornerstone of Anglo-Japanese policy in East Asia. As Professor Thomas Bailey described the Four-Power Treaty, "a four-power agreement to talk replaced a two-power agreement to fight."

The Five-Power Treaty on the Limitation of Naval Armament

(signed on the same day by the United States, Great Britain, Japan, France, and Italy) called for a ten-year construction holiday on capital ships, and for the scrapping of some ships already planned or being built. It limited capital ships to 35,000 tons and naval armament to sixteen-inch guns. The United States, Great Britain, Japan, France, and Italy were to maintain a ratio in capital ships of 5–5–3–1.75–1.75. The treaty was to remain in force for ten years, and thereafter was subject to termination on two years' notice by any of the signatory powers. All the powers welcomed the respite from the race in building expensive capital ships.

Article XIX of the Five-Power Treaty provided for the maintenance of the *status quo* in fortifications and naval bases in the Pacific. This article applied to (1) the insular possessions of the United States except (a) those adjacent to the coast of the United States, Alaska, and the Panama Canal Zone, not including the Aleutian Islands, and (b) the Hawaiian Islands; (2) Hong Kong and the insular possessions of the British Empire east of 110 degrees east longitude, except (a) those adjacent to the coast of Canada, (b) the Commonwealth of Australia and its territories, and (c) New Zealand; and (3) the following territories of Japan: Kuriles, Bonins, Amami-Oshima, Liu Ch'iu islands (Ryukyus), Formosa, the Pescadores, and any insular territories or possessions in the Pacific Ocean which Japan might hereafter acquire.

Although every gun in the United States Navy was pointed at Japan because of the heated controversies between the two countries, this agreement, promising not to fortify Guam, Pago-Pago, the Philippines, and the Aleutians, ruled out the possibility of any immediate naval action in the western Pacific. Great Britain was equally limited by its agreement not to fortify Hong Kong, although it was still free to build up the defenses of Singapore at its pleasure. Many Americans and British felt that their respective countries made disastrous sacrifices in accepting these provisions. However, these limitations removed potential sources of friction and gave Japan the additional measure of security which made the Japanese government willing to accept the inferior naval ratio.

For reasons of face, the naval contingent in the Japanese delegation agitated for parity and would have preferred no treaties at all to the short end of a five-five-three ratio. The adamant Japanese were thwarted because the people at home were war-weary, financially embarrassed, and disposed to accept a naval holiday. All the weaknesses in the Japanese bargaining position were clear to the United States, which had successfully broken the Japanese codes and could read every word of the supposedly secret communications between Tokyo and Washington.

The Nine-Power Treaty (signed by the United States, Great Britain, Japan, France, Italy, China, The Netherlands, Belgium, and Portugal) has been discussed in connection with the policies of China at the conference.

Japan looked upon this treaty as the complete triumph of the United States over Japanese diplomacy and the final blow to its drive for hegemony on the Asian continent. The Japanese delegates went back to their homeland with a feeling that they had made to China and the powers every possible concession consistent with the sense of reason, fairness, and honor. They were aggrieved by the precipitate ending of the Anglo-Japanese alliance, the apparent lack of understanding and general criticism of Japan's policies on the mainland of Asia, and above all by the vitriolic verbal attacks on Japan by the diplomats of China. The Japanese believed sincerely that their special relationship with China was mutually beneficial. They argued that China in its internal agonies should be grateful for the benevolence and restraint of Japan. In their view China should feel toward Japan as some Latin American countries felt toward the United States—not fearful and resentful but thankful because of the benefactor's contributions to law, order, and prosperity.

The Washington Conference agreements dispelled Japan's dreams of controlling China and establishing itself as the dominant naval power in the Pacific. Japan's forward march was temporarily halted, and the world was relieved for a decade from the fear of general war which might result from recurrent conflicts in East Asia.

INTERNAL POLITICS, 1923–1931

Immediately after the Washington Conference, Premier Takahashi resigned. He could not control factions within his own party, the Seiyukai; and he could not escape the consequences of the Washington agreements. The opposition party, the Kenseikai, commanded no more public respect than the party in power. In undisguised contempt for both parties, the genro named three successive nonparty governments to guide Japan through two tempestuous years of political strife. Party leaders meekly acquiesced in the genro's choice, because they preferred to see militarists or bureaucrats in power rather than their own particular party rivals.

In June 1922 Admiral Kato Tomosaburo was designated as prime minister. He had shown merit as a delegate to the Washington Conference. As a military man he was needed to withdraw troops from Siberia, to conduct negotiations with the roving representatives from Soviet Russia, pull Japanese soldiers out of China, cut back military expenditures, and implement the Washington agreements to scrap the ships which were intended to be the pride of the Japanese navy. Each of these tasks was difficult and unpleasant, and constituted an open invitation to assassination.

Admiral Kato died in office in August 1923. He was succeeded by

Admiral Yamamoto Gombei, of the scandalous notoriety of World War I. His brief tenure of office was catastrophic. It began with the terrible earthquake of September 1, 1923, which destroyed virtually the entire city of Yokohama and well over half of Tokyo. Rumors spread as fast as the raging fires that Korean nationalists, together with Japanese communists plotted to set up a revolutionary government. Many Koreans were sought out and killed by frenzied mobs or by gangs of self-styled patriotic young men. The police conducted a mass roundup of anarchists, communists, and other left-wing radicals; and their worst fears seemed confirmed by an attempt on the life of the crown prince in the heart of crowded Tokyo just after Christmas, 1923. The enormity of the crime shocked the nation—and of course toppled the cabinet of the ill-starred Admiral Yamamoto.

The third of the nonparty (or superparty) governments was installed in January 1924 under former prime minister Count Kiyoura Keigo, bureaucrat, protégé of the militarists, and member of the House of Peers. By the time of his appointment, economic conditions were on the mend and the most explosive political issues were settled. Party leaders overcame their timidity, launched a furious campaign against the highhanded and arbitrary procedures of the venerable genro and sought to restore themselves to the headship of the government. After six months of argument, they forced Count Kiyoura to resign. New elections were ordered. In accordance with the returns, Prince Saionji suggested the appointment of Kato Takaaki, leader of the Kenseikai, to the premiership.

The Kato coalition cabinet which took office on June 11, 1924, was the first of a series of party cabinets which governed Japan through 1931. It included among its members one former premier, four future premiers, and a galaxy of superior political talent. Its genius was directed toward the modernization and mechanization of the fighting services—which was to be accomplished at lower annual operating costs to the Japanese public. The army was cut by four divisions. Funds which were saved by this move were spent for a broader military training program and a more extensive campaign for military indoctrination in the public schools. Kato's program called for thrift and economy in government expenditures but without neglect of social welfare. His domestic measures included a health insurance law, factory law, labor disputes mediation law, and unemployment relief through public works. His best-known accomplishment was the universal suffrage law which was promulgated on Boys' Day (May 5, 1925). This removed all property qualifications on the right to vote and extended the franchise to every Japanese male over twenty-five years of age. The electorate was expanded by this law from 3,000,000 to more than 14,000,000 voters.

In order to prevent the extension of the suffrage from leading to radical agitation, the same diet under Prime Minister Kato passed a tighter Peace Preservation Act. It became illegal to advocate alteration of Japan's political structure or the abolition of private property. Fines and imprisonment up to ten years were decreed for membership in societies dedicated to overturning the politico-economic order. Labor was deprived of the right to strike by its obligation to submit to compulsory arbitration all disputes in enterprises directly affecting the public welfare. This was a legal euphemism for compulsory arbitration of *all* labor disputes.

Prime Minister Kato died on January 28, 1926, and was succeeded by Home Minister Wakatsuki, both as prime minister and as head of the Kenseikai. The latter's term in office was anticlimactic and ended with the first signs of an economic depression in the following year.

In April 1927 a general-politician, Tanaka Giichi, the head of the Seiyukai, became prime minister. He inherited nothing but trouble. He supported the hard line of Japan in China (which will be discussed below) and tried to minimize the effects of the world-wide depression on his vulnerable country. He tried to save the banks and to preserve the national economic strength represented by the *zaibatsu*, but he was helpless in trying to ease the suffering of the common people. Economic hardships increased political unrest, and the Tanaka cabinet took stern repressive measures. Nationwide raids put thousands of suspected communists in jail. Student associations suspected of ultraliberalism, such as the association for the study of social science, were banned. Public-communications media were subjected to strict censorship. The campaign against dangerous thoughts was stepped up, and the death penalty was decreed for serious violations of the peace preservation law. The mood of Japan began to exhibit a marked change. The exuberance and liberalism of the early party of the decade vanished; it was replaced by caution and restraint. Thoughtful Japanese worried about their future and their mission in the world.

The Seiyukai surrendered power to the newly formed Minseito, the successor in name to the Kenseikai. Its president, Hamaguchi Yuko became prime minister, and, like the Hoover administration in the United States, it tried to bring the country out of the depression by retrenchment and conservative measures. It too was unsuccessful. On November 14, 1930, the prime minister was shot by a young fanatic. While he lingered between life and death, his Minseito colleague, former prime minister Wakatsuki carried on his futile efforts to win back prosperity. At this juncture, the attention of Japan shifted overseas.

JAPAN IN ASIA

While Japan changed governments at home, it tried various tactics to preserve its position in Asia. After the armistice was signed in Europe on November 11, 1918, Japan and China continued the joint war participation board on the pretext of protection against the spread of Russian bolshevism. Japan continued to advance credit to the Peking government. It also poured money into the pockets of Chang Tso-lin in Manchuria and some of the rebel warlords in South China. It looked as if the prime Japanese interest was not in particular Chinese persons or factions, but rather in the promotion of disorder and chaos. As long as China was divided, Japan was safe. Japan never demanded collateral for its loans and registered no protests if the purposes of its financial assistance were never fulfilled. Silver bullets quieted those Chinese who might have opposed the Japanese; bribes enriched heartless officials who were completely calloused to the plight and poverty of their own people.

Japan encountered no serious opposition in Korea, Manchuria, or Mongolia during World War I, but it ran into unexpected difficulties as a result of its expedition into Siberia. The Japanese withdrew very quickly from Transbaikalia, but they remained in northern Sakhalin and the maritime provinces. They established a puppet regime in Vladivostok and tried to come to terms with the Far Eastern Republic, which came into existence in Chita in 1921. Conferences were held at Dairen during the time the Washington Conference was in session. On September 4, 1922, negotiations between the Far Eastern Republic and Japan were resumed in Changchun and on this occasion were dominated by the presence of the Soviet representative, A. A. Joffe, then on his way to China. In view of the pending incorporation of the Far Eastern Republic into the Soviet Union (accomplished on November 15, 1922), Joffe insisted that the scope of the conference should be extended to include all Russo-Japanese issues, primarily the issue of recognition. It was deemed advisable to adjourn the conference and postpone those weighty matters for later consideration. Japan chose to withdraw its troops from Siberia and to abandon its premature Siberian ambitions.

As the political situation in the U.S.S.R. stabilized, Japan had to choose between opposition and recognition in determining policies toward the new Russian regime. Japan had always feared the material and military strength of Russia; after the Russian revolution it found a new menace in the Russian-sponsored force of international communism. Viscount Goto, the mayor of Tokyo, invited Joffe to come to Japan for a rest cure after his arduous negotiations with Sun Yat-sen. Premier Kato concurred in Goto's invitation, although one Tokyo newspaper expressed its indignation against "the Soviet devil who is here to organize a communist movement and ruin us through the bonehead of a mayor fate has inflicted upon us." Joffe stayed six months in Japan, until he was recalled to Moscow. His successor in East Asia, Lev Karakhan, conducted discussions with Yoshizawa Kenkichi in Peking, and on January 20, 1925, they signed the Treaty of Peking which brought about the resumption of diplomatic relations between Russia and Japan.

The treaty provided for the exchange of diplomatic and consular representatives. The Soviet Union recognized the continuing validity of the Portsmouth Treaty, but insisted upon the revision or abandonment of all other treaties, agreements, and conventions made during the period from 1905 to 1917 between Japan and tsarist Russia. Japanese would be permitted to fish in Siberian coastal waters pending revision of the fisheries convention of 1907. Until the conclusion of a new commercial treaty, the nationals of either country were to enjoy in the territory of the other most-favored-nation treatment in matters of entry, travel, residence, private ownership of property, and peaceful pursuit of commerce and industry. Both countries pledged themselves to restrain all their officials and organizations officially subsidized from engaging in propaganda or any act, overt or covert, liable in any way to endanger the order and security of any part of their respective territories.

In protocols and annexes to the basic document Russia agreed to adjust its debts to Japan, and Japan agreed to complete the withdrawal of its troops from northern Sakhalin by May 15, 1925. Soviet authorities expressed their sincere regrets for the Nikolaevsk incident of 1920. Russia granted Japan oil, lumber, and coal concessions in northern Sakhalin for a period of forty to fifty years, subject to the stipulations that Soviet labor laws were to be observed and that half the technical staff and three-quarters of the unskilled labor were to be Soviet citizens.

Between the Japanese recognition of the Soviet Union and the Manchurian Incident, Japanese-Russian relations seemed calm and uninteresting. On January 23, 1928, the two governments concluded a new fisheries convention which reaffirmed Japan's right to capture, gather, and manufacture maritime products along the Siberian coast facing the Japan Sea, the Sea of Okhotsk, and the Bering Sea; but Russia let it be known that Russia, too, planned to expand its own activities in the vital fishing industry.

Beneath the surface of understanding, Japan and Russia nursed feelings of mutual suspicion and distrust. Each side—publicly but not officially—accused the other of espionage and sabotage. As both nations grew stronger they hurled threats at one another across the Siberian wastelands. In 1929 Japan refused to side with the United States in trying to bring pressure on the Soviet Union to stop its advance into Manchuria; and in 1931 the Russians likewise refused to take a strong stand to oppose the aggressive actions of Japan. Neither nation would take an avowed stand against the other in international actions, but no love was lost between them because of the bitter differences over international communism.

The Soviet Union was not able to utilize communism in Japan as a tactical weapon as it had done so successfully in China. Communists and fellow-travelers were not able to stand up against the Japanese police. Shortly after the Japanese Communist Party was launched in 1922, it was forcibly disbanded. Communists were among the extremists who were put in jail after the earthquake and after the attempted assassination of the crown prince. In 1924 and 1925 the Far Eastern Bureau of the Third International in Shanghai tried to reactivate the party in anticipation of the universal manhood suffrage law. Spurred on by occasional visitors from Shanghai and Moscow, the Japanese communists reorganized in 1926. They established their own propaganda organ, Akahata, or the Red Flag, and they wormed their way into virtual control of the left-wing Farmer-Labor Party. Their handbills ranged from mild slogans advocating an eight-hour day and the right to strike to extreme proposals for parliament without the emperor, confiscation of the property of the emperor and the capitalists, and dictatorship of the proletariat and the landless tenants. In 1928, as has been noted, thousands of communists were caught in police raids, and the best-known leaders were either driven underground, forced out of the country, or clapped in jail. Communists in Japan were of no help whatsoever to Russia in coping with Japan in Asia.

Japan was more baffled by its own indecision than by any overt foreign opposition in dealing with China on the eve of Chiang Kai-shek's rise to power. Japan was torn between its desire to see China peaceful, orderly, and anti-Bolshevik, and its fear of an awakened, united China determined to cast out all foreign privileges including those of Japan. All Japanese understood that China was on the move and could not be ignored. The Kenseikai, as identified with Baron Shidehara, felt that Japan would gain most by a policy of patience and tolerance. During its term in office (1924 to 1927 and 1929 to 1931) the Japanese government refused to send troops to China or to participate in international demonstrations against China such as the bombardment of Nanking on March 24, 1927. This policy became known as the "soft policy" in contrast to the "positive policy" of the Seiyukai and its leader, General Tanaka. Both policies were dedicated to Japan's hegemony in China; they represented alternative tactics. Baron Shidehara offered the velvet glove of friendship; General Tanaka advocated the iron fist. Tanaka's name was associated with the "Tanaka Memorial," which was a document purporting to contain decisions reached at an eastern regions conference of Japanese officials in Tokyo in the summer of 1927. It was often cited as evidence of Japan's blueprint for conquest of Mongolia, China, and eventually the world. If such a document actually existed, it was probably nothing more than one man's ideas of the manner in which his country could obtain its greatest security and make its maximum contribution to human welfare. Comparable state papers rest in the anonymous files of many a foreign office.

Baron Shidehara was in office during Chiang Kai-shek's northward march, and he showed admirable restraint during unfortunate incidents involving Japanese lives and property. When Tanaka became head of the Japanese government in 1928, he tried to halt the northward advance of the Chinese nationalists between Nanking and Peking. He was successful for a time, but he was obliged eventually to retire before the on-moving Chinese tide. During Tanaka's regime, Chang Tso-lin was killed on his retreat from Peking. Although the crime was committed by Japanese military units without the consent or even the knowledge of the civilian authorities in Tokyo, Tanaka was obliged to bear the responsibility for the deed.

After Shidehara returned to power, Japan again became more conciliatory. Japan recognized the government of Chiang Kai-shek as the rightful government of China in January 1929 and tried for the next two years to adjust its remaining diplomatic differences peacefully with China. Japan bargained patiently about tariff privileges, extraterritorial rights, concessions in Chinese cities, and investments in inland navigation. It promoted measures of cultural cooperation with China designed to foster sympathy and understanding between their respective peoples. But that was only one side of the medal. On the other side were the Chinese demonstrations against the Japanese and the militant uncompromising attitude of the Japanese army in Manchuria.

JAPAN IN WORLD POLITICS (1923–1931)

Although its diplomatic concentration was on the affairs of Asia, Japan was an active and leading participant in world politics during the decade of the 1920's. As one of the five great powers at the Conference of Versailles, Japan received a permanent seat on the Council, or executive committee, of the League of Nations. Japan therefore was directly concerned in the peaceful settlement of all international disputes and in the operation of the mandate system. Japanese were active in the Assembly and the Secretariat. Japan was one of the drafters of the Protocol of the Permanent Court of International Justice, and a Japanese jurist was one of its most distinguished judges. Japan paid closest attention to the work of the International Labor Office. Japan was among the first and most faithful in paying its share of the expenses of all these international agencies. Many Japanese felt their country was much too international-minded during the heyday of peace and pacifism after World War I.

The system of world organization and collective security was comforting to Japan after the Washington Conference. Japan was deprived of its particular alliance with England and in April 1923 Secretary Hughes brought about the abrogation of the Lansing-Ishii agreement. Japan lost all hope for American support for any possible revival of a campaign for "special interests" in China. With the torpedoing of its designs for naval superiority in the western Pacific by the Washington agreements, Japan had no alternative but to trim its diplomatic sails to international winds.

Within a year and a half after the conclusion of the Washington Conference, American-Japanese relations blew hot and cold. The earthquake and fire at Yokohama and Tokyo in September 1923 occasioned an outpouring of American sympathy, just as the San Francisco disaster of 1906 had elicited expressions of goodwill from Japan. The warm feelings were cooled very quickly by the American immigration actions of 1924. It will be recalled that Japan and the United States made a gentleman's agreement in 1908. According to its terms the Americans would not exclude the immigration of Japanese labor, if the Japanese themselves would curtail emigration. The agreement did not work to the satisfaction of California. Japanese immigration decreased in total numbers, but many "picture brides" were imported. American-born children (nisei) of Japanese parents showed an increase which stirred up some of the residents along the west coast.

In 1913 the California legislature passed a law stipulating that aliens ineligible to citizenship could no longer own land nor lease it for periods longer than three years. In 1920 the state took away all privileges of Japanese to lease lands, to act as guardians for their American-born children (who might own lands), and to own shares in American-controlled landowning companies. In a series of decisions between 1922 and 1925 (which were reversed in 1952 and 1953) the Supreme Court held that the land laws were constitutional in view of the fact that Japanese and other orientals were ineligible for citizenship.

A new immigration bill came before the Congress in 1924 which would deny the right of entry into the United States of persons not eligible for citizenship. Secretary Hughes opposed this measure because it seemed like an unnecessary affront to people from Asia. A quota for the Japanese on the same basis as a quota for other nations would have permitted the entry of no more than 250 Japanese per year. The secretary expressed his views to the Japanese ambassador, and in response the Japanese ambassador wrote to the Secretary of State as follows:

> I realize as I believe you do the grave consequences which the enactment of this measure containing that particular provision would inevitably bring upon the otherwise happy and mutually advantageous relations between the two countries.

This sentence was interpreted by some congressmen as a veiled threat and was cited as a further reason for oriental exclusion. The Congress, by votes of 308 to 62 in the House and 68 to 9 in the Senate, showed its determination to deal with Japan as it pleased. President Coolidge accepted the immigration bill because he approved of all its clauses except those which referred to Asians. In Japan the American exclusion act was interpreted as a personal insult, and it drained the reservoir of goodwill almost to the vanishing point.

In spite of its aggrieved feelings, Japan could not avoid close economic relationships with the United States. Japan looked eastward across the Pacific for its supplies of petroleum, cotton, and scrap iron and depended upon sales of silk, tea, and miscellaneous manufactured goods to pay its gigantic import bills. Japan relied upon American financiers for foreign loans and invited the investment of American capital in its industries. Many of the American "*zaibatsu*" established close connections with counterparts in Japan: General Electric made patent and trade agreements with Shibaura Electric and Western Electric did the same with Nippon Electric. Many American companies set up subsidiaries or branch factories in Japan—for example, Ford, General Motors, Radio Corporation of America, Victor Talking Machine, Libby-Owens Glass, Robert Dollar Steamship, Otis Elevator, Aluminum Company of America, and a half-dozen of the leading petroleum companies. The United States replaced Great Britain as the most vital foreign factor in Japan's economic welfare. Any shift in prosperity or depression in the United States was felt immediately in Japan. To Japan the West—as an abstraction—came to be more closely identified with the United States than with Europe.

Japan watched very closely the outpouring of international idealism in the United States and cooperated whenever it could do so without jeopardy to its national interests. Sentimentally, Japan wanted the right to equality with the United States and Great Britain in naval armaments, but it accepted further limitations at less than equality as a result of naval conferences in Geneva in 1927 and London in 1930. The Big Three agreed on a prolonged holiday for capital ships, a 10–10–6 ration in heavy cruisers, an approximate 10–10–7 ratio in light cruisers, and parity in submarines. Japanese diplomats seemed to share the fond hopes for peace which were frequently expressed by such statesmen as Briand and Strese-man in Europe. However, the Japanese warned that it would be impos-sible to accomplish speedily either disarmament or compulsory arbitra-tion of international disputes. They opposed hasty and imperfect defini-tions of aggression. The Japanese argued that the aggressor could not be defined as the party which struck first, because the first blow was usually the result of provocation.

Japan signed the Kellogg-Briand Treaty, or the Pact of Paris, of August 27, 1928, which contained the following provisions:

> Article I. The High Contracting Parties solemnly declare in the name of their respective peoples that they condemn recourse to war for the solution of international controversies, and renounce it as an instrument of national policy in their relations with one another.
> Article II. The High Contracting Parties agree that the settlement or solution of all disputes or conflicts of whatever nature or of what-ever origin they may be, which may arise among them, shall never be sought except by pacific means.

Japanese public opinion considered this pact as welcome as a good rice crop, but in political circles it was used as a convenient controversial issue. Critics pointed out that "pacific means" were not defined and penal-ties were not specified for violators. The government was obliged to ex-plain to the public that the phrase "in the name of their respective peo-ples" was inapplicable to Japan since the emperor was the font of sov-ereignty. It was also explained that the pact could not be considered a restriction or impairment of the right of self-defense. The sad truth was that by 1928 Japan's explosive internal situation took precedence over international agreements for the maintenance of peace. Japan was more determined to assert its right, as a have-not power, to resort to aggressive means if need be to obtain a satisfactory base for national welfare than to fulfill its obligation, as one of the great powers of the world, to limit it-self to orderly processes for the satisfaction of its needs.

On the Eve of the Manchurian Incident

In 1927 Japan experienced a preview in miniature of the world-wide depression which was to engulf the country three years later. A single bank failure released an avalanche. A number of smaller firms went into liquidation, to the advantage of the *zaibatsu* who took over residual assets. As the economic crisis deepened, neither party showed any real ability to cope with the nation's plight. The collapse of the American silk market in 1930, coupled with a short rice crop brought parts of northern Japan desperately near starvation. Premier Hamaguchi's remedy was a program of retrenchment which he called "rationalization." His aim was to boost home industries, reduce imports, and encourage exports. He tried to cut costs and depress prices. He took Japan off the gold standard. By a generous use of subsidies and bounties he diverted business from nonessential industries to key industries.

Gradually the emphasis on recovery shifted from the well-being of the individual to the welfare of the state. Japan concerned itself more with the revival of national strength than with the improvement of the level of living. A philosophy of state socialism was accepted as the only path to economic survival. It was felt that industrial potential should be coordinated with military potential to make the state as strong as possible, and taxes on subsidized industries should be so heavy that profits would accrue to the state and not to the rich *zaibatsu* owners and managers. Likewise it became national policy that foreign trade should exist entirely for the benefit of the state. Imports should be permitted not for the luxury or comfort of the individual but for the vital needs of the state. Exports should not be allowed to make profits for a chosen few exporters; rather the earnings should be put aside in special funds reserved for the use of the state. Imports were linked with exports; the former were permitted only as exchange was earned to pay for the purchases from abroad. In spite of all these stern measures, Japan was not able to balance its budget or its international income account. The nation became alarmed as it realized its utter dependence on the outside world for raw materials and markets. The alarm spread as nations not only failed to show goodwill and sympathy for Japan but also engaged in active trade wars and built high protective-tariff walls.

The economic crisis poured fuel on the rising flames of political reaction and ultranationalism. As has been noted, Japan always had a large portion of national pride, fierce patriotism, and respect for discipline in its national psyche. Even in the surge of liberalism and awakening democracy, many conservative elements seethed against the follies of modernism and argued for the superior quality of the good old days. Their voices were not heeded when times were good; they became increasingly powerful as the situation deteriorated.

As early as the nineteenth century, such ultranationalists as the picturesque Toyama Mitsuru talked exclusively about the development of national power and the expansion of Japan on the continent. They urged upon the government the need to stamp out the movement for liberty and popular rights. They provided the cloak and dagger components for Japan's activities in the Korean War, the Chinese Revolution, and every other political crisis in Asia. In 1901 they launched a society which was dedicated to the harmonizing of East and West, reinvigoration of the ancient ideals of Japan, promulgation of the Imperial Way, uplifting the peoples of Asia, and the extension of the natural frontiers of Japan to the banks of the Amur River. The society was called the Black Dragon Society, which was the literal translation of the Chinese name of the Amur River.

Nationalism of the Black Dragon variety was not very popular during World War I, but it was carefully nurtured shortly thereafter by a few colorful characters and sinister societies. In 1918 Dr. Okawa Shumei, who will always be remembered as the man who slapped Premier Tojo during the trial of the war criminals in Tokyo in 1946, organized conservatives in the intellectual circles to oppose Professor Yoshino's liberals. In 1919 Kita Ikki, a Japanese in Shanghai, wrote a remarkable book which became the bible of the ultranationalists. It was called an *Outline for the Reconstruction of Japan*. Its themes were that the nation should be reconstructed by an awakened citizenry led by no one but the military, and that it was the birthright of the weak to fight against the strong. It was imperialist, but anticapitalist. It preached national socialism. In 1924 Baron Hiranuma, a former bureaucrat who was later to become president of the privy council and premier, organized the *Kokuhonsha* or State Foundation Society to counteract the unhealthy trends of the times. Prominent politicians, students, admirals, generals, justices, and businessmen joined up, so that by the early 1930's the roster of Kokuhonsha looked like a *Who's Who* of Japan.

As ultranationalism grew, it took on the cloak of state Shinto to venerate the nation and the emperor. It had no well-defined philosophy or organization as Nazism in Germany or fascism in Italy. It tended to be anti-West, antiliberal, antisocialist, anticommunist, authoritarian, antidemocratic, antiparliamentary, anti-international (that is, anti-League of Nations), and antidisarmament. It was dedicated thoroughly to totalitarianism at home and the use of force on the Asian continent. It attracted increasing popular support although it resorted to assassinations at home and adventurism overseas. It accounted for the rigorous enforcement of the peace preservation law and the campaign against labor unions, communists, and dangerous thoughts. (Any thought was considered dangerous which questioned the position of the emperor or challenged the basic political and economic concepts of Japan's ruling groups.) The spirit of ultranationalism flourished in Japan on the eve of the Manchurian incident.

The ultranationalists looked to the army as their champion, and the true servant of the imperial will. The army was made up of peasants, and the newer generation of officers came from the common people, not the old clan leaders. Company commanders understood the distress which afflicted the families of their men; which caused fathers to sell their daughters to cafes, teahouses, and brothels in the city. The army reflected the angry emotions of the Japanese countryside. Army officers were respected as the best of the ordinary Japanese people. They were supposed to be above personal and selfish interests. They were not gelatinous like politicians nor profligate like the *zaibatsu*. In the popular mind, only the leaders of the services could be counted upon to guide the nation out of its difficulties.

The younger officers—that is younger in ideas, not in years—were not a class apart from the people, nor were they blind proponents of the past. They looked upon themselves not as feudal relics but as tools of destiny. They were austere in their way of living and deadly serious in their purposes. They were well-educated and inflexibly indoctrinated with the military spirit. They knew that Japan could not return to the past; it must go ahead. They were determined that changes in the future should be in the direction of discipline, totalitarianism, and strength, not in the direction of party brawls, indecision, and weakness. They were forbidden to take part in politics, but they were aroused to the fate of Japan.

As they saw their beloved country, it had become after ten years of bourgeois democratic-liberalism an unwholesome combination of political corruption, self-centered wealth, idle nobility, neglected peasantry, decadent culture, unpatriotic students, feckless intellectual leaders, and dangerous thoughts. It was their challenge to remove the waste from the schools, profits from the factories and corruption from political processes. They would make use of conditions and institutions created by the Meiji revolution for the spiritual regeneration of the masses. Fortunately the people of Japan were literate and susceptible to indoctrination. The program of the militarists brought far greater control over men's minds than had ever been exercised by emperor, shogun, or daimyo. As Professor Reischauer observed, the parliamentary coalition of bureaucrats, big businessmen, and politicians—with more or less active support from the urban middle classes—was pushed aside by the militarists with the noisy backing of the ultranationalistic societies and the tacit support of the rural population.

More and more younger officers in both services accepted the ideas contained in Kita's *Outline for the Reconstruction of Japan*. They were stirred to action by Japan's acceptance of the naval agreements of 1930. They thought the state was endangered and they felt that the emperor was ill-advised in accepting the antinavy recommendations of weak-kneed politicians. In late September 1930 a handful of high-ranking officers formed the *Sakurakai* or Cherry Society, dedicated to the revival of the nation's *esprit de corps*. They took the cherry blossom as their symbol, because it is fated to perish at the height of its glory. Their code was sense of duty to the state. It was embodied in the quotation from the imperial rescript to soldiers and sailors, "Death is as light as a feather, but duty is weightier than a mountain."

The members of the Cherry Society included such famous men as Generals Koiso, Ninimiya, Tatekawa, and Colonel Hashimoto. They swung into action after the attempted assassination of Premier Hamaguchi on November 1930, which in their opinion revealed the total bankruptcy of liberalism and democracy. They plotted to get rid of the diet and set up a military dictatorship. They planned to stage a *coup d'état* in March 1931 by blowing up party headquarters, staging riots, and if necessary by assassinating the entire cabinet. Their plans fell apart before the date of execution, but other plots were formulated by extremist elements within and without the army. By the end of July 1931 rumors leaked out that incidents would be provoked in Manchuria for the purpose of aggravating Chinese-Japanese relations. Other schemes were in the making for the establishment of a military dictatorship regime within Japan itself.

Conditions outside Japan contributed to the course of events inside. The trends toward totalitarianism within Russia, Italy, and Germany were looked upon with approval by Japanese militarists. The dangers of democracy and free enterprise were more heavily underscored every day because of the spreading depression and the collapse of international trade. China was regarded with the greatest apprehension. The nation was about to be unified by Chiang Kai-shek. China seemed to be in a position and mood to undertake what Japan itself had accomplished in the past fifty years—modernization and liberation from foreign influences. Japan looked like China's immediate and most vulnerable target. The climax came when Chang Hsueh-liang, the Young Marshal who had succeeded his father as boss of Manchuria, hoisted the Kuomintang flag over his palace in Mukden. Shidehara's policy of conciliation looked to the younger Japanese officers more like weakness than wisdom. It seemed to some as if the moment had come for positive action. On the night of September 18–19, 1931, units of the Kwantung army, without the knowledge or approval of either military of civilian authorities in Tokyo, blew up a section of a railroad outside Mukden and placed the blame on the Chinese. The incident was carried out which started the march toward World War II.

SUGGESTED READING

Allen, G. C., *Short Economic History of Modern Japan* (London, George Allen & Unwin, 1946).

Brown, Delmer, *Nationalism in Japan* (Berkeley, U. of California, 1955).

Buell, Raymond L., *Washington Conference* (New York, Appleton, 1922).

Embree, John, *Japanese Nation* (New York, Farrar, 1945).

Editors of *Fortune*, Japan (New York, *Time*, Inc., September, 1936).

Japanese Government, Foreign Office, *Collection of Official Documents and Releases* (nineteen vols.) (Tokyo).

Ohashi, Keishi, (ed.), *Japanese Trade and Industry in the Meiji-Taisho Era* (trans. by Okata Tamotsu) (Tokyo, Obunsha, 1957).

Royama, Masamichi, *Foreign Policy of Japan, 1914–1939* (Tokyo, Japanese Council, Institute of Pacific Relations, 1941).

Russell, Oland D., *House of Mitsui* (Boston, Little, 1939).

Scalapino, Robert, *Democracy and the Party Movement in Pre-War Japan* (Berkeley, U. of California, 1953).

Toynbee, Arnold J., (ed.), *Survey of International Affairs* (London, Royal Institute of International Affairs, annual).

Uyehara, Cecil H. (compiler, under the direction of Edwin G. Beal), *Checklist of Archives in the Japanese Ministry of Foreign Affairs.* (Washington, Library of Congress, Photo Duplication Service, 1954).

Young, A. Morgan, *Imperial Japan, 1926–1938* (London, George Allen & Unwin, 1938).

Young, A. Morgan, *Japan in Recent Times, 1912–1926* (New York, Morrow, 1929).

Young, C. W., *Japan's Special Position in Manchuria* (Baltimore, Johns Hopkins U., 1931).

16

British India in the Twentieth Century

In the early years of the twentieth century, Japan exhibited a degree of sovereignty and national vitality which was the envy of both China and India. Japan was master in its own homeland. China was nominally independent but badly bruised by the diplomatic encroachments of the foreign powers. India, on the other hand, was only a British colony. India's rulers were alien in culture, physical appearance, and way of life. The government of India was remarkably honest and efficient, and it promoted the interests of India as though India were an independent country. However, the British civil servants in India could never divest themselves of their British character, nor could they put aside the fact that they were loyal subjects of the king-emperor in London. India derived undeniable benefits from the British presence, but Indians became increasingly convinced that they could do better than the British in looking after themselves. It was no source of pride to Indians that their country was regarded as the fairest jewel in the British crown. The struggle for self-government and independence became the dominant theme in Indian history. In this respect, India was the prototype and the model for European colonies in Southeast Asia.

FROM 1900 TO WORLD WAR I

The twentieth century did not open in India as an auspicious new era. The land was parched; and the people suffered because of drought, famine, and plague. Governmental efforts to increase agricultural production by education, research, and public works fell far short of needs. Various provinces passed all kinds of laws in the interest of peasant welfare, including more generous principles of assessment, prohibition of alienation of land to noncultivators, compulsory reduction of debt to moneylenders, and legalization of financial cooperatives. Such remedial measures brought nothing more than temporary or slight relief to the poverty-ridden millions in the Indian villages who constituted more than eighty percent of India's total population. Village artisans found it increasingly difficult to compete with foreign-made factory products. Some Indians advocated protection for traditional handicrafts; others urged that old-style workers should be trained in modern techniques. The latter group, including Nehru at a later date, realized that rapid economic changes would cause fundamental social dislocations; but they argued that the benefits of modernization would outweigh the dangers.

Progress in commerce and industry at the national level was steady but inadequate. Foreign trade increased as new ports were opened and new industries established. However, the British government at home objected to Indian competition for British goods. India was not permitted to levy import tariffs in excess of five percent and was required to assess a countervailing excise tax on Indian exports of locally made textiles. The British authorities in India gave no leadership in economic planning, and they relied upon private enterprise for economic growth. British capital made substantial investments in India, but the Indians themselves preferred to put their savings in the tried and true outlets of land and moneylending. It was the exceptional Indians who invested in steel, textiles, or such new industries as glass, paper, cement, chemical products, cigarettes, matches, or large-scale sugar refining. Industrialization was bound to be slow where the home market was so limited.

Most factories and plants were built in the region of Bombay and Calcutta. This partially explains why these cities generated ardent support for antiforeign boycotts and the "Buy Indian" movement. It was a case of more profits for the entrepreneur and more jobs for the workers. The total number of jobs available in all India was ridiculously small. The pressure for such jobs as existed doomed most Indian laborers to a life of squalor. Workers, usually men, migrated from the villages and looked upon city employment as a temporary means of keeping alive until such time as they could return to their homes. They usually found jobs through some impersonal agency or calloused hiring contractor. They were disposed to accept almost any wages or conditions of work. Women or children at looms, or debilitated men in the mines, presented human tragedies worse than those which Engels had described in England three-quarters of a century earlier. The lot of the workers became even more difficult as prices climbed steadily. Up to World War I labor was almost wholly unorganized. Protests were timid and strikes were ineffective. Union leaders often thought more of their own position than the welfare of the union members. But a foundation was laid for what might happen when India's proletariat should reach substantial numbers and the conscience of India should awaken to the condition of its factory workers.

Justifiably or not, India's poverty was laid at the door of British exploitation. The overall level of living decreased as population growth exceeded the rate of economic development. As few as five percent of India's people enjoyed what might be called a middle- or upper-class way of life. Moderate socialist doctrines gained popularity with Indian intellectuals because they challenged in economic and moral terms the rule of a foreign, imperialist power. Marx and Lenin found many sympathizers who condemned free enterprise and capitalism and espoused the idea of revolt. These elements usually overlooked the substantial economic achievements which the British with their free enterprise and capitalism brought to India. The British built a solid substructure for eventual economic development. They constructed an extensive transportation and communications network and a vast system of irrigation canals. They grounded Indians in the fundamentals of private and public finance. They assisted in the establishment of banks and joint stock companies. They kept the government revenues and expenditures in balance. Taxes were high, but the national estate grew and gave a good surplus. Borrowing was limited to productive purposes, and a national debt, before World War I, was practically nonexistent. Money payments were drained from India to England, but in the British view they represented reasonable returns on services rendered or funds invested.

In addition to the economic ferment at work in India immediately after 1900, the country was aroused by social and cultural developments. A veritable mania for education swept through the nation. New life was injected into literature, drama, and music. A renaissance in art and science was shared by Hindus and Moslems alike. Organized amusements became more popular; and racial antagonisms were least apparent on the polo, cricket, football (soccer), or hockey playing fields. Larger numbers of students went abroad, usually to England; more interested themselves in political activities as they failed in their academic studies.

Economic progress and social reforms meant relaxation of the strict rules of caste. Agitation for universal primary education struck at the roots of caste distinctions, and, as the moderate leader Gokhale explained, Indians needed equality among themselves as a precondition for claims for equality among the nations. Improvements were registered in the status of women. Women were given better educational opportunities and more rights in the legal marriage relationship. The idea gained gradual acceptance that women were entitled to emerge from the seclusion of the home and to take an active share in the open life of the community. The untouchables or depressed classes were made aware of the social and economic disabilities which they had previously accepted as their lot.

Protestant missionaries taught among the untouchables, and the Salvation Army was most active in introducing to them an atmosphere of freedom and hope. Among the higher castes, some held fast to the traditions and protested against the impending changes. Others felt that the abuses of caste were slurs on their own good name, and they gave evidences of doing themselves what foreigners had pioneered in doing. Higher-caste Hindus organized philanthropic societies and took an interest in social service within the pale of their own religion.

These economic and social conditions affected India's political struggle to become a nation free in spirit and independent in status. The nationalist movement itself was not a clearly defined, isolated development, but it was a composite of many economic, social, and political factors whose only common denominator was collective self-respect. Nationalism assumed a different aspect in the princely and native states such as Kashmir, Hyderabad, and Mysore than in the provinces and territories of British India. Regional loyalties produced deep cleavages in thought and action. Separate regions, such as the Maratha country, Punjab, Madras, and Bengal, claimed their due place in the nation as a whole; it was inevitable that local pride should cause overlapping claims. It was difficult to weld regional movements into a single campaign for independence. Racial antagonisms aggravated the nationalistic conflict between the colony and the mother country. The privileged position of the British in India and the personal arrogance of many British and Anglo-Indians seemed to reflect an irritating assumption of racial superiority. Petty social quarrels or blackballs at local clubs wounded Indian sense of self-respect and gave rise to political arguments. The result was that individual Englishmen might have hosts of Indian friends, but the English as a group came to be looked upon as an exclusive lot determined to keep Indians in a second-class status from which the Indians were equally determined to escape.

Communal quarrels were unavoidable. The word "communal" designates claims which were put forward by communities or adherents of a special creed. Parsis and Christians made no communal claims, and the Sikhs only in the Punjab; however, the special claims were important to two communities, the Hindus of depressed classes and the Moslems. Members of the various communities ordinarily lived side by side in harmony in towns and villages, but the rising tide of nationalism aroused new fears and stirred up new rivalries. The tragedy of the nationalist movement was the inability to preserve harmony between Hindus and Moslems. As the Hindu element in nationalism became more pronounced, Moslem apprehensions multiplied. Moslems could not look forward to liberation, if liberation were to imply domination by fanatical Hindus. Communal differences were not created by the British for the sinister purpose of "divide and rule"; they were inherent in the faith of the respective communities, and they grew as the tide of nationalism swept forward.

In the early twentieth century, acquaintance with world politics added steam to the Indian nationalists. Their awe of British power was shattered by Boer victories in the early part of that war, and they were electrified by the victory of an oriental power (Japan) over a giant of the West (Russia). Lord Curzon remarked that "the reverberations of that victory have gone like a thunderclap through the whispering galleries of the East." The rise of Germany in Europe and the rivalry between the Triple Entente and Triple Alliance brought India into the matrix of power politics. Indians became more impressed with their own importance and more inclined to be self-assertive. They were increasingly convinced that India should not be inferior to any other nation, Asian or European.

When the viceroy, Lord Curzon, ordered the partition of Bengal in 1905, he set the stage for tremendous happenings. Indian nationalists held protest meetings in Calcutta and for the first time launched a Swadeshi or "Buy Indian" campaign. Terroristic methods gained ground as resentment over partition was coupled with student unrest and middle-class unemployment. Extremists took Kali, the block goddess of death and destruction, as their symbol and resorted to gang robberies, bombing outrages, and murder. Agitation spread to the Punjab, where fanatical Hindus, largely under the influence of the teachings of Tilak, resorted to further violence. The government passed press laws against inflammatory articles and jailed ringleaders such as Tilak for incitement to lawless actions. Terrorism was not entirely stamped out.

At least three sections of Indian opinion opposed violence as a political weapon. The princes wanted no part of fanaticism. Moderate elements within the congress, under the leadership of Gokhale, wanted to limit their activities to steady reform and constitutional action. At the Congress meeting at Surat in 1907, "chairs flew through the air, long sticks clashed and splintered and blood streamed from broken heads" before the moderate program was adopted as Congress policy. In 1908, the newly formed All-India Moslem League, organized by the Aga Khan and the brothers Mohammed and Shaukat Ali, also declared itself for nonviolence. But in the development of nationalism, the silent right was becoming infected as well as the vocal left. Landlords and merchants began to line up with the intellectuals whom their fathers distrusted. The princes also became disposed to admit that they could not remain immune to the nationalist movement forever, and they tried to readjust their own interests to accord with those of a unified independent India. The right and left elements joined in demanding as their immediate objectives more Indians in the public services, simultaneous civil service examinations to be given in

India as well as in England, and increased representation for Indians in the legislative councils.

By the time of World War I, India's nationalist movement was more than ever the private preserve of the Indian Congress, which had grown until its membership covered all parts of India. It was still an urban middle-class movement dominated by English-speaking lawyers, journalists, and merchants who were concerned only with political objectives for the nation and had little appreciation of the economic misery of the masses. Its politically ambitious members were more familiar with the struggle for democracy in England than with conditions in their own country.

The British did not dare underrate the strength of incipient nationalism as they administered their colony. While the British navy preserved the freedom of the seas and kept inviolable the route to India, the Indian army together with British forces in India and the imperial service troops (contingents under the guidance of British officers in the service of the Indian princes) guaranteed the security of India itself. The only serious challenges to law and order did not come from nationalist unrest but arose from tribal disorders on the northwest frontier. The Indian civil service was continued at a high level of competence, but a mere perpetuation of the colonial *status quo* was not sufficient to placate rising Indian tempers.

When the Liberals came to power in England in 1905, Lord John Morley, the biographer of William Gladstone, was appointed as Secretary of State for India. Liberalization was anticipated in British policies toward India, and in 1907 two Indians were appointed to the distinguished Indian Council in Whitehall. However, neither Lord Morley nor the Indian viceroy, Lord Minto (who had succeeded Lord Curzon in 1906), felt that India was really ready for democracy, although they recognized the inevitability of some concessions to India in order to forestall a disastrous swing to violence.

In 1909 the British parliament passed a new Indian Councils Act which contained the provisions known as the Morley-Minto Reforms. By this act, an Indian member was added to the former all-British five-member executive council of the viceroy, and Indian members were included in the executive councils which were forced upon the former autocratic governors in the provinces. Major changes were also made in the legislatures of India, both at the center and in the provinces. Before 1909 twelve British members of the Indian civil service, together with a half-dozen nonofficials including some Indians, acted in an advisory capacity as a kind of legislature in the central government. By the Morley-Minto Reforms a regular legislative council was set up at the center. It consisted of thirty-six British officials of the Indian civil service, twenty-seven *elected* Indians (seven by landowners, five by the Moslems, two by chambers of commerce, and the remainder by provincial legislative councils), and five appointed Indian nonofficial members. The provincial legislative councils gained nonofficial majorities who were *elected* (not merely nominated) by district and municipal boards, landowners, chambers of commerce, universities, and the Moslem community. (The franchise was granted to little more than a million voters.) These provincial councils were not given authority to pass laws but were permitted to discuss and pass resolutions on all matters. The law-making power remained in the hands of the executive.

Even after the introduction of the Morley-Minto Reforms, the administration in India remained responsible in the last resort to the parliament in London and not to the legislative councils in India. British executives were obliged to carry out policies imposed by London, no matter how hostile the reaction in India. Indian members of the various councils took advantage of their opportunity to debate and to criticize, unhampered as they were by any responsibility for policy enforcement. They put the British on the spot and by virtue of their prestige became prime movers in public opinion. They prodded the British constantly for further reforms and asked for a declaration of intention regarding the future.

Although the Morley-Minto scheme manifested a distinct advance in the recognition of the principle of election, it produced legislative councils which were hybrid collections of special interests. It contained a fatal flaw in the concession of special electorates for the Moslem community. The Moslems recognized that they could never win seats in legislatures by a general election because they would always be outvoted by the Hindu majority. Therefore they insisted upon separate electorates, with the number of seats reserved for them weighted according to the importance rather than the size of the Moslem community. Hindus protested, but the British accepted the Moslem position. In doing so they paved the way for the partition of India and the emergence of Pakistan.

In 1911 King George V and Queen Mary visited India in state, and they were wildly welcomed by princes as well as peasants. The enthusiasm was interrupted here and there by the dull thud of ineffective nationalist bombs. As boons to India, the king-emperor announced the release of some political prisoners, set aside substantial sums for education, canceled the unpopular partition of Bengal, raised the reunited region in status to a governor's province ranking with Bombay and Madras, and transferred the capital of India from Calcutta to New Delhi. As an aftermath to the imperial visit, the new viceroy, Lord Hardinge (1910–1916), went on record as a great friend of India. In his public speeches he paid frequent tribute to the qualities of Indian character, and he championed the cause of Indians against the members of the British imperial family who were guilty of anti-Indian racial discrimination. The British enjoyed a moment of enthusiastic support from their Indian colony when they declared war against Germany in the hot summer of 1914.

INDIA DURING WORLD WAR I

The action of Great Britain automatically brought India, as part of the empire, into the conflict. India rallied to British support. More than 800,000 soldiers and 400,000 noncombatants were recruited for service. Indians fought in France, Macedonia, Iraq, Egypt, and East Africa; Indians marched side by side with their British allies at Baghdad, Jerusalem, Damascus, and Aleppo. More than 26,000 Indians were killed, 70,000 wounded. In 1917 the government of India established a munitions board to develop local industries and to furnish supplies for all Allied operations in West and South Asia. The board made possible huge Indian contributions in munitions, railway tracks, uniforms, leather goods, tents, textiles, timber, petroleum, and millions of tons of wheat. Furthermore, Indian loans and taxes paid the expenses of their own troops abroad and poured gifts and cash donations into the British war chest.

Local politics declared a brief holiday—which was disregarded by some Moslem leaders and by Indian extremists overseas. The Moslems were inclined to be anti-British, because the British were at war against Turkey, the seat of the caliphate and the spiritual center of their religion. Some conspired with German agents to restore Moslem rule in India. The extremists overseas, primarily in Canada and the United States, felt that the war was their god-given opportunity to overthrow the British raj. With German money they bought arms and bribed young Indians to be smuggled into India to promote a revolution. An Indian newspaper called *Ghadr* (or *Mutiny*) was published in San Francisco, and in 1913 it contained this mock advertisement: "Wanted: brave soldiers to stir up *Ghadr* in India. Pay—death; prize—martyrdom; pension—liberty; field of battle —India." A lecturer in Indian philosophy at Stanford was dismissed for propaganda activities, and plotters were brought to trial in a federal court in San Francisco. As a cloak and dagger climax to the drama, one of the plotters shot and killed his leader on the last day of the trial and was himself slain on the spot by one of the marshals in the terrified courtroom.

The government of India was aware of the German activities throughout India—on the northwest frontier, in Bengal and the Punjab—and it introduced bills named after their sponsor, Justice Rowlatt, which were intended to stamp out subversion, curb espionage, and provide for the internal security of India at war. The Rowlatt Acts provided that in political cases judges could conduct trials without juries, and that provincial authorities could intern suspected persons without benefit of trial. The law was to be valid for three years. It was never invoked, but it stirred up a political storm.

The original war fever disappeared very quickly. The war looked more and more like the folly of the West, and it seemed to hold no glory for India. However, the intellectual currents from Europe and America reached the shores of India. President Wilson's ideas of self-determination and a world safe for democracy struck a responsive chord in the Indian psyche. A new impetus was added to the nationalist movement, and the revolution in Russia opened Indian eyes to what they considered the sure rewards of violent action.

The radical leader, Tilak, was released from jail; and the moderate leader, Gokhale, died in the early years of the war. Then, in 1916, in a pact at Lucknow, Hindus and Moslems agreed that, in consideration for the continuation of the special electorates for the Moslems, they would work together for harmonious relations with the British. Their goals were dominion status within the empire and responsible parliamentary democracy at home. Gradually a new spirit invested young nationalists. They became excited about the Irish revolt, British indifference to their feelings, the philosophy of President Wilson, and the prospect of home rule. Extremists gained control of the Indian National Congress in 1918, and they took up a surging cry for *swaraj* and *Swadeshi*. Fed by bitter resentment against what they believed to be the violation of Indian civil rights as embodied in the Rowlatt Act, they paved the way for the reappearance of riots and terroristic incidents.

Gandhi's first public act in India came on February 23, 1919, at a meeting of the Ahmadabad branch of the Home Rule League held to protest the Rowlatt Acts. Gandhi appealed to his countrymen to observe a hartal or day of national humiliation and prayer. He said, "We shall refuse civilly to obey these laws; we will faithfully follow truth and refrain from violence to life, person or property." In spite of Gandhi's idealism, a mob assembled in a protest meeting against the British in Amritsar on April 13, 1919. When the mob refused to disperse, General Reginald Dyer ordered his troops to fire—379 Indians were killed and 1200 more were wounded. In the angry reaction which followed throughout the country, titled Indians resigned their honors, students left school, Indian lawyers turned their backs on British clients, and Indians from all walks of life refused to buy British goods. The stage was set for Gandhi, who alone forged the link which joined the movement to throw off the foreign yoke with the attempt to regenerate the social, economic, and religious elements of Indian society. He combined the traits of a saint with the shrewdness of a politician to gain his tremendous charismatic power.

Gandhi was born in 1869 in Porbandar, on the Kathiawar Peninsula of western India, where his father was the hereditary prime minister of a small Hindu state. He was not a Brahman, but was a member of the Vaisya or merchant caste. As a youth he went to London to study law and was duly qualified as a barrister. He went to South Africa to follow his career and stayed there until he was 46 years old. In working among humble Indians, he developed his philosophy and proved his qualities of faith and leadership. In the Boer War, he led a corps of stretcher-bearers on the battlefield and won praise for his courage. In 1912 and 1913 he disciplined and led his people in a passive resistance movement against discriminatory racial legislation. He returned to India in 1915 and approached his teacher, Gokhale, for advice. Gokhale told him to watch and to learn for a year before venturing into speech or action. Gandhi supported the British in the war effort, but came to the parting of the ways with the passage of the Rowlatt Acts. Gradually he climbed to leadership in the National Congress. The people turned from Tilak, the aristocratic Brahman, to Gandhi, the half-naked, smiling visionary who would not hesitate to go out and clean the latrines himself when he campaigned for better sanitation. Gandhi lived with the people on their own terms, and it was he alone who joined the masses to the middle classes in the national movement.

Gandhi avoided a showdown with the British as long as the war continued. On their part, many British appreciated that further concessions were imperative. Lord Chelmsford was viceroy from 1916 to 1921, and in November 1917 Mr. E. S. Montagu became Secretary of State for India in Great Britain's war cabinet. It had already been announced in August that

> The policy of His Majesty's Government with which the Government of India are in complete accord, is that of the increasing association of Indians in every branch of the administration and the gradual development of self-governing institutions with a view to the progressive realization of responsible government in India as an integral part of the British Empire.

Secretary Montagu went to India to "get the damned bureaucracy to realize that we are sitting on an earthquake" and to listen to ideas from all classes about constitutional reforms. The Montagu-Chelmsford report was published in midsummer 1918, debated in the parliament, and became law as the Government of India Act in 1919. The franchise was extended, provision was made for a steady increase in the proportion of Indians in the civil service, Indians were given wider representation in the government and provincial assemblies were given partial responsibility for administrative action. The viceroy's executive council of seven was reconstituted to include three Indian members rather than just one. The central legislature was entirely remodeled. The former legislative council, with its official majority, was transformed into a bicameral legislature consisting of an assembly and a council of state. A larger percentage of members was elected, and the principle of special constituencies representing communities or special interests was retained. The legislature was given the usual deliberative and law-making powers, but it had no voice in the appointment or control of the government. The viceroy continued to be responsible to the British parliament, and his power to certify laws over the opposition of the legislature was preserved.

In the provinces a system of dyarchy, or dual government, was introduced. Each of the larger provinces was placed under a governor, assigned by *councilors,* responsible only to him, and by *ministers,* responsible to him *and* the provincial assembly. Councilors were in charge of "reserved" matters including police and finance; ministers were in charge of "transferred" functions such as agriculture, health, and education. In the event of an emergency or if Indian ministers were to refuse to cooperate, the governor had the power to take over a provincial administration. Like the viceroy, the governor enjoyed the right of certification and could promulgate ordinances which would have the force of law for six months. These residual powers in the hands of the executive caused many Indians to question British sincerity in the entire reform program.

Legislative authority in the provinces was vested in provincial assemblies which replaced the former legislative councils. These assemblies were unicameral and were composed of a very small group of officials and nonofficial nominees, plus a preponderant majority of elected representatives. In making the assemblies partially responsible for the Indian ministers on the staff of the governor, the British gave the Indians their first opportunity to assume executive responsibility. The act of 1919 was considered as a first step toward self-government; it was written in the law itself that further steps would be considered after ten years.

Conditions in India at the end of World War I were not conducive to the successful operation of the new constitutional measures. The country was weary at heart and disillusioned by the emasculation of President Wilson's idealistic war aims. It was depressed by the smallness of British concessions. It was in the grip of the economic doldrums which plagued the entire world. War industries were shut down, and men were thrown out of work. Prices tumbled, but no one except the rich had money to buy anything. The monsoon of 1918 failed, and starvation stalked the land. The supreme irony of the gods was that in the winter of 1918–1919 India suffered an epidemic of influenza which took millions of lives—more than had been lost on all the fields of battle during the late war. Public discontent sharpened the resentment against the British; impatient Indians showed no disposition for calm discussion of differences with their imperial rulers.

The Uneasy Nineteen-Twenties

From the point of view of the empire, the political quarrels with restless nationalists were only part of the total Indian picture. India's security and international relations continued to be British responsibilities. Treaties of friendship were concluded with Afghanistan and Nepal; trade and frontier agreements were made with Tibet. The northwest frontier was strengthened by additional military garrisons and an active program of public works. Both London and Delhi kept watchful eyes on the Middle East, where Islam was the religion of the people. Educated Moslems followed with sympathy the rejection of the Treaty of Sèvres, the rise of Mustapha Kemal Pasha, and the Turkish wars with Greece. Militant Moslems organized a party for the restoration of the sultan of Turkey as caliph of Islam, but the agitation died down when the sultan was deposed and Mustapha assumed the presidency of the Turkish Republic.

Interest in China grew as Indians emigrated to Chinese port cities and as the textile trade replaced the prewar commerce in opium. Indian army units and Sikh policemen constituted a substantial part of the British presence in China. Indians followed closely China's struggle for international equality and studied the model which Japan offered to all Asians in their efforts to achieve modernization. India strengthened commercial ties with Japan in exchanging raw cotton for cotton textiles and miscellaneous manufactured goods. A few Japanese teachers went to India, but many Indian students went to Japan for technical training or advanced education.

The government of India showed increasing concern for the welfare of Indians overseas. Agents were sent to Ceylon and Malaya to look after wages, welfare, and rights of Indian laborers. Indian delegates to imperial conferences argued with delegates from Australia, New Zealand, and Canada on behalf of Indians who suffered discriminatory treatment in the white dominions. After the constitutional changes were effected in the structure of the British commonwealth, India was accorded status as a component unit. India enjoyed a separate vote in the Assembly of the League of Nations, and it cooperated fully with such temporary commissions and special agencies as those concerned with the control of narcotic drugs. It played an active and influential part in the International Labor Organization. It was a welcome member of all international conferences on questions relating to economics, communications and transport, and military affairs. These activities brought India into the main stream of world affairs and provided many Indians with valuable training in diplomacy.

Internal political developments in the nineteen-twenties were equally auspicious for the interests of India, although Indian leaders continued their accusations against the British of "too little and too late." The British adhered faithfully to the program of Indianizing the bureaucracy and the army. Elections were first held in 1920 under the new Government of India Act in spite of the boycott of the Congress. Legislation was handicapped by nonviolent noncooperation; but new labor laws were passed, an improved labor code was adopted, and a protective tariff policy was inaugurated. The main points of conflict between British and Indians were finances and rate of progress toward self-government. Instead of trying to reach an understanding on these controversial issues, the Indian nationalists chose the tactics of opposition and agitation.

After 1919 Gandhi came to be known as the Mahatma or Holy One, and he was accepted throughout India as the embodiment of the proposition that "cooperation in any shape with this satanic government is sinful." He expressed sympathy with the Moslems and thus persuaded them temporarily to join in his program. In 1920, he influenced the Congress to boycott the elections and to take a stand for self-rule, within the empire if possible, without if necessary. At this time he displayed his profound understanding of the psychology of the Indian masses. He discarded Western clothing in favor of the homespun loincloth and dhoti. He taught that science, industry, and cities were soul-destroyers and that Indians would have to dedicate themselves anew to the simple life. He burned foreign cloth as a gesture to show the masses the meaning of *swaraj* (self-government) and *Swadeshi* (buy Indian). His religious habits and language, his poverty and vegeterianism, endeared him to the people. The charkha, or hand spinning machine, whose emblem now adorns the Indian national flag, became his chosen emblem. He was against caste restrictions, though not against caste distinctions. He championed the untouchables, whom he called *harijans* or sons of God. His favorite teaching was Christ's Sermon on the Mount, which provided him the text for his favorite requirement of the good life, which was personal service to others. Unlike other Hindus, he was not satisfied with contemplation and self-realization; he stressed action in the direction of welfare and social service.

He adopted the creed of *satyagraha* or "soul force" which he insisted was more powerful than physical strength. He translated with unerring insight effective political techniques into the Hindu idiom. Resistance to the government was noncooperation with evil; a one-day political strike was a moral protest. Passive resistance, or nonviolent noncooperation, became a campaign for truth. In 1922 recurrent popular demonstrations passed the nonviolent stage at Chauri Chaura in the United Provinces where a mob attacked a police station and burned twenty-one policemen to death. This was too much for Gandhi, who, to the dismay of some of his less idealistic colleagues, called a halt to the civil disobedience campaign. The new viceroy, Lord Reading (1921–1926) had Gandhi arrested anyway—for incitement to riot. Gandhi was sentenced to six years in prison. Jail terms became more popular than ever to Indian nationalists as hallmarks of distinction.

Following Gandhi's imprisonment, the Congress reversed its attitude toward the government. Instead of boycotting the elections, it decided to put up candidates for office and to destroy the constitution from within. The edge was taken off the militancy in the position of the nationalists. Martyrdom seemed attractive psychologically, but it failed to provide food for middle-class families. For all except the leaders at the very top it was better to work, or to serve in provincial assemblies, than to idle the days in prison. Furthermore violence alienated much public sympathy, and it became all too clear that a very thin line separated violence and nonviolence. As India overcame its economic slump, the opinion grew that it would be more sensible to abandon the public demonstrations and to adopt policies of discussion and negotiation.

After serving a little more than a year of his sentence, Gandhi was released from jail because of his frail health. He remained aloof from political quarrels and devoted his time to the welfare of the untouchables and the promotion of his hand-spinning campaign. From 1924 to 1929, C. R. Das and then the aristocratic Motilal Nehru, the father of the great prime minister, assumed the leadership of the nationalists. During these years the schism deepened between Moslems and Hindus. Occasional communal arguments culminated in ugly riots. The Moslem League was revived and intensified its demands for separate electorates, weighted representation and provincial autonomy. To counter Moslem particularism, Hindu extremists within the Congress organized a Hindu Mahasabha or association to promote their own special interests.

Until this time, nationalism was still predominantly a middle-class movement; but forces other than Gandhi came into play to broaden the base of political action. The impact of World War I disturbed the traditional way of life and released new social forces. The return of soldiers and sailors to their native villages meant the introduction of new and revolutionary ideas. The spread of education opened new intellectual horizons; radio and the moving pictures quickened new desires. Greater social movement occurred between towns and villages. Education enlivened routine lives in the countryside as well as in the mushrooming cities. Industrialization did not open up new cities; it only increased the crowding and the wretchedness of the old. Better-trained Indian leaders interested themselves in the welfare of the masses. As more Indians went abroad, they gained a better perspective on conditions in their own country. As they became acquainted with freedom and progress in the West, they determined to bring about fundamental changes in India's caste-ridden society.

Some Indians accepted the methods of ordinary reform within the limits of the constitution and the free enterprise system. Others turned to socialism and communism. The first socialist weekly was founded in Bengal in 1923. Within the Congress, there developed a youth movement in an All-India Independence League. The program of the latter included complete independence, amelioration of the condition of the masses, liquidation of the parasitic zamindars (landlords), and the introduction of a socialist state. Jawaharlal Nehru himself was the most active influence in crystallizing the socialist elements within the Congress.

The communists believed and hoped that India would be the great Asian vanguard in bringing about the world revolution. Indian revolutionaries from Bombay, Calcutta, and Delhi went to the Soviet Union in the early twenties; Russian communists, however, found it difficult to cope with Gandhiism, which did not meet the requirements laid down by Lenin for support to a nationalist movement. Communism in India attracted only the fringe of the intelligentsia, and it never gained the inside track with peasants and workers. While Indian nationalism made its most significant advances, Russian-trained Indian communists were either abroad or incarcerated in British jails.

M. N. Roy was the best-known of the Indian communists. He was influential in communist international circles, and he was active in the Comintern's anti-British program in India. He operated from Moscow, Berlin, or Paris, while communists in India organized a party of their own in Cawnpore not to conspire to deprive the king of sovereignty but "to change the present social organization and the government of India." They gave this delicate wording to their platform to keep out of the clutches of the law. For the sake of prudence the rejected affiliation with Moscow, and they called the first All-India Communist Conference in Cawnpore in 1925. Some five hundred delegates attended, elected their executive committee and transferred their headquarters to Delhi. Moscow did not show outward favor to the Delhi organization and professed greater sympathy with the noncommunist nationalists. M. N. Roy, from Moscow, favored the organization of a Workers and Peasants Party, which attracted the left-wing intelligentsia. Neither the Delhi group nor the Workers and Peasants Party could establish a claim to leadership against the personality and tactics of Gandhi. Their only effective procedure was to identify themselves with the "struggle of all classes against British imperialism."

The government of India's political problems were magnified by its financial difficulty. What good are colonies if they do not pay—and India faced continuous budgetary pressures. The convention of fiscal autonomy of 1923 established India's right to arrange its own economic affairs, and India was included in the imperial preference system.

Under the Montagu-Chelmsford scheme, the provinces were to enjoy fiscal prerogatives, but they depended upon subsidies from the center to finance their nation-building responsibilities. Money was needed if farms were to be helped or labor codes enforced. The complaint was universal that the provinces were neglected and needlessly pinched. Military expenditures were extremely high. Administrative costs, including the salaries and pensions of the civil service, looked astronomical to the ordinary Indians. Social services became more expensive as more people turned to the government for more assistance. Receipts could not keep up with expenditures. Trade fell off and the income from the customs declined. Demands for higher wages took the profits out of the government-owned utilities and railways. New sources of revenue were always needed. When the government ordered an increase in taxes—any taxes—it thought more of potential revenue than the effect on public opinion.

Time of Transition

When the Conservatives under Stanley Baldwin came to power in England, they felt that the cumbersome constitutional system of India needed drastic overhauling. In 1926 they sent Edward Wood, created Lord Irwin and later known as the Earl of Halifax, to India as viceroy. He was less brilliant than his Liberal predecessor, but he was well-known for his integrity and moral earnestness. They also appointed a royal commission under Sir John Simon to review the working of the old constitution and to make the recommendations for the "next steps" which had been promised for 1929. The Simon Commission did not include one Indian among its distinguished members. Automatically the commission, which was intended as a gesture of goodwill, became a rallying point for freedom. The National Congress, which had fallen onto dull days, at its meeting in Madras at the end of 1927 called for a boycott of the Simon Commission. It was persuaded to pass a defiant resolution which declared the goal of the Indian people to be complete independence. Gandhi was pushed into the background as two ardent leaders—Jawaharlal Nehru and Subha Chandra Bose—quickly became the darlings of politically minded youth and the radical wing of the Congress.

Nehru came from a Brahman family of ancient lineage which had migrated from Kashmir. His father, Motilal Nehru, a prominent lawyer, after 1919 devoted himself to Gandhi and the nationalist movement. The son was given all the advantages of a wealthy boyhood and was sent to England to school. He was graduated from Cambridge with an A.B. degree in 1910 and was admitted to the English bar two years later. He showed little interest in law and became completely absorbed in India's fight for freedom. He could not agree with Gandhi's ascetiscism and mysticism, nor his antagonism to Western industrialization. He turned out to be a rationalist, a foe of supernationalism, and a strong believer in socialism. He described himself as a "queer mixture of the East and the West, out of place everywhere, at home nowhere—perhaps my thoughts and approach to life are more akin to what is called Western than Eastern, but India clings to me." Bose, who was to cast his fortunes with the Japanese during World War II, showed from his earliest leadership days in Calcutta the characteristics of impatience and intolerance. He was dedicated to a program of action: "We want independence, and we want it now."

When the Simon Commission landed in Bombay in February 1928, it was greeted with the familiar signs of "Simon, go home." The fundamental pessimism of most of the members of the commission toward the political situation in India was re-enforced by their experiences on the spot. Before their report was completed, the Conservatives were turned out of office. The successors—the Labour government under Ramsay MacDonald— were inclined to take different views of India. MacDonald himself was impatient with the speed of democratic growth in India and was inclined to treat India with more consideration than his predecessors. Lord Irwin hustled back to London for consultations, and he decided that without offending his conscience he could cooperate with the new regime and serve out his five-year term (1926–1931). On his return to India on October 25, 1929, he made a forthright announcement:

> In view of the doubts which have been expressed both in Great Britain and India regarding the interpretation to be placed on the intentions of the British Government in enacting the statute of 1919, I am authorized on behalf of His Majesty's Government to state clearly that, in their judgment, it is implicit in the declaration of 1917 that the natural issue of India's constitutional progress, as there contemplated, is the attainment of Dominion status.

The issue was joined: the British declared for "Dominion status"; the Indian National Congress resolved for "complete independence." On December 31, 1929, the Congress met at Lahore and adopted a pledge of complete independence which all members were to take. The wording of the pledge declared the British government deprived Indians of freedom, based itself on exploitation of the masses, and ruined India economically, culturally, and spiritually. Therefore "we must sever all connections with the British and attain complete independence. We will prepare ourselves by withdrawing so far as we can all voluntary association from the British government and we will prepare for civil disobedience, including non-payment of taxes." On January 26, 1930, thousands of Indians signed the pledge of independence and witnessed the raising of the tricolor flag.

Gandhi called on the viceroy to make clear the Congress' position. He presented Indian demands for halving the land tax, abolition of the salt tax, cutting the government's military budget fifty percent, scaling down the salaries of the higher officials, amnesty for political prisoners, total prohibition of liquor, and the reservation of coastal shipping to Indian interests alone. Naturally Irwin turned down the demands.

On March 12, 1930, Gandhi announced defiance of the salt tax, which touched the lives of all the peasants. Colorfully reported in the newspaper headlines throughout the world, Gandhi set out on a three-week, 170-mile march to the sea. On April 6 he waded into the waves, dipped a cupful of water, and poured it onto red-hot rocks on the beach. This was his symbolic manufacture of salt from seawater, which defied the government and its salt-making monopoly. A full-fledged demonstration of civil disobedience spread throughout the nation. Indian government officials resigned, the railway employees quit. Liquor shops were picketed, and foreign businesses were boycotted. Riots broke out and police were called upon to silence the shouting, singing masses of men and women. In May Gandhi was imprisoned again, and by midsummer, 60,000 Indians were in jail on sentences of six months or more. The viceroy performed his duty, but he appreciated the strength of the feeling of nationalism. He reported to his government that more than physical force would be required to suppress the Indian threats to law and order.

It was in this atmosphere that the report of the Simon Commission was released. The report took no cognizance of the boiling political cauldron. It recommended the development of dyarchy in the provinces into fully responsible government, the extension of the franchise and the enlargement of legislatures, no change in the central executive with the government retaining special powers for national security and minority welfare, election of the members of both houses in the central legislature by provincial councils, and the ultimate creation of an All-India Federation. The report made no mention of dominion status and expressed doubt about the feasibility of a parliamentary system of government for India as yet. With the publication of the report, the British government also announced that it would assemble in London a conference representing all sections of Indian opinion, including the princes, to "consider the next steps towards Dominion."

The wholesale arrests took much of the wind out of the sails of the civil disobedience movement, and the situation in India was more calm when the round table met in London for its first session, from November 1930 through January 1931. The meetings were chaired by the prime minister himself. Ideas were presented from Indian rulers and prominent ministers of state, moderates and Moslems, the Hindu Mahasabha and Indian Christians, Europeans and Anglo-Indians, Sikhs and depressed classes—*everybody except the Indian National Congress*. It was like a wedding without the bride.

Prime Minister MacDonald adjourned the session, ordered the release of political prisoners in India, and instructed the viceroy to enter into new conversations with Gandhi. Winston Churchill, on the opposition bench, was "nauseated to see Mr. Gandhi, an Inner Temple lawyer, now become a seditious fakir of a type well-known in the East, striding half-naked up the steps of the viceregal palace while he was still organizing and conducting a defiant campaign of civil disobedience, to parley on equal terms with the representatives of the King-Emperor." An agreement was reached between the Mahatma and the viceroy, by virtue of which Gandhi himself announced that he would attend the next session of the round table as the delegate of the Congress. At this juncture, Lord Irwin was replaced by Lord Willingdon, who served as the viceroy until 1936.

The second session of the London round table assembled in the autumn of 1931. Discussion centered on dyarchy, separate electorates for communities, and the advance toward fully responsible government. Deadlocks were inevitable and insoluble, and tempers became sharper with the gnawing advance of the world depression. The session broke up in December, and Gandhi returned to an India which once again steamed like an active volcano. After the Very Important Person treatment in London, Gandhi was once more placed in a British jail. Whether Gandhi was responsible for local incidents was immaterial; his guilt stemmed from the universal recognition of his prestige as the spirit and inspiration of the Indian national movement. Thus ended the brief—and ineffective—association of the Indian Congress with the round table and the effort to formulate the "next steps" in a constitution for India.

Just before the Labour government gave way to the National Coalition, Prime Minister MacDonald announced the Communal Award. Separate electorates were decreed for all minority communities. The depressed classes were also recognized as a minority and awarded separate electorates. This communal award was obnoxious to Gandhi, who saw nothing but disaster in the deepening wedge between Hindus and Moslems and the distinction between the untouchables and the rest of the Hindu community. He vowed a fast to the death; which was broken only when Hindus worked out a scheme which gave the depressed classes a privileged status *within* the general community of Hindus.

The third and last session of the round table was held in 1932. From these discussions emerged a white paper, which after a journey through parliament became the Government of India Act of 1935. During the time of debate, the entire world moved through a period of greater transition than usual. The United States inaugurated the New Deal and Great Britain gradually muddled out of the depression. The Nazis rose to power in Germany and the Soviet Union moved toward a united front against the fascists. Japan and China squared off for battle in Manchuria. British authorities ruled India with a firm hand and tried to destroy the power of the Congress while its leaders tried in vain to get superhuman sacrifices out of the weary masses. Civil disobedience trailed off and Gandhi, after his release from prison, remained in semiseclusion. Nehru, with Gandhi's support, took over as the leader of the Congress. The Indians became more adamant for complete independence and more skeptical about British intentions.

FROM 1935 TO WORLD WAR II

The Government of India Act was not conceived by British rulers alone. It was the result of arduous negotiations between British rulers and Indian subjects and was as close to a consensus of British-Indian opinion as it was possible to achieve. It did not produce dominion status, and, as is the case with all compromises, it did not bring complete satisfaction to any of the parties. Basically, India remained a colony administered by a government responsible to the British parliament through the Secretary of State for India. However, the constitutional structure of the government was modified to the advantage of Indians. Steps were taken toward what was genuinely hoped would become a self-governing federation of India, within the fraternal framework of the British commonwealth of nations.

The act provided for the increased representation of Indians in their own government. The franchise for provincial elections was extended to 30,000,000 Indians, which was five times the previous number and one-sixth of the total adult population. Provincial legislatures were greatly enlarged, and second chambers were provided for six out of the eleven provinces. Representation was assured wherever appropriate for Hindus, Moslems, Sikhs, Indian Christians, Anglo-Indians, the "scheduled classes" (the new name for the untouchables), and for such special interests as landlords, labor, universities, chambers of commerce, and industry. The assemblies were made genuine popular bodies, without officials or nominees by the governor, and they were given full ministerial responsibility. Provincial finances were divorced completely from central control. Half the income tax collected at the center was allotted to the provinces. Provincial debts were extinguished or consolidated; grants-in-aid without strings were made according to the need for extending work in education, agriculture, and public health.

The executive power in the provinces was placed in the hands of a governor appointed by the crown, who exercised his functions through a council of ministers chosen from among the members of the provincial assembly and responsible to it. As safeguards the governor retained the right to veto legislation, to certify laws over the head of the assembly, and to promulgate ordinances having the effect of law for six months. It was his special responsibility to preserve peace and tranquillity, protect civil servants, safeguard the legitimate rights of minorities, and prevent discrimination against British commercial interests. In the event of a breakdown of constitutional machinery in the province, the governor was authorized to assume all administrative and legislative powers of the province, subject to the authority of the governor-general and not the Indian government.

For the first time, the Indian princely states were given the importance they deserved. They occupied two-fifths of the area and contained nearly one-quarter of the population of India. There were more than five hundred of these states, one hundred and twenty of whose rulers belonged to the consultative Chamber of Princes. The largest state was Kashmir; the most populous, Hyderabad. At the other extreme, the petty states were not much bigger than a large midwestern farm. They represented the greatest diversity in political, economic, and cultural conditions. Some of the states were backward; others were at least the equal of the provinces of British India in good government, economic development, and popular education.

The rajahs and princes worried about their possible fate if the firebrands in the National Congress should come to dominate a self-governing India. Therefore they supported an arrangement which was written into the Act of 1935 whereby they would surrender their power over foreign affairs, defense, and communications in exchange for a substantial voice in the central government. It was specified that their line of responsibility to the crown would go through the viceroy rather than the government of India.

The Act of 1935 provided that dyarchy, abandoned in the provinces, was to be extended to the central government. The governor-general was to rule through ministers chosen from among the members of the legislature and responsible to it. However, two important subjects—defense and external affairs—were to be reserved and administered by councilors responsible only to the governor-general. The legislature, which was to contain more Indians, including the nominees of the princes, was to have competence in everything except the reserved matters and the salaries of the governor-general, judges, and the Indian civil service. Bills relating to coinage, currency, and the constitution could not be introduced without the previous sanction of the governor-general. He retained the same constitutional safeguards at the center which the governors enjoyed in the provinces.

It was the hope of the British that the Act of 1935 would give at least temporary satisfaction to Indians in their impatient quest for self-government. The provisions dealing with the government of the provinces were implemented immediately, but it proved impossible to carry out the proposed scheme for federation at the center. The viceroy was obliged to carry on with his executive council under the rules which had been in vogue since 1919. Liberals and Moslems were inclined to accept the Act of 1935 as the best obtainable, but the Congress chose to resist. The latter became bitterly anti-British and more assertive than ever in its emphasis on social and economic reform. It reflected the attitude of Nehru who declared: "Socialism is not merely an economic doctrine but a vital creed which I hold with all my head and heart—I work for Indian independence because the nationalist in me cannot tolerate alien domination; I work for it even more because for me it is the inevitable step to social and economic change."

The Congress resolved to participate in the first elections, which were held in 1937 under the new rules. By this time, the Congress had built up an effective nation-wide organization which extended from the humblest village workers at the bottom to the president and the executive, or working committee, at the top. It boasted three million members, and its strength was in the masses as well as in the middle classes. The Congress won 711 out of 1585 seats in provincial legislatures; it also won a clear majority in five provinces and a dominant position in two others. Until World War II responsible government in the provinces was a fact, and the record of the Congress' ministries was creditable. British executives remained discreetly in the background and gave free rein to Indian lawmakers. Legislation was directed primarily toward the welfare of the masses: reduction of rents, stricter regulation of moneylenders, education reforms, campaigns against mass illiteracy, and improvement of working conditions. Moderate elements within the Congress gained an entirely new experience in politics. They had to collect taxes, restrain extremists, and enforce the laws which they previously had treated with contempt.

The term of the viceroy, Lord Linlithgow (1936–1941), was like a gathering storm. The princes turned down federation—and too many failed to get in step with the changing times. Nehru blasted the princely states as "sinks of reaction and incompetence." The left wing of the congress showed little patience with the moderates. Radical groups claimed that congressmen who cooperated with the British lost their vision and became blind imitators of their imperial masters by virtue of the sweet fruits of office. The fascistic element within the Congress, under Subha Chandra Bose, lost patience with the British and their attachment to democracy. Bose called Gandhi an "incurable, medieval mystic," spurned association with Nehru, and turned increasingly toward the tactics of Hitler and the Japanese.

Worst of all, the relations between the Hindus and the Moslems became irreparable. The Moslems brought increasing pressure to bear for more communal rights, fair representation in all cabinets, an adequate share of government posts, and a reasonable proportion of public funds for the development of Moslem cultural institutions. Who was to judge what was fair, adequate, or reasonable? Moslems proclaimed they would rather die for their rights than accept slavery at the hands of Indian infidels. They became more anticongress than anti-British.

The leader of the Moslems was Mohammed Ali Jinnah, a wealthy Bombay laywer who was a striking contrast to Gandhi. He lived in stately mansions; he was tall and elegantly groomed. He had a distinguished presence and fastidious tastes. He was not a mystic nor a pacifist; he was a fighter and a cold realist. He tried to work out a modus vivendi with Nehru in 1938 for communal cooperation, but he declared that "all hope of communal peace was wrecked on the rocks of Congress fascism." Congress refused to admit any Moslem to a post on a provincial cabinet unless he gave up his membership in the Moslem League and joined the congress. It became evident that cabinets were not responsible really to provincial legislatures but rather to the high command of the party. Moslems hated the idea of opening government meetings by singing of a Hindu national anthem, and they resented the congressional flag over government buildings. They objected to the number of good appointments which went to Hindus rather than Moslems, and they disliked the favoritism shown to the Hindi language as opposed to Urdu. Moslems declared that their children were given no opportunity to learn about the prophet, his caliphate, the saints, scholars, philosophers, poets, or heroes of Islam. Moslems began to think and to talk about territorial autonomy. The dark shadow of partition, which Gandi called "the vivisection of India," appeared over the land.

SUGGESTED READING

Bannerjee, S. N., *Nation in the Making* (London, H. Milford Co., 1925).

Chirol, Sir Valentine, *India* (London, Ernest Benn, 1926).

Cumming, Sir John, (ed.), *Political India, 1832–1932* (London, Oxford U., 1932).

Dodwell, H. H., *Sketch of the History of India, 1858–1918* (London, Longmans, Green, 1925).

Dube, S. C., *Indian Village* (Ithaca, Cornell U., 1955).

Gokhale, B. G., *Making of the Indian Nation* (Bombay, Asia Publishing House, 1960).

Hoyland, John S., *Indian Crisis, the Background* (New York, Macmillan, 1943).

Lovett, H. Verney, *History of the Indian Nationalist Movement* (London, John Murray, 1920).

Minto, Mary, Countess of, *India, Minto, and Morley, 1905–1910* (London, Macmillan, 1934).

Moraes, Frank, *Jawaharlal Nehru* (New York, Macmillan, 1956).

O'Dwyer, Sir M., *India as I Knew It* (London, Constable & Co., 1925).

Reed, Sir Stanley, *The India I Knew, 1897–1947* (London, Odhams, 1952).

Schuster, Sir George, and Wint, Guy, *India and Democracy* (London, Macmillan, 1941).

Sitaramayya, P., *History of the National Congress* (two vols.) (Allahabad, Padma, 1946).

Smith, Wilfred Cantwell, *Modern Islam in India* (London, Probsthain, 1943).

Strachey, Sir John, *India: Its Administration and Progress* (fourth ed.) (London, Macmillan, 1911).

Tagore, Rabindranath, *My Reminiscences* (New York, Macmillan, 1917).

Wernher, Hilda, *Land and the Well* (New York, Day, 1947).

Wint, Guy, *British in Asia* (New York, Institute of Pacific Relations, 1955).

Wolpert, Stanley, *Tilak and Gokhale* (Berkeley, U. of California, 1962).

17

Southeast Asia: Twilight of Empire

The travail of India, with variations, was repeated in the lesser lands of Southeast Asia. With the exception of Siam, these countries experienced similar processes of readjustment to their European imperial overlords. They struggled toward self-government and independence while they tried to raise their pitiful level of living. They clung to ancient traditions and old ways of life as they came to terms with the twentieth century. Movements for nationalization and modernization, which at first were scarcely noticeable, became dominant themes in their political history.

Internal developments in all six areas—the Philippines, Netherlands East Indies, Burma, Malaya, Indochina, and Siam—showed remarkable parallels; however, each area exercised practically no direct influence on its immediate neighbors. The Philippines knew little and cared less about the Indies, while Burma and Malaya under the British were almost without contact with Indochina under the French. Ties were strong between each colony and its particular parent, but no regional bond developed which would have made the struggle of one the interest of all.

Inside each budding nation, the people had to cope with their problems alone. They were diverse in race, language, and religion; yet they sought the oneness in spirit which is the essence of nationhood. Leaders emerged who were men and women of superior ability or achievement and who voiced the aspirations of their people. They constituted an embryo middle class and often thought more of the privileged few above them than the masses below them. None in Southeast Asia approached the vision or the spirit of Gandhi. Most of the leaders, however, became increasingly aware of the poverty of their own people and were driven to political action by a mounting sense of indignation and injustice.

The local elites were stimulated by great events and movements in distant lands. Acquaintance with the industrial revolution quickened the desire to progress beyond the agricultural stage of economy. Colonials wanted factories of their own; they were helpless as long as they were only suppliers of raw materials and markets for cheap goods manufactured by others. Their faith in themselves, as Asians, was strengthened by Japan's incredible military victory over Russia in 1905. They were deeply moved by the philosophy of Woodrow Wilson. Self-determination was as applicable to Asians as Europeans, even if it implied the doom of imperialism.

The surge toward individual freedom which followed universally in the wake of World War I challenged the concept of "second-class citizenship." Whatever rights a European was entitled to, an Asian was entitled to the same. Many Asians asked why the right to govern belonged to a European simply because of his country of origin, the color of his skin, or the course of recent history? Many Asians nurtured a silent contempt for the character or qualities of Europeans who were inferior men in spite of the garb of authority. Unfortunately, Europeans possessed power, and they could not be displaced except by greater power. Native nationalistic leaders pressed alien rulers for concessions which were never satisfied. As a result the placid landscape of Southeast Asia belied its troubled spirit.

The Russian Revolution and the spread of international communism seemed to offer hope and promise to some colonial leaders. The communists stressed anti-imperialism, and they showed a tactical willingness to accommodate the demands of the social revolution to the immediate requirements of nationalism. They made some, but not many, converts in the period between world wars. The great depression of 1929–1931 multiplied the woes of guardians in Europe and wards in Asia and added econotim intensity to smoldering colonial unrest. Then, the totalitarian regimes which appeared later in Germany, Italy, and Japan offered new models for Asians who were dissatisfied with the international *status quo*. Totalitarian procedures suggested the value of direct action to those who were already fed up with the cumbersome processes of peaceful change.

The colonial period in Southeast Asia came to a climax with World War II. Europe's tragedy was Asia's opportunity. Some Asians gave help to their alien rulers or fought bravely beside them, but the minimum price was independence. Democracy had to be made a reality for Asians as well as for Europeans and Americans. The idealism of the war aims of the allied powers practically concluded the transition from empire to nations.

The Philippines

After the Treaty of Paris was signed in December 1898 between the United States and Spain, Americans replaced the Spanish governor-general as the tenants of Malacañan Palace, the White House of Manila. Independence eluded the grasp of the Filipinos. They inaugurated the first Republic of the Philippines in Malolos and set out to win diplomatic recognition for the new government. They continued their fight for independence—but their new enemy was the United States. Malolos was taken by the Americans in March. The Philippine government took to the hills and carried on guerilla warfare which spread from one end of the archipelago to the other. Hostilities cost the Americans 10,000 casualties and hundreds of millions of dollars. Filipinos estimated their losses at 16,000 killed in action, 200,000 dead due to famine and pestilence, and untold millions of dollars in property damage. For all practical purposes the war for independence (or the insurrection, as it was labeled by the Americans) ended when Aguinaldo was captured in March 1901.

The Filipinos were introduced to novel policies with the introduction of the new sovereign. A commission under William Howard Taft arrived in the Philippines with instructions not to exploit, but to develop, civilize (!), educate and train the Filipinos in the science of self-government. A just and effective government was to be set up "not for our satisfaction or the expression of our theoretical views" but "for the happiness, peace, and prosperity of the people of the Philippine Islands." Measures adopted should be made to conform to their customs, their habits, and even to their prejudices. On the Fourth of July, 1901, civil government was installed in place of the former military administration. The representative of the United States, administratively responsible to the War Department, was to be a governor-general, assisted by a Philippine commission consisting of five Americans and three Filipinos. Throughout the islands English replaced Spanish as the language of general usage. American business enterprises multiplied, streets were given American names, and American prelates went to the Philippines to share in the work of the Church which had been carried on by the Spanish. American Protestants initiated an active missionary program. Public schools were expanded, and primary education was made universal and compulsory. Normal schools and the University of the Philippines were founded. Filipino children learned to recite the Gettysburg Address or the poems of Longfellow before they were introduced to the writings of their own heroes.

Public health was improved and highways were built. American democratic ideas and political procedures were adopted, and Filipinos were encouraged to progress toward self-government. High standards were insisted upon for the civil service, and Americans were careful to protect the rights of their new subjects. Freedom of worship was guaranteed; and much to the discomfiture of the ecclesiastical hierarchy, separation of church and state was insisted upon.

In the economic sphere, basic land laws were not altered. The gap between the very rich and the very poor continued. The only step in the direction of land reform was the purchase and redistribution of nearly a half-million acres of "friar lands" or lands in the possession of the religious orders. Public lands were protected, and natural resources were reserved for Filipinos to develop and exploit. In 1909 the American market was thrown open for free entry of Philippine products, and Americans were permitted to sell their goods in the Philippines without imposition of tariffs. The Philippines became entirely dependent on the United States from an economic point of view. Little incentive was given to Filipinos to build up industries of their own or to diversify agricultural production. The prosperity of the islands came to depend upon the duty-free privileges for sugar, Manila hemp, tobacco, and coconut products in the United States. Sound banking and currency policies were enforced, and the government of the Philippines always enjoyed a balanced budget. The costs of the government were paid for the most part by taxes collected in the Philippines. Under the Americans, a small percentage of the Filipinos continued to live in luxury (as did many Americans, Chinese, Spanish, and Spanish mestizos). The middle class expanded slightly with the progress of education, but the rural masses remained in poverty. As talk of self-government and independence spread, it was not accompanied by preparation for self-sufficiency in the economic sphere.

From the beginning Filipinos participated in government at the local level; in 1907 they were given the right to elect a national assembly, or lower house of a bicameral legislature. The American-dominated Philippine commission was converted into the upper house. At the same time the Philippines was permitted to send a commissioner to the American Congress. A Nacionalista party was organized with independence as its slogan. It was dominated by an even-tempered politician named Sergio Osmeña and a mercurial, clever man of the people, Manuel Quezon. Together they controlled the political destiny of the Philippines until the end of World War I.

When the Democrat, Woodrow Wilson, was elected to the presidency of the United States, the Filipinos expected (and received) more political favors from their American sovereign. A new governor-general, Francis Burton Harrison, Filipinized the civil service and dedicated himself to active preparation for independence. In 1916, the Congress passed the Jones Act, which pledged the United States to recognize the independence of the Philippines "as soon as a stable government could be established therein." This law provided for the establishment of a wholly elected bicameral legislature for the Philippines structured in accordance with the American model. The American governor-general retained a veto power.

All Philippine laws regarding public land, timber, mining, currency, coinage, immigration, and tariff required the signature of the president of the United States.

From 1912 until 1929 the American governors-general and the Filipino officials were in constant conflict about relative rights and privileges. The Americans insisted upon the necessity for stability, while the Filipinos pressed for greater liberality in the interpretation of the laws. In the view of Manuel Quezon, the Filipinos preferred "a government run like hell by Filipinos rather than one run like heaven by Americans."

The contest tended to be a draw until the depression in the United States convinced some American congressmen that their constituents would be better served if the Philippines were to be cut loose from the United States. Farm groups, patriotic societies, and labor organizations looked upon the Philippines as a detriment to American economic interests and advocated independence for the islands. Less influential pressure groups, such as traders, shippers, investors, and clergymen argued for the retention of the Philippines. The economic nationalism of the United States, which was sharpened by the depression, facilitated the passage of the Tydings-McDuffie or Philippine Independence Act which became law on March 24, 1934.

This law provided for a ten-year transitional commonwealth period, at the end of which time the Philippines were to be given outright independence. During the commonwealth period, Filipinos were to recognize the supreme authority of the United States and maintain true faith and allegiance to it. (This clause was later the basis of American complaints against Philippine collaborators with the Japanese.) Acts of the Philippine legislature affecting currency, coinage, imports and exports, and immigration could not become law until approved by the president of the United States. Foreign affairs were under direct supervision and control of the United States, which was responsible for the defense of the islands. The United States reserved the right to review court decisions, limit the public debt and foreign loans, maintain military reservations, keep armed forces in the Philippines, and intervene for the preservation of the government of the commonwealth or for the protection of life, property, and individual liberty. Looking toward economic independence, the act established a system of quotas and graduated tariffs to cushion the shocks of adjustment. Specified quotas on sugar, coconut oil, and abaca, for example, were to continue on the free list for five years; after that time the products of the Philippines would have to accommodate themselves to the necessities of unfavored and unsubsidized competition.

Immediately after the terms of the law were accepted by the Philippines, a convention met in Manila and adopted a constitution which was to provide for the commonwealth and the succeeding independent republic. This constitution reflected its American inspiration and gave the Philippines a head start toward a democratic form of self-government. Elections were held in the fall of 1935, and Manuel Quezon was chosen as the first president of the commonwealth for a term of six years. On this occasion the American governor-general moved out of Malacañan, and President Quezon moved in.

During the Commonwealth period, relations between Filipinos and Americans were remarkably good. As President Quezon himself phrased it: "When that starry flag finally comes down from Santiago in 1946, it will find somewhere in its folds the grateful hearts of a people—a new and vibrant republic facing with optimistic hope its rising dawn." Despite the spirit of the constitution and the meticulous devotion to democratic processes, the standards of politics deteriorated. Investments and trade expanded, but the specter of the removal of American economic supports dampened the enthusiasm for prospective independence. Filipinos were sobered by the immensity of the problems which they were about to inherit. They adopted a social justice program which was designed to ameliorate the condition of the underprivileged and remove the most flagrant causes of unrest. Further progress toward responsible administration of their own affairs was rudely interrupted by the shattering bursts of Japanese bombs.

THE NETHERLANDS EAST INDIES

The Indies under the Dutch experienced rougher traveling than the Philippines in the journey toward independence. Early in the twentieth century, the Dutch for the first time determined to extend effective control over all the islands. In 1901 they adopted the ethical policy, which announced that the new aim of colonial government would be the welfare of the Indies and not that of the mother country. Comprehensive measures were introduced for decentralized political administration and increased economic development. Credit facilities were established to keep the peasants out of the clutches of moneylenders, and rules were adopted to protect labor against exploitation. According to the new policy, the dessas, or villages, were to be treated with utmost tenderness in order to make them anchors in the storms of social change. Villagers were given opportunities to participate in public affairs at the local level as a training process for self-government.

Under the ethical policy, the Indies looked more than ever like a paradise of emerald islands in the tropical seas. Travel posters featured parks, gardens, flowers, beautiful homes, and exceptionally attractive, happy people. About two billion dollars of foreign investments, mostly

Dutch, produced spectacular economic changes. Highways and railways were improved, and interisland shipping services were expanded. The Indies became leading producers of sugar, coffee, tea, and forest and coconut products; the outer islands tasted new prosperity, thanks to the export of tin, rubber, tobacco, and petroleum. The Dutch followed the commercial theory of the Open Door, encouraging trade with all countries on an equal basis. Only twenty percent of the external trade of the Indies was with The Netherlands, in contrast to fifty percent as between Indochina and France, and eighty percent between the Philippines and the United States. The excellence of Dutch technical ability prevented a deterioration in the level of living in spite of the rapidly increasing population. Two imperfections marred the overall picture of well-being: the Dutch tended to do too much for their subjects; and, like other imperial powers, they neglected a foundation for industrialization.

Dutch political policy toward their colony was described as one of "cautious, unhurried adjustment." The Dutch preserved the native hierarchy of sultans, princes, and regents to rule over the people and to enforce the local laws and customs. They superimposed an administrative structure of Dutch and Indonesian officials who looked after the budget, the maintenance of public order, national affairs, and the social services. At the base of the political pyramid were the millions who lived in the villages; at its top was the governor-general appointed by the Crown and his illustrious Council of the Indies. The will of the Dutch was exercised by the civil service, staffed by Europeans and their native helpers. The Europeans held all the top and most of the upper intermediate jobs; scarcely an Indonesian would be found in a post which required a college education or professional training.

In 1903 a number of local councils were created by the Decentralization Act, but these councils were only advisory, and they seldom had the chance to act on their own initiative. They could not escape the ubiquitous eyes of the Dutch. The large cities were given no opportunity to manage their own affairs. It was not until 1918 that a *volksraad* or quasi legislature was set up for the entire country. It was scarcely a national representative body. It consisted of forty-eight members, half appointed by the governor-general and half elected by local and city councils. It had a European majority, and it had only the power to give advice. The governor-general could not accept its advice without the express authorization of The Hague.

The most substantial evidence of "cautious, unhurried adjustment" was the Act for the Government of the Indies, which became effective in 1927. The Crown retained the right to appoint the highest authorities in the Indies, including the governor-general and his lieutenant, the chairman and vice-chairman of the Council of the Indies, the president of the high court, the commanders-in-chief of the army and navy and the honorable members of the auditing office. The governor-general was confirmed in his responsibility to the minister of the colonies and ultimately to the states general, or Dutch parliament, for the general welfare and administration of the Indies. The *volksraad* was enlarged to sixty members, including thirty Indonesians (ten appointed and twenty elected): twenty-five Dutch; the five indigenous Asians (meaning resident Indians, Arabs, and Chinese. Japanese were considered as Europeans, not Asians.) The *volksraad* was given some legislative authority, but in the event of conflict with the governor-general it was the Dutch official who had the last word.

By the same law, the Dutch made some concessions to the growing pressures for self-government. Java and Madura were organized into three "provinces," each placed under a governor assisted by partly elected councils with a majority of non-Europeans. Councils were created for the native regents, and these with the municipal councils made up the electorate for the Indonesians in the *volksraad*. The outer islands were grouped together into three "governments"—Sumatra, Borneo, and the Great East, but were not immediately given representative institutions.

The Dutch refused to step up the pace toward self-government in spite of the mounting evidence of nationalism. After the death of the princess Raden Adjeng Kartini, her ideas were carried on by a medical doctor who also saw the way to national salvation in Western education. His activities led to the foundation of the Boedi Utomo (or Beautiful Endeavor Society) in 1908. Its members were intellectual and aristocratic. Although dedicated to the improvement of the lot of the masses, they were not geared to carry out a program of popular action. In the same year, the railway and tramway workers formed the first union in the Indies.

In 1911 the Sarekat Islam (or Islamic Association) came into being. Its goals were better economic welfare for Indonesians and the promotion of Islam; its bonds were common religion and opposition to the local Chinese. The rank-and-file of its membership were recruited from the peasants and workers; the leaders came from an extremely narrow sector of society made up of middle- and lower-rank civil servants, lawyers, doctors, engineers (some of whom were Western-trained) and the small, residual Indonesian merchant group. The Sarekat Islam conducted national meetings modeled after the Indian national congress, and in 1916 it went on record as favoring progress toward self-government under the Dutch flag. Quite understandably, it showed a certain sympathy toward socialistic ideas. None of its leaders were well-to-do persons with large landed estates (as in the Philippines), and none had great vested interests in the capitalistic system. Most were disposed to see capitalism as the tool of the affluent Dutch and their Chinese followers, and it was easy to equate capitalism with imperialism. Hostility to their colonial condition entailed opposition to capitalism.

A radical clique, headed by a Dutch communist named Henrik Sneevliet (who later became secretary to Lenin and turned up in China as an active agent of the Comintern), tried to gain control of the Sarekat Islam and to link it with the Third International. The Indonesian leadership did not favor revolutionary movements and opposed communism for religious reasons. The radical element parted company with the main body of nationalists and in 1920 organized the P.K.I., or Partai Kommunist Indonesia, the first communist party in Southeast Asia. It opposed pan-Islam as well as the Dutch and directed its appeals toward the proletariat, including the dock, government, and plantation workers.

Both Sarekat Islam and the P.K.I. grew more dissatisfied with Dutch procrastination. Between 1923 and 1926 the ordinary tranquillity of life in the Indies was disturbed by agricultural distress and industrial disputes, and the Dutch authorities used harsh measures to bring strikes to an end and to suppress every evidence of nationalistic protest. Dutch authorities learned that communist agents in Singapore maintained constant contacts between the Indies, Moscow, and Peking and supplied funds to promote lawlessness and revolution. As a direct result of a strike at the telephone headquarters in 1926, the Communist Party was banned, communist meetings were prohibited and 1300 members of the P.K.I. were exiled to New Guinea.

At this point, new leadership emerged in the nationalist movement. In 1927 Achmed Sukarno organized the P.N.I., or Partai Nasional Indonesia, which was far from a disciplined organization such as the Indian National Congress or the Kuomintang in China. It was a loose federation of groups who were linked only by common opposition to the Dutch.

Ordinary members of the P.N.I. were usually products of elementary schools, and the leaders were either graduated from Dutch schools in the Indies or educated abroad. In spite of Dutch precautions, education fanned the flames of nationalism. After 1907 the Dutch promoted a good system of village elementary schools, because they believed a little learning would make better colonial subjects. In 1919 they introduced middle schools which taught Western languages, mathematics, science, and Western literature. They shied away from curricula which would include politics or the liberal arts. The higher schools were neglected, except for a technical college and advanced schools for law, medicine, agriculture, and forestry. However, the Dutch were unable to prevent the birth of "dangerous thoughts." Some children were permitted to attend "wild schools," or unsubsidized schools, where they could absorb an unofficial point of view. Indonesian students in Dutch schools learned about politics and social action as well as their regular studies. Imaginative young people organized study clubs which paved the way for such practical activities as the formation of the P.N.I.

Shortly after the Dutch put the Government of Indies Act into effect, they set about to stamp out the "menace" of nationalism. They dissolved the P.N.I., arrested Sukarno and interned him. They exiled some of the most promising young leaders, including Mohammed Hatta and Soetan Sjahrir. These men were still in banishment or prison when the Japanese invaded the Indies. Nationalism was not given a chance to become a mass movement. Political awareness was confined to intellectuals, who were often removed in experience, feeling, and understanding from the masses. Nationalists had no outlet in politics, and those who escaped the wrath of the Dutch were obliged to confine themselves to mild activities in journalism or education.

After the depression of 1929–1931, the lot of Indonesians grew worse instead of better. Poverty was still their chief grievance. They pointed out that if the entire national income were distributed among Indonesians alone, the per-capita share would be less than twenty American dollars. They protested against poor jobs and low wages. With the depression, the world-wide demand for Indonesian goods fell off, and prices declined disastrously. People lost their jobs and in desperation returned to their native villages for food and livelihood. The Dutch policy of deflation hurt the Indies. Government expenditures were cut in half, and little money was available for public works or encouragement to private industry. Cheap Japanese goods flooded the market and forced the Dutch to abandon the commercial policy of the Open Door in favor of a system of quotas, import licenses, and export controls. The Indies were still in the throes of austerity when the Nazis invaded the Netherlands and cut the tie between the Dutch mother country and its colony.

The Indonesian cup of woe also contained a bitter political potion. Soetan Sjahrir wrote from exile that the Indies was ruled by a governor-general whose article of faith was that "we have ruled here for three hundred years with the whip and the club, and we shall still be doing it in another three hundred years." Indonesians protested against the discrimination against them in the civil service and deplored their lack of educational opportunities. They pointed out that with a population of 70,000,000, they had only 1100 students in the country's one university. In the school year 1938–1939, the secondary schools graduated a total of 777 students of whom 457 were Europeans, 204 Indonesians, and 116 Arabs and Chinese. They demanded a greater degree of economic self-sufficiency and self-government. The *volksraad* asked the Dutch government to call an imperial conference to discuss methods by which self-government should come into effect, but no response was forthcoming until after Queen Wilhelmina was an exile in London.

BURMA

Burma prospered under the British, thanks primarily to the commercial cultivation of rice in the Irrawaddy Delta. Native and Indian labor, Chettyar moneylender financing, and British governing and engineering skill converted Burma into the greatest rice producer and exporter in rice-hungry Southeast Asia. Mineral resources were developed, and substantial quantities of petroleum products were obtained. Timber (particularly teak) was a lucrative enterprise, since approximately one-third of Burma was covered by forests. Highways and railways were built, and river flotillas took care of much of the country's inland freight and passenger traffic. The seaport of Rangoon became the center of overseas trade, most of which was with India or the United Kingdom. British investments in Burma reached almost $200,000,000, which provided an annual return of almost twenty-five percent.

The British made money in Burma, so did many Indians and Chinese, but the Burmans felt they received less than their rightful share. Approximately two-thirds of Burma's workers were engaged in agriculture and animal husbandry. The crops of upper Burma were diversified, but lower Burma depended upon rice. In the rice country, the Burman worker found himself at a disadvantage in coping with the moneylender, the storekeeper, the landlord, and the rice mill purchaser. The Chettyars were liberal lenders, because interest rates were usurious and the land was good security. The Burmans were careless borrowers, and they always seemed to need cash for operating expenses or family celebrations. Because of inevitable defaults, land titles passed to the Indians. As landlords, the Indians insisted upon outrageous terms of tenancy and exorbitant rents. When the cultivators were not able to pay their bills, they frequently turned to dacoity or banditry. Jobs in commerce and industry were limited, and more than half were filled by labor imported from India. Indians helped harvest the rice and performed most of the work on the docks, the railways, and the river steamers. Wages were uniformly low, and conditions of labor usually reflected the conscience of the employers. Labor organization was rudimentary, and strikes were likely to be classified by the courts as riotous conduct. Peasant unions did not come into existence until World War II.

One of the keenest students of Burman affairs, Mr. J. S. Furnivall, described the condition of the country as "anarchy boxed in." He observed that as a result of the British laissez-faire policy, economic forces without the restraint of law "upset the balance of native economy; sapped the foundations of religious life and institutions; ousted native arts, crafts, and industries; and killed the social pastimes and recreations." (*Colonial Policy and Practice*, p. 214.) In his opinion "economic freedom merely allowed the people to pile up debt and lose their land; law multiplied litigation even at the expense of justice; education lost its spiritual content and became a means of livelihood; the departments charged with enhancing production and welfare became vehicles of oppression and corruption; democratic machinery fostered civil strife and political discontent. All these things that worked so well in Britain went awry in Burma." (*Ibid.*, p. 216.)

The British might be reasonably accused of neglect of fundamental economic and social problems in Burma, but they must be credited with the active promotion of measures for self-government. In 1897 the chief commissioner at Rangoon was promoted to the rank of lieutenant governor. He was given the assistance of a legislative council of nine; within a few years his staff was augmented by specialists in prisons, land records, education, agricultural cooperatives, forests, and public health. A system of courts was established which was intended to relieve the executive officers of their judicial responsibilities.

Burma benefited by the Morley-Minto reforms of 1909. The legislative council was expanded to thirty members with a nonofficial majority, but it was left without any authority except to ask questions and offer advice. The Montagu-Chelmsford report of 1917 recommended further special consideration for Burma, and the "dyarchy system" was extended to Burma in 1923. Burma became a governor's province, which was the highest status in the Indian system. The legislative council was increased to 103 members, of whom 79 were to be elected by all householders, without sex disqualification and with 18 as the minimum age limit. The governor's executive council consisted of two councilors in charge of reserved subjects (defense, law and order, finance and revenue) and two ministers responsible for the transferred subjects (education, public health, forests, and excise). In local government, majorities of the municipal committees and rural district committees were elected; they were given a wide range of responsibilities in maintenance of roads, public health, sanitation, maintenance of hospitals, health of cattle, establishment and control of markets, operation of ferries, and creation of school boards.

The Simon Commission, in reviewing the work of the government of Burma in 1928, reported in favor of separation of Burma from India. When the Indian round tables met in London to deliberate the destiny of India, a distinct round table met to discuss the main lines of a new constitution for Burma. The new status for Burma was incorporated in the Government of India Act in 1935; on April 1, 1937, Burma became a separate administrative entity. Its status was below that of a dominion in the British commonwealth. The Secretary of State for India became the secretary for India and Burma, and a separate Burma office was created under an Under-Secretary for Burma. The governor of Burma was made solely responsible for defense, internal security, coinage and currency, foreign affairs, and the excluded areas of the Shan States, Karenni, and the tribal hills.

General administration was entrusted to a cabinet of ten ministers, under the leadership of a prime minister and responsible to a bicameral legislature. The upper house was a senate of 36 members, half of whom were elected by the house of representatives and half nominated by the governor. The house of representatives contained 132 members, of whom 30 represented communal and special interests such as the University of Rangoon, commerce and labor. Ninety-two representatives were elected by territorial constituencies. The franchise was extended to most males over 21 and females over that age who could pass a simple literacy test. The new system was never given a fair test because it was no sooner set up than it became a casualty of war. It would have experienced great difficulties because of the attitudes which had by that time been adopted by Burma's nationalist leaders.

The nationalist movement was associated with hostility to British rule, hatred of the Indian coolie and moneylender, and conservative Buddhist opposition to Western cultural influences. Burma's nationalist leaders were not inclined to limit themselves to constitutional action, because they operated in a society whose traditions were shattered by the imposition of British rule.

Nationalists in Burma experienced difficulties in organizing themselves into political parties. In 1919 the General Council of Buddhist Associations went on record for home rule, but nothing like a concerted movement for self-government developed before the introduction of the dyarchy. In the legislative council, after 1923, a nationalist bloc led by the People's Party, voiced Burman demands for better education, more rights for Burmans, and less exploitation by the British. Extreme nationalists boycotted elections and refused to take any part in the hated dyarchy government. Burmese complaints against the British sounded like echoes from India.

Political unrest was aggravated by the economic distress of the world depression. Burma's first race riot in 1930, egged on by astrologers and led by Buddhist monks, turned into a revolt against the government. Drastic police action was needed to quell the rebellious cultivators, and the atmosphere of suspicion and distrust still lingered on when the constitution became effective in 1937.

After the separation of Burma from India, the political scene was dominated by Dr. Ba Maw who led the Sinyetha, or Poor Man's Party, and U Saw who formed the Myochit, or Patriotic Party. These men built up substantial personal followings by means of bribes and political intrigue. They were less dynamic and influential than a youthful group known as the Dobama Asiayone, or We Burmans Association. Young students insisted on the right to be addressed as *thakin,* or master, which implied that Burmans rather than the British should be masters in Burma. They did not turn their backs on Western technology, but they insisted upon economic as well as political independence. They stood four-square for nationalism, and they denounced corruption in local politics. They accepted Buddhism as an integral part of Burma's culture, but they refused to take orders from politically minded monks. They supplied the energy and drive for the national movement, which had reached critical proportions in 1939. When the war broke out in Europe, Burma's anti-British prime minister was in London on a special diplomatic mission. The former prime minister was enmeshed in the freedom bloc which he organized to agitate for complete independence. Thirty of the most ardent Thakins were in Japan—at the invitation of the Japanese consul in Rangoon—preparing to cooperate in the forceful overthrow of British rule.

MALAYA

The British were more hard-pressed in Burma than in Malaya, where colonial rule experienced a much smoother course. In 1909 the British rounded out their territory in Malaya by the acquisition from Siam of the four states of Kedah, Perlis, Kelantan, and Trengganu. These states refused to join the Federated Malay States, but they negotiated treaties with the British by which each state agreed to accept a resident adviser. In 1914 Johore, the sultanate closest to Singapore, and long under British influence, made the same arrangements with the British as the other unfederated states.

Malaya is about the size of Florida, and yet it had eleven separate governments. The Straits Settlements (Penang, Malacca, and Singapore) were organized as a crown colony, with a governor who was also the high commissioner or supervisor general of all the Malay States. The Federated Malay States (Perak, Selangor, Negri Sembilan, and Pahang) had separate state governments and a federal superstructure at Kuala Lumpur. Each of the unfederated states (Kedah, Perlis, Kelantan, Trengganu, and Johore) had its own court. Great Britain claimed legal sovereignty only over the Straits Settlements; it considered the nine states as "states protected by the British crown." Only the inhabitants of the Straits Settlements were treated in law as British subjects.

The British administration of Malaya was a benevolent despotism under the control of the Secretary of State for Colonies and the British parliament. The governor made all appointments except the justices of the high court and the auditors. He was assisted by executive and legislative councils in the Straits Settlements and by a Federal Council for the Federated Malay States. The councils were made up of officials and representatives of all the various communities, but their powers were only advisory. Advisers to sultans were given state councils with executive and legislative authority, and each of the Straits Settlements was allowed a municipal council with an Asian majority. Advisers were supposed to "advise"; actually they were obliged to give orders to sultans whose ideas of government were closer to the middle ages than the twentieth century. The day-to-day work of running Malaya was done by the civil service.

Peace and prosperity made possible the development of public works and the expansion of social services. The face of Malaya was transformed by roads, railways, bridges, telegraph lines, hydroelectric projects, and imposing public buildings. The British built hospitals and worked hard to improve public health. They provided elementary schools for Malayan boys and girls and subsidized private Chinese and Indian schools. They founded technical schools for agriculture and commerce, and they established Raffles College in Singapore. Students were eager to learn English as the magic key to a white-collar job. Malaya, like the Philippines, had a surplus of unemployed intellectuals.

The twin movements toward self-government and national independence failed to take deep roots in Malaya. The British were reluctant to accelerate the pace toward democracy. They were not unaware of the strategic and commercial value of Singapore, and they were under practically no pressure to make concessions such as they felt obliged to make in India and Burma. The economic growth of the colony and the complications of the plural society were the two main reasons for the tardiness of nationalism.

Ironically enough, the invention of the automobile and the necessity of rubber for tires was the principal factor in shaping the political destiny of Malaya. Heavy foreign investments in rubber brought unprecedented prosperity and made Malaya the greatest earner of American dollars in the British empire. Tin, palm oil, iron, pineapples, and import-export trade added to the national income. The British benefited most from Malay's strong economic position, and the Chinese shared substantially in the profits. The indigenous Malays also enjoyed better incomes because the government helped them to earn extra money from small holdings of rubber trees and coconut palms. But like other easygoing Asians, the Malays were generous spenders and careless borrowers. Like other Asians they were victimized by shrewd Chinese lenders, and they often lost their lands. Economic growth did not result in many new jobs for Malay workers. Chinese and Indians were more dependable and provided the labor for the plantations, mines, mills, stores, railways, and docks. They were also the targets for political agitators who attempted to turn every legitimate grievance into a racial or class conflict. The communists made Singapore their operating headquarters in Southeast Asia. When the great depression in 1931 knocked the bottom out of rubber prices and placed the curse of idleness on the bustling Singapore waterfront, the British were in deep trouble. However, they were able to keep the country on even keel until the economic situation was revived by the return of prosperity to the rest of the world.

The steady British hand was appreciated by all three communities —Malay, Chinese, and Indian. Each community had its own reasons to prefer the known degree of British integrity, fairness, and efficiency to an unpredictable and untested regime which might have little to offer except democracy. The Malays were not politically conscious and were not burning with any fever of nationalism. They had no concept of allegiance to Malaya as a country; their loyalty was only to their sultan. In their minds, sultans were meant to govern; common men were fated to obey. Only a few had any ideas about civil rights, and practically no one sought the responsibilities of self-government. Sultans were as backward as their subjects. As more Malays became educated, they thought more about their political future. Their desire for democracy was outweighed by their fear of the Chinese. They preferred to keep the British rather than to come under the domination of the clever Chinese.

The Chinese resented the British attitude that the Malays were entitled to special protection as the people of the country. A Chinese leader pointed out that he was not a transient—he lived in the house in Malacca which his ancestors had built in the time of Albuquerque! The Chinese wanted full rights of citizenship and equal representation with the Malays. They felt they should be given the opportunities in the civil service to which their skills entitled them. However, they left hardship behind them when they sailed from China; they were grateful for the chance to work, to save, and to make a new life in the land of their adoption. Their main interests were economic, not political. Many Chinese arrived with nothing more than the shirts on their backs, and they retired in comparative wealth. Why should they jeopardize the good fortune which the British government had brought them?

The British experienced more trouble with the Chinese than the Chinese experienced with the British. The Chinese immigrated in droves. They brought their wives, established their families, and made Singapore the largest Chinese city outside of China. They helped to build Malaya, but they never quite forgot their Chinese origin. They supported their own schools and lived as a race apart. They shared in the excitement of China's new nationalism, and they sent large sums of money back to China to support the cause of Sun Yat-sen. The cliques and political intrigues of mainland China somehow stretched to the South Seas, and the British police were determined that the anti-imperialism of the Kuomintang should not stir up dissatisfaction and riots in Singapore. It was difficult for the British to extend political privileges of any kind to native Malays, without at the same time opening the floodgates for Chinese supremacy.

The Indian community appeared quite satisfied with the British raj in Malaya. It was not a large community, but it could sway the delicate balance between the numerically equal (approximately) Chinese and Malaya. Wealthy and intelligent Indians played along and prospered with the British and depended upon the latter to protect them against discrimination from fellow Asians. Indian laborers enjoyed comparatively high wages; mostly they enjoyed the protection which a benevolent government gave to them in matters of wages, working conditions, and housing standards in the cities and on the plantations.

On the surface, in 1939 Malaya seemed to be moving in grooves which were well-defined and unchanging. British administration looked to be satisfactory in every way. Economic conditions were on the mend. Race relations were outwardly harmonious—and no one could have foreseen the cataclysmic effects of the storm which was about to burst.

French Indochina

In many respects, Indochina resembled Malaya. However, the colonial power was France, rather than Great Britain; this fact alone accounted for many deep-seated dissimilarities. The French colonial administrative system was a neat hierarchy which took shape during the term of office of Governor-General Paul Doumer (1897–1902). Theoretically the governor-general (who was usually a Paris politician and not a professional colonial servant) had nearly absolute powers, but he was under the close supervision of the ministry of colonies. He was assisted by an advisory grand council of economic and financial interests which was made up primarily of high-ranking French and Indochinese officials. Technically Cochin China was the only one of the five divisions to rank as a colony; the other four (Annam, Cambodia, Laos, and Tonkin) were all protectorates. Cochin China's government was in the hands of a governor, assisted by a privy council (with executive functions) and a colonial council (with legislative functions). The colony was divided into provinces with a French administrative officer at the head of each. The percentage of native subordinate officials was very low.

In Annam, Cambodia, and Laos the monarchs and their courts, together with the native mandarins, continued to exist side by side with the French administration. The real control in each protectorate was in the hands of a *résident supérieur* assisted by a privy council and a protectorate council. Each protectorate was likewise divided into provinces headed by Frenchmen. Actual administration was carried out by the native officials, but French control was absolute. Tonkin was administered like the colony of Cochin China.

The façade of native administration was imposing, and it made foreign rule less disagreeable. The French created a consultative native assembly to assist each *résident supérieur*. Most of its members were elected by a narrow group of officials and others of trusted loyalty. However, it was more of a showpiece than a legislature. It could not even debate political subjects and could express its views only on invitation of the French officials. French policy was in no sense to grant further self-government. The intention was to draw the dependency progressively closer to France as an integral part of a closely knit empire dominated by the mother country.

Measured in statistics of production and trade, road and railway mileage, irrigation, dikes, and land reclamation, the French record was a good one. The program of medicine and public health was good. Labor codes were adopted to control the recruiting of coolies and to establish better living conditions and shorter hours of work. Economic improvements were not shared by the peasants. The standard of living in the populous rice-growing deltas of the Red and Mekong rivers declined as the rate of population growth raced ahead of overall economic growth. Native cultivators were plunged into debt (usually to Chinese money lenders) or forced to sell their land and to hire out as workers. The French took inadequate measures to cope with a fundamental land problem which was characterized by extreme poverty, high tenancy rates, unmerciful rents, and a tax system which fell heavier on the poor than on the rich.

The effort to export French civilization resulted in a curious mixture of good and evil. Greater order and justice sometimes resulted in greater disorder and injustice. Transgressors were no longer thrown to the elephants to be trampled to death, and the worst abuses of mandarin rule were suppressed; the introduction of rules of law based on a philosophy of individualism, however, weakened the traditional family and communal ties. Individuals lost the security of family and village, without a compensating sense of dignity and equality before their alien rulers. The floating population of agricultural workers in Cochin China and industrial workers of Tonkin were deprived of the advantages of their own civilization while not yet enjoying those of Western civilization. Lives were often drab and empty. Slow reforms and improvements did not keep up with the inner resentments of insecure workers and peasants. Both nationalist and communist propaganda could thus find receptive ears.

The chief aim of French educational policy was originally to train interpreters and low-level native assistants in colonial administration. In 1906 the system of public instruction was reorganized. Elementary schools were decreed (but seldom built) in the villages for the purpose of making the children literate in Chinese or Vietnamese. Franco-vernacular grammar schools and high schools were provided, but the best families preferred to send their children to private Catholic or monastic schools. In 1939 only a half-million children attended the lower grades in the entire country. Of these only one in ten went on to grammar school and one in a hundred to high school. In 1937 the University of Hanoi had 631 students, most of whom were Vietnamese. The French were not vitally interested in vernacular education, except as it contributed to the spread of French culture. Perhaps the greatest contribution of France to Indochina in the cultural realm was the creation of the Ecole Française d'Extrême Orient in Hanoi, where a small coterie of French scholars developed one of the finest centers of oriental studies in the world.

⌈The French policy of assimilation had strangely different results from those it was intended to produce. The people of Indochina who knew the French best—admired French culture most sincerely and spoke the language most fluently—became the bitterest opponents of the French and the leaders in the national movement. It was only the French who had welded together five disparate peoples into a single entity, and it was only common opposition to the French/which made possible a concerted drive toward an independent and, if possible, unified state. The Annamese—later better known as the Vietnamese—who made up about three-quarters of the population, spearheaded the drive.⌋

The Annamese had a tradition of nationalism dating from their long struggle against the Chinese, and they never lost hope that the French would have to go. Banditry was never stamped out completely, and anti-French intrigues among the scholar mandarins were endemic. Plans for the "Restoration of Vietnam" reached a climax during World War I and were thwarted by prompt and severe French action. Leaders were executed or sent to penal settlements; for his part in the plot, the emperor of Annam was exiled to the island of Reunion in the Indian Ocean. The new emperor sent his only son—who was to be enthroned in 1925 under the reign name of Bao Dai—to be educated in France, far from the frustrations and corruption of the Annamese court at Hué.

Quiet mandarin pressure for reforms received popular and unexpected support from thousands of coolies who went to dig trenches in France during the war. Opposition to the French crystallized in two nationalist parties: the Revolutionary Party of Young Annam and the National Party of Vietnam. The parties could not agree on common leadership or a common program. The most radical resorted to terrorism and promoted an abortive mutiny in the army at Yen Bay in 1930. The repressive measures of the French were so drastic that the surviving nationalist leaders were obliged to flee the country. Agitation for independence was left in the hands of the Indochinese Communist Party, which was founded by an agent of the Comintern known as Nguyen Ai Quoc, or Ho Chi Minh.

He was born about the same time as Chiang Kai-shek. In his youth he worked as ship's steward, photographer's assistant, and assorted odd jobs. At the Conference of Versailles, he succeeded in gaining a hearing for the Vietnamese case against arbitrary French rule. He joined the French Communist Party and was an experienced hand at the communist game when he went to Moscow in 1923. He turned up in Canton in 1925 in the entourage of the Russian adviser, Borodin; he immediately organized a communist Association of Vietnamese Revolutionary Youth. Some of his colleagues were permitted to study at the Whampoa Military Academy, and others were infiltrated into northern Vietnam for subversive purposes. In 1930 the association became the Indochinese Communist Party. Immediately it took advantage of near-famine conditions in North Annam to organize demonstrations, burn tax rolls, and sack public buildings. The French reacted with vigor, with the result that in 1932 the number of political prisoners confined in Indochinese jails, penal settlements, and "special camps" was estimated at 10,000.

The Indochinese Communist Party was suppressed temporarily, and Ho found himself in and out of Russia, China, Southeast Asia, and bourgeois jails during the next few years. However, the nationalist movement was not arrested. The Emperor Bao Dai returned to his country from France in 1932 and announced his desire to reign as a constitutional monarch. Among those chosen to assist him in his reform program was Ngo Dinh Diem, a provincial governor who had gained a reputation for patriotism and integrity. The patience of the aristocrats was not matched by conspirators who formed the Vietnam Independence League, or the Viet Minh, on the eve of the Japanese invasion. Ho Chi Minh declared that its objective was to fight, not honest Frenchmen, but "the cruel domination of French colonialism . . . *corvée, gabelle,* forced consumption of opium and alcohol, crushing taxes, absolute lack of liberty, permanent terror, moral and material misery, shameless exploitation." Its objectives were clear, but its leadership was divided, and the French *securité* was strong, alert and backed by the power of the colonial army.

SIAM

Indochina's neighbor, Siam, escaped the agonies of the struggle for independence which characterized the rest of Southeast Asia. Siam entered the twentieth century as a free country under the reign of a dynasty which had been on the throne for more than a hundred years. King Chulalongkorn guided his people in a program of modernization and steered a wise if precarious course between the French and British, who exerted constant pressure on his frontiers. He was obliged to make concessions to the French in Indochina in 1904 and 1907 and to the British in Malaya in 1909. The last treaty by which Siam lost territory was also the first by which it regained some of its surrendered sovereignty: in exchange for the Siamese states in Malaya, Great Britain gave up its rights to extraterritoriality in Siam. The nations of Europe and the United States followed the British lead.

Thanks to the abundant rice crop, Siam was prosperous. It was in no hurry to industrialize, but it welcomed foreign investments. The British took the lead in developing tin, teak, and shipping; the Chinese rose to dominance in light industry, wholesale and retail trade. Ninety-five percent of Siam's industry and commerce passed into the hands of Europeans or Chinese. Siam did not suffer from such social dislocations as occurred in Burma or Indochina. No foreign conqueror was given the opportunity to displace the traditional way of life or to erect an administrative superstructure on the ancient framework of government. The infiltration of Chinese was steady but gradual, and the Siamese had ample time to absorb them without disastrous cultural shocks.

King Vajiravudh succeeded his father in 1910 and reigned until 1925. He was educated in England and was a lover of art and the theater. He sided with the Allied Powers during World War I, although he seemed to be more inclined toward the pomp and circumstance of royalty than toward democracy. He was as paternalistic toward his people as were his illustrious ancestors. He ordered all his subjects to adopt family names, and he exhorted the women to comb their beautiful black hair Western-style. In the interest of public health he decreed compulsory vaccination against smallpox, and he urged young people to go in for athletics. He made elementary education compulsory and founded the Chulalongkorn University.

King Vajiravudh was succeeded by his youngest brother, Prince Prajadhipok, who was the seventy-sixth child of his father and his last son. The early years of his reign saw the beginnings of a national radio service, the establishment of an international airport at Bangkok, and the foundation of the Royal Institute of Literature, Architecture and Fine Arts with its excellent national library and museum. The new king made significant efforts to popularize his rule by the appointment of a wider circle of advisers. He also tried to reduce the costs of the royal household, but he ran into difficulties with the slump of 1932.

The depression did not hurt Siam too badly because of the near self-sufficiency of the agricultural population. Resentment arose against the foreign influence in commerce and industry and fanned the flames of economic nationalism. Drastic cuts in the government budget inflamed the junior members of the civil service, who were already discontented because the road to promotions was blocked by the solidly princely class which monopolized all the key positions. Many of them had adopted democratic ideas through education in Europe, and they had become impatient with the working of old-fashioned royal absolutism. Many army officers were also hurt by reductions in their salaries, and they too were hostile to princely influence.

In 1932 a brilliant young law professor, variously known as Luang Pradit or Pridi Banomyong, teamed up with a military man, Phibun Songgram, to engineer a palace coup. The public took no part in the bloodless revolution. The king was obliged to accept a constitution, and the princes were excluded from ministerial posts. The army and the People's Party, as Pridi and his followers named themselves, took over the government. Siam was given a unicameral assembly—with half of its members to be elected and a council of ministers responsible to the legislature.

On the economic front, a plan for nationalization and industrialization was drawn up which was declared to be communistic. Pridi was forced into exile, but after a year he was exonerated and welcomed back to Bangkok with enthusiasm. He was obliged to share the spotlight with his military counterparts; and for the remaining years before World War II, Siam lived on the brink of crisis. The king abdicated in March 1935 in favor of his nephew, Prince Ananda Mahidol. The aristocracy lost its favored position, and the middle-class movement became divided by the growing rivalry between Pridi and Phibun.

In 1938 a new government came into power with Phibun as prime minister and Pridi as minister of finance. Its prevailing note was intensified nationalism. Much heavier taxes were levied on foreign firms. Stringent regulations were passed against Chinese, in the name of public order. Subsidies were offered to Siamese firms in the hope that British and Chinese could be displaced or driven out. Phibun started a campaign to inculcate Western manners and social practices. Both sexes were required to wear European shoes and hats in public and to dress generally in the Western fashion. The education system was brought under the strictest control. The movement to equate Buddhism with patriotism was fostered, and the rule was laid down that no official could marry an alien without special permission.

In 1939 the official name of the country was changed from Siam to Thailand, which had the connotation of the "Land of the Free." In foreign policy Phibun attempted to bring pressure on Western countries by threatening to cooperate with Japan. Japanese goods flooded the Siamese markets, and Japan discussed an aid program which included the possible construction of a canal across the Isthmus of Kra. Japan also suggested that it would help Thailand recover the territories which had been lost to the imperialist encroachments of France (in Indochina) and Great Britain (in Burma and Malaya).

The pause in the story of Siam (Thailand) in 1939 marks the transition from one period in South and Southeast Asia to another. After four centuries of colonialism, the fate of the imperial powers approached the moment of reckoning on the eve of World War II. Gracefully or forcefully they would give up their dominion over distant lands and different people. New nations were about to merge and build new states. They would recapture the memories of their ancient past and convert to their own use the contributions of their recent masters. The preparation for independence was imperfect, but the right was undeniable. The stage was set for the entry of Japan, which arrived with the plausible assertion that it had come to liberate.

It is now time to retrace the years 1931–1939 in East Asia and to analyze the events which propelled Japan on its march to the southern regions. World War II represented the merging of two historical streams: the rise of nationalism in India and Southeast Asia and the surge of Japan over China and Southeast Asia. The story of India and Southeast Asia has been told as far as 1939; but China and Japan were left on the threshold of 1931. Japan was about to make its move, and its determination made global war inevitable. Invasion, bombs, and marching armies would destroy the old order, and rob ancient Asian societies of every chance they might have had to develop in isolation. "Changeless" Asia would become dizzy with the speed of its own revolutions, and it would be integrated rapidly with the rest of the modern world.

SUGGESTED READING

Blanchard, Wendell, *Thailand* (New Haven, HRAF Press, 1958).

de Young, John E., *Village Life in Modern Thailand* (Berkeley, U. of California, 1955).

Furnivall, John S., *Netherlands India, a Study of Plural Economy* (Ithaca, Cornell U., 1952).

Grunther, Garel, and Livezey, William, *Philippines and the United States* (Norman, U. of Oklahoma, 1951).

Hammer, Ellen, *Struggle for Indochina* (Stanford, Stanford U., 1954).

Hayden, Joseph R., *Philippines, a Study in National Development* (New York, Macmillan, 1945).

Herz, Martin, *Brief History of Cambodia* (New York, Praeger, 1958).

Holland, W. L., *Asian Nationalism and the West* (New York, Macmillan, 1953).

Jacoby, Erich H., *Agrarian Unrest in Southeast Asia* (New York, Columbia U., 1949).

Kahin, George M., *Nationalism and Revolution in Indonesia* (Ithaca, Cornell U., 1952).

Kirk, Grayson, *Philippine Independence* (New York, Farrar, 1936).

Lancaster, Donald, *Emancipation of Indo-China* (New York, Oxford U., 1961).

Le Bar, Frank M., and Suddard, Adrienne, (eds.), *Laos* (New Haven, HRAF Press, 1960).

Orwell, George, *Burmese Days* (New York, Harcourt, 1930).

Quezon, Manuel, *Good Fight* (New York, Appleton, 1944).

Robequain, Charles, *Malaya, Indonesia, Borneo, and the Philippines* (London, Longmans, Green, 1954).

Sjahrir, Soetan, *Out of Exile* (trans. by Charles Wolf, Jr.) (New York, Day, 1948).

Skinner, William, *Report on the Chinese in Southeast Asia* (Ithaca, Cornell U., 1950).

Steinberg, David J., *Cambodia* (New Haven, HRAF Press, 1959).

IV

WAR IN GREATER EAST ASIA

18

The Seeds of Conflict

While the rest of the world watched a dynamic American president, Franklin D. Roosevelt, guide his country out of the depression by means of the New Deal and a powerful Russian dictator, Joseph Stalin, concentrate on the building of socialism in the Soviet Union—three nations, Germany, Italy, and Japan, embarked on aggressive careers in their respective parts of the world. Hitler in Central Europe, Mussolini in Abyssinia, and cliques of assorted militarists in Japan preferred war and the risk of defeat to what they interpreted as continued slavery to the "decadent, democratic" powers who happened to "have" the preponderant share of the world's wealth and resources.

The dynamite hidden by the Japanese Twentieth Engineers Regiment which blasted Chang Tso-lin, the Old Marshal of Manchuria, into eternity on June 4, 1928, propelled Japan on the road to Pearl Harbor. Japan's story in Manchuria (then in China), the southern regions, and the Pacific Ocean area, was the tragic record of a nation consumed with visions of greatness. The shadows of death and destruction lay heavily on succeeding generations in Asia which were required to build new nations and a new life on the ruins of World War II.

THE VIEW FROM TOKYO

With the appalling hardships of the economic depression in Japan, men of the positive persuasions of the Seiyukai interpreted the weakened condition of Japan as the product of liberal tendencies at home and soft dealings overseas. Secret societies in Japan began to whisper in the dead of night that Japan must be reborn to fulfill its divine mission of liberating the nonwhite peoples from Anglo-Saxon domination. In their view, government had to be made strong to ensure "Asia for the Asiatics." This philosophy appealed to military circles which were determined to get rid of weak-kneed elected representatives in the diet and incompetent civilian advisers to the emperor.

Propagandists in Japan spread the idea that Manchuria was Japan's lifeline. Japan had to expand into Manchuria in order to develop it economically and industrially. Japan should protect its sacred treaty rights in Manchuria as a prelude to converting that strategic region into a bastion of defense against Bolshevist Russia. The "Cherry Society" began to study Manchurian and Mongolian questions and national reformation within Japan. The ultranationalists were not long in exerting their influence upon bureaucrats within the government and the Japanese public at large.

The assassination of Premier Hamaguchi in 1930 was followed by an unsuccessful plot on the part of ultranationalistic elements—civil and military—to take over the government in March, 1931, shortly before the outbreak of trouble in Manchuria. The subsequent murder of Premier Inukai in 1932 led to the cessation of the regular processes of parliamentary government.

For the next four years, the military were in the saddle. Admirals Saito and Okada served as premiers until the incident of "two-twenty-six." On February 26, 1936, twenty-two officers and 1400 men of the Third Infantry Regiment took over strategic points in Tokyo, defied their orders to go abroad, and planned the murder of the premier and some of his cabinet officers. They remained in a state of rebellion for three days until they were induced to return to their regular status by imperial orders. Because of temporary displeasure with the superpatriotism of the military, the government was placed in the hands of an equally chauvinistic civilian, Hirota Koki, who was himself hanged as a war criminal by the International Military Tribunal for the Far East. Hirota served for one year and was followed by General Hayashi, one of the most reasonable of Japan's leaders in uniform. After four months in office, from February to June, 1937, Hayashi was dismissed because he was not considered sufficiently tough to undertake responsibility for the push into China. The militaristic cabal carried out its totalitarian schemes at home and its aggressive policies in China behind the façade of a government headed by the well-meaning but subservient civilian premier, Prince Konoye.

The psychological atmosphere on the home front became more oppressive. The liberalism of the previous decade disappeared. The diet was stripped of its prerogatives, and the press was encouraged to popularize the objectives of the new Japan. Mystic phrases, like national polity, national structure, and the Kingly Way took the place of rational political thought. Antiforeign sentiments increased, and all foreigners were looked upon as potential spies. Individual Japanese were admonished to live

Spartan lives. Ballroom dancing was frowned upon, and taxi-dance halls were closed. Golf and other luxury sports were condemned. The American words *strike, ball,* and *out* were eliminated from their beloved game of baseball. The use of English scientific and technical terms was condemned, and English names were taken off the street signs and the railway stations. The element of criticism was taken out of higher education. A witch hunt plagued the universities and forced distinguished professors to resign. Professor Minobe, a leading authority on constitutional law, was forced into dishonorable retirement because he described the emperor as an organ of the state. Labor unions were stripped of their influence, and every type of public assembly was subjected to close police scrutiny. Ultranationalism demanded conformity or silence. The molders of public opinion attacked internationalism, democracy, and capitalism. They scornfully contrasted the greed and corruption of the West with the purity and patriotism of Japan.

This psychological manipulation did not represent a popular political upheaval on the part of the masses, but it reflected the realignment of political forces behind the throne. The emperor remained as a mere symbol without real force or influence. He was a man of moderate tastes, but his views amounted to little in practical politics. Old-style moderates were pushed aside as his advisers. The military were increasingly regarded as the proper guardians of the pure Japanese spirit.

Party politicians, bureaucrats, and *zaibatsu* were obliged to play along with the military or to abandon political life. As party politicians lost their influence, they were deprived of contributions which they had customarily received from the *zaibatsu*. Political and financial leaders of the old style hated to see the passing of democracy and free enterprise. However, the new *zaibatsu* profited from defense contracts and by their actions showed that they preferred profits to political principles. They joined with the militarists in a curious sort of state socialism, whereby the large business and financial combines themselves became agencies of public administration and state control.

It could not be said that, at this early date, Japanese militarists and *zaibatsu* became co-conspirators to wage aggressive war on a global scale. Business leaders did not register substantial objections to brushfire wars in Manchuria or even in China, but they opposed and feared large scale hostilities which would increase their taxes and possibly bring about the annihilation of the value of their investments. In this situation, Japanese bureaucrats discovered a new role of importance for themselves. They were not too happy with ultranationalism or patriotism. However, they became mouthpieces for the military and spokesmen for government policy. Behind the scenes they acted as a balance wheel or as arbiters in disputes which arose between the clashing political forces. When viewed from Tokyo, Japanese in and out of government were far from undivided in their opinions when the Sino-Japanese conflict erupted in Manchuria.

CONFLICT IN MANCHURIA

Japan considered Manchuria its lifeline because of its geographic location and wealth of raw materials. After Russia was checked in Northeast Asia by the war of 1904–1905, Japan converted the Kwantung leased area into a military stronghold and developed the Kwantung army as the most legendary unit in the empire's fighting forces. Japan also used a quasi-public corporation, the South Manchurian Railway Company, as its major agency for economic development. After consolidating its legal position in Manchuria by means of the Twenty-One Demands in 1915, Japan poured millions of dollars into Manchuria and used economic penetration as a cloak for political domination. After 1917 Japan was determined that Manchuria should not fall as a prey to the spreading power of Russian Bolshevism and should not become enmeshed in the civil wars which plagued China south of the Great Wall.

No Japanese questioned that sooner or later Manchuria would be absorbed by Japan. It was only a matter of time and opportunity. Japan governed its leased territory with practically full rights of sovereignty; it administered the railway zone—including several towns and large sections of such populous cities as Mukden and Changchun—with unhampered control of police, taxation, education, and public utilities. Japan's armed forces in Manchuria, in addition to the Kwantung army, included railway guards and Japanese consular police in all the districts where Japanese consular offices were located. Japanese jurisdiction extended not only to Japanese nationals from Japan, but also to Koreans who crossed the border into Manchuria and were also Japanese subjects.

Frictions between Japan and China in Manchuria were inevitable. Japan was determined to preserve—by force if necessary—the concessions it had wrung from China in the days of China's weakness. The resurgent nationalism of China made the Chinese increasingly adamant in protesting against the validity of agreements which they claimed were signed under duress and were therefore invalid. The fundamental Chinese attitude was that the laws of the treaty might be on the side of Japan, but justice was above the law, and justice was on the side of China. Japanese treaty rights—including railway guards, consular police, extraterritoriality, and all the paraphernalia of economic exploitation—in the Chinese view were denials of justice. Consequently the Chinese adopted attitudes of opposition and obstruction to Japanese procedures in Manchuria, in spite of the fact that the Japanese carried out their policies within the letter of laws and treaties. The Chinese authorities in Manchuria annulled mining rights of Japanese, impeded the negotiation of leases to Japanese citizens, restricted Japanese rights of residence and travel, discriminated against Koreans, levied irregular taxes on Japanese, defaulted on their loans and launched a program of railway building which challenged the entire Japanese economic position in Manchuria.

The Chinese used the proceeds of loans which they had obtained from Japan to build nearly a thousand kilometers of railway lines which competed directly with the South Manchurian Railway. This made it possible for Manchurian farmers to ship their soy beans from the farm to shipside without the use of Japanese lines. The Chinese, with the help of the Dutch, built a railway terminus and deep-water dock at the port of Hulutao which challenged the commercial importance of Dairen. Japan became uneasy because it believed that time was working in favor of China. Thousands, then millions, of Chinese immigrants swarmed into Manchuria, and Japan feared that, unless extreme measures were taken, those millions of Chinese would convert Manchuria and all of its precious Japanese investments into a part of New China.

China pointed out consistently that Manchuria was always an integral part of China. It was not a dependency nor a separate area. Japan tried to substantiate the argument that Manchuria was distinct from the rest of China. Japan would have liked to set up a regime in Manchuria which would turn its back on revolutionary China and look to Japan for support. After the murder of Chang Tso-lin, Japan hoped that his undistinguished son, Chang Hsüeh-liang, would lend himself to Japanese ambitions. However the Young Marshal showed his unmistakable sympathy for Chiang Kai-shek and the Chinese nationalists. He delegated the foreign affairs of the "Three Northeastern Provinces" (the Chinese term for Manchuria) to the control of the Nanking government, and he hoisted the banner of Sun Yat-sen over his palace in Mukden. His actions spurred the Japanese into action "in self-defense" or for "defense of their rights" in Manchuria.

Events became critical in 1931. In that year, China's nationalism was assertive, but the central government of China was embarrassed and practically immobilized by floods, famine, and civil war. At the same time, the world depression deepened with increasingly disastrous results for Japan and its silk trade. The Soviet Union emerged from its crises and demonstrated a renewed interest in the Far East, especially Manchuria.

Against that background, incidents occurred in Manchuria which set the Japanese military in motion. In the early summer of 1931 a group of Koreans at Wanpaoshan, a small village eighteen miles north of Changchun, leased a large tract of land for growing rice and prepared to irrigate the land by digging a lead-in ditch which was several miles in length.

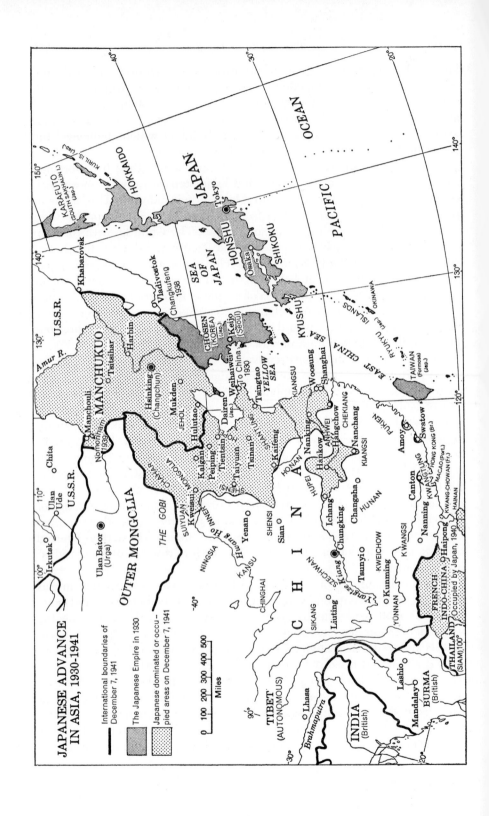

JAPANESE ADVANCE
IN ASIA, 1930-1941

International boundaries of
December 7, 1941

The Japanese Empire in 1930

Japanese dominated or occupied areas on December 7, 1941

Miles
0 100 200 300 400 500

U.S.S.R.

Irkutsk ○   Chita ○
Ulan   U.S.S.R.
Ude ○

Ulan Bator ◉
(Urga)

OUTER MONGOLIA

THE GOBI

TIBET
(AUTONOMOUS)

○ Lhasa

Brahmaputra

INDIA
(British)

Mandalay ○
Lashio ○
BURMA
(British)

THAILAND
(SIAM)

FRENCH
INDO-CHINA: ○ Haiphong
Occupied by Japan, 1940

KWANGCHOWAN (Fr.)

HAINAN

KWANGSI

○ Nanning

Canton
KWANGTUNG
MACAO (Port.)
HONG KONG (Br.)

Swatow

Amoy

FUKIEN

Kunming ○
YUNNAN

KWEICHOW

Tsunyio ○

Liuting ○
SIKANG

CHINGHAI

Chungking ◉
SZECHWAN

Yangtze Kiang

Sian ○
SHENSI

Yenan ○

KANSU

NINGSIA

Huang Ho

SUIYUAN

Kweisui ○
INNER MONGOLIA

CHAHAR

Kalgan ○

Peiping ○
HOPEI

Changsha ○
HUNAN

Ichang ○
HUPEI

Hankow
Wuchang ○

Nanchang ○
KIANGSI

Nanking ○
ANHWEI
Hangchow ○
CHEKIANG

Shanghai ○
Woosung

KIANGSU

HONAN
Kaifeng ○

Taiyuan ○
SHANSI

Tsinan ○
SHANTUNG
Tsingtao ○

Weihaiwei
1930

Peiping ○
Tientsin ○
To China

Dairen (Jap.)

Hulutao ○

Mukden ○

JEHOL

Hsinking
(Changchun) ◉

MANCHUKUO

○ Tsitsihar

Harbin ○

Nomonhan
1939

○ Manchouli

Amur R.

Khabarovsk ○

Vladivostok ○
Changkufeng
1938

CHOSEN
(KOREA)
(Jap.)

Keijo
(Seoul) ○

YELLOW
SEA

EAST CHINA SEA

TAIWAN
(Formosa)
(Jap.)

RYUKYU ISLANDS (Jap.)

OKINAWA (Jap.)

KYUSHU

SEA
OF
JAPAN

HONSHU

Osaka ○
Tokyo ◉

JAPAN

SHIKOKU

HOKKAIDO

KARAFUTO
(SOUTH SAKHALIN I.)
(Jap.)

KURIL IS. (Jap.)

PACIFIC

OCEAN

C H I N A

The ditch crossed some Chinese property, so the Chinese farmers took matters into their own hands. They drove the Koreans from their lands and filled up the ditch. Japanese consular police came to the rescue of the Koreans. They drove off the Chinese by gunfire and maintained an armed guard while the Koreans dug a new ditch. Press accounts of this Wanpaoshan incident were highly colored and provoked anti-Chinese riots in Korea and a revival of the boycott in China against the Japanese.

On August 17, 1931, the war office in Tokyo announced that in the previous June a Japanese staff officer, Captain Nakamura, had been arrested, murdered, and cremated, together with three interpreters and assistants near Taonan in North Manchuria. It was affirmed that his passports were in order and that his permit to travel in the interior was approved by the local Chinese authorities. The Chinese claimed that Captain Nakamura was put to death as a spy. He had represented himself as an agricultural expert and carried on his person patent medicines which included narcotic drugs which were to be used for nonmedicinal purposes. Japanese government officials demanded an apology, indemnity, and punishment of the murderers, but Japanese military authorities contemplated more drastic measures. One squadron of military airplanes on practice flights over Japanese cities showered propaganda leaflets calling for immediate action in Manchuria.

On the night of September 18–19, 1931, the incident occurred which was known as the "Mukden Incident." Certain Japanese military forces in Manchuria started their own war, on the flimsy pretext that a detachment of Chinese soldiers dynamited a section of the South Manchurian Railway north of Mukden. The Japanese version of the incident was that the Chinese were caught in the act by a patrol of Japanese railway guards that happened to be on night maneuvers in the vicinity. The guards opened fire on the Chinese troops, who "behaved in an insulting and provocative manner." The Chinese version was that the Japanese faked the explosion. In evidence the Chinese offered metal splinters which were of different metal than the rails. The Chinese pointed out that the southbound express from Changchun passed right over the damaged section of the track without any delay in its scheduled arrival time in Mukden.

The Japanese, in the name of self-defense, attacked the well-lighted Chinese barracks near the point of explosion. With swiftness and precision they occupied the entire city of Mukden before dawn. Within two days they installed Colonel Doihara as the city's mayor. They called their troops into action throughout the entire South Manchuria Railway zone, and they spread beyond the zone to occupy all the major cities in South Manchuria. The Chinese were not able to offer resistance. Chinese troops melted into the countryside, and the Young Marshal established a government-in-exile at Chinchow, on the Hopei-Manchurian border.

The Kwantung army took the initiative in this action and sent reports for information only to the war ministry in Tokyo. War Minister Minami was unable or unwilling to restrain the army in the field; he bore the responsibility for telling Premier Wakatsuki, ex post facto, what had actually happened in Manchuria. The premier was in an awkward position. He was obliged to defend the position of Japan against all the charges of aggression which emanated from China, the United States, and the League of Nations; yet in many instances he knew nothing of the army's actual operations or plans. The Kwantung army occupied city after city in Manchuria on the pretext of protecting life and property, while Japanese officials at home and diplomats overseas gave assurances that Japanese troops would return to their original stations as soon as the safety of Japanese nationals and investments permitted. Pressures on Japan from outside sources were to no avail. The commander-in-chief of the Japanese army in Korea sent reinforcements into Manchuria and told Prince Saionji that it might be necessary to send Japanese troops into the Yangtze Valley. When Chinchow was occupied on the morning of January 3, 1932, the Japanese were in complete military control of China north of the Great Wall, with the exception of the province of Jehol.

THE STATE OF "MANCHUKUO"

The Japanese considered their military venture as sound business, shrewd politics, sturdy patriotism, and farseeing statesmanship. Japanese military authorities took over the functions of civil government in Manchuria and the operation of all radio stations, electric light and power plants, coal mines, railways, and the postal administration. Then the Japanese gave the world an unparalleled demonstration in the art of creating a puppet state.

Provisional governments of Japanese officials and Chinese malcontents were set up in each province in Manchuria. A "Self-Government Guiding Board" was created in Mukden to correlate the activities of all elements which might express an interest in independence. A plan was set in motion to return the deposed emperor of China, Henry Pu-yi, to his ancestral home and to enthrone him in due course as the emperor of Manchuria. Late in 1931, Colonel Doihara engineered a movie thriller. With the assistance of gangsters and secret societies in Tientsin, he kidnaped Pu-yi, rushed him to a waiting launch, and spirited him away to a secret hiding place in Manchuria. In mid-February, 1932 a "Supreme Administrative Council," made up of Chinese who sold themselves to the Japanese, met in Mukden to organize a new state which would be completely independent of China. The council decided to adopt a republican form of government, under Pu-yi as regent. Parades and mass meetings were staged to impress the Manchurian populace with the power of the Japanese army. On February 29, 1932, an all-Manchurian convention was called in Mukden to inform the "public" of the proceedings to date. On March 9 Pu-yi was inaugurated as the regent of Manchukuo in the capital at Changchun, renamed Hsinking, and a constitution or organic law was proclaimed.

The Kwantung army was the stage manager of events, but the Japanese cabinet in Tokyo fell in line with the army's schemes. Tokyo decided to give all possible aid to the regency without appearing to violate the Open Door or the other treaty commitments of Japan. The Japanese government approved the organic law of Manchukuo, which placed ostensible power in Chinese officials, but which retained actual control in the Japanese administrative machinery behind the scenes. The regent and his cabinet, or council of state, were the apparent civil authorities. The ministers of state were generally Chinese, but each minister had a vice minister who was a Japanese. The entire government was at the mercy of Japanese advisers, counselors, and secretaries who received their orders from the Kwantung army's general staff. Appointments or interviews with Chinese dignitaries, even the regent himself, were dictated by the Japanese.

The Japanese tightened their grip on the new state with lightning speed. Japanese nationals were appointed to leading positions on the general affairs board; privy council; the Central Bank of Manchukuo; and in the revenue, police, banking, transportation, justice, and customs departments. The last liberal opposition in Japan to these highhanded tactics in Manchukuo disappeared when Japanese naval officers forced their way into the official residence of Premier Inukai in Tokyo and assassinated him on May 15, 1932. The new Japanese cabinet decided to go ahead with the conversion of the regency into a regular state and to endow it with all the trappings of an independent country.

On September 15, 1932, Japan signed a series of agreements with "Manchukuo" which extended formal recognition to the new state. These agreements confirmed all Japanese rights and interests and provided that the two parties should cooperate in the maintenance of law and order. According to secret notes, Japan was charged with the security and defense of Manchukuo. Japan was to take over all transportation facilities, undertake economic development, establish a Japan Air Transportation Company, develop mining concessions and appoint Japanese nationals to serve as government officials. Early in 1933 the Japanese Kwantung army —acting in its new capacity as the guardian of Manchukuo—invaded Jehol and added that province to the domain of the puppet state. The

Japanese then approached China for a truce—which was signed at Tangku on May 25, 1933—to gain time to consolidate the gains which had been won so quickly. General Araki, in explaining Japan's policies, declared that the Yamato race was in process of fulfilling its holy mission to establish peace in the orient and to make a paradise in Asia.

Japan proceeded in a very practical way to construct on the continent of Asia a "base for military operations which would contribute to the strength and glorification of Japan for ages eternal." For more than a year, the army used the façade of the regency to take over every political and economic activity in Manchuria. For a time, the South Manchuria Railway Company was permitted to manage the railways; to undertake the construction of new strategic lines; and to develop such vital industries as coal, steel, and liquid fuel. Gradually the military edged deeper into the economic hierarchy. Then the army ordered the abolition of extraterritoriality in Manchuria, which had the effect of removing Japanese individual and corporate persons from the jurisdiction of Tokyo and placing them under Manchukuo, which in reality meant under the Kwantung army. For the same reason orders were issued for the incorporation of the Kwantung leased territory into the regular government structure of Manchukuo.

On March 1, 1934, the army abolished the regency and set up an imperial form of government. Pu-yi was installed as Kang Teh, emperor of Manchukuo. The change in the form of government meant increased centralization of administration, fewer civil rights, and stricter control by local Japanese. The original four provinces of Manchuria were subdivided into ten provinces, and all local governments was placed in charge of trustworthy Japan-dominated civil servants and police. The highest Japanese official in Manchukuo was the Japanese ambassador, who was at the same time the commander-in-chief of the Kwantung army. A Manchurian Affairs Bureau, under the war minister, was established in Tokyo as an overall coordinator of Japanese policies.

The suppression of banditry was the first order of business for the new state. Where the woods were thick or the kaoliang high, influential Japanese, foreigners, or Chinese collaborators were frequently kidnaped, beaten, robbed, or murdered. Manchukuo pioneered in coping with problems which paralleled the Hukbalahaps later in the Philippines and the Communist guerillas in the jungles of Malaya. The army, police, and the home guard were called into action. When promises and reform measures failed, the government herded the farmers into protected villages and held the entire community responsible for disturbances or acts of banditry. In spite of villages which were deliberately burned and hostages who were shot, disorders were never completely stamped out.

The next priority was given to economic development. The goal was to make Manchukuo and Japan into a single bloc, according to the principle of "fit industry for suitable locality," with a common currency and without any customs barrier between the two countries. Military purposes determined economic decisions. Manchukuo was geared into the overall program of Japan. Agriculture was neglected; heavy industry was stressed. Astronomical Japanese investments produced a tremendous industrial expansion. The transportation system was improved, and key industries were nationalized. A Five-Year Plan concentrated on factories for weapons of war, airplanes, automobiles, rolling stock for railways, and such major industries as iron and steel, liquid fuel, and chemicals. German engineering skill and technical equipment were imported, power dams were built on the Yalu and Sungari rivers, new mines were opened, and many new, modern plants and mills were constructed. Industrial output was limited only by unavoidable shortages of machinery, raw materials, and management skills. Foreigners—other than the friends of Japan—were eliminated from Manchukuo; only the Japanese and their favored puppets shared the paper profits of the industrial boom. In a few short years Manchukuo was made to provide most of the war materials which Japan needed in order to sweep over greater East Asia.

Ordinary Chinese residents shared but little in the paradise which Japan claimed in Manchukuo. For a majority of the people, the level of living remained almost what it had been under Chinese warlord government. In the urban communities, it was the Japanese who prospered, while the Chinese, Manchus, and White Russians continued as hewers of wood and drawers of water. Taxes were high and commodity shortages were serious as the government diverted more and more consumers' goods into the maw of the military machine. Many Chinese businessmen were forced into bankruptcy. Black-market manipulations intensified the ordinary hardships of excessive inflation. In the country, some Chinese farmers were better off under the Japanese than they had been under the old regime. They received real money for their crops, and prices were high. Taxes were fixed and regular, and the farmers were free from the levies and extortions with which they had been plagued in the days of the warlords. On the other hand, many farmers lost their lands to Japanese immigrants, and Chinese laborers lost all their hope of a decent living by the program of low wages and compulsory savings. A labor and civil service law required all persons between eighteen and forty-five to work as a public obligation on the roads, in the mines, or in the army and navy installations.

In cultural affairs, Japan ordered the use of its own language as the medium of communication and education. Thought-control stifled all outlets of criticism because an emergency law for the preservation of peace and order enabled the Japanese to imprison anyone without trial. Education aimed at the Japanization of the youth of Manchukuo. The Japanese ideal of the "Kingly Way" became the touchstone of educational philosophy. New textbooks in all the schools played up the Confucian virtues of right conduct, propriety, benevolence, and loyalty. Formal education suffered except for vocational and civic training. All propaganda was produced by the Concordia Society, which was the creature of the army. Patriotic celebrations, national sporting contests, pamphlets, radio programs, and movies were directed toward influencing all the races of Manchuria for Japan and against China. Newspapers were mere propaganda outlets. News from the outside world filtered into Manchukuo only through the Japanese news agency and reached the people only through the official press monopoly.

According to testimony before the International Military Tribunal for the Far East in Tokyo after World War II, Japan sanctioned and developed the traffic in opium and narcotics in order to finance its operations in Manchukuo and in order to undermine the possible resistance of the Chinese. It was alleged that Japanese drug peddlers went along with the Japanese army and converted Manchukuo into a vast dumping ground for opium and its derivatives. It was undeniable that many of the Japanese civilians who followed the army to Manchuria were ruthless, buccaneering adventurers who were entirely lacking in ethical principles and often in human decency. They would hire or conscript labor, force men and women to work at a feverish pace, and sometimes fire their unfortunate victims without pay. The Chinese seethed inwardly; yet, without organization or weapons, they were obliged to submit to the police state and totalitarian regimentation.

JAPAN'S THRUSTS INTO CHINA AND CHINA'S RESPONSE

All the while Japan built its puppet empire in Manchukuo, its government kept the world guessing about its true intentions in China. In January 1932, Japanese forces occupied Shanghai after fierce fighting, but they were withdrawn voluntarily in May. Within the year the Japanese army in Manchuria seemed to accept the Great Wall as the southern limit of its operations. By the Tangku truce of May, 1933, a demilitarized zone was created in the border area between Manchuria and China proper. This zone was to be administered by China, subject to continuous Japanese aerial inspection. China was to be permitted to have only such troops in the zone as would receive Japanese approval and was obliged to close all Kuomintang offices, cease all party activities, and put a stop to all anti-Japanese activities.

Japan gave repeated assurances that it had no territorial ambitions south of the Great Wall, but it worked furiously to expand its influence westward into Mongolia and southward into North China. It strove to create an "independent" government in Inner Mongolia and to induce the five northern provinces of China to secede from the control of Nanking. Japanese military officers talked openly of stamping out the "wicked" Kuomintang and eliminating foreign interests from all of China. Japanese assumed for themselves the right to suppress all anti-Japanese activities in the major cities of North China; they imprisoned Chinese intellectuals and officials on trumped-up charges, dispersed student meetings, and intimidated those who would advocate a boycott. The Japanese in North China acted as if they were in military occupation of a conquered country.

The Hirota government in Japan, which came into power after the incident of February 26, 1936, secretly undertook the formation of a new and positive China policy. Hirota worked out three principles which were to become the basis of a new order in East Asia. According to Hirota these three principles for the establishment of peace and understanding were: cooperation between China and Japan in suppressing communism, recognition of Manchukuo by China and the formation of a Japan-China-Manchukuo economic bloc, and the cessation by China of all unfriendly acts in relation to Japan.

The diplomatic atmosphere between Japan and China was so charged for the six years between 1931 and 1937 that it seemed that at any time the secret diplomatic struggles might erupt into open war. The Japanese demanded Chinese acquiescence in Hirota's three points. In addition they insisted upon tariff revision favorable to the Japanese, establishment of an air service between Japan and China, inauguration of a special (quasi-independent political) area in North China, replacement of foreign advisers in China by Japanese, satisfaction for all anti-Japanese incidents, revision of Chinese schoolbooks to remove all traces of anti-Japanism, and extension of rights to station Japanese troops in China.

The Chinese response to these demands was to procrastinate: to hope for growing support from foreign powers and to come forth with counter demands. The Chinese demanded evacuation of Japanese troops from North China, abolition of the demilitarized zones (because of the restrictions placed upon the Chinese within those zones), abandonment of a puppet regime which the Japanese had brought into being in East Hopei near Peiping, cessation of troop maneuvers and illegal Japanese flying in North China, elimination of Japanese-tolerated smuggling and narcotic evils, and termination of undercover Japanese movements to destroy the political unity and financial stability of the Chinese government.

China followed a policy of peaceful nonresistance to Japan because it was too weak and disorganized to pursue any other alternative. At the same time, under the leadership of Chiang Kai-shek, China tried to strengthen itself for an eventual showdown with its powerful invading neighbor. As long as Japan confined itself to operations in Manchuria, the Chinese people were disappointed but incredibly apathetic. Chinese resistance stiffened as Japan thrust southward. Chiang concentrated the energies of his government on building up his armed forces, rehabilitating the national economy, and working for political unification. He hired Germans to train his armies and Americans and Italians to create an air force. He bought military equipment wherever he could establish credit, and he looked all over the world for civilian political and economic advisers. He eliminated antiforeignism from China's policies and denied by silence the venom against the foreign imperialists of earlier days. He became the model exponent of the sanctity of treaties and the orderly processes of international conciliation. He turned every phase of China's national development toward the single purpose of resisting Japan. He built roads and factories for military reasons rather than economic benefits. His anti-Japanese propaganda became vitriolic, and his party and government political machines clandestinely organized boycotts and demonstrations against the Japanese. Madame Chiang Kai-shek, who was more articulate than her husband, warned that China's undeclared war of peaceful resistance was the war of all the democracies: that if Japan conquered China, Japan would leave its footprints and bomb craters on the good earth of the territories controlled by the West.

China's tactics were, like the bamboo, to bend with the wind. Chiang's internal position was too precarious to allow him to risk a showdown with Japan. The Canton faction of the Kuomintang disputed the leadership of the Nanking faction; warlords in a half dozen provinces flouted the government's control; the Communists in south central China constituted what Chiang called "not a disease of the skin, but a disease of the heart." The Japanese failure to bring Chiang to terms exasperated their tempers and exhausted their patience. Japan complained that Chiang continued to help the bandits in Manchukuo and to tolerate Communists at his council table and urged him to change his ways by suppressing anti-Japanism, dissolving anti-Japanese societies and student movements, enforcing stricter control of the press and public opinion, and giving wider circulation and greater credence to Japanese statements and advertisements. Because of the responsibilities of his position, Chiang tempered his personal sentiments with official caution, but he shared the national preference for suicide rather than the galling spectacle of Japanese troops on Chinese soil.

Chiang Kai-shek and the Communists

Chiang's greatest problem was to discover the best way to deal with the Communists. During the years 1927–1931 Mao Tse-tung and Chu Teh managed to convert the ragtag of workers, peasants, stragglers, and bandits into a Red army and to survive in the rugged hills of Hunan and Kiangsi. On November 7, 1931, the anniversary of the Bolshevik Revolution in Russia, the Communists convened the first All-China Soviet Congress in Juikin. They established a central government for the first "Chinese Soviet Republic," adopted a constitution, and promulgated laws which reflected their doctrines and their policies. The principle of party leadership was clearly established, and the masses were whipped into line by all kinds of popular organizations. Both sexes were given equal right to vote and to hold office, but they were also charged with equal obligations to work and to serve in the army. "The people are the sea, we are the fish; as long as we can swim in that sea, we will survive." Little assistance was received from Moscow.

The Communist government did not control large areas of China, but its procedures offered a preview of conditions under the subsequent Chinese People's Republic. Communist propaganda glorified the workers, peasants, and the army. Economically, the scale of living was crude but self-sustaining, except for salt. Agrarian reforms were carried out to eliminate the landlords as a class and incidentally to improve the lot of the peasants. Lands were confiscated and redistributed. Deeds were destroyed in public bonfires at the magistrate's office, and such evidences of private property as field markers or corner posts were publicly removed. Debts were canceled, and usurers were shot on the spot. The enemies of the people were tried, condemned, and punished summarily by the people's courts. Stores of grain were commandeered, and the personal property of the wealthy (anyone who had more than one hundred dollars was considered wealthy) was taken over by the state.

The Communists made every effort to perfect their techniques of warfare. The regular Red armies were supplemented by a mobilized reserve of young farmers and by the local militia. Soldiers were taught to sing, shout slogans, and practice war cries. Primarily they were taught to fight. "When the enemy advances, we retreat; when the enemy halts and encamps, we trouble him; when the enemy seeks to avoid battle, we attack; when the enemy retreats, we pursue." When the Red army entered a town, it looted the banks and public buildings. It plundered the grain stores and extorted as much money as it could from the members of the chambers of commerce. It usually treated the common people with great deference and tried to win their support and cooperation. Its rules of discipline called for exemplary behavior toward the masses: "Don't take a single needle or piece of thread without paying for it; don't hit or swear at people; don't take liberties with women; speak politely, pay fairly for what you buy, return everything you borrow and pay for anything you damage." For the substantial middle-class farmers and the wealthy, the Reds were a scourge; for the poor, the Communist regime represented a promise of less work and a brighter future. The details of ideology were meaningless.

Still, the Kuomintang could not afford to ignore the social ferment produced by Communist propaganda. The government was obliged to undertake an agrarian reform program of its own and to rival the Communists in matters of rural education, health, afforestation, cooperatives, rent reduction, and relief from the heavy burdens of debts. But it was more important to exterminate the Communist menace than to try to outdo it in social reform. In fighting against the Communists, the government faced baffling handicaps. More of the local people in Kiangsi seemed to favor the Communists than the Kuomintang. The morale of the Kuomintang troops left much to be desired. It was reported that their commanders could not give the soldiers more than five rounds of ammunition or the soldiers would sell the surplus. Money and propaganda flowed freely to get troops to switch sides; time out during the fighting often offered opportunities to barter salt, cigarettes, opium, and even rifles. For four years the Communists outmaneuvered the best Kuomintang generals, but they succumbed eventually to a combination of superior military force and an economic blockade.

As the noose of the Kuomintang tightened about the Soviet republic in Kiangsi, the party leadership undertook the desperate "Long March" from South and Central China to the northwest. After more than a year and six thousand miles across mountain passes, rivers, and grasslands; after fighting against half the armies of Chiang Kai-shek and the local warlords of a half-dozen provinces—the Communists reached Yenan, northern Shensi, in October, 1935, and established their base in that part of China closest to the Soviet Union. During this period, Mao Tse-tung rose to a position of undisputed command within the party. He overruled unrealistic theoreticians from Moscow and overcame his personal rivals for power. Mao asserted his leadership in the civil war against the government of Chiang Kai-shek, and at the same time he strengthened the position of the Communists in international affairs.

From the moment of the Mukden Incident, the Communists referred to that event as a "warning signal for the world proletariat, the harbinger of a second world war—of a war against the Soviet Union." They accused

Chiang of groveling before Japan in a most shameful manner, and in their haven in the hills in Kiangsi they adopted a strong platform in foreign policy. They called for the overthrow of imperialism in China and for the formation of a united revolutionary front with the world proletariat and all oppressed nations. After the Japanese attack on Shanghai in 1932, the Chinese Communists declared war on Japan. They called upon the masses of the Chinese people to join them, and they offered to enter a fighting alliance with any army or body of troops against the Japanese invasion and against the treachery and sabotage of the Kuomintang agents. The Communists assumed a bold stance in resistance to Japan.

While Chiang's government was bound by restrictions which flowed from responsibility for the conduct of foreign affairs, the Communists organized mass meetings and aroused the popular hatred of Japan. During the time the Communists played cat-and-mouse with the government armies, they agitated for a second united front. Their argument was that brothers should not fight one another while they were both endangered by a foreign enemy. After the Long March, they redoubled their efforts to end the civil war. They infected the bandit-suppression troops with their ideas, and they caused two of Chiang Kai-shek's own subordinates (Chang Hsüeh-liang and Yang Hu-cheng) to kidnap him at Sian at Christmastime in 1936. They held Chiang a prisoner for two weeks, and released him only when he agreed to call off the war against the Communists and to lead a united nation against Japan. The Communists could have put the generalissimo to death, but it was decreed (perhaps by Stalin himself) that Chiang would be more useful as a living symbol of his nation.

By 1936 the entire Chinese nation seemed to demand war against Japan. Opposition to Japan became synonymous with patriotism, and the dynamic sentiment reached beyond the treaty ports into the highways and byways of rural China. Chinese were keenly aware of the hardships and suffering which were in store; but they rallied behind such slogans as "Boycott Japanese Goods," "Recover the Lost Territories," "Wipe Out the National Disgrace," and "Fight Japan to Save China." In was in this atmosphere that the second united front was born. In February, 1937, the Chinese Communists (in keeping with Communist policies throughout the world) agreed to a truce with their immediate enemy in order to concentrate against fascist aggression as represented by Japan.

By the terms of the second united front, the Communists promised to abandon the policy of armed insurrection against the Kuomintang and to stop their program of land confiscation. They promised to give up their propaganda warfare and to strive for the realization of the three principles of Sun Yat-sen. They agreed to abolish their autonomous border governments and to place their armies under the command of Chiang Kai-shek.

On its part, the Kuomintang agreed to assume responsibility for the Communist armies, to assign them to particular areas of operation and to subsidize them to the approximate extent of a half million dollars per month. The Kuomintang also promised to call off the civil war, release political prisoners, and accept the Communist demands for civil liberties, land reform, and a constitution. On the surface it looked as if the Communists and the Kuomintang were ready to fight shoulder to shoulder in resisting the Japanese as the latter moved from Manchuria into the provinces of China proper.

WORLD REACTION TO JAPAN'S ADVANCE

China seemed tragically alone in standing up against its powerful neighbor except for the sympathy of friendly powers. From 1931 to 1937 the rest of the world was too preoccupied with economic woes, too divided in diplomatic attitudes, and too weak in terms of military armaments to think of a concerted stand against aggression. Within hours after the Mukden Incident, China appealed to the League of Nations to halt Japan. The League passed an ineffective resolution advising both sides to withdraw their troops. Japan objected to intervention by the League and pressed for direct negotiations with China. However, China refused to engage in bilateral negotiations as long as Japanese soldiers occupied Manchurian territory outside the railway zone. In November, 1931, the League decided to send a commission of enquiry under Lord Lytton to investigate the facts of the Sino-Japanese dispute.

While the League pursued its own course of action, Secretary of State Henry L. Stimson tried to generate more active opposition to Japan's aggression. Athough not a member of the League, the United States sent an observer to Geneva to indicate unity in spirit if not in action. Secretary Stimson urged Great Britain and other European nations to take a firm stand for the sake of peace. He appealed to both China and Japan for moderation. He framed his protests to Japan in terms of mildness in the hope that he would not embarrass Japanese liberals and play into the hands of the militarists. When his efforts for conciliatory measures failed, he addressed identical notes to Japan and China on January 7, 1932, which stated his policy of nonrecognition. These notes said:

> The American government cannot admit the legality of any situation de facto, nor does it intend to recognize any treaty or agreement entered into between those governments, or agents thereof, which may impair the treaty rights of the United States or its citizens in China, including those which relate to the sovereignty, the independence, or the territorial and administrative integrity of the Republic of China, or to the international policy relative to China,

commonly known as the Open Door policy; and that it does not intend to recognize any situation, treaty, or agreement which may be brought about by means contrary to the covenants and obligations of the Pact of Paris of August 27, 1928, to which Treaty both China and Japan, as well as the United States, are parties.

The United States had neither the intention nor the means to back the nonrecognition doctrine with force, and other nations—mindful of their obligations to the League—were not disposed to support the implied condemnation of Japan. They gave moral support to the United States just as the United States professed moral support for the League. After more than a year of study and investigation, the Lytton Commission submitted its report to the League which in effect failed to support the arguments of Japan. On February 24, 1933, the Assembly of the League shied away from sanctions or punitive measures against Japan but it adopted a resolution according to which the member states of the League pledged themselves not to recognize Manchukuo either *de jure* or *de facto*. Japan turned its back on the collective security system, and its delegate dramatically walked out of the League, never to return.

The question of Manchukuo faded into the background. Memories were short and convictions were hollow. One by one, El Salvador, Germany, Italy, Franco's Spain, and others accorded recognition to Manchukuo. The British sent a trade mission to Manchukuo, but its recommendations did not eventuate in recognition. The U.S.S.R. treated Manchukuo with all the formalities short of *de jure* recognition. The United States, Australia, and Canada carried on direct and indirect trade relations without surrendering their firm position against recognition. Chiang Kai-shek himself negotiated postal pacts, through-train arrangements, and telephone and telegraph agreements with Manchukuo. These accords testified to a tendency to forgive and forget, which might have become more prevalent had it not been for Japan's further surge into China.

Japan became increasingly intransigent in its international relations, and its actions in China together with those of Germany and Italy split the world into hostile camps. Japan blamed the Western powers for aiding Chiang Kai-shek and thus prolonging the "hellish agonies of war." On April 17, 1934, a spokesman for the Japanese foreign office, Amau Eiji, declared that Japan would object to any joint operations undertaken by foreign powers in China in the name of technical or financial assistance. Supplying China with warplanes, building airdromes in China, detailing military instructors or military advisers there, and contracting loans to provide China with funds for political uses would tend to disturb the peace in East Asia, and would therefore be opposed. The United States, Great Britain, Germany, and Italy had been doing things to which the Amau statement objected.

Japan looked upon opposition to its program as denying Japan's right to live. The United States in particular regarded Japan's program as illegal, unjust, and catastrophic. Japan's relations with the Western powers went from bad to worse because of trade rivalries, competition in merchant shipping, and arguments over the limitation of naval armaments. On December 28, 1934, Japan denounced the Washington Naval Treaty effective as of the end of 1936.

Japanese militarists conceived their mission in China to be to purge China—as Japan had purged itself—of liberalism, democracy, socialism, and communism as the "rotten fruits" of the West. Even Chiang Kai-shek was accused of being a pro-Communist, a participant in the united front against Japan. Japan wanted to eliminate all the poison in China, as represented by the Kuomintang and the Communists, and to enlist China in an "Asia for the Asiatics" campaign against the West. Asia should be governed by the ideology of Confucius based on the ancient virtues of loyalty, filial piety, benevolence, and propriety. Asia should be emancipated from the tyranny and highhandedness of the white people and the material civilization of the West should be rectified by the moral civilization of the East.

Japan talked of a holy war and considered itself above treaty-breaking. For Japan any means were justified in seeking the ends of righteousness, self-defense, and the accomplishment of a new order in Asia. Japan's bellicosity toward the powers seemed to fluctuate in rhythm with its program on the Asian mainland. When Japan seemed to make progress in China, its attitudes were adamant and hostile; when Japan was baffled, its diplomacy became more conciliatory. Japan discovered that its anti-Western or Pan-Asian campaign was impossible because of China's unwillingness to cooperate. Japan therefore stressed anticommunism as the motive for its aggression in China, but even this failed to attract Chiang Kai-shek. However this tactic gained the friendship and cooperation of Germany and Italy, pinpointed the hostility of Japan against the Soviet Union, and influenced the United States and Great Britain toward benevolent neutrality. On November 25, 1936, Japan and Hitler's Germany signed an anti-Comintern Pact which provided for a mutual exchange of information about Communist activities and discussion of cooperative measures to be taken in mutual defense against communism. A secret article provided that if either party were attacked without provocation or menaced by the Soviet Union the other would not carry out any measure which would in effect relieve the position of the Soviet Union. In such event both parties would immediately consult on measures to preserve their common interests.

The Japanese thrust into Manchuria seemed to presage a direct attack against the Soviet Union. In 1931 the Soviet Union was weak on its eastern flank, and was constrained to adopt a policy of accommodation to the advances of Japan. Stalin had no faith in the efficacy of collective security, and he chose not to cooperate with the League of Nations. He tried appeasement, offering the Japanese a nonaggression pact, which they spurned. Then he concentrated on building up his military forces in Siberia and directed a large part of the Second Five-Year plan toward the industrial development of his Far Eastern territories. He harbored no illusions about Japan's pretensions to arrest the spread of communism, and he appreciated the Japanese desire to weaken or destroy if possible the geographic base of Russian strength in Asia. In 1935 the Soviet Union concluded the sale of the Chinese Eastern Railway to Manchukuo. In 1936 it signed a defensive alliance with Outer Mongolia and announced for the particular benefit of Japan that it would fight for Outer Mongolia exactly the same as if Outer Mongolia were an integral part of Russian territory. With the adoption of the world-wide united front between communists and capitalists against Fascists, the Soviet Union repaired its diplomatic fences in Europe, the United States, and China.

Gradually the policy of strategic retreat was abandoned and Russian diplomats took a firmer stand against Japan. Disputes flared along the boundary areas of Manchukuo and arguments developed perenially between Japan and the U.S.S.R. over their respective fishing rights in the Sea of Okhotsk. Russians accused the Japanese of intriguing with White Russians to incite counterrevolution in Siberia, plotting to acquire the maritime provinces, and developing Manchukuo as a base for an attack on the U.S.S.R. itself. Japanese accused the Russians of giving aid to bandit forces in Manchukuo and to Chiang Kai-shek, of spreading the poison of communism, and militarizing Siberia to an alarming degree. Russian radio stations at Khabarovsk and Vladivostok carried on a relentless battle of the air waves with Japanese stations in Mukden, Dairen, and Hsinking.

Each side was convinced of the justice and necessity of its own case and of the menace to its own existence in the acts of the enemy. Either nation had ample opportunity and excuse to start a war against the other had it been inclined to take the risk. Neither believed the local conflicts sufficiently vital to justify all-out hostilities. Russia believed that Japan conspired to wage aggressive war but preferred to postpone a showdown. Time was on its side. Japan could not seem to make up its mind whether to move against the Soviet Union, plunge deeper into China, or perhaps play for its greatest stakes against the United States and Great Britain in the southern regions.

Japan might have come to terms with Great Britain and the United States at almost any time between 1931 and 1937 had it so desired. Great Britain had no cause to be happy with chaotic China and its anti-imperialism. The British, with their emphasis on trade and investments, sympathized with the aspirations of Japan. Everybody would profit if the Japanese were successful in their objective of bringing peace and stability to East Asia. However, the British had their deep-seated differences with the Japanese. Japan cut deeply into Britain's textile trade, menaced its naval supremacy, and threatened to oust its firms from the China market. Most of all, the British were worried about Hitler in Europe. They dreaded the growing cooperation between Germany and Japan, and they hoped for the continuation and strengthening of the League of Nations and the system of collective security.

Japan was certain to encounter stiffer opposition from the United States than from Great Britain. The succession of President Franklin D. Roosevelt and the Democrats after the election of 1932 made no appreciable difference in American policy. China was the traditional friend of the United States in East Asia, and the United States was disposed to help its friend. American companies helped to develop China's commercial aviation and American fliers helped to train Chinese pilots and crews. Loans and advice were made available. But a modest amount of assistance to China was insufficient to cope with the serious situation which arose when Japan and Germany united in what President Roosevelt called an "attempt at world conquest unparalleled alike in boldness of conception and in brutality of operation." The United States was slow to react to the magnitude of Japan's challenge in Asia. Americans were deeply involved in the New Deal and more concerned about isolation and neutrality than they were in opposing the aggressors. Furthermore, Hitler seemed much more menacing than the government of Japan, although Ambassador Grew reported from Tokyo that the Japanese military machine was built for war, felt prepared for war, and would welcome war. He warned of Japan's swashbuckling mood and advised the United States to make itself strong. He said that a situation of strength was the only cold fact that the militaristic chauvinists of Japan could understand. Neither warnings nor countermeasures were sufficient to stop the Japanese as they went ahead with their plans.

SUGGESTED READING

Bassett, Reginald, *Democracy and Foreign Policy, A Case History, the Sino-Japanese Dispute, 1931–1933* (New York, Longmans, 1952).

Bertram, James, *First Act in China* (New York, Viking, 1938).

Hsiao, Tso-liang, *Power Relations within the Chinese Communist Movement, 1930–1934* (Seattle, U. of Washington, 1961).

Hudson, Manley O., (ed.), *Verdict of the League: China and Japan in Manchuria* (Boston, World Peace Foundation, 1933).

International Military Tribunal for the Far East, *Judgment* (Washington, D.C., Department of the Army, November, 1948).

Jones, F. C., *Manchuria Since 1931* (London, Royal Institute of International Affairs, 1949).

Kawakami, K. K., *Manchoukuo, Child of Conflict* (New York, Macmillan, 1933).

League of Nations *Report of the Commission of Inquiry and Supplementary Documents* (Geneva, The League, 1932).

MacNair, Harley F., *Real Conflict Between China and Japan* (Chicago, U. of Chicago, 1938).

Presseisen, Ernest L., *Germany and Japan: A Study in Totalitarian Diplomacy, 1933–1941* (The Hague, Martinus Nijhoff, 1958).

Smith, Sara M., *Manchurian Crisis 1931–1932* (New York, Columbia U., 1948).

Snow, Edgar, *Red Star over China* (New York, Grove, 1944). (P)

Wales, Nym, *Red Dust* (Stanford, Stanford U., 1952).

Wang, Ching-chun, *Japan's Continental Adventure* (London, George Allen & Unwin, 1940).

Willoughby, Westel W., *Sino-Japanese Controversy and the League of Nations* (Baltimore, Johns Hopkins U., 1935).

Yakhontoff, Victor A., *Chinese Soviets* (New York, Coward, 1934).

Yoshihashi, Takehiko, *Conspiracy at Mukden* (New Haven, Yale U., 1963).

19

Undeclared War in China

Internal conditions in Japan, frustration on the Asian mainland and the international political atmosphere in 1937 combined to push Japan faster and further along the road to war. While Hitler and Mussolini commanded most of the world's attention with their behavior in Europe, Japan's militarists relentlessly pursued their aggressive policies in Asia. When Manchukuo failed to produce the paradise which it promised, the control of China looked more important than ever to Japan in the fulfillment of its self-imposed mission in Asia.

Japan was baffled because it could neither force nor attract China toward its way of thinking. As the troops of Japan spread throughout North China, they had little difficulty in winning military victories. However, they failed to win Chinese political cooperation, and they could not find a magic way to make their conquests pay economic dividends. The more pressure the Japanese applied, the greater resistance they encountered. Special service officers tried to bribe or cajole Chinese warlords into cooperation or declarations of autonomy.

Japan sought unsuccessfully to create regimes in North China which would duplicate the power of Manchukuo, but which would avoid the irritating features of blatant puppetry. Japanese diplomats presented Chinese officials with a constant stream of political and economic demands which the Chinese managed to evade or oppose. At the national level, the two governments settled their immediate differences peaceably if not amicably.

At the local level, tempers blazed. The Japanese military in China behaved with an arrogance usually associated with an alien conqueror. Chinese (and foreigners) were ordered about with complete disregard for legality or decency. In retaliation Kuomintang party workers did all they could to inflame public opinion and to organize secret boycotts against

Japan. Where Chinese were helpless to defend themselves against the strong Japanese soldiers, they vented their anger on hapless Japanese civilians. In 1936 bloody attacks on Japanese nationals took place in such widely separated places as Chengtu, Canton, Hankow, Shanghai, Swatow, Taiyuan, and the outskirts of Peiping. Any future looked bleak for the Japanese in China, short of the assertion of overwhelming force.

The formation of the united front between the Kuomintang and the Communists at the end of 1936 promised to unify China to resist the further encroachments of Japan; it also increased Japan's sense of urgency. Japan felt that it would have to act in China *at that moment* or it might forever be too late. From 1937 to 1941, Japan and China engaged in a contest of wills, variously called the Sino-Japanese Controversy or the Sino-Japanese Incident. Japan invaded China, blockaded the coast, and showered bombs on China's defenseless cities. It was four years of war in everything but name.

INSIDE JAPAN

Japan's primary move was to place itself on a practical war footing. Prince Konoye, a man without rigid ideas of his own, but with prestige because of his distinguished family, became premier. Hirota took over the ministry of foreign affairs. The new cabinet established an inner circle or advisory council, a planning board for the integration of economic policies, and an imperial headquarters for centralized direction of the army and navy. In accordance with Japanese tradition, the real decision makers in the military services remained behind the scenes. Scarcely any one in the Western world even heard of General Tojo in 1937.

Economic mobilization was carried forward in a thoroughgoing manner. The diet passed in 1937 an emergency capital adjustment law which was intended to channel all available funds into necessary industries. The next year the national general mobilization law practically put Japan on a wartime economic footing. Each industry was authorized to take care of its own production, materials, labor, capital, prices, and markets, subject to the strict control of the state. By subsidies, licenses, quotas, protective tariffs, or tax concessions strategic industries were fostered; smaller or nonessential enterprises were either squeezed out of existence or forced to merge. Priorities were given to munitions, aircraft, automobile, engineering, machine tool, iron and steel, liquid fuel, coal, nonferrous metals, shipbuilding, electric power, and railway equipment industries because of their obvious military value. In 1941 a key industries control ordinance set up series of "control associations." A control association was held responsible for all activities within its own industry. It was subject to the supervision of the planning board, which was in turn under the thumb of the military.

Government control of finance was as tight as the control of production. The flow of money and credit from banks to industries was determined by the nation's strategic needs, and the money market was kept in bounds by taxes and forced savings. The control of foreign exchange was absolute. Imports were prohibited, or permitted only if "linked" to specific exports. As in any inflationary situation, Japan seemed to be prosperous. Jobs were plentiful and yen were abundant. Beneath the apparent prosperity was the dearth of consumers' goods, the prohibitive level of prices, and the pouring of the products of Japan's booming factories into the insatiable maw of the war machine. Not one-third of Japan's production was being used in China; more than two-thirds was being stock-piled for later adventures.

While the Japanese should have been enjoying prosperity, they were instead subjected to onerous restrictions and fantastic propaganda. In May, 1938, General Araki Sadao became minister of education and ordered revision of textbooks and improvement of the curriculum. Military training was expanded to include drills, marches, and handling of weapons for everybody. History, civics, geography, and ethics were made to contribute to aggressive militarism. Schools and universities were dedicated to indoctrination of the idea that Japan was on the way to fulfillment of its destiny in Asia.

All the media of mass communications were given over to ultranationalistic propaganda. Foreign motion pictures were excluded, and Japanese productions were designed to move their audiences to anger and hate. War in the films was shown as glorious, not sad; Japan was always portrayed as a righteous nation struggling for its life, never an aggressor. The Japan Broadcasting Company made the radio an extremely effective instrument in whipping up patriotic spirit. Newspapers were censored and editorials were supervised. Foreign language newspapers were forced out of business or reduced to inanity. All government publicity handouts were screened by a board of information, whose president was given cabinet status. Any writer who submitted an article with an overtone of peace was sure to receive a visit from the police. If public meetings were held, the police had to be there; if public addresses were to be made, copies had to be submitted to the police and approved in advance. The ministry of interior had a national thought and activities headquarters which was responsible for thought control and for repression of subversive ideas.

Foreigners in Japan experienced difficult times. Businessmen saw their enterprises ruined by Japan's economic nationalism. Missionaries were hurt to see their churches diverted to political ends and their schools nationalized. Individuals were subjected to the most meticulous scrutiny

by the local police. As a group, foreigners were blamed for Japan's fri-
volities. The militarists called for a return to native purity and the elimination of the evils of the West. The pendulum went into reverse: the previous rush to copy the West gave way to an unreasoned frenzy to rid
Japan of every association with the West.

The heavy hand of totalitarianism crushed the tender seeds of individual freedom which had struggled to show signs of life in Japan. In the
villages the neighborhood associations watched over the activities of every
family and forced them into conformity or silence. In the cities the *mogas*
and the *mobos*, the modern girls and modern boys, were forbidden to have
their parties and discussion groups and were pushed into the grim business of preparing for war. Tokyo walked with heavy tread and talked with
frightened voice. In 1941, before Pearl Harbor, the peace preservation law
was tightened. A national defense security law, military secrets protection
law, and defense resources secrets protection law were placed on the
statute books. Only in silence were there safety---unless the occasion was
a patriotic mass meeting, the dedication of a new factory, or the departure
of another troop train heading ominously toward the China front.

The conviction grew that political parties based on liberalism, democracy, and socialism were not appropriate for the Japanese nation.
Patriotic organizations like the Black Dragon Society or the Cherry Blossom Society talked more and more of Japan's divine mission. The Ex-
servicemen's Association and the Imperial League of Young Officers became the liveliest spokesmen for the doctrine that the military were the
purest interpreters of the imperial will. In 1940 all political parties, labor
unions, and associations of whatever sort were abolished. They were
gathered up into a huge Imperial Rule Assistance Association dedicated
to the service of the emperor. The entire country was groomed to "move
as a cannonball of fiery resolution."

JAPAN IN CHINA

Japan was haunted by its fears of population pressure, political discrimination, and economic inequity, and determined to take whatever
action seemed to be required for self-defense. It would strike out—toward
Siberia, deeper into China, or in the direction of the South Seas—wherever the opposition seemed weakest. China was the initial target.

On the night of July 7, 1937, the Japanese troops while on night
maneuvers at Lukouchiao (Marco Polo Bridge) near Peiping, reported
the disappearance of a soldier. While the Japanese searched for the missing soldier, firing broke out between the Japanese and local Chinese
troops. Reinforcements were rushed in and war clouds hung low. The

Chinese were jumpy and in a mood to shoot any Japanese on sight; the Japanese were tactless but firm in the conviction that they were embarked upon a mission of righteousness. The missing soldier was found and the firing died away, but Japan poured thousands of troops into north China by land, sea, and air from Manchukuo, Korea, and Japan itself.

The Japanese ambassador in Nanking gave Chiang Kai-shek a new list of demands. Chiang continued to procrastinate, but his followers became more restive. In spite of his awareness of China's weakness, he stiffened his posture against Japan. In the summer of 1937, Chiang attained magnificent stature as the leader of his people and the symbol of Chinese nationalism. He called publicly for the last ounce of strength in the struggle for existence. He gave his opinion that surrender to Japan in North China would be an "unpardonable sin against our race." He asked, "If Peiping could become a second Mukden, what is there to prevent Nanking from becoming a second Peiping?" He realized that hostilities would demand sacrifices and he declared, "We will trade space for time—once the fighting begins, we will never surrender." Through his foreign office, Chiang notified the world that "if actual hostilities break out between Japan and China in North China, they will spread until they encompass the whole of China." His spokesman warned, "It will not be just a case of some soldiers in the north fighting against certain Japanese troops, but it will be a case of the Chinese nation against the Japanese nation. Trouble will surely arise in Kwangtung, Fukien and the Yangtze Valley, but everywhere it will receive the attention of the Chinese forces."

China insisted upon the diplomatic negotiations at the national level for the settlement of disputes, but Japan preferred to carry on discussions between military commanders in the locality where disagreements occurred. Argument continued and incidents in the Peiping area multiplied. Large-scale fighting broke out in Tientsin and Peiping and the Japanese commanding general in North China declared that the time had come to "beat China to its knees so that it may no longer have the spirit to fight." On August 8, he took over Peiping and set up a military government there.

Hostilities also took place in Shanghai. Trivial incidents provoked large-scale action. On August 13 a Japanese landing party was fired upon, and the entire delta area of the Yangtze River became the scene of heavy fighting. The Japanese cabinet issued a statement, condemning Chiang Kai-shek for arousing public opinion and treating Japan with contempt. Japan declared that Chiang, overconscious of his power and in league with the Communists, increasingly adopted an insulting and arrogant attitude toward Japan. Therefore it became imperative for Japan to take drastic measures to chastise the lawless Chinese. Japan expressed its determination to eradicate antiforeignism and anti-Japanism and to bring about true harmony between Japan, Manchukuo, and China. Japan said that it harbored no ill will toward China's masses and no designs against Chinese territory. It gave assurances that it would spare no efforts to safeguard foreign rights and interests in China.

China again appealed to the League of Nations, and the League stated flatly that the military operations by Japan were out of all proportion to the incident that occasioned the conflict. At an international conference at Brussels under the auspices of the League in November 1937, the member nations pronounced Japan the aggressor in the conflict and promised to refrain from any action which would weaken China's power to resist. Again the goodwill of the League—and the United States—were powerless against the sweep of Japan through China.

By the end of 1937, Japanese armies spread throughout North and Central China. The capitals of Chahar, Hopei, Suiyuan, Shansi, Chekiang, and the capital of China itself fell to invading forces. Japan continued to treat its campaign in China as an "incident," not a "war," and repeated that its purpose was not to occupy territory, but to annihilate, smash, and kill all Chinese national armies. General Matsui, commander of the Shanghai expeditionary force, stated that the mission of his troops was to fulfill all its duties of protecting Japanese residents and interests, and to chastise the Nanking government and the outrageous Chinese. When he entered Nanking in triumph, he ordered special studies to be made so as to dazzle China with Japan's military glory. For six weeks after December 17, 1937, the Japanese army dazed the world with one of history's most brutal orgies of robbing, raping, looting, burning, and shooting. The American vice-consul reported, "It would seem that the soldiers were let loose like a barbarian horde to desecrate the city." From elsewhere in China came stories of the water treatment, electric shocks, cigarette burning, and worse, which cast grave shadows over Japan's pretensions for a new order.

Chiang moved his government first to Hankow and then to Chungking, deep in the heart of China's interior. As the Chinese soldiers retreated, they made many gallant but futile stands against the Japanese. Millions died and tens of millions lost their homes. The Chinese preferred to scorch their good earth rather than surrender it to the hated enemy. The Chinese grew grimmer in their determination to fight to the end. Chiang became more and more the symbol of resistance and he issued blast after blast against Japan. He defied the invaders to come into his new capital—Chungking, in free China—to dislodge him.

In 1938, the year of Munich, Japanese forces reached as far as Hankow and Canton. It was not a dress-parade penetration. Chinese guerrillas harassed the Japanese regulars and taught the Japanese that they could conquer the country on horseback, but they could not rule it on horseback. The Japanese controlled the major cities, the coast and the routes of communication, but they had neither the ability nor the manpower to take over the villages and the farm lands. When it became clear that Japan could make no further headway against Chiang Kai-shek, the Japanese government announced that in the future it would ignore Chiang and cooperate only with those Chinese who shared Japanese ideals and aspirations. Japan then pushed on to Hainan Island and to Nanchang, the capital of Kiangsi. In 1939 the Japanese took Nanning, the capital of Kwangsi, and this marked the extremes of their advance until the later stages of World War II. As definitive military victory eluded them, the Japanese devised political and economic stratagems which would bring at least partial rewards for their costly conquest in China.

OCCUPIED CHINA: WANG CHING-WEI

The Japanese invasion divided all China into three parts. The first part, or occupied China, consisted of the cities, towns, and communications routes which lay east of an approximate line extending from Peiping through Hankow to Canton. The second part, or free China, was identified with Chungking and Chiang Kai-shek, and it lay to the west. The third China was the vast hinterland, which contained hundreds of millions of wretched, poverty-stricken people who were the victims sacrificed to the gods of war. It was in the vast stretches of this no man's land that the Communists gained the experience which was later to bring them victory in civil war and put them in control of the entire country.

Just as political manipulations accompanied the military adventure in Manchukuo, so politics went hand in hand with the military advance in China. When the Japanese commander set up the military government in Peiping on August 8, 1937, he threatened with death any Chinese who would defy its orders. Japanese forces created peace maintenance organizations in various localities in North China, and the Japanese high command brought an elderly Chinese ex-official, Wang K'eh-min, from Hong Kong to Peiping by way of Japan to head up a provisional government. This government was inaugurated on December 14, 1937, and was a carbon copy of the puppet creation in Manchukuo.

On March 28, 1938, a renovation government was formally set up in Central China. It was also staffed by puppets and supported by local peace maintenance committees in Shanghai, Nanking, and Hangchow. The residual influence of Chiang Kai-shek in Central China was sufficiently strong to make it difficult for the Japanese to find Chinese of stature who would cooperate openly with them. The Japanese army and its special service sections were obliged to maintain a great degree of control and accept overt responsibility for the renovation government.

The Japanese also created in northwest China an autonomous federation of Mengchiang (Mongolia and Sinkiang) with the Mongolian Prince Teh at its head. Chahar, Suiyuan, and Shansi were organized as separate local governments under the federation, but none of these organizations became effective realities because of military necessities. The Japanese had to devote their energies to fighting the guerrillas, particularly the Communists.

The government in Tokyo effected coordination of its assorted Chinese puppets through the *Ko-a In,* or China Affairs Board. The board was directly under the prime minister and was in charge of all politics, economics, cultural activities, and administrative affairs in China conducted by any Japanese government agency. The board maintained its own branch offices throughout China and worked closely with the Japanese army and the Chinese collaborators.

All Japanese efforts to form a respectable political façade in China came to nothing until Wang Ching-wei, vice-chairman of the Kuomintang and vice-chairman of the National Defense Council—second only to Chiang Kai-shek—left Chungking and cast in his lot with the Japanese. Wang was a proved patriot, a respected revolutionist, and one of the most brilliant of the Chinese intellectuals. He was convinced that China could not win a war against the Japanese and that cooperation was the only alternative to disaster. He was not an overly ambitious man; he would have been satisfied to continue as a follower of Chiang Kai-shek, if Chiang had been willing to negotiate with the Japanese. Wang hated the Communists and the idea of a united front, even against a common enemy. He felt that "cooperation with communists would be tantamount to drinking poison to quench one's thirst." He believed that if Chiang were to exhaust himself in fighting the Japanese, the country would fall to the Communists. Some of the best-known Kuomintang leaders shared Wang's views and joined up with him in his puppet organization.

Wang's opponents called him a thoroughly selfish and incompetent traitor. Chiang Kai-shek labeled Wang's government "a government of slaves of utter moral depravity and an insult to the will of the Chinese people." The Japanese hailed Wang as a "harbinger of spring, like daffodils which comes before the swallow dares."

After secret meetings between Wang's friends and Japanese agents, Wang was spirited away from Chungking to Indochina and to Shanghai. On December 22, 1938, Wang announced that he would lead the Chinese in coming to terms with the Japanese. Some Japanese, even at this late date, hesitated to accept Wang except as a last resort. They would have preferred a China federation including Chungking, if only Chiang would give up his anti-Japanese and pro-Communist policies. Chiang was under constant pressure to surrender.

Japan was obliged to hesitate, and to vacillate in its attitudes toward China during 1939 because of the general international situation. Within a period of four months, between the end of August 1939 (when Hitler and Stalin signed a nonaggression pact) and the middle of January 1940, Japan suffered two cabinet changes which were motivated more by events in Europe than in China. Even before the startling victories of its German ally in the Low Countries in the spring of 1940, Japan decided to go ahead with its formation of a new national government of China under Wang Ching-wei. On March 30, 1940, the new government was inaugurated at Nanking, the capital of occupied China and was recognized by Japan as the legitimate successor to the stubborn Chiang Kai-shek.

The other puppet governments were not abolished but were made subordinate to the new regime. Perhaps the Japanese army units which manipulated their own local marionettes in Peiping and elsewhere were not willing to surrender their creatures to their own colleagues in central China. Local Japanese commanders retrained responsibility for peace and order in their particular theaters of operation. They sought out local Chinese who would join the peace maintenance committees or serve in the model peace zones. Special Service officers acted in a permanent liaison capacity in every city ward and county seat and saw to it that the Chinese carried out the ordinary government functions of conscription, tax collection, and local administration. The Japanese did not have the manpower to extend their control into China's countless villages or boundless countryside. Wherever and whenever the Japanese army advanced, they took the authority of Japan temporarily with them. When the Japanese withdrew from any locality, the power of Japan went along with the troops.

Wang Ching-wei in Nanking, like the emperor of Manchukuo in Hsinking, was surrounded with Japanese advisers and given the protection and guidance of the Japanese army. The government in Tokyo then spelled out its basic policies toward its newest puppet in a basic treaty and associated documents which were signed in Nanking on November 30, 1940. The treaty pledged amity and economic cooperation between China and Japan and joint defense against communism. It granted Japan the right to station troops, naval units, and warships in China until two years after the return of peace and stability. One additional secret agreement pledged the two countries to concerted action in diplomacy and obligated China to comply with Japan's demands regarding railways, communications, and waterways in areas where Japanese troops were stationed. A second secret agreement gave Japan wide latitude in naval operations in Chinese waters and laid down nominally favorable conditions for joint development of China's resources. In a separate letter, Wang promised that as long as Japan carried on military operations in China, his government would cooperate toward the full attainment of Japan's war purposes.

The long-range effect of this treaty was that Japan gave up its imperialist privileges in China. Extraterritoriality, tariff control, and territorial concessions in Chinese cities and spheres of influence were thrown into the scrap heap of history. The joker was that the gesture for the abolition of imperialist privileges was replaced by a situation infinitely more sinister for China's future. Japan threatened to reduce all China to a condition of utter colonialism. On the same day the agreement between Japan and Wang Ching-wei's China were concluded, the governments of Japan, Manchukuo, and China (occupied China) issued a joint declaration providing for mutual respect of each other's sovereignty and territory, general cooperation as good neighbors, common defense against Communist activities, and economic cooperation.

Japan's techniques of aggression were economic and social as well as military and political. Japan expected that its conquests would bring jobs and profits and looked to China for greater economic returns than had been gained from Manchukuo. Japanese businessmen, in the wake of the army, worked out trade agreements with Chinese merchants and pushed the ordinary channels of trade to the limits. The Japanese used "official" methods to augment their profits. They condoned tax evasion and smuggling, and they diverted revenues from the constituted Chinese authorities or the maritime customs to their puppet regimes.

Economically, the war shattered the basis of China's prosperity. In Shanghai alone, Chinese losses included five-sevenths of their cotton mills, five-sixths of their rubber factories, three-fourths of their silk filatures, one-half of their establishments for flour, tobacco, lumber, soap, paper, cement, and vegetable oils. Factories and machines were destroyed or looted. Thousands upon thousands of laborers were thrown out of work. International trade was stopped except that which contributed to the needs of the Japanese army in China. Other coast cities, railways, highways, and industries were crippled because of the ravages of war. Millions of Chinese were deprived of every means of subsistence. Banking and commercial life were stifled and agriculture became a hand-to-mouth occupation. Nepotism, corruption, rack rent, usury, and bribery bedeviled the lives of the miserable masses.

These conditions also plagued the ambitious Japanese militarists. How could conquests bring profits when they produced such misery? Furthermore the old established Japanese companies in China—Mitsui, Mitsubishi, and the Yokohama Specie Bank—resented the loss of their traditional markets and distrusted the military's interference in their regular business. They cautioned against the reckless overinvestment of Japanese resources in China which dissipated Japan's material wealth and brought nothing but paper profits and inflated egos. They warned that soldiers were not workers and that the costs of military campaigns coupled with the loss of China's goodwill would lead to disaster.

Their advice was wasted on policy makers who believed that a Japan-China-Manchukuo economic bloc would form the basis of a Greater East Asia Co-Prosperity Sphere. The official program was to make the Japanese empire a self-sufficient unit in coal, iron, cotton, timber, tin, tungsten, and vegetable oils, with exportable surpluses to exchange for petroleum, wool, rubber, bauxite, potash, and steel alloys. According to the proposed co-operation between Japan and its satellites, Japan would make all the decisions with regard to industrial activity, labor, finance, banking, exchange, communications, and transport. In Northeast Asia, fullest use would be made of a combination of the know-how of Japan, the water power of Korea, the resources of Manchukuo, and the manpower of China.

The China Affairs Board planned to develop China as a contributor, not a competitor, to Japan's national economy. In April 1938 two national policy companies were created: the North China Development Company and the Central China Promotion Company. These were giant holding companies to supervise a multitude of subsidiary operating companies in their respective areas. In North China, subsidiaries were formed for communications, telephones and telegraphs, aviation, iron mines, coal mines, and salt production. In Central China, companies were organized for mining, municipal utilities, and sericulture. But because of the terrible local conditions, the Japanese economic program in China never got off the ground. The Chinese saw through the hypocrisy of joint companies, where they provided the work and the Japanese took the profits. In spite of Japan's best efforts, all economic activity in China became bogged down in a morass of inflation, black marketing, and general insecurity.

Japan's social policies in China were equally unsuccessful. With all its propaganda, Japan convinced few Chinese of its sincerity or good intentions. The Japanese created a *Hsin Min Hui*, or New People's Society, as the only recognized political party. It organized popular demonstrations, conducted mass meetings, and victory parades, but never won the loyalties of significant numbers of Chinese. Some Japanese were accused of undermining the foundations of Chinese mores by acting as the worst breed of gangsters, kidnapers, girl-snatchers, drug peddlers, and carpetbaggers. A sad Chinese victim of the Japanese lamented: "They created a desert and they called it peace."

Japan ascribed a large measure of its patent failures in occupied China to the existence of the foreign concessions and settlements in the large cities and port areas. Japan intimated that with the abandonment of its own unequal privileges in the treaty with Wang Ching-wei, it would expect the other powers to follow suit. At times, the Japanese practically ignored the special status, for example, of the International Settlement in Shanghai. They landed their troops in the international area, marched their men through its streets on the way to battle, and even destroyed large amounts of property in the actual fighting. Japanese military authorities interfered constantly in the work of the police. They accused foreigners of offering anti-Japanese elements a privileged sanctuary for intrigue and espionage. Foreign newspapers published in China were the most bitter critics of Japan's new order. Japan became increasingly baffled and infuriated as it tried in vain to use its Chinese puppets to undermine the settlements and concessions. The powers gave in to Japanese and puppet demands when they had no alternative to the use of force. However, they lodged protests to keep their legal position clear and they brought in as many army reenforcements as their embarrassments in the rest of the world permitted.

FREE CHINA: CHIANG KAI-SHEK

Wang Ching-wei was the symbol of collaboration with Japan; Chiang Kai-shek was the soul of resistance. After he decided to fight in 1937, he never wavered. For three bloody months in the Yangtze Delta, he hurled Chinese bodies against Japanese steel. All his plans for modernization and nationalization were consumed in enemy flames. His best troops were slaughtered and his capital ravaged.

After the rape of Nanking, the Chinese conducted a fantastic mass migration to the west. The rich bought airplane or boat tickets to Hankow, the poor traveled by junks or walked. They salvaged only what they could carry with them. Students left the universities, and coolies dragged heavy machines through swamps and over mountains hundreds of miles into the interior. The sick and wounded died on the way. Government officials burned their files, took only their brains and their problems with them, and in early 1938 set up shop in Hankow. Kuomintang generals who survived the Japanese holocaust made pathetic efforts to keep their remnants intact. Some set up temporary headquarters in inaccessible areas; others clustered about Chiang Kai-shek in his new and temporary capital. Ordinary soldiers sold their guns, hid them or threw them away, and disappeared among their fellow countrymen in the chaotic countryside. Millions of refugees stumbled aimlessly toward the setting sun, with no emotion save to curse the Japanese and no hope except to survive.

Chiang Kai-shek was given only a brief respite in Hankow. Japanese re-enforcements pushed relentlessly forward in spite of scorched earth, breached dikes, and one magnificent military victory which will forever in Chinese history be associated with the tiny village of Taiehrchwang. In order to establish a broader basis for his government, Chiang organized a people's political council of some two hundred leaders which adopted a program of resistance and rehabilitation as its bible for the war against Japan. Then the generalissimo divided China into nine war areas, but unfortunately he was obliged to place eight out of the nine under commanders who had either fought or offered to fight against him in the course of his checkered career. To show his faith in the united front with the Communists, he permitted Communist members in the people's political council and in the high military command. He continued to pay the agreed-upon subsidies to the Eighth Route Army (Communist) in Shensi, and he ordered the formation of a new Fourth Army in South China which was to be made up of the Communists who had been left behind at the time of the Long March. Both Communist armies were ostensibly under the ultimate command of Nationalist generals.

Hankow fell to the Japanese on October 25, 1938. Free China moved to Chungking. The roads were longer, and the trails more steep. The Yangtze was no longer the quiet waters of the delta; it was a dragon which roared through the gorges. The new capital on its banks tossed with the fever of war. Housing was inadequate or nonexistent, as hundreds of thousands of refugees straggled into the flimsy haven of shelter. Food was scarce and drinking water had to be paid for, even for tea. Sanitation was primitive, and disease was endemic. Not enough goods were to be had for the barest necessities of life. Chungking was a city of misery, but it was a psychological experience. It was the heart of free China.

It was immune from Japanese attack by land or river, but it was battered by incessant bombing attacks. Because the city was without air defense, the Japanese bombers could fly low and kill mercilessly. Thousands of Chinese perished. The Japanese took the lives of the Chinese people, but they created the Chinese nation. They could not bend its will or destroy its spirit.

Chiang organized the most effective government he could in the midst of circumstances which would have thwarted a lesser leader. It was not democratic; perhaps it was less democratic than it might have been. His object was not to create a viable democracy; it was to conduct a viable government. Chiang was obliged to deal with unsympathetic elements in Chungking—those who sided more than he with Communists or with the Wang Ching-wei puppets—and with quarreling cliques in his own party. The Kuomintang was plagued with factions—old revolutionaries like the two brothers Chen Kuo-fu and Chen Li-fu who made up the "C.C." clique; Whampoa graduates like the militarists Hu Tsung-nan and Ho Ying-chin; moderates like Sun Fo, the son of Sun Yat-sen; modern "capitalists" like T. V. Soong and his brother-in-law H. H. Kung; and political radicals who led such extremist organizations as the Blue

Shirts or the San Min Chu I youth corps. Elections were impossible, and Chiang felt that he had no alternative to government by political tutelage, as the exclusive prerogative of his own party. This was in accordance with Dr. Sun Yat-sen's program for the Kuomintang.

Chiang held dozens of positions. He was responsible for every phase of the fighting against Japan, and his jobs were impossible. He had no economic resources. He could not provide food for his people, let alone build an industry which could sustain a national war effort. He was not allowed to create wealth; he was forced to destroy China's existing assets to keep them out of the hands of the Japanese. He was practically isolated from the rest of the world. The only routes to Chungking were over the hump or along the hazardous mountain road from Burma; the long desert road from the Soviet Union by way of China's northwest; the railroad from Indochina to Kunming and thence by a rickety bus over a bumpy interior highway; or by air from Hong Kong. Chungking was also in constant touch with the Chinese coastal cities through one of the most fantastic smuggling rings in history. It was masterminded by General Tai Li, the cloak-and-dagger specialist on the staff of Chiang Kai-shek; it operated through lines which were manned by puppets, Communists or the Japanese themselves. The Chinese conducted a regular mail service between occupied China and free China all through the fighting.

Chiang's army was a mixed bag. He lost his best, modern-trained units at Shanghai. Many of the old warlords, often in desperation, turned their troops over to him. Liu Hsiang in Szechwan, Han Fu-chu in Shantung, sundry Kwangsi warlords, Sheng Shih-tsai in Sinkiang, and Lung Yun in Yunnan were among those who pledged cooperation with the Kuomintang. Their loyalty was not an unmitigated blessing. Their soldiers were of doubtful quality, and they would expect rations, supplies, and pay from the generalissimo. They could not be grouped in any scientific way to mount a counteroffensive. Chiang's practical procedure was to recognize each heretofore independent army as a unit of the nationalist army and to authorize each one to act in his own locality in the name of the regular army of free China. The Kuomintang had no facilities for training; it had no supply lines or medical service.

The record of each outfit which wore a Kuomintang uniform or protested loyalty to the Kuomintang depended upon local conditions and not upon orders from Chungking. Some commanders fought heroically, others surrendered. Some treated the peasants with consideration, others were brutes. Soldiers were forced to live off the land and to fend for themselves in search of food and shelter. In any district where an army was stationed, it was the army which collected the taxes and enforced law and order. Chiang Kai-shek could not possibly have been held accountable for the behavior of units with whom he could scarcely communicate. Chungking, with its wartime singleness of purpose, was a vastly different place from the free China of the interior where chaos and the survival of the fittest were the order of the day.

COMMUNIST CHINA: MAO TSE-TUNG

Mao Tse-tung came to personify Communist China in the same way than Chiang Kai-shek was identified with free China. When Mao and his ragged band of Communists arrived in Shensi, they were received as a band of adventurers with a strange ideology and with few interests in common with the poor farmers and mountaineers of China's northwest. Those ideas were changed as the Communist presence attracted the opposition of the local warlords, Chang Hsüeh-liang's displaced Manchurian forces, and the armies of Chiang Kai-shek. With the Sian kidnaping, it was evident that the Communists had come to Northwest China to stay. In writing their own history, they gave the name "War of Resistance against Japan: Phase I" to their early years at Yenan in Shensi from 1937 to 1941.

Although the Communists had declared war on Japan in 1932, they were in no position to do any actual fighting until the Japanese advanced into North and Central China in 1937. After the formation of the united front, both Communists and Kuomintang adopted new policies of re-

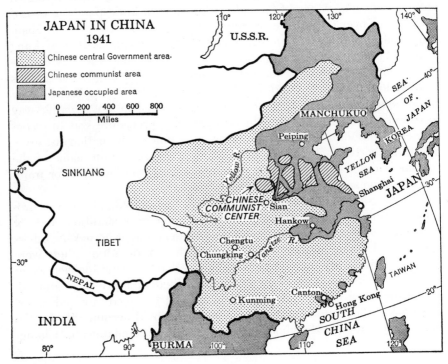

sistance against the Japanese. Chiang Kai-shek called off his annihilation campaigns; Mao Tse-tung agreed to end the insurrection. Mao said he would place the Communist armies under the command of the National-ist government, abandon their Soviets in Northwest China, and modify the more radical of their land reform measures. Instead of confiscating the land of landlords and rich peasants, the Communists declared they would content themselves with reduction of rents and rates of interest on bor-rowed money.

The united front held up for a very brief time. 1940–1941 was the year of confusion unlimited in interior China, when the Japanese pene-trated as deeply into China as they ever went. The traditional social fabric of China was torn to shreds as officials, landlords, and merchants evac-uated their homes and left the peasants to fend for themselves. Every hamlet and farm in China became fair game for anyone who had a gun. Secret societies, bandits, and local bullies competed with puppets of Wang Ching-wei, the soldiers of Chiang Kai-shek, and Communist guerrillas for the food and loyalty of the helpless peasants. In this triangular strug-gle, the puppets lost out very quickly. Wang was despised as a traitor and hated as a contributor to the suffering which they ascribed to his Japa-nese masters.

Nationalists and Communists fought each other as consistently as they fought the Japanese. Many of the clashes occurred without any ref-erence to differences in policy, but most resulted from the widening gap between the official attitudes of Chungking and Yenan. Many Kuomintang leaders preferred Wang Ching-wei or even the Japanese to the Commu-nists, and they accused the Communists of using the war against Japan as an excuse to expand their own area of influence. The Communists said they were always afraid that the Kuomintang would "sell out" to Japan. Communists charged that Nationalists failed to deliver the money and subsidies which they had promised; Nationalists replied that they would be foolish to give Communists weapons and ammunition which would be turned against the giver.

As supreme commander of all Chinese forces, Chiang Kai-shek or-dered the Communists to confine their fighting to their bases in the moun-tains, swamps, and moors. Instead, the Communists asserted that the only way to beat the Japanese was to go out and meet them. The Communists sent their guerrilla columns all the way from Shensi to the China coast, and they established some twenty bases of operations behind the Japa-nese lines in practically every province of North and Central China. Local Communist leaders fought against local Kuomintang commanders, and the latter usually lost. In defeat they deserted to the Japanese or to the puppet forces. Often the generals made their way to Chungking and left their men to make the best bargain they could with anyone who would give them food and pay.

In 1941 the united front came to an effective end because of the Fourth Army incident. The Fourth Army was a Communist group under General Yeh T'ing, but like other Communist armies it was subject to the ultimate command of a Nationalist super-general. Half of the army operated north of the Yangtze River, and half south of the river—all in the vicinity of Nanking. When Wang Ching-wei was inaugurated as the puppet president, the detachments of the Fourth Army south of the river stepped up their political activities. The Nationalist super-general ordered the transfer of all detachments south of the river to join the detachments in the north. When all but the headquarters detachment had departed, the Nationalists attacked the isolated stragglers. Many were killed, including the chief of staff; many were captured, including Yeh T'ing himself. On January 17, 1941, Chungking announced that the Fourth Army was dissolved.

However, the Fourth Army remained very much alive. It established new headquarters north of the river, and it flourished in spite of Kuomintang opposition and Japanese mopping-up campaigns. Its new commander was Ch'en Yi, later the Foreign Minister of Communist China, and its political commissar was Liu Shao-ch'i, later chairman of the People's Republic. It kept seven divisions in action in four provinces and created a situation of political strength among the local people from which it was never dislodged. After the Fourth Army incident, the united front disappeared, and open hostility characterized the relations between the Kuomintang and the Communists. As a political party, the Communists went underground, except for open bureaus which were permitted in Sian and Chungking itself. Traffic between Chungking and Yenan came to a standstill. Wherever possible, the Kuomintang threw a blockade around Communist strongholds. However, in their own bailiwicks the Communists continued to preach that all Chinese must fight Japan and must not surrender like the Kuomintang.

The Communists organized their forces into the regular army, guerrillas and militia. The regulars were uniformed and built around the seasoned veterans of the Long March. The two armies—the Eighth Route Army and the Fourth Army—were subdivided into brigades, regiments, battalions, companies, platoons, and squads. Guerrillas were not uniformed, but they were disciplined and directed by an ordinary military command structure. They were organized into columns and detachments and were restricted to the area where they were mobilized. The militia were local people who were mobilized for service only in the place where they lived. They acted as a great intelligence network, provided food and lodging for the fighters, served as a transport corps for the army in the field, performed whatever services they were asked, and supervised an ingenious system of passports and identity cards. It was reported in

1938 that the Eighth Route Army had about 45,000 effectives and the Fourth Army 30,000. In spite of losses, the ranks were increased constantly by the addition of peasants, students, and soldiers from former warlords, the Kuomintang or Wang Ching-wei puppets. By the end of 1941 the Communist armies might have contained as many as ten times the number with which they began the war of resistance against Japan.

Mao Tse-tung worked out six principles which in his opinion constituted the strategic program for victory over the Japanese. Guerrillas must (1) "on our own initiative," with flexibility and according to plan, carry out offensives in a defensive war; (2) coordinate with regular warfare; (3) establish base areas; (4) undertake tactical defensive and strategic offensive; (5) develop into mobile warfare and (6) establish a correct relationship of commands. The Communists worked on the assumption that it would be a *protracted war* against Japan; that the Japanese could never subjugate China; and that the Chinese could not achieve a quick victory over Japan. Mao recognized that war would be total and it would be brutal. He wrote: "We are not Duke Hsiang of Sung and we have no use for his stupid scruples about benevolence, righteousness and morality in war." He thought the war would pass through three stages: retreat, stalemate, and counteroffensive; eventually the Chinese would be preserved and the Japanese annihilated.

Only once did he launch a massive assault on the Japanese. In the summer of 1940 he ordered the hundred regiments offensive which lasted for five months and struck at the Japanese control of the railways in five northern provinces. The results were disastrous for the Communists. The Japanese retaliated with their "three-all's" campaign: kill all, burn all, and destroy all. Scarcely a village in Hopei and Shensi escaped the smoke and flame of Japanese fires. Thousands of soldiers and civilians were slaughtered.

The standard Communist guerrilla procedure was to stay out of the reach of the enemy or to "sting them like hornets." A Japanese commander said that the "guerrillas were like flies on your face: if you brush them away, they come right back." Another Japanese officer said: "If we send out small patrols, they never come back; if we send out larger detachments, they never find the Communists." From 1938 until the end of the war, the Japanese army mobilized massive forces and sent them into areas believed to contain Communists. Their mopping-up campaigns made terror and devastation a constant ingredient in Chinese rural life. When the Japanese approached, the Communists simply melted into the countryside; when the Japanese departed, the Communists returned.

Guerrilla warfare was not so much a military technique as it was a political condition. Its success did not depend upon favorable geographic conditions, or mobility at the expense of supply trains, or adroit employment of commando tactics. The key to success was the support of the population. The Communists and the masses perceived a common interest in resisting Japan, and the Communists outsmarted the Kuomintang in achieving the leadership of masses who were ready to follow anyone who would take up their cause against their persecutor.

In Hunan, many years earlier, Mao Tse-tung had learned the value of the Chinese peasants. He perceived that guerrilla warfare could not flourish without the sympathies and cooperation of the masses. Their near-perfect intelligence contributed to the success of surprise ambushes and to the complete bewilderment of the Japanese. He stated flatly, "No one who is in any way opposed to the people can ever hope to win a guerrilla war." The Communists did not have to teach the people to hate the Japanese; their job was to find the techniques to make the most efficient use of the people's disposition to fight against the enemy invader.

All the while the Communists fought, they struggled to perfect their autonomous, distinctive way of life in their base areas. Primarily they looked after the welfare of the army because "every Communist must grasp the truth—political power grows out of the barrel of the gun." Mao wrote: "Whoever wants to seize the political power of the state and to maintain it must have a strong army." The Communists strengthened the party because "the Party commands the gun, and the gun shall never be allowed to command the Party." Unquestioned party leadership was the first principle of their political creed. They subjected party workers to rigid discipline; they sharpened their indoctrination methods by self-criticism, intensive study, and public confession meetings. They established schools for the training of party leaders (cadres) and government officials. They set up their own version of democratic government and studied how to adapt Moscow theories to Chinese realities.

During this Yenan period in the evolution of Chinese Communism, Mao Tse-tung laid down its philosophical basis in a celebrated pamphlet entitled the *New Democracy*. He said the revolution would be accomplished in two stages: first, the current stage, or the new democracy; and later, the second stage, or the stage of pure socialism. The first stage in development necessitated practical compromises which the Chinese chose to adopt and implement in all areas which were subject to the direction and control of Yenan.

Economically, the Communists continued their program of land to the tiller, but at a moderate pace. In the main, they lived up to their promise to stop the confiscation of land. They needed food, and they did not want to alienate any skilled agriculturalist, even though he was a landlord or a rich peasant. They enforced the reduction of rents and interest rates, but they made the peasants pay their legitimate levies. They did not condemn all capitalism, but they controlled what they called its worst monopolistic aspects. They accepted almost any arrangement which contained the hope of increased production. They encouraged cooperatives, but they tolerated private ownership and management in smaller enterprises. The Communist "state" owned and operated all banks, mines, utilities, railways, and trading companies.

Politically, the Communists developed the idea that their government was a dictatorship of all classes, not just the proletariat. They considered peasants, workers, intellectuals, petty bourgeoisie, and national bourgeoisie as "people" whose strength was based on the alliance of peasants and workers and whose hope of victory lay in the leadership of the Communist Party. They experimented with various forms of "democratic centralism" in the government of their base areas, and they perfected administrative techniques which they utilized when they took over—at a later date—the government of all China. A party-directed council took over every *hsiang*, or borough, and every *hsien*, or district, and a regional council administered the affairs of the larger government units.

In seeking to implement the doctrine of a "united front of all people," the Communists adopted their 3–3–3 formula. Elective posts were filled one-third by Communists, one-third by the non-Communist leftist progressive elements, and one-third by such middle-of-the-roaders as the Kuomintang. Top jobs were given to civilians and often to young student leaders. The chief functions of political officers were to spread anti-Japanese propaganda, to learn the rudiments of public administration and to organize the masses as a military auxiliary. Their training manual makes practically no mention of the word *communism*.

The supreme achievement of the Communists from 1937 to 1941 was the organization of the masses. Mao insisted that no one could be a good Communist if he did not love the masses and listen attentively to their voices. They were entitled to schools and hospitals, to all the advantages of culture and education. For the enlightenment of the masses the Communists published newspapers and conducted literacy campaigns. Every individual, regardless of age, occupation, or sex, was mobilized into some kind of national salvation association—either a National Salvation Association for Youth, a National Salvation Association for Peasants, a National Salvation Association for Women, or something of the sort. These organizations gave the humblest and loneliest individuals a sense of "belonging" and laid a broad base for the burgeoning sentiments of nationalism.

During this period, Mao Tse-tung came to be accepted as the one individual who could represent and lead Communist China. He had no rivals whom he found it necessary to purge. He was the philosopher, spokesman, statesman, and foremost military leader of the Communist Party. He led the troops in battle, and he shared their hardships. He was the most-wanted man on the list of the Japanese, and it was his life that was in greatest personal danger. He was constantly on the move; yet he found time to read and, in a fashion, to keep up with world affairs. He studied, he wrote, and he delivered lectures at the Ynan Anti-Japanese Military and Political College. He lived the simple life of one of the masses. He even found time to compose poetry in classical Chinese styles.

A cursory glance at the political clock in 1941 might have indicated that for the Chinese Communists it was still "five minutes to midnight." The Communists were the first enemies of the Japanese and their Chinese puppets. The Communists were also the basic foes of the Kuomintang, as evidenced by the dying agonies of the united front. A closer study of the situation might have indicated that it was five minutes to high noon instead of five minutes to midnight.

The Japanese invasion destroyed the old order in China and liberated the underprivileged masses. This pleased the Communists, but it shattered the strength of the Kuomintang. The Kuomintang, as the party in power, was obliged to bear the responsibility for China's losses and to suffer the pain of China's defeat. Every weakling who had taken refuge under the banner of the Kuomintang sullied that banner when he surrendered to Wang Ching-wei or the Japanese. When the Japanese inched a little deeper into the territory of China, it was the Kuomintang which bore the brunt of positional warfare. Kuomintang troops perished, or saved themselves in flight or surrender. When the Japanese pulled back to their bases of greater security—as they inevitably did—it was the Communists who rushed in to fill the vacuum.

While the fortunes of the Kuomintang tobogganed, the Communists in the third part of China laid the foundations for a more auspicious future. According to their critics, the Communist policy was "ten per cent resisting Japan, twenty per cent dealing with the Nationalists, and seventy per cent expansion." The Communists launched an effective challenge to Chiang Kai-shek for the leadership of the nationalist movement. Communists were not looked upon by the masses in North and Central China as traitors, but as heroes and national martyrs. In China, at that time, Communism did not belie patriotism; on the contrary, it offered itself in the service of the Chinese nation-state.

In looking ahead, Mao Tse-tung expounded theories which would fit Communism into Chinese molds. He concerned himself less with the Russian experience than the Chinese popular will. He wanted to get rid of the influence of Chinese Communists whose expertise lay merely in familiarity with Russian-style Communism and to discover the most effective way of applying the teachings of Marx and Lenin directly to his own country and his own people. He wanted the Chinese to learn more of Chinese communism than mere anti-Japanism. Mao created an ideology which was not particularly brilliant or original, but it was communist (universal) and Chinese (nationalistic). Such a theoretic blueprint was badly needed at the end of the war. Perhaps more important, Mao designed the political stratagems and provided the indomitable will which sparked the Communists on the road to power.

SUGGESTED READING

Bisson, T. A., *Japan in China* (New York, Macmillan, 1938).

Borton, Hugh, *Japan Since 1931* (New York, Institute of Pacific Relations, 1940).

Byas, Hugh, *Government by Assassination* (New York, Knopf, 1942).

Carlson, Evans F., *Twin Stars of China* (New York, Dodd, 1941).

Chamberlin, William H., *Japan over Asia* (Boston, Little, 1939).

Griffiths, Samuel, *Mao Tse-tung on Guerilla Warfare* (New York, Praeger, 1961).

Hahn, Emily, *Chiang Kai-shek* (New York, Doubleday, 1955).

Johnson, Chalmers, *Peasant Nationalism and Communist Power* (Stanford, Stanford U., 1962).

McLane, Charles B., *Soviet Policy and the Chinese Communists, 1931–1946* (New York, Columbia U., 1958).

Payne, Robert, *China Awake* (New York, Dodd, 1947).

———, *Forever China* (New York, Dodd, 1945).

Quigley, H. S., *Far Eastern War, 1937–1941* (Boston, World Peace Foundation, 1942).

Rosinger, Lawrence K., *China's Wartime Politics, 1937–1944* (Princeton, Princeton U., 1944).

Royal Institute of International Affairs, *China and Japan* (London, The Institute, 1938).

Selle, Earl Albert, *Donald of China* (New York, Harper, 1948).

Storry, Richard, *Double Patriots* (Boston, Houghton, 1957).

Taylor, George E., *Struggle for North China* (New York, Institute of Pacific Relations, 1940).

United States Department of State, *Foreign Relations of the United States* (Washington, Government Printing Office). Annual volumes dealing with the Far East.

20

From Marco Polo Bridge to Pearl Harbor

At the same time it fought an undeclared war in China, Japan became a major propellant toward World War II. It contributed to international conflicts which were not settled until all the major nations were caught in the web of war. The issues between Japan and China first exploded in the railway incident on the outskirts of Mukden; they were not resolved until Japan signed the surrender instrument on the decks of the battleship "Missouri" on August 14, 1945.

Aggressors in Europe marched in step with the armies of Japan in China. In Manchuria, Japan successfully challenged the flimsy structure of collective security. Italy followed suit in Ethiopia while Germans, Italians, and Russians sharpened their military claws in the civil war in Spain. Hitler rebuilt the German army, tore up the Locarno agreements for peace in western Europe, and refortified the Rhineland. He wrecked the disarmament conference and dealt the *coup de grâce* to the League of Nations. While Japanese hobnailed boots tramped into Hankow and Canton, Germans rode their shrieking tanks into Austria and Czechoslovakia. Aggression fed upon appeasement, and in 1938 at Munich the Germans seemed to get every concession they demanded from the staggering British and French. Only Russia stood aside and suggested that if the "democracies" would stand up against the "fascists," Russia would take its stand with England and France against Germany and Italy.

Between 1938 and 1941 the major shifts in European diplomacy and the attitudes of the United States were at least as important as the fortunes of Japan in China in determining the destiny of Asia. Cabinets in Japan were made and unmade by the vacillations in German policy and by the cynical shifts in nonaggresison pacts which were negotiated by Russia. While Germany and Russia were at odds in Europe, Japan could afford to take risks against the Russian position on the Siberia-Manchukuo border. When Germany and Russia settled their differences and war broke out in Europe, Japan backtracked in Northeast Asia. Japan was scared that the "treacherous" German-Russian pact provided such security for Russia on its European front that Russia would feel free to take strong measures against Japan in Asia. What a sense of relief swept over Japan when the German armies invaded Russia!

As long as Germany appeared strong in Europe, Japan did not hesitate to flaunt the rights of Britain and its allies in Asia. Great Britain was helpless in Asia because of its vital menace in Europe. Japan gambled heavily, and fatally, on the disinterest of the United States. Never for a moment was Japan unaware of the importance of the situation in Europe and America on its own future, so it was with eyes wide open that it chose to expand the undeclared war in China to the declared War of Greater East Asia.

The events of 1937–1941 have been analyzed as they appeared only in Japan and China; it is time to re-examine them in the broader context of world affairs. The scene opened with the Japanese at Marco Polo Bridge; it closed with Japanese bombs at Pearl Harbor.

JAPAN AND THE POWERS IN CHINA

The Japanese army in China perpetrated deliberate incidents against British, French, and Americans which embarrassed their respective governments. In 1937 the British ambassador was shot under circumstances which could scarcely be described as accidental. River boats were machine-gunned from the air. An American gunboat, the "Panay," was sent to the bottom of the Yangtze River. Missionary properties were bombed and destroyed; foreign nationals were insulted, slapped, beaten, or killed.

The Japanese rode roughshod over foreign rights and interests in the treaty ports. Foreigners were humiliated and squeezed out of their rights at Hankow, Canton, Amoy, and Tientsin. Japan blockaded the China coast and closed the inland rivers to shipping other than Japanese. The Japanese undermined the integrity of the maritime customs with consequent losses to foreign bondholders. The new Sino-Japanese joint business ventures knocked long-established foreign commercial firms out of business. At Shanghai—the pride of Western traders on the China coast—the Japanese used the International Settlement as a military headquarters, took over law-enforcement, and passed out strong hints that the future of Shanghai would have to be changed. Japan robbed Shanghai of its sparkle and profit and converted the flourishing metropolis into the strongest base for Japan's attack on the position of the treaty powers in China.

The British and the Americans were berated as the "real snakes in the bosom of Chiang Kai-shek." Great Britain was blackened as the pillar of the Chinese temple and the fiendish enemy of the new order. Bitter propaganda stirred up popular demonstrations against the British on the streets of Tokyo and Peiping. Because of their preoccupation in Europe, the British were obliged to shift their forces out of China and to seek an understanding with Japan. A strong stand such as would have been the pride of the British lion a generation earlier was obviously impossible. The British extended the hand of friendship to Japan as well as to China.

On January 14, 1939, Great Britain sent a note to Japan which placed itself alongside the United States in flat opposition to Japanese expansion. British financial aid was extended to Chiang Kai-shek, and British activities were speeded up on the Burma border. The Japanese struck back with a campaign of hate and vilification. They declared "unless Japan peels off the thick skin of the British for all Orientals to see, eternal peace will not dawn in Eastern Asia." In the wave of bitterness which followed, a British businessman was kidnaped, a British foreman in a Shanghai mill was fatally stabbed, and British missionaries were wounded by Japanese bullets which "went astray." A British journalist in Tokyo was arrested in an espionage drive, and he jumped to his death before he could be questioned by the *kempeitai,* or constitutional police. The "Tuckwo," the queen of the Yangtze River steamers, was sunk; British business houses in China were looted and burned.

The whole tenor of British life in China became a nervous dread of what the Japanese military might do next. At Tientsin in the early summer of 1939 the Japanese cut off the food supply and electrified the barriers of the British concession. On the pretense of searching for bombs, the Japanese sentries stripped British subjects, ridiculed them and slapped their mouths with confiscated passports. The sport came to an end with German-Russian rapprochement in Europe. Then the British ambassador in Tokyo drew up, with the Japanese foreign minister, the "Craigie-Arita" formula, according to which the British recognized the actual situation in China, admitted the special needs of the Japanese forces, and undertook not to countenance acts prejudicial to those needs. The British government then advised British subjects to evacuate Japan and Japan-occupied China. British military impotence in Europe was an inescapable fact, and on September 3, 1939, war broke out between Germany and the Allied Powers. After the fall of France the British assented to the Japanese demand to close the Burma Road for three months (July 17, 1940 to October 17, 1940)—they could do nothing else while the bombs dropped every night on London. By the time the road was reopened, the Battle of Britain had been won, and the danger of a German invasion had disappeared. And the Japanese had shifted their attention from China to the larger areas of the southern regions.

Japan experienced little difficulty with Germany in China. German businessmen resented the pro-Japanese policies of their own government, and they had established many profitable enterprises in Nationalist China. German military advisers helped to build the armies of Chiang Kai-shek. German businessmen and German military advisers would have liked to see peace between Japan and China, but they were overruled by the Nazi party extremists. The German position in China was sacrificed to the demands of the anti-Comintern alliance. The Japanese program in China received German support in exchange for Japanese endorsement of Germany and Italy in Europe.

On September 27, 1940 (after the fall of France), Japan, Germany, and Italy signed the Tripartite (or "Axis") Pact by which they agreed to recognize one another's leadership in their respective spheres and to assist one another with all political, economic, and military means in the event that any one of the three contracting parties should be attacked by a power at present not involved in the European war or in the Sino-Japanese conflict. This of course meant the United States. The pact affirmed that "aforesaid terms do not in any way affect the political status which exists at present as between each of the contracting parties and Soviet Russia." The Japanese looked upon this treaty as a means of helping in the solution of the China incident and of preventing the spread of the European war to East Asia. General Tojo himself declared that "there was no thought whatever of dividing the world among the signatory powers nor of world conquest."

The Japanese were as hostile to the French as they were friendly to the Germans. The first clashes between Japanese and French took place in the French concession in Tientsin. In July 1937, French authorities refused to permit Japanese soldiers to pass through the concession on their way to the destruction of Nankai University in the Chinese part of the city. The next month the French joined the British in the effort to preserve the neutrality of the International Settlement and the French concession in Shanghai. The French consul-general ordered the Annamite troops to man the concession barricades and to shoot to kill if the Japanese tried to penetrate the defenses. The French were equally tough in the protection of their concession in Hankow. The French held out against the Japanese until their weakness in Europe became more apparent. Then they had to give in to Japanese pressures. They accepted the Craigie-Arita formula for their own policy in China: namely, that they would countenance no acts or measures prejudicial to the special requirements of the Japanese forces. The French concessions were practically surrendered to the Japanese, and French troops were withdrawn from China. When in 1938 the Japanese troops captured Nanning in South China, they built an airfield from which their bombers frequently attacked the railway from Indochina to Yünnan—a major supply route for Chiang Kai-shek.

The Japanese showed no more respect for the sensibilities of Americans than they showed for the rights of Europeans. However, the Americans were in a position to protect the rights of all foreigners in China, and in 1937 they continued desperately to hope that their traditions of isolation and neutrality would keep them out of war. The Germans seemed more menacing than the Japanese, but the Americans entertained a baffling sentimental attachment toward the Chinese. The American doctrine of nonrecognition constituted a psychological check to Japan, and a succession of American notes and protests kept the legal record unmistakably clear. The United States was concerned about its rights in China, but it was infinitely more perturbed about the progressive breakdown of the international system of collective security. The Japanese scrapped the agreements of the Washington Conference and by their actions in China served notice to the world that they no longer intended to pay any attention to the Open Door.

Shortly before the incident of the Marco Polo Bridge, the United States amended its neutrality policy. It shifted from an embargo on shipments to all belligerents to the doctrine of "cash and carry." The Congress sought by this measure to discriminate in favor of Great Britain as against Germany, but it neglected to consider the effect of its legislation in Asia. Chiang Kai-shek's China had no cash, and Japan had the ships which could come to California to haul away their precious cargoes of petroleum products and scrap iron. Immediately after the hostilities broke out in North China, Secretary of State Cordell Hull issued a statement obviously aimed at Japan which reaffirmed American dedication to fundamental principles of "orderly processes" in international affairs. The Japanese government commented that it too concurred in these principles but it felt that they could be fully attained in the Far East only by full recognition of the particular circumstances in that region. The repeated reference to "principles" on the part of the United States was looked upon in Japan not as high-mindedness but as a technique for the protection and promotion of American national interests.

The sympathies of the United States were for Chiang Kai-shek, but the government moved slowly toward action against Japan. The United States had no standing army to speak of, so it could not dispatch large numbers of troops to China to stand up against Japan. American citizens in China were warned to evacuate China or to stay at their own risk. American opinion was outraged by Japanese military brutalism in China, and pressure groups within the United States called for an economic blockade of Japan. On September 14, 1937, President Roosevelt ordered that "merchant vessels owned by the Government of the United States would not be permitted to transport to China or Japan any arms, ammunition or implements of war." This mild order worked against China more than against Japan, but it set a precedent for subsequent executive orders which engaged the United States in practical economic warfare against Japan.

President Roosevelt awakened the American public to a sense of danger in Asia as well as Europe. On October 5, 1937, he delivered the famous quarantine speech in which he suggested that all peace-loving nations should quarantine those nations which were responsible for the existing reign of terror and international lawlessness. Significantly he began a build-up of the army (which the chief of staff reported ranked eighteenth among the standing armies of the world) and stimulated the growth of vital industries by defense contracts. He joined with the League of Nations in condemning Japanese action in China as a violation of treaty obligations and participated with eighteen other nations in a futile conference at Brussels under the League of Nations to consider peaceable means to hasten the end of the conflict between China and Japan.

As a moral embargo, the United States opposed the sale of airplanes and aviation equipment to countries which bombed civilian populations. It also discouraged the extension of credit to nationals of Japan. On frequent occasions it protested against Japanese interference with the rights of its nationals in China. It objected to the closing of the China market to American competition, Japanese control of China's foreign exchange, alterations in the tariff and the administration of the customs, the setting up of special companies and monopolies, the censorship of American mail, restrictions upon residence and travel rights of Americans in China, and interference with trade and shipping. The Japanese replied that the new order created a new situation, and any attempt to apply to the conditions of today and tomorrow the inapplicable ideas and principles of the past would not solve the immediate issues. Diplomatic notes to Japan were supported by modest actions of aid to China. On July 11, 1939, the United States gave notice of the termination of the 1911 trade treaty with Japan. Six months later the termination was to become effective, and legal obstacles would be removed should the United States wish further to clamp down on trade with Japan.

JAPAN AND THE SOVIET UNION

While Japan challenged the Europeans and Americans in China, it kept an eagle eye on its relations with the Soviet Union. Japan was well aware of the growing military strength of Russia under Stalin and satisfied itself that Russia would not intervene in China before it diverted its attention from Manchukuo southward to China. It tested Russian intentions by precipitating a clash with Russian patrols on two separate disputed islands in the Amur River. The clash occurred on June 30, 1937, exactly a week before the move into North China. Japan was prepared to fight should the need arise. However Russia backed away and Japan felt that its northern flank was secure as it committed so much of its strength to the conflict in China.

As a response to the Japanese advance into China, Russia negotiated a nonaggression pact with free China. Russia retained its ideological sympathy with the Communists in China, but sent aid and advisers to Chiang Kai-shek. In the incipient civil war in China, the Soviet Union had a foot in each camp. But Russia's capacities in Asia were limited because of the overwhelming and immediate menace of Hitler's Germany on Russia's western frontier. Communist Russia's united front with the capitalist democracies and the renewed cooperation with the League of Nations in defense of collective security were dictated by the demands of Europe. These facts were well-known in Japan. The Japanese government counted on its German ally to pin down the Russians in Europe, and thus relieve the Japanese from the worry of a possible attack from Russia while the Japanese were enmeshed in China.

Border incidents in Manchukuo continued to embitter the official relations between Japan and Russia. During the months of July and August 1938, Japan demanded the cession of an important hill, Changkufeng, west of Lake Khasan, which overlooks the rail and highway approaches to Vladivostok. Russia said no. The Japanese brought up an entire division of their army from Korea and attacked the Russians in force. The Russians did not retreat. They put up a stiff fight and forced Japan to accept a truce. Both sides agreed to mediation of the dispute by a bilateral commission.

In the summer of 1939, Japan and Russia fought over disputed territory east of the Khalka River in the Nomonhan district east of Lake Buir. Russia again accused Japan of utilizing a frontier dispute as a pretext for an aggressive attempt to secure an advanced military base for further war against the Soviet Union. The Japanese attacked the border guard and for four months carried on large-scale hostilities involving aircraft, artillery, and tanks. According to Russian figures, Japanese-Manchukuoan casualties exceeded 50,000; Russian-Mongolian losses were more than 9,000. The operations were on a front of fifty to sixty kilometers wide and twenty to twenty-five kilometers deep. The Japanese abandoned the attack with the announcement of the German-Soviet nonaggression pact in Europe in August, 1939.

The suddenness of the pact caused the overthrow of a Japanese cabinet while a new stopgap government took time out to reassess the situation. Japan feared that Germany had sold out Japan, had bought salvation for itself at the cost of releasing Russia's energies for an instantaneous mighty blow against Japan. Japan feared communism and air raids from Siberian bases against its flimsy wood-and-paper homeland. It was a shattering blow to have the Germans and the Russians come together. In a kind of panic, Japan relaxed its campaign against the Western powers in China. New plans had to be drawn up to take care of possible action from the direction of Siberia. General Tojo admitted that he conceived Russia to be Japan's implacable enemy but he confessed that he never intended to invade the Soviet Union. Rather Japan was "bent on defense against Russian aggression in a very timorous manner."

It came as a quick relief to Japan that Russia had no intention of letting down its guard against Germany. Stalin continued to strengthen his military position against Hitler; the two conspirators divided the body of Poland for their mutual advantage. The Japanese showed willingness to take Stalin at his word when he said he preferred an arrangement with Hitler to an understanding with Great Britain "which grinds in the dust Hindus, Arabs, blacks in Africa and workers at home." They believed Stalin when he said that he had nothing but contempt for France which "deserted Czechoslovakia in its hour of need" and for the United States which "hates Communism as much as Fascism." The Japanese also chose to accept Hitler's explanation that he needed a pact with Stalin in order to concentrate on the western front against France and England. As Russians became involved more deeply in Finland, some Japanese again began to talk about "planting the flag of the Rising Sun in the Urals" or "rolling all over Asia like a ball of fire."

In the spring of 1940, the Germans drove through the Low Countries. The Russians were worried lest the Germans turn and strike like lightning against Russia. The Russian discomfiture and the demonstration of German might restored the confidence of the Japanese. The caretaker government of Japan was cashiered, and Prince Konoye was brought back as premier. Japan decided to forget the German "treachery" and to conclude the Axis Pact with Germany and Italy. This enabled Japan to postpone a showdown with Russia and to prepare immediately for an attack against the helpless attractive remnants of empire in the southern seas.

To continue the story with Russia (and to leave the story of the southward advance of Japan until the next section): Germany then approached Russia with a proposition to join the Axis Pact. Molotov was invited to come to Berlin to explore the possibilities of a four-power world. Russia and Germany were unable to reach agreement on the delineation of respective spheres of influence in the Balkans and the region of the Black Sea. Russia also showed increasing interest in the growing antagonism between Japan and the United States in the Pacific. Russia did not wish to tie itself up in an understanding with Japan if the United

States were to bring itself to the necessity of stopping Japan even at the cost of war.

The new Japanese foreign minister, Matsuoka Yosuke, took off for Europe in March, 1941, seeking a truce with Russia. After preliminary talks in Moscow, he proceeded to Rome and Berlin. He learned of Germany's military preparations against Russia, and he had not the slightest doubt that Germany would quickly dash Russia to pieces. He had visions that, while Germany fought Russia, Japan could make a quick move to the south and then return to take Siberia. Neither England, France, nor the Netherlands could offer any effective resistance, and in his opinion the United States was not prepared—psychologically or physically—for war. He became more enthusiastic for a neutrality pact with Russia. He reasoned that if Germany should attack Russia, then the Russians would be inclined to withdraw forces from the east. Russia's eastern flank would be exposed to Japan. A neutrality pact would afford breathing space for Japan to ponder over its future policies. Matsuoka returned to Moscow and on April 13, 1941, concluded a Neutrality Pact with Stalin. Russia gained the promise of Japan's neutrality if Germany should attack Russia; Japan received assurance of Russia's neutrality should war break out between Japan and the United States. The pact was to remain valid for five years. At the same time Russia and Japan signed a supplementary declaration of mutual respect for the territorial integrity and inviolability of the Mongol People's Republic and Manchukuo, so as to eliminate the perennial source of friction between Russia and Japan. Russia also canceled the Japanese concessions in northern Sakhalin so as to reduce the danger of spies. Stalin and Matsuoka were immensely pleased with their diplomatic coup. Stalin himself went to the train to see Matsuoka off on the Trans-Siberian Express, and the two men embraced warmly as they said good-by.

On June 22, 1941, Germany attacked Russia. Japan had diplomatic commitments to both nations: the Axis Pact with Germany and the neutrality pact with Russia. It had ample legal justification for any course it might pursue. Should it join with Germany and close the pincers on Russia by an attack on Siberia? It was tempted because Russia seemed as ready to fall on the ground as a ripe persimmon. As long as Germany felt confident of victory over Russia single-handedly, it told Japan that it did not want any help with the harvest and advised the Japanese to concentrate on Singapore. This was Japan's other alternative. Should it honor the neutrality pact and move to the south? It never occurred to Japan to stand still: it had to move in one direction or the other. None but the most ardent chauvinists believed that Japan could move in both directions at the same time, and almost all Japanese believed that the China affair would be brought to a speedy conclusion once Japan launched out beyond the frontiers of China either to the north or the south. Japan did not consider that its paper commitments could possibly interfere with any course which it chose to follow in the name of self-defense.

Japan gave a limited amount of aid to Germany in the war against Russia, primarily in the form of valuable economic, political, and military intelligence. Through Russian spies on the staff of the German embassy in Tokyo, Russia knew exactly the nature and extent of Japan's help and often learned of Japan's intentions. Japan interfered with Russian shipping in the Far East, particularly with Lend-Lease supplies which were destined to go from the American west coast to Vladivostok. (The United States adopted a policy of aid to Russia after the German attack.) Japan closed the Sangar Straits and obliged Russia to use the La Perouse Straits or the Korean Straits. When the former froze over and the latter became too dangerous because of submarines, the Russians had to take the long, foggy route through the Aleutians and the Kuriles. Japan was treaty-bound to observe neutrality toward Russia, but the neutrality was far from benevolent.

It was not one world and one war when Japan bombed Pearl Harbor. In Europe, Germany was at war with England and Russia; Japan became a co-belligerent against England, but it was neutral as between Germany and Russia. In Asia, Japan became a belligerent against the United States and England, but in that war Russia was neutral. The Russians were in an anomalous position in Asia. They were exposed and ineffective in their own Siberian homeland. They were actively allied with Outer Mongolia. They were sympathetic to the Chinese Communists, bound to do nothing directly or indirectly to hurt Chiang Kai-shek; yet they were committed to observe neutrality toward Japan. They developed an air supply route from the United States and Canada through Alaska to Siberia. Through the grudging tolerance of "neutral" Japan they maintained a trickle of supplies by sea from their ally the United States. Every ton of aid over the distant, icy North Pacific contributed to Russia victory over Germany and the return of Russia to the Asian scene after its temporary eclipse during World War II. The Russians were in no position at any time after the outbreak of the war in Europe to cause any embarrassment to Japan, as Japan turned its attention away from Russia and the north and toward the position of the colonial powers in the southern regions.

Japan's Moves to the South

When Hitler's armies crashed through the Allies on the western front, Japan decided irrevocably that Germany represented the wave of the future. Therefore Germany's enemies would become the enemies of

Japan, and Germany's drive for a new order in Europe would be matched by a Japanese scheme for a co-prosperity sphere of all peoples in greater East Asia under the leadership of new Japan.

Japan's first target was the French position in Indochina. The Japanese were angry about the stream of supplies which moved out of Hanoi over the railway to Yünnan and ultimately to Chiang Kai-shek in Chungking. Intermittent bombing after 1938 failed to put the railway out of commission, but the Japanese warned the French that all-out bombing raids would take place unless the traffic was stopped. The French government agreed to embargo military cargoes, and supplies which were badly needed by the Chinese piled up at Hong Kong, Haiphong, and Hanoi. Guns, munitions, and airplane parts deteriorated as they lay idle on the wharves or in the warehouses. Trucks, medical supplies, and petroleum products were held up because they were considered as "military cargoes."

In 1939 the Japanese occupied Hainan and small neighboring islands. Hainan is fifteen miles south of the China coast, fifty miles from the French leased territory of Kwangchowwan, and one hundred miles east of Indochina. It is 320 miles south of Hong Kong, 800 miles northwest of Manila, and approximately midway between Japan and the Netherlands East Indies. Hence its strategic value. The French realized that the Japanese agreement of 1907 to respect the rights of France in South China and Indochina was worthless when, early in 1939, the Japanese foreign minister told the diet: "France is nothing but an independent state which depends on the great powers of Britain and America. She has nothing of her own and is bound to take a most sneaking, foxy attitude towards this country."

On February 9, 1939, sixteen Japanese vessels took over Hainan. The Japanese foreign minister explained that the operation was "for the purpose of exterminating the Chinese military forces on the island and is therefore an affair which has nothing to do with the question of assuring peace and security as envisaged by the Japanese-French agreement." The duration of the occupation would depend upon strategic necessities, and the Japanese would make no statement as to the future status of Hainan.

As the Japanese loomed beyond the horizon of Indochina, the French, rather on the frantic side, studied measures for the protection of their frontiers and naval bases. Some 40,000 Frenchmen in Indochina suddenly found themselves sandwiched in between a hostile indigenous population and the troops of aggressive Japan. The French put into jail all known Communists and forced reformist elements and non-communist revolutionaries underground. They realized too late that any successful defense of their colony would necessitate arming the native inhabitants. This step was too risky because the guns might be turned against the French. With the declaration of war in Europe, France was obliged to abandon Indochina to its own devices. With the collapse of French resistance and the installation of the Vichy government, Indochina lay helplessly exposed to the increasing Japanese pressures.

The Japanese sent a military mission to Hanoi, in northern Indochina, to arrange for air bases, artillery, stations, and the transportation of Japanese troops on Indochina's railways. The Japanese put an end to all traffic to Chiang Kai-shek and took over all the accumulated goods on the docks and in the warehouses. The military mission signed the Hanoi convention on September 22, 1940. Japan agreed to respect French rights and interests in Indochina and the Far East, and France consented to the placing of its military facilities in northern Indochina at the disposal of the Japanese. The Japanese quickly landed troops at Haiphong and took over the harbor, railway, and highway facilities and the air bases. They acted as if they had come to stay.

The Japanese extracted new economic agreements which in effect guaranteed that the products of Indochina would be made available exclusively to Japan. Then the Japanese moved toward southern Indochina. On July 22, 1941, exactly a month after the German invasion of Russia, they forced Vichy France to conclude a mutual defense pact. As a result, they occupied Saigon as completely as they had previously established themselves in Hanoi. The French were helpless and could only look to eventual victory in Europe to restore their position in Asia. A Vichy appointee, Admiral Decoux, replaced the De Gaullist, General Catroux, as governor-general. Under painful duress, he agreed that the French administration would do nothing to interfere with Japanese plans.

Meanwhile, Japan displayed affectionate attention toward Thailand. Japan advertised itself as a "guide" or "trail blazer," without any idea of subjugation or domination in Southeast Asia. On June 12, 1940, Japan and Thailand concluded a treaty providing for mutual respect of territory and consultation on questions of mutual interest. Japan said this treaty was an expression of gratitude to Thailand, because the latter refused to share in the general condemnation of Japan in the League of Nations. Japan was interested in the military bases of Thailand, and the use of Thai territory to protect the flanks in the event of operations against Singapore and the Malay peninsula. The Japanese gave their blessing to rising Thai nationalism which pretended that all territories populated by Thai peoples should be united under the political rule of Bangkok. This included parts of Burma, Malaya, and Indochina. Thailand immediately "demanded" rectification of the border with Indochina and implemented its demands with an undeclared war in January, 1941. An "armistice" was negotiated between the Thais and the French who represented Indochina on board a Japanese cruiser in Saigon harbor. A treaty signed at Tokyo on May 9, 1941, turned over to Thailand all the border territories which had been demanded. Japanese prestige was naturally unlimited in Thailand; French humiliation in Indochina was complete.

The Dutch were the next to feel the sting of the Japanese lash. The Dutch were always hopeful that the Chinese-Japanese controversy would be confined to China's mainland, and they were not pleased with the prospect of a complete victory for either China or Japan. If the Chinese should win, it might stir up illusions of grandeur in the minds of the million and a quarter Chinese residents of the Netherlands East Indies. If the Japanese should win, Japan would surely expand into the attractive Dutch colony.

Japanese residents in the Indies lived in self-contained communities —ideal for espionage purposes. They were primarily engaged in trade. The rising flood of Japanese imports was carried in Japanese ships, financed by Japanese banks, stored in Japanese warehouses in the coastal towns of Java, and sold to Javanese consumers through Japanese middlemen and tiny Japanese bazaars. Japanese buyers of native products for export to Japan penetrated into the deepest interior of most of the islands. Japanese fishermen sailed at will in strategically important seas, and Japanese businessmen bought mining, lumber, and agricultural rights of doubtful economic value in localities of military importance. Thus Japanese antagonized the Dutch in the Indies, as well as the local residents of Chinese racial descent.

After the outbreak of the war in Europe, the Netherlands was without effective means of giving protection to the East Indies against possible aggression from Japan. After the occupation of the mother country by the Nazis, Netherlanders in the Indies had to depend entirely upon themselves for defense. The Dutch government-in-exile in London treated its overseas "orphans" with unbelievable callousness as those orphans faced the approaching shadow of Japan.

The Japanese acted with speed in the Indies once they received the official German assurance of Germany's lack of interest in Dutch territories. German parachute troops were still landing in the streets of The Hague when the Japanese minister called at the Dutch foreign office to offer condolences and to make suggestions about Japan's requirements in the Indies. In August, 1940, Japan sent to Batavia a diplomatic mission to obtain peaceful assurance of cooperation between Japan and the Indies. The Japanese were insistent upon huge quantities of petroleum products and the control of finance and shipping. The Dutch procrastinated as best they could, but they could not thwart Japan's obvious determination to acquire the wealth of the Indies as an aid to the conquest of the southern regions.

A second mission to the Indies in 1941 increased Japanese pressure on the Dutch. The Dutch argued that they must consider the welfare of the people of the Indies, and must not dispense the resources of the Indies to a foreign power to the detriment of the native population. Negotiations dragged on while the whole world watched. Secretly, Japan planned military action if diplomacy failed. Japanese military authorities drew up details for military government of the Indies and went so far as to print occupation currency. In June, 1941, negotiations broke down. Japan decided to postpone immediate action vis-à-vis the Dutch in the Indies in favor of concentrating on the French in Indochina. At the same time, the crisis atmosphere in relations between Japan and the United States prevented the Japanese from embarking upon uninhibited, reckless adventures which would have precipitated total and immediate A-B-C-D (American-British-Chinese-Dutch) retaliation. The Japanese talked about the dangers of A-B-C-D encirclement all the while they conducted diplomatic negotiations with the Americans in Washington.

JAPAN AND THE UNITED STATES

The policies of the United States contained the key to the tempo and limits of Japanese expansion. When Japan made its firm decision to move to the south, it anticipated trouble with the Anglo-Saxon powers. It was not prepared for the firmness of the American response. The United States immediately initiated a program to stockpile strategic materials and adopted a license system for the export of military equipment, munitions, and machine tools. Great Britain and China could buy these items; Germany and Japan could not. The United States then prohibited foreign sales of strategic minerals and chemicals, aircraft engines, aviation gasoline, lubricating oils, and iron and steel scrap. President Roosevelt laid before the Congress a complete defense program covering the requirements of the army, navy, air force, and American industry. He also set up a National Defense Research Committee, with a uranium sub-committee, which became the parent of the atomic bomb.

In the summer of 1940, the president was nominated for a precedent-breaking third term. He was acutely aware of the necessities of domestic politics while conducting foreign policies in Asia and in Europe. To make America strong he obtained the passage of a Selective Service Act. To strengthen Britain, he concluded a deal which exchanged fifty over-age American destroyers for the use of British bases considered vital to American defense. He believed that a British victory was essential for the preservation of the American way of life, but he assured the electorate he would not send "our boys" to take part in foreign wars.

President Roosevelt felt constrained to avoid an open rupture with

Japan during the dark days of the Battle of Britain. As indications of his sentiments, he extended new credits to Chiang Kai-shek as he applied economic pressures on Japan. He advised the 16,000 Americans who remained in Asia to come home. He shifted the Pacific fleet from its base in San Diego westward to Pearl Harbor, and he sent new draftees to Hawaii or the Philippines for training. He backed down on no issues with Japan and caused a succession of diplomatic protests to be registered against each new forward thrust of Japan. He let it be known that he would not be provoked into war in Asia as long as the critical menace existed in Europe. After the election was over, President Roosevelt announced to the world that the United States would become an arsenal for the democracies, and his words were as electric in Tokyo as they were in Berlin or Rome.

World War II grew out of inseparable antagonisms in Europe and in Asia. Japan was not led or even advised by Germany, but it was encouraged by the psychological effects of German successes. The United States was driven along the road to global war by twin forces—Japan in Asia and Germany in Europe—and was obliged to do everything in its power to defend itself on both fronts at the same time. In the Atlantic and the Pacific it faced a common danger.

On January 6, 1941, President Roosevelt defined the four freedoms—freedom of speech and expression, freedom of every person to worship God in his own way, freedom from want, and freedom from fear—and declared that American self-defense no longer called for neutrality but for total resistance to tyranny. In March Congress passed the Lend-Lease Law which "would move the products from the assembly line of our factories to the battle line of the democracies—now." On May 27, 1941, the president proclaimed the existence of an unlimited national emergency. He warned Americans that if in modern times you "wait till you see the whites of their eyes, you will never know what hit you."

One more paragraph will complete the European background for the crisis which built up in Asia. After Germany attacked Russia, the president met with Prime Minister Churchill on board the "unsinkable" battleship, "Prince of Wales," in the North Atlantic. On August 12, 1941, they drew up the Atlantic Charter, which expressed the war aims of Great Britain and the diplomatic principles of the United States. Specific objectives included no territorial aggrandizement, self-determination, equal access to trade and raw materials, greater economic collaboration, peace and freedom from want after the destruction of Nazi tranny, freedom of the seas, and the abandonment of the use of force in international relations. Incidents in the Atlantic brought the United States and Germany to the very brink of war, and on Navy Day, October 27, 1941, President Roosevelt concluded his address with the declaration, "We Americans have cleared our decks and taken our battle stations." By the time of Pearl Harbor, American entry into the war in Europe seemed imminent at any moment.

The relations between the United States and Japan in 1941 rocked from crisis to crisis, in rhythm with the metronome in Europe. The Japanese had faith in themselves and their destiny. As General Tojo said, the duly constituted Japanese authorities believed that Japan's policies involved neither aggression nor exploitation. The moment had arrived for Japan to decide the "fate of our nation," a war of self-existence seemed to be its only alternative. The Japanese hoped to strike swiftly, entrench themselves in a limited area, and force a quick compromise settlement. The Japanese war machine was in gear; public opinion reached a fever pitch. The Japanese government decided to make a reasonable effort to accomplish its ends by diplomacy—if diplomacy should fail, Japan would resort to war.

As early as January, 1941, Ambassador Grew cabled from Tokyo that reports were current to the effect that Japan planned a mass attack at Pearl Harbor, perhaps some Sunday morning after the sailors had spent a typical Saturday night ashore. However, rumors in Tokyo were a dime a dozen, and the cable was filed away. It was Prime Minister Churchill's fear that the Germans might persuade the Japanese to attack the British in Asia at the same time the Germans battered the British in Europe. He believed that neither Germany nor Japan desired a war with the United States; therefore he urged President Roosevelt to do anything he could to curb the Japanese short of war. He also used his influence with the Japanese ambassador in London to dissuade the Japanese government from taking up arms in alliance with the Germans.

In January, 1941, Japan sent affable, poker-playing Admiral Nomura as its ambassador to the United States. His instructions were to persuade the Americans not to meddle in Japan's sphere of interest in East Asia. It was commonly, but erroneously, believed that his sole function was to "pull the wool over the eyes of Americans" while Japan carried on its military program. Admiral Nomura was a sincere man, an ardent patriot, and a hard-working diplomat. He met with President Roosevelt eight times and with Secretary Hull some fifty or sixty times. He made constant proposals for a peaceful understanding between Japan and the United States, but the American position was that all his efforts would be totally unnecessary if Japan would only live up to its treaty obligations. Secretary Hull told the Japanese ambassador that the United States had no intention of sitting quietly by while the militarists of two or three nations threatened to conquer the balance of the earth, including the seven seas and all trade routes and the other four continents.

Japan wanted the United States to acquiesce in its advance into

Southeast Asia, abandon Chiang Kai-shek and give its blessing to the Japanese program in China, take no notice of Japanese cooperation with Germany under the terms of the Axis Pact, and restore normal economic relations with Japan. The United States wanted Japan to withdraw from Southeast Asia, pull out of China, and stay out of the European war. In the meantime the United States sent a steady stream of supplies to Great Britain and Russia and tightened its economic measures against Japan. Export bans were expanded, and shipping restrictions were multiplied. Careful watch was kept by American diplomats for cleavages within Japan in order to detect local circumstances which might in any way be favorable to the United States. Diplomatic messages between the Japanese foreign office and the Japanese embassy in Washington were intercepted and decoded. Secretary Hull often knew Admiral Nomura's instructions more quickly than the Japanese representative himself.

On July 24 (after the Americans learned of the Japanese strike at Saigon) President Roosevelt invited Admiral Nomura to the White House to tell him that if Japan would call off its move in Indochina the United States would enter into a neutrality guarantee for Indochina which would assure Japan continued supplies of rice from that area. Then the president mused tactfully that so far he had refrained from an embargo on petroleum products because of the risk of provoking Japan to war. It had been his desire to keep war out of the Pacific area, but he intimated that his desire might be altered. Two days later he issued orders freezing the assets of Axis nationals. By these decrees, which also applied to the Philippines, an effective economic blockade was established against Japan. At the same time the president created USAFFE—the United States Armed Forces in the Far East—and recalled General MacArthur to active duty as its commander in chief. A military mission under General Magruder was sent to assist Chiang Kai-shek, and American troops and gunboats were shifted from China to the Philippines. American shipping to the orient was provided with cruiser escorts, and merchant ships were routed through the Torres Strait north to Australia to avoid Japanese waters.

It was in the midst of this determined opposition to Japan, that President Roosevelt and Prime Minister Churchill in their Atlantic Conference met to discuss their future policies. It was decided to warn Japan that further use of force would compel the United States and Great Britain to take all steps to insure their safety and security. War clouds hung lower; negotiations threatened to give way to hostilities. Prince Konoye and Admiral Nomura suggested a Japanese-American summit conference to overcome the diplomatic stalemate. Ambassador Grew strongly supported the Japanese suggestion, but the official American attitude was negative. It was held that unless prior understandings were reached, a meeting of the heads of states would only lead to deeper cleavages.

On September 6 (Tokyo date—September 5, Washington date) the Supreme War Council in Tokyo, intoxicated by the spectacular German drive into Russia decided that if its demands were not met by Great Britain and the United States, "we will make up our minds to get ready for war." Admiral Nomura presented Secretary Hull with a new version of his old proposals, only to be told on October 2 (after nearly a month's delay) that diplomacy was useless unless Japan got out of Indochina first.

Americans took their time, but the Japanese became more impatient. On October 17 General Tojo replaced Prince Konoye as prime minister. The Japanese military took over complete command of Japan's policies and went full speed ahead with its preparation for war. On November 20, the Japanese fleet rendezvoused at its base in the Kuriles in preparation for an attack on Hawaii. Secretary Hull informed his cabinet colleagues that negotiations were deadlocked and said that Japan might at any time start a new military movement of conquest by force. Ambassador Grew again cabled warnings of a possible tactical surprise by the Japanese. On November 24 Admiral Kimmel in Hawaii and Admiral Hart in Manila were advised that a "surprise attack in any direction is a possibility."

On November 26 Secretary Hull handed the Japanese representatives (Admiral Nomura and Ambassador Kurusu who had come to assist him) a note which the Japanese called an "ultimatum," but which the Americans considered as a recapitulation of their constant position. This note proposed that both Japan and the United States pledge themselves to a treaty system and recognize the traditional principles of international conduct. They should enter into a series of agreements covering nonaggression in the Pacific area, the status of Indochina, aid to Chiang Kai-shek, and normal economic relations. The Japanese were to withdraw their troops from Indochina and China, and it was assumed that the United States would be free to proceed in Europe in accordance with the requirements of its own defense. Since it was known from Japanese intercepts that "things were automatically going to happen in three days," the American government adhered to its rigid diplomatic stand in spite of the imminence of Japanese military action. Secretary Hull repeated his warning to the Secretaries of the Army and Navy that diplomacy was exhausted, that the next steps were in the hands of the military.

On December 6 President Roosevelt telegraphed the emperor of Japan a personal appeal to prevent further death and destruction in the world. In answer to the president's appeal and to the American demands of November 26, the Japanese sent their final diplomatic communication which was to be delivered in Washington, Sunday, December 7, at 1:00 p.m. Washington time. The note was delayed until after Japanese bombs were to be dumped in Hawaii and, in Secretary Hull's view, was worse than an insult. It charged that the American proposals ignored Japanese sacrifices during four years of the China affair, menaced the existence of the Japanese empire itself, and disparaged the honor and prestige of Japan. It accused the United States of conspiring against the new order and said that in view of the attitude of the United States, the Japanese government could not but consider it impossible to reach agreement through further negotiations.

In spite of President Roosevelt's statement that Japan's sneak attack constituted a day of infamy that would live forever, the Americans and their allies had not neglected their own military measures in East Asia. They had received Churchill's assurance a month before Pearl Harbor: "should the United States become involved in war with Japan, the British declaration will follow within the hour." American strategists worked out with their British and Dutch opposite numbers plans for the defense of Southeast Asia, the Philippines, and the Indies. Allies—and potential allies—held military conferences in Washington, Singapore, and Manila and moved their newest and best bombers into the Far East. Airfields were developed in Rabaul and Port Darwin, American marines were withdrawn from Shanghai, Canadian reinforcements were sent to Hong Kong, and the waters of Manila Bay were mined. The signs of impending hostilities were as "plain as though they were written on the blackboard for children."

At approximately the same time that the Japanese struck at Pearl Harbor, they swung into action in Shanghai, and dropped their bombs on Kota Bahru in Malaya and on Manila. The emperor of Japan then released the imperial rescript on December 7 (December 8 Tokyo time) which stated: "Eager for the realization of their inordinate ambition to dominate the Orient, both America and Britain, giving support to the Chungking regime, have aggravated the disturbance in East Asia . . . For existence and self-defense Our Empire has no other recourse but to appeal to arms." The Japanese action climaxed the seething hostility between the two camps in world affairs and merged the separate wars in Europe and Asia into one vast global conflict. The day after Pearl Harbor, Great Britain, the Netherlands, and China declared war on Japan. Within a few days the European members of the Axis alignment joined Japan and declared war on the United States. Of the great powers, only the Soviet Union—overwhelmed as it was in Europe—remained as a neutral in Asia.

SUGGESTED READING

Beard, Charles A., *President Roosevelt and the Coming of War* (New Haven, Yale U., 1948).

Churchill, Winston, *Second World War* (six vols.) (Boston, Houghton, 1948–1953).

Butow, Robert J. C., *Tojo and the Coming of the War* (Princeton, Princeton U., 1962).

Feis, Herbert, *Road to Pearl Harbor* (Princeton, Princeton U., 1950).

Grew, Joseph, *Turbulent Era* (two vols.) (Boston, Houghton, 1952).

Hull, Cordell, *Memoirs of Cordell Hull* (New York, Macmillan, 1948).

Japanese Government Foreign Office, *Collection of Official Documents and Releases, 1922–1940* (nineteen vols.) (Tokyo, Japanese Government, 1940).

Langer, William L., and Gleason, S. Everett, *Challenge to Isolation, 1937–1940* (New York, Harper, 1952).

————, *Undeclared War, 1940–1941* (New York, Harper, 1953).

Maki, John M., *Japanese Militarism* (New York, Knopf, 1945).

Millis, Walter, *This Is Pearl* (New York, Morrow, 1947).

Morison, Samuel E., *Rising Sun in the Pacific* (Boston, Little, 1948).

Shigemitsu, Mamoru, *Japan and Her Destiny* (New York, Dutton, 1958).

Togo, Shigenoru, *Cause of Japan* (New York, Simon, 1956).

Trefousse, Hans Louis, *What Happened at Pearl Harbor* (New Haven, College & University Press, 1958). (P)

United States Department of State, *Foreign Relations of the United States, Japan: 1931–1941* (two vols.) (Washington, Government Printing Office, 1942).

Wohlstetter, Roberta, *Pearl Harbor: Warning and Decision* (Stanford, Stanford U., 1962).

21

Japan's War of Greater East Asia

COURSE OF THE WAR

While the United States groped for a dramatic name for World War II, Japan gave it the label of The War of Greater East Asia. Japan announced immediately that its aim was to consolidate its position in China and to destroy Anglo-Saxon domination in Southeast Asia and the western Pacific. The Japanese general staff estimated that five months would be required to isolate Chiang Kai-shek; to conquer the Philippines, Malaya, Burma, and the Netherlands Indies; and to establish a defense perimeter extending in a giant arc from the Kuriles, through the Marshall Islands, the Bismarck Archipelago, New Guinea, Timor, and past the tip of Sumatra to the borders of India. Within this area Japan planned to create an impregnable military fortress and a self-sustaining economic co-prosperity sphere. Japan hoped that the United States would accept a compromise peace rather than pay the price to dislodge Japan from its conquests. It was taken for granted in Japan that Germany would smash Russia, defeat Great Britain, and make itself supreme in Europe. Then Germany could expand eastward and join hands with Japan in Central Asia or India.

When Japan attacked the American fleet at Pearl Harbor, its objective was to disable the striking arm of the navy. No hopes were entertained for a landing on Hawaii. The operation was fantastically successful, as capital ships were put out of action and 3000 American fighting men were killed. Within hours of the attack on Pearl Harbor, the Japanese struck at the Philippines. Within a single day airfields, army forts, and naval bases were rendered useless. Submarines were sunk at dockside and the American B-17 bombing fleet was destroyed on the ground. Before Christmas Guam, Wake Island, and Hong Kong fell to the Japanese.

The main Japanese force which moved into Southeast Asia was ridiculously small. Japan's early conquest was accomplished by a mere thirteen divisions, 1,175 land planes, 475 carrier planes, and a handful of marines. The Japanese forces fanned out from their recently acquired bases at Saigon and Camranh Bay and landed at Kota Bahru in Malaya. Some Japanese units drove into Thailand—which offered no resistance. On December 21 Thailand signed a treaty of alliance with Japan and on January 25, 1942, declared war on the United States and Great Britain.

The Japanese then approached Singapore from the land side—out of the range of the British guns which were aimed toward the sea. In a march of fifty-five days, the Japanese defeated British, Australians, Indians, and Malayans and on February 15, 1942, planted their flag at Singapore. In the first days of battle, Japanese airplanes sank the capital ships "Repulse" and "Prince of Wales." Japanese forces sent spearheads into Burma to cut the route of supplies to Chiang Kai-shek. On March 10, 1942, Rangoon fell; and by the end of April the Irrawaddy Valley was in the hands of the invaders. The Japanese gave what General Stilwell called a "hell of a beating" to the British, Indian, and Chinese forces who were forced to retreat through the jungles.

Meanwhile, in the Philippines the Japanese landed on Luzon Island —north and south of Manila—before the end of December, 1941. Manila was bombed repeatedly. The American army evacuated Manila—which was declared an open city by the retreating Americans—and took up prepared positions at Bataan and Corregidor. The Japanese occupied Manila on January 2, 1942. They took Bataan on April 9, 1942, and accepted the surrender of Corregidor less than a month later, on May 6. In the meantime, the Japanese pressed toward the Netherlands East Indies with their precious reserves of petroleum, bauxite, and rubber. Japanese parachute troops operating out of Malaya landed in Sumatra so quickly after the fall of Singapore that the Dutch had no time to destroy the oil derricks and set fire to the wells at Palembang. Organized resistance in Java ended with the capitulation of Batavia on March 9, 1942.

So far, so good for Japan. Almost according to schedule the Japanese reached the limits of their anticipated expansion. All too quickly, they began to suffer the consequences of their miscalculation of American recuperative power. Without diminishing the major military effort in Europe, the Americans set to work to contain Japan in the Pacific. They determined to hold Hawaii at all costs and to safeguard the supply line to Australia. Small hit-and-run bombing raids were carried out against the Japanese in the Gilbert and Marshall Islands and in New Guinea. On

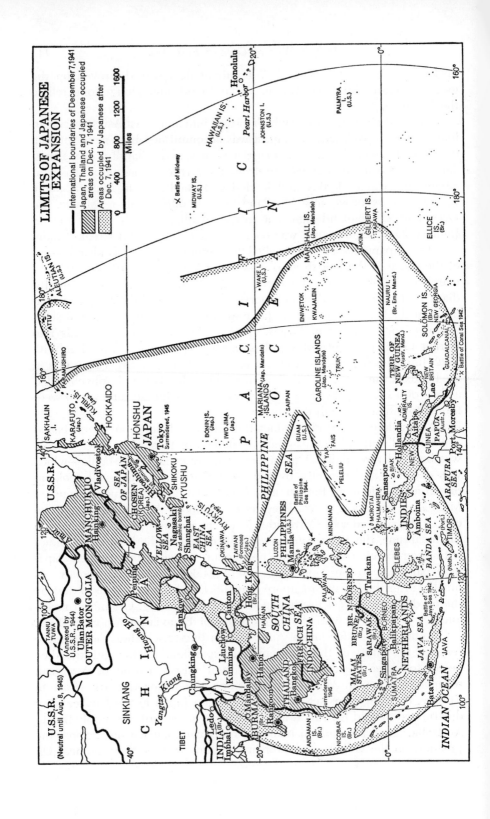

LIMITS OF JAPANESE EXPANSION

International boundaries of December 7, 1941
Japan, Thailand and Japanese occupied areas on Dec. 7, 1941
Areas occupied by Japanese after Dec. 7, 1941

Miles
0   400   800   1200   1600

April 18, 1942, Lieutenant Colonel James Doolittle carried out a spectacular, if ineffective, raid on Tokyo itself.

The Japanese then decided to stretch their defense perimeter to the Aleutians, Midway, Samoa, Fiji, New Caledonia, and the whole of New Guinea. Landings were made in the Aleutians; however, on June 4, 1942, efforts to occupy Midway were thwarted. The naval battle of Midway was the turning point of the war in the Pacific. The Americans unleashed a two-pronged counteroffensive—under Admiral Nimitz in the central Pacific and under General MacArthur in the southwest Pacific. In the latter theater of war, the Americans seized beachheads on Guadalcanal and Florida islands in the Solomons and occupied Tulagi on August 7, 1942. They fought bitterly against the Japanese at Port Moresby in New Guinea, and they stopped the advance of the Japanese navy toward Australia in the battle of the Coral Sea. No fewer than five major naval engagements were fought between August 1942 and November 1943 before Japan yielded the mastery of the southern seas. Then the Solomons became the forgotten battlefields, with Americans holding beachheads and airfields in spite of disease, tropical downpours, and the occasional artillery shells from the beleaguered Japanese who were holed up in the hills.

By November 1943 the American forces launched the relentless attack against the Japanese-held islands in the central Pacific, the Philippines, Formosa, and the Japanese mainland. The navy prepared to seize the more important islands and to leap-frog over the rest, leaving the marooned Japanese garrisons on the bypassed islands to wither on the vine; Tarawa and Makin in the Gilberts were retaken, followed by Kwajalein, Majuro, and Eniwetok in the Marshalls. In the Carolines, the Japanese strongholds at Truk and Ponape were bypassed; and in the Marianas, Saipan, Tinian, Rota, and Guam were captured in the summer of 1944. That one colorless sentence sums up an operation that demanded the lifeblood of thousands of young men and consumed a month's total economic output of an entire nation at work.

Early summer, 1944, was most noted for the Normandy invasion, but it was equally fateful in signaling the doom of Japan. The fall of Saipan (July 19) led to the dismissal of the Tojo government. The ultimate defeat of Japan was evident to all but the most diehard of the Japanese militarists. For a long time, American submarines had preyed upon Japanese tankers and merchantmen and had thrown an effective blockade around the Japanese homeland. The Japanese army was scattered in remote regions a long way from home and was entirely cut off from reinforcements and supplies. Battle lines extended over one-fifth of the globe. The flower of the Japanese race was driven by hunger, disease and superior odds to fight with a fanaticism born of despair. The soldiers' greeting to each other was "Until we meet in Yasukuni" (the sacred shrine for the spirits of the dead). Atrocities were more commonplace than qualities of mercy. The navy was in a precarious position, and in the defense of the Marianas the sea-borne air power of Japan was practically destroyed. With the loss of the airfields on Guam and Tinian, all of Japan became an exposed target for the America B-29's, or heavy bombers.

Meanwhile, General MacArthur accomplished the arduous return to the Philippines. From Port Moresby his men crossed over the Owen Stanley Range and occupied town after town along the northern coast of New Guinea. "What hellish fighting it was—with the Japanese only a few yards away in the ten-foot-high Kunai grass and with deadly snipers in every banyan tree!" One GI said: "The South Pacific is the only place in the world where you can be in mud up to your waist and wipe the dust out of your eyes." General MacArthur gained command of New Britain, bypassed Rabaul, and occupied Morotai, north of Halmahera, in September 1944 in readiness for the jump to the Philippines.

The two prongs of the American counteroffensive converged at Leyte on October 19, 1944—the first occupation point in the Philippines. Battles by sea and air knocked out the Japanese and opened the entire Philippine Archipelago for the American return. The Leyte campaign was over by Christmas, and Manila was in American hands within a month. The bombardment and destruction were appalling. Island after island, town after town, fell to the liberating forces; but the mopping-up operations cost as many casualties as the original landings.

Iwo Jima and Okinawa were the last bloody stops on the road to Tokyo. Iwo was secured in February, 1945, and Okinawa in April. Okinawa provided an advance base for operations against the Japanese in China and Korea and against Japan itself. By March, 1945, prior to heavy air attack on the home islands, Japan was reeling. Its navy had been sunk or immobilized, and its merchant marine had been annihilated. Japan's casualties were catastrophic. Only the unique willingness of the Japanese soldiers to face death and to endure hardships preserved their lingering effectiveness as a respectable fighting force. The conventional air power of Japan had been reduced to kamikaze, or suicide tactics; and the strangulation of Japan's economy was well under way before the devastating rain of bombs from "Mr. B-29." The Twentieth Air Force, in charge of strategic bombing, flew over 1,000,000 miles, made more than 32,000 sorties and dropped nearly 170,000 tons of bombs to reduce Japan's cities to ashes and to destroy Japan's will to fight. The job of defeating Japan was practically completed before August 6 when the atomic bomb blew Hiroshima into history.

JAPANESE HOME FRONT

The account of military expansion and contraction was only part of the story of Japan's War of Greater East Asia. The home front was as important as the field of battle. At the beginning of the war, Japan considered Korea and Formosa as part of the home front. War plans treated Manchukuo and North China as the "inner zone" and South China and the southern regions as the "outer zone." As the fortunes of war turned against Japan, the assets of the outer zone were lost and communications with the inner zone became difficult. Toward the end of the war, it became evident that areas under Japanese control outside Japan could not be expected to bear the strains of defeat in the same manner as Japan itself. Fifty years of overlordship had not converted Koreans and Formosans into Japanese. It was up to the people in the home islands alone to provide ambitious leaders for the soldiers, the fighting spirit, and the military supplies which the program of conquest demanded.

Japan's political institutions stood the tests of war although political procedures had to be modified. The emperor retained his position as the state incarnate. His prestige was not affected, but his views did not prevail. He did not prevent the coming of war, but he did make possible the making of peace. All decisions were made in the name of the government, headed by the premier. General Tojo continued in office as premier until July 1944, when he was replaced by General Koiso. Koiso's cabinet weathered impending disaster until April 1945, when the air raids began in earnest. An eighty-year-old patriarch, Admiral Suzuki, was made premier. He was looked upon as the one last leader who might bring victory. After the awful reality of defeat only a prince of the imperial family was entrusted with a government which could be expected to preserve Japan's national existence.

The constitution was not set aside, and the forms of representative government were not abandoned. The diet met in abbreviated sessions and retained its right of interpellation. Only one election was held—in April, 1942, when Japan rode the crest of the wave. Election ground rules were formulated so that candidates were elected who had the approval of the militarists. The diet became increasingly outspoken in its criticism of the government as war conditions grew worse; and new elections were scheduled for September, 1945, which turned out to be the moment of surrender. For the first time during the war, representatives were named to the Japanese diet from Korea, Formosa, and Karafuto (Sakhalin).

The government, that is, the premier and his cabinet, received all the criticism for Japan's reverses; yet it was powerless to make vital decisions. The premier was seldom consulted by the general staff, and he was never asked his opinion about the value of impending campaigns or actions. Ordinary cabinet officials were treated with little consideration. They were never more than advisers or administrators. Only selected cabinet members were asked to discuss policy matters. They were less influential than the boards, commissions, and advisory councils of ex-party leaders, bureaucrats, and businessmen whose utmost support was deemed essential for the war effort. When administrative chaos threatened to stifle production, the premier named a minister of munitions to act as an economic tsar. The foreign minister was reduced to a puppet, and he was overshadowed by a minister for greater East Asia. It was only when the soldiers failed that the diplomats and civilian officials were called in to clean up the debris of the debacle.

While the premier and his cabinet carried out their function as a political front, the Japanese sought new agencies to bear the vital responsibilities of government behind the scenes. The privy council and the officials of the imperial household (lord keeper of the privy seal, grand chamberlain, and minister of the imperial household) retained their importance. With the passing of the last genro, Prince Saionji, in 1940, a new and informal organization rose to prominence. It was referred to as the "senior statesmen" and it was composed primarily of former premiers. The emperor called upon the senior statesmen more frequently for advice as the crisis deepened. However, real policy makers were the officers of the imperial headquarters. They often announced their decisions through liaison conferences which were held between the high command and government officials in the imperial presence. In August 1944 a supreme council for the direction of the war, dominated by the military, was established as the highest policy-making body.

Local government was of secondary importance in wartime Japan. To improve administration, prefectures were grouped into nine (later eight) special administrative districts. Each region was placed under a chairman and a regional council. These chairmen worked closely with the army, and they were called together once a month in Tokyo. At the local level, the people were regimented into neighborhood associations in the villages and into block or war associations in the cities and towns. Similar associations had been used in Tokugawa times to collect taxes and apprehend criminals. In wartime Japan they were re-created to register labor, carry out air-raid defense, supervise rationing, and control the people's thoughts. These small organizations were invaluable for staging patriotic rallies, collecting scrap metal in the form of old pots and pans, and selling war bonds.

Political parties did not perish, although they ceased temporarily to operate. Political bosses kept their gangs around them, but they buried their identity in Prince Konoye's Imperial Rule Assistance Association. Although this large amorphous association, to which practically everybody belonged, contained cells which reached down into every village and hamlet, it was not a totalitarian party in the sense of the Communists in Russia, Fascists in Italy, or Nazis in Germany. The Japanese preferred to keep their own small groups under the tent of a giant body whose only common interest was the determination to be of assistance to the throne. Mass meetings were held, and propaganda slogans were shouted. With many serious-minded Japanese, the association was a great deal of nonsense. It was scorned by the army until in desperation Premier Tojo himself took over the association and tried to use it as a means of whipping up patriotic sentiment and stimulating production. The Imperial Rule Assistance Association gave way to an Imperial Rule Assistance Political Society (bolstered by a National Youth Corps) and eventually to a Greater Japan Political Association. None of these Japanese-style single parties developed into instrumentalities of effective political control.

Japan suffered under severe ideological handicaps during the war. Prince Konoye campaigned constantly for national spiritual mobilization and argued that Japan's great ideal was to bring the moral principles of the East and the civilization of the West into perfect synthesis and harmony. But Japan was not in a position to fashion its ideology as total anti-West or as total pro-East. Japan entered the war as a partner with two Western nations (Germany and Italy) against two other Western nations (Great Britain and the United States). Japan was therefore pro-*some* of the West and anti-*some* of the West. Its propaganda could be against the bad features of the West—"inefficient democracy, decadent liberalism, barbarous communism and Anglo-Saxon imperialism"—but it could not be indiscriminately leveled against *all* Westerners or *all* whites. Japan was equally handicapped in trying to represent itself as the spokesman of the East. It talked about its new structure dedicated to the new order in East Asia. However, Japan's most devastating psychological opponent was China, also a symbol of the East. China repudiated Japan's claims to ideological leadership and, by its war of resistance, exposed the hypocrisy and insincerity in Japan's major propaganda theme "Asia for the Asiatics."

Economically, Japan was no match for its enemies. In 1941 the authorities were carried away by their apparent progress. In spite of a decade of fighting in China, they had built up a respectable industry and accumulated a substantial stockpile of raw materials. They hoped that Manchukuo and China would supply vital resources and labor to do the coolie work for the Japanese forces and Japanese industry. They banked on a quick victory before the Americans and the British could get their production into high gear. Contrary to Japanese calculations, their own economy reached a peak and began to decline in 1942 when the American economy entered a period of staggering growth. At its peak, Japan produced 5000 airplanes per month; at war's beginning President Roosevelt called upon the Americans to produce ten times as many.

Japan was short in practically every essential of modern industry. It depended upon imports for petroleum, coking coal, rubber, nickel, tin, cotton, phosphate, potash, magnesite, graphite, and nonferrous metals. When some of these materials became available in the southern regions, Japan had neither the shipping, skilled labor, or plant facilities to take advantage of their conquests. Shortages of iron and steel deprived Japan of ships, guns, artillery, tanks, and armored cars. Stockpiles were exhausted with frightening speed. Although all production was mobilized for war purposes, Japan was never in the same league with the United States.

The Japanese man in the street experienced austerity which was unknown in America. Housewives worried about the thinness of the soup for breakfast and the availability of rice or its substitute for the next meal. They spent most of their time in queues for rations or working in their minuscule vegetable gardens. Every inch of land was devoted to food. People at home went hungry in order to ship rice to the boys overseas. Belts were tightened as rice disappeared from the stores and fish became scarcer each day. Not a single item of food could be purchased on the open market, and all restaurants and geisha houses were closed due to wartime austerity. Prices were fixed, but consumers' goods were not to be had at any price. The government did its best to distribute food fairly, but there was simply not enough to go around. Japan had its share of speculators, hoarders, bootleggers, and black-marketers; but as a rule cabinet members could not live much better than farmers or factory workers. Families sold their treasures or heirlooms for food, medicine, or something special for the children. Clothes were shabby and made of synthetic fiber which deteriorated rapidly. The men wore a kind of civilian uniform and women garbed themselves, as an economic necessity, in unattractive blouses and pants. Shoes were made of pressed paper, or anything but leather. People made money (yen) but most of it went into taxes or compulsory savings in the form of war bonds. In 1941 a yen was worth approximately a quarter of a dollar, but in 1945 an exchange quotation was meaningless.

Early in 1945 it was apparent that Japan was on the verge of economic collapse. The shortage of raw materials reduced the most ingenious of Japan's planners to despair. Steel was produced at the rate of a mere million tons per year, and it was doubtful if that level could have been maintained for long. As coal supplies dwindled, the coking ovens turned out less than one-third of the amount of toluol, which was needed for TNT. Petroleum was so short that the population was urged to dig up pine roots as a possible source of gasoline. By April 1945 only five Japanese battleships were afloat; of these only one, the "Yamato," was able to get sufficient fuel to sortie for the battle at Okinawa. The Japanese air force did not have gasoline for training purposes, reconnaissance flights or anti-submarine patrols. When a kamikaze pilot was ordered to take off with his bomb load, he was given enough gas to take him to his target, but not enough to bring him back. Oil tanks all over Japan were empty and were dismantled for scrap metal. Refineries were already out of operation when in the spring of 1945 they became major targets of American air attacks.

Japan's economic decline had reached the critical stage before Japan was subjected to the full force of the bombing raids. Due to the submarines and the blockade of the home islands, Japan was beaten months before the surrender. Of ten million tons of Japanese merchant shipping, eight and a half millions had been sent to the bottom. Ships sent from Japan to the southern regions with their precious cargoes of men, munitions, and supplies seldom reached their destination; not a shipload of supplies on the return journey from the southern regions reached Japan after January, 1945. Thousands of victims were sacrificed to the fury of the flames and the atomic bomb on Japan's divine land before the stubborn leaders would recognize the facts of defeat. It was only then that the people, heart sick and hungry, were granted relief from their heavy burdens.

Psychologically, the Japanese home front changed in much the same manner as any other home front might be expected to change in similar circumstances. The Japanese were stern-minded, cohesive, and patriotic, but they were not superhuman. By 1941 the whole populace was "brainwashed" until "100,000,000 hearts beat as one." The Japanese were told repeatedly that they were discriminated against, exploited and threatened by the Americans, and that there was no salvation, no hope of peace or common prosperity for all mankind except in war in which Japan would "kill or be killed, devour or be devoured." They believed but they did not understand. They were told that their ultimate triumph was the indisputable rule of heaven.

In the first stages of the war, the crowds shared the frenzy of Japan's first victories. An enthusiast wrote:

> From the icy rocks of the Aleutians, across the vast expanse of the Pacific and among its countless islands, down the littoral of the Asiatic continent, through the fabled lands of the Indies to the very gates of the Antipodes, and then around into the Indian Ocean, the undisputed power of Japan has been established. The sting of Japan's lash has been felt as far afield as the mainland of America, in the harbors of Australia, off the coast of Africa, and even in the Atlantic. Over tens of thousands of miles, from the Arctic to the tropics, over the seven

seas and on five continents, the land has rumbled to the tread of Japan's legions and the skies have thundered to the roar of Japan's winged knights of the air.

Another writer declared that "we will plant the Rising Sun flag, dyed with our life blood, on the farthest corners of the earth, in the far desert with its twinkling stars, and where the lion roars beneath the trees." He went on to say: "Our grandchildren shall raise a monument to us in a Chicago purged of gangsters, and when our time comes to cross the Styx, we will wrestle with the shades themselves." The masses were called upon to reflect the spirit of *Bushido* as bravely as the soldiers at the front. Fishermen dragging their nets out at sea, woodcutters burning charcoal deep in the mountains, and widows earning a living for their fatherless children were told that they were as beloved by the emperor as the soldiers who were enshrined in Yasukuni and worshiped as the patron gods of their divine land. The gentle, artistic, and esthetic side of Japanese culture was shunted aside by the demands of the nation at war.

All the media of communications were dedicated to the war effort. Movies were battle epics of the saga of heroes. They were the great molders of patriotic thought. The radio was a perpetual bearer of good military tidings, a director of calisthenics, or a reminder to eat less and work hard. The newspapers were official propaganda sheets fashioned by the minister of information. The war was treated as something inevitable, like a storm, and its purpose was seldom mentioned. The enemy was not personalized as someone to be hated. The Japanese were exhorted to offer their lives in the service of the emperor, and if need be to die properly and heroically with *banzai* on their lips.

Exultation disappeared from Japanese masses as the enemy roads converged on Tokyo. Tiny chinks appeared in the Japanese armor, and the "other side" began to emerge in Japanese behavior. The Japanese were not totally absorbed in affairs of the emperor and the state; they showed an increasing concern over their own fate and the future of their families. "Was it really better 'to die or to live to fight another day'?" Correspondents from the front wrote that "our men are shedding tears over their vain efforts before the inexhaustible stream of enemy bullets from the air"; more remarkably, their stories were printed in the daily press. Whispers were heard of draft-dodging and desertion. Tales of jumping ship became more frequent, and at least one feature article urged young Japanese sailors not to be afraid of American submarines.

War-weariness was the inevitable companion of suffering. The Japanese longed for lights and gaiety on the deserted, blacked-out streets of Tokyo. They resented the "hero's life" and the relentless austerity. They registered the same disgust as people in Germany or Great Britain against the inequities of rationing and the black market. Their patience wore thin, and they sought escape from their pent-up emotions in bootleg sake. They dreaded the air raids as much as people everywhere. Some met death quickly, bravely, and stoically. Others screamed in fear or pain and wept hysterically because of the tragedies to themselves or their loved ones. However, no mass of people ever suffered more than the Japanese. They were spiritually numb and psychologically exhausted when the emperor informed them that hostilities had come to an end.

DIPLOMATIC WARFARE: THE UNITED NATIONS

In time of actual fighting, diplomats on both sides of the Pacific were less assertive and less important than generals. However the diplomatic tug-of-war continued quietly and unspectacularly until hostilities ended. Then the pendulum reversed. Military leaders faded into the background, and the conference tables again took the place of battlefields as the main arena of international conflict.

On January 1, 1942, the representatives of twenty-six nations at war against the Axis signed at Washington the Declaration of the United Nations. The signatory governments, "convinced that complete victory over their enemies is essential to defend life, liberty, independence, and religious freedom and to preserve human rights and justice in their own lands as well as in other lands, and that they are now engaged in a common struggle against savage and brutal forces seeking to subjugate the world," pledged themselves to employ their full resources, military or economic, against the members of the Tripartite Pact and its adherents and not to make a separate armistice or peace with any enemy.

A major diplomatic conference was held in January 1943, at Casablanca, when President Roosevelt suggested that it would be very desirable to get a definite engagement from Russia that it would join in the war against Japan once Germany was defeated. At a subsequent meeting between Roosevelt and Prime Minister Churchill in Quebec in August 1943, the question of Russian participation in the Pacific War again came up for discussion. The Southeast Asia Command, under Lord Mountbatten, was created at Quebec, and separated from the China theater, under Chiang Kai-shek. In October, the Council of Foreign Ministers met at Moscow. During the course of the conference, Stalin astonished Secretary Hull by saying unequivocally that the Soviet Union would join in the war against Japan after the defeat of Germany. He made no mention of the Russo-Japanese neutrality pact.

President Roosevelt and Prime Minister Churchill could not arrange a meeting with Chiang Kai-shek and Stalin at the same time as long as Russia was formally a neutral in Asia. In November 1943, they met with

Chiang in Cairo; at the conclusion of their talks Roosevelt and Churchill proceeded to Tehran to meet with Stalin. On December 1, Great Britain, the United States, and China issued the Cairo Declaration:

> It is their purpose that Japan shall be stripped of all the islands in the Pacific which she has seized or occupied since the beginning of the first World War in 1914, and that all territories Japan has stolen from the Chinese, such as Manchuria, Formosa, and the Pescadores, shall be restored to the Republic of China. Japan will also be expelled from all other territories which she has taken by violence and greed. The aforesaid three great Powers, mindful of the enslavement of the people of Korea, are determined that in due course Korea shall become free and independent.

At Tehran Stalin gave his approval to the Cairo Declaration. He reaffirmed the Soviet plan to join in the Pacific war, an act which gladdened the President, the prime minister and their staffs. Stalin showed himself less eager to move rapidly against Japan than the Allies would have liked. It was also clear that Stalin in his own good time would come forward with the price tag which the Soviet Union would demand for its participation. Almost all the Soviet demands which were later accepted at Yalta were discussed in a provisional way at Tehran.

President Roosevelt and Prime Minister Churchill next met Stalin at Yalta, in February 1945, immediately after the president's inauguration for a fourth term. The Big Three exchanged views about Germany, Poland, Austria, and Yugoslavia; thoughts on treatment of states liberated from the Nazis; and plans for the United Nations, the Council of Foreign Ministers, and the Far East. They sketched their grand design for a postwar world, and the Far East seemed to be the least important component. They met from Sunday to Friday, and they did not reach Far East problems until Thursday afternoon. They wanted a formal agreement on China as a precondition of Stalin's entry into the Pacific war. It was accepted policy that Soviet assistance against Japan was eminently to be desired because it would shorten the war and save countless American lives. (See below for the text of the Far East provisions of the Yalta agreement.)

When President Roosevelt left Yalta, according to Harry Hopkins, "we really believed in our hearts that this was the dawn of the new day we had all been praying for and talking about for so many years." No new day appeared for Chiang Kai-shek, who was not even shown the text of the Yalta agreement. The brightest new day came for Stalin, who proceeded to interpret the European clauses of the Yalta agreement according to his own pleasure and to move on to the Far East for the kill. On April 6, 1945, Russia informed Japan that the neutrality pact had lost its meaning and that continuance of the pact was impossible. It was supposed to be in effect for another year.

On April 12, 1945, President Roosevelt died. On May 1 Hitler disappeared from the scene, and one week later German resistance ended. The Russians began to transfer their troops to the east, and the diplomats of the Western world met in San Francisco to organize the United Nations. From July 17 to August 2, Truman, Churchill (later Attlee), and Stalin met at Potsdam to discuss the unsettled business of the war against Japan. Decisions had to be made about the terms of surrender for Japan, Soviet entry into the Pacific war, and the Sino-Soviet treaty. The news of the successful explosion of the atomic bomb forced a new appraisal of the factors for victory, but it was too late to bring about any fundamental change in the agreements of Yalta. Truman was soberly impressed with the news of the bomb, Churchill called it "the second coming in wroth," but Stalin seemed uninterested. For at least a month the Soviet intelligence service had had full knowledge of the bomb and the coming first test.

At Potsdam the American and Soviet chiefs of staff worked out a synchronized plan of military action against Japan. The line delimiting the Soviet area of operations ran from the interior of Asia through Manchuria down to Busui Tan (Cape Boltina) on the Korean coast, then through the Sea of Japan to a point on the La Perouse Straits, between Sakhalin and Hokkaido. Part of South Manchuria and practically all of Korea were assigned to the Americans. On July 26 the Potsdam Declaration was released, defining the conditions for Japan's surrender:

> There must be eliminated for all time the authority and influence of those who have deceived and misled the people of Japan into embarking on world conquest . . .
>
> . . . Points in Japanese territory to be designated by the Allies shall be occupied . . .
>
> The terms of the Cairo Declaration shall be carried out and Japanese sovereignty shall be limited to the islands of Honshu, Hokkaido, Kyushu, Shikoku and such minor islands as we determine.
>
> We do not intend that the Japanese shall be enslaved as a race or destroyed as a nation, but stern justice shall be meted out to all war criminals. . . . The Japanese Government shall remove all obstacles to the revival and strengthening of democratic tendencies among the Japanese people. Freedom of speech, of religion, and of thought, as well as respect for the fundamental human rights, shall be established.
>
> Japan shall be permitted to maintain such industries as will sustain her economy and permit the exaction of just reparations in kind.

DIPLOMATIC WARFARE: JAPAN

Before considering the impact of these surrender terms in Tokyo, attention must be drawn to the diplomatic battle with the United Nations as it had developed from the viewpoint of the Japanese. Japan did not achieve the cooperation and close liaison with its partners which the United States enjoyed with Great Britain and Russia. Japan gave no warning of Pearl Harbor to Germany or Italy, but the initial successes of and Japanese gave a tremendous lift to German and Italian morale. Exultant Japan and its equally exuberant friends in Europe concluded a military alliance on December 11, 1941; however, misunderstandings followed quickly in the wake of stalemate and defeat. Germans and Japanese were not able to work out coordinated attacks against their common enemies. "One world" at war was in reality "one world in two wars"; one in Europe and the other in Asia and the Pacific. Germany wanted Japan to shift its attack from the southern regions to Russia. Japan urged Germany to cut its losses in Europe and to come to the aid of Japan in the East. After its original expansive drive, Japan would have been most receptive to almost any peace on compromise terms. Hitler had no sympathy for Japan's desire to make peace. Japan showed little interest in Italy, and after Italy's surrender Italians were interned the same as enemy aliens in Japan.

In the earliest stages of the war, Premier Tojo disdained diplomacy as a useful weapon for the furtherance of Japan's national interests. He considered greater East Asia as the only region which mattered, and he chose not to deal with it through the normal channels of the Japanese foreign office. He named his own henchmen as minister for greater East Asia and minister of foreign affairs, and he expected them to do nothing except to serve the will of the Japanese military. The inadequacies of his prescription became apparent as soon as the first flush of victory disappeared. He then called upon an experienced diplomat, Shigemitsu Mamoru, former ambassador to Russia, Great Britain, and China, to take charge of Japan's foreign relations.

Shigemitsu felt that his first duty was to define Japan's war aims in East Asia. He would convince China and all neighboring nations that Japan genuinely stood for liberation from imperialism and for the birth of a New Asia. He insisted upon recognition of equality for all nations of Asia as a basis for permanent peace. He knew better than the Japanese militarists that China could not be scorned and abused, and he felt that a settlement with China on an equitable basis was the only hope for a reasonable future in East Asia. In the broader picture Shigemitsu saw clearly the relative weakness of Japan. He had lived abroad, and he appreciated the strength of the enemy nations. He knew that the army was determined to fight to the bitter end, but he also knew that the emperor longed for peace. As foreign minister, Shigemitsu believed that his most important duty was to bring about peace with honor. If Japan should fail, it must rise again.

Peace talk in Japan was considered treason. The secret police watched carefully cabinet members, senior statesmen, diet members, and ordinary people of a liberal turn of mind who might conceivably be prepared to accept peace short of victory. Officials like Shigemitsu were obliged to work amid extreme difficulties in an atmosphere of pervading suspicion. A very select coterie of Japanese, through sources of information from such neutral capitals as Stockholm, Lisbon, and Buenos Aires, were well-informed about conditions abroad. They knew that Stalin intended to participate in the Pacific war in spite of the neutrality pact; yet they had insufficient bait to induce Stalin to stay a neutral throughout the war. The Japanese hastened to come to agreement with Russia whenever misunderstandings arose—as was the case with fisheries, the North Sakhalin concessions, transit of aid supplies from North America to Siberia, and the Russian grant of asylum to American flyers who were downed in Russian territory after having dumped their bombs on Japan. It was the Japanese dream to make peace between Russia and Germany, so as to win Russia over to the side of the Axis.

Japanese premiers in wartime were inclined to conduct their own foreign affairs and to ignore the diplomats whenever possible. Koiso was as adamant as Tojo. Koiso shared Shigemitsu's determination to settle the China affair, but the premier failed to appreciate his colleague's insistence upon fair and equitable treatment. His diplomacy was to detach Chiang Kai-shek from his Anglo-Saxon allies and to smash the united front in China between Chiang Kai-shek and the Communists. Koiso wanted Chiang to desert Mao and join up with Wang Ching-wei on a platform of anticommunism. Koiso used businessmen in Shanghai or secret agents at Chungking as go-betweens and resorted to bribes and fantastic offers in his vain efforts to attract Chiang to the Japanese side. Elsewhere in greater East Asia, Japan tried to cut its military losses by giving support to free India and by encouraging independence for Burma, the Philippines, and Indonesia. In Indochina, Japan tolerated the French (Vichy) regime until De Gaulle entered Paris. When Governor-General de Coux swore allegiance to De Gaulle early in 1945, Japan had no alternative but to replace the French administration with a Japanese military government.

Even greater East Asia became a side issue as the realization grew in Japan that compromise or further temporizing would be impossible. After the Japanese disasters in the Marianas in July, 1944, the focal point in all Japanese policy became the protection of the home islands and the future of the Japanese nation itself. Fears deepened with the success of the American campaign in the Philippines. Iwo and Okinawa were the last barriers to invasion. All the while the air raids converted Japanese cities into seas of flame, diplomats struggled to find an acceptable way to end the war.

DEFEAT AND SURRENDER

Iwo fell in February, and in March the attack on Okinawa loomed just beyond the horizon. The senior statesmen—including Wakatsuki, Okada, Hiranuma, and Prince Konoye—asked Foreign Minister Shigemitsu secretly if there was any way by which Japan could be rescued from its hopeless position. The talk of the time was that the loyal Japanese masses would lure the enemy ashore and fight to the last man with wooden guns and bamboo spears if necessary. Shigemitsu felt that the people were too exhausted to think clearly and that the wish deepest in their hearts was that the war would end. He told the senior statesmen that the worst was yet to come because Russia would probably join with the United States and Great Britain. He suggested that discreet inquiries might be made in Sweden as to the peace terms the allies had in mind. Perhaps overtures looking to an end to hostilities might be made to Russia—as a neutral mediator—or messages might be addressed directly to the United States and Great Britain broaching the subject of peace.

No immediate action was taken. Okinawa fell early in April and Admiral Suzuki succeeded General Koiso as premier. Togo Shigenori replaced Shigemitsu as foreign minister, and Togo was known as an advocate of closer relations with Russia. At this juncture Russia announced the termination of the neutrality pact. Togo authorized Hirota and Prince Konoye to approach Jacob Malik, the Russian ambassador in Tokyo, with an offer to transfer to Russia certain Japanese rights on the continent as an inducement to peace. Malik was interested; Moscow was not. However, Molotov assured Ambassador Saito in Moscow that Russia still intended to honor the neutrality pact during the remaining year—although secretly Russia was rushing its troops eastward across Siberia.

On June 8 Marquis Kido, the lord keeper of the privy seal, received imperial assent to embark upon a project to bring the war to an end. Or as the Supreme War Council put it, "to carry on the war under more favorable circumstances." Things moved slowly, and on June 22 His Majesty summoned the entire Supreme War Council to a tea party and in its presence gave instructions to the premier to prepare plans for terminating the war. The emperor stressed the need for haste, but the army would not countenance anything that looked like surrender. The premier decided on July 7 to send Prince Konoye to Moscow with a letter from the emperor asking Russia to mediate. While Ambassador Saito strove to get Russian permission for Konoye to make this trip, Stalin and Molotov took off for Potsdam. All the while the Potsdam conference was in session, the Japanese were at Stalin's door as suppliants for peace.

Diplomats in Tokyo were anxious for peace, and only the military extremists showed determination to protect the emperor by fighting to the
death.

In these circumstances, the Japanese received the radio transmissions
of the terms of the Potsdam Declarations. The terms were severe: Japanese territories would be restricted to nineteenth-century limits. Korea
would become independent, Formosa and the Pescadores were to be
restored to China, and the mandated islands given up. Reference was
made to reparations, a ban on the manufacture of munitions, the punishment of war criminals, and the adoption of democracy. Still it was provided that Japan should be permitted to have a viable economy, and the
fate of the emperor was not specified. Tojo's reaction to the Potsdam
Declaration was one of indignation, and Premier Suzuki ordered that it
should be treated with contempt.

Then came the most fatal ten days that Japan had ever experienced.
An atomic bomb fell on Hiroshima, and President Truman said: "If they
do not accept our terms they may expect a rain of ruin from the air, the
like of which has never been seen on this earth." The Soviet Union entered the war, and a second bomb shook Nagasaki. The army suggested
acceptance of the Potsdam ultimatum subject to four conditions: the position of the emperor must be retained as a national institution, the enemy
must not land on Japan or attempt to occupy it, Japanese forces abroad
should be withdrawn on Japan's own initiative, and war criminals were
to be tried by the Japanese themselves. The government, in distinction to
the army, showed willingness to accept the Potsdam Declaration on the
single condition that the emperor institution should be preserved. The
emperor himself ruled in favor of the government, but his secret decision
in the air raid shelter of the imperial palace did not serve to eliminate the
ominous rumbles of civil war in Tokyo.

On August 10, the Japanese government cabled its conditional acceptance of the Potsdam Declaration to the United States by way of
Switzerland. While the Japanese awaited their reply, the Russian army
drove deeper into Manchuria and the American navy ploughed closer to
the shores of Japan itself. After an eternity of twenty-four hours, the Japanese received the following telegram from Secretary Byrnes: "From the
moment of surrender the authority of the Emperor and the Japanese Government to rule the State shall be subject to the Supreme Commander of
the Allied Powers, who will take such steps as he deems proper to effec-
tuate the surrender terms." Did this mean, or did it not mean, that the
Japanese would be permitted to retain their sacred emperor? For three
days the army and the government argued.

On August 14, Tokyo time, in the small hours of a moonlit morning,
the emperor solemnly told the Supreme War Council that he had decided

to "end the war." He prepared a record which would announce his decision to his people at noon the following day. Premier Suzuki submitted his resignation. The emperor himself summoned his senior commanders responsible for home defense and explained his position. They consented to obey his will. War Minister Anami disemboweled himself in ceremonial fashion rather than submit to the disgrace of surrender.

On the morning of August 15 (Tokyo date), when crowds were delirious with joy in San Francisco and London, the Japanese were brought to the brink of civil war. Army units burned the residence of the premier and ransacked the palace in search of the emperor's record, which they intended to destroy. General Tanaka, in command of Tokyo defense, put down the uprising. The rebellious officers committed suicide en masse. Then General Tanaka satisfied himself that the broadcast would take place as scheduled and that Tokyo was in no further danger of civil war. Having fulfilled his heavy responsibilities, he destroyed himself with his own sword.

At midday, the high-pitched imperial voice told his people that he had issued an imperial rescript ending the war. He told his good and loyal subjects: "We declared war on America and Britain out of Our sincere desire to ensure Japan's self-preservation and the stabilization of East Asia, it being far from Our thought either to infringe upon the sovereignty of other nations or to embark upon territorial aggrandizement." He went on to say that after nearly four years of fighting, "the war situation has developed not necessarily to Japan's advantage." Moreover, he said: "The enemy has begun to employ a new and most cruel bomb, the power of which to do damage is indeed incalculable. Should we continue to fight, it would not only result in an ultimate collapse and obliteration of the Japanese nation, but also it would lead to the total extinction of human civilization." In conclusion, he said: "It is according to the dictate of time and fate that We have resolved to pave the way for a grand peace for all the generations to come by enduring the unendurable and suffering what is insufferable." He warned against outbursts of emotion and fraternal strife: "Let the entire nation continue as one family from generation to generation . . . Unite your total strength to be devoted to the construction for the future. Cultivate the ways of rectitude; foster nobility of spirit; and work with resolution so as ye may enhance the innate glory of the Imperial State and keep pace with the progress of the world."

To the masses who had been indoctrinated with the psychology of fight to the death, the emperor's broadcast was a bolt from the blue. When it dawned on them that the emperor had decided to spare them further suffering, their hearts were filled with gratitude. The emotional relief was about the only good thing in Japan's desperate situation. Prince Higashikuni was ordered to head the new government which would be responsible for carrying out measures for ending the war. It was necessary to persuade troops in the field to accept the order to cease fire, to bring Japanese troops home, and to carry out the terms of the Potsdam Declaration. General Kawabe was sent to Manila to receive directions for the accomplishment of the formal surrender.

On August 14 (Washington date)—at approximately the same time the imperial record was played over the Japan Broadcasting Station in Tokyo—President Truman announced that the war was over and that General Douglas MacArthur was designated Supreme Commander for the Allied Powers (SCAP) to accept Japan's surrender and to carry out the occupation of Japan. General Order Number One, issued by Mac-Arthur as soon as his appointment was made official, ordered the Japanese in China (excluding Manchuria), Formosa, and Indochina north of sixteen degrees north latitude to surrender *only* to Chiang Kai-shek. Japanese within Manchuria, Korea north of the thirty-eighth parallel, and Sakhalin were to surrender to Russia. Japanese elsewhere were ordered to surrender to the United States and its allies.

Late in August, American naval units steamed into Tokyo Bay, and small advance units of the Eleventh Airborne Division landed without incident at Atsugi Airport near Yokohama. On September 1 the main forces of the United States Eighth Army landed, and with the cooperation of Japanese officials, assumed control of Japan's "divine land" in the vicinity of Tokyo and Yokohama. Formal surrender ceremonies took place the next day aboard the flagship of the American fleet, the U.S.S. "Missouri."

Perhaps the emperor himself summed up best the mood of Japan in a brief poem:

> Man should be like the manly pine
> That does not change its color
> Though bearing the fallen snow.

Shigemitsu wrote that Japan had experienced death in order to have a fuller life. He was among those who saw the last twenty years of Japan's national existence as a horrible nightmare. He hoped that Japan would follow literally the emperor's admonition to "work with resolution so as to enhance the innate glory of the Imperial State and keep pace with the progress of the world."

SUGGESTED READING

Amrine, Michael, *Great Decision* (New York, Putnam, 1959).

Butow, Robert J. C., *Japan's Decision to Surrender* (Stanford, Stanford U., 1954).

Cohen, Jerome B., *Japan's Economy in War and Reconstruction,* Minneapolis (U. of Minnesota, 1949).

Congdon, Don, (ed.), *Combat, the War with Japan* (New York, Dell, 1962). (P)

Feis, Herbert, *Between War and Peace* (Princeton, Princeton U., 1960).

Feis, Herbert, *Japan Subdued* (Princeton, Princeton U., 1961).

Hachiya, Michihiko, *Hiroshima Diary* (Chapel Hill, U. of North Carolina, 1955).

Hersey, John, *Hiroshima* (New York, Knopf, 1946).

Jones, F. C., Borton, Hugh, and Pearn, B. R., *Far East, 1942–46* (New York, Oxford U., 1955).

Kase, Toshikazu, *Journey to the Missouri* (New Haven, Yale U., 1950).

Leahy, William D., *I Was There* (New York, Whittlesey, 1950).

Lee, Clark, *They Call It Pacific* (New York, Viking, 1943).

Sherwood, Robert, *Roosevelt and Hopkins* (New York, Harper, 1948).

Toland, John, *But Not in Shame* (New York, Random, 1961).

Truman, Harry S., *Memoirs* (two vols.) (New York, Doubleday, 1955).

Tsuji, Masonobu, *Singapore, The Japanese Version* (Sydney, Australia, Ure Smith, 1960).

United States Department of State, *Foreign Relations of the United States. The Conferences at Cairo and Tehran, 1943* and *The Conferences at Malta and Yalta, 1945* (Washington, Government Printing Office, 1961 and 1955).

Yoshida, Shigeru, *Yoshida Memoirs* (London, Heinemann, 1961).

22

World War II and China

Nothing contributed more to the downfall of Japan than its frustration in China. Japan was neither able to force China to surrender nor to win China's support for the new order. On the broader stage, Japan never had a chance to win the race with the Western powers because one leg was always deeply mired in the mud of China. China pinned down thousands of Japan's best troops and drained away Japan's resources. Every Japanese scheme for control of China or destruction of China's unity was shattered by Chinese resistance.

It was a miracle that after ten years of invasion and nearly four years of global war the Chinese nation survived. The key to survival was the Chinese peasant. He supplied the food and the manpower which were the only resources which China possessed. He worked in wartime the same as in peace "tilling the sod and harrowing the clod," except that the work was harder and the returns were less. Wandering soldiers—Chinese or Japanese—conscripted or killed his able-bodied sons, stole his mule or his ox, and walked away with his grain. He had barely enough to eat. Millions died but more millions lived. The peasants remained as the foundation on which the new Chinese nation would have to be built.

Throughout the entire course of the war, the Japanese were forced to contend with the same complex "Chinas" which their invasion had created. The legal government of China in the eyes of most of the world was that of Chiang Kai-shek at Chungking. That government bore the brunt of the Japanese attack. The second China was occupied China—the cities, coastal areas, river valleys, provincial centers, railways, and highways—under the rule of enemy guns. The third China, perhaps the most difficult of all, was that vast hinterland beyond the long reach of the Japanese military. In that area where local law or no law prevailed, the peasants survived by their own brawn and brains. In that area also the

461

Communists expanded their power at the expense of the Kuomintang. In all three Chinas, the spirit of nationalism hardened. Each in his own way—Chiang Kai-shek, Wang Ching-wei, and Mao Tse-tung and the millions which each one symbolized—felt that he opposed Japan in the most effective fashion. Chiang did not feel that he was a dictator, Wang that he was a traitor nor Mao that he was a rebel. Each believed that he contributed to China's ultimate future as a strong and great nation.

If Japan's War of Greater East Asia did anything for all China, it made China one of the most confident and assertive exponents of nationalism in East Asia. China emerged from the war bloody and devastated, economically exhausted and torn by internal dissensions. But its huge mass was ready to be molded into a form and energized with a spirit capable of fulfilling what all its leaders conceived to be China's rightful destiny as one of the "great" powers of the entire world.

NATIONALIST CHINA—CHIANG KAI-SHEK

When the bombs fell on Pearl Harbor, the echoes in Chungking brought a great sense of rejoicing. The Chinese knew that they would not have to continue the fight alone. The bitterness of neglect momentarily disappeared. Too long the Chinese felt they had been unappreciated and overlooked, and the slight tokens of sympathy and assistance from the United States were no more than a sop to their wounded feelings. Early in 1941 the Americans made China eligible for Lend-Lease, but a great time gap separated the promise of help and actual delivery of the goods. A technical mission was dispatched to increase the tonnage over the Burma Road, and the organization of General Chennault's Volunteer Air Group with official American blessing climaxed a series of measures intended to bolster China's air strength. Such small measures seemed insignificant in the light of the substantial American program of help to its friends in Europe. With the entry of the United States into World War II, the government at Chungking believed that its star was bound to rise. Humiliation and suffering became more bearable because ultimate victory was assured.

Immediately after Pearl Harbor, the Japanese aimed to complete the encirclement of the Chinese nationalists by cutting the Burma Road. To thwart the Japanese, the allied high command set up the China-Burma-India (C-B-I) theater, with Chiang Kai-shek as commander-in-chief and with the American General Joseph Stilwell as his deputy. Chiang offered to send two armies to Burma to fight alongside the British, but General Wavell was not eager for Chinese assistance. British pride seemed to be at stake, and the Burmese officials did not relish the prospect of poorly fed and ill-disciplined Chinese troops in their country. Anglo-Chinese relations were cool from the beginning. Chiang visited India in February, 1942, to call attention to the plight of South Asia; Prime Minister Churchill, however, would not assent to a proposed conference between Chiang and Gandhi.

The campaign to hold Burma against the Japanese, with General Stilwell in command, was a disaster for the allies. British Indian contingents were speedily driven out of the Rangoon area, and the Chinese expeditionary force in north Burma was routed. By mid-April, 1942, all of Burma was in Japanese hands. The British and Americans made their way through the jungles to India, and the Chinese remnants straggled back to their own borders ahead of the advancing Japanese. Stilwell said curtly that the Japanese "gave us a hell of a beating." He explained that the defeat was due to bitter antagonism between British, Chinese, and Americans; a hostile Burmese population, which was as willing to put knives in the backs of the British as the Japanese; superior Japanese initiative, which enabled their soldiers to march three hundred miles in eighteen days; "stupid, gutless leadership" on the part of the officers; and defeatism on the part of the soldiers. It became Stilwell's obsession to reorganize the Chinese army and to recapture Burma as a prelude to a drive across brutal, mountainous territory into China itself. He was in constant conflict with the British (who wanted to fight back across Malaya instead of Burma), with the Chinese (who wanted to spare their soldiers from fighting in Burma so they could be used at home in China); and with General Chennault (who thought it was stupid to rely on the foot soldiers for jobs which could be accomplished so much easier by air power). General Stilwell could not get allotments of supplies for his campaign. He confided to his diary that "The Peanut (Chiang Kai-shek) and I are on a raft with a sandwich between us, and the rescue ship is headed in the other direction."

The Allies set up a training center for Chinese troops in Ramgarh, central India, after the Burma debacle. Some 60,000 Chinese soldiers, subject to the command of Chiang Kai-shek, received modern training in India, where they were better fed and more efficiently equipped than they ever imagined a Chinese army would be. At the same time, some thirty Chinese Nationalist divisions were trained, largely by American advisers in southwest China, and were equipped with materiel which was flown in over the mountainous "hump" between Burma and China. At a fantastic cost in manpower, Americans helped the Chinese build bases in China which were immediately useful for air attacks on Japanese shipping. It was hoped that in due course these bases would serve as take-off points for attacks against the Japanese army in China and ultimately for massive raids on Japan. These bases, and the whole C-B-I theater, declined in importance as the Americans drove spectacularly against Japan across the Pacific.

The dreary work of training and waiting continued through 1943, while diplomats on the world stage talked about China's promising political future. Lacking the landing craft, tanks, guns, and planes to meet the needs of Russia, the Italian campaign, the second front, and the C-B-I, the Allies tried to use diplomatic encouragement to divert Chinese attention from its military plight. Chiang demanded assistance and action and permitted hints to leak out that some Chinese might understandably be attracted by persistent Japanese overtures for peace. In December, 1943, Stilwell launched his "back to Burma" drive from headquarters in Assam. The going was rough, but the British and Indians drove successfully through Arakan on the west, while the Chinese hammered away at the Japanese on the upper Salween in the east and north of Burma. In August, 1944, Myitkyina in upper Burma was recaptured. The Allies were poised for a major thrust to retake the Burma Road and to clear the way to reestablish communications between the outside world and beleaguered China.

Then the Japanese began to stir in China. While fatally engaged in the central Pacific and Southeast Asia, the Japanese remained comparatively quiet in China. In the summer of 1944—as the Japanese faced the realities of global defeat—they adopted new tactics in, and tightened their grip on China. Some militaristic hotheads in Japan talked of the possibility of becoming so strong that they might fight on in China and the entire inner zone should their beloved home land "suffer unforeseen catastrophes." The Japanese launched new offensives in China. They occupied many smaller, previously ignored cities along the rivers and the coast. It was their belief that the smaller cities would become very important if Chinese from the interior should try to link up with possible American landing parties on the coast.

The Japanese launched major offensives along the railways north and south of Hankow toward Peiping and Canton. It was the Japanese intention to cut China in two and to isolate Chungking. This would deprive Chiang of any possible source of help should the Japanese decide to press on toward the Nationalist strongholds in Kunming, Sian, or the capital, Chungking. In 1944, when allied fortunes were brightest in Normandy, in the Marianas, and in the Philippines, the Chinese came nearest to collapse. The Japanese advanced practically as they pleased. They caused Chinese armies to evaporate and destroyed most of the Sino-American airbases, which had been built with superhuman efforts. A half-million Chinese soldiers were lost. Eight provinces and a population of 100,000,000 Chinese were ripped from the ostensible control of Chungking. Changsha, Hengyang, and Kweilin were taken by the Japanese as they swept on to the Indochina border. The entire front in China was threatened. The China war effort lost its vitality as panic and war-weariness contributed to the demoralization of the Kuomintang. At this point General Stilwell suggested that the only remedy for the situation was to combine all Chinese forces—Kuomintang, Communist, or bandit—under the command of an American general.

Stilwell was not afraid of a coalition between Kuomintang and Communists. He said that he judged both parties by what he saw. He saw the Kuomintang as indifferent to the war effort, filled with the cynical sentiment that the Kuomintang had shed far more than its share of blood. He saw corruption and chaos—hoarding, black-marketing, and trading with the enemy—as the hallmark of the Kuomintang. On the other hand he gave the Communists credit for practicing what they preached—reducing rents and taxes, raising production and the standard of living, giving the people a chance to participate in government, and supplying a burning spirit to resist Japan. He would not hesitate to give American help to the Communists, and he threatened to cut off help from the Kuomintang unless they turned over a new leaf. He believed that if American support were given to the Communists in their war effort, they might become independent of Moscow and favorable to the United States. In any event he saw the Kuomintang as a decadent, reactionary faction, and the Communists as a rising, dynamic force. Stilwell's ideas were not accepted, either in Chungking or in Washington. He was recalled, and his position was given to the affable General Wedemeyer.

At this juncture the fortunes of war turned more drastically against the Japanese and inferentially more favorable for the Chinese. It became perfectly plain that the Japanese would never be able to capture Kunming, Sian, or Chungking. The quality of the Japanese army deteriorated as the best troops were pulled out of China. The certainty of defeat shattered the famed Japanese spirit. Allied ground troops recaptured the Burma Road, and the Fourteenth Airforce stepped up its deliveries over the hump. Since Europe no longer made so many demands, more American supplies became available for the war in Asia. As Americans gained control of the air in China, the Japanese learned what it meant to be strafed, bombed, and marooned without communications. The Chinese regained their bravado vis-à-vis the Japanese, and there was no more talk about an American commander for all Chinese forces.

Nevertheless, Nationalist China could not contemplate its future with optimism. It was clear that Japan would be beaten but that China would not receive the glory of defeating Japan. China had become a sideshow, which was held in low esteem by most of its own allies. Nationalist China, headed by Chiang Kai-shek, was numbered among the powers which won the war, but it deteriorated to a pathetic condition because of its frightful ordeal. Its territory was chiseled away, and its military prestige was lost. Such allegiance as any province or war zone gave to Chungking at the war's end rested on the flimsy basis of personal interest. The determining factor was the relationship between the local commander or the local official and Chiang Kai-shek.

World War II as fought between Japan and Nationalist China was a peculiar kind of war. The Chinese kept control of such strategic positions as the Yangtze gorges, the bend of the Yellow River at Tungkuan, the southwest flank in Yünnan, and the rice bowl of southeastern China. Hundreds of ill-organized divisions under semi-independent commanders held large areas which the Japanese chose not to attack. These Kuomintang units paid most of the cost of resisting Japan. The Japanese confined themselves to defensible positions under the protection of light artillery and machine guns. Japanese equipment more than compensated for the Chinese advantages in numbers and geography. There were no fronts or major engagements, and consequently there were no thrills of victory. The Japanese seemed contented to subject Chungking to slow strangulation or to force the government to wither on the vine. Japanese offensives before the last desperate stage of the war were designed to keep the Chinese off-balance and to keep the countryside in terror.

The Nationalist army was a jerry-built affair. The commanders were loyal Kuomintang members in the top echelons. In the field, however, many generals were of shifting loyalty; they acted precisely as the warlords of former days. They usually received a money subsidy from Chungking, but no supplies, medicines, arms, or ammunition. They were expected to fend for themselves. They raised and paid their own armies as circumstances demanded. Their command status implied a license to loot. They held civilian as well as military power in their hands, so they were supreme beyond question in their own bailiwicks. They levied taxes, requisitioned grain, commandeered draft animals, and conscripted recruits at their pleasure. They treated their humble soldiers as so much dirt. The ordinary soldiers were underfed, and they suffered from disease and malnutrition. Armies had no such thing as a medical corps or a commissary. Whole divisions moved on their bare feet, regardless of terrain or weather. The death rate among the Chinese soldiers reached as high as thirty percent without any enemy action whatever. Chinese soldiers never had air support, tanks, guns, or heavy armor; yet they fought bravely against unmerciful Japanese hammering.

The most serious charge against the forces of the Kuomintang was their careless or brutal treatment of the peasants. They failed to establish bonds between the common people and themselves—to convince the common people that the Kuomintang battle was also the battle of the masses. No decent man in some areas would join the Nationalists if he could possibly buy his way out. Only the most wretched entered the ranks. Too many generals prospered while the people suffered. The Kuomintang forces gained the reputation of preferring to trade with the puppets rather than fight the Japanese. In Honan, it was reported that the people believed in two slogans: "Better the soldiers of Japan than the soldiers of Tang En-po (the Nationalist general)" and "China has two sorrows—the Yellow River and Tang En-po." When the Japanese launched their fatal offensive in that province, the peasants, who had suffered two years of horrible famine under their own officials, used the Japanese advance as an excuse to turn against the Kuomintang. At the end of World War II, Chiang Kai-shek's army, in spite of American training and American supplies, exposed itself as a military machine of doubtful quality both in structure and performance.

Nationalist China also suffered because of its political problems. The government at Chungking was a one-party organization. The Kuomintang —the party of Sun Yat-sen—ran the show. Decisions were made by the party, which was organized along the Communist lines. It was made up of less than one percent of the population; yet it regarded itself as the sovereign power within the state. It controlled the army, the government, and public funds. Theoretically it was still in the stage of "political tutelage," which entitled it to govern in the name of the people. The party was represented by a national congress, which had been elected in 1935 and whose members were all "down-river" exiles temporarily in refuge in Chungking. The decision-making group was the central executive committee or its small standing committee led by Chiang Kai-shek. The government—as distinguished from the party—was the creature of the party. It was made up of the five Yüan—executive, legislative, judicial, control, and Examination—which in turn were subordinate to a state council and supreme national defense council. Chiang presided over the government as well as over the party. He was known as the "generalissimo" and was granted full emergency wartime powers.

Various political cliques struggled for power within the party hierarchy. Former warlords, landlords, bureaucrats, and merchants clustered about two politically minded, reactionary, brothers, Chen Kuo-fu and Chen Li-fu, who stood high in the generalissimo's favor. Some individuals cast their lot with the Whampoa clique, which consisted of Chiang's subordinates who were high in military circles. The Liberals, who were usually identified as the returned students, patriotic young officers, and lower bureaucrats depended upon the leadership of Sun Fo. None of these cliques had any hope of implementing its program without the support of the man in charge.

The reactionary circles who exerted the dominant influence on Chiang Kai-shek felt that the times demanded a dictatorship. The conduct of the people should be regimented and their thoughts controlled. It was not the moment for free thought or free speech. As a result of their pressures, two secret police outfits—one attached to the national military council and the other to the party—placed in jeopardy the small amount of democracy which China enjoyed. A strict authoritarian control over internal politics was an essential part of the right-wing credo.

The left-wing Liberals pressed for more civil rights and a broader-based government as a means to restore the national morale and effect economic reforms. The more the Liberals—or foreigners in Chungking—argued for their program, the more rigorous became the reactionary oppression. It was a vicious circle. As conditions deteriorated, the stronger became the urge to complain. The louder the rumblings, the more ubiquitous the secret police. The more difficult his personal problems appeared to be, the more petulant the generalissimo became in his manner and attitudes. Dissatisfaction in Chungking was matched by incipient revolt at the grass roots. Uprisings in Kweichow, Kansu, Fukien, and Hupei threatened the solidarity of Nationalist China when it was rescued by the happy circumstance of victory.

Economic difficulties compounded Chungking's political troubles. China survived only because it produced its own food. China entered the war without any stockpiles of raw materials or any substantial industries. The Chinese did not posses munitions factories capable of equipping a single division of a mechanized army. The maximum output of bullets made in China was four per man per month; uniforms and boots were out of the question. The government's move to the interior plus the Japanese blockade paralyzed the internal economic system. Transportation was stalled. The busiest highway in Nationalist China in 1944 clocked only 125 vehicles—jeeps, trucks, and buses—going in both directions daily. Essential supplies were brought into Chungking by one of the most fantastic smuggling rings in history. Nationalists sold tungsten, tin, and antimony (for example) to pro-Japanese puppets for gasoline, cloth, rubber tires, or medicines. On occasions, Chinese nationalist troops brought rice from Chinese peddlars who had acquired their supplies from Japanese-controlled areas in Indochina. Sometimes it was possible to land cargoes from American submarines on lonely spots along the Chinese coast and, by a judicious use of bribes, to transport some of the cargoes through Japanese and puppet lines all the way to China's deepest interior.

China's greatest economic scourges were local famines and the general inflation. In March 1943, Honan starved. Of 30,000,000 people in the province, two or three million fled while another two or three million died of hunger or disease. No trucks were available to move food or raw materials. The sad truth was that China had few assets of any kind. There were no sources of revenue, only the printing press. Salaries were fixed, but prices skyrocketed. A month's salary for a white-collar worker in Chungking would not buy a day's supply of coal. Prices at the end of the war were two thousand times as high as they were in 1941. Chicken rose to four dollars a pound and fish to a dollar an ounce. Peanuts were a dollar apiece and a single egg cost fifty dollars. Paper currency, in spite of the thousands of bales of it which were printed in New York and flown into China over the hump, was worthless. The only things of value were sacks of grain.

Thousands of nameless, heroic government functionaries struggled to make ends meet. They sold their scrolls, works of art, and pieces of jade to get enough to eat. People worked in crowded offices and lived in primitive conditions. Inflation gave rise to corruption. However, a bit of squeeze, a small theft, or a little white lie did not seem like corruption—they were better alternatives than death. The little man could not be expected to forego petty crimes when he saw the ostentatious living and comparative luxury of some of the officials at the top. Morale was bound to suffer. It was utterly hopeless in Nationalist China where graft and misery destroyed the will to fight. Only the unswerving leadership of Chiang Kai-shek held the creaking ship of state together and kept China in the war.

OCCUPIED CHINA—WANG CHING-WEI

Pearl Harbor caused a different kind of war in occupied China than it produced in Nationalist China. Occupied China was that part which extended from the northern border of Manchukuo and Mongolia, through the cities, congested areas, and communications routes of North and Central China to the border of Indochina. It included the great river valleys, but it extended no further inland than the city of Hankow. It was not a continuous land mass, entirely subject to Japanese control. It was more like a Swiss cheese, with more holes than solid food. In the "holes," the Japanese were engaged in unrelieved conflict with Kuomintang, Chinese Communists, bandits, or perhaps "disloyal" Chinese puppet forces.

The Japanese administered Manchukuo for their exclusive benefit. The emperor Kang Teh was completely under the thumb of the Japanese. He later confessed that if he had dared to oppose them, he would have been murdered. The premier and state council, the general affairs board, and the administrative bureaus were guided and manipulated by Japanese. At first only the most innocuous elements in Manchukuo collaborated with the Japanese, but gradually more capable Chinese were attracted into government service. They had no other way to make a living. The Japanese raised and trained an army of a half-million men in Manchukuo. There was no fear of armed revolt because of the presence of the Kwantung regular army with the general-ambassador at its head. The Japanese *gendarmerie* or military police made law and order doubly certain.

The Japanese looked to Manchukuo as an economic reservoir for their war effort. They forced the exploitation of coal, iron, and electric power and concentrated on steel, ordnance, transportation equipment, chemicals, and munitions. Huge dams were built, including one on the Yalu River forty miles upstream from Antung. The army took over industrial development as a state monopoly, and with the assistance of some of Japan's most capable *zaibatsu* it made an impressive record. Factories for the production of machine tools, engineering equipment, aircraft and automobiles, explosives, rubber products, cement, and explosives sprang up in the neighborhood of Mukden and Dairen. The industries of Manchukuo and Japan were treated as a single unit, and trade between the two countries was carried on without the formalities of international customs regulations or tariffs. The currency of Japan was used interchangeably with the money of Manchukuo.

The Japanese achievement in Manchukuo was the building up of an industrial structure which was far ahead of anything elsewhere in China. This was the great attraction for Russians, Chinese Communists, and the Kuomintang at the time of Japan's collapse. However, the economic value of Manchukuo was not the same at war's end as it was at war's beginning. As Japan suffered, so did Manchukuo. Machines in both countries wore out. Factories were idled and rolling stock was depleted. Labor productivity declined along with industrial output. Some of the best industrial installations in Manchukuo shivered with the blasts of American bombs before the Soviet army invaded the area in August, 1945. Russian destruction of machinery was accompanied by indiscriminate looting on the part of the Chinese populace. The basic structure of Manchukuo industries, together with the rich sources of raw materials remained intact, but the physical plant was a shambles.

The morale of the Chinese in Manchukuo disintegrated with the fortunes of war. They accepted Japanese propaganda only as long as there was physical improvement in their lot and a reasonable hope of victory. Continued defeat for Japan wiped out the spirit of collaboration. The native population of Manchukuo suffered from food shortages as much as did the people of Japan. They had the land to grow more food, but they also had the ubiquitous Japanese army as tax gatherers. The political and social effects of Japanese rule vanished with the disappearance of Japanese military power from the scene in Manchukuo.

The spectacular victories of Japanese arms in the opening stages of World War II marked the high point in the relations between Japan and its puppets in China. Political resistance was at its lowest ebb. The Japanese enrolled as many as a million Chinese in their armed services for garrison purposes and for special duties. Economic conditions were hopeful as the currency was momentarily stabilized. Trade flowed between Tientsin, Shanghai, and Tokyo without interruption. Japanese victories in Southeast Asia caused many Chinese to line up with Wang Ching-wei and to disavow Chiang Kai-shek. The Japanese ousted the "white men" from their privileged positions in the concessions and settlements in Chinese cities and interned the foreigners themselves. In the eyes of occupied China, imperialism was discredited for all time, and the prestige of Europeans and Americans was destroyed with their property rights.

Complications multiplied as Chiang Kai-shek refused to surrender. Japan was too preoccupied in the Pacific to mount an offensive against Chungking, and Chiang spurned Japanese offers of peace. Japan would have been glad to desert Wang Ching-wei in favor of Chiang. Such a switch seemed a possible solution to Japan's growing problems. From an economic point of view, China was a costly proposition to Japan. Resources of coal, iron, salt, and cotton were useless without capital, manpower, factories, and transportation to convert raw materials into implements of war. China could not feed itself let alone produce a surplus for the Japanese army in China and for the hungry people of Japan. Most seriously, attitudes of ill will and contempt threatened to obliterate the little confidence and respect which remained in China for Japan.

The Japanese military authorities relied upon stricter application of traditional measures to whip the Chinese into line. They ordered more attacks against the guerrillas, and they dealt with the people in more brutal ways. They burned homes and entire villages. They built pillboxes along the roadside and dug trenches parallel to railways for better protection. They established more protected areas and model peace zones as control devices, and they made short shrift of any Chinese who refused to bend to the Japanese will.

Ambassador Shigemitsu in Nanking was among those who saw the bankruptcy of Japanese procedures. He argued that military supremacy was futile unless it led to cooperation in the cause of peace. He insisted that the Chinese would have to be treated as equals and their country would have to be recognized as an independent, genuinely sovereign state. He wanted peace on terms which the Chinese would accept and respect, after which Japanese soldiers should be pulled out of China as soon as possible. He persuaded the emperor, Premier Tojo, and many of the officials in Tokyo of the soundness of his program. For its implementation, he was obliged to wait for an auspicious moment in the military situation.

In December 1942, Wang Ching-wei was invited to Tokyo; while there, on January 9, 1943, he formally declared war on the United States and Great Britain. Thus, occupied China took its stand *against* the Allies while Nationalist China fought *on the side of* the Allies. As a reward to occupied China for its action, Japan promised to give up its unequal rights and privileges in China and to turn over to the Nanking (Wang Ching-wei) government the former International Settlements in Shanghai and Kulangsu, and the Legation Quarter in Peiping, as well as all enemy properties in China which had been seized by Japan. This action was synchronized with the treaties of January 11, 1943, between Great Britain and China, and between the United States and China, by which those powers also agreed to give up their unequal privileges. The great difference was that Japan made its engagements with Wang Ching-wei's China while the British and American accords were signed with Chiang Kai-shek's China. In either case, no matter who won the war, one China or the other was assured that the end of imperialism was in sight.

The Japanese handed over their concessions in Tientsin, Hankow, Shasi, Soochow, Hangchow, and Amoy without compensation. The Chinese took over police and administrative duties, and Premier Tojo felt obliged to visit China in order to assure the Japanese residents there that they were not being deserted by their government. Before the end of the summer in 1943, the Japanese transferred to China their rights in the International Settlement in Shanghai and persuaded Vichy France to give up its rights in the French concession. On October 30, 1943, Wang's China and Tojo's Japan signed a treaty of alliance, according to which they agreed to cooperate as equal and independent neighbors in the establishment of greater East Asia. Japan undertook to withdraw its forces from China when general peace should be restored and the state of war should cease to exist. Japan also renounced its treaty right to station troops in China—undoubtedly as a lure to attract the attention and possibly the support of Chiang Kai-shek.

At the same time, Japan proceeded to return to China properties which had been seized by the Japanese army. Steps were taken to remodel the Central China Promotion Company and the North China Development Company to make them Chinese concerns in outward appearance. Japan took the new propaganda line that misunderstandings between Japan and China had been fomented by the United States and Great Britain, but fortunately were erased by Japan's new policies. Since Japan conceded Chinese sovereignty and integrity, the Japanese argued that there was nothing left to fight about. Various Japanese officials expressed their regrets for the China affair and urged a new formula for lasting peace. They wanted Chiang to abandon the United States and his united front *with* the Communists, and to join up with Japan and Wang Ching-wei in a united front *against* the Communists. The Japanese warned that the Communists were bent on expanding their influence in China and that public opinion in the United States appeared to support the Communists rather than Chiang Kai-shek.

The new policy failed to bring the desired results, so Japan was obliged to launch its offensive against Chiang Kai-shek in the summer of 1944. The puppet troops were not faithful allies, although they performed behind-the-scenes chores which released Japanese soldiers for the actual fighting. The Japanese declared that their military operations were not to punish the Chinese but simply to frustrate American and British attempts at aggression and domination. The Japanese said "the Chinese people are our friends and even the armed forces under the Chinese regime who are opposed to the United States and Great Britain are not our enemies." The Japanese sent men of influence, including the brother of Prince Konoye, to Shanghai to make contacts with Chinese businessmen and secret agents of the Chungking government in the interest of peace. This was the very moment of the Chiang-Stilwell crisis over the control of Chinese troops. It may be that if President Roosevelt had tried to force Stilwell on Chiang, or had agreed to send supplies to the Chinese Communists, Chiang might have been more responsive to Japanese overtures.

Late in 1944 Wang Ching-wei, the most illustrious of the collaborators, died and his place was taken by Chen Kung-po, one of Wang's less distinguished followers. As Japan was battered and beaten, occupied China became the major casualty in the collapse of Japan's house of cards. The government at Nanking was doomed to an inglorious fate. It lost all claim to the loyalty of the Chinese people who survived the Japanese invasion. It had gambled on the side of Japan; and, when it lost, it was reduced to chaos and despair. For the peasant there was always the land. For other Chinese, there was nothing. Pride and spirit vanished. The economy was in ruins, and the shattered social organization had nothing but the strength of its ancient traditions to hold it together. Chen Kung-po and other remnant leaders of occupied China were executed as traitors to their country by a Kuomintang firing squad after the Japanese surrender.

COMMUNIST CHINA—MAO TSE-TUNG

World War II closed the book on occupied China; it wrote but a single chapter in the career of the Chinese Communists. Wartime in China's great interior created ideal conditions for the Communists to carry on their type of hostilities against Japan, win the leadership of the masses and groom the party for its ultimate conquest of China's national government. After Pearl Harbor, Communists and Kuomintang carried on the pretense of the united front. Although they lashed one another with bitter speeches, they continued to talk about the necessity of unity. Both jockeyed for larger allotments of American aid. The Communists protested that they were not tools of Moscow or the Comintern and said that they would as soon cooperate with the United States as with Russia. They struggled to give the impression that they were closer than the Kuomintang to American ideas of democracy. Both sides stationed their troops with an eye to a favorable position in the event of civil war. Chiang used ten divisions to erect a blockade which interdicted the movement of all supplies into Communist territory. For two years he refused to allow visits to Yenan by foreign correspondents in Chungking. Although the Communists representative in the Chinese capital was supposed to have a voice in national affairs, he was as effectively isolated from official circles as the ambassador of a foreign power.

The Communists did not do all the fighting against the Japanese, as was sometimes believed; but they did a large and important share. After the failure of the "Hundred Regiments" campaign in 1940—which was a large simultaneous attack against Japanese positions in five provinces—the Communists depended entirely upon guerrilla tactics. Without arms except those which they captured, and without munitions except mines or grenades which they made themselves, they took a heavy toll of Japanese troops. Their hit-and-run raids prevented the Japanese from making capital out of the occupied territory. They usually operated in small bands, but they could quickly muster a striking force of thousands. All movements were directed by divisional headquarters and coordinated by the general staff in Yenan.

Within four months after the outbreak of World War II, Communist troops moved as much as 700 miles from their home base. They infiltrated seventy percent of the territory behind Japanese lines. They established a string of bases which stretched from Manchuria to the lower Yangtze Valley, and they created pockets of resistance on the outskirts of seaports where ultimate American landings were anticipated. Communists entrenched themselves in the interior of Hainan Island and established cells inside such major cities as Canton, Shanghai, and Tientsin. Month after month Communist power and influence grew as Japanese mopping-up campaigns ended in failure.

Partisan warfare as practiced by the Communists was not a matter for the wealthy or the elderly who were associated with the Kuomintang. Consequently when the Japanese attacks were most vicious, the Kuomintang officials tended to run away. Thus the idea grew that the Communists were patriots, or the real Chinese nationalists. In the countryside, the people knew nothing of Chungking or the heroic struggle of Chiang Kaishek. To peasants in the interior, the Kuomintang meant the local soldiers and officials who gained the reputation of abusing the common people, trading with the puppets, and refusing to fight the Japanese. They saw the Communists fight the Japanese—therefore the Communists were patriots. The Communists were the "good guys" and the Kuomintang were the "bad guys."

During the war the Communists established close links with the masses. There was no need for ideological persuasion or totalitarian methods of mass manipulation. For self-preservation people banded together as they hid in caves or tunnels or ran away from ruined homes. The masses needed leaders, and the Communists met the need. The people provided the army with food and formed militia units which bolstered the strength of the regular guerrilla fighters. Ordinary villagers acted as indispensable intelligence agents and kept a constant watch over enemy movements. The Communists armed the peasants and converted the war of resistance against Japan into a genuine people's war.

The union between the Communists and the masses was also effected in the nonmilitary sphere. The Communists discovered that they automatically won a man's loyalty when they gave him a voice in electing officials, fixing tax rates, and collecting grain. They taught him to read and write, gave him a gun and helped him to fight off Japanese who raped his wife or tortured his mother—he had little need for further indoctrination. Most of those who joined up with the Communists, or merely followed them, had never heard of communists or communism before the war. The Communists assumed the leadership in mass organization, and therein lay the sources of their future strength.

The Communists never lost sight of the concept of their party as a highly centralized, highly disciplined elite, nor their confidence that they were the wave of the future. They would be the creators of a strong, modern, unified, and communistic China. They adopted a program to "fight the enemy, improve the army and administration, unify leadership, support the government and love the people, increase production, correct wrong tendencies, realize the 'Three Thirds' system, reduce rent and interest, investigate cadre workers (for incorrect activities) and educate the masses about current affairs." While in Yenan they conducted a *Cheng Feng* or Rectification Campaign to correct undesirable and erroneous tendencies in the party, army, and administrative units. The party wanted to make sure that its mass of new converts held "correct thoughts." Methods of study and review, public discussion and self-criticism were employed to guarantee orthodoxy. A correct version of party history was compiled, and the thought of Mao Tse-tung was made the infallible guide for the interpretation of Marxism-Leninism in China. When Mao was asked whether he was first a Chinese or first a Communist, he replied: "Might as well ask which came first, the parents or the children—without the Chinese nation, there would be no Chinese Communist party." A young and vigorous group of disciplined leaders was trained—which added new life and energy to the veterans of the Long March.

At this juncture, Mao's economic ideas were the products of his fight for existence. He was less worried about dogma than survival. He wrote that people were mistaken who thought then that Communists were against the development of individual initiative, private capital, and private property. He gave his approval to trade for personal profit so long as there was no hoarding, profiteering, or dealing with the enemy. No one was allowed to become rich. Officers and enlisted men, elite and masses, lived at the same level of austerity. Mao urged that the most effective use should be made of labor; he insisted that every school, army, and administrative unit should become self-sufficient. Marshal Chu Teh hoed his own cabbage patch, and Mao himself grew the tobacco which he smoked. Mao accepted temporarily the bourgeois slogan of land to the tiller, but he reminded his people that they should not overlook the ideals of agricultural cooperatives and socialist collectivization. He tolerated reasonable landlords and rich peasants because of the need to increase production as a means of overcoming the Kuomintang blockade. Only one tax was assessed—a progressive tax on agriculture—and it was paid in grain. The rate was fixed by the vote of the people, and the tax gatherers were elected. Peasants were obliged to pay rents up to thirty-seven-and-a-half percent of the crop, and borrowers were held responsible for legal obligations on their debts. Mao's objective was to eliminate economic injustice, but he warned that no one must doubt his faith in Marxism or his determination to head China for socialism and communism.

When Japanese military activity slackened in China late in 1944, the Communists were given an opportunity to reappraise the united front with the Kuomintang. Victory for China was assured, what should be the role of the Communists? The Communists no longer feared the Kuomintang; rather, they held it in contempt. They had witnessed the collapse of Kuomintang armies; and they possessed unbounded faith in their party, the Communist fighting machine and their future in China. The Communist party had increased its membership to more than a million in spite of the war. The Communist army boasted of 900,000 regular soldiers supported by 2,200,000 militiamen. Nearly 100,000,000 Chinese lived in the Communist-liberated area, and in the Communist view, they too should play a substantial part in the fulfillment of what Chiang Kai-shek called "China's destiny." The Communists were not ready for a test of arms with the Kuomintang, but they demanded a voice in the affairs of China commensurate with their strength. Through the American ambassador in China, General Hurley, the Communists communicated to Chiang Kai-shek their specific terms for continued cooperation.

The Communists demanded that the existing Nationalist government in Chungking should be replaced by a coalition government of all anti-Japanese parties and political groups and that all the armies of China should be placed under a new military council on which all parties should be represented. The Communists were not about to put their fate into the hands of Chiang Kai-shek. Specifically the Communists demanded that the Kuomintang should end the blockade, furnish supplies for sixteen Communist divisions in the field, recognize the legality of all Communist governments in liberated areas, release political prisoners, put an end to secret service activities, abolish all regulations restricting the people's freedom, and recognize the Communists as a legal political party. Naturally the Kuomintang would not consent to relax its fundamental control of the government or the army and would not compromise its right to govern all Chinese territory whether or not some of its territory happened to be under the temporary jurisdiction of the self-styled Communist liberators.

The diplomatic deadlock between Communists and Kuomintang dragged on through the spring of 1945. Both sides played for time, hoping that the inevitable victory over Japan would improve their respective bargaining positions. The Communists did not rest on their oars. They called a party conference in Yenan which tightened their discipline and aroused their spirit. They adopted a new party constitution which was drafted by Liu Shao-ch'i, the general secretary of the party. They also approved, on June 11, 1945, a program of action which was submitted to them by Mao Tse-tung in the form of a long speech which he entitled "On Coalition Government."

According to this program, which would destroy foreign and feudal oppression in China, the Communists would thoroughly annihilate Japanese aggressors and make no compromise. They would forego a one-party dictatorship and establish a democratic coalition government as the best means of unifying the people and bringing about the type of freedom which was envisaged by Sun Yat-sen. With regard to the people's army, the Communist position was "first give us the right kind of state and then we will turn over our army to it." The program for agriculture would be the continuation of "land to the tiller" with the gradual and voluntary organization of producers' cooperatives. In industry, the great problem was to create an industry rather than to argue about theoretic questions of types and procedures. In matters of culture and education, the Communists stressed the elimination of illiteracy and the building of a national culture which would not exclude foreign, alien, or modern elements, but would reflect the genius of the Chinese as accumulated through the ages. The Communists renewed their pledges of respect and assistance to their national minorities. Finally in the realm of foreign policy, they expressed approval of the Atlantic Charter and the correct decisions of the conferences of Moscow, Cairo, Tehran, and Yalta. They were in accord with the effort to create an organization of the United Nations. Thus the Communists, in contrast to the Kuomintang, showed effective teamwork in arranging their internal affairs as they prepared themselves to burst out of their shell at the moment of China's victory.

CHINA'S WARTIME DIPLOMACY

In seeking solutions for its internal problems, China was bound to take into account its position in world affairs. Although Chiang Kai-shek was the leader of China on the side of the United Nations, he shared the universal Chinese resentment against the record of all foreign powers in China. In his book, *China's Destiny*, he flayed the imperialists for making China weak and despised. He blamed them for warlordism, prostitution, gun-running, opium-smoking, gangsterism, and political chaos. The young Nationalists with whom he was surrounded, even many who had gone to school in the United States, were Western in their thinking; yet they felt an inner shame and hatred because they were often treated as coolies or second-class citizens in their own country. In addition, the Chinese felt that they had been neglected during their ordeal of fire with the Japanese. They were dismayed by the American slogan of Europe first. They had a fundamental feeling that any help or assistance which was given to them was only a shadow of their just due and a feeble effort to undo the wrongs which had been perpetrated against China throughout the years.

In the United States, after Pearl Harbor, public sentiment tended to glorify the heroic role of China in the war. President Roosevelt insisted that Chiang should be treated as one of the Big Four. He and Secretary Hull went so far as to suggest that China should regain all the territory which it had lost during the past century, including Hong Kong. Prime Minister Churchill registered his rigorous dissent. Both he and Stalin felt that the American estimate of the importance of China was strangely out of proportion.

China signed the declaration of the United Nations against a separate peace but was not invited to participate in the Allied conferences at Casablanca, Washington, and Quebec. It was argued that there were no military secrets at Chungking: any information to Chiang filtered immediately to the agents of Japan. China had the feeling that it was overlooked until it was invited to appear as one of the signers of the Declaration of Principles adopted by the Moscow Conference of Foreign Ministers in October 1943. By this declaration, the governments of the United

States, the United Kingdom, the Soviet Union, and China declared that after the war their united action would be continued for the organization and maintenance of peace and security. Chiang also participated in the Cairo Conference and signed the communiqué which announced that "all the territories Japan has stolen from the Chinese, such as Manchuria, Formosa and the Pescadores shall be restored to the Republic of China."

In 1943 Chiang received further diplomatic bonuses in the form of new treaties concluded on the basis of equality and reciprocity. On January 11 the United States and Great Britain agreed to terminate their rights under the Boxer protocol of 1901, to transfer the control of the International settlements at Shanghai and Amoy and the British concessions at Tientsin and Canton to China, and to relinquish extraterritorial, consular, and related privileges. The contracting powers agreed to negotiate a comprehensive modern treaty of friendship, commerce, navigation, and consular rights after the cessation of hostilities. Then on December 17, 1943, President Roosevelt signed an act which removed longstanding legislative discriminations against the Chinese. The act repealed the Chinese Exclusion Laws, established an annual immigration quota and made legally admitted Chinese eligible to naturalization as American citizens.

The crux of China's wartime diplomacy was the relationship between Nationalist China and the Soviet Union. Chiang was willing to agree to anything not detrimental to Chinese sovereignty which would forestall Russian support to the Chinese Communists. Chiang was not afraid to deal with Stalin, because the Russian record of cooperation with Nationalist China had been good during the period of the Kuomintang-Communist united front. From 1937 to 1941 Russia sent five times as much aid to Chiang Kai-shek as the United States sent to him. The Russians sent trucks, airplanes, and gasoline to China while the Americans sold scrap iron and petroleum to Japan. During the course of the estrangement between the Communists and the Kuomintang after 1941, the Russians did not send so much as a single plane, a ton of gasoline, or a crate of munitions to the Communists. When Russian observers went to Yenan, they first obtained the permission of Chungking. In Yenan at the end of the war, there were three Russian civilians—a doctor and two newspapermen—and there were five American military observers for every Russian.

Stalin was on record as approving Chiang Kai-shek as the best leader for united China. Neither he nor Molotov was willing to admit that Chinese Communists were anything more than agrarian reformers. He denied that Russia had any territorial ambitions in China, and he said he would always respect China's sovereignty. He declared that his policy would be to support the United States in China, since he would need all his own strength and assets to rehabilitate his devastated homeland.

Chiang became increasingly anxious to reach a formal understanding with Stalin before Russia should enter the Pacific war. Roosevelt and Churchill were as eager as Chiang for an agreement with Stalin covering the Far East.

The Big Three—Stalin, Roosevelt, and Churchill—met at Yalta to discuss a peacetime settlement for the entire world. Chiang Kai-shek was not invited, although he had a fairly accurate idea of the provisions referring to China. The secret agreement regarding the Far East concluded at Yalta February 11, 1945 read as follows:

> The leaders of the three Great Powers—the Soviet Union, the United States of America and Great Britain—have agreed that in two or three months after Germany has surrendered and the war in Europe has terminated the Soviet Union shall enter into the war against Japan on the side of the Allies on condition that:
> 1. The status quo in Outer-Mongolia (The Mongolian People's Republic) shall be preserved;
> 2. The former rights of Russia violated by the treacherous attack of Japan in 1904 shall be restored, viz:
> (a) the southern part of Sakhalin as well as all the islands adjacent to it shall be returned to the Soviet Union,
> (b) the commercial port of Dairen shall be internationalized, the preeminent interests of the Soviet Union in this port being safeguarded and the lease of Port Arthur as a naval base of the USSR restored,
> (c) the Chinese-Eastern Railroad and the South-Manchurian Railroad which provides an outlet to Dairen shall be jointly operated by the establishment of a joint Soviet-Chinese Company it being understood that the preeminent interests of the Soviet Union shall be safeguarded and that China shall retain full sovereignty in Manchuria;
> 3. The Kurile islands shall be handed over to the Soviet Union.
> It is understood, that the agreement concerning Outer-Mongolia and the ports and railroads referred to above will require concurrence of Generalissimo Chiang Kai-shek. The President will take measures in order to obtain this concurrence on advice from Marshal Stalin.
> The Heads of the three Great Powers have agreed that these claims of the Soviet Union shall be unquestionably fulfilled after Japan has been defeated.
> For its part the Soviet Union expresses its readiness to conclude with the National Government of China a pact of friendship and alliance between the USSR and China in order to render assistance to China with its armed forces for the purpose of liberating China from the Japanese yoke.

The contents of the Yalta agreement were not communicated officially to Chiang Kai-shek until June 15. Chiang seemed "disappointed" with the terms, but he took comfort in the Charter of the United Nations, which was then in process of adoption at San Francisco. China was recognized as one of the Big Five, together with the United States, Soviet Union, United Kingdom, and France. It was given a permanent seat on the Security Council, which carried with it the power of veto. At the conclusion of the San Francisco Conference, Chiang sent his brother-in-law, T. V. Soong, to Moscow at Stalin's invitation to negotiate a treaty.

On the very day the Japanese surrendered, August 14, 1945, Russian and Chinese delegates affixed their signatures to nine Sino-Soviet agreements, including a treaty of friendship and alliance. These agreements were between Stalin's Russia and Chiang Kai-shek's China. The two nations agreed to help each other in prosecuting the war against Japan and not to conclude without mutual consent any armistice or peace treaty with any Japanese government which did not renounce aggressive intentions. They promised mutual assistance in the event of a renewed Japanese attack. They agreed to work together after the coming of peace and to act according to the principles of mutual respect for their sovereignty and territorial integrity and of noninterference in each other's internal affairs. The government of the U.S.S.R. agreed to render to China moral support and aid in military supplies and other material resources, such support and aid to be entirely given to the Nationalist government as the central government of China.

By notes and agreements the government of the U.S.S.R. recognized the territorial and administrative integrity of the three eastern provinces, commonly known as Manchuria, and reaffirmed its respect for China's full sovereignty there. China agreed to recognize the independence of Outer Mongolia if a plebiscite after the defeat of Japan should confirm that such was the desire of the Outer Mongolian people. Dairen was to become a free port under Chinese administration, but half its port facilities were to be leased to the Soviet Union. Port Arthur was to be used jointly by China and the U.S.S.R. as a naval base, and the Manchurian railways were to be jointly owned and operated by the two powers. Detailed measures were accepted for the reoccupation of Manchuria, whereby authority would be originally vested in the commander-in-chief of the Soviet forces and gradually transferred to the representatives of the Nationalist government.

Chiang expressed himself as "generally satisfied" with these arrangements. Actually he was under the gun as Soviet troops were already streaming into Manchuria. Chiang could not be sure that the Red army would honor Russian commitments and he could only hope that Russians on the spot would not support the Chinese Communists, give them arms, or use them to set up an independent local government in Manchuria and North China. On their part, the Chinese Communists were distressed by the Stalin–Chiang Kai-shek agreements. Their distress did not prevent them from pressing their claims on the Kuomintang and surging forward to force the surrender of Japanese units to the Communist army.

The Tragic Hour of Victory

Neither the Kuomintang nor the Chinese Communists showed the slightest confidence in each other. The Communists continued to offer one hand of friendship to the Kuomintang—but in the other hand they held on to the gun. Chiang persevered in his attitude that the Communists were worse than the Japanese. He still felt the Japanese were a disease of the skin, whereas the Communists were one of the heart. He told the world that the Communist problem was one which could be solved only by political means; yet he maintained that no agreement with them was possible because they were so untrustworthy. He refused to relax his blockade against them.

Diplomatic conversations and hostile actions between Communists and Kuomintang came to a dramatic climax on V-J Day. General Mac-Arthur's General Order Number One ordered the Japanese in China to surrender only to Chiang Kai-shek. The Communists paid no attention. They felt that they earned the right to accept the Japanese surrender and to take part in all the formalities of victory. Within forty-eight hours, Marshal Chu Teh launched a general Communist offensive to disarm all enemy troops and to take over all Chinese territory in the hands of the Japanese. Communists swept across North China and established themselves in two cities, Kalgan and Chefoo, which were excellent take-off points for Manchuria. Communists in the pockets behind the Japanese lines threw off their cloak of secrecy and emerged to take charge of the areas where they had hidden for their lives. Almost immediately after the surrender of the Japanese, the Communists were in *de facto* control of the hinterland of North and East China.

Chiang was in a difficult situation. He accepted the surrender of between a half-million and a million puppet troops and incorporated them into his own army. Six puppet generals who fought against the Communists and for the Japanese were taken back into the Kuomintang fold. Chiang summoned the commander-in-chief of the Japanese forces to Chungking and warned him not to surrender to the Communists, but to give over his arms only to soldiers of the Kuomintang. Unfortunately Chiang's soldiers were all in South and Central China. Chiang called on the United States to move his divisions toward Shanghai, Nanking, Hankow, and Peiping; by the time they arrived at their destination, the Communists were already in charge. The Communists were not able to hold on to the metropolitan areas. Over 50,000 American marines were

landed in North China to maintain law and order and to help in the repatriation of the Japanese. They helped the Nationalists accept the surrender of most of the Japanese units, but they could not prevent the flow
of great quantities of Japanese arms and munitions into Communist hands.

While Communists and Kuomintang troops raced to gain control of
North China, their representatives continued political discussions in
Chungking. Ambassador Hurley brought Mao to Chungking in his own
private plane on August 28, but Mao was not very happy about the situation which he found. He felt that the American airlift of Kuomintang
troops amounted to interference in China's internal affairs; he intimated
that if the Americans continued to help the Kuomintang, he might turn to
the Russians. Telephone connections had been established between
Yenan and Moscow, and more Russian personnel put in appearance at the
Chinese Communist capital. Mao charged that all Chiang's diplomatic
discussions with him were mere pretenses to stall for time while he,
Chiang, consolidated his military position in North China. Mao resented
American aid to the Kuomintang. Nevertheless, on October 11, 1945, Mao
and Chiang announced agreement on general principles to preserve peace,
secure a national army, create an all-party political consultative conference, and prepare for the inauguration of genuine democratic government. No agreement was possible on the administration of the liberated
areas, and an unbridgeable gap separated the general principles and the
specific measures which would be required for their implementation.

In spite of American pressures to bring the Kuomintang and the
Communists together, and in spite of American determination to prevent
the outbreak of civil war, neither side would make adequate concessions
for the establishment of peace. The Kuomintang attacked the Communists
in their interior strongholds; the Communists destroyed the railroads on
which the Kuomintang depended for the movement of their troops. Fighting spread over eleven provinces and reached into the key area of Russian-
held Manchuria. The Communists made it appear that they stood for
reform and the Kuomintang stood for the restoration of the old order.
Only one thing was certain: Communists and Kuomintang locked in
savage combat for the control of the body of China. American policy was
to stay out of civil war and to offer its aid only to a China which would be
"free, united, strong and democratic." The Americans wanted to save the
leadership of Chiang at any cost, but they discovered that the Communists were more adamant and more powerful than they assumed. All
too soon China moved away from its moment of victory over Japan and
plunged into the tragedy of fratricidal war.

SUGGESTED READING

Band, Claire, and Band, William, *Two Years with the Chinese Communists* (New Haven, Yale U., 1948).

Chennault, Claire L., *Way of a Fighter* (New York, Putnam, 1949).

Chiang Kai-shek, *Collected War Time Messages of Generalissimo Chiang Kai-shek, 1937–1945* (two vols.) (New York, Day, 1946).

Chien Tuan-sheng, *Government and Politics of China* (Cambridge, Harvard U., 1950).

Compton, Boyd, (trans.), *Mao's China, Party Reform Documents, 1942–1944* (Seattle, U. of Washington, 1952).

Epstein, Israel, *Unfinished Revolution in China* (Boston, Little, 1947).

Forman, Harrison, *Report from Red China* (New York, Holt, 1945).

Liu, F. F., *Military History of Modern China, 1924–1949* (Princeton, Princeton U., 1956).

Lohbeck, Don, *Patrick J. Hurley* (Chicago, Regnery, 1956).

Peck, Graham, *Two Kinds of Time* (Boston, Houghton, 1950).

Romanus, Charles F., and Sunderland, R., *Stilwell's Mission to China* (Washington, Department of the Army, 1953).

——, *Stilwell's Command Problems* (Washington, Department of the Army, 1956).

Rowe, David Nelson, *China Among the Powers* (New York, Harcourt, 1945).

Stein, Gunther, *Challenge of Red China* (New York, Whittlesey, 1945).

Stilwell, General Joseph, *Stilwell Papers* (edited by Theodore White) (New York, Macfadden, 1962). (P)

United States Department of State, *United States Relations with China (The White Paper)* (Washington, Government Printing Office, 1949).

Utley, Freda, *China Story* (Chicago, Regnery, 1951).

Wedemeyer, General Albert C., *Wedemeyer Reports!* (New York, Holt, 1958).

23

The Southern Regions

India and part of Southeast Asia were dragged into World War II by events which occurred in Europe more than two years before the Japanese attack on Pearl Harbor. When Great Britain declared war on Germany, India was implicated. So were the British possessions, including Hong Kong, North Borneo, Singapore, Malaya, and Burma. When France and the Netherlands took their stand against fascist aggressors in Europe, the "mother countries" gambled the fate of their colonies in Asia.

INDIA

As the shadows of war lengthened in Europe in the spring of 1939, the Indian Congress served warning on England that it would not fight in other people's wars. The impending war between England and Germany came under the category of other people's wars. The Congress held that it was for the people of India to determine whether India would join in a war or not and resolved that India should resist any decision imposed upon India by England.

In the British view, England's war was also India's war. On September 3, 1939, the day that England declared war on Germany, the viceroy of India proclaimed that India was at war. The central legislature of India (with the Congress members absent) gave its approval to a defense of India bill. The provincial premiers of Bengal, Punjab, and the Sind pledged their support to the war effort. The Indian princes pledged every possible assistance in men, money, and materials. The Moslem League promised support on condition that no constitutional changes be made without its consent and approval. Only the Indian Congress opposed. The Congress condemned Naziism and fascism; however, since England had

485

declared war without seeking or obtaining the consent of the Indian people, the Congress could not associate itself with the war effort unless India was declared an independent nation. All members of the Congress who held official positions resigned—and the Moslems celebrated the event with a day of thanksgiving for deliverance from Hindu tyranny.

The viceroy let it be known that demands for independence or immediate self-government were impractical, but he repeated the British offer of dominion status after the war. He offered to expand the government to include more Indians in the management of the war effort. The Congress continued to be hostile. It demanded an immediate assembly to draft a constitution for independent India. Jinnah opposed the Congress position, fundamentally because he rejected the idea that the Congress alone should speak for all India. In the view of the Moslem League, India never was the name of a single country or a single culture. As Moslem opinion hardened against the Congress, the Moslems stated firmly that they wanted no part of a federation which would result in majority-community rule under the guise of democracy and a parliamentary system of government. In the spring of 1940, Jinnah said that Moslems were not a minority, but a distinct nation—with distinctive culture and civilization, language and literature, art and architecture, customs and calendar, history and tradition, aptitudes and ambitions. The Moslems took an unshakable stand for autonomous and sovereign Moslem states in areas where Moslems were in the majority, as in the northwestern and eastern zones of India. This was the root idea of Pakistan, "the land of the pure."

For nearly a year, India gave little thought to the war. The "phoney war" in Europe caused no great stir in India. Some Indian troops were sent to East and North Africa and eastward to the British base in Singapore. Recruitment was increased casually. India became the supply center for the Middle East; war orders produced substantial increases in such industries as iron and steel, cotton and jute, cement and aluminum. With the blitzkrieg in May 1940, a profound change occurred in Indian psychology. In spite of Gandhi, a deep sympathy stirred in India for the heroic spirit of the Battle of Britain. Many Indians admired the bulldog defiance of Winston Churchill, the new prime minister, although they could hope for no concessions from him in the direction of full self-government as long as the British people themselves were engulfed in the struggle for their own existence. Gandhi persisted in his pacifism and suggested that as India should be defended by nonviolence so should the British homeland be best preserved in the same manner.

In Britain's darkest hour, August 8, 1940, the government repeated the offer of full and equal partnership in the British Commonwealth *after the war*, with full weight to the views of minorities. It ruled out the possibility of constitutional changes during the war, but declared that at the conclusion of the war it would set up a body representative of all elements in India's national life to devise a new constitution for themselves. In the meantime it invited all parties and communities to cooperate more fully in the prosecution of the war. To that end it offered immediately to expand the viceroy's council by adding more Indian members and to create a war advisory council consisting of some thirty representatives of British India and the princely states. The Congress remained obdurate. It would not help the British with men or money; it advocated nonviolent resistance to all war. Thousands of Indians, including all the prominent leaders of the Congress, were sent to British jails.

When Japan entered World War II, India was obliged to make an agonizing reappraisal of its position. India was sandwiched between Germany on the west and Japan on the east. It was menaced from both sides. It was given a breathing space by the defeat of the axis armies in Africa, but it was subjected to a new crisis of nerves by the Japanese conquest of neighboring Burma. Indian troops had shared the glory of victory in the west, only to taste the bitterness of defeat in the east. Indians were among those killed and captured at Singapore, and among those who left their blood stains on the steaming jungle trails which led out of Burma into Assam. As eager as the Indians were to get rid of the British, they were not disposed to listen to the siren songs of the Japanese. The cure would be worse than the disease.

In March 1942, the British sent Sir Stafford Cripps, a prominent English socialist long associated with the cause of India's freedom, to India in order to rally all Indians to guard their land from the menace of the invader. He announced the British aim "to create a new Indian Union, which shall constitute a Dominion, associated with the United Kingdom and the other Dominions by a common allegiance to the Crown but equal to them in every respect, in no way subordinate in any aspect of its domestic or external affairs." He made four proposals: upon cessation of hostilities, an all-Indian constitution-making body was to be set up; a union should be established, with any province free to join or not to join; obligations of the British government, including the protection of racial and religious minorities, would be safeguarded by treaty; and until the new constitution might be framed, the British would be responsible for the defense of India, with the full cooperation of the Indian peoples. No group in India showed complete satisfaction with the Cripps program. The Congress passed a resolution in August 1942, that the British should "quit India" and demanded that a national government with real responsibility and power should be established immediately. The government replied by declaring the Congress an unlawful association and putting its leaders back in jail. Riots and sabotage spread throughout India as telegraph wires were cut, railway lines torn up, air strips destroyed, post offices and railway stations burned. Meanwhile British and Indians built up their forces in India, thousands of Americans came to India as a base for operations looking to the return to China, and more thousands of Chinese received their training from allied officers on Indian soil.

The Japanese tried hard to inspire Indians overseas to join in efforts to "liberate" their native land. The Japanese sponsored an Indian independence league and an Indian national army, headed by Subhas Chandra Bose, a former president of the Indian Congress who was brought to Southeast Asia from his place of exile in Germany. A provisional government of "free India" was established at Singapore with Bose at the head. He was expected to rally all Indian support for the Japanese as they launched their invasion attempt against India. The Indian support fell apart when the Japanese themselves were defeated. Bose himself was killed in an airplane accident in Formosa in 1945 as he tried to make his way back to Japan from the scene of the abortive liberation effort which, in his view, was to be the first step to India's freedom.

In the autumn of 1943, Lord Wavell was named viceroy to India. In his dogged way, he carried on the effort to obtain the cooperation of all parties—primarily the Congress and the Moslem League—in the prosecution of the war. Hindu-Moslem antagonism was the stumbling block to unity. It was clear that there would be no alternative to an independent Pakistan, the only questions were the extent of territory, the nature of sovereignty, and the timing of the establishment of the Moslem state. After the fall of Germany, Lord Wavell lifted the ban on the Congress party. In June 1945 he invited Indian leaders of all persuasions to participate in a conference at Simla to discuss a national administration to carry on the war and a constituent assembly to draw up a constitution at the end. It was expected that the war against Japan would last another year, and it was noted that there were many foreign troops in the country who would preserve internal order in spite of anticipated political disputes. The Congress insisted on its exclusive right to speak for all India; the Moslem League demurred. The problem was no longer the transfer of power from Great Britain, but into whose hands should the power be given.

The conference ended in stalemate. Then the elections in Great Britain in July 1945, showed that the British were in no mood for further sacrifices and adventures abroad, even in their own colonies. The platform of the victorious Labour government called for "self-government for India in friendly association with Great Britain." On August 14, Japan surrendered. With the end of the war, both the British and the Indians were obliged to come to grips with the seething demand for self-government and independence.

World War II had caused profound changes in the development of India. Its military record belied any image of pacifism. Indian troops fought honorably in North Africa and Somaliland, Italy and Iran, Syria and Iraq, Malaya and Burma. Of a million men in the Fourteenth Army who participated in the reconquest of Burma, sixty percent were from India. Casualties during the war amounted to 180,000 of whom one in six was killed. Indian defense forces at the end of the war numbered more than two millions, including the army, navy, air force, and women's auxiliary corps. The commissioned officers were mostly Indians, not Europeans. Furthermore, India became largely self-sufficient in war supplies. It became a vast arsenal for most kinds of arms and ammunition.

The pattern of India's economic and social life was irrevocably altered. Indians formed new contacts with thousands of Americans and Chinese, and learned more about their ways. Many Indians left their villages for the first time, and many served overseas. As millions of people came together in new associations, customs changed. The air force and the navy set aside the caste distinctions in food and touch. Village boys were taught new trades and given new skills. Manual labor lost much of the social prejudice against it. As industry and trade increased, many thousands achieved a new middle-class status which came along with their wealth. Women enjoyed new privileges. They were accepted into the auxiliary corps and given office or clerical jobs where they could work for money of their own.

The farms and villages shared in the general upsurge of economic activity. Food was basic, and peasants received better prices than ever for their crops. The country demanded more and more raw materials of all kinds: cereals, tea, coffee, cotton, jute, oil seeds, timber, mica, and manganese. Higher incomes meant that debtors paid off a good share of their obligations.

Prosperity was uneven. While some people and some areas flourished, others suffered. Rationing could not make up for actual shortages in things to eat. Bengal suffered a terrible famine in 1943. Harbors, roads, and railways were expanded, yet all India seemed to be bogged down in a perpetual traffic jam. Inflation hurt the white-collar groups; higher taxes and savings drives siphoned off the extra profits into the coffers of the government. Thanks to its own careful financial procedures and to the huge expenditures of the United States and Great Britain, India during the war repaid the whole of its sterling debt, bought out British shares in a number of Indian railways, and accumulated a credit balance of some five billion dollars in London. Such peripheral effects as these were more important than the bare military record of World War II in determining India's future.

Japan's Program in the Southern Regions

Outside of India, World War II meant little in South and Southeast Asia before the entry of Japan. The inactivity of 1939 and the blitzkrieg of 1940 gave little opportunity to European powers to get the most out of the manpower and resources of their colonies. Then the sweep of the armies of Japan throughout greater East Asia brought the war to everybody's doorstep. The marching feet of Japan's soldiers trampled the old order out of existence and speeded up the process of integrating Asia into the modern world system on a basis of equality and reciprocity. Many Asians were killed and their meager property destroyed; those who survived were fired by new ideas of prosperity, freedom, and national independence.

By the end of the summer, 1942, the Japanese flag flew over every capital and important city in Southeast Asia. Japanese armies occupied enormous territories stretching from Manchukuo to New Guinea. They settled down to problems of administration and exploitation. The entire economy of the occupied areas was adjusted to meet the needs of Japan. Normal trade patterns between Asia and Europe or between Asia and the United States were destroyed. Only trade with Japan was permitted until it too was brought to an end by the shortage of ships. Stockpiles were looted, and movable goods were sent back to Japan on the return trips of Japanese transports and troop-carriers. Long-established economic patterns were uprooted as Japan decreed that each area should readapt itself to the military needs of Japan or the achievement of self-sufficiency. Rubber plantations were neglected or abandoned, sugar was ploughed under for rice, or cotton was coaxed out of conditions which were next to impossible.

Rice was short in most areas; it was a glut on the market in others. Transportation was the problem. Japanese soldiers had to be fed, whether or not the native inhabitants were hungry. Help the Japanese or starve! Labor had to be recruited and mobilized as a service corps for the Japanese army. Nonmilitary jobs were scarce, and the pay was worthless. The only money was the military scrip which was ground out by Japanese printing presses. Everywhere prices rose to fantastic heights, but nothing was available at any cost. Shortages in food, salt, medicines, clothes, and soap from one end of the "co-prosperity sphere" to the other gave rise to hoarding, speculation, and black markets.

The Japanese pretended to respect the sublime culture and mature customs of the occupied areas, but they spread their own language, educational ideas, and way of life. They determined to bestow upon all Asia the Yamato Damashi or spirit of the immortal race. English, French, or Dutch were forbidden as official languages, and the study of Japanese was made compulsory. Local papers, magazines, and radio programs featured daily lessons in Japanese. National languages—for example Tagalog, Burmese, or Malayan—were tolerated but pushed aside. Street names and shop signs were printed only in the unfamiliar Japanese script.

Local schools were closed as soon as the Japanese took control. Educators from Japan were imported to remold curriculums, revise texts, and train native teachers. Liberal subject matter was expurgated and emphasis placed on Japanese-style ethics, calisthenics, and vocational training. Southeast Asians, like Koreans, would be taught their rightful place in the Japan-arranged "eight corners of the world under one roof." Special students were sent to Japan for training or conferences so that they could return to their homes to spread stories of Japan's strength, benevolence, and cultural advancement.

In all occupied areas, the Japanese sought to establish strong social controls. They instituted the neighborhood association system which made an entire community responsible for the actions of its individual members. The neighborhood associations were used to encourage informing, suppress dangerous thoughts, and administer the rationing of food. The Japanese set up women's service associations, youth societies, and single-party systems as means of Japanization. They were careful not to attack indigenous religions and to propitiate Asians of all faiths. They brought Japanese preachers and priests along with the fighting forces in order to explain to their new flocks the principles of the co-prosperity sphere. Prayer meetings were conducted for the ultimate victory of Japan. Japanese Christians, Buddhists, and Mohammedans were used as tools to strengthen Japan's claim to political leadership. The Japanese hoped eventually to persuade Asians of other nationalities to abandon their former ties to the "decadent" West and to accept the superiority of Japan's culture.

According to the Japanese political program, Japan must be the center and leader of Asia. Each nation and people should be encouraged toward "independence" modeled after the precedent of Manchukuo. Such independence had nothing to do with liberalism or self-determination, but implied inseparable attachment to Japan. The weak needed the protection of the strong. Japan would crush the forces of imperialism which kept millions of Asians in economic and spiritual poverty; Asians themselves "must fight, fight, fight with all their heart and soul until Great East Asia is completely and forever their own."

Japan took native leaders who had been neglected, imprisoned, or exiled by their former overlords and placed them in charge of puppet governments. Once installed in office, they were eulogized as beacon lights of Asia. In November 1943, the most distinguished among them were assembled in Tokyo in a Greater East Asia Conference. They drew up a Declaration of Principles which was advertised as Asia's answer to the "meaningless" Atlantic Charter. These principles for the construction of a greater East Asia were: stability and common prosperity should be ensured through mutual cooperation; countries in the region should respect one another's sovereignty and independence and practice mutual assistance and amity; they should respect one another's traditions and develop their creative facilities; they should accelerate economic development through close cooperation on a basis of reciprocity; finally, the countries of greater East Asia should cultivate friendly relations with all the countries of the world and work for the abolition of racial discrimination, the promotion of cultural intercourse and the opening of resources throughout the world.

Aside from issuing the Declaration of Principles, the conference was used as a sounding board for well-established propaganda lines on the general theme of Asia for the Asiatics. Theoretically Japanese propaganda exercised a strong appeal to local pride and the sense of nationalism. Actually it was nullified by the brutal behavior of the Japanese soldiers and the obvious imperialistic intent in Japan's program. To the end of the war, Japan's leaders were deliberately blind to their country's faults and loyal to its pretensions. During his defense before the International Military Tribunal for the Far East, Premier Tojo testified: "Never could we imagine that such a policy (as ours) should be construed as the planning of conquest, the domination of the world, or aggression."

Implementation of Japan's Program: the Philippines

The Philippines was the first country in Southeast Asia to receive the full impact of the Japanese thrust. When the bombs dropped and the fires raged, the American troops withdrew from the open city of Manila to Bataan and Corregidor. President Quezon accompanied the American high commissioner and General MacArthur to Corregidor and took the Philippine government-in-exile with him. While under fire on Corregidor, President Quezon urged the Americans to agree to a plan for the neutralization of the Philippines which would imply the withdrawal of all American and Japanese forces. Washington refused. Quezon was taken to Australia, and thence to Washington where he remained as the head of the legitimate Philippine government until his death in August 1944.

Filipinos, who had looked upon the Americans as supreme and invincible for forty years, could scarcely believe the evidence of the Japanese invasion. White men were whipped and disgraced, and the native population was left without its accustomed protector. Some Filipinos fled to the countryside to join their relatives or ran away to hide in the hills. Others had no place to go. They had no alternative except to stay at home, match wits with the conqueror, and hope for the best in the struggle for existence.

The Japanese declared that Americans—not Filipinos—were their only enemies. The tone of the Japanese psychological warfare was indicated in the first propaganda leaflets which were dropped from enemy planes. They were addressed to Filipinos:

> Dear friends! Folks at home.
>
> Do you realize what you are fighting for. You probably sincerely believe that you are defending democracy from the aggressor but nothing could be further from the truth. Open your eyes and see what America has done to you so far. In order to advance their imperialist cause, they seized your country forty years ago and since then you have been abused, exploited, neglected and what is worse, you have been treated as an inferior race.
>
> The best sections of Manila, as you all know, have been seized by Americans and they own the best clubs, the best stores, the best residences in utter disregard of your just rights. You are scorned in public and made fun of in their exclusive clubs where you are not allowed admission. This is true in camps as well as in civilian life. Americans are better paid although they are no good as soldiers. Most of them come from the farms in the mid-west and manners and courtesy are not their forte. How can you expect such crude creatures to respect the rights of womanhood and the ideals of Filipino civilization? . . . .
>
> The present fighting has been caused by America's greed to place Asia under its control. They could not do this as long as Japan, the most powerful nation in the Orient remained; so America and England formed a conspiracy to blockade Japan economically. We knew of this long ago, but not desiring to start a war in the Orient, we have restrained ourselves, but now the hour for us to act has arrived. . . .

The Japanese expressed indignation that "the great soul and spirit of the true Filipinos have been maliciously perverted and debilitated by long years of hypocritical exploitation under the American regime." It was charged that Americans camouflaged their real aims under sugar-coated labels of justice and democracy and gave the Filipinos, in exchange for their birthright of independence and virile existence, the ephemeral benefits of cheap materialism and a false sense of economic stability. Therefore the Japanese would de-Americanize the Philippines. Dewey Boulevard in Manila was given a Japanese name, and Taft Avenue became the Road of Greater East Asia. American flags were destroyed, textbooks were scissored, postage stamps were defaced or overprinted, American holidays were tabooed, American films were banned, and lively music was condemned. American citizens were interned and humiliated. After two years of intensive anti-Americanism, the Japanese ambassador was obliged to admit that the program was a failure, because the Filipinos were too steeped in the American way of life.

The Japanese treated Filipinos with inexcusable brutality. For psychological effect, the Japanese exhibited looters and petty thieves in cages, or tied them to telephone poles, drenched them, and left them to agonize in the tropical sun. Japanese soldiers ordered the scared Filipinos around and slapped them as so many slaves. The death penalty was decreed for political crimes, and warnings were issued that hostages would be taken and shot in any area where offenses were committed against the imperial forces.

The Japanese military administration set up a puppet government at the outset of the occupation. This government consisted of a Philippine executive committee (cabinet) and a state council including most of the former Nacionalista politicians. Japanese dominated the entire administrative machine, including the provincial governors and the municipal mayors. They controlled legislation and took over the police and the courts. They organized a new political party, totalitarian style, which they called the *Kalibapi,* or Association for Service to the New Philippines. In the fall of 1943 a national assembly was called together which elected Jose P. Laurel as president of the Independent Republic of the Philippines. The "independent" government entered into an alliance with Japan. The two countries agreed to respect each other's territory and independence and to collaborate in the prosecution of the war. No formal declaration of war against the United States was made by the Philippines until September 23, 1944, and by that time it was an idle formality. The Philippines refused to conscript their manpower, to force their soldiers to take an oath of loyalty to the Japanese, and to order their army into the field against the Americans.

The Philippines was the great Japanese problem child in Southeast Asia. The Japanese were so exasperated that they labeled all Filipinos as "ninety-five percent pro-American and five percent liars." Collaborators could not be trusted, and guerrillas made life unbearable for the invaders. A constant stream of weather information poured into the Australian headquarters of General MacArthur from secret radios. Different guerrilla groups were coordinated by radio orders from Australia or by secret instructions hand-delivered by American submarines. One effective guerrilla band known as the *Hukbalahaps,* or People's Liberation Army against Japan, which included Communists among its leaders, did a lot of killing both of Japanese and of feudal landowners—primarily in northern Luzon.

The bloodletting which accompanied the American return to the Philippines was the climactic legacy of the Japanese. The Americans landed in Leyte in October 1944, and in Luzon shortly after the new year (1945). Thousands of Filipinos were tortured and slaughtered by the Japanese in their hour of doom. Manila was razed and sacked during the last horrible artillery duel between the Americans and the Japanese. The remnants of the Japanese army were driven to the mountains, where they dug in to make the American mopping-up campaigns as costly as possible. The Japanese commander, General Yamashita, obeyed the imperial order to surrender on August 14, 1945, but some stragglers from the Japanese forces eked out a defiant, miserable existence in the mountains and jungles for days and months.

After the liberation of Manila and before the end of the war, the Americans spent all their energies in converting the Philippines into a vast staging area for the anticipated invasion of Japan. President Osmena returned to the Philippines with General MacArthur and brought the commonwealth government back with him. It was immediately restored to power. The puppet government was dissolved, and some of its leaders were taken to Japan. Others were arrested and placed in Filipino jails to await judicial trial for their acts as collaborators. As for the ordinary Filipinos, they emerged from the war bruised in body and battered in spirit. Their ordeal could not fail to result in a deep hatred of Japan.

BRITISH TERRITORIES: MALAYA AND BURMA

The outposts of the British Empire in Asia—Hong Kong, Borneo, Singapore, Malaya, and Burma—escaped none of the fury of the Japanese attack. Hong Kong and the British possessions in Borneo were taken over and administered as integral parts of the territory of Japan. Singapore, renamed *Shonan* (or Light of the South) became the chief Japanese operating base in the southern regions. Malaya was given little political consideration; Burma, like the Philippines, was treated as a worthy "independent" nation. The British government took the position that its possessions were only temporarily in the hands of the enemy. Prime Minister Churchill insisted that British colonialism was not obsolescent, still less in liquidation. He declared:

We mean to hold our own. I have not become the King's first minister to preside over the liquidation of the British Empire. . . . I am proud to be a member of that vast commonwealth and society of nations and communities gathered in and around the ancient British monarchy. . . . Here we are, and here we stand, a veritable rock of salvation in this drifting world.

Great Britain suffered a grievous blow on February 15, 1942, when General Percival surrendered at Singapore; British prestige was damaged beyond hope of immediate repair. The Japanese created a military administration for Malaya. They divided the country into eight provinces and put an end to the former distinction between Straits Settlements, Federated, and Unfederated States. They added Sumatra to Malaya and handed over to Thailand the four northern provinces of Malaya which had been placed under British protection in 1909. They designated the sultans as heads of bureaus of religious affairs and reduced their salaries. There was no promise of independence for Malaya, although some consultative councils were inaugurated. Toward the end of the war, the Japanese hinted at the possibility of a "New Malai" which, with Indonesia, might become the homeland for all peoples of the Malay race. Nothing happened beyond the talk stage.

The Japanese were too busy with the militarization and exploitation of Malaya to take fullest advantage of communal rivalry which might have been utilized for Japanese advantage. Malays might have been attracted to the Japanese cause on account of their rivalry with the Chinese, and Indians might have been induced to support Japan completely because of their desire to weaken the British. Instead the Japanese drove the three communities—Malays, Chinese, and Indians—closer together in common opposition to tyranny and oppression The seeds of Malayan nationalism flourished in the rich soil of the Japanese occupation.

The resistance movement was also an important by-product of Japanese policies. Special "stay-behind" groups left by the British became the nucleus of the underground in Malaya. Its moving spirit was the Malay Communist Party which organized the Malaya People's Anti-Japanese Army and its political counterpart the Malaya People's Anti-Japanese Union. Its membership was entirely Chinese. The British air-dropped arms and ammunition to the guerrillas on the basis of an agreement that they would harass the Japanese and cooperate with the Allies at the time of liberation. It was the British understanding that the guerrillas would work under British direction and would be disarmed after the fighting was over. The British were fully aware that the Communist program aimed at the expulsion of the British and the creation of a Communist-controlled Republic of Malaya. Such worries were relegated to the postwar future.

The surrender of Japan and the return of the British was comparatively unspectacular in Singapore. The surrender edict was not made known to the public for a week. Then General Itagaki published the emperor's rescript simultaneously with a statement that the Japanese army had lost none of its honor and dignity, since it was quite ready to engage in decisive battle. He explained that Japan called off the war in order to spare the people of Southeast Asia from the disaster of the atom bomb. He thanked the people of Malaya for their cooperation and declared this was not the end of the struggle of Japan to establish greater East Asia. He made no effort to set up an independent regime for Malaya in the three weeks which elapsed before the return of the British troops. The Japanese retired to the towns outside of Singapore and kept order with their own guns, which they were allowed to retain. Much of the interior fell into the hands of the guerrillas who gave the impression that it was they who defeated the Japanese. When the British returned, they were escorted on the road to Singapore by a red-starred guard of honor. They awarded an O.B.E. to the Chinese Communist leader, Chin Peng, who was hailed as "our most trusted guerrilla" and invited to London to participate in the victory parade.

The experience of Burma was more traumatic than that of Malaya. When the war with Japan broke out, Burma's prime minister, U Saw, was in London seeking a better political status for his country. He was told that article three of the Atlantic Charter which guaranteed the freedom to choose one's own government did not apply to the British Empire in Asia. He was told further that self-government for Burma would be the measure of cooperation with Great Britain in the war effort. Full dominion status within the British Commonwealth might be attained after the war. On the way home U Saw stopped in at the Japanese embassy in Lisbon, and from cable intercepts it was learned that he assured the Japanese that he would help them should they decide to invade Burma. U Saw was arrested in Egypt and detained in British Uganda for the duration of the war. A pro-British Burman in Rangoon was nominated as prime minister; with several associates he constituted the Burmese staff of Governor-General Dorman-Smith, who technically administered the affairs of Burma from temporary wartime headquarters in Simla.

The Japanese expected that the fiery young Thakins would provide all the native help that was needed, but they were disappointed. The Thakins had no desire to turn their country over to the Japanese; they only wanted Japanese help in driving out the British. Immediately after the Japanese established themselves in Rangoon in March 1942, they discovered that Aung San's Burma independence army was not much of a military force. Its ranks were filled with rabble who, under the protection of their new masters, settled old political scores against Karens and Indians and led the country toward civil war.

The invaders then turned to Ba Maw, a former prime minister and leader of the anti-British "Freedom Bloc," to do their bidding. He was put in charge of a Burmese executive administration and on August 1, 1943, was named *Adipadi,* or leader of the "independent" Republic of Burma. The Japanese-drafted declaration of independence was dedicated to "One Blood, One Voice and One Leader." The ethnic Burmans were given authority over all minority groups, including Karens, Arakanese, Shans, and Kachins. The territory of Burma was fixed without regard to the rights of neighboring China. In due course, Burma signed an alliance with Japan and a declaration of war against the United States and Great Britain.

Ba Maw's cabinet and Privy Council included practically all the nationalistic Thakins except those who were Communists. One prominent Communist fled to India where he established contact with the British and another joined the resistance movement in its earliest stages in the Irrawaddy Delta. Ba Maw, under Japanese prompting, abolished the old British-style administrative structure and the courts of justice. To show his contempt for democratic forms he revived some of the ancient customs of the Burmese kingdom. However, he was not a complete automaton. In most difficult circumstances he warned the Japanese that they should not mix in internal Burmese matters and should not stir up popular feelings against his administration.

Next to the Philippines, Burma suffered more than any other country in Southeast Asia because of the Japanese invasion. Burma was a constant battlefield. When the British first retreated, they pursued a scorched-earth policy. They scuttled ships; burned oil wells; wrecked railways and port installations; and destroyed mines, factories, and power plants. The fighting in the north, involving Chinese and Americans, added to the destruction of ricelands, towns, and villages. Because Burma was the Japanese base for the ill-fated India campaign, Burma's cities and transport systems were targets for continuous allied bombing. When the Japanese retreated, the devastation was made complete.

Burma's scars were psychological as well as physical. As a Buddhist country, it resented Japanese acts of defilement against the pagodas and temples. According to local complaints, the Japanese used monks' robes to bind horses' feet, hung their laundry on altars, destroyed images and scrolls, and used temples as latrines. Perhaps the darkest blot on the Japanese record was the death of thousands of prisoners of war and Asians who died of disease and exhaustion while forced to work on the fatal railway between Burma and Thailand.

When the tide of battle turned against Japan, Ba Maw kept up the façade of collaboration. He looked the other way as his associates secretly organized the Anti-Fascist People's Freedom League (AFPFL) as the core of resistance against Japan. Aung San and his communist brother-in-law, Than Tun, linked together the communist-led underground, socialist peasant and worker's associations, patriotic Karens, the East Asia Youth League (a lawful service association), and eventually the Burma national army in a broad national union dedicated to the expulsion of the

Japanese and the establishment of democracy and independence. The flag of the AFPFL—a large white star on a solid red background—eventually became the flag of Burma. In this manner, most of Burma's young leaders made a timely shift in their behavior. They turned from the Japanese to the British. As leaders of the underground, they received weapons and supplies by parachute from the British and Americans. They emerged from the war as full-fledged members of the winning side.

While Chinese and Americans swept across northern Burma, the Fourteenth Army of British and Indians drove into the deltalands of Lower Burma. It was tough fighting all the way, in contrast to the return to Malaya. At the end of April 1945, the Japanese evacuated Rangoon and retreated to the hill country in the north and east. Mopping-up campaigns continued for months; and Burma's army, renamed the People's Volunteer Organization, joined in the fighting. The puppet government was dissolved, and Ba Maw fled to Tokyo. His associates, including the Thakins Mya and Nu, retreated in comparative obscurity to Moulmein. Aung San and his colleagues in the AFPFL were the lions of the hour, and they asserted their exclusive right to speak for all Burma in the difficult days ahead.

INDONESIA AND INDOCHINA

The Dutch in Indonesia and the French in Indochina experienced the same shocks at the hands of the Japanese as the Americans in the Philippines and the British in Burma. Although Japan failed to establish a new order, the old order collapsed. After World War II the hands of the political clock could never be turned back any where in Southeast Asia.

The Dutch in Indonesia were doomed by the fall of the Netherlands to the Nazis. The islands were unable to offer effective resistance to the Japanese, who raised their flag over Batavia in March 1942. All the Indies with their rich resources came under effective Japanese control. Batavia was renamed Djakarta and made the headquarters for the Japanese military administration. The Japanese navy took over Borneo, Celebes, and the Lesser Sunda Islands. The Dutch administrative structure was done away with and the sultans were deprived of their glamour and prestige. New and severe laws were introduced, and police affairs were placed in the hands of the Japanese *Kempeitai* who recruited native assistants.

The Japanese advertised themselves as the "Three A's—the Protector of Asia, Leader of Asia and the Light of Asia." They told the Indonesians that the Japanese had come to drive out the Dutch, and they expressed regret that they were compelled to wage a war that was caused "by the aggression of the Netherlands." They carried out the usual propaganda campaign through newspapers, radio, moving pictures, and the schools; they decreed death for anyone caught listening to short-wave broadcasts. Old political associations were disbanded, and all political discussions were tabooed. The religious ideas of the Japanese encountered difficulties with the Moslem faith of the Indonesians. Moslems were determined to bow toward Mecca, not toward the imperial palace in Tokyo. Moslems would not tolerate Japanese interference with religious fasts and feasts. The Moslems worshiped one God—Allah—and they would not accept the multiplicity of divinities in the Shinto pantheon. Moslems refused to eat "unclean" pork when it was served up with Japanese rations.

Most Indonesians approved harsh Japanese measures against the Dutch and Chinese, but the approval disappeared when the Japanese seized the meager food supplies, conscripted labor, and requisitioned raw materials. The Japanese seized Dutch plantations, factories, and mines; but they failed to transfer the assets to Indonesians. The lowly native people lost their jobs as shipping stopped and trade dried up. The only available employment was service for the Japanese armed forces, and that was all sweat and no pay. Even the Japanese at the end of the war appeared ragged and undernourished. The wealth of the Indies was reduced to the common poverty of the co-prosperity sphere.

Indonesians were regimented into neighborhood associations and special service organizations for women, youth, or religious groups. A home guard, or volunteer corps, was organized to help put down resistance and defend the islands in the event of allied invasion. Arms were permitted only during the long, hot hours of actual drill. The customary totalitarian political party in the Indies was called Putera, or Concentration of People's Strength, and was dedicated to the elimination of Western influence and the promulgation of the ideals of East Asia. Sukarno was the director, and its membership was not open to Eurasians or Chinese.

Sukarno proved to be the most able of the prewar nationalist leaders. He and Hatta chose to collaborate with the Japanese; Sjahrir and Sjarifoeddin were among those who preferred to work with the underground. The Communists, including Tan Malakka and Semaun, also participated in the resistance movement. In the Indies—in contrast to the Philippines, Burma, and Malaya—guerrilla warfare played a minor role in the defeat of the Japanese.

Until the tide of war turned against Japan, the Indies resembled an armed camp. The Japanese ran the government, and they made no definite promises of independence. They showed little respect for their Indonesian collaborators, who were restricted to ineffective, advisory roles in the administration. The Japanese were never satisfied with the amount or the quality of Indonesian assistance. In March 1944, the Putera was dissolved because it was "insufficiently cooperative and too nationalistic." A substitute was created in the form of the Hokokai, or Corporation for Communal Services, which reached down into all the villages and aimed at total mobilization.

When Koiso succeeded Tojo as premier of Japan, he changed the tone of the relationship between Japan and the Indies. He gave shadowy promises of independence, and he gave Indonesians more responsibility in administrative affairs. He allowed the Indonesians to fly their red and white flag on certain occasions and permitted them to sing their national anthem at public gatherings. He authorized Sukarno and Hatta to tour the Indies and give speeches playing up the theme of "One Nation, One Language, One People." Koiso pursued new tactics, but his objective was still to make the Indies and Japan one and inseparable.

As defeat approached, Japanese officials gave thought to the creation of a "political time bomb," a national state which would have cause to be anti-Dutch and friendly to Japan. In the spring of 1945 a group of Indonesians, Eurasians, and Chinese under the leadership of the Japanese was called together to draw up a draft constitution and to issue a declaration of determination to fight to the death for the Japanese against the allied enemies. In July, after the Japanese defeat at Okinawa and the first land-ings in Borneo, the independence movement snowballed. Early in August, the Japanese commander in chief of Japanese forces in the southern regions summoned Sukarno and Hatta to his headquarters in Saigon. He informed them than independence would be granted in September.

Political events moved faster than Japanese intentions. On August 15, 1945, the 120 members of the Indonesian committee of national independence learned of the Japanese surrender. They drew up a statement of principles for their new state and they adopted a constitution. On August 17 they proclaimed their independence. Sukarno, Hatta, and Sjahrir were great popular heroes; the fiery Sukarno was the living symbol of victorious nationalism.

The Japanese were supposed to keep order throughout the Indies until the return of the victorious allies. In defeat, all but the top leaders were gripped by indecision and a certain amount of fear. They had no desire to help their former enemies and many were hungry. They bartered or gave away arms and ammunition to Indonesians and permitted the excited native people to do largely as they pleased. Indonesian guards took over the internment camps of the Dutch and atrocities were frequent. The radio brought a futile message "be prudent and cautious and await the return of the Dutch." It was tragically clear that the Dutch would not return, at least in their former glory. Indonesian nationalists were in the saddle. They would not surrender easily what they had won through years of pain and humiliation.

The experiences of Indonesia were paralleled by the war years in Indochina, except that it was the French rather than the Dutch who watched as their empire was chipped away by the Japanese. The Japanese had an effective grip on Indochina *before* Pearl Harbor, so the ordinary man in the street there escaped the fires and the slaughter which went with air raids and naval bombardments. The French-Japanese convention of July, 1941, gave the Japanese complete control of the ports, harbors, and transportation facilities which served as the main base for Japan's advance into the southern regions. That agreement served the purposes on both sides. The French colonial officials saw the political understanding as the only means of preventing complete Japanese conquest. For their part the Japanese did not trust the French, but used the French to maintain internal order while the Japanese concentrated on external military operations. The French were obliged to give the Japanese economic privileges in Indochina, and to make the rich resources of the French colony available for the exclusive use of the Japanese war machine.

Underground resistance to the Japanese represented a new turn in the expression of communism and indigenous nationalism. Before 1941 local patriots were primarily against the French; after 1941 they opposed the Japanese. Such Communist leaders as Ho Chi Minh, Vo Nguyen Giap, and Pham Van Dong set up the Vietnam Independence League, known from a shortened version of its Annamese name as the *Viet Minh*. The Chinese across the border were as anti-Japanese as the Viet Minh, but they disliked seeing Communist leadership in opposition to Japan in Indochina. They launched a rival organization called the Vietnam Revolutionary League, but it could not get off the ground without the dynamic Ho Chi Minh and his Communist associates. The Viet Minh and the Revolutionary League combined to form a coalition in 1943 dedicated to resistance to Japan *and* independence from France. The Communists were the recognized leaders of the coalition, but, because they kept their ideology in the background, they received the support and cooperation of the allies, particularly the Americans.

A new element entered the picture in October, 1943. De Gaulle and his French Committee of National Liberation in North Africa announced that Indochina would not be alienated to a conqueror nor placed eventually under an international trusteeship as President Roosevelt suggested. De Gaulle promised that after the war Indochina should be given a new status within the French Empire. A De Gaullist representative came to Chungking, and Chiang Kai-shek broke off relations with Vichy France. The free-French representative in Chungking organized his own resistance movement. At the same time American airplanes raided Indochina, but they did more damage to civilians and food supplies than to Japanese troops or military installations.

After the Americans returned to the Philippines and De Gaulle entered Paris, the Japanese anticipated an attack on Indochina. On March 9, 1945, the Japanese demanded that the French should turn over all military, administrative, and police functions to the Japanese. Admiral Decoux was arrested, French troops were disarmed, and French civilian officials were interned. The next day the radio announced that the colonial status in Indochina had ended and support would be given to local independence movements. In the city of Hué, the emperor of Annam, Bao Dai, proclaimed his independence. His sovereignty over Annam and the "National Federation of Tongking" at Hanoi was recognized by the Japanese. His dominions were renamed Vietnam, which means the "country south of China." On March 13 the king of Cambodia at Phnom Penh declared his independence. In Cochin China, which was a French colony and not a protectorate, there was no king to assert independence. Therefore the Japanese named a Japanese civil governor for Saigon and its vicinity. After a month of wait-and-see, the pro-French king of Luang Prabang belatedly declared his independence, and the Japanese were very displeased with his delay. The Japanese also seized the former French-leased area of Kwangchowwan and turned it over to the Chinese government in Nanking.

The Japanese scarcely inaugurated the new system before it was time to surrender. Ho Chi Minh's underground refused to have anything to do with Bao Dai's "independent" government and liberated seven provinces in the north. The Viet Minh controlled resistance pockets throughout the countryside and established strongholds in and around Saigon. When the Japanese house of cards came tumbling down, there was no French organization to replace it. In the north the Japanese handed over their arms to the Viet Minh. The emperor Bao Dai abdicated and became supreme adviser to his compatriot Ho Chi Minh.

On September 2, 1945, in the hills beyond Hanoi near the Chinese border, the congress of the Viet Minh severed all connections with France. In a document reminiscent of the Declaration of Independence of the United States, the Viet Minh declared the independence of Vietnam. A provisional government was proclaimed, and Ho Chi Minh was elected president. The government was then transferred to Hanoi, where banners on the street carried the slogans "Down with Imperialism" and "Independence or Death." No French troops were anywhere in evidence, and no voices were heard for the return of the French. Ho Chi Minh felt that the nations which had recognized the principle of equality at Tehran and San Francisco could not fail to recognize his government of Vietnam. Meanwhile in Saigon, a pro-Viet Minh national committee assumed power. That committee preserved order and kept the public services functioning while the French, who were still in custody, awaited the appearance of the liberating forces.

THAILAND

When the Japanese tide engulfed Southeast Asia, the independent kingdom of Thailand gambled its fate on the side of Japan. Believing that Japan would win, Thailand determined to be on the winning side. In January 1942, its leaders declared war on Great Britain and the United States. Seni Pramoj, the Thai ambassador in Washington, refused to deliver the document to the American authorities, and for four years the United States regarded Thailand not as an enemy but as a country to be liberated from the enemy. However, American planes bombed Thailand because of the great numbers of Japanese troops which were stationed there.

Thailand relished the friendly Japanese action which added 100,000 square miles to Thai territory and increased its population by more than 3,000,000 persons. Thailand acquired borderlands from Laos and Cambodia, Burma, and Malaya. In exchange, Thailand permitted its territory to be used by Japan for its military purposes and turned over the national economy for the service of the invaders. Thailand paid a heavy price for its shotgun decisions. The Thai army was pushed into the background and restricted to the unglamorous duty of frontier defense and maintenance of public order. The economy was wrecked, as Japanese requisitioned rice and supplies, cut off international trade, and flooded the country with worthless currency. Thai society was guided by the whims of its political leadership and subjected to an abortive attempt to remodel Thailand according to the pattern of Japan. A constant exchange of goodwill missions, students, films, and educational materials failed to establish intimate links between the Thai people and the Japanese. The Thais saw no reason why they should bother to learn the difficult Japanese language or substitute Japanese culture for their own beloved way of life.

During the war, the king of Thailand remained in Switzerland and was spared the embarrassments of his nation's subservience to Japan. Decisions in his name were made at the beginning of the war by Premier Phibun Songgram, one of the military leaders who had exercised political power since the revolution of 1932. Phibun's position became more precarious as the war progressed. His paternalistic decrees about popular behavior disgusted his people, and they blamed him for their unaccustomed hardships. He also antagonized the Japanese as he tried to look after the interests of his own country and his own people. The mounting allied victories made it clear that Thailand had backed the wrong horse. The Thais decided that Phibun would be made the sacrificial victim as they sought for ways to disassociate themselves from Japan and court the good-will of the Allies.

Phibun's long-time colleague, Luang Pradit (also known as Pridi Banomyong), became the chosen instrument of the new policy. He was minister of finance in Phibun's cabinet when the war began. When the Japanese entered Thailand, Pridi resigned and tried to establish an independent government in northern Thailand. He organized an underground which established contacts with British and Americans in India and China. He was impatient to show his hand, but he warned of the dangers of premature uprising. He was told to "lay low" until the allies could muster sufficient strength to return with a liberating force.

In July, 1944—after the resignation of Tojo in Japan—the Thai legislature, under the domination of the friends of Pridi, forced Phibun's resignation. Pridi himself was named as sole regent of the absent king; and Pridi's friend, Khuang Aphaiwong, was designated as the new premier. It was a curious situation. Thailand was the ally of Japan, and its government was daily in closest association with the Japanese. It was common knowledge that the Thais merely awaited a favorable moment to turn against the Japanese. Allied agents established themselves in Bangkok and sent out a constant stream of information about Japanese military strength and troop movements. The Japanese were aware of such anomalies but were helpless. The strongest political figure in the Thai capital was Pridi, who was not even in Bangkok, but was the leader of the resistance movement somewhere in the north. He was the regent, the man behind the premier and the contact man between the Thais and the Allies.

This confusing situation still obtained when the war ended. The Japanese surrendered before a native uprising became feasible. Political power was restored to the Thais without their having to fight to win it. A mere shift in government was sufficient to restore Thailand to the good graces of the victorious powers. Pridi was accepted as the man to talk peace, but he reasoned that it would be more acceptable to the Allies if he designated Seni Pramoj as premier. Seni was the head of the "free Thai" government in Washington throughout the war. He was in good favor with the United States and was never in any way compromised by collaboration with Japan.

Thailand came out of the war with fewer problems than any other country in Southeast Asia. It escaped the ravages of war at the end as at the beginning. The resistance movement was not the major factor in victory, nor were the Communists the leaders to whom the success of the resistance was due. Thailand had no colonial regime to overthrow and no returning "imperialistic" armies to oppose. It did not face the necessity of profound political changes because it was quite contented with the structure of its kingdom. It had less need than others for great economic changes. Thailand had plenty of rice. The great desire of the Thai people was for the restoration of the old order, with improvements. They were not fired up with the urge for revolution.

The end of the war in Southeast Asia compounded the tragedies which Japan had suffered in Manchukuo, China, and the homeland itself. The dream of empire was gone. The planes of Japan were knocked out of the skies, and the ships of Japan were sent to the bottom of the seven seas. Its armies were destroyed. The flower of Japanese manhood died in the service of the emperor. A sad chapter was closed in Japanese history. Broken in spirit, devastated and helpless, surrounded by enemies, Japan was forced to cope with the wreckage of the past and to struggle to build a new life in the Asia which emerged from World War II.

SUGGESTED READING

Benda, Harry J., *Crescent and Rising Sun* (The Hague, W. van Hoeve, 1958).

Chapman, F. Spencer, *Jungle Is Neutral* (London, Chatto & Windus, 1952).

Coast, John, *Railroad of Death* (London, Commodore Press, 1947).

Considine, Robert, *General Wainwright's Story* (New York, Doubleday, 1946).

Cripps, Sir Stafford, *Lord Privy Seal's Mission, Statement and Draft Declaration* (London, H.M.S.O., 1942).

Donnison, F. S. V., *British Military Administration in the Far East, 1943–1946* (London, H.M.S.O., 1956).

Eldridge, Fred, *Wrath in Burma* (New York, Doubleday, 1946).

Elsbree, Willard H., *Japan's Role in Southeast Asian Nationalist Movements, 1940–1945* (Cambridge, Harvard, 1953).

Grenfell, Russell, *Main Fleet to Singapore* (New York, Macmillan, 1952).

Jones, F. C., *Japan's New Order in East Asia, its Rise and Fall 1937–1945* (London, Royal Institute of International Affairs, 1954).

Mook, Hubertus J. van, *Stakes of Democracy in Southeast Asia* (New York, Norton, 1950).

Mosley, Leonard, *Gideon Goes to War* (New York, Scribner, 1955).

Mountbatten, Louis, Earl, *Report to the Combined Chiefs of Staff* (London, Her Majesty's Stationery Office, 1951).

Nu Thakin, *Burma under the Japanese* (London, Macmillan, 1954).

Ogburn, Charlton, Jr., *Marauders* (New York, Harper, 1959).

Percival, A. E., *War in Malaya* (London, Eyre & Spottiswoode, 1949).

Prasad, Brisheshwar, (ed.), *Official History of the Indian Armed Forces during Second World War, 1939–1945* (five vols.) (New York, Longmans, 1960).

Recto, Claro M., *Three Years of Enemy Occupation* (Manila, People's Publishers, 1946).

Rose, Saul, *Britain and Southeast Asia* (Baltimore, Johns Hopkins, 1962).

V

THE SHAPING OF NEW ASIA

24

Japan: Occupation and Peace

Japan, the most utterly beaten nation in World War II, was the first to regain its bearings. In a remarkably short space of time (six years), it passed through a period of alien occupation and laid the foundations for a new and independent existence. It paid the price of defeat and negotiated a favorable treaty of reconciliation. From surrender on August 14, 1945, to treaty of peace on September 8, 1951, unbelievable changes occurred in the history of Japan.

When Japanese soldiers were brought back to their beloved homeland after the surrender, they were as bewildered as the wretched relatives or friends who lived to greet them. The people were numb and dazed, exhausted spiritually as well as physically. The country was prostrate. It was an anomaly that the diplomacy of the victors should be concentrated on the Potsdam formula that "Japan should never again be a menace to the peace of East Asia." How could such a desert of desolation be a menace to anyone? More than half of Japan's cities were in total ruin, and Tokyo was in ashes. Japan's farmlands were neglected, and its fishing fleet was depleted. Food was so scarce that a Japanese family had less to eat in a day than an American GI was rationed at a single meal. No jobs were to be had because industry and commerce were at a complete standstill. Misery was everywhere, and winter was just around the corner when Japan began life under the occupation.

The occupation was nominally an Allied enterprise but actually an American operation. The interests of the Allies were safeguarded by an eleven-nation policy-making body in Washington called the Far Eastern Commission and a four-nation Allied Council for Japan which met in Tokyo. This council consisted of representatives of the United States, the Soviet Union, China, and the British Commonwealth; it was empowered to advise the occupation authorities on the implementation of the terms

of surrender. It never amounted to much. Its meetings were often carica-
tures of international gatherings and served only as opportunities for re-
crimination and propaganda. The sole authority for the occupation was
the Supreme Commander for the Allied Powers (SCAP), originally General Douglas MacArthur.

An elaborate bureaucracy grew up in Tokyo at the general headquarters of SCAP. As many alphabetical agencies flourished as in Washington, and they gave employment to more than 3000 American military
officers and civilians. The names of the sections indicated the scope of
their responsibilities: diplomatic, economic and scientific, legal, public
health and welfare, natural resources, government, civil information and
education, civil transport and civil communications. Their offices occupied
most of the buildings which were left standing in the ruins of downtown
Tokyo. The American Eighth Army, with troops from the British Commonwealth, acted as the police agent for the occupation. Civil affairs
teams carried out the tasks of military government in the prefectures and
in the local communities.

The victors chose not to depose the emperor of Japan nor to destroy
the framework of the Japanese government. They decided to use the
Japanese rather than to install a direct military administration. They
created a central liaison office which served as an intermediary between
various Japanese government offices and their counterparts in the hierarchy of SCAP. A certain number of Japanese bureaucrats carried out
duties assigned them by instructions or directives from their American
"bosses." Prince Higashikuni, as post-surrender premier, relied upon his
prestige as a member of the imperial family to weather the first shocks of
life in a kind of national servitude. The elderly Baron Shidehara took over
the delicate task of cooperating with occupation authorities; by the time
he resigned (April 22, 1946), procedural routines were clearly established.

The objectives of the occupation as defined in the initial post-surrender policy for Japan were to insure that Japan would not again become
a menace to the peace of the world and to bring about a peaceful and responsible government in conformity with the principles of democratic
self-government. These objectives were to be achieved by the following
means: limiting Japanese sovereignty to Honshu, Hokkaido, Kyushu,
Shikoku, and such minor islands as might be determined; effecting Japan's complete disarmament and demilitarization; encouraging the Japanese to desire individual liberties, respect fundamental human rights, and
form democratic organizations; and affording the Japanese the opportunity to develop a viable economy.

This basic document of the occupation listed the detailed measures
which should be taken: war criminals should be tried, political parties
should be encouraged, unpalatable legislation of prewar Japan should be

abolished, secret societies should be broken up, and political prisoners should be released. Economically, industry should be demilitarized and democratized; organizations in labor, industry, and agriculture should be favored; trusts should be dissolved; appropriate production and trade should be resumed and controlled; identifiable loot should be restored; and occupation expenses and reparations should be collected. The philosophy was that Japan's internal maladjustments should be cured so that Japan could follow the paths of peace.

The Period of Rapid Reform

The Americans set to work with zeal to carry out their instructions. More than 1000 directives from SCAP to the Japanese government in a single year ordered the remolding of Japan. Demilitarization was the first order of business. The imperial general headquarters and the ministries of war and the navy were abolished. All Japanese troops and civilians were brought home from overseas, and the last of Japan's soldiers and sailors were demobilized. No more arms, ammunition, and implements of war were to be made in Japan, and no research was permitted into such dangerous subjects as nuclear physics and aerodynamics. By the fiat of the occupation, Japanese guns were thrown into the sea and thousands of samurai swords were sent home to the United States as souvenirs. Japanese war criminals were placed on trial and punished for their crimes against peace and humanity. The emperor was excused; so were officers of the victorious nations who might have been suspected of atrocities or crimes against the peace.

SCAP's demilitarization program exerted relatively little permanent influence on the Japanese. Real demilitarization both in spirit and in the physical sense had taken place before the occupation with the collapse of the Japanese military machine. All that was left for the occupation was to dispose of the debris. The suffering of the Japanese during the bombing raids added a new sense of pacifism to the Japanese psyche. The Japanese felt that at any cost they should never give occasion again for air raids. They cynically came to believe that military strength was useless unless it was the greatest. They saw the evidences of insufficient strength all around them. Alien forces occupied their divine land, while enemy tanks and guns rattled over their streets. Occupation troops rode in comfort in first-class trains while Japanese people jammed through the windows to find standing room in old wooden cars. A weak power was worse than no power. The Japanese were beaten by superior forces, not by a better way of life.

It was difficult for an autocratic military organization like SCAP to strengthen democratic tendencies in Japan. Exponents of militarism or militant nationalism were "purged" from public life. Such ultranationalistic organizations as the Reserve Officers Association and the Black Dragon Society were dissolved.

A new constitution was drafted by the Americans for Japanese adoption, going into effect in May 1947. The emperor was transformed into a symbol of the state, deriving his position from the will of the people, "in whom resides sovereign power." Japan was converted into a parliamentary democracy with a bicameral diet elected by universal adult suffrage. The upper house, or House of Councilors, consisted of 250 members; the lower house, or House of Representatives, was made up of 466 members. The diet was vested with real control of the budget, and the House of Representatives was given responsibility, British-style, for the prime minister and his cabinet.

The longest chapter in the constitution was devoted to civil rights, which were conceived of as inalienable human rights and no longer as concessions from a gracious sovereign. Unconditional guarantees were given for the usual rights of free speech and freedom of assembly and in addition for rights to work, to bargain collectively, to receive protection against economic exploitation, to maintain the minimum standards of wholesome and cultural living, and to enjoy complete social equality. The constitution also provided for separation of church and state, more local autonomy in government, and for an independent judiciary with the right of judicial review. The famous article nine contained the revolutionary provision by which the Japanese people forever renounced war as a sovereign right of the nation and the threat or use of force as a means of settling international disputes, and pledged themselves never to maintain land, sea, and air forces, as well as other war potential. The words were inspired by Americans who believed that Japan would never be able to protect itself by its own strength.

Perfunctory changes were easy to make; enforcement was another matter. In the direction of effective democracy, the emperor issued a decree on New Year's Day, 1946, that the people should no longer believe in the myths of divine origin of the emperor institution. He adopted a program intended to humanize his position. He moved freely among the people, and he welcomed their cheers. He visited the scene of mine disasters and even took his wife to the ball game. Old-line politicians struggled to adapt themselves to the demands of the new democracy, but the institutions, attitudes, and procedures of prewar days needed drastic overhauling to make a success of the new form of government. The Japanese did not move forward as fast or as far as the Americans would have liked, but they demonstrated their ability to operate the new political machine in a creditable manner.

Japan held its first postwar elections in April 1946, when for the first time women were allowed to vote. The old Minseito and Seiyukai parties, with well-phrased conservative platforms, appeared before the voters as "Progressives" and "Liberals." The Social Democrats and the Communists campaigned for the left-wing votes. Yoshida Shigeru, who had been associated with the prewar Seiyukai positivist, Baron Tanaka, emerged as the winner. He was the leader of the Liberals and became the foremost politician of Japan under the occupation.

The American authorities discovered that they could not teach democracy to hungry people, and they were forced to cope with the economic devastation of defeated Japan. In Tokyo alone, a million and a half persons stood in line every noon hour to purchase a skimpy bowl of porridge or a crust of bread. Bread was more important than directives or propaganda. Men were hungry; they talked about food, and they thought about food. SCAP brought in emergency supplies and tackled the job of "helping Japan up instead of keeping Japan down."

At first, SCAP accepted no responsibility for Japan's economic plight and took no official interest in the scandals of graft, corruption, and bribery which were commonplace. The Americans contented themselves with directives, while production lagged, trade came to a practical standstill, and prices skyrocketed. Gradually the Americans gave increasing attention to reparations, *zaibatsu*-busting, industrial development, labor unions, and agrarian reform. Bitter critics talked about the unholy trinity of the military mind, the New Deal, and the Japanese bureaucracy. In spite of criticisms and blunders, Japan gave the world an unprecedented record of steady economic achievement.

The nations which suffered most at the hands of Japan expected reparations and were grievously disappointed to discover that no reparations were available. A realistic appraisal of Japan's assets showed that gigantic international efforts would be required to give Japan the basic means to sustain itself. Practically nothing in the way of factories or machine tools could be salvaged to ship as reparation to those who had lost their property at the hands of the Japanese. Southeast Asians at first had high hopes of collecting damages from Japan; ultimately they were obliged to settle for a pittance.

The Americans were eager to take Japan off the American dole and therefore spearheaded the drive for rehabilitation and economic reform. In the interest of a democratic basis for Japan's future economic activities, the United States determined that the *zaibatsu* should be broken up. The assets of the largest holding companies were frozen, and their stocks were forcibly exchanged for nonnegotiable, noninterest-bearing, taxable government bonds. Members of the Mitsui, Iwasaki (controlling Mitsubishi), Sumitomo, and Yasuda families were ordered to resign and to cease to influence the management of their companies. Their properties were to be sold to workers, trade unions, cooperatives, and private purchasers outside the families. The diet passed two laws—the Anti-Monopoly Law of 1947 and the Trade Association Law of 1948—designed to abolish monopoly practices, but the laws were quickly outmoded. The Americans discovered that the *zaibatsu* were not such ogres as they were imagined to be, and these companies turned out to be important factors in Japan's recovery. The *zaibatsu*-busting program was discreetly abandoned.

Trade unions were encouraged as means of building a positive democratic force in Japan's economy. Seven million workers—nearly half of Japan's labor force—were organized into 35,000 unions. These were integrated into two giant federations: Sohyo or the General Council of Trade Unions; and Zenro or the All-Japan Trade Union Congress. They rushed into politics and became malleable tools in the hands of left-wing Socialists and Communist leaders. A spate of laws defined the rights of labor; fixed labor standards for men, women, and minors; regulated rates of pay and working conditions; provided for workmen's compensation, unemployment insurance, vocational guidance, and public employment exchanges; and fostered conciliation, mediation, or arbitration in the event of industrial disputes.

The honeymoon period between organized labor and the occupation came to an end in February, 1947. Labor threatened a general strike. General MacArthur ruled that he would not permit the right to strike to jeopardize the general purposes of the occupation. A transportation tieup would make it impossible to bring rice to the cities from the farms, so a general strike was forbidden. Labor was resentful and adopted an attitude of sullen opposition until the occupation ended.

The most enduring economic reform of the occupation dealt with the ownership of land. An ambitious program of land redistribution was put into effect. Absentee landlordism was abolished, and the size of farms was limited to two and a half acres for noncultivators and seven and a half acres for owner-cultivators. Excess lands were purchased by the government and sold to tenants. Due to the terrible inflation, an acre of land sometimes brought less than a carton of cigarettes on the black market. Five million acres were transferred, and three out of four tenants acquired some land of their own.

Economic and Social Foundations of New Japan

With the advent of the cold war in 1948, the Americans took decisive action to put Japan back on its economic feet. A bastion of democracy in

East Asia required a solid economic foundation. SCAP gave more generous assistance to farmers and fishermen and imported raw materials to put the Japanese to work. Private trade and foreign investments in Japan were encouraged. Corporate taxes were reduced. The merchant marine was rebuilt, and Japan was helped in its search for export markets. Under the auspices of SCAP "Made in Occupied Japan" became a familiar trademark in a hundred countries from Argentina to Zanzibar. Japanese industries again turned to the production of machinery, ships, rolling stock, autos, and machine tools, and they found ready markets. By 1950 the 1930–1934 level of production was reached, real wages were boosted, and the price level was stabilized. Exports were increased to balance imports. Japanese payments on occupation costs had reached the point where they exceeded by twenty percent the American grants-in-aid. On the somber side, it was to be noted that Japan at the end of the occupation had twelve more millions of people to take care of than it had at the beginning.

A hard-headed economic policy refused to permit Japan to squander its rapidly mounting income. In 1948 the nine-point Economic Stabilization Program worked out for the occupation by a Detroit banker, Joseph Dodge, obliged Japan to balance the budget, enforce tax collections, limit extension of credits, stabilize wages, strengthen price controls, improve foreign trade and foreign exchange controls, improve the allocations and rationing systems, increase the production of raw materials and manufactured goods, and improve the food collection program. The distinctive feature of the program was the rigor of its enforcement rather than the novelty of its provisions.

The Japanese government discharged nearly 500,000 excess employees, and the banks cut down drastically on their easy loans. Americans helped Japanese collect rice assessments in the country and taxes in the city. The entire Japanese nation displayed the energy, ambition, and discipline which made the free-enterprise system a distinctive success. By the end of the occupation, impressive new buildings were erected; and a new industrial structure was built. Shops were filled with goods of every description, and the streets were crowded with the worst traffic jams in the world. People dressed well and seemed to have money to spend for pleasure. The spiritual heaviness of defeat gave way completely to the buoyancy of progress.

The social effects of the political and economic reforms of the occupation were enormous. The disappearance of the power of the military, the change in the status of the emperor, the forced introduction of parliamentary government, accelerated industrialization and urbanization, and the leveling in the structure of rural society created a new Japan.

Furthermore, the occupation tried to revamp Japan's traditional educational system, with profound social consequences. The spirit of ultranationalism and militarism in the schools was eliminated. Courses in morals and ethics were replaced by civics and social studies. Teachers were screened, and school administration was recast in the image of that of the United States. Public schools were placed in control of local communities instead of the autocratic ministry of education at Tokyo. Public education was made coeducational and compulsory through the junior high school. Some Japanese said that education was made equal for all, but equally unsatisfactory for all. In Japan, as in the United States, progressive education bore the brunt of the blame for social insecurity, moral anarchy, and juvenile delinquency.

In the field of higher education, the occupation had neither the time nor the talent to do more than dabble with some of Japan's most flagrant problems. Again the emphasis was more on organization than on content. Universities were remodeled into four-year institutions with American-style graduate schools. Junior colleges were stressed, and orders were issued that every prefecture, ready or not, should have its own college. Academic freedom was to be respected, but the occupation violated its own principles by cracking down on alleged Marxists and Communists. Efforts made to induce the Japanese to copy the American idea of nonprofessional boards of trustees for university control but without great success. The Japanese felt that American "amateurs" did more harm than good to their system of higher education, and expressed open relief when the Americans were gone.

The occupation made no substantial impact on Japanese religious institutions except to stress the separation of church and state. However, the ideas of individual rights associated with democracy cut deeply into the social fabric by their influence on Japanese concepts of hierarchy. In the Japanese family and throughout Japanese society, equality is less important than one's proper status. The *oyabun-kobun*, "father-like, child-like," relationship existed as between lord and vassal, boss and henchman, and patron and protégé, whether in business or politics. Traditional ideas persisted and even pervaded such creatures of the occupation as the labor unions and the black-market gangs. The Japanese social code of loyalty suffered modifications by the introduction of new concepts of individual rights regardless of social status.

It was difficult to judge whether the period of occupation in Japan was more remarkable for the magnitude of change or for the persistence of tradition. Americans and Japanese developed feelings of mutual affection which were a complete reversal of the wartime enmities. Goodwill was almost universal in spite of the thousands of Americans of all types who were obliged to work with the best and the worst of the Japanese in the difficult relationship of conqueror and captive. The Japanese were thrown off-balance temporarily by the sheer weight of the reforms to which they were subjected, but they never lost control of the direction of their progress. They had no alternative except to bow to the will of the victors.

Most Japanese looked upon the reforms of the occupation as a continuation of the modernization process. Social changes in Japan under the occupation were not considered different in kind, only in degree, from changes which took place during the Meiji era. Trends toward liberalism which had been interrupted during the thirties were resumed at increased tempo. Many of the best accomplishments of the occupation were possible only because of the groundwork which had been done in the past by the Japanese themselves. Intelligent Japanese felt no sense of shame because of the wholesale borrowing of Western ideas because they believed their nation and their people were improved by the vigorous branches which were grafted on to their own root stock. They rejoiced that the occupation helped them to achieve in six years what otherwise might have taken sixty. They were sufficiently wise to know that they could discard such innovations as they found to be useless and undesirable, and they could nurture those things which they discovered to be of value.

PREPARATION FOR PEACE

Both SCAP and the Japanese government wanted to bring the occupation to an end as soon as possible and to restore Japan to its sovereign place in the community of nations. Americans were reduced in force, and Japanese were given rapidly increasing responsibilities in the management of their own affairs. Japanese were given permits to travel abroad, and the Japanese government was allowed to establish overseas agencies which did the work of ordinary diplomatic and consular establishments. Japanese delegations were sent to meetings of such international bodies as the International Labor Organization, the World Health Organization, and the United Nations Educational, Scientific and Cultural Organization.

The problem of rearmament arose to plague the Japanese. The demilitarization program had seemed like utopia because it was so cheap to have no taxes for armies, navies, and airplanes. The Americans began to regret article nine and wanted Japan to bear some of the cost of self-defense. It was suggested that Japan might create a national police reserve, with light arms, "to crush subversives." Ironically enough, the occupation's program of political emancipation provided an opportunity for the Communists to become a significant force in Japanese politics. Communists supported the reforms and gathered with other Japanese in front of the general headquarters to shout "MacArthur *Banzai.*" When the occupation adopted its conservative program of economic rehabilitation, the Communists resorted to sabotage, riots, and denunciation of the occupation. In retaliation, the Japanese government deprived Communists of public position, suspended their newspaper, *Akahata,* or *Red Flag,* and forced party leaders into hiding. These actions, taken with the approval of the American authorities, seemed to conflict with the guarantees of civil liberties and aroused memories of thought control by the hated constitutional police. In September, 1949, General MacArthur expressed his satisfaction that "the threat of Communism as a major issue in Japanese life is past."

At the beginning of 1950, Japan looked like an "oasis of tranquillity." Then the outbreak of the war in Korea shed new light on Japan's helplessness. Japan reluctantly departed from its ideal of a disarmed country as contemplated by article nine of its new constitution. Enlistments were stepped up in Japan's national police reserve and maritime safety board (a kind of coast guard). General MacArthur reflected that the ideal of the renunciation of war must give way to the inalienable right of self-defense against unprovoked attack. To the Japanese he said: "It will become your duty within the principles of the United Nations in concert with others who cherish freedom to mount force to repel force." The specter of a rearmed Japan alarmed its neighbors who reminded the United States, "You have ideals, but we have memories."

The war in Korea sent a wave of fear over Japan. The Japanese believed that Korea was no more than a preliminary to the main attack which the Communists would launch against Japan. Therefore Japan placed all its strength, such as it was, at the disposal of the United Nations. The great lesson which was made clear was that the occupation had reached the end of its usefulness. The time had come for the Japanese to make their own decisions and resume full responsibility for their own nation and its role in world affairs, particularly peace in Asia.

Since 1947 President Truman and General MacArthur had agreed that a peace treaty with Japan was desirable. They wanted to put American relations with Japan on such basis that Japan would of its own free will ally itself with the United States as opposed to Russia. However, treaty-making was an international matter because of the United Nations' declaration of January 1, 1942, which pledged all the signatories to "no separate armistice or no separate peace." Neither Russia nor Nationalist China was in a hurry to end the *status quo* in Japan under the occupation.

President Truman voiced the American demand for peace with Japan —with Russia if possible, without Russia if necessary. He ignored accusations of violating the Declaration of the United Nations, and he risked open war on the part of Communist China and the Soviet Union. On February 14, 1950, those nations announced their treaty of alliance pledging mutual assistance in the event of aggression by Japan or any power in concert with Japan. On September 8, 1950, President Truman named John Foster Dulles as his special ambassador in charge of peace-making with Japan; the State Department assigned a distinguished career officer, John Allison, as his assistant.

The Americans explored the ideas of all interested parties with regard to peace with Japan. The United States favored easy terms; Russia clung to the punitive aspects of the Potsdam Declaration. Russia was determined that the United States should derive no special benefit from peace with Japan and insisted that the Communists should speak for China in all discussions. The United States countered that only the Nationalists could speak for China. Nationalist China argued that it had suffered most at the hands of Japan and wanted a settlement which would "exact no revenge but would brook no coddling." It wanted substantial reparations, permanent elimination of Japan's militarism, reduction of Japan's industrial capacity, and outside control of Japan for fifty years. Communist China shared the sentiments of Nationalist China; however, it demanded that Peking and not Taiwan should participate in the preparation, drafting, and signing of any peace treaty.

The Philippines, Australia, and New Zealand sought a treaty which would guarantee their protection against possible renewed Japanese aggression. They feared a new and strong Japan. India, Pakistan, and Indonesia insisted on having their views respected in peacemaking. Korea was never consulted but publicly presented its case that after forty years of tragedy, humiliation, sorrow, and misery it was entitled to all Japanese property in Korea. The British had minor differences of opinion with the Americans, and they favored the Communists rather than the Nationalists as the representatives of China.

Japan itself had nothing to say about the shape of the treaty except by the courtesy of the American negotiators. Japan's officialdom objected to the words *violence and greed* as used in the Chiro Declaration, because, in their opinion, Japan's acquisitions in Asia were made by processes in vogue and confirmed by universally recognized treaties. Some Japanese began to wonder—in private—whether they might not suggest the return to Japan of special interests in Korea, Manchuria, or Formosa as the price of Japanese cooperation in a possible future war. Japan wanted a general peace pact with as many nations as would sign, and let it be known that it was "definitely and irrevocably committed to the side of the free world."

Dulles and his staff spent nearly a year in reconciling conflicting points of view. They visited Japan twice and conducted negotiations in ten world capitals. Sometimes they talked with Russians; sometimes they exchanged notes; but they never gave in to Russia's filibustering tactics. After a series of drafts and amendments, the Americans and the British reached agreement on a final text of a treaty. In August 1951, this text was circulated to nations invited to a peace conference in San Francisco. This conference was not to be a discussion conference, because the discussions were concluded before the conference was called. The powers were invited to come and to sign, to accept or reject the treaty with which they were confronted.

THE PEACE SETTLEMENT WITH JAPAN

The peace settlement with Japan was not limited to the single treaty of peace signed at San Francisco on September 8, 1951. It also included properly a prior mutual assistance treaty between the Philippines and the United States signed in Washington on August 30, 1951; a mutual security pact between Australia, New Zealand, and the United States (the ANZUS Pact) signed in San Francisco two days later; a bilateral security pact between the United States and Japan signed at the Presidio in San Francisco on September 8, 1951; an exchange of notes on the same date between the United States and Japan pledging Japanese support to the forces of the United Nations in the Far East; and an administrative agreement concluded on February 28, 1952, between the United States and Japan implementing the bilateral security pact.

The treaty of peace was nonpunitive and nondiscriminatory, and it restored Japan to dignity, equality, and opportunity in the family of nations. In the preamble, Japan declared its intention to apply for membership in the United Nations; to conform to the principles of the Charter; to adhere to the new ideals of human rights and freedoms which were implanted in the constitution and laws of Japan; and in international trade, to conform to internationally accepted fair-trade practices.

Chapter one of the treaty ended the state of war and recognized the full sovereignty of the Japanese people.

Chapter two dealt with territory. It ratified the Potsdam surrender terms which limited Japan's sovereignty to the four main islands and such minor islands as might be determined. Without providing for the disposition of territories taken from Japan, it obliged Japan to renounce all right, title, and claim to Korea, to Formosa and the Pescadores, to the Kurile Islands and southern Sakhalin, to its former mandates, to the Antarctic area, and to the Spratly and Paracel Islands. With regard to the Japanese islands south of twenty-nine degrees (including the Ryukyus), Japan retained the sovereignty but recognized the American right of administration. Japan expressed its concurrence in any proposal to place these islands under the trusteeship system of the United Nations, with the United States as the sole administering authority.

Chapter three was entitled "Security." It bound Japan to the peaceful principles of the United Nations. It obligated Japan to refrain from the use of force in its international relations, but it recognized that Japan possessed the inherent right of individual or collective self-defense. All occupation forces were to be withdrawn after the coming into force of the treaty, but some of these forces might be retained and stationed in Japan in consequence of a bilateral or multilateral agreement between one or more of the Allied Powers and Japan. Dulles was a skillful lawyer, and this was his formula to keep American forces in Japan after the formal end of the occupation.

Chapter four contained political and economic clauses. Japan was not to be subjected to any permanent discriminations. Its economy was to be unrestricted and its right to trade unlimited. Pending permanent agreements regarding trade and commerce, fishing on the high seas, and international air transport, each Allied Power would be entitled to most-favored-nation treatment in customs duties—on a basis of reciprocity—and to national treatment with respect to shipping, navigation, and imported goods.

Chapter five, "Claims and Property," covered the controversial matter of reparations. It was implied that that those who suffered at the hands of Japan were entitled to reparations, but that Japan *presently* simply could not afford to pay. It was recognized that Japan should pay reparations, and it obligated Japan to make available the service of the Japanese people in production, salvaging, and other work for those Allies who wanted Japanese help. The Allied Powers were also entitled to take over Japanese property in their jurisdiction. Allied property in Japan was to be restored to its original owners or to be compensated for in blocked yen. Japan affirmed its liability for prewar external debts and for debts arising out of prewar contracts.

Although Korea was never at war against Japan, and although China was not represented at the San Francisco Conference, the treaty made special provision for the interests of Korea and China. Korea's independence was to be recognized by Japan, and Japan was obligated to enter into negotiations for the transfer of large holdings of Japanese property to Korea. With regard to postwar trading, maritime fishing, and other commercial arrangements, Korea was given the same rights which accrued to the Allied Powers. China was given the right to a separate peace treaty with Japan on the same terms as the present treaty, with the assurance of the renunciation of all Japan's special privileges in China.

The final chapters of the treaty provided that any dispute concerning the interpretation or execution of the treaty should be referred to the International Court of Justice and defined the process of ratification.

The realities of the Korean War and the menace of international communism to American interests in East Asia seemed to require additional security arrangements. Japan and the United States signed a bilateral security pact on the same day that they signed the treaty itself. The security pact granted the United States the right to dispose forces in and about Japan. Such forces might be used for maintenance of peace and security in the Far East and for the security of Japan against armed attack from without, including assistance given to the Japanese government to put down large-scale internal riots and disturbances in Japan caused by an outside power. During the exercise of this right, Japan would not grant, without the prior consent of the United States, any bases or any military rights whatsoever to any third power. The security pact would expire whenever alternative arrangements should come into force which would satisfactorily provide for peace and security in the area of Japan. The Americans made it clear that without the security pact there would be no peace settlement.

Delegations from fifty-two nations came to San Francisco to give vent to their opinions and to sign the document which the Americans and the British had agreed upon. Surprisingly, the Soviet bloc decided to attend. The neutrals and ex-enemies of World War II were not invited. Burma and India chose not to attend: Burma, because it believed the treaty to be too liberal to Japan, and India, for the opposite reason. The only compromise solution on the matter of China's attendance was to agree that neither China should be represented.

The Russian delegate offered a series of objections to the treaty and proposed a number of amendments. He saw no reason why Japan in Asia should be treated better than the defeated Axis Powers in Europe. His specific objections were that the treaty:

(1) gave no guarantee against the rebirth of Japanese militarism or the renewal of Japanese aggression

(2) did not provide for the withdrawal of American troops

(3) did not prevent Japan from joining in an aggressive bloc in the Far East against China or the USSR

(4) did not provide for the continuation of democratization, nor prevent the rebirth of Fascist organizations in Japan

(5) did not restore to China territories including Formosa

(6) did not carry out the terms of the Yalta agreement regarding the Kuriles and southern Sakhalin

(7) made Japan's economy the slave of foreign monopolies

(8) ignored the legitimate claims of some nations for reparations, yet imposed upon Japanese labor a slavery-like obligation

(9) constituted not a treaty of peace but a preparation for a new war in the Far East

The proposed Russian amendments included territorial adjustments in favor of China and the Soviet Union; exclusion of foreign troops and bases in Japan; provision for a conference on reparations; guarantees of continued democratization; prohibition of resurgence of fascistic organizations in Japan; prohibition of any coalition or alliance against any of the ex-Allies; limitation of Japan's armed forces to 150,000 for the army, 25,000 personnel and 75,000 tons of ships for the navy, 20,000 personnel and 150 planes (no bombers) for the air force, and 200 medium and heavy tanks for the armored forces; limitation of military training; prohibition of atomic weapons, guided missiles, long-range guns, mines, and torpedoes; the right to unrestricted development of trade, peaceful industry, and equal access to raw materials; and demilitarization of the straits between the Japanese islands and the entire Japanese coast.

Other nations aired their grievances, and voiced their hopes that "the fangs of hatred would be buried." The Australian delegate expressed the idealistic mood of the San Francisco Peace Conference when he said because of "agreement on one or two of the issues which divide the world, little by little we may reach upward to the stars and find peace for humanity." No one at the conference felt that the treaty was perfect, yet all but the Soviet bloc signed. Premier Yoshida took the floor for Japan. He paid his respects to "this fair and generous treaty" and then referred with diffidence to certain points which caused him pain and anxiety. He mentioned territorial losses, international economic prospects, and the 340,000 Japanese prisoners still in the hands of the Russians. He expressed Japan's keen determination to establish international relations of mutual trust and to work with other nations for the advancement of world freedom. He talked about the sinister thoughts of totalitarian oppression and tyranny whose forces were sweeping over half the Asian continent and breaking out into open aggression at the very door of Japan. He declared that it was imperative for "our very existence" to take adequate security measures, and he suggested this should not raise a bugbear of a new Japanese peril. He said that the Japanese were purged of all untoward ambition and "burn now with a passionate desire to live at peace with their neighbors in the Far East and in the entire world and to rebuild their society so that it will in ever greater fulness yield better life for all."

RESUMPTION OF NORMAL INDEPENDENT EXISTENCE

When the newspapers, radio, and moving pictures brought to Japan the news of the completion of the peace settlement, Japan reacted with consummate restraint. The Japanese were happy to regain their independence, but they were aware of its responsibilities. There would be no more occupation, but there would also be no assurance of American economic assistance. Japan was to be free, but the Japanese were fearful lest that freedom be marred by depression. A clear majority in Japan, perhaps as many as two to one, felt that Japan's treatment in the restoration of peace exceeded reasonable expectations; but a vocal minority expressed grave doubts. A leading newspaper said: "Japan intends neither to antagonize unduly the so-called totalitarian nations nor aggravate the antagonism between the two worlds by joining the ranks of the free nations—our resolve for peace is much stronger than that expressed by Mr. Yoshida."

President Nambara of Tokyo University thought that to abandon the renunciation of war and neutrality at its first real test was immoral and spiritually shattering. Hashimoto Tetsuma, a right-wing commentator, in referring to Japan's lost territories, said: "We got our independence—84,000,000 people crowded into a prison with life sentences—and if American wisdom is limited to crowding us into such narrow confines expecting birth control to answer our problems, then I doubt whether Americans are intelligent enough to stop a third world war." The Socialists continued to talk about their three-point program (overall peace with all nations, permanent neutrality, and no foreign troops or bases in Japan), although in the aggrieved tones of a lost cause. The Communists were loud in their condemnation of the peace settlement as the inevitable cause of another capitalistic war. Some economic interests brought up the problem of trade with Communist China and suggested being excused from reparations because of their own hardships. Some Japanese expressed concern over the fate of their "loyal Ryukyuan brothers" and others tried to elicit sympathy for Japanese aspirations for the recovery of the Kuriles and southern Sakhalin.

The sharpest Japanese criticisms of the peace settlement were aimed at the security pact. All Japanese except the very young—regardless of any alleged penchant for discipline and the glitter of military uniforms—suffered much because of the sword, and they rejected the vague feeling that revived militarism would bring economic prosperity. They accepted alignment with the United States only because there was no possible alternative for self-defense. They did not want to take sides in the world conflict or to accept American troops in Japan, but it was the only way to protect themselves against the "confirmed rapaciousness of the Communists." Most Japanese were neutralists at heart, but pro-American in their heads.

The former president of Keio University, Koizumi Shinzo, defended the security pact as the guardian of the interests of Japan as well as those of the United States. He admitted that it was by no means an honor for such a big country as Japan to defend itself with foreign troops, but he believed that such conditions must be tolerated for the sake of peace. Japanese worried about the costs, dangers, and inadequacies of rearmament. Premier Yoshida said in private conversation that it would wreck Japan's budget even to build one warship, and he expressed grave uncertainty about the constitutionality of a rearmament program. To him, the security pact, "under which American forces at our request will be stationed in and about our territory," was the only means to defend unarmed Japan and to join in a common defense of the Pacific against the menace of communism.

President Abe Yoshishige of the Peers School (which has scions of the most illustrious families in Japan as its students and alumni) argued that "the treaty is not so much a peace treaty with Japan as a war treaty against other peoples." His colleague, Professor Shimizu Ikutaro, deplored the alliance with the United States, alleged that the militarists would soon be back again, and asserted that Japan would be the first target of a Russian A-bomb. He reflected the bitter Japanese conviction that an atom bomb is a personal device of the devil. Yamakawa Hitoshi accused Dulles of driving Japan to rearmament and war by means of a false illusion. To him rearmament was more dangerous than the threat of invasion. He said that the maximum army which Japan could afford would be so many toy soldiers and "rearmament is more an excuse for invasion than protection against it." A respected magazine, featuring criticism of the peace settlement, sold five editions of its 272-page publication the first month. It was advertised as the stifled voice of the Japanese people. The articles bore such titles as "Abuse of Peace," "Avoid Rearmament," "Do Not Send Our Students Again to the Battlefields," "The Security Pact Does Not Guarantee Peace," and "We Must Now Cast Away Our Cowardly Silence."

In spite of opposition, both houses of the Japanese diet approved the treaty of peace and the security pact by overwhelming majorities. The emperor signed the treaties on November 9, 1951, and sent his special envoy to deposit the Japanese ratifications in Washington on November 25. The British House of Commons and the American Senate approved the treaties with a mere sprinkling of negative votes. Australia ratified the peace treaty in April 1952, in spite of the vigorous opposition of Mr. Evatt and the minority Labour party. Indonesia and the Philippines delayed ratifications pending a settlement of reparations. But in accordance with the provision that the treaty would become effective upon the ratification of the majority of the signers, including the United States, the treaty entered into force on April 28, 1952.

On the same day Japan made peace with Nationalist China. China registered its faith that Japan had abandoned its imperialism and became an outpost for the world's defense against communism. Japan recognized Chiang Kai-shek as the sovereign authority in Formosa, the Pescadores, and the territories which might in future come under his control. Japan was not willing to endorse Chiang's claim to sovereignty over the entire mainland. On June 9, 1952, Japan made peace with India. The two countries officially renewed their "ancient ties," dedicated themselves to peace and security within the framework of the United Nations, and granted each other reciprocal most-favored-nation treatment in commercial matters. On November 5, 1954, Japan came to terms with Burma. Only the Soviet bloc remained technically at war with Japan and Communist China reserved the right to negotiate a settlement with Japan on its own behalf.

As a "national symbol" on the day that the peace treaty became effective, the emperor penned two stylized poems:

> As I see pigeons playing in my garden peacefully
> I hope the world we live in will be like that.

and

> Winter with bitter cold wind has gone,
> And much-waited spring comes round
> With double cherry blossoms.

It might have been like spring, with its double cherry blossoms, for Japan to resume its normal existence as a sovereign, independent nation. However, difficult tasks which stemmed from the war were still to be faced. Japan was obliged to reconstitute its diplomatic machinery and negotiate new treaties of friendship, amity, and commerce. Japan wanted new international agreements on reparations, international fisheries, and civil aviation. It desired most of all to prepare for entry into the United Nations and to resume its place as a great force in international affairs. Japan wished to associate itself with those nations which were determined that mankind's path of progress should be marked by a decent respect for all who wanted to live in freedom and prosper in peace.

SUGGESTED READING

Ball, W. MacMahon, *Japan: Enemy or Ally?* (New York, Day, 1949).

Clifton, Alan, *Time of Fallen Blossoms* (New York, Knopf, 1951).

Cohen, Bernard C., *Political Process and Foreign Policy Making of the Japanese Peace Settlement* (Princeton, Princeton U., 1957).

Dore, Ronald P., *Land Reform in Japan* (London, Oxford U., 1959).

Dunn, Frederick S., *Peace-Making and the Settlement with Japan* (Princeton, Princeton U., 1962).

Feary, Robert A., *Occupation of Japan, Second Phase, 1948–1950* (New York, Macmillan, 1950).

Gayn, Mark, *Japan Diary* (New York, Sloane, 1948).

Hankey, Lord, *Politics, Trials and Errors* (Chicago, Regnery, 1950).

Kawai, Kazuo, *Japan's American Interlude* (Chicago, U. of Chicago, 1960).

Lewe van Aduard, Baron E. J., *Japan from Surrender to Peace* (New York, Praeger, 1954).

Martin, Edwin M., *Allied Occupation of Japan* (Stanford, Stanford U., 1948).

Supreme Commander Allied Powers, Government Section, *Political Reorientation of Japan, Sept. 1945 to Sept. 1948* (two vols.) (Washington, Government Printing Office, 1949).

Swearingen, Rodger, and Langer, Paul, *Red Flag in Japan* (Cambridge, Harvard U., 1952).

Textor, Robert B., *Failure in Japan* (New York, Day, 1951).

United States, Department of State, *Occupation of Japan, Policy and Progress, Publication 2671, Far Eastern Series 17* (Washington, Government Printing Office, 1946).

Vining, Elizabeth G., *Windows for the Crown Prince* (Philadelphia, Lippincott, 1952).

Whitney, Courtney, *MacArthur, His Rendezvous with History* (New York, Knopf, 1955).

Wildes, Harry Emerson, *Typhoon in Tokyo* (New York, Macmillan, 1954).

25

Transition in China

The transformation in Japan after World War II proceeded toward its happy climax like a well-ordered novel. The transition in China was in stark contrast. China was doomed to four years of civil war (1945–1949) which ended in the collapse of the Kuomintang and the succession of the Communists to the control of the government in Peiping. In Japan, the United States was on the winning team; in China, it was on the side which lost.

The contrast between Japan and China resulted as much from international factors as from internal conditions within the two countries. Japan lined up with the United States, China chose to lean to the side of Russia. In Japan, American armed power was dominant; the United States enjoyed the approval of friendly Allies in its policy of assisting Japan to rise above the ashes of defeat. During the occupation, Russian strength was nowhere in evidence. Russian armed forces were not introduced into Japan, and Russian civilians lived and worked in obscurity. General MacArthur refused to tolerate Russia's attempted obstructionism, and Russia was too preoccupied with domestic rehabilitation and European problems to try to improve its anomalous position in Japan. Japanese Communists did not constitute an armed menace and had no cause to look to Russia for anything more than moral support and tactical advice. Whatever the Japanese needed for reconstruction, they obtained in ample quantities from the United States.

INTERNATIONAL ASPECTS OF CHINA'S CIVIL WAR

In China, conditions were exactly the opposite. As long as the war continued, the United States cooperated in every possible way to bolster the war effort against Japan. The Kuomintang made no charges against the United States for interference in internal affairs, except when American officials intimated the possibility of direct aid to the Communists who also fought against the Japanese. With the transition from World War II to civil war, all American aid to China took on the character of interference in internal strife and one-sided assistance to Chiang Kai-shek. The movement of Nationalist troops to the north and the stationing of American marines in the Tientsin-Peiping area were of incalculable assistance to Chiang although they were accomplished under the guise of helping China's legitimate government and national army accept the surrender of the Japanese. The Nationalist government of China and the government of the United States felt that their measures were just and, they hoped, sufficient to put down the Communists and prevent the extension of Russian power in East Asia.

Both Chinese and Americans were guilty of grave miscalculations. The Kuomintang lost and the Communists won. In the eyes of millions of Chinese—all who eventually came under the sway of the Communists —the Chinese civil war was made in America. The Communists alleged that the fighting would have ended quickly had it not been for the American marines and American supplies. In their view, the Americans were the architects of the strategy of Chiang Kai-shek and they provided him with every weapon, round of ammunition, airplane, ship, tank, truck, and gallon of gasoline which he used in the civil war. When he lost, the Americans shared the odium of defeat. The Communists came to power with all the traditional Chinese anti-imperialist hatreds focused on the Americans, in addition to the new grievances which followed from American association with the Kuomintang. In Communist propaganda, the United States became the successor to Japan as the symbol of reaction in East Asia.

American power disappeared in Asia, as in Europe, immediately after victory because the troops were called home and demobilized. Quite apart from the wisdom of attempting to do so, the United States lacked the physical strength to impose a "Made in U.S.A." solution in China. Americans offered advice; the Chinese could take it or leave it. The material aid given to China accomplished little beyond prolonging the conflict, but it is doubtful if any government could have led the American people to make an all-out effort to aid the Kuomintang.

Stalin, on his part, was committed officially to help Chiang Kai-shek by the treaty of August 14, 1945, but he was not disposed to let his commitment damage his long-term interests. He predicated his neutrality in the China situation upon the continuance of American neutrality. Stalin was not convinced that the Chinese Communists were capable of winning in an all-out struggle for control of China, but as Americans shifted to greater support of the Kuomintang, Russians countered with support to the Communists. At first the Russians spoke softly to the Nationalists and winked at the Communists. Toward the end of the conflict, Stalin left no doubt of his attitude toward his fellow communists. Nevertheless, as late as the spring of 1949, when the Nationalists moved their seat of government from Nanking to Canton, the Soviet Ambassador to China accompanied the Nationalists.

As soon as Russia declared war on Japan, Russian troops poured into Manchuria, the richest part of China. They accepted the surrender of the Japanese in Manchuria; then they held on to Manchuria while the Kuomintang and the Communists scrambled for military advantage. Both sides wanted to have the honor of recovering the lost provinces and to gain possession of Manchuria's extensive economic assets. When it looked as if the Kuomintang might win the race, the Russians destroyed and looted much of Manchuria's industrial wealth. With Russian tolerance, many of the puppet troops of Manchukuo were absorbed into the Communist army along with most of the arms and ammunition left behind by the Japanese. The armed Russian presence was vital to the Communists in Manchuria, and Manchuria was vital to the rest of China. The Communists had reason to resent the Russian action in depleting much of the wealth of Manchuria, but they also had cause for gratitude to Russia in the vital military assistance which they received.

The world was heartily sick of war in the autumn of 1945. Yet the old alignment of "fascist aggressors" and "antifascists" no sooner disappeared than the specter of a new alignment rose up to take its place. In Europe and in Asia the skeleton emerged of what Prime Minister Churchill labeled the "cold war." By words and actions, the Communist powers headed by Soviet Russia let it be known that they intended to make their power and ideology dominant throughout the world. Therefore the situation in China took on a new importance. The immediate stake in the civil war was the control of the Chinese government and the Chinese people; the ultimate importance of the situation in China was its influence on the cold war. Chiang Kai-shek was identified as the champion of the "free world"; Mao Tse-tung carried the banner of the Socialist camp. The shape of the entire world between World War II and the conflict in Korea was determined to a large extent on the battlefields of China.

Civil War as a Chinese Internal Affair

The continuation of hostilities prevented the government from tackling age-old problems of economic development and social change. The Communist victory at arms determined fundamentally that it would be the Communists, not the Kuomintang, who would be given the opportunity and the responsibility for the pace and direction of China's interrupted program of modernization.

Economic planners in Chungking, even at the height of the war, produced utopian blueprints for factories and transportation systems which theoretically could make China prosperous and self-sufficient. It was clear that China's success in the postwar world would depend upon economic development and a solid social structure. Whichever party or person held political control—whether Kuomintang or Communist— would have to open mines, build roads and highways, repair railways, deepen rivers and canals, construct dams, improve harbors, and expand shipping. It would have to lay the foundations for modern industry, while undertaking the gigantic tasks of increasing agriculture production to meet the needs of China's burgeoning population. Changes would have to be made in Chinese society to eliminate the worst abuses of the past and to produce a reasonably happy people. In spite of the utter exhaustion of the individual Chinese, they would have to be aroused to work for the good of the nation. It would be up to the party in power to find ways to enable Chinese children to escape the miseries of the present generation.

China's leaders (the Communists more clearly than the Kuomintang) discovered the basis for an integrated modernization program in every province, county, and village in China. The strait jacket of the traditional way of life went up in the smoke of the Japanese invasion. Millions of families were broken up as countless widows and orphans wandered aimlessly in the countryside. Millions had little food, no place to sleep, and insufficient clothes to cover their half-naked, emaciated bodies. Those who managed to survive cared little for social restraints imposed by landlords, government officials, and feudalistic army officers. For centuries law, morality, and power had been on the side of the well-mannered aristocrats who constituted China's gentry. For the first time the scales of social justice tipped toward the common men because of the ordeal of invasion. Peasants were given a chance to live not as second-class citizens but as dignified individuals.

The welfare of the peasant became the critical test in the struggle between the Kuomintang and the Communists. The future belonged to the side which would provide the best solution to the problems of land-holding, high rents, exorbitant interest rates, and modernization of agricultural methods. The Kuomintang leaders understood the situation. They wrote scholarly monographs and passed excellent laws dealing with agrarian reform. Unfortunately, the Nationalist government failed to implement its own program. It feared the masses, and it refused to supply guns to the peasants. It resisted change in the countryside and hoped to restore the agricultural *status quo* as approximately as possible. It relied upon the landlords and their allies, the village elders, the bureaucrats, and the local militia. When the landlords returned from their places of war-time safety, they frequently demanded payments of back rents and extra compensation for damage caused to their property by the hazards of war. They were greeted with sticks and stones—or worse—especially in the areas which had experience with communists.

On the other hand, the Communists in time of civil war gave the same close attention to the lot of the peasant that they gave during the Japanese invasion. They tightened their control over the land and showed less consideration for landlords and rich peasants. They de-emphasized "production" and reverted to previous policies of "redistribution." They continued to stress the idea of "land to the tiller." The Communists understood that their chief political support would come from the peasantry and they used the simplest propaganda methods to explain their program in terms which were meaningful to the peasants.

The war-weary people wanted peace, food, and human rights; the Communists centered their program about peace, food, and human rights. They stressed that the object of their revolution—the only revolution—was a new life for the masses of China. According to the Communists, economic improvement could be achieved only by political means, and political power could be obtained only by a disciplined party, working in secret and backed by a strong armed force. The Communists insisted that they would guide the revolution at every step according to the needs of the peasant. "Leaders of the masses must draw their sustenance from the masses." Party cadres would eat the food of the masses, share their hardships, and live in the villages on a common level of austerity. The Communists spoke of their movement as the "Liberation"—the freeing of the peasants from the bonds of exploitation and ignorance. It was not a revolt against established government or a civil war. The Yenan paper was called the Liberation Daily, and the Communist army became the People's Liberation Army. A town was never captured; it was liberated, so the followers of the Communists were given the feeling of participation in a movement of freedom and reform.

The Kuomintang was out-maneuvered in the towns and cities as well as in the cities. As soon as the armies of Chiang Kai-shek were returned to Nanking, Shanghai, and Peiping, the civilian bureaucrats and their followers began the reverse trek from Chungking toward the coast. The capital of the Nationalist government was returned to Nanking. Kuomintang appointees were installed in every province, county seat, and municipality, except in the local areas under Communist control. The nation breathed sighs of relief in getting rid of the Wang Ching-wei traitors and hoped that the arrival of the Kuomintang would usher in a brighter day. Shanghai greeted the returnees with flags, bands, celebrations, and a victory parade.

Disillusionment followed very quickly. After courts-martial executed a few of the leading Japanese puppets, others bought, bribed, or intrigued their way back into positions of responsibility. Within six months of their re-establishment, the Kuomintang were uniformly condemned for their venality and incompetence from Peiping to Canton. Selfish officials worked hardest to feather their own nests. They did not even try to improve the lot of the undernourished and the underprivileged. They alienated the sturdy business groups who before the war had been their chief support. Greedy politicians drove thriving business concerns to the wall by taxes and illegal extortions, and they allocated all new industries or possibilities for profitable trade to themselves and their relatives. One observer wrote that "it was sickening to see the Kuomintang fatten on the cities and provinces in their control." Licenses and privileges were sold disgracefully, foreign relief supplies were mismanaged, and speculation was fostered while prices soared. Bureaucrats danced at night clubs while beggars died of starvation within sound of the music.

Extravagance and corruption besmirched the record of some—but not all—Kuomintang officials. Chiang Kai-shek himself was above reproach, and so were many of his loyal followers who discharged their duties with the same honor and integrity which they had displayed at Chungking. However, the Kuomintang behavior in the cities alienated the support which might otherwise have sustained them when the civil war finally reached the cities. In the early stages of the war, the Communists were helpless in the metropolitan centers. Communist agitators were suppressed, and labor unions had no appeal to hungry people for whom any job was a blessing. Chiang's soldiers in the cities were well-supplied, well-housed, and well-fed, but they too were callous to the poverty with which they were surrounded. When the cities were "liberated" by the Communists, the masses joined the victorious Communist armies in the Yang Ko, or Liberation Dance.

In the appeal for popular support, the Kuomintang called the civil war a struggle between freedom and slavery. They insisted that they offered ultimately to the Chinese the only hope of freedom, and they promised national construction along the lines of the principles laid down by their founder, the venerable Sun Yat-sen. The Communists also said the civil war was a struggle between freedom and slavery, but they argued that only the Communists offered the way to freedom and "the New Democracy." They charged that the only freedom under the Kuomintang would be the freedom for the rich and the privileged classes. Words and arguments were meaningless to most Chinese. They might have had a theoretic power of choice as to whether the Kuomintang or the Communists offered the lesser police state or the greater hope of survival; but in fact decisions were determined by a factor entirely beyond individual control, the outcome of the civil war.

The Kuomintang called the Communists the stooges of a foreign power; the Communists returned the compliment. The Communists admitted freely that their ideology was the heritage of Marx and Lenin, but they contended that their political program was entirely Chinese. It did not depend upon Russian help for its implementation or its success. The Communists insisted that World War II erased any doubts about their title as the true exponents of Chinese nationalism. From the time the civil war began until it ended, the Communists offered themselves to the Chinese people as the heirs of Chinese history and Communist ideology. They would develop China's economy according to their own blueprints and would reshape Chinese society for the benefit of the "people," which meant the peasants, the proletariat, and their friends. In the Communist view, the success of the program depended absolutely upon the indispensable leadership of the Communist Party.

COURSE OF CIVIL WAR

Although the breach between the Kuomintang and the Communists seemed to be beyond repair in December 1945, President Truman sent his most-trusted military adviser, General George C. Marshall, to China to assist in the establishment of a strong, united, and democratic government. Chiang Kai-shek, as the head of the legal government of China, was recognized to be the proper agency for unification. The American objectives were to help the Chinese bring civil strife to an end and to set up a coalition government in which all the major political groups would have fair and effective representation. Such a coalition government would close out the Kuomintang's period of political tutelage and usher in a multiparty system in which the Communists would have the right to compete openly for political support. The Americans also wished to assist in the elimination of autonomous armies, primarily the Communists, and the creation of a single national army which could maintain law and order and fulfill China's international responsibilities. Economic aid was promised on the condition that China should move toward peace and unity; the Chinese were warned that American aid would not extend to intervention in China's internal strife.

It was not the American intention to support Chiang Kai-shek at all costs and under all circumstances, nor to sell him out to the Communists. The Americans were aware of the risks which they took. They knew that the Communists and the Kuomintang would continue their rivalry for power, but they felt that Chiang had better cards for the game of political negotiation than for the game of guerrilla war which the Communists played so well. The Americans continued to supply Chiang with all the forms of aid which had been instituted during the war. Furthermore, they proceeded with the transfer of Chiang's troops to the north, and turned over to him more naval vessels and surplus war supplies. The Communists were infuriated and argued that such activities compromised any attempt of General Marshall to pose as an honest broker.

Soon after General Marshall went to China, Secretary of State James Byrnes went to Moscow, where he discussed the China question with the foreign secretaries of Great Britain and the Soviet Union. The three nations in Moscow joined in a declaration on December 27, 1945, which called for an end to civil strife and for the formation of a democratic government in China under the Nationalists. Russia and the United States promised to withdraw their troops from China as soon as possible. Stalin treated the China problem as relatively unimportant because of his tremendous task of rehabilitation at home. Russia showed no disposition to retreat from its treaty position of giving assistance to China only through Chiang Kai-shek and it seemed content to accept American leadership in seeking the best way out of China's troubles.

Meanwhile a political consultative conference (PCC) consisting of delegates from the Kuomintang, the Communists, the Democratic League and nonpartisan groups met in Chungking to chart a course to peace and unity. It was not easy to reach agreement because the major antagonists were cocksure of themselves and suspicious of each other. The Communists felt that because they held one-third of China and dominated the same proportion of China's people they deserved a voice in government commensurate with their power. They argued that such problems as restoration of communications and the incorporation of the Communists into a national army could only be taken up *after* the Kuomintang should give up its political monopoly. The Kuomintang position was that *first* the Communists must submit to the legitimate power of the government, then the two sides could proceed to work out agreements on matters of detail.

The PCC agreed to a cease fire on January 10, 1946, and permitted the creation of an executive headquarters in Peiping to direct American participation in the enforcement of the truce. Troop movements were halted except to permit Nationalists to make transfers in South China and to move more men into Manchuria. Resolutions were passed dealing with government organization; a program for peaceful national reconstruction; military problems; a new national assembly, and a constitution. Agreement was reached that the national army should be reorganized on a basis of five Nationalist divisions to one Communist division and the total number of divisions should be reduced to sixty within eighteen months. As a side benefit to the Chinese, the Americans agreed to set up a military advisory group which would assist in the modernization of thirty-nine divisions and the creation of an eight-and-one-third-group air force.

For a time the China skies seemed peaceful and sunny, but storm clouds soon appeared in Manchuria. Chiang's troops were airlifted into Changchun and Mukden, while the Communists established themselves along the railroads. The Kuomintang were not able to exercise more than an uneasy jurisdiction over their cities due to the ill-will generated primarily by corrupt officials and carpetbaggers. On the other hand, the strength of the Communists in the countryside increased as they accepted former Manchukuo troops into their ranks. The Communists converted masses of people and swelled their arsenals with guns and ammunition which were left behind by the Russians. By the time the Russians withdrew from Manchuria, in the spring of 1946, Communist forces seemed well on the way toward control of the entire northeast. The Kuomintang occupation of Manchurian cities and railways, justifiable on political grounds, spread their military forces too thinly to permit flexibility of maneuver.

The PCC resolutions for peace and unity proved to be as fragile as all former Kuomintang-Communist understandings. The military truce was negated by endless clashes, and the political agreements were vitiated by subsequent arguments over the interpretation of the resolutions. Both sides agreed upon the creation of a supreme policy-making body in a proposed new coalition government to be known as the state council, which should be made up of forty delegates. The Kuomintang insisted upon the right to name twenty-seven of the forty delegates; the Communists would permit the Kuomintang to designate no more than twenty-six. The difference of one delegate was vital because decisions were to be made only on the basis of a two-thirds vote. The Kuomintang wanted the kind of an assembly and constitution which would preserve unlimited authority for the majority party; the Communists sought safeguards which would make minority representation effective. The Kuomintang became more convinced than ever that the Communists used dilatory oratorical tactics as a screen behind which they could build up military strength. Chiang felt that a genuine understanding with the Communists was impossible and that he had better use force against his enemy while the odds were overwhelmingly in his favor.

In October 1946, the Kuomintang took two Communist strongholds —Kalgan in Inner Mongolia and Antung on the border between Manchuria and Korea. Skirmishes occurred throughout North China and signaled the approach of general civil war. The Kuomintang put an end to political discussions and ordered the convocation of a national assembly on the basis of its own rules of election. The Communists and the Democratic League (representing third-party liberals) refused to have anything to do with the entire procedure. The new national assembly, representing only the Kuomintang, adopted a new constitution on Christmas Day, 1946.

General Marshall, noting the growing number of "Yankee Go Home" signs among the Kuomintang as well as among the Communists advised President Truman that his usefulness as a mediator had come to an end. He asked to be recalled. On his return to the United States, he explained to the American public that his failure to stop civil strife and to "create a coalition government in which all major groups would have fair and effective representation" resulted from the "complete, almost overwhelming suspicion with which Kuomintang and Communists regard each other." He said that extremists on both sides made it impossible for "a splendid group of men" of moderate and liberal persuasion to salvage the situation. The American marines were withdrawn from North China at the same time (January 1947), leaving their ammunition behind for the use of the Kuomintang.

Foreign Minister Molotov of Russia suggested that the China question should be placed on the agenda of the Council of Foreign Ministers, which in the immediate postwar period acted as a kind of steering committee for world affairs. Americans refused because of tightening tensions between communists and anti-communists everywhere. The Truman Doctrine and the Marshall Plan were adopted by the United States as methods of extending assistance to all nations, including China, which were in danger of attack by Russia or communists. As the cold war progressed, the United States rejected the feasibility of any coalition government containing communists. The United States became more desirous than ever of seeing a victorious Kuomintang under Chiang Kai-shek in China, but it also became increasingly conscious of the limitations upon its power to shape the course of events.

In 1947 Chiang was sublimely confident of ultimate victory. His armies captured much territory from the Communists and occupied the Communist capital at Yenan. But Chiang ignored the conditions which threatened his rule from within. His officials handled rice riots, strikes, and student demonstrations with strong-arm methods. In Formosa they perpetrated a disgraceful massacre of political opponents. Throughout China well-known liberals were jailed or assassinated, and liberal organizations were banned. The Kuomintang alienated the non-Communist third parties and their sympathizers. Chiang's American friends, including General Wedemeyer, warned him of the dangers of lethargy and corruption and stressed the need of reforms. Toward the end of the year, former ambassador to Russia William Bullitt visited China and sounded an alarm that without substantial American help China was doomed to become a satellite of Russia. Bullitt recommended that General Mac-Arthur, in addition to his duties in Japan, should be given the task immediately of working with Chiang Kai-shek in devising ways and means to keep China out of Russia's hands.

Feeling confident of his military position in 1948, Chiang turned his major attention to political maneuvers. He asked for and obtained a large American loan. He accepted a Joint United States Military Advisory Group (JUSMAG) to assist in the training of his troops. In March he convened the national assembly, which inaugurated the new government of China. As everyone anticipated, Chiang Kai-shek was elected president for a six-year term and Li Tsung-jen, one of the better types of China's former warlords, was chosen vice-president. In his inauguration speech the new president presented an optimistic military report and promised his followers that he would annihilate all the Communists south of the Yellow River within six months. Within six months it was Chiang who was fighting for his life. An American congressional mission visited China in November and reported that nothing could save China from communism except extending direct military aid, exercising American authority in China's military operations and "taking the cost of the China war out of the Chinese budget and putting it in our own." The report said saving China was no longer a piecemeal matter: "It is now an all-out program or none, a fish or cut-bait proposition."

In the meantime the Chinese Communists were active. Mao Tse-tung called for general mobilization and assured his followers they would win victory in the civil war as they had won victory over Japan. In April the Communists reoccupied their capital in Yenan. The Communists laid plans for the eventual control not only of Manchuria or North China, but all of China's territory. In August, a meeting of the All-China Labor Federation was convened in Harbin and a committee was established in Shihchiachwang (a strategic railway center between Yenan and Peiping) to prepare for a People's Government for All-China. Military victories in North China and Manchuria began a drive which ended in disaster for the Kuomintang.

Collapse of the Kuomintang

Internal rot helped to account for the rapidity of the debacle of 1948–1949. The cost of war ate into government reserves and military operations constituted ninety percent of the government budget. China was crippled by inflation which brought universal despair. From January to July wholesale prices in Shanghai went up 4500 percent. Economic production practically ceased in China, and for everything except food the nation was obliged to exist on imports provided by foreign aid. Supplies were short and commodities were rationed. The government tried a strict price-control scheme; when it failed, the people lost all confidence in the economic viability of the Kuomintang.

While the reputation of the Kuomintang went down, that of the Communists went up. The high life of the privileged classes under the Kuomintang seemed wicked in comparison with the austerity of the Communist leaders; the dejection of the masses under the Kuomintang contrasted with the hope of a better future, which the Communists seemed to represent. Frightened landlords, disgruntled businessmen, and disillusioned liberals shifted away from the Kuomintang and joined with the young students, peasants, and proletariat in a popular united front. The Communists did not stress their ideology and welcomed anyone on their team who would join in the fight against the Kuomintang.

From September 1948 to January 1949, city after city fell to the Communists in Manchuria and North China: Mukden (Shenyang), Tientsin, Peiping, and Tsinan. The Nationalists lost tanks, guns, and ammunition beyond estimation and watched millions of their men desert their ranks and join the Communists. American-trained regiments surrendered as quickly as provincial levies. The commanding general of JUSMAG reported: "No battle has been lost since my arrival due to lack of ammunition or equipment." In his opinion the military disaster of the Nationalists was due to "the world's worst leadership and many other morale-destroying factors that lead to a complete loss of the will to fight." The defeat was due not so much to superior striking power of the Communists but to the galloping collapse of the Kuomintang. Nevertheless, the fact that the Communists were able to shift to positional warfare and conduct three major campaigns (Liaohsi-Shenyang in Manchuria, Huai-Hai in East Central China, and Peiping-Tientsin in North China) proved the growing strength and competence of the People's Liberation Army (PLA). By spring 1949, the Communists were in control of North China and poised to strike toward the Yangtze Valley.

The Communists displayed their discipline and efficiency as they moved into the larger cities. They established administrative machinery in some cases and invited skilled and irreplaceable technicians to join them. They permitted the people to go about their normal business with as little interruption as possible, and they fostered good relations between the local residents and their new military masters. In Peiping the Communist troops paraded under the banner, "Liberation from the Kuomintang Reactionaries and the American Imperialists"; and as they marched down the glacis in front of the Imperial Palace they showed the populace the greatest array of American weapons and materiel which had been assembled in one place since the Manila staging for the Japanese invasion. When the Communists entered the city, some residents were enthusiastic and others appeared only moderately hopeful or acquiescent. However, in the words of a qualified observer, "almost everyone at the time accepted the Communists as the wave of the future."

In a New Year's message to the nation in 1949, while still holding his capital at Nanking, Chiang announced that he would be willing to enter into peace negotiations with the Communists regardless of his personal fate. He then asked the American, British, French, and Soviet governments to act as intermediaries for renewed Kuomintang-Communist discussions. When they refused, Chiang made public his decision to retire to his birthplace in Chekiang Province and to turn over the government to Vice-President Li Tsung-jen. Before he left Nanking he ordered that the gold which belonged to the Chinese government should be shipped to Formosa and all deliveries of United States aid destined for Shanghai should be delivered to Taipei. He made his son, Chiang Ching-kuo, the head of the Kuomintang on Formosa and named his trusted lieutenant, Chen Cheng, the governor of the province. High civilian and military officials commandeered every available means of transportation to take them to Formosa, although most of the government offices were in process of transfer to Canton.

Early in January, 1949, the Chinese Communists published an eight-point program which would have to be accepted as the price of peace:

> Strict punishment of war criminals.
>
> Abolition of the constitution.
>
> Abolition of the Kuomintang legal system.
>
> Reorganization of Nationalist troops according to democratic principles.
>
> Confiscation of "bureaucratic" capital.
>
> Reformation of the land system.
>
> Abolition of "reasonous treaties."
>
> Convocation of a Political Consultative Conference with non-participation of "reactionary elements," establishment of democratic coalition government, taking over all authority of the "Kuomintang reactionary government" and all its strata.

Acting President Li Tsung-jen sent peace delegates to Peiping in April, but discussions were fruitless. The delegates did not even return, but stayed in the north to join the Communists. The Communist armies then resumed their southward march and with ridiculous ease crossed the Yangtze. They took Nanking (April 24), Hankow (May 16–17), and Shanghai (May 25). Shanghai greeted the Communists as it had greeted the returning Kuomintang four years earlier, with embroidered signs of "welcome to the Liberators" and "ten thousand years of happiness to the victorious troops."

The turnover to the Communists in the cities of Central China was marked by the same discipline and methodical efficiency which had been experienced in Peiping. The Communists then pushed on and merely entered the power vacuums which were left as the Kuomintang disintegrated. Cities up and down the coast, and in the far interior surrendered in rapid succession. With the exception of a few rugged leaders in isolated resistance pockets, the Kuomintang commanders who were not able to retreat to Formosa cast in their lot with the communists. The Communists gained control of the entire Chinese mainland.

Nothing was left for the Kuomintang except Formosa and the offshore islands. Li Tsung-jen sought sanctuary in the United States. Chiang Kai-shek left his home in Chekiang and undertook to reconstruct the remnants of his shattered political machine in Formosa, which the Chinese preferred to call Taiwan. In December 1949, the exiled Nanking regime announced that it would continue to operate from Taipei as the legally constituted government of the Republic of China (GRC).

SUCCESSION OF THE COMMUNISTS TO POWER

Mao Tse-tung refurbished his political program to keep pace with the speed of his military triumph. By early 1949 the Communists had formed an All-China Students' Federation, an All-China Women's Congress, a new Democratic Youth League, a League of Writers and Artists, and a host of other useful mass organizations. The central committee of the party, meeting at Shihchiachwang, planned the shift of major attention from rural to urban areas and called on party leaders to concentrate on municipal and industrial affairs. It was a tremendous leap for the Communists from the hills to the cities, and the party would sink or swim depending upon its ability to master the staggering problems of China's complex, crowded cities. The Party would have to rally the proletariat as it had roused the peasants and to mold a massive united front to carry forward the work of the proposed new communist state.

In March, 1949, Mao Tse-tung formally transferred his headquarters to Peiping. On July 1 he published his political ideas about China's future in a definitive article which he entitled *On the People's Democratic Dictatorship*. He declared that the Party was no longer a child, but after a tortuous course of hardship and bitter experience had become an adult. It would continue to strive hard to create conditions in which classes, state power and political parties would disappear; but, in Mao's words,

"Our past work is only the first step in a long march of ten thousand li." Mao's plan was to set up a people's democratic dictatorship which would be "united in a common struggle with those nations of the world which treat us as equals."

The Communists organized a Sino-Soviet friendship association, and it became clear immediately that Mao intended to place China unequivocably in the Socialist camp. He wrote: "You are leaning to one side. Exactly . . . all Chinese without exception must lean either to the side of imperialism or to the side of socialism. Sitting on the fence will not do, nor is there a third road." He admitted that because of the existence of imperialism in this epoch, it was impossible for a genuine people's revolution to win victory without various forms of help from international revolutionary forces. "Internationally," he said "we belong to the side of the anti-imperialist front headed by the Soviet Union." With regard to domestic and foreign reactionaries, Mao entertained no worries about being "too irritating." He considered imperialists and their running dogs as wild beasts, to be dealt with accordingly. "Either kill the tiger or be eaten by him—one or the other."

Mao made no apologies for the people's democratic dictatorship: "You are quite right, my dear sirs, that is just what we are." In his view all the experience of the Chinese people through several decades required the enforcement of a democracy for the people and a dictatorship for the reactionaries. Who were the people? At that stage in China, they were the working class, the peasantry, the urban bourgeoisie, and the national bourgeoisie, or those merchants and industrialists who had escaped the taint of the imperialists. These classes, led by the workers and the Communist Party, should unite to form their own state and elect their own government. They alone should enjoy freedom of speech, assembly, association and so on and should possess the right to vote. Who were the reactionaries? They were the landlord class and the bureaucrat-bourgeoisie, as well as the representatives of those classes, the Kuomintang reactionaries and their accomplices. They should be suppressed, allowed only to behave themselves and not be unruly in word or deed.

Mao reaffirmed his Marxian desire to abolish state power eventually but declared "we cannot do it yet because imperialism still exists, because domestic reaction still exists, because classes still exist in our country." Therefore the state apparatus had to be strengthened—mainly the army, the police, and the courts—in order to consolidate the national defense and protect the people's interests. Under satisfactory conditions China could develop from an agricultural into an industrial economy, from a new democratic into a socialist and communist society, and could abolish classes and realize the great harmony. Mao pledged himself to apply a policy of benevolence toward the people but not toward the reactionaries.

The people should be protected, educated, and remolded by democratic methods, by persuasion and not compulsion. As for the reactionaries, as long as they did not rebel, sabotage, or create trouble, they might be reformed through labor into a new people.

As a temporary expedient, Mao said that the Communists would control capitalism rather than eliminate it. The national bourgeois could do a great deal of good, but when the time should come to realize socialism, that is, to nationalize private enterprise, "we shall carry the work of educating and remolding them a step further." In handling the serious problem of the peasantry, Mao realized that the socialization of agriculture would require a long time and painstaking work. He stated frankly: "Without socialization of agriculture, there can be no complete, consolidated socialism"; he proposed to coordinate the socialization of agriculture with the development of a powerful industry having state enterprise as its backbone.

In September, 1949, the Communists convened a people's political consultative conference (PPCC) consisting of 662 delegates, including the best known names on the Chinese mainland. Party stalwarts were kept in the background, but they determined the policies and wrote the legislation which the Conference accepted as its own. The PPCC established a new state thenceforth to be known as the People's Republic of China (PRC, in contrast to the GRC or Government of the Republic of China on Formosa). It also set up a new government structure called the Central People's Government. It relocated the capital of China at Peiping, which was given its former name of *Peking* (or northern capital). The red flag of the Communists, which was flown all over Peking, showed four yellow stars clustered in a crescent about a larger star. The smaller stars represented the classes of the people and the larger star symbolized the leadership of the Communist Party.

The PPCC adopted a common program which was a declaration of policy and principles in amplification of the democratic dictatorship. The common program consisted of a preamble and seven chapters covering general principles, the organs of state power, the military system, economic policy, cultural and educational policy, policy toward nationalities, and foreign policy.

Many of the clauses were of particular interest. As a general principle, the war of liberation was to be carried on until all Chinese territory (including Taiwan) was liberated and China completely unified. All organs of state power, that is, people's congresses (legislatures) and government councils (executive organs) at all levels, were to practice democratic centralism and to enforce a revolutionary working style embodying honesty, simplicity, and service to the people, and punishing extravagance and corruption. Military forces were to be strengthened and used in agricultural and industrial production when not actually engaged in defense activity. The economic system envisaged was a mixed one composed of various categories—state-owned, cooperative, individual peasant and handicraft, private capitalist, and state capitalist. The chief economic emphasis was on encouraging production and as soon as possible a general economic plan was to be adopted. Agrarian reform was considered essential. The stated goal of such reform was not nationalization of the land, but peasant ownership and the development of voluntary "forms of mutual aid and production cooperation."

Culture and education were defined as "New-Democratic, that is national, scientific and popular." Education was to be universal with emphasis on technical education. The main tasks of the government were to be the raising of the cultural level of the people; the training of personnel for national construction work; the eradication of feudal, comprador, and fascist ideology; and the development of the ideology of service to the people. The clauses on nationalities guaranteed the equality of all nationalities in China and the exercise of regional autonomy for all minority groups, including Tibetans, Mongolians, and the mountain people of Southwest China. Acts involving discrimination and oppression were prohibited and minorities were promised the opportunity to preserve and develop their own language and customs.

Under the heading of foreign policy, the common program stated that the main principle for China was the protection of the independence, freedom, integrity of territory and sovereignty of the country, upholding of lasting international peace and friendly cooperation between the peoples of all countries, and opposition to the imperialist policy of aggression and war. The Communists enunciated their principle of recognition: China may "on the basis of equality, mutual benefit and mutual respect for territory and sovereignty, negotiate with foreign governments which have severed relations with the Kuomintang reactionary clique and which adopt a friendly attitude towards the People's Republic of China, and may establish diplomatic relations with them."

The framework of the new Communist government was patterned upon the Soviet Union. At the head of the new government were a chairman, five vice-chairmen, and a government council. The position of the chairman and the vice-chairman were honorific, much as in the Russian system. The government council was to supervise its subordinate arm, the government administrative council, which in ordinary Western terms, would have been called the cabinet. Although political appointments were to be made in the name of the government council, all jobs and responsibilities were allocated by the Polituro, or the inner circle of the party. Actually it made little difference whether the powerful group of men at the heart of the Communist regime operated in the name of the

PPCC, the party organs, or the government council. The same men dominated both the party and the government, and the military council and the courts as well.

On October 1, 1949, the government council announced the birth of the Chinese People's Republic. Mao declared: "Our nation will from now on enter the large family of peace-loving and freedom-loving nations of the world . . . Our nation will never again be an insulted nation. We have stood up." At three in the afternoon at Tien An Men square, before more than 300,000 people, Mao himself hoisted "the majestic new national flag while many salvos of guns made the earth tremble." The next day, Russia extended recognition to China and the two states exchanged ambassadors. The new China was not recognized by the United States, nor was it admitted to the United Nations. It was not a new Chinese state that was created on October 1, 1949—only a new government. It was the same old ship of state, but it was under a new captain and a new crew. By the end of October all the Communist ministries, commissions, and councils were in operation.

LAUNCHING THE NEW GOVERNMENT

The immediate problem facing the new government was the completion of pacification and the cleansing of the party machine. The Kuomintang claimed that a million "freedom fighters" remained on the mainland, but the Communists insisted that no more than 200,000 "bandits" were left behind by the flight of the Kuomintang. Guerrilla actions were uncoordinated and constituted a nuisance—but not a threat—to the central government. The Communist army developed into a respectable fighting force entirely capable of wiping out lawless elements. The Communists needed to raise the educational level of their troops and to find the cadres who could provide leadership in local areas where political guidance was more of a problem than pacification. The top Communist hierarchy was obliged to examine carefully into the quality of its lower-level party machine. The party had grown from 1,210,000 in 1945 to more than 5,000,000 in 1950. Such rapid growth left insufficient time for thorough indoctrination and for casting away the bad seed. Further difficulties were anticipated because of the necessity of raising the proportion of the city workers as compared to the peasant membership.

The party labored mightily to indoctrinate the masses. Every segment of the population was regimented into some organization for purposes of the state. Thought-control was deemed necessary to erase the last vestiges of counterrevolutionary ideas. Every medium of communication became a propaganda tool. No views except official ones could be brought to the attention of the Chinese masses and no news unfavorable to China could reach the outside world from Communist Chinese sources. The arts were placed at the service of the revolution. Drama and literature were encouraged, but only to serve the soldiers, peasants, and workers. Thousands of drama circles, theatrical troupes, vaudeville artists, and ballad singers used Communist themes for the plots of their songs and stories. With regard to the movies, the Communists, disgusted with the crudities and reactionary viewpoints of Hollywood, set up their own studios for documentaries and feature films.

The government proceeded with caution in the social realm. Mission schools were re-examined; the public schools took on an immediate pro-Soviet, pro-Marxist orientation. Although freedom of religion was guaranteed, it was inevitable that the unsympathetic regime would sooner or later attack the religious elements in Chinese society. The most significant new social law which went into effect in the early days of the Communist regime was the Marriage Law (May 1, 1950). The press hailed it as the Magna Carta of Chinese womanhood. Freedom of choice in marriage was granted to both sexes, and divorce was to be the same for women as men. Concubinage and child marriages were prohibited. Men and women were to have exactly the same rights and obligations in the marriage relationship and in the home.

China's greatest problems were in economic affairs. The government was forced to deal with land reform, industrialization, transportation, relations of state and private enterprise, labor and finance on a vast national scale. With a pitiful shortage of competent personnel, it was obliged to clean up the wreckage of the war, get the trains running, and restore agricultural and industrial production. A famine threatened in 1949, and strict measures were required to insure "equality in hunger." Jobs had to be found for men in the cities and wages paid in terms which would guarantee purchasing power for starving families. The Trade Union Law of 1950 ordered that the All-China Federation of Labor should be the single voice of organized labor, but it warned that unions should not be formed exclusively to look after the rights of labor. The unions were to be the transmission belts between the party and the workers and were to think primarily of increasing production. Urban industry was the Communists' most baffling problem. Factories were small and industrialization far away. Public speeches mentioned the heavy industry which the state would control some day and the light industries which in the future would produce consumers' goods for China's empty cupboards. But for the present the Communists could only dream—and work for a five year plan that would put them on the path that had been pioneered by Russia. International trade came to a standstill, except for barter arrangements with the Soviet bloc. However, by deflationary measures—rigorous taxation, forced sale of government bonds, rationing, and control of the market by state trading companies—the Communists were able to halt the inflation which had brought economic catastrophe to the Kuomintang.

In June 1950, the Communists passed their first nation-wide Agrarian Reform Law. It was intended to preserve the rich peasant economy and, further, to restore agricultural production. The land and property of rich peasants were not to be disturbed. The land, draft animals, farm implements, and surplus grain of the landlord class were to be confiscated and distributed to the poor. After the completion of the distribution process, the government was to issue title deeds to all owners so they could manage, buy, sell, or rent their land freely. It was expected that this law would hold until conditions were ripe for widespread mechanized farming and collectivization. Nationalization was treated as a matter for the distant future.

Foreign policy was no less important than economics. Mao Tse-tung took his first trip out of China in 1949 and spent nine weeks in Moscow. On February 14, 1950, Russia and China abrogated their old treaties and concluded a new set of agreements. A treaty of friendship, alliance, and mutual aid, valid for thirty years specified that "in the event of one of the contracting Parties being attacked by Japan or any state allied with her, thus being involved in a state of war, the other contracting Party shall immediately render military and other assistance by any means at its disposal." Russia agreed to transfer to China without compensation its rights in the Chinese-Changchun Railway, Dairen, and Port Arthur and agreed to extend long-term credits to China for much-needed economic construction. Exchanges of notes provided for the complete guarantee of the independent status of the Mongolian People's Republic and arranged for the return to China of properties acquired by Soviet business organizations from the Japanese in Manchuria and buildings of former Soviet military settlements in Peking.

On March 27, 1950, agreements were signed for the establishment of joint stock companies to exploit oil and nonferrous metals in Sinkiang and to organize and operate civilian airlines between Peking and Chita, Peking and Irkutsk, and Peking and Alma-Ata. A series of agreements at later dates provided for details of trade—through-rail connections, through-tickets and through-bills-of-lading—and further shipments of Russian machinery. Russia was an indispensable factor in China's industrialization.

After Russia recognized China, other nations followed suit. By the time of the Korean War, seventeen nations had recognized China and nine others expressed their willingness to exchange diplomatic representatives. The United States followed a policy of waiting for the dust to settle. In January 1950, President Truman announced that the United States would not follow a course leading to involvement in China's civil war or give military aid or advice to the Nationalists on Formosa. The door was slammed on any possible *modus vivendi* between the Communist Chinese and the Americans when in February the Chinese ordered all American officials out of Chinese territory. The Communists tried to gain admission to the United Nations, but they were rebuffed. In the Security Council, the Soviet representative proposed that the Kuomintang delegate should be expelled and the Communist accepted as a replacement. When his proposal was rejected, the Soviet representative walked out of the meetings. His empty chair proved to be more of a detriment to himself than to his colleagues.

What happened in China during the transitionary period from 1945 to 1950 exercised a profound influence on the rest of Asia. Overseas Chinese—twelve millions of them—and China's neighboring nations watched the progress of China's two battles. The first battle was to drive out the imperialists. All Asians were tired of second-class status and rejoiced in the death throes of imperialism in China. The second battle was the internal one. It was between the landed and the landless, the privileged and the under-privileged, the rich and the poor within the society. It was a revolution and was destined for certain victory. The Communists identified themselves with the forces of change, and in China they emerged as the champions of nationalism and the agents of social transformation. They usurped such words as democracy and freedom and convinced the villagers that their system would provide the most effective remedy for the age-old ills of poverty and tyranny. With the mastery of the present, they obtained a mortgage on the future. No Asian leader, whether Indian or Indonesian, Burman or Filipino, Vietnamese or Thai, could afford to overlook the directions which were written on the signboards of China.

SUGGESTED READING

Barnett, A. Doak, *Newsletters on China* (New York, Institute of Current World Affairs, 1952).

Belden, Jack, *China Shakes the World* (New York, Harper, 1949).

Beloff, Max, *Soviet Policy in the Far East, 1944–1951* (New York, Oxford, 1953).

Bodde, Derk, *Peking Diary, Year of Revolution* (New York, Schuman, 1951).

Chiang Kai-shek, *Soviet Russia in China* (New York, Farrar, 1957).

Kuo, P. C., *China: New Age and New Outlook* (New York, Knopf, 1956).

Lapwood, Ralph and Lapwood, Nancy, *Through the Chinese Revolution* (London, Spalding & Levy, 1954).

Lattimore, Owen, *Situation in Asia* (Boston, Little, 1948).

Lauterbach, Richard, *Danger from the East* (New York, Harper, 1947).

Levi, Werner, *Modern China's Foreign Policy* (Minneapolis, U. of Minnesota, 1953).

Mende, Tibor, *Chinese Revolution* (London, Thames & Hudson, 1961).

Moorad, George, *Lost Peace in China* (New York, Dutton, 1949).

Payne, Robert, *Portrait of a Revolutionary, Mao Tse-tung* (New York, Abelard, 1961).

Peck, Graham, *Two Kinds of Time* (Boston, Houghton, 1950).

Rigg, Robert, *Red China's Fighting Hordes* (Harrisburg, Military Service Publishing Co., 1952).

Sprenkle, Otto B. van der, (ed.), *New China, Three Views* (New York, Day, 1951).

Strong, Anna Louise, *Chinese Conquer China* (New York, Doubleday, 1949).

Stuart, J. Leighton, *Fifty Years in China* (New York, Random, 1954).

Utley, Freda, *Last Chance in China* (Indianapolis, Bobbs, 1947).

26

Partition in South Asia: India, Pakistan, and Ceylon

At the end of World War II, Japan's problem was to arise from the ashes of defeat and to resume the paths of internal progress and international harmony from which it had so disastrously departed. The challenge of China was to survive the civil war which was fought to mold the future of the greatest underdeveloped nation on earth. The tasks of the rest of Asia were of a different nature. The restoration of world peace signaled the beginning of a great period of transition and creation in South and Southeast Asia. The era of Western supremacy in the East was gone; what kind of a political system would appear to take its place? Subject peoples needed no longer to fight for freedom and independence, but they had to demonstrate the capacity to shoulder the responsibilities of the goals which they had achieved. For some, imperialism died hard; for others, it faded away without resistance and without lament. But in every case, the passing of the power of the white man in Asia meant violent shocks to the old order. New leaders emerged who were called upon to carry the burdens of self-government and self-development.

LAST DAYS OF BRITISH INDIA

India was the prime example of the many difficulties involved in the transition from colonialism to independent nationhood. India hated British rule, but Indians never despised the British people: "They have done too much for us." More important than the roads, railways, canals, factories, and public buildings which the British placed on the Indian landscape were such ideas as individual equality before the law, interests in

the welfare of one's fellow man, the value of science and industry and political democracy which the British instilled in the Indian psyche. When
the British raj came to an end in South Asia, it left as its heritage the skills
and building materials for political and economic freedom. India was
neither exhausted nor resentful when the British pulled out, but it was
full of vigor and high expectations. Independence was greeted as the dawn
of the millennium.

As soon as the Labour government entered office in London in 1945,
it pushed forward with plans for the attainment of Indian self-government. Its first decision was to hold fresh elections in India for the central
and provincial legislatures. The results were that the Moslem League won
practically all the seas reserved for the Moslems. Moslems were repudiated
who advocated anything less than Pakistan or a separate Moslem state.
The Indian National Congress was equally successful in the non-Moslem
or general constituencies. The Congress campaigned exclusively for immediate independence. The Hindu extremists who wanted strong anti-
Moslem measures were emphatically rejected—independence was all that
mattered. The next steps decided upon by the British were to set up an
all-Indian executive council and to convene a national assembly to draw
up a new constitution. England's problem was not *whether* to grant independence or self-government to India; it was rather a question of to whom
and on what terms should the new status be conferred.

The burning issue was communalism, which reached crisis proportions as between the Moslems and the Hindus. These two communities
were not the only special interest groups in India, but they were the
most irreconcilable. The sense of communal identity permeated groups
which enjoyed either a common religion, language, or historical origin; or
worked in the same occupation or lived in one distinctive geographic region. But it was only in the field of religion that feelings became too inflamed for followers of the two major faiths to try to live together under
a single political regime. The Moslems professed a fanatic belief in one
God, one last prophet, and one holy book which revealed the true standards of faith and conduct. The Moslems were bound together by a strong
sense of community, with a long tradition of aristocracy and imperial
rule behind them. Collectively, they wanted a religious state, entirely
and uniquely their own, which would accept as its highest duty the conversion to Islam.

To the Hindus this intolerance was irrational and immature; this
desire for a religious state was impossible of fulfillment. In their religion,
the Hindus did not require uniformity or strictness. They permitted unlimited variation in belief concerning the nature of God, and a corresponding diversity in cult and standards of behavior. Let man believe
anything he pleased, there was still a place for him in Hinduism. Nothing

seemed more futile or unrewarding to a Hindu than a concerted effort for conversion or spreading the faith by means of the sword. In the matter of the state, the Hindus wanted a secular government. Since the Hindus were in the majority in South Asia, they felt they had the right to a dominant role in determining the nature of the political system which would succeed the British rule.

The antagonism between the two largest communities in India sharpened as economic and political divergencies added their weight to the religious conflict. As has been noted, Moslems and Hindus before the coming of the British lived together in the same villages, used the same speech, shared identical customs, and celebrated each other's religious festivals. Peoples of both faiths were of the same ethnic stock, and they were distinguished only by such externals as dress and eating habits. Rivalries seemed unimportant at the top and the bottom of the social pyramid. Rulers of one religious persuasion often hired civil administrators and generals of the other. Moslem princes frequently made alliances with Hindu princes against other Moslems, and vice versa. At the bottom of the scale, peasants and workers shared common hardships regardless of their religion. However, the inevitable arguments between peasants and landlords or between workers and employers were always worse in areas where either class was Moslem and the other Hindu.

With the coming of the British, the divisions deepened—so much so that the British were accused of a deliberate policy of divide and rule. The Hindus were quick to take advantage of British education and to learn the English language. They took clerical and political jobs in the British employ, and they made up the rising middle class. As the British transformed tax gatherers into legal landlords, it was the Hindus who benefited. Hindus and such astute non-Moslems as the Parsis became the wealthiest of India's businessmen. On the other hand, the Moslems tended to shun the British infidels as they had stood aloof from the Hindu infidels. The Moslems had enjoyed the rich plums of conquest under their own dynasty, but they lost progressively their exclusive privileges and their quasi-monopoly on the sources of wealth. They blamed their fate on what they saw as the unholy British-Hindu alliance.

As the British tried to keep a political balance between Moslems and Hindus, each group accused the British of favoring the other. The Moslems took exception to the principle of majority rule, and the Hindus objected to British insistence on protection of minority rights. The idea of communal representation seemed valid as a compromise method at the time of its adoption, but through the years it seemed to intensify rather than to modify intercommunal disputes. As Hindu politicians exercised control in the various organs of government, the Moslems hurled mounting charges of "atrocities." In the Moslem view, Hindu atrocities consisted of favoritism in appointments to public office, exclusive use of the Hindi language, Hinduization of the public schools, acceptance of the spinning wheel Congress Party emblem as the national flag and adoption of a Hindu hymn as the national anthem. At the time of the 1945 elections in India, the great Moslem leader Ali Jinnah declared in fury, "Only over the dead bodies of Moslems will the Congress Party flag fly in the northern provinces."

The ideological cleavages between the Moslems and the Hindus culminated in the showdown battle after 1945 between the respective gladiators for the two communities: the Moslem League and the Indian National Congress. These were no longer mere office-seeking political parties; they were life and death organizations motivated by cultural and religious forces. They sought sympathy and support where they could find it. Moslems outside of India were lukewarm in their endorsement of the League. They too hated British rule, but they believed the Congress to be a more effective instrument than the League to deal the *coup de grace* to the British in India. Communists inside India leaned toward the League, not because they believed in its objectives, but because they saw the League as a valuable ally in their own contest for power against the Congress. Third parties in India, for example the Sikhs, Christians, and Anglo-Indians, showed no particular love for either the League or the Congress. The leaders of the scheduled castes often indicated their sympathy toward the League because they felt that almost anybody would be better for India than the upper-caste Hindus.

PROCESS OF PARTITION

These schisms complicated the British program in India. Some conservative opinion in England suggested that the existing chaos was scarcely a proper background for independence and argued for a prolongation of the period of transition. But the Labour government reflected the popular feeling that the game of imperialism was no longer worth the candle, and it estimated correctly the power of the underlying Indian sentiment of nationalism. The masses in India were touchy and prone to demonstrate their antiforeign sentiments. The trial of Indian officers who had associated themselves with Subhas Chandra Bose and his pro-Japanese "Free Indian" army stimulated a perverse train of thought. Bose was an Indian patriot, revered by thousands of his Bengali followers, and he cooperated with Japanese (also Asians) in trying to overthrow the British. Those who followed him ought to be praised, not punished, so the argument ran. Indian workers went on strike in foreign-owned mills, and demonstrators smashed windows in foreign stores. Sailors of the Indian navy mutinied at Bombay and laborers refused to work at air force bases. Mobs milled around the offices of the United States Information Service and tore down the American flag. Indians were in an ugly anti-imperialist, anti-British, and anti-Western mood. Only the presence of the army preserved order.

On February 19, 1946, the British cabinet sent a three-man mission consisting of Lord Pethick-Lawrence, the secretary of state for India, Sir Stafford Cripps, then president of the board of trade and A. V. Alexander, first lord of the admiralty, to India to assist in the framing of a constitution. The prime minister made it clear that England was in dead earnest to make India completely free. It was up to India to make its own future in the world. Mr. Atlee said, "I hope that the Indian people may elect to remain within the British Commonwealth. . . . But if (they) so elect it must be by their own free will." The British were war-weary and broke, and they faced the appalling job of rehabilitation at home. In view of Indian opposition, it was impossible to carry on in India. Many British soldiers were fed up fighting for the empire and let it be known that "they did not give a damn for India."

The mission tried to reconcile the opposing points of view of the League and the Congress, but it was up against a stone wall. The Congress demanded a strong central government; the League wanted a loose federation with real political strength in the units of local government. Jinnah told the British, "You divide India, then quit"; Nehru's position was "you quit, and we'll divide India if any division is to be made." The British were reluctant to admit the necessity of partition. They reasoned that no partition could be so perfect as to erase all minority problems. Partition would disrupt the economy of the divided sectors, since economic development, transportation, post, and telegraph had been built on the basis of a united continent. Armed forces had been trained for the security of the country as a whole. Furthermore, the proposed Moslem homeland would consist of two halves hundreds of miles apart. To the British it seemed that partition would not heal religious schisms, but would extend religious, commercial, and political rivalry into the field of international relations. The threat to peace would be magnified if two mutually suspicious nations were to take the place of united India.

The mission recommended a scheme of its own for peace and unity which it called the "Three-Tier Proposal." The first tier was to consist of a central government with powers over defense, foreign affairs, and communications. No communal matter could be acted upon by the first tier save by a majority vote of both major communities. The second tier would be made up of voluntary groups of provinces: group A, the Hindu majority area of Madras, Bombay, United Province, Bihar, Central Provinces, and Orissa; group B, the Moslem majority area of Punjab,

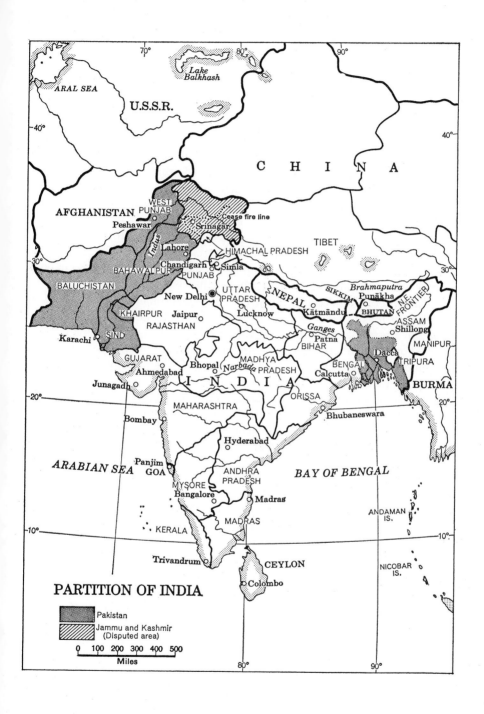

PARTITION OF INDIA

Pakistan

Jammu and Kashmir
(Disputed area)

0   100 200 300 400 500
Miles

Northwest Frontier, and Sind; and group C, the weak Moslem majority area of Bengal and Assam. Each group was to work out its own constitutional arrangements. The third tier, or the solid foundation of the governmental pyramid, was to remain the local governments, namely the provinces of British India and the princely states. Both the League and the Congress gave tentative approval of the scheme, but they made approval meaningless through their objections and qualified interpretations of the grouping formula.

The viceroy, Lord Wavell, was harried to form an interim government, preferably one which would represent both the major factions. To make sure that the viceroy would not bend to the will of the Congress, Jinnah decided to demonstrate the Moslem capacity for political action. He designated August 16, 1946, as "Direct Action Day" which became in effect the day of farewell to hope of achieving harmony through peaceful methods. Wild riots broke out in Calcutta, and the massacres spread throughout eastern and northern India. Thousands were murdered in communal hatred during the months which followed.

In spite of the blood in the streets, the government went ahead with its plan to make India free. An all-India constitutional convention was called in December 1946, but the Moslems refused to attend. The country swayed on the brink of civil war. Mr. Attlee seemed mild in demeanor but he acted with iron nerve. On February 20, 1947, he announced that come what may Britain would withdraw from India—government and soldiers —by June, 1948. By fixing an ultimate date, he determined to make the Indians look beyond their legalistic arguments to the assumption of administrative responsibility. He named the meteoric Lord Mountbatten (who was described as "a heart of gold, a lad of life, an imp of fame") as the new viceroy.

Within three months, Lord Mountbatten decided that no plan for preserving the political unity of India would be acceptable. He discerned that the Congress would be receptive to partition; that the League would settle for less territory than it demanded; and that the Sikhs and the Bengalis could be persuaded to the division of their respective territories. He also became convinced that the pace of transition must be faster than London anticipated, and that the changeover of power would have to take place within the next few months. On June 3, 1947, he announced his plan of partition, which was adopted as the official government policy. If the areas with a majority of Moslem population so desired, they should be allowed to form a separate dominion. Bengal and the Punjab would be divided. A referendum would be taken in the Northwest Frontier province to ascertain whether it should join Pakistan or not. The district of Sylhet in Assam would be joined to the Moslem area in Bengal, if approved by popular referendum. Boundary commissions would be set up to divide Bengal and the Punjab. Legislation would be introduced in the current session of parliament for conferring dominion status on India— or India and Pakistan if partition was decided upon.

The actual date for the transfer of power was fixed as August 14, 1947. Haste became the order of the day. Within two months the assets of the country had to be divided between the two new dominions, and the army and the public services had to be reassigned according to religious and regional affiliations. It was necessary to reach agreement on the apportionment of the public debt and to inaugurate new systems of exchange, currency, and coinage. Such items as files, office furniture, and public automobiles had to be earmarked for Karachi or New Delhi. Details were turned over to ten expert committees made up of senior Indian officials. These bodies in turn presented their recommendations to a supreme partition council which was responsible for fundamental policy and administrative decisions. A commission under Sir Cyril John Radcliffe undertook the touchy job of boundary demarcation.

The partition was ratified in legal form by act of parliament in July, 1947. India and Pakistan were to become dominions within the British Commonwealth, and the princely states were to join whichever dominion they chose. The heady wine of independence brought roseate dreams of freedom and prosperity; it also produced an orgy of pillage, fire, and slaughter. In West Punjab and the Northwest Frontier, Moslems murdered Sikhs and Hindus; in East Punjab and the Sikh states, Sikhs and Hindus murdered Moslems. In the United Provinces, Hindus and Moslems murdered each other. Delhi itself was engulfed in cruelty as incoming Sikhs led gangsters and goons in attacking miserable Moslem artisans. The Punjab became a sea of anarchy as an endless stream of refugees—Moslems fleeing westward, Hindus and Sikhs eastward—staggered along on foot, crawled by oxcarts, or chugged slowly by in filthy, thirsty, bloody trains. Maybe as many as 12,000,000 joined the trek of death; maybe as many as a million died.

Against this background of utter madness, a constitutional assembly in New Delhi on August 14, 1947, declared India a dominion within the British Commonwealth and chose Lord Mountbatten as the first governor-general of India. In Karachi, Pakistan was also proclaimed as a dominion, with Ali Jinnah as governor-general and Liaquat Ali Khan as prime minister. In the festive atmosphere of New Delhi Nehru said: "Long years ago we made a tryst with destiny and now the time comes when we shall redeem our pledge, not wholly or in full measure, but very substantially." Rajendra Prasad, the president of the constitutional assembly declared: "While our achievement is in no small measure due to our own sufferings and sacrifices, it is also the result of world forces and events, and last though not least, it is the consummation and fulfillment of the historic tradition and democratic ideals of the British race." The Indians hailed the day of independence as the beginning of a new era when their relations with Britain would rest on a basis of equality, mutual goodwill, and mutual profit.

A New Nation-State: the Union of India

Before the new Union of India could address itself to any of its long-range problems, it was forced to calm the fears and assure the safety of the Moslem minorities. In spite of steady migrations, Moslems still comprised about eleven percent of India's population after partition. India was also obliged to look after the welfare of Hindus who, as evacuees from Pakistan, were crowded into special camps without money, jobs, food, or any hope of a decent future. These refugees demanded that their new homeland should recover their lost property and wealth, thereby creating complex legal questions and severe emotional strains. Similar conditions—only worse—existed in Pakistan. Inflammatory claims and threats in the press, and mutual recriminations between governments led to a war scare in March 1950. Taut nerves were relieved temporarily by an agreement to protect minorities, curb propaganda, and set up commissions for refugee welfare. This agreement did not solve festering problems nor stop all movement of minorities. But it eased the crisis atmosphere and reduced bitter issues to manageable proportions.

The worst personal loss in these tragic times was the assassination of Gandhi, who spent his last years working for communal harmony. On January 30, 1948, he was killed at a prayer meeting by a Hindu extremist. His life was a monument to his people. He did not want any sect of Gandhiism to live after him. He did not claim to have originated any new principle or doctrine: he simply tried to apply eternal truths to everyday living. He insisted that his opinions and conclusions could not be taken as final. He said, "I may change them tomorrow. I have nothing new to teach the world. All I have done is to try experiments in truth and non-violence on as vast a scale as I could." In death he was more powerful than in life. His sacrifice, in a way that nothing else could approximate, convinced the masses of the incredible folly of terror and revenge.

Without Gandhi, India was the poorer in launching its ship of state. The union of India was a country of some 340,000,000 people at the time of independence, five-sixths of whom were Hindus and 50,000,000 of whom were untouchables. The first task was to determine the physical make-up of the state, to join the former provinces of British India and the princely states into a new national structure. Under the direction of Deputy Prime Minister Sardar Valabhbhai Patel, some six hundred states were consolidated into thirty units by absorbing some, merging others, and leaving a few intact. The autocratic rule of the princes came to an end. The personal problems of the princes were solved by the gift of pensions free of income tax. Rajahs became mere landed gentry. Descendants of hardy adventurers or seasoned warriors effaced themselves and abandoned their palaces for the biblical thirty pieces of silver, and a few privileges.

Troubles arose in three states—Junagadh, Hyderabad, and Kashmir. In Junagadh, four-fifths of the population was non-Moslem, but the ruler was Moslem. He tried to accede to Pakistan, but the Union of India occupied his capital city and took over his state to prevent administrative breakdown. A plebiscite resulted in an overwhelming vote to join India. In Hyderabad also, the masses were Hindu, but the Nizam, or prince, was Moslem. The masses lived in medieval conditions, but the landlords and officials were prosperous. The Nizam was one of the wealthiest men in the world. He tried to isolate his domain from modernism, but in banning the Indian National Congress he unwittingly exposed his people to the influence of communal extremists and Communists. Armed Moslem irregulars terrorized the populace, and Communists claimed to exercise real power in more than 2,000 villages. The Nizam wanted to continue his independence so he could handle his state in the same old despotic way. India said this was impossible and suggested a plebiscite (which would certainly have approved accession to India). In June 1948, India invaded Hyderabad in the name of national security. The prince took his case to the United Nations, but swift Indian action solved the situation before the international machinery could start in motion. Indian troops restored order, and an Indian military administrator initiated steps to liberalize the government. The Nizam was not deposed, but Hyderabad became an Indian state.

The case of the Jammu and Kashmir state, or Kashmir, as it is usually called, was more complex and without the decisive ending for India. Kashmir was of major strategic, political, and economic significance to Pakistan and of great prestige value to India. Exactly the reverse of Hyderabad, Kashmir's population was seventy percent Moslem; the ruling elite was Hindu. The Moslem population suffered repression and religious discrimination at the hands of the Hindu autocracy. Reforms were attempted by a Congress-sponsored Kashmir people's conference, headed by a pro-Indian noncommunal Moslem named Sheik Mohammed Abdullah, who was in jail in 1947 for his political activities. The maharajah, who was not sophisticated in the affairs of state, disliked Pakistan because of its religion and India because of its democracy. He wanted to remain independent, but neither India nor Pakistan would let him. India built a new road into Kashmir from the south over which Sikh and Hindu refugees streamed, bringing their inevitable communal quarrels with them. In the northern part of the state, tribesmen, with at least the moral support of Pakistan, entered Kashmir well armed with machine guns, rifles, mortars, and light artillery. They burned and looted as they approached Srinagar the capital. They took control of most of the north country and set up a government of Azad (Free) Kashmir. The maharajah appealed to India for help (which India promptly gave) and offered accession of his state to India. He then resigned in favor of his son, and turned over the government of Kashmir to the former gentleman in jail, Sheik Mohammed Abdullah. This man, as prime minister, was a Moslem in religion but a pro-Indian in his politics and, much to the disgust of Pakistan, was guilty of repression of his own coreligionists.

Disorders flared continuously, and at the end of 1947 the Kashmir question was first placed by India on the docket of the Security Council of the United Nations. The United Nations resolved that the Pakistan-supported troops should be withdrawn from northern Kashmir, that the Indian troops should be withdrawn from the central and southern parts of the state, and that a plebiscite should be arranged with the help of the international organization to determine Kashmir's political destiny. A cease-fire line across Kashmir was agreed upon in July 1949, and direct relations were established by the respective divisions of Kashmir with India and Pakistan. No progress was made on synchronization of troop withdrawal, on terms for the proposed plebiscite, or on the composition of a state government which would be acceptable to both sides. Kashmir receded in world importance at the time of the Korean War, but the question lost none of its complexity or bitterness. In July 1952, Sheik Mohammed Abdullah signed an agreement with India which fell short of accession but which established a special relationship with the Union. It was agreed that Kashmir should elect its own chief of state and pursue economic and social reforms at its own pace regardless of the constitution of India.

India's first major political achievement in internal affairs was the adoption of a constitution which became effective on January 26, 1950. The constitution, as printed, emerged as a book of 251 pages written in the spirit of justice, liberty, equality, and fraternity for all. India was made a secular state, meaning absence of discrimination for or against any religious group. No religious instruction was to be permitted in institutions supported by state funds, and no student was required to attend worship except with his own or his guardian's consent. It was provided that no citizen on grounds of religion, race, caste, sex, or place of birth should be subject to any disability, liability, restriction, or conditions, with regard to access to shops, public restaurants, hotels, and places of public entertainment, or the use of wells, tanks, bathing ghats, roads, and places of public resort. The practice of untouchability was abolished. Restrictions on civil liberties were to be made only in the interest of public order, morality, or health. The constitution was a liberal, democratic document dedicated to the dignity of the individual and the unity of the nation.

The constitution summed up the aspirations of India in the social and economic sphere. It contained "Directive Principles of State Policy" which ranged over the field of economic justice and social security. They included broad injunctions against undue concentration of wealth and productive power. They stressed the need for decent working conditions, equal pay for equal work by men and women, and for old-age and disability benefits. In the field of education, the constitution promised that the state would provide free education for all children under fourteen within ten years.

The structure of the government was a reflection of its Anglo-Saxon model. The federal Union of India was set up as a parliamentary democracy with an independent judiciary. The head of state was a president, elected by an electoral college for five years. He was regarded more as a unifying symbol than a political power, except that he was given the supreme command of the defense forces. The president was to be aided and advised by a council of ministers headed by a prime minister responsible to the lower chamber in the legislature as in the British system. The lower chamber was given the name of House of the People and was composed of 500 members, elected for five years by universal adult suffrage. The upper chamber was called the Council of States, and it consisted of 250 members. Twelve members were to be appointed by the president for distinction in literature, art, science, and other fields; the rest were to be elected for six-year terms by the lower chambers of the state legislatures.

In the various states, the governors were appointed by the president. Each state was to be administered by a council of ministers responsible to the state legislature or to the lower chamber in bicameral legislatures. Unlike the American federal structure, all powers not mentioned in the constitution were to reside in the union government, not in the states. Union and states were given concurrent powers over economic and social planning, commercial and industrial monopolies, employment and social security. In cases of national emergency, the president of the Union was given temporary powers to suspend the bill of rights, concern himself with subjects ordinarily restricted to the states and issue administrative orders with the force of law. However, the states assumed greater importance in the Indian political picture than the constitution would seem to suggest. They controlled the various programs of land reform. Because of their long tradition of political responsibility, they addressed themselves to emergency situations which were not specifically covered by the provisions of the constitution.

India, like China, discovered that the making of a constitution was no more than the first step in a long journey. It was not too difficult to build the framework and to lay down the ground rules for a democratic system. The real problem was to make the system work. Could India find the men and the means to convert its goals into reality? Could the Congress Party transform itself successfully from a monolithic fighter for freedom into a first-among-equals in a multiparty system for independent India? The Congress had ridden to glory on two issues—anti-imperialism and communalism—which were no longer meaningful. A small group of men, whose mettle had been tested as leaders of the opposition, was called upon to assume positive leadership in the constructive tasks of running the government and raising the standard of living for the masses.

The Congress adopted a new platform. It repudiated religious conservatism and communalism and came out for a secular, socialist state. It gave first priority to economic progress in order to bring the masses freedom from want. It directed its appeals to the depressed classes, displaced persons, labor, and the peasants. It advocated a mixed economy, with some opportunity for the private sector, but with basic industries owned and controlled by the state. It was strong for economic equality and social justice. It was jealously nationalistic, but it staunchly advocated world peace. The new platform of the Congress Party expressed well the general mood of Asian leaders, and it attracted three-quarters of India's electorate. Prime Minister Nehru, concurrently president of his party, was India's most influential vote-getter, spokesman, and statesman.

It was entirely in keeping with India's new status that other parties rose to challenge the Congress. Opposition appeared from the right and the left. The old parties of the right which were based on Hindu communalism—the Hindu Mahasabha, or People's Association, and the Rashstriya Swayamsevak Sang, or National Volunteer Association, came under a cloud with the murder of Gandhi. Their followers were rallied into two new associations—the Bharatiya Jan Sang, or Indian People's Party, and the Ram Rajya Parishad, or Rule of God Party. However, conservatism was not very popular because the masses demanded change and reform. The Congress met its greatest challenge from the left. The Federation of All-India Scheduled Castes agitated for faster action in favor of the untouchables. The Socialist Party and the KMP, or Peasant, Workers, and People's Party, broke off from the Congress because they wanted more, not less, attention to the needs of their followers. These parties were categorically anti-Communist both in methods of internal "revolution" and foreign policy.

The Communists in India were not accepted as leaders of the nationalist movement. They never worked wholeheartedly with the Congress and during World War II cooperated with the British. In much Indian opinion, the Communists were regarded as the tools of a foreign country. No foreign country was welcomed as a participant in India's internal affairs, whether it was Britain, Russia, or (later) China. In February 1948, the Communists called an Asian Youth Conference in Calcutta to plan their strategy for all of South and Southeast Asia. They adopted a program of extreme social reform including abolition of landlordism and rural indebtedness, nationalization of industry, minimum living wages and an eight-hour day for labor, equal democratic rights for women, and the guarantee of free, universal education. Their tactics were to be to arm the people, stir up strikes, and rouse the peasants, students, youth, women, and untouchables against the Congress and the Socialists. Internally they would cooperate in a democratic front against imperialism, feudalism, and the middle class; on the international scene, they would lean to the side of the Soviet Union and China. Naturally, they attracted the wrath of the government, which put thousands of Communists in jail. Prime Minister Nehru was "neutralist" in foreign affairs, but he was anti-Communist at home. In 1951 the Communists, much-reduced in strength, abandoned their tactics of violence and began to act as an ordinary political party.

The crux of all political rivalry was the control of the continuing revolution for economic and social improvement. Independent India was forced to take up the burdens which had been set aside by the former British administration. India was still one of the most poverty-stricken, disease-ridden countries in Asia. At the time of independence, nine-tenths of its people lived in rural areas with an annual income of fifty-seven dollars per capita and a life-expectancy of twenty-six years. Reform was essential because conditions were getting worse. Population increased faster than wealth, and it was estimated that by the year 2,000 India would have one-third the world's population. Birth control promised no remedy. India had no religious scruples against family planning, but Hinduism and the agricultural nature of the economy placed a premium on children.

The Congress was not particularly active for the peasants until the Communists and the Socialists beat the drums for agrarian reform. The Congress came out for modest restrictions on the rights of landlords and limited improvements in the welfare of tenants. Measures were passed in various states to limit future acquisitions of land, protect the tenant from arbitrary eviction, enable the tenant to make improvements at the landlord's expense, and to grant tenants the right to purchase land they cultivated at prices fixed by revenue courts. The government reclaimed large tracts of wasteland, promoted irrigation and rural electrification projects, and made provisions for financial assistance which would alleviate the crushing weight of high taxes, excessive rents, and perennial debts. Community development schemes were introduced to increase agricultural production, eliminate the worst evils of land tenure, and protect landless agricultural workers. India saw the necessity of agrarian reform and moved ahead without the violence which accompanied reform in China.

Industrialization was no less urgent than agricultural development. Jobs, millions of them, were essential for substantial progress. The Congress abandoned Gandhi's spinning-wheel philosophy and turned to machinery. India had raw materials, but practically no factories. The crying need was to build—anything and quickly—and a horde of planners turned out a spate of blueprints which were more utopian than realistic. India adopted socialistic methods, not because of a hatred of the capitalist system, but because of the greater promise of fast results from planned action. The state did not attempt to destroy existing private enterprise but laid down strict rules for future cooperation between the public and private sectors of the economy. The government would monopolize the manufacture of armaments and atomic energy, the railways, and any industry vital to defense in times of emergency. It would initiate all new undertakings in coal-mining, iron and steel, aircraft production, shipbuilding, communications equipment, and the exploitation of fuel oil resources. All other enterprises would be left to private initiative, provided they showed a record of satisfactory progress. The law required that fifty-one percent of any company formed in India should be owned by Indians, and the company should be Indian-managed.

Such rules as these reflected the latent fears of economic imperialism and scared away new investments of private capital. India needed foreign financial assistance and received its most substantial help from the Colombo Plan for cooperative economic development of South and Southeast Asia. According to this plan, jointly devised by the commonwealth governments in Colombo in March 1950, five billion dollars would be made available to underdeveloped countries in the area during the following six years. Five-sixths of the money was to be advanced to India and one-seventh to Pakistan. Even these huge sums represented a small beginning in the new home-grown attack on poverty and outmoded social conditions.

The Indian government was hard-pressed to continue the social revolution which was well under way during the British regime. No conqueror in India ever tried to destroy the Hindu pattern of society, because it supplied the only enduring element of stability and unity throughout Indian history. But Hindu society was subject to continuous change, and at an ever-accelerating rate. Under the independent government of India, the caste system was exposed to further pressures. The radio, moving pictures, and the spread of education weakened ancient barriers and gave people the courage to demand the enforcement of laws removing restrictions on the untouchables. High caste candidates for office strained social customs in seeking low caste votes.

The government showed vigorous leadership in looking after the welfare of the underprivileged masses, or to put it another way, shouldered courageously the burdens of carrying on with the social revolution. It could boast of little immediate accomplishment; however, it showed that it recognized the problems and undertook programs which might bring results in the long-range future, if at all. The first task was to provide food and jobs for the depressed millions; next, to look after the conquest of disease. How could the government bring decent standards of existence to the villages and to the miserable, burgeoning city slums? Scarcely less vital was the matter of education, the key to a better life. How could a new and impoverished administration provide even the most elementary education for most of the half-million villages which had no schooling facilities at all? Who would pay for the schools and the teachers for the free, compulsory education which the constitution said would be made available for all children in ten years?

In a less obvious way, the government was obliged to tackle more sophisticated problems which were equally vital to the freedom of the individual and the welfare of the nation. How should it proceed in guaranteeing equal rights for women and preventing the exploitation of children? It passed mining acts, factory acts, and plantation acts for the benefit of workers; yet how could these acts be translated into realities? How could government officials persuade labor unions to concentrate more on the welfare of their two and a half million workers rather than upon the political activities of their respective sponsors? How could the central government rise above national pride or provincial loyalties and find a common language which would overcome India's linguistic chaos? English was to be the accepted language for fifteen years, but after that the nation was committed to the use of Hindi for official communications. Finally, the Indians themselves faced the classic problem of reconciling the conflicting claims of individual freedom and public order. Such English traditions as free speech and a free press were also precious in India, but with self-government the Indians could no longer enjoy these privileges without accepting the consequent responsibilities.

The national elections of 1951–1952 gave India the occasion for taking stock. These elections marked the end of the transition period in India, and the real beginning of the history of contemporary India. Of 176,000,-000 voters—eighty-five percent of whom were illiterate—more than 100,000,000 went to the polls. This was democracy in action, and it offered thoughtful Asians an alternative to communistic methods which had seemed successful in China. The Congress Party was obliged to submit its program to the test of the polls. It captured the majority of the seats contested, but it attracted only forty-five percent of the voters. A substantial opposition came from the Socialists and the Communists, who recruited new strength from those for whom democracy appeared to be unsatisfactory and inadequate. Although the Congress itself took a strong position left of center, it was too conservative for millions who wanted the government to move faster, not slower, in the direction of development and reform.

CREATION OF PAKISTAN

The tribulations of India looked small compared to those of Pakistan, because Pakistan as a state did not even exist at the time of partition. It had little beyond the determination to work for God and country. The agonizing effects of the great migrations in 1947 extended over a few parts of India, but they reached down to practically every family in Pakistan. Every province in Pakistan before partition had a sizable minority of Hindus or Sikhs, but almost all fled in the mass exodus. Pakistan lost many of its bankers, traders, officials, doctors, teachers, and technical personnel, and received in exchange millions of miserable, hungry peasants and workers. It was touch and go whether political chaos could be averted and economic collapse could be prevented. It was a miracle that Pakistan survived as creditably as it did.

Pakistan, or "the Land of the Pure"—with *P* for Punjab, *A* for Afghanistan (or the Northwest Frontier Province), *K* for Kashmir, *S* for Sind, and *TAN* for Baluchistan—began life as the seventh largest nation state in the world. It contained eighty million people, or one-fifth of the population of India, living on one-fourth of its land area. It was composed of two separate sections hundreds of unbridgeable miles apart. West Pakistan, or the territories listed above, and East Pakistan, including East Bengal and a portion of Assam, had little in common except religion and their solid opposition to the Hindus. Karachi, in West Pakistan, was established as the national capital even though it lacked houses and public buildings, except those which had been used for the former provincial government of Sind. A handful of ex-British officials and their devoted but inexperienced associates undertook the imposing job of creating a new state and launching an entirely new system of government.

A constitutional assembly was chosen in 1947 to serve as a federal legislature pending the adoption of a new constitution, until which time Pakistan was shared by the governor-general, the central government gates to the Constitutional Assembly were chosen by provincial legislatures on the basis of one delegate per million inhabitants, and the selection was controlled by the Moslem League. Temporary political power in Pakistan was shared by the governor-general, the central government headed by the prime minister, and the provincial legislatures. The smooth functioning of the political apparatus depended upon the successful manipulation of a few dozen professional politicians, who were backed by landlords and influential lawyers in their respective localities. The basis for successful democratic procedures was too flimsy to expect incorrupt or efficient administration. In 1949 the province of Punjab experienced the first taste of what became a chronic condition—the suspension of parliamentary government and the assumption of authority by the executive. The army was the usual instrument to preserve law and order.

Two insoluble problems made it impossible for the new state to get off to a good start. The first problem was the place of religion in politics. The red-hot communalists wanted an all-out religious state based on Allah, the Law, and the Prophet. But eleven million non-Moslems remained in Bengal alone, and they refused to be treated as second-class citizens. They had sufficient voting strength in the constitutional assembly to block any measure which would deprive them of full rights of life, property, and participation in public affairs. The second problem was the relationship between the two "wings" of Pakistan. East Pakistan was only one-sixth the size of West but it contained more than half the population. Through East Pakistan's export of raw materials, it earned most of the foreign exchange; however, West Pakistan received most of the nation's subsidies for economic development. East Pakistan felt isolated from the heartbeat of politics in Karachi. It resented the domination of the government by the men of West Pakistan and protested against the use of Urdu rather than Bengali as the favored language in the transaction of public business. East Pakistan was rocked by constant rumbles of autonomy or possible separation.

Pakistan was torn by recurrent political crises which stemmed from dissensions within the Moslem League, from opposition parties, and from personal rivalries for leadership. In December 1947, the All-India Moslem League became the Pakistan Moslem League. It tried to be the party of the masses although it was dominated by landlords and the political elite. It was open to all Moslems over eighteen years of age, and its annual dues amounted to something like twenty cents a year. Its organization extended from the national level down through the provinces and districts to the smallest villages. Like the Kuomintang in China, the Moslem League conceived its role to be that of guardian and trustee for the state. Party and government were so intimately intertwined that it was impossible to tell whether one or the other was more responsible for maladministration and prevalent irregularities. The League did not take kindly to opposition. Jinnah, as long as he lived, appealed for unity, faith, and discipline. His successor, Liaquat Ali Khan, used different tactics toward his opponents—he branded them as "traitors, liars and hypocrites" and fought them tooth and nail.

Opposition groups in Pakistan accepted the position of the Moslem League in castigating imperialism and advocating united effort for raising the level of living. All parties agreed to some sort of socialism or planned development of irrigation, power resources, and industries. However, vocal minorities repudiated the mildness of the Moslem League and argued strenuously for an outright Islamic state or a pan-Islamic bloc. Some demagogues sought to increase their personal prestige by emotional appeals to the refugees or their "suffering brethren in Kashmir." Another opposition group agitated for an independent "Pakthunistan" as a potential homeland for the Pathans who lived near the Afghanistan border. The scheduled castes maintained their own party organization, and the Socialists tried without success to make inroads into the monopoly political position of the Moslem League. The *Azad Pakistan* of Free Pakistan Party used the word *Free* for its propaganda appeal, but it appeared actually as a Communist front.

The Communists were less successful in Pakistan than in India. As early as 1934, the Communists of India went on record as supporting autonomous regions for all sections of the Indian people who have common historic traditions, common language, culture, psychological make-up and common economic life. On this basis the Communists defended Pakistan; they joined with the Moslem League against their mutual enemy—the Indian Congress—on Direct Action Day (August 16, 1946). But the cooperation between the Communists and the Moslem League was nothing more than a marriage of convenience. The Communists gained some sympathy and open support by their intellectual position in favor of reform, but they lost public favor by an abortive plot to assassinate the existing leaders and to set up a military dictatorship in 1951. Communists in East Pakistan carried on active campaigns through cheap books and magazines, and they constantly stirred up demonstrations and riots. They harped on the achievements of Russia and China and incessantly belabored the United States. In 1954 they overreached themselves, goading the government into outlawing the Communist party and forcing it underground.

Most of Pakistan's political problems were deeply rooted in desperate poverty. Pakistan was poorer than India. Ninety percent of the people derived their living from agriculture, and after partition they needed everything for economic development. They needed water for their parched lands, factories for their raw materials, and improved transport facilities to enable them to earn a little money from international commerce. In West Pakistan, the critical need was water.

Kashmir was of great strategic importance because of its location near the source of some of Pakistan's important rivers. Pakistan was at the mercy of India, which controlled the upstream territory in the valley of the Indus and its tributaries. Arguments between the two countries over water rights might have led to blows had not the World Bank stepped in with generous plans to assist both countries in the development of dams, reservoirs, and irrigation canals.

In East Pakistan, the vital challenge was to establish a new trade pattern which would enable Pakistani farmers and Calcutta mill owners to cooperate for their mutual profit. Before partition, cotton, jute, and wheat moved easily from the countryside to the factories of Calcutta; after partition, the growers and processors of raw materials were in different countries, and they engaged in unremitting economic warfare. Furthermore, it was the agricultural surplus of East Pakistan which enabled Pakistan to pay for factory products for which it was entirely dependent upon India or the outside world. Pakistan naturally wanted an industrial system of its own; yet how could it raise the money, apart from foreign loans? Pakistan placed a special levy on exports of jute, and in retaliation India raised still higher the price of finished jute products. Pakistan then placed export duties on cotton, hides, and skins; India came back with added charges on shipments of machine-made cloth, cotton yarns, oil seeds, vegetable oils, and coal.

A crisis occurred in 1949 when sterling-bloc countries, including India, devalued their currency. Pakistan did not devalue, which had the effect of reducing the value of the money owed by Pakistan to India, reducing the value of India's exports, and increasing the purchasing power of Pakistan. India severed trade relations, but both countries suffered. Coal piled up in India, and factory workers in Calcutta lost their jobs. Pakistan was unable to market its crops. The situation was saved by the Korean War, which boomed the demand for all raw materials. A dark crisis changed to mad prosperity, and Pakistan adopted grandiose plans for industrialization. But the affluence disappeared as suddenly as it came. The end of the Korean War meant that the bottom dropped out of the jute market, and this happened in a sad harvest season. Hunger in Pakistan reached famine proportions in 1952. The demonstrations of hungry people forced the army to take over to keep the peace. It was open to grave doubt whether Pakistan could survive as a democracy and whether it was ready in a democratic way to cope with problems of government and development.

In such circumstances the government was unable to show substantial progress by way of social change. Peasants were too preoccupied with getting enough to eat to worry about their rights vis-à-vis the landlords. Workers were thankful for jobs, whatever the working conditions. Embryo labor organizations had no economic bargaining power; they only jockeyed for political position by joining one side or the other in the tug of war between the communistic Trades Union Congress and the non-Communist All-Pakistan Confederation of Labor. Religious battles were fought outside the arena of politics. Although social modernists were indignant about such inequalities as the seclusion of women, the zest for reform had to be sidetracked while the country wrestled with the fundamental problem of survival.

South Asia in World Affairs

When India and Pakistan achieved their independence, they elected to stay within the British Commonwealth. On February 4, 1948, they were joined by their smaller neighbor to the south—Ceylon—and the three nations as component members of the Commonwealth gave South Asia a new and influential voice in world affairs.

In many respects, Ceylon is to the subcontinent what the island of Formosa is to the mainland of China. At the time of independence, it was a nation of some eight million people. Its constitution provided for a parliamentary form of government, complete with governor-general, prime minister, and bicameral legislature. Actual power was contained in the hands of a high-caste, economically prosperous, English-speaking elite. Ceylon enjoyed a higher level of living than its neighbors thanks to the cinnamon, rubber, tea, coconut, and cocoa plantations which were superimposed on its small-scale peasant rice economy. Like other nations in Asia, Ceylon noted the gap between the rich and the poor and the lack of a middle class which was needed as a foundation for democracy and bourgeois prosperity. Therefore Ceylon determined to create an economic structure which would be in keeping with its newly won status of political independence. Its problems were complicated by personal rivalries between its various leaders and by the cultural diversity of its people. Bitter feelings prevented satisfactory cooperation between the Buddhist, Singhalese-speaking majority and Hindu Tamil-speaking, Moslem Urdu-speaking, or Christian English-speaking minorities. Fortunately for its own future Ceylon boasted a seventy-percent literacy rate and was endowed with an English-type educational system which offered free education to every young Ceylonese from the village primary schools to an excellent national university.

All three nations experienced common problems because of their membership in the commonwealth. They were new. Consequently they were concerned about matters of status and fiercely jealous of their prestige. They resented every evidence of racism or "Jim Crowism." They disapproved the policies of South Africa—or anyone else within or without the commonwealth—which granted non-whites less than complete equality in immigration, or rights of domicile, franchise, trade, or intermarriage. The respective governments expressed their deep moral convictions on these issues at every opportunity although they refused to become enmeshed in diplomatic arguments on behalf of their overseas nationals. In general matters of international politics, India tended to look toward the east, particularly toward Southeast Asia. On the other hand, Pakistan concerned itself more in the West because of its interest in the welfare of the Moslem world.

India quickly assumed leadership in speaking for "Asia," whose common denominator was anti-imperialism and poverty. As soon as Nehru was released from jail in 1945, he visited Indonesia and Singapore and expressed his conviction that these areas should be self-governing. In September, while the flames of World War II were still burning, the Indian National Congress passed a resolution asking for freedom from imperial domination not only for India but also for Burma, Malaya, Indochina, and Indonesia. In 1947, before India was partitioned, Nehru called an Asian Relations Conference of twenty-eight countries from all parts of Asia including the Central Asian republics belonging to the Soviet Union. The agenda included such topics as national movements for freedom, national problems and inter-Asian migration, transition from colonial to national economy, agricultural reconstruction and industrial development, labor problems and social services, cultural problems, and status of women and women's movements. The leaders of Asia who attended the conference stressed the advantages of Asian solidarity against any encroachment from the West, but some statesmen, including Nehru himself, reminded Asians that they were also human beings with obligations extending beyond Asia to all mankind.

In December 1948, after a Dutch police action against Indonesians, India convened a second conference, sometimes called the Second Asian Relations Conference, with focus on Indonesia. Nineteen nations attended, but no delegates came from Soviet Central Asia. The conference called the Dutch action "naked and unabashed aggression" and declared that Asia which was too long submissive to others "would no longer brook any interference with her freedom." The resolutions of the conference were passed on to the United Nations for consideration, and in this action can be seen the beginnings of an Arab-Asian bloc as a pressure group in international organizations. Some Asian nations, under the inspiration of India, imposed sanctions on the Dutch by denying them transit facilities for men and supplies by land, sea, or air.

As soon as possible, India gave its full attention to international matters at home. India wished to rid itself of the embarrassing establishments of France in Pondicherry and of Portugal in Goa. After British sovereignty was withdrawn from Indian soil, it was inevitable that the French and Portuguese anachronisms of empire should follow. India was eager to define its position with states with whom it shared a common border. Kashmir was impossible, and the dispute dragged on. India signed a treaty with Bhutan in 1949 by which India agreed not to interfere in internal affairs of Bhutan and in exchange Bhutan agreed to be guided by the advice of the government of India in regard to external relations. In 1950 a treaty with Sikkim provided that the latter should be a protectorate of India. Indian troops were to be stationed in Sikkim and all its foreign relations were to be conducted through India. The prime minister of Sikkim was to be an Indian official appointed by Delhi. In 1950 India also came to terms with Nepal. Both India and Nepal recognized each other's complete territorial integrity and sovereignty, but India exerted great influence in democratic movements against the Rana family, which had exercised unchallenged power in Nepal for more than one hundred years. India adjusted its boundaries with Afghanistan on the west and Burma on the east, but it made no progress in locating the precise frontiers with China—which extended over a thousand miles of jungles, jagged mountains, and deserts.

Neither India nor Pakistan expressed undue alarm because of the victory of the Communists in China. Both recognized the new government of China at an early date and advocated its admission into the United Nations. They discarded Chiang Kai-shek in favor of Mao Tse-tung when the former lost his grip on the Chinese revolution. They were willing that China should become united and strong, even under the Communists; they did not fear that China would become a Russian satellite. Nehru's only quarrel with China was over questions relating to the border. He was apprehensive when Chinese troops invaded Tibet in October 1950, but his protests were fruitless. The Chinese argued that India could not properly concern itself with Tibet, because Tibet was an integral part of Chinese territory. Nevertheless, India and China began a long series of negotiations which were to cover the entire gamut of trade, boundaries, and peaceful relations.

India and Pakistan felt that they had a vital interest in every situation in Asia which contained the seeds of misunderstanding, although India was far more active than Pakistan in the perpetual "brush-fire wars" in East Asia. India warned the United Nations that China would enter the war in Korea, if the UN forces should cross the thirty-eighth parallel. India also refused to brand China as an aggressor and worked incessantly for the return of peace. In spite of strong anti-imperialist feelings India refused to become involved in civil war in Vietnam or the emergency in Malaya. India wanted all Asians to get together. It refused to sign the peace treaty with Japan because it believed Japan was immediately entitled to full and complete sovereignty. For the sake of peace in Asia, India urged Japan and China to strive to find a new basis for political and economic cooperation.

India, in particular, became identified with the international procedure known as "nonalignment" or "neutralism." India refused to commit itself either to the communists or anti-communists in the cold war, and refused to choose between one ideology or another when the quarrels stemmed from roots which were not Indian. India suggested that some communist ideas, such as anti-imperialism, equality in racial relations, planned economic development, and social justice might be more useful for India than American-style democracy, private capital, and free enterprise. Nehru said that he was far from being a communist and that he was too much of a bourgeois and a liberal to stand for dogmatism, regimentation, and heresy hunts. He could not accept the atheism of communism, and he declared that India would never pay the price which China and Russia paid for progress. Nehru condemned India's Communists for looking abroad for orders and inspiration and castigated them as India's worst reactionaries and counterrevolutionaries.

India did not share the American alarm that communists—Russian, Chinese, and every other variety—were out to conquer the world. India saw the rivalry between Russia and China, on the one hand, and the United States on the other, as primarily a power struggle. Nehru believed that the national interests of India could best be promoted by an active, independent foreign policy which would not align India with one military bloc or the other. He said that his tactics of neutralism did not indicate neutrality of belief or convictions, but should be interpreted as George Washington's type of neutrality or Thomas Jefferson's doctrine of no entangling alliances.

India had little real knowledge of the United States because, until World War II, Indians from India were comparative strangers in the United States, and few Americans tried to make themselves or their country understood in India. After the war, India was convinced that Americans concentrated too much on the cold war and consequently the United States made unwise decisions everywhere in Asia: in China, Korea, Indochina, Indonesia, Formosa, and Japan. India was quick to point out the paradox between the American refusal to recognize the People's Republic of China and the precipitate recognition of Israel. Indian leaders pointed out that Americans were prone to champion the imperial European powers in their last struggles in Asia, and were inclined to favor landlords and capitalistic entrepreneurs to the detriment of peasants and workers. Americans were charged with timidity in taking an uncompromising stand for racial equality and the welfare of the underprivileged. It was a common complaint that the United States forgot its own revolutionary background and favored the *status quo* rather than the necessity for change.

India, representing a large segment of Asia's thoughtful leaders, considered that the greatest motivating forces in international affairs were the psychological aspirations for equality, dignity, and self-respect and the economic drive for a better life for Asia's millions. On these premises it selected its friends and associates. Nehru said "We are not going to join in a war if we can help it, and we will join the side which is to our interest when the choice must be made." He wanted war with none, friendship with all. "Peace, freedom and racial equality—for the rest we will not interfere with others and we will not permit them to interfere with us."

SUGGESTED READING

Binder, Leonard, *Religion and Politics in Pakistan* (Berkeley, U. of California, 1961).

Bourke-White, Margaret, *Half-Way to Freedom* (New York, Simon, 1949).

Bowles, Chester, *Ambassador's Report* (New York, Harper, 1954).

Brown, W. H. Norman, (ed.), *India, Pakistan, Ceylon* (Ithaca, Cornell U., 1951).

Callard, Keith, *Pakistan, Political Forces in Pakistan* (New York, Macmillan, 1959).

Campbell-Johnson, A., *Mission with Mountbatten* (London, R. Hale, 1952).

Jeffries, Sir Charles, *Ceylon: Path to Independence* (New York, Praeger, 1963).

Markandaya, Kamala, *Nectar in a Sieve* (New York, Signet, 1956).

McKim, Marriott, (ed.), *Village India* (Chicago, U. of Chicago, 1955).

Menon, V. P., *Story of the Integration of Indian States* (Princeton, Princeton U., 1956).

———, *Transfer of Power in India* (Princeton, Princeton U., 1957).

Moon, Penderel, *Divide and Quit* (London, Faber & Faber, 1961).

Nehru, Jawaharlal, *Independence and After* (Delhi, Publications Division, Ministry of Information and Broadcasting, Government of India, 1949).

Sayeed, Khalid Bin, *Pakistan, the Formative Phase* (New York, Institute of Pacific Relations, 1960).

Singh, Khushwant, *Mano Majra* (New York, Grove, 1956).

Symonds, Richard, *Making of Pakistan* (London, Faber & Faber, 1950).

Talbot, Phillips, (ed.), *South Asia in the World Today* (Chicago, U. of Chicago, 1949).

Tuker, Sir F., *While Memory Serves* (London, Cassell, 1950).

Vakil, C. N., *Economic Consequences of Divided India* (Bombay, Vora, 1950).

27

The New World in Southeast Asia

Events in India and Pakistan foreshadowed the transition which occurred in Southeast Asia after World War II. It was apparent that the day of imperialism had come to an end. Neither Great Britain, the United States, France, nor the Netherlands could have restored their previous position of power, even if they had so desired. It was a moment of rampant nationalism, with shouts of freedom and independence in the air. Burma, immediately, and Malaya, after a painful interlude, cut their close political bonds with Great Britain. The Philippines assumed its new status as a fully independent country as scheduled on July 4, 1946. The peoples of Indochina, under the leadership of Ho Chi Minh, fought for eight long years against the French. The Indonesians likewise chose war rather than submission to the stubborn Dutch. They would not be cheated out of the "independence" which they felt the Japanese had brought them. Thailand had no colonial yoke to throw off, but it had to cast out its old leaders in order to resume a place of honor in the seething new world of Southeast Asia.

Throughout the entire region, the pain and ashes of war seemed to matter less than the quiet hope of a kinder future. A new generation of leaders tolerated no such words as hardship and responsibility, but they charmed their followers with wild assurance that everything would be better—much better—with the end of imperialism and feudalism. The war destroyed old standards of value and symbols of prestige. Stability, law and order, and jobs with the foreigners were no longer prized. It was important only to put an end to treatment as "second class citizens" and to achieve full recognition of nationhood and absolute sovereignty. Nothing less would relieve their psychological frustrations or satisfy their yearning for self-respect. Without permitting any questions about ability or readiness, the new leaders demanded full and complete equality in the family of nations. The gap between the leaders and followers must be underscored. Fewer than five percent of the people constituted the sophisticated elite, with any awareness of the deep significance of political events. Ninety-five percent were the masses—the "wonderful goddam peasants" as a Filipino writer bitterly called them—with no interests beyond their personal lives and no political fate except to patter the line of their accepted spokesmen.

In a sense, the situation was revolutionary. The goals of political independence, economic prosperity across the board, and social justice were not new; the spirit of "no delay and no compromise" was so unaccustomed and so determined as to be revolutionary. The tempo of the revolt of Asia speeded up; Asians wished to do the work of a century in a single day. This did not mean that conditions were tailor-made for the communists. Turmoil would have been prevalent had there been no communists around. The communists, too, bore the stigma of "imperialists" because they were either citizens or tools of a foreign power. But the communists proved themselves to be more adept than their rivals in utilizing conditions of chaos, inequality, and poverty for their own advantage. They concentrated not on the leaders, but on the masses. They organized the neglected and the underprivileged—peasants, laborers, soldiers, women, students, low-grade civil servants, and teachers—and tried to convince these groups that communism was the wave of the future. They posed as apostles of peace and called imperialists the "warmongers." They talked little about internationalism and the withering away of the state; they worked hard to gain control of nationalist movements.

Nationalism was the dominant theme in the history of Southeast Asia after World War II—unbridled, assertive nationalism—late by a hundred years in a world which was being rapidly driven into cooperation and interdependence. When independent nationhood was not complete, the first order of business was to make it so. Lesser themes were the quest for a workable form of government; agricultural improvement and economic development; and continuing change, or modernization in the social structure. The record of each country—Burma, Malaya, Philippines, Thailand, Indonesia, and the component parts of Indochina—can be best understood by stressing those themes and their local variations.

Union of Burma

Immediately after the liberation of Burma, the British returned with ideas for the future of Burma incorporated in a White Paper of May 17, 1945. They intended to re-establish civil government, hold elections, and

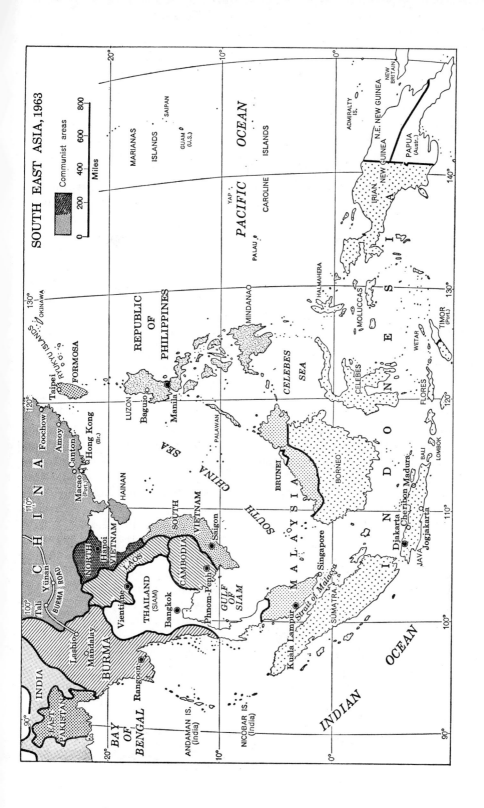

SOUTH EAST ASIA, 1963

Communist areas

Miles
0   200   400   600   800

to begin to draft a constitution which would assist Burma to attain complete self-government within the commonwealth as soon as circumstances permitted. The British were vitally interested in the immediate reconstruction of Burma's economy, particularly the profitable British business firms in Burma. The Burmese were not satisfied with any such selfish Fabian program. Aung San emerged from the war as a national hero and the unquestioned leader of the Anti-Fascist People's Freedom League (AFPFL). He insisted upon a major voice in Burma's future, and he came out for complete independence. Strikes and banditry increased throughout Burma, and only speedy measures on the part of the Attlee government in London averted a civil war. London agreed to the immediate election of a constitutional assembly and to negotiation for independence within or without the commonwealth.

In July 1947, Aung San and six of his colleagues were machine-gunned in cold blood by assassins hired by U Saw. Political responsibility passed into the hands of Thakin Nu, or U Nu, as he was subsequently known. Under his leadership a constitution was drawn up in September 1947 for the republic of the Union of Burma. *Union* was the key word because the new state was composed of Burma proper and the Shan, Karen, and Kachin states. Real unity was difficult to achieve because of the divergent minority groups, many of whom lived in the strategic frontier areas. The constitution provided for a French-style president and a British-style cabinet. It called for a bicameral legislature—a Chamber of Deputies and a Chamber of Nationalities. The former was made up of 250 members elected by all citizens over eighteen. The latter consisted of 125 members representing the various ethnic groups of Burma. The constitution guaranteed customary human rights and civil liberties and laid the foundations for a socialized welfare state.

The constitution of 1947 reflected the philosophy of socialism. It guaranteed private property and private initiative, but it gave the state the right to limit foreign property and to expropriate with due compensation. The constitution permitted nationalization of natural resources, water transport, rice export, and national financial institutions. Provision was made for national economic planning, state ownership of public utilities, and state aid to economic organizations "not working for private property." The state was to concern itself with the raising of the standard of living of its peoples and to be the most active agent in converting Burma into *Pyidawtha*, or a happy welfare land.

Supported by the new constitution, U Nu journeyed to London to sign with Prime Minister Attlee a treaty by which Great Britain recognized the complete independence and full sovereignty of its former colony. The Nu-Attlee agreement also covered matters of citizenship and finance. Great Britain conceled many of Burma's debts but insisted upon payment for British properties lost by nationalization. A supplementary defense agreement, extended in 1954, stipulated that Great Britain would send appropriate military missions to Burma and would provide needed military supplies and assistance. On January 4, 1948, at 4:20 a.m.—the exact moment determined by Burmese astrologers—the independent Union of Burma came into existence.

Chaos followed independence. Law and order disappeared with the removal of British economic power and the British army. The inherently unstable social order collapsed. Burmese and minority groups went after each other like fighting cocks. The governing elite—which was smaller and younger in Burma than in other countries of Southeast Asia—splintered into irreconcilable factions. U Nu kept his hand on the Socialist Party, which was the dominant force in the AFPFL. But part of the former freedom fighters, calling themselves the People's Volunteer Organization (PVO), rebelled. The Communists divided themselves into Stalinist and Trotskyite factions and separately resumed civil war. To cap the climax, the Karen national defense organization, with some of the best soldiers in Burma, took up arms against the government. The countryside was unsafe and travel impossible. Only four or five cities, including Rangoon, were secure.

U Nu's government was sorely tried. Fortunately its enemies were as bitter against each other as against the central authority. Slowly the government extended its fiat beyond Rangoon and subdued the rebellious factions, one after another. U Nu built up the army and created the Union's military police. He activated village defense forces to fight bandits. He refused to listen to the "demands" of insurgents, but he promised good treatment to all who would surrender. He proceeded on the assumption that pacification could not be achieved by arms alone but would inevitably have to be followed by reforms in every field.

He began by sponsoring religious revival among the Buddhists. He established the bureau of special investigation (BSI) to weed out graft and corruption in the government. He advocated educational improvement, better public health, and cheaper housing. He set up the Burma translation society for foreign books. He popularized the slogan, "Love Burma, Speak Burmese, Encourage Burmese Literature." He tried to put his doctrinaire socialism in practice to remove economic abuses and social injustices. He proclaimed programs for redistribution of land, better tenancy conditions and easier credit, reclamation and irrigation, and amelioration or elimination of debts. His words were grandiose, but they were empty. Nevertheless, by 1951 he felt that he had made sufficient progress to risk a general election. Highways and rivers were not completely safe, villages were not free from payments of protection money, and ministers in Rangoon lived behind armed guards; yet the integrity of the state was no longer in question.

The government distinguished itself for its moderation. It was tempted to expropriate all foreign property, but it appreciated the need for foreign capital. Therefore it treated foreign investments with consideration and announced as its immediate aims joint operation rather than nationalization. However, it followed a disastrous policy in the marketing of its great export crop—rice. Burma set up a state agricultural marketing board which bought rice from the peasants (thus putting the Chinese middlemen out of business) and sold the rice abroad for four or five times its purchase price. The profits were welcome, but eventually the gouging led to disaster. When the bottom fell out of the rice market, as it did in 1954, the Communists used the economic calamity for their political advantage. They spread tales among the rice growers that the rice monopoly was corrupt and inefficient, and they urged the peasants to switch their support from the Socialists to the communistic Burma Workers' and Peasants' Party.

Ideology was not for the masses, but only for the political elite. Ideology as it developed in Burma was a combination of Buddhism, with its desire to escape from the world, and socialism, with its determination to improve the world. Burmese socialism consisted of prewar Marxism plus a devotion to the welfare state adopted from the British Labour Party. Burmese leaders did not consider socialism as disguised communism or as a step toward communism. They rejected any marriage of convenience with the Communists. They committed themselves to the support of democracy, as an internal political system, and they rejected communist amoralism on the issue of means and ends. In opposing the old imperialism of the Western powers, they showed equally fervent hostility to the new imperialism of the Communists. They considered the Soviet type of imperialism even more degrading and dangerous, because it was "more ruthless, more systematic and more blatantly justified in the name of the world Communist revolution." The government handled its internal Communist problem as a domestic matter, well within the government's power to regulate and control. In spite of the Communists' seductive slogans of "No Rents, No Taxes and No Foreign Landlords," they were hopelessly divided by their own opportunism. They were a disruptive force, using all their wiles and strength in underground deviltry and open dissension. But they were unable to gain control of the government or to capture the leadership of the national movement. The Burma Communist Party was outlawed in 1953.

Burma, from the beginning, sought to promote its national interests by the policy of "neutralism" or noncommitment to either side in the cold war. It was the first nation outside the Soviet satellite bloc to extend recognition to the People's Republic of China; but it maintained cordial, correct relations with the United Kingdom and the United States. Burma was not overfriendly with Thailand, with which it had waged centuries of bloody wars, but was sympathetic to the new and struggling Republic of Indonesia. Burma looked with approval on the nationalism of Ho Chi Minh but showed no concern for the fate of Chiang Kai-shek. Because of common interest in socialist activities, Burma was especially cordial in its relations with Israel and Yugoslavia.

Sponsored by the United States and Great Britain, Burma was admitted to the United Nations in 1948. It supported the original UN resolutions to take action in Korea, but it voted against branding Red China as a participant in aggression. It joined the Colombo Plan in 1952 and (until 1954) agreed to accept economic aid from the United States. Burma refused to attend the San Francisco Peace Conference with Japan and took until 1954 to make its own peace and reparations settlement with its former enemy. Although Peking labeled U Nu as an "imperialist stooge," the Burmese prime minister avoided close identity with the policies of the United States or Great Britain. He wanted no part of America's crusade against communism, but he insisted upon no diminution of the fight against colonialism. He stood firmly against attachment to any alien ideology and declared his main objective to be "coexistence and concentration on Asia's real war, the war against want."

MALAYA, SINGAPORE, AND BORNEO

The transition from colonialism to nationhood was slower in Malaya than in Burma, because it was delayed by the twin obstacles of communalism and communism. For six months after the Japanese surrender, the British governed Malaya with a military administration which restored law and order, but not without charges of corruption, illegal commandeering of property, gunplay against unarmed civilians, and sale of arms to gangsters. Late in 1945 a British diplomat, Sir Harold Mac-Michael, induced all the sultans to sign treaties which surrendered to the king of England sovereignty and the right to make future constitutional arrangements. On the basis of these treaties, the British set up a protectorate which was to be called the Malayan Union. It was to consist of the nine Malay States, together with Penang and Malacca; it was to exclude Singapore. Sovereignty was transferred formally from the sultans to the British Crown, and a common citizenship was created for Chinese and Malays.

The establishment of the Union aroused a storm of protest. Malays disliked the shabby treatment of the sultans and the grant of citizenship to the Chinese. The Chinese objected to the separate status of Singapore. Indians in Malaya lamented that they were overlooked. In an astute strategic retreat, the British transformed the Malayan Union into a new federation of Malaya, which was inaugurated on February 1, 1948, by the joint action of King George VI and the nine sultans. The king retained complete control of defense and foreign affairs, and the sultans, although restored to nominal sovereignty, engaged to rule in accordance with British advice. The federation was to be governed by a high commissioner, assisted by executive and legislative councils. Malayans were given special consideration and citizenship rules were tightened to discriminate against the Chinese. Singapore was not included in the federation; it was continued as a separate crown colony with its own British governor. Any advance toward self-government or dominion status within the British Commonwealth for Malaya would not necessarily include Singapore, but Singapore was given the option of joining the federation with the mutual consent of both parties.

Upon their return to Malaya, the British gave prior attention to economic affairs. Rubber and tin were important dollar earners for the commonwealth, and the British firms were eager to re-establish the profitable position which they had enjoyed before the Japanese invasion. The British government entered into international agreements for price control and marketing which the Malayans felt were to their detriment. However, Malayan feelings were pacified by a development program which represented a practical compromise between government planning and private enterprise. This program called for a balanced growth in agricultural production and industrialization and for expansion in education and the social services. The interests of Malayan farmers, poor Chinese shopkeepers, and Indian plantation workers were taken care of, including the health and education of their children. Good prices for tin and rubber brought a substantial dollar income to Malaya, but prosperity was elusive because of the guerrilla warfare commonly known as the "Emergency."

After 1948 the Communists shifted their major operations from strikes and riots in Singapore to terrorism in Malaya. The Communists were anticapitalist and antiforeign. They killed and kidnaped rich Chinese and prosperous British planters. They ambushed travelers, wrecked trains, and destroyed rubber trees. Those who had won British approval as the Malaya peoples' anti-Japanese army transformed themselves into a Malayan races liberation army, dedicated to the destruction of the British economy and the expulsion of British political control. A hard core of some six thousand guerrilla fighters in the jungle, aided by the *min yuen,* or Chinese villagers, cost Malaya one-fourth of the national income for pacification. It took the regular army, the air force, the home guards, and the volunteers to beat the terrorists. More important, it was shown that military measures alone could not beat the communists. The government was obliged to supplement its military measures with a vast resettlement program for Chinese squatters. Final victory was not achieved until all the communities in Malaya were convinced that their interests were served by good government, and that good government was synonymous with self-government. As an antidote to communism, the British adjusted themselves to the swelling tide of Malayan nationalism.

The demands for nationhood in Malaya as elsewhere came from the Western-educated elite, not from the fishermen, farmers, workers, or small shopkeepers. A graduate of Cambridge, Tengku Abdul Rahman, took the leadership in organizing an alliance of Malays, Chinese, and Indians dedicated to freedom for Malaya. When the various communities decided to bury their differences for the sake of unity and independence, their progress was spectacular. They obtained a cabinet system for Malaya and more Malayan representation in the federation government. Elections were authorized on the local and then on the national level. In the first elections of 1955, the Malayan-Chinese-Indian (MCI) alliance party won fifty-one of fifty-two contested seats in the legislature and polled eighty-four percent of the votes. After that, the British conceded there was no future in Malaya except in retirement; and with the Malayans they worked out a scheme for transition to self-rule.

A joint commission of distinguished jurists formulated a constitution which provided for independence within the Commonwealth. The actual process of transferring sovereignty was an exemplary demonstration of successful statecraft. In August 1957, a paramount ruler was selected by the various sultans; he signed an agreement with the high commissioner which ended British jurisdiction in Malaya. Arrangements were entered into which provided for continuing military cooperation and economic assistance. On the last day of August, the duke of Gloucester, representing the queen, formally transferred power to Tengku Abdul Rahman, the chief minister of Malaya, who read the declaration of independence of Malaya to the crowd assembled in Kuala Lumpur for the festivities. At midnight the lights in the stadium went out (eight minutes late) and then came on again to signify the beginning of the new regime. *Merdeka,* or freedom, was announced by the roll of drums, the unfurling of the flag, the 101-gun salute, and the Moslem call to prayer.

Self-rule for Singapore was longer delayed. The problems were more difficult because of the Chinese make-up of the city, its commercial importance, and the value of the British naval base. The state of Singapore—distinctly separate from Malaya—was launched in 1959. It was given full internal self-government and a Singapore citizenship. Singapore was granted the right to choose its own head of state and legislative assembly.

The first election, held on May 30, 1959, resulted in an overwhelming victory for the People's Action Party, which won forty-three out of fifty-one seats. A third-generation Straits Chinese, son of a prosperous merchant family and a law graduate from Cambridge, named Lee Kuan-yew, became the state of Singapore's first prime minister. His powers extended only to internal affairs—not to defense or external relations—and in security matters he was obliged to confer with representatives of Great Britain and Malaya. As long as such limitations as these existed, it was sure that further adjustments would be required in relations to the federation of Malaya and the rest of the commonwealth and in the independent status of Singapore itself.

A short distance across the South China Sea, the British possessions in Borneo showed signs that they too expected a future beyond the confines of colonialism. At the beginning of World War II, Britain had four separate regimes in Borneo: Sarawak, under British protection and ruled by the third of the "White Rajahs" of the Brooke Dynasty; North Borneo, also a British protectorate and ruled by the British North Borneo Company; Brunei, embedded in Sarawak and also under British protection; finally, the island of Labuan, directly administered from Singapore. After the war, the British made separate crown colonies out of Sarawak and North Borneo. The latter absorbed Labuan. Brunei resumed its status as a protectorate in 1946 with the assistance of the British Resident. All three areas showed unmistakable signs of political unrest and the urge toward self-government. The idea of amalgamation of the British territories in Borneo, or the more ambitious project of federation with Malaya and Singapore, seemed feasible and reasonable to British colonial administrators—but not so to the oil-rich sultan of Brunei nor to Borneo's neighbors in Indonesia and the Philippines.

REPUBLIC OF THE PHILIPPINES

Never were birth pangs more agonizing than those of the republic of the Philippines. President Quezon had died in exile and President Osmeña succeeded him. Osmeña had waded ashore at Leyte with General MacArthur; and in February, 1945, he returned his government to Manila. In June he reconvened the congress. Of twenty-four senators, seven were dead, and seven were in the hands of the counterintelligence corps. Of ninety-eight representatives, seven had been arrested, twenty had been in the puppet assembly, eleven had taken jobs under the Japanese, and the others were dead or missing. The government was helpless. Important decisions on all matters were made by the American army, which was preparing for the invasion of Japan. With only token authority, President Osmeña prepared for independence.

He relied upon American policies as personified by the new high commissioner, Paul McNutt. The major problems were agrarian unrest, disposal of ex-enemy property, investigation and trial of collaborators, reorganization of the Philippine constabulary, restoration of economic activity, and preparation for new elections. There was no starvation— the army took care of that—but otherwise chaos reigned. Time was required before the American promises for reconstruction and rehabilitation could be fulfilled. The American Congress passed two acts—the Tydings or Philippine Rehabilitation Act and the Bell or Philippine Trade Act—in 1946. The first made $620,000,000 immediately available for rehabilitation, and the second provided for preferential trade arrangements until 1974. The trade act contained a controversial clause, known as the "parity clause," which guaranteed Americans parity with Filipinos in the development and utilization of public lands and natural resources in the Philippines for the duration of the period of trade privileges.

Elections were held in the Philippines on April 23, 1946, while many parts of the country were still under the control of the military. The candidates were President Osmeña and Eulogio Rodriguez for the old-time Nacionalistas, and Manuel Roxas and Elpidio Quirino for the newly-formed Liberals, or liberal wing of the Nacionalistas. The Liberals, energized by the younger, more dynamic Manuel Roxas, gained the support of most Americans, the press, the landlord class, the church, and the civil service. The issues were collaboration, personalities, and alleged influence with the United States; but the election was won by the simple fact that the Liberals controlled the ballot box. Shortly after the elections, independence became a fact. On July 4, 1946, the American flag came down; and the republic of the Philippines was born.

President Roxas did his best to utilize the vast sums of American aid for the benefit of the nation as a whole. But government functionaries became too engrossed in the game of making quick profits. Humble people who received money wanted to buy petty luxuries of which they had been deprived for years. Imports raced ahead of exports, and dollars siphoned back into the United States. Production lagged and taxes fell off. Danger signals warned of hard times ahead.

As an issue, collaboration disappeared. In January 1948, President Roxas granted a general amnesty. His great problem was agrarian unrest. The peasant movement had fallen into the hands of the Communist-led *Hukbalahap,* or Anti-Japanese People's Liberation Army, which was renamed simply The People's Liberation Army. The Huks protested against the fraternization between the Americans and the *haciendéros,* and they opposed the Roxas administration as a mere puppet of the American imperialists. The Huk leaders adopted a program which went far beyond the requirements of agrarian reform. The Huks supported the losing ticket of the Nacionalistas in the elections of 1946; they were successful, however, in electing seven of their candidates, including their leader Luis Taruc, to the congress. They were refused their seats by the committee on elections. Violence ensued, and President Roxas ordered the constabulary to give them neither rest nor quarter. He branded them as Communists and as such refused to allow them a place in the government.

The Huk situation went from bad to worse. The rice-bowl provinces were kept in a state of constant uneasiness as ordinary farmers were victimized both by Huks and the constabulary. In March, 1948, the Huks were outlawed, and their forays became increasingly brutal. Robberies, kidnapings and daylight assaults on buses, trucks, and trains were daily occurrences.

President Roxas remarshaled his forces. He initiated a land reform program and launched a new move for industrialization. He sought to cure unrest by removing its causes. He launched financial reforms which led to the creation of the central bank and the imposition of import and exchange controls. He introduced legislation which discriminated against aliens, particularly the Chinese, in seeking a greater share for Filipinos in the economic life of the nation. Before these measures could be completed, President Roxas died. He was succeeded by his vice-president, Elpidio Quirino, who lacked the ability to cope with his economic tasks. President Quirino devoted himself to politics and to re-election. He defeated his opponent, largely due to terroristic methods and mass frauds. Quirino's victory only served to alienate the people further from the government. The economy continued to deteriorate. At the time of the invasion of Korea, the republic of the Philippines faced political and economic bankruptcy.

In the summer of 1950, President Quirino invited the all-American Bell Economic Survey Mission to the Philippines. The mission sounded an alarm for immediate action. The Philippines and the United States agreed to an improvement program. The Philippines would reform land legislation and the tax system, and would pass a minimum wage law. The United States would grant $250,000,000 in loans over a five-year period.

The local law and order situation took a turn for the better when the dynamic Ramón Magsaysay—former guerrilla captain, trucking operator, and congressman—was made secretary of defense. Magsaysay demonstrated his vigor and his political acumen in a successful campaign against the Huks. He brought a new sense of responsibility to the army. When he went after the Huks, he destroyed them or he won them. He under-stood the harsh realities of poverty which drove men to rebellion. He held out hope for new life to those who would surrender. He broke the back of the Huk movement by means which were more effective than mili-tary force.

He soon overshadowed President Quirino with his popularity. The Quirino administration took credit for the restoration of order, but it could not live down its reputation for graft and corruption. The press regularly headlined scandals in real estate deals, school supplies, Chinese immigra-tion quotas, surplus property, crop loans, and import licenses. Whether from jealousy on the part of Quirino, or disgust or ambition on the part of Magsaysay, the two men came to a parting of the ways. Magsaysay left the Quirino cabinet to become the president of his country—and the herald of a new era in the history of the republic of the Philippines.

Before that era began, the Philippines was obliged to make funda-mental readjustments in its foreign relations. Invasion and liberation gave the Filipinos a new appreciation of their own nationalism. Henceforth it was not enough to be anti-Spanish or anti-American or anti-Japanese. They would have to be pro-Philippines. They could not afford to be exclusively a passenger on an American ship; they would have to navigate their own craft. In Asia, this meant they had to make peace with Japan, to learn to live with China, and to forge closer links with their Asian neighbors, whom they had largely ignored. Filipino delegates attended the New Delhi conferences on Asian Relations and on Indonesia; and they con-vened, in 1950, an inter-Asian conference on cultural and economic affairs at Baguio. They participated actively in the world of the Economic Com-mittee for Asia and the Far East and other United Nations agencies in Southeast Asia. President Quirino explored with Syngman Rhee and Chiang Kai-shek the possibilities of a united anti-Communist stand in Asia.

The Philippines faced its most troublesome dilemma in relations with the United States. Close ties were welcome—in economic assistance and mutual security—but not subservience. The Philippines signed agree-ments with the United States for military assistance in 1947 and for eco-nomic cooperation in 1950. In addition the two countries entered into a treaty for mutual defense in 1951 at the time of the San Francisco Peace Conference with Japan. Above all, Filipino officials worked to prevent a sharp clash between chauvinistic young nationalism and American friend-ship. President Quirino quarreled with the United States over such mat-ters as Japan policy, trade preference, and interference in local affairs; but he refused to let his differences of opinion harm the fundamental Philip-pine-American relationship of goodwill and cooperation. In matters of collective security and opposition to communism, the Philippines rejected the ideas of neutralism and stood vociferously on the side of the free world. The Philippines became one of the most active Asian members of the United Nations.

THAILAND (SIAM)

The transition from war to peace in Thailand was different in practically every respect from the experience of the Philippines. Traditionally known as "the island of smiles in a sea of tears," Thailand was obliged to do penance for its unwise decision in taking sides with the loser. The Thais ousted their hapless prime minister, Phibun Songgram, and detained him in polite house arrest. The ruling clique used the regent and guerrilla leader, Pridi Banomyang, to negotiate peace. He denounced the declarations of war and volunteered to return to Burma and Malaya the territories which Thailand had annexed in the early days of the war. He suggested that the boundary disputes with the French should be referred to the United Nations. He relaxed restrictions on the minorities in Thailand and, in a burst of national humility, changed the haughty name of Thailand back to Siam. Thus when the war finally ended, Siam was under a government which had already begun to mend its fences with the victors.

The United States chose to ignore the Thai declaration of war and brought pressure on Great Britain and France to treat Thailand with gentleness. In treaties of peace, Thailand was required to expel the Japanese from Thailand, give up its recently acquired territories, make its rice surplus available for distribution elsewhere in Southeast Asia, restore prewar economic rights of foreign nationals, and renew its promises regarding a possible canal across the isthmus of Kra. The Thais came to terms with the Kuomintang government of China, promised most-favored-nation treatment to the United States and, in an understanding with Russia, agreed to legalize the Communist party in Thailand and to exchange ambassadors with Russia. In 1947, Thailand (or Siam as it was called at that moment) became the first ex-enemy country to be admitted to the United Nations.

Siam's postwar political situation was a constantly shifting contest for power within the framework of the constitutional monarchy. The kingship received none of the onus for Siam's difficulties, but in 1946 the youthful king was found dead in his palace. An investigating commission ruled that it was "murder, suicide or accident." His younger brother, Rama IX, or Phumiphon Aduldet, succeeded to the throne. He enjoyed the sincere respect of his people as the ceremonial chief of state and the head of the Buddhist religion. The ordinary people were aware of the king and his position, but they were indifferent to the tightly knit little group of army officers and civilian intellectuals which fought to control the government.

In theory Siam was supposed to be democratic, with a British-style cabinet responsible to a unicameral legislature. Actually power resided in the hands of a few thousand people who controlled the bureaucracy, the army, and the police. Cabinets rose and fell, not according to the will of the people, but according to intrigues, cabal, and turns of personal wheels of fortune. In the three years after 1945 nine governments came and went before Phibun—the former collaborator with the Japanese—re-established himself in authority. One of his first official acts was to restore the official name of Thailand. He sent his chief rival, Pridi, into exile in China because of alleged complicity in the death of the former king. Phibun survived one attempted *coup d'état* after another. Once he escaped death because he was a good swimmer; again, because of a convenient stomach pump; and the third time, because his assailant was an incredibly bad shot.

Thailand's social stability and economic prosperity kept the country on an even keel in spite of political and diplomatic storms. Thai institutions—the family, the village, the social hierarchy, the church, and the monarchy—had not been touched by foreign administrators nor shaken by alien ideas. In spite of the poverty in the hills of the northwest, on the plateau of the northeast, and in the extreme south on the Malayan border, the Thais of the river valley lived well under their own system of government. Food was abundant and land was available for all who wanted to own it. Landlordism was not a blight, debts were not excessive, and taxes were not unreasonable. The Thais felt no compulsion for a mysterious something which the West called democracy. Similarly they had no predilection for communism—native style, Russian, Chinese, or Vietnamese. They were prosperous, orderly, and pleased with their lot in life. Their existence was identified with a city, a fishing village, a forest clearing, or a plot of rice land. Their spiritual needs were filled by Buddhism. In their relations with one another, the Thais were dignified and easygoing. Their social safety valves were unrestrained and frequent celebrations.

The ordinary Thai farmers saw little need for agrarian reform, except perhaps from improved irrigation and transportation facilities. They looked to the government for protection against the Chinese buyers, millers, and distributors of rice and for financial help which would keep them out of the grasp of usury. On the other hand, the Thai political elite was infected by the love of wealth. It wanted the profits earned by Chinese and Westerners. To this end it adopted a philosophy of national socialism and used the state as its instrument. The government took the lead in stimulating trade and industry, with more benefit to insiders who got the contracts than to the consuming public.

The Thais turned against the Chinese as the major cause of their economic ills. In 1948, while the Kuomintang was still in power in China, the Thais reduced the annual immigration quota of Chinese from ten thousand to two hundred. They restricted the Chinese embassy in its functions and closed the Chinese consulates. They exercised careful control over the Chinese schools and Chinese newspapers. With the coming of the Communists to power in China, the Thais increased their anti-Chinese pressures. They tightened the naturalization laws and assessed a high registration fee for aliens. Thais and Chinese avoided serious troubles because they both exhibited consummate skill in the subtleties of compromise. Thais and Chinese were useful to each other. The political elite was Thai in citizenship, but partially Chinese in its blood. It had prestige, but it needed rich relatives, Chinese or otherwise, to pay the bills. To a Chinese, it was an advantage to have a son or daughter married to a highly placed Thai or his relative. There was an endless payoff between Thai politicians and Chinese merchants. Further down the scale, there was a standard operating procedure of squeeze and bribery. Many shops displayed the limited partnership sign—which indicated a nominal Thai ownership with Chinese relatives or brains behind the business.

Aside from the repressive treatment of minorities, the government of Thailand was prone to disregard problems of the masses in pursuing its own interests. This divergence in outlook between the government and the people contained elements of strength and weakness. Changes in government did not mean changes in policy, but popular indifference bred corresponding irresponsibility within the governing elite. The United States recognized all of Thailand's postwar cabinets as quickly as they were constituted, but it resented the return of Phibun Songgram. However, everything was forgiven by the American government when Phibun achieved status as the staunchest anti-communist in Southeast Asia. Although his people were not interested in the cold war, Phibun strengthened his military forces, pushed forward plans for economic development, and took an uncompromising stand against the Communists, who virtually surrounded him. Phibun feared communist agitation among dissident elements in his own country and he was sensitive to China's promotion of a Thai People's Republic, or a greater Thailand for all Thai ethnic groups in Southeast Asia.

After the outbreak of the war in Korea, Thailand sent a small expeditionary force to fight on the side of the United Nations. Phibun quietly permitted the development of a regular underground railway funneling supplies to the Nationalist Chinese troops under General Li Mi, which set up an anti-Communist guerrilla base in the Thailand-Burma border area. In return for this cooperation, Thailand received extraordinary assistance from the United States, the International Bank for Reconstruction and Development, and the whole alphabet of United Nations agencies.

REPUBLIC OF INDONESIA, FORMERLY THE NETHERLANDS EAST INDIES

The recovery of Thailand progressed like a success story, but the process of independence of the Netherlands East Indies required four years of anarchy. On August 17, 1945—while still under the Japanese—the Netherlands East Indies declared independence and took the name of Indonesia. However, the declaration was meaningless without the assent of the Dutch. Because the Dutch had no troops of their own for service in Indonesia, the Southeast Asia command under Lord Mountbatten dispatched British troops to disarm and repatriate more than 200,000 Japanese and to protect the Dutch internees. The Dutch followed as they could, but they encountered stiff and sullen Indonesian resistance as they tried to restore their former empire. Incidents and skirmishes threatened to turn into open warfare.

In March 1947, the Dutch and the Indonesians accepted a formula which recognized the authority of the new "Indonesian republic" in Java and Sumatra. The outer islands were to be administered separately but joined with the Indonesian republic to form the united states of Indonesia —which in turn would be part of the Dutch Commonwealth. This arrangement broke down within three months, and the Dutch initiated "police action" to restore order. It was a losing battle, both against the Indonesians and against world opinion. Pressure from the United Nations forced a new truce agreement, signed aboard the American cruiser "Renville." Peace eluded the Dutch, who lost their homes and their places of business. The last ties of friendship between Dutch and Indonesians tended to disappear. In September 1948, the Communists at Madiun, Java, in phase with Communists elsewhere in Southeast Asia, made an unsuccessful bid for political leadership; the Communist leaders were overpowered and shot by the Nationalist leaders. In the confusion which followed, the Dutch tried a second futile police action to eliminate terrorism. The Dutch then resigned themselves to negotiations as a means to salvage anything possible from their investments of three and a half centuries in the Indies. As a result of the "Round Table Agreements" of

The Hague in November 1949, they transferred sovereignty over all but West Irian (New Guinea) to the new state of Indonesia. In June, 1950, Indonesia was admitted to the United Nations.

On August 17, 1950—five years to the day after nominal independence—Indonesia proclaimed a new, provisional constitution. During those five years, cabinets rose and fell with great frequency. However, political power remained in the hands of the small group of nationalistic leaders who had distinguished themselves under the Dutch and under the Japanese. These men were not wealthy. They had no connection with landlords, as the oligarchy in the Philippines, and no direct stake in the capitalistic system. To them, capitalism meant Dutch colonialism. They were favorably disposed toward socialism, but not toward communism. They were without top-level administrative experience as they undertook to run their own complex, independent state.

The constitution provided that the republic of Indonesia would be a unified state, with a president, cabinet, and a legislature. Sukarno kept the presidency, and the self-constituted central national committee assumed the role of a national assembly. Elections were contemplated for 1953, and in the meantime party organizations mushroomed. The Party-Nationalist-Indonesia (PNI) continued as the rallying point for the fanatical nationalists. The Moslems divided into many subgroups, chief of which were the Masjumi, or Council of Indonesian Moslem Associations, and the Nahdatul Ulama (NU), or Association of Islamic Scholars. Another Moslem group, Darul Islam, or the Moslem World, consisted of extremists who advocated an out and out Moslem state. The Darul Islam group sheltered guerrillas and bandits and permitted their movement to degenerate into sheer terrorism. The Catholics formed their own political party, and so did the Socialists. The Party-Kommunist-Indonesia (PKI) grew rapidly and took its policy cues from Moscow or Peking. A small proletarian party (Partai Murba) followed the Communist line internally, but refused to accept foreign direction.

With such political division, and such a small reservoir of political talent, the archipelago was wracked by political instability. Cabinets were never more than weak temporary coalitions. The elite was not accustomed to the self-imposed limitations of democracy, and it did not display the same spirit of sacrifice which characterized the earlier freedom fighters. It was difficult to shift from the time-honored techniques of opposition to the techniques of rapid decision required by a party in power. Blundering and inefficiency gave way to bribery and corruption. Men from the outer islands complained about the Javanese monopoly of the bureaucracy. The army gained in prestige and political power.

The Communists took on new life. After the failure at Madiun, they shifted their tactics along with Communists throughout the world. They renounced rebellion in favor of peaceful conversion of peasants, labor, soldiers, students, youth, and women. They built a strong grass-roots organization and campaigned openly and peacefully for members. Communist headquarters were the best-marked buildings in many Indonesian villages. They gained substantial control of the urban workers, estate laborers, and the farmers' union, and succeeded in planting sympathizers, if not actual party members, in sensitive government positions. The Communists in their propaganda were careful not to offend the sensibilities of the Moslems. They never criticized Moslem leaders for their religious beliefs nor referred to religion as the opiate of the people. They set out to demonstrate that they could act constitutionally in times of peace, as well as subversively in times of crisis. They declared that while they were friendly both to Moscow and Peking, they were servants of neither. They clothed their program in such phrases as "peace," "nationalism," and "cooperation against the imperialists." As long as they refrained from violence, the government was content.

Indonesia's political problems were complicated by a condition of perennial economic crisis. The prewar trade patterns which brought prosperity to the Dutch in Indonesia were destroyed, and the large plantations were neglected. While all local political parties united to vent their spleen on the evils of colonial capitalism, business went to rack and ruin. Tea leaves were not picked, rubber trees were untapped, and sugar mills were idled. Government revenues fell off and poverty increased. Agriculture—seventy percent of the economic life of Indonesia—suffered most. Peasant farmers could not produce enough to eat. An extra million tons of rice per year were needed to feed hungry mouths. Debts increased; and without Dutch protection, tiny family farms were further subdivided or sold to landlords. Plantations were abandoned or left to the mercy of squatters. The benefits of years of scientific management were dissipated. As export prices became more unstable, smuggling outstripped legitimate trade. Shipping, which under the Dutch had been the pride of the archipelago, became a national disgrace.

The situation in industry was equally dark. The nationalists were nonplused when nationalism failed automatically to bring prosperity. They underestimated the damaging effects of their policies of nationalization and socialization. Foreign companies could not afford to take risks of further investments for plant expansion or modernization. Heavy taxes, exchange restrictions, and irregular exactions handicapped private enterprise. Endless forms slowed up and complicated every process of trade. Laborers developed more and more antipathy toward working for foreigners. To individual brigandage and thievery were added organized idleness and sabotage. Indonesia plunged toward bankruptcy as it squandered its accumulated reserves. The government produced grandiose plans for economic expansion; but the only solidity in its planning was provided by foreign grants, loans, and trade agreements. The United States, the United Nations, the World Bank, some nations in the Colombo Plan, the Netherlands, and the Soviet Union contributed substantially to Indonesia.

Economic confusion aggravated deep-seated social problems. Farmers were moved to new fury by tax collectors and landlords, and even began to ask embarrassing questions about rich sultans. Men and women in small villages—through their enormously expanded schools—learned of teachers and doctors in the cities and wanted the same for themselves. The government opened schools and taught the national language with amazing energy, and it could not escape the social demands which are the by-products of education. Much of modern Indonesia continued to live as it had in the sixteenth century, but a large part of its society began to move in new channels. The momentum of eighty million people in flux became the determinant factor in Indonesia's future.

With so many problems at home, Sukarno characterized his foreign policy as being against colonialism and for peaceful coexistence. He insisted that communism and democracy could coexist, but not colonialism and peace. Following Burma, he took the path of neutralism, but he preferred to call it "active independence." He used West Irian as a battle cry against the Dutch but stated that he had no legal claims to Portuguese Timor or British Borneo. Indonesians boycotted the Dutch, took over their business enterprises, closed their consulates and ordered fifty thousand Dutch passport-holders to leave the country. This brought to an end every special relationship between the Indonesians and the Dutch.

Sukarno showed little consideration to foreign capitalistic enterprises within his country—Dutch, British, American, or Chinese—but he adopted a moderate tone in matters of less immediate diplomatic importance to him. He spoke of injecting the voice of reason in international affairs and of mobilizing all the strength of Africa and Asia on the side of peace. He felt few bonds of sympathy with Australian conservatives, who in turn looked upon Sukarno as a crypto-communist. He made many trips abroad and seemed to exhibit genuine enthusiasm over the communist countries. He established diplomatic relations with the Soviet Union and with the People's Republic of China. Sukarno considered himself as a sincere peaceloving member of the international community, willing to cooperate with all regardless of social systems. He made peace with Japan. Then he told the world that he would welcome aid—without strings—from anyone who would help his people in trade, commerce, technical development, and national social reconstruction.

In 1955 Sukarno paused to reappraise his international position and to fix a new course for his internal policies. He ordered a general election, and that election might be taken as the end of the period of Indonesia's transition into the contemporary world. An approximately the same time, Indonesia's neighbors in Indochina approached the end of the road in their struggle against the French.

NEW STATES OF INDOCHINA

The peoples of Indochina faced the same opportunities and the same problems as the Indonesians confronted at the end of World War II. But, if anything, the difficulties in Indochina were greater. The French were at least as adamant as the Dutch—and the clash between colonials and returning imperialists reached the proportions of civil war. The struggle lasted longer; and it was three states, not one, which had to learn to walk alone.

Before the battered French could muster sufficient strength to return to Indochina, it was British troops in the south and Chinese in the north which took charge of repatriating Japanese and restoring law and order. By February 1946, the French were back with their protectorates re-established in Cambodia and Laos. With Vietnam it was different. Fighting was scattered in Saigon, and it ended quickly in favor of the French. North of the sixteenth parallel, in the vicinity of Hanoi, Ho Chi Minh was the man of the hour. He sent Bao Dai, ex-emperor turned private citizen, as his representative on a vague mission to Hong Kong. But Bao Dai wrote to De Gaulle, saying, "You must see to understand the desire for independence which is in everyone's heart. If you re-establish French administration, it will no longer be obeyed. Each village will be a nest of resistance. Your officials and colonists will themselves ask to leave this atmosphere which they will be unable to breathe." Ho overcame his rivals, who were supported by the Chinese Kuomintang, and set up a government within which he could carry out his own ideas. He expressed his program in words of one syllable which appealed to the peasants. He advocated less taxes, lower rents, and no forced labor. He promised more food, better health, and better schools. The subtleties of ideology were left to the intellectuals. He replaced the Indochina Communist Party with an association for the study of Marxism.

In February 1946, Ho and the Chinese came to terms, whereupon the Chinese, with a black record of rape and loot, left Vietnam. Within a week, on March 6, Ho obtained from the French an agreement by which France recognized Vietnam as a free (but not independent) state within the French union. As French troops began to return to North Vietnam, Ho went to France to conclude a working arrangement with the French on the details of reoccupation. Ho signed a *modus vivendi* at Fontainebleau which was the last agreement between Ho, as the representative of the Viet Minh, and France until 1954.

Shortly after Ho's return, war broke out between the Vietnamese and the French. Each side blamed the other for causing it. Ho said the Vietnamese would cooperate with the French if the latter would do as the Americans had done in the Philippines or the British had done in India. The French were determined by that time (1947) to keep Vietnam out of the hands of Ho Chi Minh, who, in their opinion, had become a tool of Moscow. Unfortunately, Communist or not, Ho was the acknowledged leader of the nationalist revolution. Ho's men were not mere agitators or convicts: they represented the nationalist cause.

The French were halfhearted in their fight to crush Ho until after the Communist victory in China. Then the little local war took on the aspect of the next spot in the global conflict between Communists and anti-Communists. The French tried to split the Vietnamese. They enticed Bao Dai to desert Ho and to head up a rival government. After December 30, 1949, when Bao Dai took over the reins in the south, the name *Vietnam* had two meanings. Ho clung to his use of Vietnam as meaning his Democratic Republic of Vietnam (DRV) in the north; Bao Dai and the French appropriated the word as referring to the new government in Saigon. Bao was no match for Ho as the exponent of Vietnamese nationalism. His white sharkskin suits, fluent French, clumsy Vietnamese, and corpulent fondness for French cooking contrasted sharply with Ho's wispy frame and plain clothes of black or khaki.

The unequal contest had serious international implications. By February 1950, Ho gained the recognition of the Soviet bloc but spurned the overtures of Tito. Bao Dai received the backing of nations represented by France, the United States, and the United Kingdom. In June 1950, the Korean War broke out, and President Truman immediately stepped up American aid to the Vietnam of Bao Dai and France. American influence in policy grew with the expanding proportion of the military bills paid by the United States.

From 1950 to 1954—from the Communist conquest of China to the Geneva agreements—the character of the civil war in Indochina changed. Ho tightened up his own command. In 1951 he changed his study group into the Lao Dang, or Working People's Party, and he used it as the nucleus of a Lien Viet or united front of the Vietnamese. He declared his war was an integral part of the world revolution led by Russia. He formulated new military tactics: first win the people; then the supply lines; then attack the forts. Vo Ngyuen Giap, a former history teacher, with outside aid and assistance transformed the ragged guerrillas into a capable army.

On the other side, Bao Dai entrusted local administration of affairs to the mandarin class of wealthy, French-educated, Vietnamese. He left the fighting to the French. In France, between escapades, he negotiated vainly for "more independence." While diplomats procrastinated, soldiers died. The northern Vietnamese (henceforward called simply Viet Minh) killed French officers faster than St. Cyr could graduate them. Supplies were exhausted faster than France and the United States could provide them. The bloody pathy ended in the mountain town of Dien Bien Phu —and the conference tables at Geneva.

In the meantime, the other states of Indochina, Cambodia, and Laos, strove for improved status within the French union. These states were as foreign to the Viet Minh and the Vietnamese of the south as the latter were to France. The youthful king of Cambodia made and unmade his prime ministers, and he determined his own policies. He was anti-Communist, and also anti-Vietnamese. He was plagued by the Issarak, or "free" dissidents in his own territory, and was haunted by fears of invasion from Vietnam. He wanted to conduct his own foreign affairs, and he objected to being a pawn of France. He proved himself to be an expert in the game of playing both ends against the middle, and he used his neighbors and the United States in his efforts to win more concessions from France, which was his official protector. He took advantage of France's embarrassment in Vietnam in 1953 to negotiate a series of protocols giving Cambodia full sovereignty in military, judicial, and economic matters. This was still short of complete independence.

In October 1953, France and Laos signed a treaty declaring Laos to be fully independent, but within the French union. Laos was threatened directly by the fighting in North Vietnam, and it lay directly over the mountain, almost in the shadow of Dien Bien Phu. In addition to the threat from the Viet Minh, Laos also had its pro-Communist insurgents. Therefore all three states—Vietnam, Cambodia, and Laos—were eager participants at the Conference of Geneva in the summer of 1954 when France officially wrote "finis" across its balcony on the Pacific.

By the agreements signed at Geneva, hostilities were ended. All three states were granted recognition of their sovereignty, independence, unity, and territorial integrity. But Vietnam was partitioned after the manner of Germany and Korea, and the possibility of unity was left for elections fixed for the summer of 1956. France accepted these arrangements; so did the Viet Minh. But South Vietnam felt that it had no voice in its own fate and withheld its signature. The terms of peace for Cambodia provided for the withdrawal of foreign troops and for the incorporation of the Issarak rebels into the national army. Cambodia agreed to undertake no military alliances, give no military bases, and receive no military assistance except in actual defense of the country. Laos fared equally well. Troops were withdrawn, and Laos was estopped from receiving all types of armaments except as necessary for the defense of Laos. Laos also agreed not to join military alliances so long as its security was not threatened. Laos permitted the French to continue their military mission and retain their bases at Xien Khouang and Seno. Rebel troops of the Pathet Lao, or the country of Lao movement, were to be assembled in two provinces in the northeast—Phong Saly and Sam Neua—pending final understandings between the leader of the rebels and the royal government.

This marked the final step in the creation of the new world of Southeast Asia. Within approximately ten years from the end of World War II, the rule of the imperial powers had practically disappeared. In its place had arisen a battery of new nations including Burma, Malaya and Singapore, Thailand, the Philippines, Indonesia, Vietnam, Cambodia, and Laos. Although infants in terms of political independence, they were called upon to assume full responsibility for their own growth and development, and to carry a share of the load in solving the problems of the contemporary world.

SUGGESTED READING

Abaya Hernando, *Betrayal in the Philippines* (New York, Wyn, 1946).

Bernstein, David, *Philippine Story* (New York, Farrar, 1947).

Buttinger, Joseph, *Smaller Dragon* (New York, Praeger, 1958).

Cole, Allan B., *Conflict in Indo-China and International Repercussions, Documentary History, 1945–1955* (Ithaca, Cornell U., 1956).

Fall, Bernard B., *Viet Minh Regime* (rev. ed.) (New York, Institute of Pacific Relations, 1956).

Fifield, Russell H., *Diplomacy of Southeast Asia, 1945–1958* (New York, Harper, 1958).

Fischer, Louis, *Story of Indonesia* (New York, Harper, 1959).

Giap, General Vo Nguyen, *People's War, People's Army* (New York, Praeger, 1962).

Jumper, Roy, and Hue, Nguyen Th'e, *Political and Administrative History of Vietnam, 1802–1962* (Saigon, Michigan State U. Vietnam Advisory Group, 1962).

Kennedy, J., *History of Malaya* (New York, St Martin's, 1962).

King, Frank H. H., *New Malayan Nation* (New York, Institute of Pacific Relations, 1957).

Lancaster, Donald, *Emancipation of French Indo-China* (New York, Oxford U., 1961).

Mills, Lennox A., *Malaya, A Political and Economic Appraisal* (Minneapolis, U. of Minnesota, 1958).

Purcell, Victor, *Malaya: Communist or Free?* (New York, Institute of Pacific Relations, 1954).

Pye, Lucian, *Guerrilla Communism in Malaya* (Princeton, Princeton U., 1956).

Pye, Lucian, *Politics, Personality and Nation Building* (New Haven, Yale U., 1962).

Smith, Robert A., *Philippine Freedom* (New York, Macmillan, 1958).

Starobin, Joseph, *Eyewitness in Indo-China* (New York, Cameron & Kahn, 1954).

Thompson, Virginia, and Adloff, Richard, *Minority Problems in Southeast Asia* (Stanford, Stanford U., 1955).

Wolf, Charles Jr., *Indonesian Story* (New York, Day, 1948).

28

Korea: Police Action and After

The dawn of the new world of Southeast Asia was stormy, but it was no worse than the dawn of Korea as an independent state. Koreans welcomed liberation after thirty-five years under the heel of Japan. Patriots who had known the hardships of Japanese jails or who in exile had kept the lamps of freedom burning flocked back to the land of their fathers. They were fired with determination to do great things for their native country. Because of their lack of political experience and because of the frustrations of the international situation, they were doomed to disappointment.

Korea was divided. It was occupied by the Soviet Union north of the thirty-eighth parallel and by the United States to the south of the fateful line. The will of the Koreans was subordinated to the needs of the great powers, and, through circumstances beyond Korean control, their homeland was flooded with propaganda, torn by civil war, and exposed to foreign invasion. Korean soil was soaked with blood in the battles between North Koreans and South Koreans, between enemy aggressors and the forces of the United Nations. Instead of happiness and prosperity, the Koreans received more than a full measure of sorrow and destruction. The curse of fate and history hung heavy over a small, half-forgotten nation which more than any other in contemporary Asia faced a long and difficult road to political stability and economic improvement.

From the date of its opening by Japan, Korea was the helpless victim of great-power conflicts and ambitions. The geographic location of Korea made it attractive to China, Russia, and Japan, and the internal rot of its politics doomed it to the control of its strongest neighbor. From 1910 until Pearl Harbor, no one challenged Japan's position in Korea. Japan gave Korea a stable, ultracolonial administration and exploited Korea's rich agricultural and mineral resources for the benefit of Japan's economic and military machine. Korea's fundamental problems of land, livelihood, and population expansion were obscured by Japan, and the persistent demands by Korean leaders for personal consideration and political rights were ignored by militant Japanese overlords.

For Japan, Korea became the chief base for further penetration into the Asian continent. The entire Korean nation was treated as a cog in Japan's imperial machine. Korea was a training ground or staging area for Japanese troops. Korean farms were made to produce rice for Japan, and Korean factories were built solely to fill the gaps in the burgeoning industry of Japan. Korea's children were taught the language and lore of Japan, and its adults were given only such jobs as suited Japanese purposes. The Japanese treated Korea as a permanent possession and made no pretense at preparing its people for independent existence.

Japan's paternalism partially accounts for the difficulties of Korea at the end of World War II. When Japan lost the war, all the Japanese were unceremoniously repatriated, leaving behind them their investments and personal property. The victorious allies failed to make adequate provision to fill the vacuum created by the departure of the Japanese. Certainly the Koreans themselves were in no position to solve the problems of their prostrate country, so contemporary Korea's troubles stemmed primarily from the circumstances of the great war itself.

World War II and the Destiny of Korea

The Cairo Declaration of November 1943 stipulated that "in due course Korea shall become free and independent." The Soviet Union accepted this proposition on entering the war against Japan. As a result of a military understanding first discussed at Potsdam, Russia accepted the surrender of the Japanese and occupied Korea north of the thirty-eighth parallel while the United States accepted the surrender of the Japanese and established military government south of the dividing line. The division served an immediate, useful, military purpose, but it destroyed the political unity and the economic viability of the Korean nation.

Korea was not severely damaged by military action during World War II, but its economic life was shattered. At the moment of cessation of hostilities, Korea was helpless. With the bisecting of the country, recovery seemed impossible. North Korea, with a population of seven million contained most of the nation's raw materials, power installations, and industrial potential. South Korea, with three times as many people, contained the capital city, the best seaports, and most of the productive agricultural acreage. North Korea shared a common border with the Soviet Union and with China. Its railways, harbors, factories, and sources of power constituted a vital link in an economic chain which the Communist powers hoped to forge in northeast Asia.

In the interim between the end of hostilities and the installation of occupation regimes, Koreans in north and south set up local people's committees to maintain order. In the north, the Russians utilized these committees and imported Korean Communists from China and the Soviet Union to strengthen them. In the south, the Americans (who were six weeks late in arriving) ignored the committees and unwisely permitted the Japanese to remain temporarily in control. The Americans brought with them some well-known Korean leaders—Kim Koo, Kim Kiusic, and Syngman Rhee—who had spent years in exile. In short order, the American fighting men who were given responsibility for government in their zone of occupation found themselves to be completely baffled by the factions and intrigues of Korean politics.

Korean affairs were referred to the Council of Foreign Ministers, which, at its meeting in Moscow on December 27, 1945, agreed to establish a U.S.–U.S.S.R. joint commission to assist in the formation of a provisional Korean "democratic" government. It was provided that in preparing suggestions the Commission should consult with "democratic" parties and social organizations throughout Korea. It was further provided that it should be the task of the Commission to work out a four-power trusteeship for Korea for a period of up to five years, after which Korea was to be given a fully independent government.

Toward an Independent, Democratic, and Unified Korea

Koreans, north and south, reacted violently against the insulting trusteeship arrangement. They wanted independence, not a shoddy substitute. Early in 1946 representatives of the people's committees in North Korea assembled at their capital in Pyongyang to lay plans for an "independent government" under the leadership of a Soviet-trained Communist, Kim Ilsung. At the same time in Seoul, South Koreans paraded in protest against the proposed trusteeship. In the midst of a seething political situation and a critical economic impasse the U.S.–U.S.S.R. joint commission made no progress toward either a trusteeship or a provisional "democratic" government.

In North Korea the Russians acted as they pleased. They ran the country as a police state through their Korean puppets. They built up the North Korean army and strengthened the Communist party. In August 1948 they ordered elections for a supreme people's assembly, which created the Democratic People's Republic of Korea. The government was installed in Pyongyang, and it claimed sovereignty over all of Korea. Kim

Ilsung was designated prime minister, and he was accorded immediate recognition by the Soviet Union and its satellites. The Russians withdrew their troops and entered into agreements with North Koreans for economic assistance and cultural relations. The most eloquent testimonial to the quality of the regime in North Korea was the daily stream of refugees to the south.

In South Korea, the United States took cautious steps to admit more Koreans into administrative and judicial positions. An interim legislature was established with a partially elected membership. But because of the inability to reach an understanding with Russia, the United States placed the Korean question on the agenda of the United Nations. On November 14, 1947, the General Assembly passed a resolution which recognized the rightful claims to independence on the part of the people of Korea. This resolution established a UN commission to facilitate a program for a national government of Korea and for the withdrawal of all occupation forces.

On May 10, 1948, elections were held for a national assembly in South Korea. Almost 1,000 candidates contested for 200 seats. Issues were inconsequential—except that everybody stood for immediate independence. Parties were based on personal loyalties. The Hankook Democratic Party, headed by Kim Songsoo (an influential landlord and industrialist) captured the most seats, followed by Syngman Rhee's National Association for the Rapid Realization of Korean Independence. The Korean Independence Party, led by Kim Koo, ran third. Various "youth" groups won a few seats, but extreme leftists, including the South Korean Labor Party, either boycotted the elections or went underground. In the summer of 1948, Korea had two governments—one in the north and one in the south, one backed by Russia and the other by the United States—each of which insisted that it was the only government for all Korea.

The assembly of South Korea chose Dr. Rhee as the president of the Republic of Korea and on August 15, 1948, he was inaugurated in Seoul. The American military government transferred its authority to the new administration, and Americans prepared to withdraw their troops as the Russians had done in the north. On December 12, 1948, the General Assembly of the United Nations passed another resolution which declared that the government in South Korea was the only lawful government in Korea, recommended the withdrawal of troops as early as practicable and created another commission to help to bring about the unification of Korea and the further development of representative government.

On New Year's Day, 1949, the United States extended full recognition to the Republic of Korea in Seoul. The United States launched a broad program of relief and economic assistance and undertook to withdraw its troops. The arguments for and against withdrawal were formidable. Some Americans warned of the risks involved, because withdrawal would look as if the United States was prepared to write off Korea and possibly all of East Asia to the Communists. Others pointed to the embarrassing realities that American forces throughout the world were pathetically weak and were overwhelmed by responsibilities in China and Central Europe. It was hoped that South Korea would be able to cope with its own internal Communist problems and to handle the threat of an invasion from the north. The American government, with Truman as president and Eisenhower as chief of staff, felt that the strategic interests of the United States were not sufficient to justify the continued maintenance of American troops and bases in Korea. Consequently all tactical units were withdrawn by June 30, 1949; the only American military presence in Korea was a small military advisory group of a hundred officers and men for the advice and training of Korean security forces.

After the retirement of the American army of occupation, the Republic of Korea strengthened its ties with the United States but it made discouraging progress toward prosperity or democracy. South Korea rejected Communist overtures for unification and nurtured a growing confidence in its ability to overcome North Korea in the event of a fight. Economic difficulties multiplied as prices spiraled and food production failed to keep pace with the increasing population. Tenants agitated for land reform, and farmers begged for fertilizer, which had previously come from the north. Textile mills and other light industries closed down for lack of power which the North Koreans refused to transmit. Korea suffered from the lack of trained technicians to take the places previously filled by competent Japanese. The national budget showed mounting deficits, and the printing presses turned out bales of paper money to pay for salaries and public services. Korea appealed to the United States for aid and $160,000,000 was authorized for the fiscal year ending July 1, 1950.

President Rhee ruled with a strong hand. He dominated the cabinet and bullied the assembly. He herded his docile supporters into the Il Min Hoi, or People's Party. Reports of police brutalities were commonplace, and assassinations were distressingly frequent. Criticism was silenced by the National Security Law. Korea was on the side of the democracies, but it was far from democratic. In new elections in South Korea on May 30, 1950, Rhee lost some of his support, but he was able to continue as president. He was, however, confronted with a deeply discontented and perennially hostile assembly.

On the eve of the invasion from the north, President Rhee hinted that in answer to the cries of his brothers in distress beyond the thirty-eighth parallel, he might strive to reunite the country by forceful means if necessary. Americans in Seoul feared that he would do just that. They were less interested in unification than in solving economic problems and broadening the base of democracy. They were uneasy about their cantankerous Korean ward, but they were determined not to stop halfway through the work begun in Korea. On January 12, 1950, Secretary Acheson omitted Korea from his delineation of the defense perimeter of the United States in the western Pacific; he stated that in the event of aggression in Korea it would be a matter for the United Nations.

Meanwhile in North Korea, the People's Democratic Republic passed under the complete control of the Communists. North Koreans conducted raids across the strategic thirty-eighth parallel and carried out their subversive activities in the south. Radio Pyongyang, in the spring of 1950, called for a conference between north and south to unite all Korea and announced that the the north would hold elections *in the south* sometime in August. The Russians continued to control the build-up of the army and the North Korean economy. No one paid any attention to China, which was knee-deep in the inauguration of its own People's Republic in Peking. Within a week after Special Ambassador John Foster Dulles assured the South Korean Assembly, "You will never be left alone so long as you continue worthily your part in the great design of human freedom," the Communist army of North Korea spilled across the frontier and launched its military drive against the south.

"Cynical, Brutal, Naked Attack"

On Saturday afternoon, June 24, 1950, which because of the fourteen hour time differential between Seoul and Washington was daybreak Sunday, June 25, in Korea, tank columns slushed through the mud and the rain on the way to Seoul. The United Nations Commission in Korea called this invasion an act of aggression, without warning and without provocation, in execution of a carefully prearranged plan. Within twenty-four hours, the United States asked for an emergency session of the Security Council of the United Nations and authorized General MacArthur in Tokyo to make military supplies available to South Korea. With the Russian delegate absent and the Yugoslav delegate abstaining, the Security Council immediately passed a resolution calling upon North Korea to cease hostilities and to withdraw the invasion forces.

On Sunday night, June 25, Washington time, President Truman called his senior advisers together in Blair House (the temporary White House) and told them the time had come to put an end to drifting and to bickering. A thoroughly aroused president spelled out the reasons why successful resistance to the Communists in Korea was required. In his view it would serve to demonstrate that aggression would not be accepted by

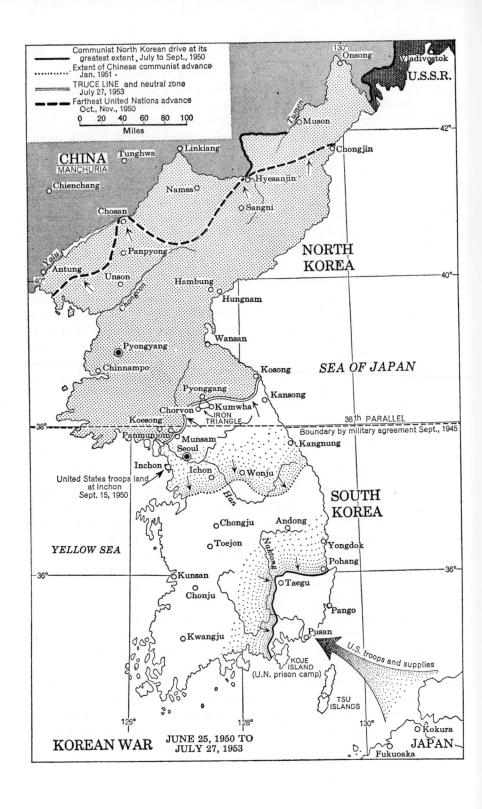

Communist North Korean drive at its
greatest extent, July to Sept., 1950
Extent of Chinese communist advance
Jan. 1951
TRUCE LINE and neutral zone
July 27, 1953
Farthest United Nations advance
Oct., Nov., 1950

0   20   40   60   80   100
Miles

CHINA
MANCHURIA

Tunghwa
Linkiang
Chienchang
Namsa
Chosan
Panpyong
Antung
Unson
Hambung
Hungnam

NORTH
KOREA

Onsong
Vladivostok
U.S.S.R.

Muson
Chongjin
Hyesanjin
Sangni

Wansan
Pyongyang
Chinnampo
Kosong
Kansong
Pyonggang
Chorvon
Kumwha
IRON
TRIANGLE
Koesong
Panmunjom
Munsam
Seoul
Kangnung

SEA OF JAPAN

38th PARALLEL
Boundary by military agreement Sept., 1945

38°

United States troops land
at Inchon
Sept. 15, 1950

Inchon
Ichon
Wonju

SOUTH
KOREA

YELLOW SEA

Chongju
Andong
Toejon
Yongdok
Pohang

Kunsan
Chonju
Taegu

Pango

Kwangju
Pusan

KOJE
ISLAND
(U.N. prison camp)

U.S. troops and supplies

TSU
ISLANDS

Kokura
JAPAN
Fukuoka

126°
128°
130°

KOREAN WAR   JUNE 25, 1950 TO
                    JULY 27, 1953

the United States or the United Nations, provide a rallying point for the free world against the threat of the Soviet Union, deflate the exaggerated political and military prestige of Communist China, give assistance to the organization of non-Communist resistance everywhere in Asia, carry out commitments of honor to South Korea, make possible a far more satisfactory peace settlement for Japan, lend resolution to countries who were living within the shadow of Communist power and let them know they need not rush to come to terms with communism, inspire those who might be called upon to fight against great odds if subjected to a sudden onslaught by the Soviet Union or Communist China, lend point and urgency to the rapid build-up of the defense of the Western world, bring the United Nations through its first great effort in collective security, and alert the peoples behind the iron curtain that their masters were bent upon wars of aggression and that this crime would be resisted by the free world.

The next day (June 26) the president ordered the evacuation of American citizens from Seoul and directed General MacArthur to send his air and sea forces into action. On June 27 President Truman made an announcement which General MacArthur said "lighted into flame a lamp of hope throughout Asia that was burning dimly toward extinction." The president sent combat forces into action in Korea, ordered the Seventh Fleet to prevent any attack on Formosa, re-enforced American bases in the Philippines, and stepped up military aid to Indochina. That one exciting day had its clouds as well as sunshine. Seoul capitulated. The South Korean army collapsed and seventy percent of its personnel disappeared as casualties, prisoners, or deserters. Thousands of innocent civilian refugees joined the government in the long trek toward the southern tip of the Korean peninsula. That night, the Security Council, with Russia still absent and with only Yugoslavia voting in the negative, passed a second resolution which branded North Korea as an aggressor and recommended assistance to South Korea.

The United States sent a direct appeal to Russia to call off the North Koreans, but Russia merely replied that the situation in Korea was an internal affair—beyond the competence of the United Nations. Russia took the attitude that all UN activities were illegal because of the absence of the Russian delegate and the presence of the wrong Chinese delegation. Not to be thwarted by diplomatic maneuvers on the part of Russia, the United States pushed ahead with a vigorous program. Congress appropriated $6,000,000,000 to oppose what Secretary of State Dean Acheson called "the most cynical, brutal, naked attack by armed forces upon an undefended country that could occur." In order to avoid legal complications, President Truman told the American people they were not at war but were engaged in "police action" under the United Nations. War or not, on June 30 the president authorized the air force to attack specific military targets in North Korea, committed American ground troops to the fighting, and ordered a naval blockade of the entire Korean coast.

The UN Security Council asked President Truman to establish a unified command for all the forces fighting in Korea, and the president appointed General MacArthur. All these steps were possible because of the voluntary absence of Russia, which was in a temporary boycott of the UN as a protest gesture against the refusal to accept the new Communist regime as the representative of China. Most of the UN troops in Korea —nine-tenths of the non-Koreans—were American, so the appointment of an American seemed entirely in order. By mid-July 1950, some sixteen nations had offered ground troops, naval units, or aircraft to participate in the fighting, and a dozen others had contributed food, clothing, or medical supplies. The Nationalist Chinese offered soldiers, but General Mac-Arthur rejected the offer for reasons of military and political expediency.

Hostilities in Korea lasted for a year and four months. In the first six weeks the Communist blitzkrieg drove the UN forces almost out of the peninsula. For another interminable month they clung desperately to a tiny toehold around the port city of Pusan. On September 15, General MacArthur staged a brilliant amphibious landing behind the Communist lines at Inchon, near Seoul, and launched a counterattack which swept the enemy back beyond the thirty-eighth parallel. The general felt that the war would be over by Thanksgiving, and he comforted his shivering soldiers with the hope that they might be home by Christmas. He gave the same assurance to President Truman in a dramatic series of face-to-face meetings on Wake Island. The UN troops captured the North Korean capital at Pyongyang on October 19, and they pushed on to the shadow of the Manchurian border. Then the Chinese entered the war in force. They rolled the UN forces back and recaptured Seoul in January 1951. Once again the UN armies regrouped, rallied, and liberated Seoul for a second time. They advanced to the thirty-eighth parallel and dug in, while the diplomats took over the task of settling the fate of Korea.

The fighting took a terrible toll of lives and reduced much of Korea to ashes. The Republic of Korea army, or the "Roks," lost 50,000 killed; the Americans, half that number; and the others counted 2500 dead. Wounded and missing were numbered in tens of thousands. Factories, homes, and entire cities were blasted to rubble, to say nothing of the physical damage in North Korea due to thousands of bombing attacks. Korea paid a ghastly price for its preservation, but it emerged from the war with the strongest, best-trained army which the anti-Communists had at their disposal in Asia.

The position of the United States among the United Nations with regard to Korean policy was no more than *primus inter pares*, although it carried the heaviest burdens and practically directed the action. The others followed of their own free will, and they went only as far as they liked. The British agreed to the moral condemnation of aggression, but they refused to impose embargoes or apply sanctions to China. They were eager to restrict the area of conflict and to bring the fighting to an end as soon as possible. France never felt any enthusiasm for Korea because of its own problems in Indochina. Of the Asians, the Philippines, Thailand, and Japan were most cordial toward American purposes and procedures. Japan in particular expressed its gratification at American action. Premier Yoshida stated that in two worlds in conflict, it would have been suicidal for the democracies to stand idly by. The Arab-Asian bloc considered the United States as "precipitate and injudicious" in Korea and strove unceasingly for a cease-fire or negotiated settlement. India advocated peace, localization of the conflict, and more consideration for the views of Mao's China.

All the while that fighting progressed, the General Assembly and the Security Council addressed themselves to the problems of Korea. The various commissions of the United Nations poured a steady stream of useful information into headquarters at New York and the commander in chief of the UN army in Korea reported regularly about military affairs. The members of the political delegations naturally echoed the official policies of their respective countries, with the result that the rights of the rostrum were often used for propaganda purposes. Russia denounced the United States for aggression in Asia, manipulation of the UN, germ warfare, and indiscriminate bombing. American speeches denounced Russia for unleashing aggression, blocking action in the UN, and for trying to maneuver the Peking government into the world organization for nefarious purposes.

On October 7, 1950, in the flush of victory, the General Assembly passed a basic resolution on Korea. It recommended that steps be taken to ensure conditions of stability throughout Korea; that all constituent acts be taken, including the holding of elections, for the establishment of a unified, independent, and democratic government; that UN forces should not remain in Korea except for achieving the above objectives; and that all necessary measures be taken to accomplish the economic rehabilitation of Korea. The resolution side-stepped the issue whether UN forces should drive on to the Manchurian border, but in the course of the debate the Indian delegate warned that crossing the thirty-eighth parallel would jeopardize the strategic interests of China and provoke Chinese intervention. General MacArthur assumed that the phrase "ensure conditions of stability throughout Korea" constituted all the authority he needed to advance to the Yalu River.

After the Chinese intervened in force and reoccupied Seoul (January

4, 1951), the UN explored the possibility of a cease-fire and proposed an international conference on "Korea and other Far Eastern problems." The Chinese proved recalcitrant on both ideas. Therefore the General Assembly, on February 1, 1951, passed a resolution which condemned China for engaging in aggression in Korea. It was up to each member to implement the resolution according to its own lights.

At this time, General MacArthur repeated his admonition that there was no substitute for victory and that victory would entail the risk of total war. He recommended four further measures as essential for victory: reconnaissance flights over the coast of China and Manchuria; bombing Chinese supply routes, coastal cities, and their privileged sanctuary in Manchuria; an economic and naval blockade of China; and the use of the troops of Chiang Kai-shek for diversionary pressures on the mainland of China. Washington rejected these recommendations on grounds of political—not military—strategy. Some allies of the United States doubted the value of the recommendations and feared the possible moral repercussions on the part of Asians. The secretary of defense opposed the risk of provoking the Soviet Union and China to further action and the chief of staff said that a war against China would be "the wrong war in the wrong place at the wrong time against the wrong enemy." President Truman said simply, "General MacArthur was ready for total war, I was not."

Denied, in his judgment, the possibility of victory, General Mac-Arthur sought to arrange a military truce with his adversary. He wrote letters to political friends in the United States elucidating his position. President Truman believed General MacArthur to be uncooperative and insubordinate and relieved the distinguished general of all his posts in the Far East. The resulting political furor in the United States scarcely interfered with the continuing process of exerting political pressures on the enemy and probing for a possible armistice. On May 18, 1951, the General Assembly recommended an embargo on the shipment of arms, ammunition, and implements of war to North Korea and Communist China. After invitations and taunts, the Soviet delegate to the United Nations told an American radio audience on June 23, 1951, that "the Soviet peoples further believe that the most acute problem of the present day—the problem of the armed conflict in Korea—could be settled." He suggested that discussions should be started between the belligerents for a cease-fire and an armistice providing for the mutual withdrawal of forces from the thirty-eighth parallel. Thus the American pressure for peace bore fruit, and within a month a long bitter struggle for an armistice began in the primitive, isolated tent cities of Kaesong and Panmunjom. Battle lines and truce teams were within sounding distance of each other.

ARMISTICE AND THE STRUGGLE FOR PEACE

Incidents occurred and casualties mounted while discussions dragged on. Neither side was victorious in the fighting, so neither side could impose its will on the other at the conference table. It took months to reach agreement on measures to prevent renewed outbreak of hostilities. These measures included the definition of the demilitarized zone, provision for neutral inspection teams, construction of airfields, rotation of troops, and designation of ports of entry. It required more months to discuss political implications of the armistice and to set up satisfactory procedures for exchange of prisoners of war. The deadlock was broken only after a new administration came into power in the United States and after Malenkov succeeded to the position of Stalin in Russia.

When in the spring of 1953 both sides indicated a genuine inclination to compromise, President Rhee showed concern lest he be deserted by the United States and the United Nations. He demanded a defense pact with the United States, a positive commitment of American aid and guarantees of unification, and the withdrawal of Chinese troops as prerequisites for an armistice. On June 6 President Eisenhower laid down the law to President Rhee. He said that the United States would negotiate a defense pact with Korea *after* the armistice. He also declared that matters of Korean unification and withdrawal of Chinese troops were not within the competence of Korea and the United States alone—they would have to be discussed by a political conference. President Eisenhower said bluntly that the armistice was *required* of the United Nations and of the Republic of Korea.

President Rhee looked upon an armistice as a death warrant for the Korean nation. He believed that it was a breach of faith to quit the fight before victory, and he opposed bitterly any compromise or agreement with the Communists. He permitted noisy mobs in Seoul to shout, "Go Home, Damned Yankees" and to chant "Buk Chin," or "Drive on to the North." He released 25,000 prisoners of war on his own responsibility. In anger he warned that he would pull Korean troops out of the UN command if the armistice were concluded against his will.

In spite of President Rhee's objections, the armistice was signed on July 27, 1953. It provided for (1) establishment of a neutral zone; (2) a cease-fire; (3) withdrawal of forces from designated coastal islands and waters; (4) no reinforcements; (5) a military armistice commission to supervise the armistice; (6) a neutral nations supervisory commission composed of officers of Sweden, Switzerland, Poland, and Czechoslovakia; (7) a neutral nations repatriation commission to supervise exchange of prisoners of war; (8) the convening within three months of a political conference to negotiate on the withdrawal of foreign forces and the peaceful settlement of the Korean question, "and so forth."

On the same day the sixteen nations which provided troops for the UN command declared formally that they would support efforts to bring about a unified, independent, and democratic Korea and world work with the United Nations in assisting the people of Korea to repair the ravages of war. They affirmed that "if there is a renewal of the armed attack . . . we should be prompt to resist. The consequences of such a breach of the armistice would be so grave that in all probability it would not be possible to confine hostilities within the frontiers of Korea."

President Rhee disliked these measures which to him savored of appeasement. He set out immediately to obtain guarantees for Korea's security, which he believed was in jeopardy as long as a Communist regime existed in the north. On October 1, 1953, the United States and the Republic of Korea (South Korea) signed a mutual defense treaty which required the parties to consult together whenever either one "is of the opinion that the political independence or security of either is threatened by external armed attack." Each party recognized that an armed attack in the Pacific area on either party would be considered as dangerous to its own peace and safety and declared that "it would act to meet the common danger in accordance with its own constitutional processes."

The treaty was mild and limited in scope. It was worked in such manner as to restrain South Korea from initiating any forceful moves toward unification. At the same time it took cognizance of the desirability of unification by peaceful processes. The treaty accorded the United States the right to dispose of land, sea, and air forces in and about the territory of Korea. It contained no obligation for Americans to participate in the internal security of the Republic of Korea or to take any military measures as a result of a violent overthrow of the government of a *coup d'état*. There was, in fact, *no obligation* for the United States to maintain any armed forces whatsoever in Korea.

President Rhee had more urgent need for immediate economic assistance than for long-term guarantees of security. The facts of economic destruction overshadowed the spiritual stimulation of "liberation." During the hostilities in Korea, more than a million Korean cilivians died. Hundreds of villages went up in smoke. Two and a half million people became homeless refugees, and twice that number depended upon relief. The details of economic chaos duplicated the worst features of postwar China. Retail prices increased 7200 percent from 1947 to 1954 with all the suffering, bribing, and black-marketing which that ugly fact implied.

Battered Korea looked to the United States for help. The latter undertook a five-year billion dollar assistance program. Ships bound to Korea carried cargoes of building materials, machinery, plants, and food in the hope of assisting Korea to provide a sound economic basis for a brighter political future. President Rhee was a hard man to help because he demanded so much. In his opinion, his position was justified because he was deserted in midstream. He had carried the major burdens of fighting Communists and was left with nothing but rubble and ruin in his beloved land. He wanted a strong army which would not have to depend upon the goodwill and support of the United States in the event of future hostilities. Such an army would be costly, and he expected the United States to pay all its bills for at least ten years. He wanted the United States to underwrite all economic-development plans for Korea. He saw no reason why Korea should not have, at American expense, new factories, a modern highway system, a good merchant marine, respectable tourist hotels and a steady stream of food supplies and consumers' goods for his underprivileged people.

President Rhee was equally adamant in his views on foreign affairs. He looked upon negotiations with Communists as a waste of time, and he saw no hope for peace in Korea short of defeating the Communists in battle. Therefore he scorned the article in the armistice agreement which called for a political conference "to settle the Korean question 'and so forth.'" Nonetheless, the foreign ministers of the United Kingdom, France, the United States, and the Soviet Union in February 1954, jointly agreed that a conference should meet in Geneva to reach a settlement of the Korean question (and at the same time to discuss the problem of restoring peace in Indochina).

Negotiations for peace in Korea were less fruitful than the earlier efforts to reach the armistice agreement. Delegates from the Soviet Union, the People's Republic of China, and North Korea met in Geneva on April 26, 1954, with the delegates from South Korea and those United Nations members with interests in Korea. Both sides said they wanted peace and unification, but neither side was willing to depart from its own proposals. The North Korean delegate suggested a plan for nationwide elections which the American representative called a Chinese copy of the Soviet scheme for the unification of Germany. The South Korean repeated his firm opposition to any "sell-out" or "Munich-style" appeasement and called for an uncompromising stand against any surrender of the freedom for which so many fought and died. The British cochairman of the conference, Anthony Eden, suggested that because of no possible agreement on the authority of the United Nations and the principle of free elections, the Korean question should be returned to the United Nations. Thus the war, which was not a war but a "police action" and which never had a formal beginning, never reached a technical end. It was laid to rest on the tables of the United Nations in New York. Those who died in Korea were totally unaware of such subtleties.

President Rhee visited the United States by official invitation in late summer, 1954. He appealed to the American Congress and the American people to support his call for an immediate military crusade against the Communists. He would begin in North Korea. He wanted to fight, fight, fight against the Communists everywhere—in Indochina, on the China mainland and in Central Europe. In his view, the salvation of humanity depended upon the defeat of the Communists, and his Koreans would do their share.

KOREA'S TROUBLES

Politics within Korea clouded the prospects for an independent, unified, and democratic government. Both North and South Korea became more confirmed in their positions with the passing years. Neither half of Korea was granted admission to the United Nations, but the world body faithfully discussed the problem of Korea at every annual session. Until 1960 the UN operated a substantial assistance program. It continued the work of the Commission on Unification and Rehabilitation and maintained its forces along the thirty-eighth parallel. Periodically it reaffirmed support of the armistice agreement and its intention to preserve peace in the area. Whenever a resolution in favor of South Korea was introduced into the General Assembly, the United States and its friends voted "yes," the Soviets and their allies "no," and a large number of Afro-Asian states abstained. In 1961 the pro-Korea faction in the UN was obliged to admit that prospects of unification, on which a full measure of stability and sound economic progress depended, seemed as remote as ever.

North Korea became a hard core member of the Communist bloc, friendly both to the Soviet Union and the People's Republic of China. Treaties and assistance programs were negotiated with both, and Korean officials exchanged goodwill visits with their counterparts in both Moscow and Peking. Kim Ilsong in North Korea was accorded a personal position which was as supreme as that of Stalin in the heyday of the cult of the individual in Russia. The Korean Workers' Party (the Communists), with a million and a half members, dominated the political scene and corralled one hundred percent of the votes in any popular election. The army was toughened, and its officers were placed in key political positions. For a time General Nam Il became North Korea's foreign minister. Economically, North Korea claimed progress "with the speed of a winged horse." Agriculture was collectivized; mines, utilities, transport systems, and heavy industries were placed under state ownership and management. Cities were rebuilt, and new houses were constructed. The seven-year plan launched in 1961 covered the whole gamut of food, fabrics, steel, power, coal, and housing, and was apparently intended to make North Korea a Communist showcase in Asia.

Because of its experience in the war, and because of affinity with China, North Korea was bitterly anti-American. It objected to Khrushchev's overtures for peaceful coexistence with the United States and it tried to disrupt relations between the United States, Japan, and South Korea. North Korea pursued a soft line toward South Korea in spite of South Korea's belligerence. North Korea supported Soviet proposals for another international conference on Korea and, after the withdrawal of Chinese troops from Korea in 1958, announced its own program looking toward unification. It suggested that north and south should enter into agreements for trade and cultural exchange and should undertake discussions for "free and democratic elections." North Korea would be willing to permit neutral nations—but not the United Nations—to supervise elections, if first the UN troops would be withdrawn. Its fundamental position was that, if the United Nations should first withdraw, progress might be made toward unification. On the other hand, South Korea said that if North Korea would show progress toward real democracy and permit genuinely "free" elections, then the UN forces could gladly go home.

The political troubles in South Korea stemmed from the undemocratic regime of Syngman Rhee. President Rhee was first elected in 1948, then re-elected in 1952 and again in 1956. He seemed to consider himself as Korea's indispensable man. In his advancing age (he was eighty-four in 1960) he became more autocratic and intolerant. As 1960 approached, it became clear that he intended to run for a fourth term, and he used relations with North Korea as his chief campaign material. He said "our brothers in the north call for rescue, their only hope must come from us."

He asserted that the North Koreans violated their armistice engagements every day. He accused them of importing the fastest Soviet planes and the latest military equipment, expanding their air strips and enlarging their ground forces. He alleged that the North Korean army was twice as strong in 1960 as it was in 1953, and he insisted that the ostentatious withdrawal of Chinese troops was merely an artful dodge. He maintained that the Chinese kept a strategic reserve at full strength just across the border on the Manchurian side of the Yalu River. In his opinion, the North Koreans stimulated and paid for subversive activities in South Korea. He said that his men had arrested more than 13,000 Communist agents, guerrillas, and underground saboteurs apart from the military spies which they had captured between 1953 and 1954. Thus he needed tough laws, and he inspired the assembly to pass them. Antisubversion legislation made it a criminal offense to disseminate "false" or "distorted" news—which meant that every medium of communication in South Korea was placed at the mercy of the administration. The police became increasingly bold and oppressive of human rights.

President Rhee's totalitarian methods precipitated a showdown in the spring of 1960. He ordered elections on March 15, and his henchmen in the ministry of the interior and in every town and village in South Korea saw to it that he won. The students seethed, and after a month they burst forth in riots. President Rhee's own army refused to disperse the demonstrators. There was no doubt what the students wanted—the resignation of President Rhee. He had no alternative. He retired, for the good of the country, and took refuge in Hawaii, his former home in exile. New elections were decreed. In July 1960, a comparatively mild regime came to power headed by John M. Chang (Chang Myun) as prime minister.

The pendulum swung from severity to carelessness. Politics became dangerously unstable, and economic conditions deteriorated. Some army officers alleged that they could stand by no longer because the "devil's hand of the Reds reached into the cabinet of John M. Chang." On May 16, 1961, they completed their organization of a military junta and staged a *coup d'etat*. They ousted Chang and his easygoing aides, cleared the streets of hoodlums, and raided the lounging placers of loafers in dance halls and cheap hotels. They declared martial law, imposed a strict curfew, censored the press and—to ease the shocks—distributed rice to the poor. General Park (Pak) Chung-hi emerged as the power within the junta. He received his early education and training in Japan, but he was greatly influenced by American ways and American ideas. He said that the students had brought the country to chaos; it was time the army stepped in to restore order.

The army junta organized a supreme council for national reconstruction which was ultranationalistic and ardently anti-Communist. Its master mind and driving force was the head of the central intelligence agency— General Kim Chongpil—who perfected an organization which placed his operatives in every ministry and agency of government. General Kim's job was to nip subversion; prevent assassination; watch the students and servants, intellectuals and foreigners; check corruption; control the left; and exercise strict surveillance over every aspect of life which was in any way connected with public affairs. The press was muzzled, and ordinary politics were suspended. The junta published a little booklet, called *Our Nation's Path,* which admitted that Korea had no experience with democracy and would have a very difficult time finding the way to democracy and progress. Nevertheless the army expected every Korean citizen to learn about duty and responsibility, so that the army could hand back the control of the government to civilians.

The first act of the junta was to bring crooks and criminals to trial. Former political insiders were arrested for illegal importation of Japanese automobiles, manipulation of the stock market, and using information or contracts involving foreign aid for personal gain. The worst scandal was the erection of a swank tourist hotel resort in Walker Hill, a notorious section of poverty-stricken Seoul. Thirteen businessmen, who amassed fortunes during Chang's administration, were convicted of evading almost $33,000,000 in income taxes. Chang himself was put on trial for his life and was sentenced to ten years in jail.

The junta then took steps to prepare the way for the return of "democratic government," which was promised for the end of 1963. General Park instructed his associates to organize a Democratic-Republican Party, which he anticipated would become a vehicle for him to transfer his regime from a military to a civilian basis. In December 1962, the country was asked to vote on constitutional amendments which would give Korea a political structure roughly comparable to that of the United States. The amendments called for an American-style president and separation of the powers of the various branches of government rather than the British system of ministerial responsibility to the legislature. The amendments were approved by a four-to-one vote, and General Park congratulated the public on its "clever judgement."

The junta discovered that the return to democratic processes was not as easy as expected. Therefore, the junta hedged on its promise and announced that it would continue its tenure as a military regime for four more years. Civilian politicians protested, and the American State Department added its restrained comment that "prolongation of military rule could constitute a threat to stable and effective government." The junta was caught on the horns of the classic dilemma—how to be strong and effective yet tolerant and democratic. National elections were held in November, 1963. By a surprisingly narrow margin, General Park was elected president and his party was given majority control in the national assembly.

The prestige of the junta suffered. Army officers split into a dozen factions, and their excursion into politics weakened the morale and the power of the fighting services. Men who emerged in the public spotlight with good reputations were charged with corruption, dictatorship, and inefficiency. Some of the original members of the junta were themselves clamped behind bars, and others were sent abroad on convenient "inspection trips." General Kim Chongpil, the genius of the organization, was named as a roving ambassador. Korea teetered on the edge of a political volcano. The army became a hothouse for intrigue. Political parties proliferated as old-style leaders struggled to build up their personal machines. Students grew restive and angry. The air was charged with the danger of anarchy or civil war, and Koreans of every persuasion were all too ready to place the blame for their difficulties on their friends abroad.

Meanwhile, no progress was possible on the only diplomatic question which was of importance to South Korea—relations with Japan. Geography made Korea and Japan neighbors; history made them enemies. As long as President Rhee was in power, he nursed the idea that every Japanese kimono hid a dagger intended for a Korean heart. An understanding was impossible. Arguments between the two countries centered about claims and debts, fishing rights, definition of territorial waters, jurisdiction over controversial islands, trading rights and boycotts, the whole range of subversive activities, and the repatriation of Japanese in Korea and Koreans in Japan. With the accession of the junta, the official Korean attitude toward Japan became more reasonable. Negotiations were conducted in a more favorable atmosphere, and hope was held out for the restoration of normal diplomatic relations. Those hopes subsided as the junta looked less promising to the Japanese as the Korean wave of the future.

The junta encountered its greatest difficulties in the sphere of economics. Generals were not good economists. They had no blueprints for national development, and, like their predecessors, they were handicapped by lack of capital, resources, and management talent. Korea was poor to begin with, and every year the situation got worse. Economic growth took place at an approximate rate of two percent annually; the population increased half again as fast. In spite of all the assistance from the United States and the United Nations, agricultural improvements and the new factories could not keep up with the demands of the expanding population. As assistance tapered off, Korea's economic problems multiplied. Unemployment stood at a steady level of nearly twenty-five percent of the labor force. Of the men who were demobilized from the armed services each year, or who were graduated from one of Korea's fifty-five colleges and universities, only one in three could find a job. Of 4300 students who went to the United States between 1953 and 1960, only one in ten returned. Half of those were unemployed. For each job in private industry or in the government, there were at least twenty applicants.

The economic picture had its bleak points and its hopeful aspects. The junta came up with a five-year plan in 1962 which concentrated on electric power, agriculture, and public works. How could it be implemented? The government's budget was in the red, and the prospect was that income would go down and expenditures would go up. The army accounted for fifty percent of the total cost of government, and that figure could not be reduced. As a matter of fact it was bound to increase as Americans insisted on greater cuts in their heavy programs of military and economic assistance.

The future of South Korea was not entirely dark. South Korea was capable of producing a surplus of rice, which could pay for advice and assistance from Japan. Trade between the two countries was possible at a greatly expanded level. At first glance, South Korea's economy appeared to be gloomier than that of the north. But North Korea was not prone to publicize its difficulties, and it gave out only such information as tended to create an optimistic impression. South Korea's difficulties were well-known and advertised to its friends and foes. The patent fact was that the greatest economic indicator of all—the movement of people in search of better conditions—was overwhelmingly from north to south. The Korean people possessed energy and skills which if utilized properly could increase the nation's productive output and consuming power. Most of all it was entirely likely that Korea's allies would continue to search for the most effective way to lend a helping hand.

SUGGESTED READING

Berger, Carl, *Korea Knot* (Philadelphia, U. of Pennsylvania, 1957).

Clark, Mark W., *From the Danube to the Yalu* (New York, Harper, 1954).

Fehrenbach, T. R., *This Kind of War* (New York, Macmillan, 1963).

Goodrich, Leland M., *Korea* (New York, Council on Foreign Relations, 1956).

Joy, Admiral C. Turner, *How Communists Negotiate* (New York, Macmillan, 1955).

Kyung, Cho Chung, *New Korea* (New York, Macmillan, 1962).

Leckie, Robert, *Conflict, History of the Korean War, 1950–1953* (New York, Putnam, 1962).

Marshall, S. L. A., *River and the Gauntlet* (New York, Morrow, 1953).

McCune, Shannon, *Korea's Heritage* (Rutland, Charles E. Tuttle, 1956).

Oliver, Robert T., *Syngmann Rhee* (New York, Dodd, 1955).

Osgood, Cornelius, *Koreans and Their Culture* (New York, Ronald, 1951).

Riley, John W., *Reds Take a City* (New Brunswick, Rutgers U., 1951).

Rudolph, P., *North Korea's Political and Economic Structure* (New York, Institute of Pacific Relations, 1959).

Russ, Martin, *Last Parallel* (New York, Rinehart, 1957).

Spanier, John W., *Truman-MacArthur Controversy and the Korean War* (Cambridge, Harvard, 1959).

Stone, I. F., *Hidden History of the Korean War* (New York, Monthly Review Press, 1952).

United States Senate, *United States and the Korean Problem, Documents, 1943–1953*, Senate Document 74, 83rd Congress, First Session (Washington, Government Printing Office, 1953).

Vatcher, William H., *Panmunjom* (New York, Praeger, 1958).

Whiting, Allen S., *China Crosses the Yalu* (New York, Macmillan, 1960).

VI

THE CONTEMPORARY SCENE

IV

THE CONTEMPORARY SCENE

29

The New Japan

Within seven years of the signing of the instrument of surrender, Japan resumed its place of importance in the society of nations. With the coming into effect of the treaty of peace with most of its former enemies in April, 1952, Japan became once more the strongest of the free nations of Asia. A chastised—but proud—generation undertook the reconstruction of the New Japan. The nation emerged from the occupation, not pro-American, pro-British, or pro-anything, except pro-Japan. It was recognized immediately as a leader among its neighbors. It was a pioneer and a model for other Asians.

The new Japan was a remarkable combination of the traditional and the ultramodern. Jet planes roared over ancient-type fishing vessels on the approach to the international airport at Tokyo. New department stores and giant office buildings rose above the myriads of flimsy, delicate, unmistakably Japanese wood-and-paper homes. The finest electric trains in the world raced from modern city to modern city through countryside which looked as if it might have been lifted out of an eighteenth century print. The famous cone of Mt. Fuji was usually obscured by the eye-stinging smog, the curse of modern industry in Japan, as well as England or the United States. In the new Japan, symphonies competed with *no* plays, movies with the kabuki theater, and baseball with Japanese-style wrestling. The girls clung to kimonos but imported the latest creations from Paris, Rome, or New York. Tokyo preserved its geisha houses but livened the old "floating world" with pin-ball machines, coffee houses, strip-tease joints, and spectacular night clubs.

Yoshida Shigeru, premier during the crucial years 1949–1955, presided over the transition from the occupation to independence. More than any other person, he was the architect of the new Japan. He endeavored to keep Japan on the democratic road and to lay solid foundations for economic development. He was responsible for lining up Japan with the anti-Communist group of nations, and he was a zealous guardian of the nation's prestige and diplomatic integrity. He steered a wise course between the "old guard" and the "renovationists," identifying himself with the conservatives but giving sufficient rein to his opponents to prevent social chaos. He deserved a large share of credit for the stability and progress of contemporary Japan. Those who followed him in office found it extremely difficult to live up to his example.

GOVERNMENT AND POLITICAL PARTIES

The government structure of the new Japan was determined by the constitution of 1947. The emperor was the symbol of the state rather than the source of sovereignty. He enjoyed new prestige because of the humanization of his position. The marriage of his son, the crown prince, in 1958 promised greater popularity for the imperial institution in the years ahead. The parliamentary system of government functioned effectively in spite of occasional lapses from dignity in the diet. The six-year 250-member upper house, or House of Councilors, added the expected measure of stability to the legislative process, and the 467-member lower house, or House of Representatives, reflected in a satisfactory way the diverse interests of the broad masses of the people. The lower house, which was elected at least every four years, was the supreme lawmaking authority and it exercised control over the public purse. By its power to name the prime minister, it was the ultimate authority over the armed forces. Japan created a national defense agency with self-defense forces in 1954. This was its way of getting around the constitutional prohibition on an army, navy, and air force. The police were placed under the jurisdiction of a diet-controlled national public safety commission. Because of bitter experiences in the past, the Japanese showed extreme care to prevent the return of totalitarian practices.

The democratic practices initiated by the occupation were carefully preserved, and they seemed to take deep root in the unfamiliar soil of Japan. Free elections were held whenever a government lost its majority in the House of Representatives. Freedom of speech, freedom to assemble, and even freedom to riot were protected from undue government interference. At times Japan seemed almost to err on the lenient side, permitting demonstrations which called for stronger measures than the police were able or willing to take. New rights and freedoms, new responsibilities and opportunities, coupled with unprecedented economic prosperity, gave millions of Japanese a tangible stake in the preservation of the democratic system of government.

Most, but not all, of the responsibility for making the democratic system work rested on the political parties which came back into prominence after their near-extinction at the hands of the militarists before World War II. The parties were like mutual-aid organizations of politicians in the manner of exclusive clubs, without too many ties going down to voters at grass-root levels.

The prewar Seiyukai reappeared as postwar Liberals, and the Minseito came to new life in the Democrats and Progressives. In spite of their labels—Liberals, Democrats, and Progressives—these three parties were conservative. They merged to form a coalition popularly called the Liberal Democratic Party (LDP). Their members consisted of bureaucrats, businessmen, and farmers. Their leaders came from ex-officials or graduates of the national universities who passed higher civil service, judiciary, or foreign service examinations. They were linked by school, ministry, or family ties, and they often enjoyed the backing of influential persons in the various professions. The conservatives recruited strenuously among professional associations and such trade groups as barbers and cosmeticians, laundrymen and dry cleaners, theater managers, innkeepers, public-bath operators, and restaurant proprietors. They paid close attention to chambers of commerce and the powerful agricultural and fishing cooperatives.

Instead of forming their own local party cells, the conservatives used the ample funds at their disposal to make deals with local bosses. In exchange for votes, candidates for national offices distributed cash and promised support for pet local projects in which the bosses were interested. Local bosses carried as many as ten million names on their rolls, but the LDP listed fewer than a half-million as regular party members.

The conservative leadership was divided sharply by individual loyalties and personal rivalries. Within the party it was a constant battle to forge a combination of men who could gather sufficient strength to form a government. Factional leaders who became prime ministers included Ishibashi, Kishi, and Ikeda; the price of their leadership was the judicious distribution of key administrative posts. Factions temporarily in step with the government were known as "mainstream" or "main-current" factions, while those out of power or out of favor were dubbed "anti mainstream" or "anti main-current." These small groups pulled apart or coalesced as personal interests dictated, and they waged a never-ending struggle for advantageous position. Whenever a government appeared to be rocky, a wholesale reshuffle took place. Diet members of the majority party scrambled to disassociate themselves from the apparent loser and to line up with the prospective winner. Since the conservatives always polled approximately two-thirds of the popular vote and elected two-thirds of the lower house in the diet, it was factional bickering rather than the strength of the opposition which determined the succession of cabinets and prime ministers.

The platform of the LDP called for peace, in conformity with the spirit of the United Nations, and for the active development of peaceful diplomacy. The party did not wish to permit the opposition to monopolize the issue of "peace." The conservative platform was against war, but it advocated limited rearmament for the sake of honorable self-defense. It opposed the use of atomic or hydrogen bombs and supported the idea of trade expansion even with Communist China. It desired the normalization of relations both with the People's Republic of China and the Soviet Union.

The Liberal Democratic Party was more concerned with internal policies than with international relations. It was the party of internal stability and prosperity. It did not go so far as to suggest the return of emperor-worship, the reconcentration of wealth under the *zaibatsu,* or the re-creation of a totalitarian, single-party state. It was dedicated to democracy and the free-enterprise system. It did not subscribe to laissez-faire economics because it wanted the government to take such measures as might be required to "rectify" the labor movement, rationalize international trade, and to promote a cautious, conservative welfare state. Ideologically, the LDP was the bitter foe of left wing-ism and Communism.

The heart of political opposition in Japan was the Japan Socialist Party (JSP) which was the heir of prewar proletarian movements. *Socialist* was not a bad word in Japan: it was warm and imaginative. It represented the hopes for a better way of life on the part of the underprivileged. Until recently, the great mass of Japanese fell into that category. With burgeoning prosperity, many people became too well off to nurse a grievance against the social order. Socialism retained its appeal as a utopian philosophy, but lost its attraction as a practical method for political action. Economic progress was an inhospitable environment for Socialists.

Prewar proletarian parties never won a majority in the diet nor got a chance to choose a government. In 1947 Katayama Tetsu became Japan's first Christian and first Socialist prime minister. His regime was no more distinguished than the administrations of the conservatives for honesty or perspicacity. In the contemporary period, Socialists of all varieties ordinarily polled slightly more than one-third the popular votes and elected a similar proportion of the members of the diet. This figure of one-third plus one was important because it was the number required to block any conservative attempt to bring about rearmament by an amendment to the constitution. The majority party could never quite muster sufficient strength to produce the required two-thirds vote for the amendment process. The opposition was in an anomalous position. It could block action but could not implement a program of its own. The opposition groups had no reasonable prospect of winning much more than their accustomed thirty-five to forty percent of voter support.

The strength of the Japan Socialist Party came from the large cities, organized labor, and the intellectuals. Students were inclined to be doctrinaire Marxists, and half the JSP diet members were college or university graduates. Party fortunes depended almost exclusively upon the status or condition of the two large federations of labor unions: Sohyo, or the General Council of Trade Unions, and Zenro, of the Japan Trade Union Congress. The former, inclined further to the left, represented the interests of about four million members. The latter was only about one-quarter as large. The JSP was healthy when the unions were cooperative and expansive; it suffered when the unions were indifferent or enmeshed in personal vendettas.

The JSP itself was in many respects a ghost party. Funds were scarce, and nationwide issues lack much importance for candidates who fashioned their campaign strategy according to local conditions. National headquarters ordinarily gave little assistance or support to their individual standard-bearers. It demanded a lively imagination to link the Hokkaido miners and the Marxist study groups of the large universities in a single political structure. Perhaps it would be more meaningful to describe the JSP as a movement than as an organization. Only a few thousand members considered themselves as active party workers, and they were subject to no such discipline as characterized the Communists. Yet they turned out in the neighborhood of fourteen million votes. The greatest weakness of the Socialists was to neglect the middle classes, both in the country and in the cities. After land reform eradicated the worst evils of tenantry in Japan, most farmers were immune to the ordinary rabble-rousing appeals used by Communists elsewhere in Asia. But the farmers of Japan still had their problems, and they might have been attracted to the JSP by promises of justice and equality. Likewise the small businessmen needed political allies, but they were courted more ardently by Conservatives than by Socialists.

If anything, factions were worse in the Japan Socialist Party than in the Liberal Democratic Party. Factions represented every shade of opinion from extreme right—near-capitalists—to extreme left—the near-Communists. Leadership in the JSP enjoyed precarious tenure. It gravitated usually toward men of the center, temporarily in good favor with the main stream of Sohyo. The cleavages within the ranks of the JSP were so sharp that in 1959 a faction of rightists under Nishio Suehiro defected from the main party to set up a separate party. These men called themselves the Democratic Socialist Party (DSP), and they controlled a substantial bloc of votes in both houses of the diet. They cooperated with their fellow socialists in opposing rearmament, but they differed in practically every other aspect of their program.

The right wing of the JSP refused to accept a statement which

Asanuma, the leader, made in Peking in 1959 to the effect that "American imperialists were the common enemy of China and Japan." This incident caused the party split and the formation of the DSP. The main difference between the right and the left—both doctrinaire Marxian Socialists—was that the right was more concerned with the conflict between democracy and Communist totalitarianism while the left was more preoccupied with the struggle between capitalistic and socialistic society as represented by the free world and the Communist group of nations. Whenever right-wing Socialists wanted to cooperate with a nonsocialist party, they looked toward the Liberal Democratic Party; by way of contrast, the left wing looked toward the Communists. The right wing wanted to step up its activities on behalf of the middle class; the left wing was more interested in the proletariat, particularly in the labor unions. The right wing opposed, the left wing condoned, the Communist sympathy which existed in the labor movement.

Sharp differences characterized the views of right and left in foreign affairs. The right did not think the United States was too bad, although it opposed Japan's sole dependence on its American ally. It favored gradual elimination of all military ties between the two countries, including the controversial bases. It rejected categorically the Communist view of the world. The left was more bitterly anti-United States and demanded immediate American withdrawal from its bases in Japan. It looked more kindly toward China and Russia, but it wanted no more commitment to Communists than to the democracies. Right-wing Socialists in their propaganda literature used such mild words as *peace, neutrality,* and *nonaggression.* The leftists used such vitriolic phrases as "cannon fodder," "atomic guinea pigs," and "cheap Japanese blood in a new imperialist war." Socialists of all shades won popular approval for their stand on independence and neutralism but alienated public opinion by their ideological affinity with Russia and China.

After the defection of the right wing, the JSP drew up its platform in such manner as to make it easy for the dissidents to return to the fold. In foreign policy, the JSP came out for adoption of neutralism, termination of the American security treaty, and acceptance of a four-nation nonaggression pact to include Japan, the United States, the Soviet Union, and Communist China. It urged the recognition of Communist China and its admission into the United Nations. In domestic policy, the party called for the preservation of the constitution without change, and it advocated the progressive disbandment of the Japanese defense forces. It urged the closing of the gap between the rural and urban areas, enactment of a national minimum wage, active opposition to increased prices, and the improvement of the national pension and health systems.

Platform-making was no more than the first step in answering questions which plagued the Socialists. How far should they go in ideological orthodoxy? To what extent should they make ideological compromises for the sake of practical politics? One faction suggested that an admirable slogan would be "American Material Progress, Soviet Social Security, British Parliamentary Democracy and Japan's No-War Constitution." Some leaders urged closer study of the British Labour Party and its political tactics. Others felt that the whole emphasis of the Socialist movement should be on improved conditions for the workers rather than upon the acquisition of political power. Socialists could not agree on the merits of demonstrations and riots. Some insisted on sticking to parliamentary procedures; others argued that the only answer to defeat in the diet was to "take to the streets."

Communists were less powerful than Socialists but they made a little headway with their campaign to make themselves a "lovable party." Communists basically were not popular in Japan because of their association with Russia and their opposition to the institution of the emperor. They were more out of tune with the times than the Socialists because of the widespread prosperity. Their only trump card was the close relationship between their bitter anti-Americanism and the more strident variety of Japanese nationalism. The police kept the Communists under strict surveillance so the party failed to win the open support of great numbers of Japanese. The bad behavior of the Communists among the Japanese repatriates from Russian territory added to their unattractive popular image.

In 1949 the Communists won ten percent of the votes; in 1963 they dropped to four percent. They placed five members in the lower house and only one (Nozaka Sanzo, the party chairman) in the upper house. Card-carrying membership in the party fluctuated around 100,000, but 1,775,000 votes were cast for the Communists in the elections of 1963. The party confined itself to underground activities until Khrushchev's speech in 1956, although it aired its views publicly in its daily newspaper, *Akahata* (the Red Flag). The first national convention of the party in eleven years was held in 1958. Japanese Communists showed a closer sympathy with China than Russia in the ideological rift, but they preferred to hold themselves as aloof as possible from intraparty quarrels. They preferred to concentrate on Japanese domestic matters, although they realized that short of an economic depression or a major war they could never be more than an opposition party or a protest faction.

DEMOCRACY IN ACTION

Aside from the major parties—the Liberal Democrats, Socialists, and Communists—some groups achieved a certain amount of political influence in contemporary Japan. Extreme rightist groups, with names like the Japan Reconstruction League, Patriotic Youth Volunteers' Committee, and National Martyr's Youth Corps, received world-wide attention when a young fanatic coolly stabbed the Socialist leader, Asanuma, to death in 1960 in full view of the television cameras. A Buddhist-affiliated *Sokka Gakkai,* or Value Creation Society, emerged as an example of a Japanese organization which was not, strictly speaking, a political party, but which exerted a significant amount of political influence. It boasted of three million households in its following, and in 1962 it elected all nine of its candidates to the House of Councilors. Its appeal was religious and emotional. It appeared to be a ready-made instrumentality which might be used by a rising demagogue.

Political behavior in Japan approximated the patterns of the more experienced democracies of the West. Six general elections were held between 1952 and 1963. The results were usually slightly less than two-thirds Liberal-Democratic, one-third Socialist, and a sprinkling of Communists and others. Not one in three Japanese voted a strict party line. Japanese, like their more sophisticated counterparts in the West, listened respectfully to campaign speeches and cast their ballots for the candidates they liked the best. Radio and TV, newspapers, electioneering pamphlets, family conferences, and "advice" from the landlord or the boss counted for no more and no less in Japan than in the United States. The candidate who polled the highest vote in the elections of 1962 was a panelist on the Japanese "What's My Line?" He was followed closely by an ex-general, the head of the Tobacco Marketing Corporation and the president of the Midwives Association. In those elections, two and a half million ballots were ruled invalid because they were marred by handwritten phrases "scornful of politics." As life became more complicated and more interesting, Japanese tended to show increasing indifference to the privilege of the polls. But apathy vanished in times of crisis.

Not many issues captured nation-wide attention in the early years of contemporary Japan. A Subversives Activities Prevention Law was passed (1952) which gave special powers to the government for the preservation of public safety. This law was reminiscent of the hated "peace preservation laws" of prewar days, so it was not invoked in the first decade of its existence. Teachers in the public schools were constant subjects of legislative attention, but actual legislation was impossible because of the conflict between public security and civil rights. Premier Kishi, in 1958, threw the diet into an uproar when he tried to push a police bill through the legislative mill. He wanted to give the police more power, but he was forced to retreat before a storm of protest. The Japanese would not permit the slightest step in the direction of the return of tyranny.

A crisis occurred in May and June 1960, in connection with the diet's consideration of the revised Japan–United States security treaty and the anticipated visit of President Eisenhower. Students, officials, teachers—including Socialists, Communists, and anti-mainstream Conservatives—participated in riots which were anti-American, antigovernment, and anti-Kishi. Procedures in the diet degenerated into a parody on democracy and the snake dances in the streets turned the clock back to mob scenes in the heyday of militarism. Leaders of the Zengakuren, or Federation of Student Self-Government Associations, spearheaded the demonstrations. They accepted money wherever they could get it (no money, no demonstrations), and they admitted some of their funds came from anti-Kishi rightist industrialists. The nation's business came to a standstill. In due course, the treaty was ratified. President Eisenhower's visit was canceled, and the rioters cooled down. Premier Kishi resigned, and new elections were ordered. On July 18, 1960, Ikeda became premier.

In spite of occasional lapses into disorder, contemporary Japan displayed a creditable amount of political stability. Its time-honored institutions kept pace with the rapid changes in the nation's economy and social structure. Japan made democracy an essential part of its social fabric and proved that democracy could flourish in Asia as well as in Europe or America. Everybody loved the atmosphere of freedom. The existences of disputes merely underscored the strength of the body politic. Parliament and parties showed weaknesses which were serious, but not fatal. Japan's internal political strength was entirely adequate for the successful fulfillment of international obligations which flowed from Japan's high place in the world.

JAPANESE-AMERICAN DIPLOMACY

After the peace treaty of San Francisco restored Japan's political independence, Japan made a new inventory of its national interests. Deprived of its possessions on the mainland of Asia and in the South Seas, Japan was confined to its four main islands. It retained residual sovereignty over the Ryukyus and hoped for recovery from Russia of two tiny fog-bound islands off the shores of Hokkaido. This was an extremely limited area for a country which anticipated an eventual population plateau of perhaps 120,000,000 inhabitants.

Japan's primary concern was its national security. The nation was saddled with a constitution which outlawed armed forces and the method of war for settling disputes, and it was committed to a policy of dependence upon the United States for protection against extreme aggression or internal disorders. The majority of the Japanese people remembered what war was like, and they were determined never to experience it again. More than 200,000 Japanese bore the marks of atomic bombing, and thousands more carried the scars of burns or bullets. Japan was aware that its population was concentrated heavily in urban centers which were "sitting ducks" for planes or missiles from Sino-Soviet bases. The feeling was general that war was futile, since no one could entertain a hope for meaningful victory. Pacifism was deep and genuine, particularly in the hearts of the older generation. Pride and self-reliance called for a modicum of rearmament, but Premier Yoshida voiced the sentiments of his people when he said the idea of rearmament seemed to him on verge of idiocy. Rearmament would risk the return of militarism and would threaten the death of the infant democracy. Besides, Japan was poor; and it preferred rice to guns.

The Americans exerted pressure for greater Japanese efforts in the direction of self-defense and in 1954 entered into mutual assistance agreements according to which Japan undertook to expand its self-defense forces. It agreed to put approximately 250,000 men in service. Japan promised to equip its ground forces with tanks and medium and heavy artillery and to create an embryo navy with destroyers, submarines, mine sweepers, and auxiliary craft. The air force was limited to fighters which were trained for ground support and interception. Most of the bills were paid by Americans, and the United States provided a military advisory group of seven hundred officers for purposes of advice, assistance, and training in all branches of military activity. The government of Japan showed no enthusiasm for these measures. It refused to consider conscription for its youth, and it would have nothing to do with atomic weapons. Atomic missiles were not permitted on Japanese bases, and atomic submarines were not allowed to put in to Japanese ports. In 1957 Japan and the United States formed a bilateral committee for security affairs.

Japanese attitudes on foreign relations, as distinguished from defense measures, stemmed from Japan's strategic location between the Communist-dominated Asian mainland and the American-dominated Pacific Ocean. In the event of a clash between the two giant-power combinations, Japan was caught in the middle. It was linked with the United States by practical politics, but it would have preferred nonalignment as an intellectual ideal. Neutralism was appealing to the heart, but association with the free world was dictated by the head. Japan did not share the pathological American fear of communism. It was determined not to be a pawn of the United States because it was haunted by the possibility of desertion by the Americans in a moment of crisis. American vacillation and isolationism were traditional. Japan appreciated its own importance as a vital cog in the machinery for collective security in the Pacific, especially after its admission to the United Nations in 1956.

Japan considered itself not as an American puppet but as an indispensable pillar of prosperity and stability throughout East Asia. Japan believed that it had more power to mold the future, and to determine the destiny of communism, than the combined military potential of South Koreans, National Chinese, and Vietnamese. Japan remembered that Stalin once said that if communism could capture Japan, communism throughout the world would be made invincible. Japan knew that it was vulnerable and needed the United States; it also realized that Japan itself was the strongest bastion of democracy in Asia. These ideas were not confirmed to the Japanese elite. The "man in the street" was surprisingly well-informed and interested in foreign affairs; and it was worthy of note that the city people, the youth, and the better-educated often favored attitudes which Americans considered less correct and less desirable.

Japan and the United States showed a basic difference in their approach to problems of world affairs. To Japan, the essential role of diplomacy was to improve the level of living; to the United States, the overriding objective of international relations was to contain, deter and, if possible, eliminate, the menace of communism. In bilateral negotiations, Japan steered the conversations and agreements into channels of finance and trade.

Much of Japan's prosperity was built on good economic relations with the United States. Americans spent huge sums in Japan during the occupation, and bought vast quantities of Japanese goods during the Korean War. After Japan became independent, Americans invested heavily in Japanese industries. Eighty percent of more than a billion dollars in foreign investments in Japan was represented by American capital. Scarcely a day went past without some agreement between a Japanese firm and a private American firm for the use of patents on the payment of a satisfactory royalty. One-third of Japan's trade was conducted with the United States as Japan became the second-best customer of the United States. More than a billion dollars in goods flowed annually in each direction; but Japan bought more than it sold. All the transistor radios, cameras, plastic raincoats, shirts, cotton textiles, and baseball gloves which Japan exported to the United States could not pay for the rice, wheat, dairy products, cotton, scrap iron, and petroleum which Japan imported from American sources.

Arguments arose between the two countries which took on the familiar coloring of economic nationalism. Americans complained of the huge quantities of Japanese imports which threatened the "American standard of living." Whispers were heard of quotas, tariffs, or even boycotts to keep out the "shoddy products of cheap Japanese labor." Japanese denied the American charges and stoutly defended the quality of Japanese goods. They pointed out that America's most famous astronaut carried a Japanese-made camera with him on his trips around the earth. Japanese told Americans that labor in Japan was not cheap when measured in terms of productivity, that labor costs *per unit of product* in the United States were perhaps the cheapest in the world. They also reminded Americans that the Japanese were heavy purchasers of agricultural commodities and raw materials which were surplus on the American market. Such problems as these prompted the formation of a cabinet-level Japan–United States committee on trade and economic matters which met annually for an exchange of views.

Security issues seemed more vital to the United States than economic matters, and the security issues generated an excess of emotional steam on both sides of the Pacific. The most bitter controversy raged around the Japan–United States security treaty which was negotiated in 1951 and renewed in 1960. The original agreement provided that the United States should retain primary responsibility for the defense of Japan. American troops—and no other—would be stationed at bases in Japan to deter armed attack and to put down internal riots. More and more Japanese came to the conclusion that the bases were useless, over costly, outmoded, insulting, and immoral. Because the bases were used for U-2 reconnaissance flights and for troop deployment to third countries in Asia, many Japanese felt that the American bases were an invitation to disaster. Thus the demonstrations of "Yankees Go Home."

The government was not prepared to demand the abolition of the bases in 1960, but it negotiated a new agreement which gave Japan improved status with regard to the bases. Japan for the first time was recognized as an equal partner in the preservation of the peace in the Far East. An armed attack on either partner would be regarded as a danger to both, and the two would consult together whenever the security of Japan or peace in the Far East was threatened. To that end, Japan renewed the American bases for another ten-year period, with the agreement subject to termination on a year's notice. Japan was relieved of financial obligation to contribute to the payment of American troops and was given the right of consultation whenever substantial changes in manpower or equipment were contemplated. The clauses in the original treaty which provided that American forces could be used to put down large-scale riots and that Japan was forbidden, without American consent, to give any military rights to a third power were eliminated. The new treaty was ratified by the Japanese, but the public demonstration of disapproval served unmistakable notice that the days of the American bases in Japan were numbered. Nothing less than complete American withdrawal would satisfy Japan.

The Japanese made no effort to include Okinawa in the general category of bases in Japan. The conservative government was not too displeased with nuclear weapons in Okinawa and with the security which was afforded to Japan by the substantial American base in the Ryukyus.

Before the war, the Ryukyus were under the undisputed sovereignty of Japan. So long as that sovereignty was recognized, Japan was not disposed to press the issue of reversion. The Japanese accepted the reality of an American military government in Okinawa with full administrative rights. They made a mild suggestion, by way of compromise, that a Japanese civil administrator might be appointed exclusively for nonmilitary matters.

The Okinawans themselves were ambivalent. They protested against the American overlordship but they liked its economic benefits. Americans gave the Okinawans as many democratic rights as military necessity permitted, including the right to elect some members of the legislature. Anti-American elements, presumably Communists, agitated for more local autonomy. They wanted the right to choose their own government, including a chief executive. Frequent demonstrations took place which were usually sparked by quarrels over acquisition of more lands for added length to airplane runways. Feelings ran high between some Okinawans and the American military administration. As a gesture of goodwill on the day before Christmas, 1953, the United States relinquished its rights over the Amami-Oshima group in the northern Ryukyus. On June 9, 1962, the Americans appointed a civil administrator for Okinawa, but they let it be known that they expected to retain Okinawa as a base under their own jurisdiction for as long as there was threat to the free peoples of Asia or tension in the Far East. That sounded like nothing short of forever.

RELATIONS WITH OTHER NATIONS

Although Japan disliked its unhappy status as junior partner in relations with the United States, it derived a certain amount of satisfaction and strength from its American tie when dealing with its Communist neighbors. Very few people in the New Japan felt sufficient resentment against American policies to advocate a switch to the Communist camp. Neutralism was as far as most Japanese wanted to go.

Relations with Russia failed to reach a point of cordiality. The government of Japan disapproved of Moscow's interest in Japanese Communists and protested repeatedly against Russian treatment of Japanese prisoners of war. Repatriated prisoners brought back lurid tales of forced labor and brainwashing. At the same time, Russia treated Japan with little consideration. Russian aircraft flew over Japanese territory at will, and Russians seized Japanese fishing vessels which ventured beyond the three-mile limit. Russia complained of the satellite position which Japan assumed in the American world.

As long as Stalin lived, he stressed the idea of peaceful coexistence with Japan. In a New Year's message in 1952 to the people of Japan, he wished them freedom, happiness, and full success in their gallant struggle for the independence of their homeland. He said that Russians, too, understood the horrors of foreign occupation. He wished the Japanese workers deliverance from unemployment, low wages, and high prices. He wished the Japanese peasants deliverance from landlessness and high rents. He wished the entire Japanese people full victory for the democratic forces in Japan, revival and advancement of the country's economic life, and flowering of national culture, science, and art, and success in the preservation of peace. This goodwill message was sent from Russia to Japan in spite of Russia's refusal to subscribe to Japan's general treaty of peace.

Russia and Japan maintained limited economic relations until both sides determined to expand the basis of their contacts. In 1954 Russia invited the members of the science council of Japan—210 of them—to visit the Soviet Union for intensive all-expenses-paid study of Russian scientific methods, and Japan opened its doors for a Soviet trade mission. The two nations undertook negotiations which led on October 19, 1956, to a joint declaration of peace. It was agreed to terminate the state of war, open diplomatic and consular relations, repatriate the remaining Japanese prisoners in Russia, waive reparations claims against each other, and to carry on talks for a future trade agreements, fisheries conventions, and a formal treaty of peace. Russia said that it would support Japan's entry into the United Nations and, after the conclusion of the treaty of peace, would surrender the small islands of Habomai and Shikotan to Japan. This declaration was a useful device whereby the two nations established *de facto* relations, although they were not ready to follow the standard international procedures of treaty-making or formal recognition.

In accordance with the declaration, more Japanese prisoners were repatriated. Annual agreements were entered into for the regulation of the fisheries off the Siberian coast. Trade was expanded as the Japanese made strenuous efforts to sell their wares in Russia. In 1963 Japan and Russia signed a pact which provided for the exchange of $700,000,000 in goods over a three-year period. Japan would sell ships, textiles, machinery, rolled steel, paper, and pulp and would buy raw materials, primarily petroleum. Commercial expansion did not result in better political climate. The Japanese hated Russia's nuclear testing as much as they hated the American tests. The Russians sent Deputy Prime Minister Mikoyan to Japan in 1961 on a goodwill mission. During his visit he remarked that Japan would be well-advised not to renew the security treaty with the United Sates. He was told in no uncertain terms that Japan would brook no interference in its internal affairs, and after his departure, Russia still ranked at the bottom of all the nations in Japan's popularity polls.

Next to the United States and Russia, Japan paid closest attention to its relations with China. The Japanese felt they understood the Chinese, and they did not want a permanent rift to develop between the two neigh-bors. Most Japanese wanted a full measure of political peace and commer-cial intercourse with China, in spite of that country's Communist regime. They felt that "ideology is ideology, but business is business." Japanese businessmen, union leaders, and leftist politicians trekked to Peking to promote their point of view. Trade grew steadily until 1958. Then the Communists cut off commercial intercourse because the Japanese refused to grant diplomatic status to their trade mission. Trade stopped for four years. In November 1962 Japan and Communist China signed a new memorandum calling for a total trade of $500,000,000 in five years, based on an exchange of fertilizer, machinery, and manufactured products for coking coal, iron, and salt. In 1963 Japanese interests concluded arrange-ments for a huge textile mill in China.

In dealing with Peking, the government of Japan avoided giving offense to the government of the United States. The Japanese disapproved of American inflexibility toward Commununist China, but they could not afford to register any strenuous protest. The Japanese procedure was to maintain official silence, but to keep their ships moving. They would have been much happier if they—and the Americans—had been able to work out a mutually satisfactory formula for recognition and the restoration of normal diplomatic relations.

At the same time Japan was not willing to turn its back on the Chinese government in Taiwan, which it consistently supported in the United Nations. Japan negotiated a Treaty of Peace with Chiang Kai-shek's China in 1952 and opened an embassy in Taipei. Japan sent economic advisers to Taiwan and worked hard for close cultural understanding. Japan was aware of its heritage of distrust in Chinese hearts, and it tried to win Chinese friendship. Annual trade pacts between Taipei and Tokyo pro-vided for the barter of as much as $100,000,000 in machinery, fertilizer, textiles, metals, and marine products for rice, raw sugar, bananas, salt, and coal. Japan was not in a position to have any official opinion about the des-tiny of Taiwan, but it could not be separated from its memories. It could not hope for the return of Taiwan to Japan, nor could it accept the pros-pect of Taiwan's absorption into the system of mainland China. Its un-official preference was not for "Two Chinas" but for "One China and One Taiwan."

Japan searched to re-establish harmonious relations with all coun-tries which showed a willingness to forget the past. Japan discovered new bonds of sympathy with India. Both countries felt that they had much to teach the rest of Asia without succumbing to communism. Both were at-tracted to the practicality of "nonalignment," and they shared a deep aversion to war. Both sought to improve the welfare of their respective peoples and insisted upon the treatment of communism as an internal

matter. Both believed in the virtues of expanded trade with China and refused to accept the thesis that Peking was no more than Moscow's helpless
satellite. Japan lost a large share of its prewar market in India, but it found
new opportunities for technical assistance and cultural exchange. Japan
also realized that if India ever entered the game of balance of power
politics in Asia, Japan and India together could make themselves a pair
of pincers to squeeze China. And in Pakistan Japan found even more
sympathy than in India.

Because of the deep scars of war, the Japanese ran into rough sailing
in their efforts to rebuild their political fortunes. Korea was the worst case.
When the Japanese were defeated, the Koreans insisted that the Japanese
should go home and never come back. Koreans preferred to let their
fields lie fallow, their mines and railways be idle, rather than to utilize
Japanese skills. Koreans even resisted Japanese help to the forces of the
United Nations during the fighting in Korea. In the Japanese peace settlement, it was stipulated that the disposition of Japanese property in Korea
and claims, including debts, should be the subject of subsequent bilateral
arrangements. Japanese nationals had owned eighty percent of all commercial and industrial property in Korea and more than half the farmland.
Japan wanted credit or compensation for as much of this property as
possible. Korea took the position that if Japan were to surrender every
dollar of the property of its nationals in Korea, it could still not pay for one
percent of the suffering and humiliation which Japan had inflicted upon
Korea. The two nations also argued about the rights of 600,000 Koreans
living in Japan, the sovereignty over some disputed islands and the right
of the Japanese to fish in Korean territorial waters.

Progress toward mutual understanding was impossible as long as the
rabidly anti-Japanese Syngman Rhee was president of Korea. In 1952
Rhee announced that he would follow the American precedent and assume Korean sovereignty over the continental shelf. He claimed that
Korea's offshore jurisdiction extended 150 to 200 miles out to sea, almost
to the shores of Japan. The edge of the area was known as the Rhee Line.
He ordered Japanese fishing boats to leave his territorial waters and captured all those which refused to obey him. President Rhee was infuriated
by the United States' policy of reconciliation toward Japan, and he
vowed that the republic of Korea should never have an army which
would in any way be inferior to the reconstituted forces of Japan. After
President Rhee's displacement, the Japanese still experienced difficulty
in coming to terms with the Korean military junta; but individual Japanese gradually were invited to return to Korea for limited economic
activity.

Japan also discovered that it was no easy task to regain the confidence
which had been shattered in Southeast Asia and Australia. The nations

in those areas were uneasy because of the rapid recovery and the possible rearmament of Japan. They wanted to make sure—as was stated at Potsdam—that Japan would never again become a menace to the peace of East Asia. Japan entered into a series of agreements by which it paid more than a billion dollars in goods and services as reparations to its former enemies in Southeast Asia. Then Japan concluded formal peace arrangements and re-established its prewar network of diplomatic and consular posts. In 1954 Japan joined the Colombo Plan and began to participate in international programs of economic assistance to underdeveloped countries. It built up an extensive trade on the basis of bilateral, short-term, barter agreements. The peoples of Southeast Asia welcomed the cheap price of Japanese goods, but they were wary lest Japanese competition should thwart their own plans of industrialization. Psychological attitudes improved remarkably. Immediately after the war, any Japanese returning to some countries in Southeast Asia would have experienced danger to life and limb. Within a generation, the Japanese flag was back in the stores, the harbors, and airports. Crowds cheered for Japanese athletes and turned out to welcome Japanese movie stars.

Australia found it most difficult to bury the hatchet. Australia opposed the expedition of Japanese whalers to the Antarctic and showed no enthusiasm for Japanese entry into the Colombo Plan. Because of the prewar activity of Japanese pearlers in providing vital information for the Japanese air force, Australia passed strict rules for the renewal of pearling by Japanese in northern Australia waters. However Australians could not forever blind themselves to the value of improved relations with Japan, because Japan became Australia's third-best customer. Japan purchased eight times as much from Australia as it sold "down under." Yet it would have been very difficult to persuade Australia that an overall Pacific pact, including Japan, might have more value for the world at large than the limited Australia–New Zealand–United States (Anzus) Pact or the Southeast Asia Collective Defense Treaty which was signed at Manila in 1954.

Japan quickly placed its relations with the United Kingdom on a satisfactory basis. The Japanese and the British had been allies for many years, and both peoples showed a willingness to consider World War II as an unpleasant interlude. The architects of the new-style monarchy in Japan were inclined to study the traditions and etiquette of the Court of St. James as their model. Aristocratic Japanese were prone to copy the manners of the British and to teach their children British English rather than the American idiom. Economic relations were close in spite of commercial rivalries. The British wanted to protect their home market from the competition of Japanese goods, and they wanted to keep as much as possible of the markets of Southeast Asia for themselves. Nevertheless, an enormous trade grew up between Japan on the one hand and all the members of the commonwealth on the other. The existing trade pattern, of which Japan was an important part, provided an attractive alternative for those British who were lukewarm toward the European Common Market.

ECONOMIC CONDITIONS AND SOCIAL CHANGE

The new Japan measured its diplomatic achievements in terms of economic progress. No matter how spectacular Japan's rehabilitation and recovery, its leaders could not forget for a single moment the haunting reality of too many people on too little land. Japan had ten times as many people as the state of Texas, living in half the area. Population increased at the rate of a million per year and created a constant demand for new jobs. Under such pressures as these, Japan registered an impressive record of growth. In 1962 per-capita income reached $500 per year, and industrial production attained a level three times greater than the prewar peak. The gross national product climbed steadily by almost ten percent per year, and the government adopted plans to maintain that rate for at least ten years.

Prosperity was a necessity for the Japanese government. Caught between the pressures of inflation and austerity, the government balanced its budget. It was helped by the small cost of national defense—less than six percent of the total expenditures. It reduced some taxes and paid off a substantial part of its public debts including prewar financial obligations. It built up a strong financial position and joined the International Bank and Monetary Fund. Even the conservatives in power were obliged to take cautious steps in the direction of a welfare state. The government spent heavily for roads, highways, and public housing and promised a social security system which was intended to equal any in the West. The government's attitude toward the masses was "you never had it so good, but we will make it better."

More than half of Japan's national income came from the manufacturing segment of its economy. Japan's industrial organization was made up of two distinct components—the small enterprises and the large factories. The former, accounting for more than sixty percent of industrial workers, were usually individual or family activities. They paid low wages and demanded long hours. They were not unionized and were not subject to the ordinary industrial laws. The large factories, on the other hand, were as modern and as fully automated as comparable establishments in the United States. This industrial organization placed Japan in the front rank among all nations in the manufacture of textiles, textile machinery, precision instruments, electrical apparatus, radios, cameras, bicycles, cement, ceramics, and toys. The Japanese were able to compete successfully in most lines which were once the pride of American, British, or German workers.

Japan experienced the same kind of labor problems which complicated the economic life of the advanced countries of the West. Sporadic strikes or short-term work stoppages occurred in power, transportation, and communications industries. The threat of a general strike always clouded the economic horizon. Japanese management argued that it was saddled by the occupation, with American labor standards and without American wealth, and that it would go bankrupt if it met all of labor's demands. It urged the government to take a strong stand against strikes and warned of the dangers of communism in the labor movement. Labor, working through the Socialists, attacked the government for using organized labor as the whipping boy for its own political advantage. It denied the menace of communism. Union leaders argued that more than four million workers had no steady jobs and earned less than a subsistence wage. They insisted that their demands were modest. They pointed out that half the workingman's income went for food and that six months' savings were required for a suit of clothes. They produced figures to show that the workers did not benefit proportionately from Japan's forward spurt and warned that workers could not be expected to suffer in silence even in the interest of cheaper production costs or expanded export markets.

Foreign trade was not a luxury for Japan; it was a necessity. No matter how much prosperity in the nation, Japan was obliged to import eighty percent of its raw materials and twenty percent of its food. Japan re-established its credit abroad and invited foreign investment in its own domestic market. Plants were modernized, and trading methods were invigorated. The *zaibatsu* were permitted, even encouraged, to recover their prewar dominance. Cartels and trade associations were considered better for Japan than cutthroat competition. The government revived a whole series of controls over importation and marketing. Foreign automobiles, Scotch whiskey, American cigarettes, and other luxuries were taxed out of competition, and imports were limited so far as practicable to such essentials as petroleum, coal, iron, and textile fibers. Japan looked for the cheapest sources for its raw materials and combed the world for new markets.

Trade was expanded by a series of barter arrangements. Bilateral agreements covered the world: whale oil and silk went to Germany for chemicals and machinery; capital equipment to India for cotton; textile machinery to Burma for rice; machine tools to the Philippines for logs and timber; iron and steel products to the Argentine for wheat and wool. Neatly dressed, well-mannered Japanese salesmen with heavy brief cases competed against all comers in the markets of the Middle East. Southeast Asia, Africa, and Latin America. Japanese fishermen, technical experts, and financiers negotiated contracts to render technical assistance in underdeveloped countries. The Japanese offered the oil-rich monarchs of the Middle East unbelievably favorable terms in an effort to displace Americans and British in the production, refining, and transportation of the fabulously rich petroleum reserves of the Arab lands.

It was not easy for the Japanese to beat their competition. Sometimes their annual sales fell short of their overseas purchases by as much as a billion dollars. Japan was effectively barred from China; and it was limited in Southeast Asia by political instability, low purchasing power, and local industrialization programs. Japan encountered stiff sales resistance in the United States and Great Britain. Although a member of GATT (General Agreement on Tariff and Trade), Japan was not able to obtain most-favored-nation treatment from some nations except on a temporary basis. The Japanese were forced to impose ceilings on their own exports for fear of reprisals. Japan's fishermen were excluded from many of their old fishing grounds and Japanese shippers faced insuperable obstacles in trying to capture their prewar share of the carrying trade. Japanese plans for maritime expansion prompted some American organizations of shippers, shipbuilders, maritime labor, and veterans to register emphatic objections. In presenting its case for a greater share of international trade, Japan placed constant stress on two facts: first, that it bought more than it sold, and second, it had to export or die. Self-preservation was the basic law of life. Japan would have to seek its raw materials and markets wherever it could find them—either in the East or in the West. Japanese businessmen, like businessmen everywhere, cared nothing about the religion, ideology, or personal idiosyncrasies of their customers.

Although the overall standard of living increased in Japan, it was inevitable that some shared less than others in the general prosperity. Some people clipped coupons while others tightened their belts. Golf courses were crowded, but so were the cheap restaurants. Tokyo displayed magnificent new hotels and office buildings, but reported a shortage of three million ordinary dwellings. The Japanese spent a billion yen per year on research, but they bet fifty times that amount on the horses. The rich passed the week ends at Karuizawa in the mountains or at Atami by the sea, while common people were glad to scrape enough money together to buy their beloved rice instead of barley or other substitutes for lunch.

Social changes occurred in contemporary Japan which were as sweeping as those of the Meiji revolution. Television, jet planes, coffee parlors, and traffic jams became as common place as geisha performances, sumo wrestling, or the kabuki theater. Japan raced toward the future, but clung to the past. The rising-sun flag continued to wave in the breeze, and the old national holidays were restored. The Meiji Imperial Rescript on Education was brought back to the public schools, and the *kimigayo,* or the national anthem was given its former place of honor in public ceremonies.

New patterns appeared in Japanese society. Farmers changed from downtrodden peasants to responsible landowners who harvested bumper crops year after year. The labor force of 43,000,000 found new confidence in the strength of its 7,000,000 organized members. Big businessmen could no longer behave as the autocrats of the old days. They were forced to act as ordinary corporation managers with recognized responsibilities to stockholders, workers, and the general public. University professors emerged from their ivory towers and agreed to deliver lectures or write articles on matters of public concern. Public-school teachers joined their unions and insisted upon their rights of academic freedom. They defied the officiousness of the ministry of education, but they courted trouble if they fell out of step with the spirit of the local communities. In former premier Yoshida's home town, the townspeople barred the school doors against what they considered leftish teachers. One or two were thrown into the community fountain with the warning that "you should go to Russia, you bandits."

Perhaps the most marked difference between old Japan and new Japan was the attitude toward government and public officials. The feeling grew that the government was not something above and beyond the people, but was primarily their servant. The greatest decline was in the status of the military and the police. Bureaucrats lost strength and prestige to party bosses. Women, with newly enforced equality, took their political responsibilities seriously. Defeat came easily to any candidate who overlooked or spoke against the rights of women.

Profound changes took place in the nation's behavior patterns. Easygoing American ways were made familiar to Japanese in rural areas as well as in the cities. Every other home in Japan had a television set, and they all enjoyed the baseball games. Between innings the viewers were charmed with American-style commercials about soft drinks, tooth powder, or lipsticks. The advertisers appealed to the growing sentiment that life should be enjoyed. Housewives urged their husbands to buy washing machines, refrigerators, and modern kitchens; and the men began to think of hand tractors, motor bikes, or even automobiles for their own pleasure. The high level of mass consumption made it possible for Japanese industry to shift partially from exports to products for the home market. The Japanese worked hard and they played hard. They kept the industrial boom going, but they enjoyed a multitude of holidays. The Japanese spent as much time in touring, sightseeing, drinking, dancing, and "living it up" as any people in the world. They loved the Olympic games.

An intense spirit of freedom permeated the Japanese way of life. Experimentation and expression were unlimited in the arts, music, and the theater. Tokyo ranked with any European capital for the variety and excellence of its cultural life. It was forever Japanese, but it was as cosmopolitan as its smaller rivals, London and New York. Freedom gave birth to excitement. The demonstrations of 1960 bordered on the psychotic. An eyewitness wrote: "It was as if some ocean of inner feeling which had been dammed up for a long time had broken loose and was gushing forth in torrents." The privilege of freedom also brought to the social surface those who were unable to bear its responsibilities—the mobsters, lawbreakers, hoodlums, and juvenile delinquents. Japan had its share.

The mass of Japanese seemed to enjoy the new order and would not willingly surrender its benefits. Few would want to go back to the "good old days," although many writers warned their people of the necessity of giving constant thought to the preservation of their traditional qualities. The Japanese psyche bore one ineradicable scar—Hiroshima. The very word could cause a shiver or spark a demonstration from one end of Japan to the other. The Japanese deliberately cherished and preserved the horror as a token of peace and a prod to the conscience of man. The central memorial arch in the formerly stricken city bore the inscription, "Rest in Peace for the Error shall not be Repeated." All Japanese felt deeply that never again should an atomic bomb or an H-bomb be used as an implement of war, and never should nations devote their money and their energies to the building or testing of nuclear weapons.

No nation—communist or democratic—accomplished more spectacular progress than Japan, and none had greater handicaps to overcome at the end of World War II. The face of Japan changed, and so did its way of life. But whatever it was that made Japan distinctive remained constant in spite of those changes. The Japanese who enjoyed modern music, or attended cocktail parties or drove to the office in large automobiles, or cheered hoarsely at baseball games were just as Japanese as their ancestors who delighted in court poetry or took pride in their samurai swords. They were part of Asia, but they were also part of the modern world.

SUGGESTED READING

Allen, G. C., *Japan's Economic Recovery* (New York, Oxford U., 1958).

Asahi Shimbun Publishing Company, *This is Japan*. Annual.

Beardsley, Richard K., Hall, John W., and Ward, Robert, *Village Japan* (Chicago, U. of Chicago, 1959).

Cary, James, *Japan Today, Reluctant Ally* (New York, Praeger, 1962).

Cohen, Jerome B., *Japan's Economy in War and Reconstruction* (Minneapolis, U. of Minnesota, 1949).

Colton, Kenneth, Colton, Hattie K., and Totten, George O., (eds.), "Japan Since Recovery of Independence," *Annals of the American Academy of Political and Social Science*, vol. 308 (Philadelphia, 1956).

Dore, Ronald P., *City Life in Japan* (Berkeley, U. of California, 1958).

Ike, Nobutaka, *Japanese Politics* (New York, Knopf, 1957).

Kurzman, Dan, *Kishi and Japan, Search for the Sun* (New York, Obolensky, 1960).

Leng, Shao Chuan, *Japan and Communist China* (Kyoto, Doshisha University, 1958).

Maki, John M., *Government and Politics in Japan* (New York, Praeger, 1962). (P)

Maraini, Fosco, *Meeting With Japan* (trans. by Eric Mosbacher) (New York, Viking, 1960).

Morris, Ivan I., *Nationalism and the Right Wing in Japan* (New York, Oxford U., 1960).

Olson, Lawrence, *Dimensions of Japan* (New York, American Universities Field Staff, 1963).

Quigley, Harold S., and Turner, John E., *New Japan* (Minneapolis, U. of Minnesota, 1956).

Scalapino, Robert A., and Masumi, Junnosuke, *Parties and Politics in Contemporary Japan* (Berkeley, U. of California, 1962).

Taeuber, Irene B., *Population of Japan* (Princeton, Princeton U., 1958).

30

The People's Republic of China

While Japan moved along in high gear, the People's Republic of China (called China here) forged ahead in a massive effort to assert itself as one of the greatest powers in world affairs. Comparisons between Japan and China are impossible. Japan made great progress in a few years, but so did China. Such problems as Japan encountered were magnified a dozen times in China—and China was in a stage of development approximately a century behind Japan. One China makes eight Japans, either from the standpoint of size or population. A nation's difficulties increase geometrically with added bulk and greater diversity.

Japan accepted the rules of the modern world and worked to adjust itself to the established framework of the society of nations. China was a revolutionary state which condemned the rules of the international community. China refused to be bound by the injustices of the past. It reserved the right to transform traditional cultural values to accord with its Communist concepts. China was so massive that the shape of things to come in all the modern world would depend in large measure on the success or failure of the Chinese revolution.

The establishment of the government of China at Peking in October 1949, was like the opening scene of a great drama. What happened in China's past was only prologue. The ideology of Marx and Lenin and the revolution of Russia were contributions to the understanding of the plot. The founding of the Chinese Communist Party, the split with the Kuomintang, the struggle for survival in Kiangsi, the Long March to the northwest, the united front, and the war of liberation against Japan were incidents which helped to determine the mood of the play. The tragedy of the civil war and the exultation of victory were the last episodes which set the stage. As the curtain went up, the stage was littered with dead and dying, and the air was heavy with smoke. The hero, Mao Tse-tung, posed in triumph over the shattered image of his departed rival, Chiang Kai-shek. After appropriate orations and gestures, the scene shifted to Korea. As the drama developed, one could only follow the action—imperfectly. It became clear that the play would be a long one, and one could only guess at its ending.

PARTY GOVERNMENT AND POLITICS

The Chinese Communist Party was the heart and the head of the People's Republic. A small group of men exercised absolute command. By 1950 the rank-and-file of the party (7,000,000 members) was made up of peasants, workers, and soldiers who had flocked to the Communist banners merely to escape starvation. Who could be sure of their ideology? Within the party were also hundreds of thousands of landlords, successful businessmen, shopkeepers, merchants, rich peasants, and Kuomintang ex-officials who joined the Communists to salvage something of their past. The job of the high command was to purify the ranks and make the party a fit instrument of authority.

At the time of the war in Korea, Mao ordered a *san fan* or "three anti" campaign against corruption, waste, and bureaucracy. He followed this with a *wu fan* or "five anti" campaign against bribery of government personnel, tax evasion, theft of state property, cheating on government contracts, and stealing state economic information for private speculation. These campaigns were prosecuted at the same time that extreme land reorganization measures were put into effect. The result was compulsory labor, imprisonment, or death for millions who were given summary judgments by bamboo courts, those people's tribunals where emotion and hysteria wreaked vengeance in the name of justice.

The purification of the old party members was accompanied by a search for new recruits. The emphasis shifted from the country to the urban areas. Qualifications for party membership included good social status, enthusiasm, good example for the masses, and determination to stick to the party through thick and thin. Training programs were rigorous and exacting. The Communist Party was not a collection of social misfits or riffraff, but it became a well-trained thoroughly disciplined elite. All party members were enjoined to conduct themselves with military discipline, bearing in mind "we Communists never enjoy special privileges, we only undertake heavier responsibilities." Techniques of study and review, group meetings and self-confession molded a party monolithic in doctrine and unswerving in action.

At the national level the party hierarchy dominated the government. The real power in the party organization was centralized in a national party congress of more than 1,000 members. The hard core of party leadership was the standing committee of the Politburo. The group installed in 1956 consisted of seven men, all born around 1900, whose acknowledged leader was Mao Tse-tung. The group included Liu Shao-ch'i, ex-labor organizer and chairman of the government after 1958, and Chou En-lai, suave diplomat and perennial premier. The party had its committees at every level of government and its cells in every village, township, city block, factory, and school. According to the theory of democratic centralism, orders for political action were transmitted downward to each local unit from the party secretariat in Peking where the party line was fashioned.

The government of China was given permanent form by the constitution which was adopted in 1954. According to it, the state continued to be a New Democracy, based on the principles of class struggle, party rule, and democratic centralism. The National People's Congress was designated as the legislature and the highest organ of state power. The Central People's Government (the official name of the government) was made the supreme executive. The congress was to meet once a year. It was given the duty of choosing the chairman and vice-chairmen of the government, and of selecting from among its own members a standing committee to carry on between plenary sessions. Thus the standing committee of the congress was the supreme legislative authority during eleven months of the year. The congress was also to elect the council of state (super-cabinet) composed of premier, vice-premiers, heads of ministries and commissions of cabinet rank. In every respect the government was made subordinate to the party.

For local government, the country was divided into provinces, autonomous regions, and municipalities directly subordinate to the central authority. The provinces and autonomous regions were further subdivided into *chou,* or districts, counties, and municipalities. The counties were administratively divided into *hsiang,* or groups of villages and towns. Every unit of local government was to be ruled by an elected people's congress which chose its own administrative agency or people's council. Only the deputies to the congresses at the lowest levels were elected directly by the people.

A supreme people's court, local people's courts, and special courts were empowered to exercise judicial authority. A system of people's assessors was adopted and all trials were to be public unless otherwise provided by law. The courts were not independent, but were responsible to the people's congresses at the various levels. A procurator-general, responsible to the National People's Congress, exercised supreme supervisory power over all cabinet offices, local administrative organs, personnel organs of the state, and all citizens "to ensure observance of the law." The judiciary, instead of being a bulwark against tyranny, was designed to serve as an effective agency of the totalitarian apparatus.

The constitution contained a bill of rights which guaranteed ordinary civil rights, and some extra ones, for those who hewed to the Communist line. No rights were guaranteed for traitors or counterrevolutionaries. The government assumed the obligation to protect Chinese abroad and to offer asylum to any foreign national persecuted for supporting a just cause. Citizens were enjoined to abide by the constitution and the law, preserve labor discipline and public order, respect social ethics, respect and safeguard public property, pay taxes, defend the homeland, and perform military service.

The constitution was scarcely a fundamental law. It was not the result of deliberation on a nationwide scale; it was the expression of the will of the party. It was a blueprint by which China's leaders, regardless of their posts, could carry forward the work of the revolution. Mao Tse-tung was the chairman of the national party congress, the central committee, the political bureau, and the central secretariat in the party hierarchy; at the same time, he was the chairman of the People's Government. In addition he was chairman of the national defense council. China's most influential leaders held responsible positions in both party and government. Interlocking directorates prevailed from top to bottom in the political structure throughout China. There was no grass-roots democracy or local autonomy in China. The principle of democratic centralism was a substantial guarantee of totalitarian control.

Political power in China depended primarily upon the command of the armed forces. The exact relationship of the military committee of the Communist Party, the ministry of defense in the government, the national defense council, and the general staff made little difference. Actual command was exercised by a few individuals, whatever their posts. The People's Liberation Army, as it was officially called, consisted of approximately 2,500,000 men, backed by 700,000 in the security forces and at least 10,000,000 in the militia. After 1955 it was on a conscription basis; about one young man in ten was drafted upon reaching age eighteen. When not in actual training, soldiers were used in public works. Every adult Chinese was supposed to know something of military affairs and to spend some time on active duty.

China's rulers paid close attention to minority problems. Six percent of China's population, occupying nearly half of the total area, consisted of racial minorities, including the mountain people of Southwest China, Tibetans, Mongols, and the Turkish peoples of eastern Sinkiang. China was less interested in their cultural autonomy than in the creation of a secure frontier, after the manner of Russia in eastern Europe. China organized autonomous regional governments in Inner Mongolia, Ningsia,

Sinkiang, and Kwangsi; started one in Tibet; and established hundreds of autonomous districts with special status under various provincial governments. Local nationalism on the part of any minority was discouraged because of its threat to Chinese unity.

Tibet was China's most difficult minority area. The primitive but hardy men of the towering Tibet mountains had their own distinctive way of life, dominated by the Buddhist religion, the Dalai Lama, and a feudalistic hierarchy of nobles and monks. They resisted the introduction of Communism. On May 23, 1951, China signed an agreement with Tibet which promised Tibetan autonomy. China continued to recognize the spiritual authority of the rival lamas—the Dalai Lama and the Panchen Lama—but assumed control of Tibet's foreign relations. By 1954 China sent more than 100,000 soldiers into Tibet. Resentment smoldered into rebellion because of tough administrative policies and the drafting of labor for work on highways and military installations. In 1959, the Dalai Lama, with thousands of his followers, took refuge across the border into India. The Chinese reminded the world that Tibetan affairs were internal affairs; that Tibet was as essentially a part of China as California was a part of the United States.

The Chinese also insisted that the liberation of Taiwan was an internal affair. They called the Americans intruders on Taiwan. In 1954 the Communists began to lob artillery shells onto the offshore islands (Quemoy and Matsu) at some points less than two miles from Communist territory. The Communists coupled their military measures with a double-barreled propaganda campaign. On the one hand they declared that Americans were enemies of all Chinese and should be driven out of Taiwan. On the other hand they repeated their desire for peace and understanding with their blood brethren on Taiwan. They were frustrated by their continued inability to conquer Taiwan by force or to overthrow the government of Chiang Kai-shek by subversion.

In spite of its problems, the Communists set up the strongest government on the mainland which China had known in a century. Taiwan, with all its propaganda and guerrilla activities, was helpless in its efforts to encourage sabotage and revolt. A large measure of Communist success was due to vigorous programs of regimentation and indoctrination.

ORGANIZATION AND CONTROL OF CHINESE SOCIETY

The Communists carried regimentation to unprecedented extremes. Every segment of the population—peasants, workers, youth, women, and students—was regimented into its own interest group for party purposes. Millions of the Sino-Russian Friendship Association or the Women's League for Democracy could be turned out for such diverse public purposes as "Swat the Fly" or "Support to Castro."

In 1956, after Khrushchev's anti-Stalinist speech to the Twentieth Congress of the Communist Party of the Soviet Union, Communist leaders in China felt that the Chinese people "groused too much" and should therefore be purged of their jealousies and conflicting interests which Mao called contradictions. On February 27, 1957, he delivered an off-the-record talk to the party congress which he labeled, "On the Correct Handling of Contradictions among the People." His message, which was dutifully leaked to the press, was "Let the Hundred Flowers Blossom, Let the Hundred Schools of Thought Contend."

He invited political criticisms, but the criticisms turned out to be more vehement than he anticipated. Some critics blasted Mao and the party, others wrote bitter things about "stagnant Marxism" and China's ally—Russia. The party chose to counterattack. It launched a new rectification campaign—not a bloody purge, but a serious campaign to be conducted as "gently as an autumn rain or a mild breeze." Guilty offenders were expelled from the party or reformed through labor. The flowers were treated as weeds, and "turned under as fertilizer." By the new year

(1958), the discontented were cowed into silence. In the renewed confidence, the party undertook a new membership drive and enrolled seventeen million members by its fortieth anniversary on July 1, 1961.

The party then decided to concentrate on ideological remolding. The twin objectives were to stamp out counterrevolutionaries, and to get the masses to think positively as revolutionaries. The army, militia, and police kept public order. The bureau of social affairs of the party and the ministry of public security in the government were responsible for public security and they placed their secret agents in every village and on every city street. "Vigilant and patriotic citizens"—as they called informers—constituted "people's supervisory organs." Block leaders, or the chairmen of street committees, could enter any home any time and ask any question. Everyone was organized and supervised; every act was subjected to the microscope of the authorities. Permits were necessary for all meetings of five or more persons, and police notification was required if family members went away for a night or entertained overnight guests.

Ordinary citizens in groups of six to twelve were brought together practically every day to hold discussions or receive instructions. In meetings of criticism and self-criticism, brow-beaten individuals confessed faults and crimes, whether guilty or not, and vied with one another in accusing friends and relatives of wrongdoing. It was all deady serious; no joking and no pleasantries. No one could get by with passive conformity; no one had the freedom of silence. Nothing was acceptable short of complete and enthusiastic acceptance of the party line.

All of China's cultural resources were geared to the creation of proper thoughts, which theoretically would produce right actions. The apparatus for positive thinking was directed by the party's committees on propaganda and cultural and educational affairs. The government's arm was the ministry of culture, and people's participation was achieved through organizations like the All-China Federation of Literary and Artistic Circles and a network of literary and artistic institutes and colleges. All talents —theater, drama, opera, ballet, and dance—were to be devoted to the furtherance of the revolution. Motion pictures scorned stories of human love and passion. Documentaries and feature films played up propaganda themes, usually the defeat of the imperialists and their lackies. Art was dedicated to the class struggle; literature was mobilized to serve the party and the state.

Religion was subjected to heavy attacks as the "opiate of the people." The Taoists were treated as counterrevolutionaries; their priests and astrologers were forced to take up productive labor. Buddhists had their lands and temples confiscated, their schools closed. Monks and nuns were ordered to return to the laity with a warning to cleanse themselves of feudalism and foreign influences. The Islamic minorities were obliged to give up education in Arabic and to accept such reforms as the abolition of veils for women.

Christians received especially harsh treatment. Foreign missionaries were sent home, Chinese Christians were brainwashed or imprisoned. Churches, schools, hospitals, and orphanages were closed. Protestants and Catholics were told that they had to organize native churches, purge themselves of all foreign loyalties, and achieve the three self's: "self-administration, self-support, and self-propagation." Christian dogma was reinterpreted to make it a blend of Christ and Marx. The faithful were exhorted to pray for Marx and Mao, and to venerate Christ, the son of a carpenter and a great proletarian leader.

The education system was continuously revamped to respond to social needs. Western concepts—except those of Russia—were entirely rejected. Education was to consist of ideological training, productive physical labor, and scientific research. The schools were expected to provide mass leaders who would be "red and expert." Special schools for adults mushroomed with the commune system. By 1960 nine out of ten children of school age were reported to be in attendance in primary schools. More than twelve million youths, age thirteen to seventeen, were supposedly in the middle schools on a curriculum of half-study and half-work. Iron discipline and a Spartan schedule took care of problems of juvenile or teenage delinquency. Nearly a million students were in the universities, technical and professional colleges. Students were told exactly what courses they had to take and what jobs they were to fill after graduation. Excellence for a few distinguished leaders was considered less important than an improved level of training for the masses.

The Communists used mass media as effective agencies of social control. The Chinese sifted foreign news and manipulated domestic news releases to suit their political purposes. The gathering, publication and distribution of news was the monopoly of a single official agency—the New China News Agency. The *Peking People's Daily*, the *Peking Review*, or *Red Flag*, as mouthpieces for the government, always carried the correct editorial line which other Chinese papers were obliged to copy. Newspapers were supplemented by the official radio, but the Communists denied themselves the luxury of TV. However, the state owned and operated more than sixty publishing houses and printed a half-dozen times as many books and magazines as the prewar Kuomintang. Chinese papers and periodicals which were intended for foreign circulation were subjected to strict censorship, and foreign reporters in China were severely limited in their work by the strict rules and subtle pressures of the totalitarian regime.

Economic Development and Hungry People

Nothing made the Chinese government more careful in its handling of the news than the fear of unfavorable interpretation of the perennial economic crisis. In China the battle for survival was always difficult; with the burgeoning population it became more so. China's population grew at the rate of fifteen million per year (which is about the rate of three thousand in the time it takes to read a chapter in this book). Only total mobilization of people and resources would do. The new regime in its first few years made remarkable progress in removing the debris of war and rebuilding the nation's shattered economy. It rehabilitated and expanded the transportation system, particularly the railways. It provided food—if only at a bare subsistence level. With abounding enthusiasm, it launched plans to expand agriculture and to industrialize.

The Peking administration undertook a transition to socialist society by three five-year plans. At the outset it was planned to concentrate on heavy industries—not so much to raise the level of living of the masses as to create a base for industrialization and military power. Russia agreed to provide the necessary technicians, tools, machinery, and financial assistance. In the first five years, 1953–1957, China reported that its industrial production doubled and the share of industry in the national income rose from eighteen to twenty-six percent. Old plants were renovated and expanded; new plants were built in the interior cities. The railway system was improved for easier movement of grain to the cities and for speedier transportation of soldiers to danger spots on China's frontiers or coastline. A new rail line was built through Mongolia which cut 700 miles off the distance from Peking to Moscow, and construction was begun on the trunk line over the desert road to Turkestan. Light industries were considered as less important than heavy industries, and consumers' goods were dismissed as unnecessary. In socializing the economy, the government organized small businesses and handicrafts into cooperatives. Eighty percent of private commercial and industrial firms were converted into state or joint state-private enterprises. Nine-tenths of all industrial assets passed into the hands of the state. The socialized sector of the economy accounted for eighty percent of the retail and ninety percent of the wholesale trade. The state monopolized all foreign trade. Any foreign businessman in Hong Kong, for example, could trade with China only in goods which China's state organizations designated and only through such channels and on such terms as China prescribed.

The second five-year plan for the period 1958–1962 was announced in an atmosphere of optimism. Target figures for 1962 would place China among the leading industrial nations of the world. The will to progress was fanatical. China hypnotized itself with the slogan "The Big Leap Forward." The new line was to make the big leap from agricultural backwardness to modern industrialization as quickly as possible. Overall production was to be boosted one hundred percent in a single year. China would turn out countless trucks and tractors; expand light industries as well as heavy; build thousands of miles of new railways and highways —and surpass Britain in fifteen years. Small blast furnaces appeared like beehives on the landscape, and millions of people devoted themselves to the smelting of pig iron. Cadres sent fantastic reports of their achievements to Peking, and Peking in turn told a shaken if somewhat skeptical world of China's unbelievable accomplishments.

For a brief moment, China enjoyed the publicity. Even before the end of the first year, Peking admitted that things were going wrong. Much of the backyard iron was totally unusable, and half the coal could not be hauled away from the mines. Railway jams were blamed for food crises in the cities, and many of the spectacular reports of crop yields turned out to be pure fiction. Production targets were revised downward; administrators and cadres were punished.

The rest of the five-year period was increasingly bitter for the regime and the people. Forced-draft industrialization lost its momentum. New construction was limited; the rate of development in heavy industry was reduced. Steel fell off by fifty percent, and general cutbacks were ordered right down the line. Overambitious projects and uneconomical ideas (like home blast furnaces) were abandoned. Laborers looked for more food or better wages, instead of which they received only meaningless advice to buy bonds and increase their savings. For the "Big Leap Forward," China substituted the modest slogan "Walk on Two Legs." The government talked of such generalities as readjustment, fulfillment, consolidation, and improvement.

In 1962 Chou En-lai did not come forward with the expected third five-year plan. Instead he told the national party congress that China faced many urgent economic tasks, which included increasing the supply of food, cotton, and oil-bearing crops; rationalizing the production of light and heavy industries; and improving the distribution process. His major themes were work hard, go back to the farm, and above all produce more food.

Agriculture was the key to China's economic development, and the Chinese determined to collectivize agriculture in rhythm with industrialization. Collectivization seemed, from socialist reasoning and Russian experience, to promise sufficient food for China's millions. It also offered a formula for shifting a large proportion of China's work force from agriculture to industry.

The broader basis of land ownership accomplished by the Agrarian Law of 1950 did not bring about a substantial increase in agricultural production. Farming was just as difficult no matter who owned the land. The shift in ownership did not provide money for better seeds, chemical fertilizers, or improved machinery. Furthermore, Mao always believed that "land to the tiller" was a proletarian concept; and he made it clear that additional steps toward collectivization were in order. In 1955 he decreed the organization of higher-stage producers' cooperatives, varying in size from a few dozen to a few hundred families. This decree was a real shocker. Except for a small plot of land for personal use, the peasant had to surrender the title to *his* property—his land tools and draft animals —to the cooperative. He was told that joining up was entirely voluntary, and that he could always pull out of the cooperative if he wanted to. But he was also told that the cooperatives would make him more prosperous and would serve the interests of the state. By the end of 1956, ninety-five out of a hundred households were members of the higher-stage producers' cooperatives. At the same time Mao organized 120 collective farms on an experimental basis and launched a thorough-going propaganda campaign for further collectivization.

In August 1958, Mao established the people's communes; groups of cooperatives were merged into communes which varied in membership from 10,000 to 100,000 and which ranged in size from a few square miles to the area of a large Western country. The average commune contained about 5,000 households and controlled a labor force of about 10,000 workers. All the peasants' shares in the cooperatives, and their tiny garden plots as well, were taken over by the communes. Private property in rural land disappeared, with the temporary exception of homes, courtyards, and trees. The peasant became an ordinary wage earner, paid partly in cash and partly in supplies. In a few hectic months, 99 percent of China's 126,-000,000 households were organized into 26,000 communes.

It was intended that each rural commune would be a self-sustaining economic unit, complete with its own agricultural land and small factories. On the social side, life was revolutionized. Living quarters were reshuffled, and new dormitories were built. Some 4,000,000 dining halls were set up to take care of the meals for three-quarters of China's population. Kindergartens and crèches were provided for the youngsters, and homes were made available for the aged and the infirm. Women were "released from the drudgery of housework," so they could be put to work for the community. Their lot was made no easier—they merely changed jobs. The commune was organized along military lines, all the way from squads at the bottom to brigades at the top. Every man became a soldier "with one hand on the hoe, the other on the rifle."

Urban communes were also established, but at a slower pace. A specific urban area, a large factory, a street, or a group of government offices was utilized as the nucleus of an urban commune. Members of the commune made shoes or clothing, furniture or household utensils; or they worked in mess halls, dormitories, kindergartens, or "service stations" for washing, cleaning, and sewing. Occasionally, communes were established to operate garden plots in the neighborhood of a large factory, in the interest of getting the most labor out of all men and all women. The urban communes were effective for making the best use of the limited supply of grain. Management committees could enforce the rations and see to it that the mess halls made two meals do the work of three. The tight organization of the commune eased the jobs of education for the very young and thought control for the adults.

The original regulations for the communes proved to be too rigorous. In time the peasants were permitted to keep their furniture, bedding, clothing, and their small farm tools, as well as their homes. Working conditions were eased, and workers were paid not according to their need but according to their work. The communes proved to be too big and too cumbersome for good management so the emphasis was shifted gradually back to the smaller producers' cooperatives and mutual-aid teams. The communes were not abandoned but were reduced in importance. Each cooperative was made responsible for the best use of its own labor. Nobody could be taken off a farm to work on roads or dams without the consent of the cooperative. Communes were ordered to plant crops according to local conditions, regardless of the general rules which were laid down by Peking.

By way of further concessions to individuals, cash incomes were increased. Fewer meetings were to be held. Plots of land were returned to the peasants and peasants were to be given free time to work their own plots. It was conceded that peasants would work harder if permitted to work for personal profit. And they were permitted to sell their surplus vegetables on the newly sanctioned free market. Such concessions as these were made in the grim battle against hunger and starvation.

For four successive years, 1959–1962, China experienced unfavorable harvests; 1963 was not much better. Natural disasters—floods, typhoons, droughts, and insects—were aggravated by the faults of China's economic high command. The Communists were guilty of many mistakes: too much emphasis on heavy industry, destruction of all personal incentive, excessive centralization, and incompetent management. Food production in 1962 regained the level of 1957, but China was obliged to feed sixty million more people on the same amount of grain.

A certain amount of weariness and grumbling set in, but nothing worse. Although outside observers wondered about the possibilities of civil disobedience, the Communists kept the situation under control.

Mao had warned his people very early in the game that "revolution is not an invitation to a banquet." Since Mao and his colleagues shared the austerity and the privation of the masses, there was no large-scale resentment against the government. Taking no chances on disorder, the authorities declared war upon "bad elements guilty of sabotage, upon slackers and ideological sluggards." They warned of rectification campaigns which would be conducted every year or two.

By 1963 it was apparent that China had weathered its immediate crisis. It was equally apparent that decades would be required for China to attain the rank of a modern economic and industrialized state. Evidences of food shortages were unmistakable. As peasants hoarded their grain, the city people were forced to do with less. Dining halls cut down drastically on their meals. Restaurants became more scarce, and prices even for simple meals climbed out of reach. Rationing was tightened and long queues formed at food stores. Poultry and fish practically disappeared from the market; milk and eggs were reserved for children. Refugees and letters to the outside world told an unrelieved tale of hunger and hardship. Millions of food packages were sent from Hong Kong to the mainland, and Chinese visitors to their ancestral homes were most welcome for the food which they brought with them.

In spite of its own food shortages, China shipped huge quantities of rice to such places as Cuba, Ceylon, Albania, and East Germany. Some shipments were deemed essential for political reasons. Others were carried out in fulfillment of contractual obligations or were used to pay for China's minimal needs in imports. Nevertheless, China's domestic food needs were so great that it was obliged to dig deeply into its financial reserves to pay for the millions of tons of grain that were purchased from Australia, Burma, Canada, and France. Apparently, China preferred to use its precious gold for ordinary commercial purchases from the West rather than appeal to Russia and the satellite bloc for help.

CHINA AND RUSSIA

From the beginning of its existence, the People's Republic of China acknowledged its great debt to Russia and recognized its obligation to the Soviet bloc. As long as Stalin lived, he was Russia to the Chinese Communists. It was Stalin who first recognized the Communist regime and entered into a treaty of alliance with it. He supplied the technicians and the advisers for China's industrialization. He provided the tanks, guns, and planes which made possible the Chinese war in Korea. He furnished the muscles with which China could make military gestures against the offshore islands and could keep the Indochinese peninsula in turmoil. Stalin treated China as a junior partner, not a satellite; and thanks to Stalin's support, Mao rose to be the great individual leader in China.

China saw the first of Khrushchev when, with Marshal Bulganin, he visited China in 1954. He came as an apostle of peace—good-natured and bearing gifts. He was cordially welcomed and lavishly entertained. After a year he was regarded differently. In his speech to the Twentieth Congress of the Communist Party of the Soviet Union in February 1956, he announced new directions in party doctrine which the Chinese did not like. He declared that because of the acceleration of imperialist decay and the growth of socialist strength, war was no longer fatalistically inevitable. He became the great apostle of peaceful coexistence.

Without warning to the Chinese, Khrushchev denounced Stalin and the cult of individualism. The Chinese had a high regard for Stalin. They felt that he was a great revolutionist, an implacable foe of the imperialists, the architect of Soviet greatness and a true defender of Leninism. Mao saw his own position in China weakened by Russian attacks on the cult of the individual. As Khrushchev made overtures for understanding with the United States, China became more unhappy. An ideological rift developed which was exploited in the daily columns of the officially inspired press in Moscow and Peking. The differences of opinion came out into the open in 1961 when Khrushchev gave up the quest for unanimity in the world-wide Communist camp. He read the Albanians out of the party and used them as a front to attack the Chinese. The Chinese retaliated by assailing Tito, but when they said Tito they meant Khrushchev. International Communist meetings sometimes turned into name-calling, booing, stamping, whistling mob scenes.

Khrushchev argued for economic competition and peaceful coexistence with the archimperialist—the United States. Mao stuck with the Leninist formula on the inevitability of war as long as imperialism were to exist. He wanted peaceful coexistence only with nonimperialist nations, such as those in Asia. Mao wanted no compromise between Russia and the United States on disarmament or nuclear weapons. He believed that Russia was the superior military nation after the launching of the first satellite, Sputnik, in 1957. He thought that "the East Wind had already prevailed over the West Wind," and that the Communist bloc should proceed full speed with revolutions and aid to liberation movements regardless of the danger of war. China had less respect than Russia for the retaliatory power of the United States. Mao insisted that the United States was a paper tiger, but Khrushchev warned that the paper tiger had nuclear teeth and "just might use them." Mao's feeling was that war would bring about the downfall of imperialism and should not be feared; Khrushchev's response was that war might mean the end of all mankind and should be avoided.

Chinese and Russians reached identity of views in 1957 on certain cardinal problems of social revolution and social construction. They agreed that variant roads to socialism and communism were entirely permissible. They admitted that revisionism and opportunism (Khrushchev's alleged faults) and dogmatism and sectarianism (Mao's "heresies") were equally dangerous to the success of the communist movement. They declared that the working class and its vanguard—the ninety communist parties with forty-two million members throughout the world—were to seek to achieve the socialist revolution through peaceful, parliamentary means, but should keep in mind the possibility of nonpeaceful methods.

As Russia gained confidence in its growing power to meet the West on its own terms, and as China's economic difficulties grew more serious, the ideological rift deepened. Mao took a strong stand against summit conferences and argued that it was useless to negotiate with imperialists. In his view no imperialists were liberal, sober-minded, or sensible—as Khrushchev contended—because they were all reactionary and war-mongering. Mao argued that struggle (or war) was essential for communist victory; he felt that Khrushchev talked nonsense in his interpretation of Leninism.

Khrushchev, in return, scorned China's concept of "an alternate road to socialism." China could have communes instead of state farms, and a united front of all classes as its form of the dictatorship of the proletariat. It might even offer itself as a model for the other underdeveloped nations of Asia. But it was still only in the stage of a democratic republic. It had not discovered any magic short cut to socialism. Only Russia, which had blazed the trail to socialism, stood ready to advance to communism. Furthermore, Russia did not want the hollow glory any longer of being called the "head of the socialist camp." This empty title implied at least partial responsibility for possible Chinese recklessness, or adventurism, in foreign policy. Russia did not want to invite nuclear destruction of its own homeland as a result of some rash Chinese action.

World Communists, meeting in Moscow in 1960, issued a "statement" of their position on at least some of the most bitter issues. Said the statement, "It is possible, even now, to free mankind from the nightmare of another world war." All Communists were to be for peaceful coexistence with stress on the search for avenues of cooperation rather than the class struggle. The hope of peace was the strength of the Socialist camp; the danger of war was in American imperialism. Peaceful existence did not rule out unreserved support for wars of liberation. Such wars were not really wars, they were popular uprisings.

In the statement Russia was not referred to as the "head of the Socialist camp." Russia was recognized as the first among equals and the Communist Party of the Soviet Union was admitted to be the "vanguard of free and independent national communist parties." As Khrushchev explained later, it would be impossible to lead all socialists from a single center. Russia could not accept responsibility for every decision in every communist party. China agreed, but insisted upon the clause, "Every Communist Party in power bears historic responsibility for the destiny both of its own country and the entire Socialist camp."

In the years which followed, Russia and China continued their skirmishes. China demanded that Albania be restored to the ranks of the faithful, that Tito be outlawed from Communist ranks, and that the policy of peaceful coexistence be softened. Mao accused Khrushchev of "appeasement" in Cuba, and praised Castro for refusing to beg for peace. Khrushchev said his policies in the Caribbean represented a victory for "sanity"—it was just good sense not to go to war. He likened the United States and Russia to two goats, with locked horns, on a footbridge over a chasm—if they struggled, they would both plunge to their death. Khrushchev, on his part, expressed no enthusiasm for China's "adventures" on the Indian border. In 1963 both Mao and Khrushchev talked about the necessity of harmony and understanding but they attacked one another with the bluntness and venom which they had previously reserved for their capitalist, imperialist enemies.

While the ideological rifts occupied first place in relations between Peking and Moscow, economic and political matters were blurred. Up to 1959 Russia reportedly made loans to China of more than $2,000,000,-000 which were to be repaid in currency and trade. In 1959, the two countries agreed upon a nine-year program calling for an additional $1,250,000,000 for further industrial development. Thousands of Russian engineers and technical assistants came to China. Millions of dollars in rolled steel, trucks, and machinery were traded for tin, wool, silk fabrics, clothing, soybeans, tea, and rice. It was hoped that economic assistance and bilateral trade would help to spur China's economic progress. Russian-Chinese trade, at its peak, amounted to nearly $2,000,000,000 per year and was a give-and-take, unsentimental, commercial proposition. Each year, trade missions negotiated amounts and terms of trade, and entered into agreements for "economic, scientific and technical cooperation." But China's bargaining position weakened as its internal crisis deepened. Gradually Russia reduced its share in China's total trade (fifty percent in 1960; forty percent in 1961) and limited its credits to China. Then Russian economic assistance to China came to a halt. Russian technicians were recalled from China and Chinese students in Russia were sent home.

Both China and Russia declared their undying friendship on appropriate public occasions, but they carried their ideological feud into the realm of political relations. Ceremonial exchanges of greetings on national holidays became perfunctory affairs. The Chinese accused the Russians of tearing up hundreds of contracts and in retaliation closed Russian consulates in leading Chinese cities. Each nation accused the other of espionage, sabotage, and fomenting border incidents. Diplomats were snubbed and journalists expelled. Taunts and jibes flew back and forth across the airways. Mao called Khrushchev an appeaser for signing the nuclear test ban treaty and chided him unmercifully for backing down in Cuba. Russia retorted that China should look to its own appeasement in accepting the *status quo* of Taiwan, Macao, and Hong Kong. China's reply was that someday China might choose to discuss with Russia the rectification of the boundary with Siberia along the Amur River, the recovery of the maritime provinces, and the control of the strategic mountain passes which led from China into Central Asia.

China was at a great disadvantage in its duel with Russia. It had no nuclear weapons and no military potential apart from Russia. Except for Russian assistance, it was an economic giant only in terms of its sprawling size. But Mao was not without trump cards in his own hand. Chinese pressures in Asia made Russian-provoked crises in Europe (Berlin and Germany) doubly effective. China had prestige in Asia which Russia could never hope to match. Mao warned the Western powers not to rejoice prematurely over the Peking-Moscow disputes. His foreign minister warned, "Our differences will exist forever, but we will have no fundamental disagreement on the building of socialism." On another occasion he said, "Should anyone touch a hair of the Chinese peoples, he would surely be smashed to pieces by the mighty power of the Soviet-Chinese alliance." In 1963, Khrushchev echoed with almost the same words. He declared, "He who dares to attack the Chinese People's Republic will meet a crushing rebuff from the great Chinese people, the peoples of the Soviet Union, the entire Socialist camp." In a reception in the Kremlin for the visiting king of Laos, he announced in tones the world could hear, "The Soviet Union and the People's Republic of China will join in the final act of burying capitalism."

CHINA IN WORLD AFFAIRS

China based its action and determined its policies in international affairs on the assumption that its best friends were Communists and that communism was the wave of the future. Imperialism, the last stage of capitalism, was looked upon as the source of all the world's troubles but fortunately it was supposed to be in its last dying kicks. Anything which could be done to help the Communists—even war—was considered "just" because good ends justified any means. According to their double standards Russian aid to China was good; but American aid to Chiang Kai-shek was bad. The revolution toward a Communist-dominated world was the supreme good—in their view—and deserved the strongest support, in spite of all their poverty, hunger, and economic embarrassments.

The constitution of 1954 changed none of the basic concepts of the common program announced at the time the government was founded. The fundamentals of their doctrine could not prescribe the exact course of day to day operations of foreign policy. Their tactics shifted according to circumstances and stemmed from the dynamic factors of security, defense, geography, enhanced welfare, and the objective realities of the immediate international situation as well as from the intellectual acrobatics of the party theorists. Many things which Chinese Communists credited to the excellence and infallibility of their doctrine were things which Chinese governments before them had attempted to do and which other Chinese governments after them—Communist or not— would be constrained to follow.

Communist China's determination to assert its leadership in the Asian region followed the classic patterns of strong dynasties in the past. The Communists insisted upon secure frontiers and demanded control of some neighboring territories which it claimed rightfully as its own. It gave aid to its allies, North Korea and North Vietnam, and made substantial investments in Russian-dominated Outer Mongolia. In long-range perspective China saw Asia, not necessarily as a world to be ruled over by Chinese generals or commissars, but as a community of socialist states with China at the center. It conceived of itself as the major influence in Asian communism and in all Asian liberation movements. China was firm in its demands that Western interference in the internal affairs of Asian nations should be stopped.

Until 1957 China was the great champion of peaceful coexistence in Asia. In 1955 Chou En-lai was the star of the Bandung Conference of Asian and African nations, where he preached his principles of non-aggression, mutual respect, and peaceful coexistence. He enshrined these principles in solemn treaties with India and Burma, and offered to accept them as a basis for negotiation with any nation throughout the world. After 1957 China's campaign of peaceful coexistence faded into the background in Asia. China resorted increasingly to military pressure, political action, ordinary diplomacy, psychological warfare, economic competition or subversion, as the occasion demanded, to pursue its own ends.

China looked upon Japan as the most important country in Asia— after China—because of its industrial know-how and military potential. If China was ever to have an Asian alternative to Russia in military and economic assistance, it would have to be Japan. It was therefore China's objective to detach Japan from the United States. China expanded its trade with Japan, suggested new fishing arrangements, offered to repatriate Japanese prisoners of war, and opened the way for hundreds of unofficial Japanese delegations to visit China. It played upon common Asianism and hatred of militarism as common bonds of friendship.

The Chinese courted the left-wing and middle-of-the-road Socialists. China offered to sign a peace treaty with Japan any time Japan became "independent, democratic and free." It promised to go along with the proposal of the Japanese Socialist Party for a multilateral collective security treaty for the entire Pacific area. Through 1963, China continued an anti-Japanese–conservative campaign but welcomed a resumption of economic and cultural relations. China was not able to have everything its own way in dealing with Japan—Japan was too powerful.

China was in a more favored position in negotiations with the nations of South and Southeast Asia. Those nations were not as strong as Japan. They were, therefore, more amenable to Chinese overtures. Since the new countries in the area were eager to assert their complete independence, they accepted help and sympathy wherever obtainable.

China's policies in Southeast Asia were complicated by the twelve million Chinese emigrants resident there. The overseas Chinese possessed economic power out of proportion to their numbers, and they were more interested in making money than in politics. They were split in their ideas about communism, but they shared a common pride in their racial origin. From the establishment of the People's Republic, Peking adopted a vigorous policy toward the overseas Chinese. The Communists said, "Once a Chinese, always a Chinese," and they promised to protect the legal rights and interests of all Chinese living abroad.

On the surface, the Peking government pursued moderate policies. It set up a national commission on overseas Chinese affairs and invited prosperous merchants to visit their native land. The government gave special privileges to relatives in China and set up scholarships for their children in the Communist schools. On the other hand, the Chinese foreign minister publicly urged the overseas Chinese to respect the laws and customs of the countries where they lived. He would have the Chinese come to terms with local nationalism without giving up their ties to their native land. He gave specific assurance to the various countries that China would not use the overseas Chinese for subversive purposes. But he recognized the value of the overseas Chinese as instruments of foreign policy. He would use them for friendship or troublemaking, depending upon the prevailing emphasis in the ideological line.

Chinese diplomacy made no headway whatever in the Philippines, South Vietnam, Thailand, or Malaya. These nations felt their self-preservation lay in the policy of resistance to China, with the help of the West.

China's record was not much better with the neutralists, including India, Indonesia, Burma, Nepal, Ceylon, Cambodia, and Laos. Originally China denied their right to be neutral: they were either openly for the Communists or inferentially against them. Then China changed the line. If they were not openly with the imperialists, they could be considered as friendly to the Communists. During the period 1951–1957 formal diplomatic relations were established with the uncommitted states, and generous grants of economic assistance were given them. Chou En-lai roamed through Southeast Asia as a very persuasive salesman of the principles of coexistence.

After 1957 China became less tolerant of neutralism. China would have been quite happy with neutralist leadership in pro-American countries like Thailand or Japan, but it had no patience with neutralism in a state which China felt should be unreservedly in the socialist camp. When neutralism was tolerated, it was as a tactical measure. Chinese opinion—like much American opinion—held that no country could be genuinely neutral in a divided world.

These variations were evident in China's dealings with individual countries. Sometimes China applauded Burma's genuine spirit of neutrality; at other times it condemned the warmth in Burma-American relations. China blew hot and cold with Nepal. The bitter arguments with Indonesia over dual nationality were followed by a joint declaration that "China supports Indonesia in West Irian, and Indonesia supports China's claim to Taiwan and to membership in the United Nations." Pakistan and China changed from hostility to friendship as a result of the clash between India and China. The one country among the neutralists which China consistently treated with care was Cambodia, perhaps because of Prince Sihanouk's firm resolve to maintain his independence in spite of the friendliest of overtures from the United States. China even gave open support to the neutrality of Laos. It seemed content to keep Laos out of the control of either the United States or Russia.

China also vacillated in its relations with India. China was suspicious of the sentimental bonds between India and England, but in 1954 China negotiated an agreement with India which was the classic expression of coexistence and which ironed out difficulties in Tibet. Then the revolt in Tibet in 1959 and the border troubles between India and China made peaceful coexistence a dead issue. During the Tibetan revolt, the Dalai Lama and 13,000 refugees sought asylum on Indian soil. As a consequence, the Chinese took aggressive measures to rectify the Chinese-Indian frontier. The frontier is more than two thousand miles long, comparable to the frontier between the United States and Canada. Disputes flared in three sectors as widely separated as the states of Washington, Minnesota, and Maine. China maintained that the boundary was never delimited; India insisted on the legality of documents inherited from the British Empire.

The rugged borderlands on the roof of the world are isolated, and inhospitable, barren and well-nigh impassable; remote and relatively underpopulated; but they have strategic and psychological value. In the northwest (Ladakh) the Chinese built outposts and constructed a highway from Turkestan into Tibet which crossed disputed territory. In the middle sector, each country charged the other with murder, indignities to its citizens, and violation of its territory by overaggressive border patrols. India feared that Chinese incursions would undermine its privileged position with Nepal, Bhutan, and Sikkim. Most of all it feared the consequences of the proposed road from Lhasa to Katmandu, Nepal gateway to the exposed Indian plains. In the northeast, the arguments between China and India hinged on the legality of the MacMahon line, which was negotiated by Sir Arthur Henry MacMahon of the British regime in India. Some 50,000 square miles of frontier lands were at stake.

The Chinese advanced militarily at will and withdrew their forces to a cease-fire line which they held while they offered negotiation. The Chinese press turned on and off an anti-Indian, anti-Nehru campaign like a water tap. Sometimes the tone was mild. At other times, Nehru was labeled an American puppet, a cheap politician, a thief, and an Indian rabble-rouser. The Indians closed Chinese consulates in India, sent ordinary Chinese citizens back to China, and girded up their loins for the menace of invasion and war. Chou En-lai denied any aggressive intent upon Indian territory, but insisted on the recognition of China's historical and strategic claims. In the meantime, he preached the official line: "There is no conflict of basic interests between the Chinese and Indian peoples; we will be friendly to each other for generations to come." He gave enthusiastic support to India's action in chasing the Portuguese out of Goa, and the Indians continued to be champions of Peking in the United Nations.

Outside of the Soviet Union and the nations of Asia, most of China's relations with the rest of the world hinged upon its struggle with the United States. By 1964 China was conducting regular diplomatic relations with some forty nations, and economic and cultural relations with more than one hundred countries and regions. But it was handicapped in its negotiations even with friendly nations by the American factor. For example, China could not take full advantage of the traditional British willingness to deal with anyone regardless of political ideology because of British sensitivity to American opinion. The British gave full diplomatic recognition to China early in 1950, but the Chinese refused to restore regular relations with the British because of arguments over the position of Taiwan and alleged discrimination against Chinese in Hong

Kong. The Chinese made limited purchases of airplanes, trucks, and miscellaneous goods from Britain on a barter basis, but full and unencumbered trade relations were impossible, largely because of the lack of political confidence.

The Chinese were treated as a Communist pariah in Western Europe out of deference to the American position in NATO until the cooling of Sino-Soviet relations. Then Chinese overtures to the European common market became less unwelcome and seemed less fraught with political danger. West Germany, France, Italy, and Belgium had been important in China before World War II, they might become so again. China was obliged to choose between its desire for trade and its zeal in exporting revolutionary ideas.

China was extremely active in Latin America, which was promoted in China's thinking from the backdoor of American politics to the front line in the anti-imperialist struggle. Naturally China concentrated on Castro's Cuba, establishing formal diplomatic relations, negotiating commercial agreements, and working on local Chinese in Cuba to spread propaganda. Of 100,000 persons of Chinese racial origin in Latin America, 35,000 lived in Cuba. The Chinese organized associations for Sino–Latin-American friendship, and they passed resolutions pledging "undying support for our brave Cuban brothers." They flooded Latin America with propaganda and invited hundreds of Latin-American scholars, students, painters, writers, and politicians to take guided tours of China. China played up the "anti-Yanqui" bias of Latin Americans and professed sympathy for the weak and the oppressed. Cuba was extolled as the first exhibit of successful revolution; it should be followed by Chile, Brazil, Venezuela, the Argentine, and Mexico.

China was also determined to carry the torch of Marxism-Leninism to Africa. China was not willing to surrender Africa either to the imperialists or to the Soviet Union. China offered to recognize each new African nation as it was created, and it made overtures for trade pacts and loans. Chinese leaders, like Africans, were nonwhite, and China professed a special kinship for the newly emerging nations. China—not Russia—should be the model for all underdeveloped areas. China used the same propaganda techniques in Africa that it used in Latin America, but with less success. African students were far less noticeable in Peking than in Moscow or on the campus of almost any large American university.

Nearly all China's efforts in foreign affairs were directed against the United States. China fought against the latter in Korea and after the truce engaged in a decade of cold war. The Chinese made no distinction in their hostility to Democratic and Republican administrations, but they drew a distinction in their propaganda between the

American government and the American people. Chou En-lai went so far as to say, "There is no conflict of basic interests between the peoples of China and the United States, and friendship will eventually prevail."

China kept open a channel of official communication in the absence of formal recognition. First at Geneva, then at Warsaw, the two governments conducted marathon talks on the release of Americans in jail in China and all other matters in dispute. No agreement was reached on such topics as the use of force in the Taiwan Straits, meeting of foreign ministers, lifting of the embargo, exchange of correspondents, or a cultural pact. Neither side seemed anxious for "recognition." In Peking's view, there could be no mutual recognition, or resumption of regular diplomatic intercourse, until the United States withdrew from Taiwan and gave up its support for Chiang Kai-shek. China would accept no halfway recognition and would entertain no solution of the Taiwan problem based on two Chinas, or one China and one Taiwan. There was one China, and Peking was its symbol.

Peking was in no hurry to reach a settlement with Washington. According to Peking, sooner or later the United States would lose out in Laos, Vietnam, and Korea. Peking reasoned that after the first breakthrough, there would be a chain reaction which would undermine and destroy the entire American position in the western Pacific. Let the United States continue not to recognize China, argued Peking: China would not topple. Peking poured forth incessant propaganda against the United States. Street parades, demonstrations, posters, rallies, stage plays, broadcasts, and movies—the theme was always the same. Americans were "monsters threatening freedom" or "ferocious and cunning butchers as busy as malignant beavers in Asia."

China held the United States primarily responsible for its fate in the United Nations. Sometimes China did not seem to care whether it was admitted to the United Nations; other times it expressed great indignation. China never ignored the United Nations, and set up a UN bureau in its own foreign office. China felt the sting of the United Nations in Korea and refused to cooperate with the world organization after the Korean affair in the maintenance of peace.

Two governments—the Republic of China on Taiwan and the People's Republic of China at Peking—claimed the right to occupy the seat allotted to "China" in the United Nations. Largely due to the efforts of the United States, the question of Chinese representation in the General Assembly was consistently resolved in favor of Taiwan. As many new and smaller states sent delegations to New York, a vague sentiment grew that it was unwise for the United Nations to deprive itself of the representation of the world's largest nation. China felt that the UN had greater need of China than China had of it. Therefore China was confident that it would be admitted in due course. But Chou En-lai warned solemnly that his government would never take part in the United Nations if the Taiwan clique were to appear in the world organization in any form or any manner.

Chou also told the world that China would shoulder its responsibilities for peace whether or not the United States recognized China, whether or not China was received into the United Nations. He refused to adhere to the nuclear test pact signed by the United States and Russia in 1963 and he argued consistently for complete and total disarmament. He intimated that it was only a question of time until China would have nuclear bombs and "then there would be less chance of war than now when only a few nations belong to the nuclear club." In support of his stand for peace he cited China's record of nonaggression pacts, statements on peaceful coexistence, and campaign for a nuclear-free zone in the Pacific. In supporting a multilateral nonaggression pact, he said that such a pact would be impossible without diplomatic relations between the United States and China, and that it was "inconceivable to have diplomatic relations between the United States and China without settling the Taiwan dispute."

Although China did not want war, according to Chou, he admonished his people not to fall into the "mire of bourgeois pacifism." Communists must always be ready to fight just wars. Therefore China must keep up its military strength. To the rest of the world it was evident that there could not be any effective agreement on disarmament—nuclear or otherwise—without diplomatic relations between China and the major powers, or without China in the United Nations.

China undoubtedly wanted "peace," or the least troublesome condition of world affairs, in order to devote its major attention to its overwhelming problems at home. Ordinary folks within China could not but be worried about the future. Leaders like Mao Tse-tung, Chou En-lai, and Liu Shao-ch'i struggled to whip up flagging spirits and to keep alive the people's confidence in a better future. They had reason to be proud of China's undoubted achievements, but they were sobered by the immensity of China's problems. As Chou En-lai remarked to Edgar Snow, his American visitor in 1960: "Don't ever quote me as saying anything is easy here. Ten years ago, all China began a Long March. We have taken the first step, that's all, *the first step.*"

SUGGESTED READING

Barnett, A. Doak, (ed.), *Communist Strategy in Asia* (New York, Praeger, 1963).

Boyd, R. G., *Communist China's Foreign Policy* (New York, Praeger, 1962).

Center for International Affairs and the East Asian Research Center, *Communist China, 1955–1959* (Cambridge, Harvard U., 1962).

Chen, Theodore H. E., *Thought Reform of the Chinese Intellectuals* (Hong Kong, U. of Hong Kong, 1960).

Hudson, G. F., Lowenthal, Richard, and MacFarquhar, Roderick, *Sino-Soviet Dispute* (New York, Praeger, 1961). (P)

Hughes, T. J., and Luard, D. E. T., *Economic Development of Communist China, 1949–1960* (second ed.) (New York, Oxford, 1961).

Kirby, E. Stuart, *Contemporary China* (Hong Kong, U. of Hong Kong). Annual.

Lewis, John Wilson, *Leadership in Communist China* (Ithaca, Cornell U., 1963).

Mao Tse-tung, *Selected Works* (four vols., to date) (Peking, Foreign Languages Press, 1961). Obtainable in the United States from China Books and Periodicals, 334 W. Schiller St., Chicago 10, Ill.

Mende, Tibor, *China and Her Shadow* (New York, Coward, 1960).

Mu Fu-sheng, *Wilting of the Hundred Flowers* (New York, Praeger, 1962).

Nossal, Frederick, *Dateline-Peking* (New York, Harcourt, 1963).

Pentony, DeVere E., *China, Emerging Red Giant* (San Francisco, Chandler, 1962).

Union Research Institute, *Communist China, 1949–1959* (two vols.) (Hong Kong, The Institute, 1961).

United States Department of State, *Publications of the American Consulate General, Hong Kong.*

Wilson, J. Tuzo, *One Chinese Moon* (London, Michael Joseph, 1960).

Wint, Guy, *Common Sense About China* (New York, Macmillan, 1960).

31

The Republic of China: Taiwan

While the People's Republic of China at Peking took its first steps on the long march toward socialism, the legally constituted government of the Republic of China undertook to reconstruct its shattered remnants at Taipei, the provincial capital on the island of Taiwan. The former was the "China" represented by Mao Tse-tung and the Communists; the latter was the "China" of Chiang Kai-shek and the Kuomintang. Both claimed to be the only rightful representative of China; both dismissed as wishful thinking the idea that "two Chinas" could be accepted as a compromise basis for peace.

When Chiang Kai-shek was driven from the mainland in 1949, some two million Chinese—ranging from defeated soldiers to wealthy citizens who were able to buy passage by airplane, ship, or junk out of Shanghai —came with him. Families were divided as women and children remained at their homes. The pilgrimage was tragically reminiscent of the earlier flight to Chungking to escape the Japanese. Some of the men looked to Taiwan (or Formosa) as the last possible haven of refuge beyond the reach of the Communists. Others accepted the retreat as a strategic incident which would give them time to regroup their forces. They believed the Communist regime would fail or fall apart. At the propitious moment, the national army of the Kuomintang would return to the mainland and take over the government which was legitimately theirs.

Such was the thinking of the Kuomintang in 1949; such were its hopes as the years rolled by. It clung to the dream of reconquering the mainland. The government on Taiwan expected confidently that the Communist regime would bring about its own downfall, or that the indignation of the free world would lead to a concerted military campaign to defeat the Communists and restore the Kuomintang. Both expectations led to disappointment. The exciting prospect of a triumphal return gave way to the more prosaic task of organizing and conducting an ordinary government on Taiwan. Such a government was to be national in scope and attributes. It would carry on the cultural traditions of China. It would assume the treaty obligations undertaken by previous governments of China and would take over the role assigned to "China" in the United Nations. Men of the stamp of Chiang Kai-shek would never surrender their dream, but they could not escape the grim reality that the future of the government of the Republic of China on Taiwan would depend on the success or failure of Peking. The only alternatives would be international diplomatic agreement or the armed strength of friendly powers.

GOVERNMENT AND POLITICS

The legal status of Taiwan was still cloudy in 1949. According to the Cairo Declaration and the Japanese surrender terms drawn up at Potsdam, Formosa and the Pescadores were to be restored to China. Neither document constituted a legal transfer of title. General MacArthur's General Order Number One of August 15, 1945, gave Chiang Kai-shek *de facto* control of Taiwan and the Pescadores by granting him power to accept surrender of the Japanese forces there. In the absence of a Japanese treaty, Nationalist authorities administered the islands as an army of occupation. When Chiang moved his government to Taiwan, he did so in spite of his lack of clear title. The Japanese peace treaty, effective April 28, 1952, merely stripped Japan of all right, title, and claim to Formosa and the Pescadores. It did not establish present or future legal claims to sovereignty over these islands. Both the People's Republic of China and the government of the Republic of China agreed that the islands should belong to "China," but which China remained a matter of dispute.

The structure of the Nanking government was transferred to Taipei without significant modifications. The form of the government remained intact. The same men who ran the government in Nanking set up shop in Taipei and conducted office affairs as if they were still in charge of the entire mainland. The national assembly, with a scant quorum present, met in 1954 for the first time in six years and re-elected Chang Kai-shek as president for another six-year term. The same national assembly, with its members older in years and reduced in numbers, met again in 1960 and re-elected Chiang for his third six-year term. Chen Cheng, a comrade in arms to the generalissimo for many years, was named as vice-president. Chiang exercised all practical executive responsibilities by virtue of his threefold position as party chief of the Kuomintang, president of the national government, and commander in chief of the armed forces. He controlled the national purse and the secret police and he dispensed patronage. He appointed premiers and cabinets at his discretion and surrounded himself with personal followers of proven loyalty. It was difficult to see how any individual could succeed to the position of total power which Chiang held.

The national government had no roots in Formosa. It had no mass support. It was imported and set up as a disconnected superstructure on top of a flimsy provincial base. It was manned by mainlanders. A galaxy of admirals and generals, together with the entire bureaucracy of all China, converged on Taipei and continued to exist on the government payroll. Men whose competence was in the administration of foreign affairs, immigration, taxes, or customs on the huge mainland scale had to be fed, housed, and clothed out of the meager resources of the island of Taiwan. Ex-governors, customs inspectors, and district magistrates were maintained in offices where responsibilities were more fictitious than real. The national government took care of such important matters as foreign relations, internal security, and the armed forces—but it kept a China-size organization for a Formosa-size job.

It was important to energize the provincial government which kept the responsibility for local affairs, including taxation, land reform, road repairs, education, and social welfare. It was essential to attract the cooperation of as many Formosans as possible. A provincial assembly, with advisory powers only, was established. The governor of the province of Taiwan was appointed, and he was assisted by a provincial council on which seventeen out of some twenty provincial commissioners were ordinarily Formosans. Local officials, including district magistrates and municipal mayors and their respective legislative councils, were elected by the people. More and more Taiwanese (alternatively called Formosans or islanders) were chosen for government service, usually at the provincial level. Elections were reasonably free. Any Formosan—whether or not a member of the Kuomintang—was entitled to run for office; however, local party cells were sure to keep an attentive eye on personalities, police, and election procedures.

The Formosan people, with the exception of a tiny minority of aborigines, were Chinese in race and culture but were distinct from the mainlanders in recent political experience. From 1895 to the end of World War II, Formosa was a part of Japan. Formosans, like Koreans, were made to learn the Japanese language, attend Japanese schools, and work wherever the Japanese provided jobs. Japan brought comparative prosperity to Formosa, giving it the highest level of living in Asia outside of Japan itself. The islanders, in spite of their Chinese ancestry and because of their recent Japanese orientation, looked upon the mainlanders as alien intruders. Their fears and prejudices were reinforced by the first of the nationalistic mainlanders, who treated Formosa as a conquered territory. When Chiang Kai-shek arrived he improved relations, but he could not gloss over or eliminate some of the most deep-seated grievances. Formosans were pushed into the economic and political background by their unwelcome guests; yet Formosan farms were expected to provide the rice and the taxes for the cumbersome government and the exaggerated army. As one Taipei businessman expressed it: "We Taiwanese have been made to feel like slaves to the Nationalists; we represent four-fifths of the population and have little or no say in setting our policy or choosing our leaders."

Nationalists crowded the island and brought with them an air of superiority. They found it hard to understand the Fukien dialect which Formosans spoke and consequently ordered the substitution of the official Mandarin tongue for schools and official correspondence. Mainlanders took the best jobs, even outside the government circles. All but two or three presidents of colleges and universities were mainlanders, and the faculties were staffed by professors in exile. Principals of high schools and elementary schools likewise were chosen from the displaced persons. Almost all the bankers, industrialists, and merchants who had any chance at all for a share in government contracts were selected because of their former mainland connections. Formosans and mainlanders tended to have different ways of life. The mainlanders lived in a frothy, temporary atmosphere, expecting to go back home at any moment. They took over the clubs and the former Japanese quarters and created a social way of life which was entirely unknown to the native residents whose entire life and concept of the future was wrapped up in their city and their island. However, fusion of the two groups began almost immediately as lonesome men married local girls and raised new families.

The relationship between the government and the party in Taipei remained as it had been at Nanking. The Kuomintang—like the Communist Party—was Russian-style in its organization. It enjoyed a political monopoly except for miniscule opposition parties which were tolerated for the sake of window dressing. The national congress of the Kuomintang elected a central committee of some thirty members which in turn elected a ten-man steering committee. Working committees in the party were set up for finance, planning, discipline, party affairs, information, intelligence, and affairs of overseas Chinese. Total party membership was reduced to fewer than 500,000 members. Self-criticism and "rectification" campaigns purged many opportunistic and unsavory elements. The cliques which had wrecked party efficiency in Nanking disappeared in Taipei; however, it was still Chiang Kai-shek who provided the ideology, leadership, and inspiration which held the Kuomintang together. Party cells were spiritless and under the complete domination of party elders. The same men who had been with Chiang in China for many years, with the significant addition of his elder son, Chiang Ching-kuo, made up the senior statesmen and the inner council of advisers. Their standards of administration rose immeasurably, perhaps because their decisions and actions received so much publicity. Taiwan was a very small place.

In spite of its size, Taiwan had its share of political difficulties. Compared with free China during the early years of World War II, Taiwan was stagnant for lack of ideas, enthusiasm, and individual initiative. The spirit declined as year after year passed without the promised return to the mainland. The sole *raison d'etre* for the national government on Taiwan and its huge military establishment was the hope of reconquest of China. Every holiday produced speeches whose theme was "We shall return." Sometimes the hope seemed like a possibility—when for example reports trickled into Taiwan about food shortages and unrest on the continent, when a rift between Peking and Moscow seemed imminent, or when Western tempers blazed over crises in Berlin or Cuba. At other times, the hope seemed forlorn. The spirit of Taiwan dipped as conditions on the mainland seemed to improve or as the crusade for peaceful coexistence promised to be successful. Any truce or understanding between Communists and anti-Communists was an anathema in Formosa. Responsible leaders in the government of the Republic of China managed to present a bold front, but they realized they had no real prospect for return to glory without a massive popular revolution in China or global war.

As the leaders grew older, they became more desperate in their calculations. They felt that if they could put one division ashore, they might spark a general explosion. They hoped that revulsion against the excesses of the Communist regime would prompt the masses to welcome the Kuomintang as the leaders of a reconstruction crew. Admittedly this was a desperation gamble, and it would have to be taken—if it were to be taken—without the approval of American allies.

Time would not wait. As Nationalist army ranks thinned out, replacements were conscripted from among the Formosans. The army on Taiwan in 1953 was made up of mainland veterans; in 1963 more than half the enlisted men and a third of the officer corps were Taiwanese. The same thing happened in the party. As veterans died, young Taiwanese were selected to fill the vacancies. This produced a tremendous gap between desperate leaders and cautious followers. The young people who were recruited into the party or conscripted for the army had no personal memories of the mainland. It was not their home, and they could not "return" to a place they had never been. Youth was not infected by the crusading spirit. In the party and in the army, Formosa-mindedness grew to be more important than mainland-mindedness.

Trying to stage an invasion of the Chinese mainland from Formosa seemed as impertinent as "trying to launch an invasion of the United States from Staten Island or Catalina." Chinese forces numbered approximately 600,000 well-equipped and well-trained effectives. They were the best of the free world in Asia. But it was "no contest" when they were compared to the Communist forces. The military organization itself could not escape its ancient heritage—personal favoritism, persistence of traditional military concepts, indifferent morale, too many of the old guard and top-heavy organization. Surplus admirals and generals by the hundreds were kept on the active list on the grounds that they would be needed for instantaneous action once the drive to the continent was launched. In the meantime they enjoyed the pay and prerogatives of senior officers.

Furthermore the army in Taiwan could not concentrate on military matters because it was too deeply enmeshed in politics. Chiang himself was a traditional blend of general and politician, and he rose to prominence in party affairs because of his power in the army. In Taiwan, anyone who showed potential rivalry to Chiang was quietly cashiered or maneuvered out of the limelight. Anyone who hoped to succeed Chiang —including the most likely candidates Chen Cheng and Chiang's own son, Chiang Ching-kuo—needed the support of the army.

The inevitable consequence of the militarization of Taiwan was the creation of a quasi police state. The ever-present threat of Communist invasion plus the continuous dangers of infiltration and subversion complicated the ordinary problems of security. It was inaccurate to speak of *free* China, because the secret police were everywhere. The army, party, various cabinet ministries, and the president's office had their own secret agencies of investigation and control. They did not attempt a strict regimentation of life such as prevailed on the mainland, and their existence was unknown to most people. Criticism of the government was not permitted; it was considered tantamount to subversion.

Civil rights were ignored. Former governor of Formosa, K. C. Wu, who broke with the regime, testified: "I did my utmost to inculcate the principles that arrests cannot be made without sufficient evidence of crime and searches cannot be conducted without due process of law. But as my powers were limited, even now (1955) I can hardly tell how many people were, and have been, illegitimately held and molested." News was censored, at least informally; and the schools were kept under strict surveillance of the authorities. Woe to the journalist or the educator who was considered dangerous. The unwary deviationist was liable to be whisked away for an unpleasantly long course in political education. The press was anything but free. Lei Chen, the publisher of a fortnightly "independent" journal called *Free China*, was arrested in the fall of 1960.

He was charged with defeatism and subversion, but his real crime was very simple. He and his companions were in process of forming a new party, which was anti-Communist, but was also predominantly Taiwanese in membership and viewpoint. Lei Chen was given summary trial by a military court and sentenced to ten years imprisonment. His influential friends were powerless to help him.

The tragedy of Taiwan was that it had neither the stimulation of political freedom nor the ruthlessness and efficiency of totalitarianism. The regime forced conformity, but it did not inspire confidence. Loyalty was given without enthusiasm and as a kind of ritual. Whatever inclinations might have existed for democracy, the atmosphere of emergency and crisis was an uncompromising taskmaster. Formosa had one government, one party and one leader. The walls of government buildings, the arches on the street corners, and the sides of the sports stadium were plastered with the familiar portraits of Sun Yat-sen and Chiang Kai-shek. Gates, doorways, and public buildings were splashed with blue and white Kuomintang slogans, the most prominent of which were "Obey the Leader" and "Resist Russia and Recover the Mainland."

ECONOMIC AND SOCIAL CONDITIONS

The miracle of Taiwan was that it was able to survive and—after a fashion—to register progress. The island was completely dependent on American assistance, which exceeded a billion dollars in the first decade of its existence. The Nationalist forces received all their hardware from the United States, and in addition obtained raw cotton for uniforms together with construction materials for barracks, airfields, and harbor works. The army also received medical supplies, food, trucks, and countless items which might have been useful either for military or civilian purposes. The civilian economy was shored up by construction of roads, bridges, dams, facilities for the distribution of electric power, and exploitation of natural resources. Such activities were justified on the American side by military necessity. Large quantities of wheat, soy beans, raw cotton, and machine tools were shipped practically free to Taiwan from the United States, ostensibly to bolster military morale, but actually to balance the budget and keep the economy moving. Education, exchange and training programs for Taiwanese were paid for by the United States out of funds appropriated for technical assistance. On a per-capita basis, Taiwan probably received from the United States more assistance than any other area in the world.

Thanks largely to this American aid, Taiwan's economic record was impressive. Taiwan was essentially an agrarian society, with most of its people making a living off the land. Virtually all the cultivable land was placed in production, and the output per unit of land was as high as anywhere in the world. Agriculture accounted for two-thirds of the island's gross national product and provided ninety percent of its foreign exchange. Four out of five families owned all or part of their land and their real income increased in proportion to the rise in the general level of living. In a decade (1951–1961) the gain was more than a third.

Farm prosperity began with a fundamental program of agrarian reforms. Rentals were reduced to maximums of 37.5 percent of the crop, and a law guaranteeing minimum tenure of six years was enacted to protect tenants against eviction. Large landholdings of the Japanese were confiscated by the government and redistributed to tenants. In 1953 a Land-to-the-Tillers Act was passed which affected three out of four farms in the entire country. Landholdings were limited to eight acres of average-grade land. The surplus was sold to tenants on generous terms. The former owners received compensation in the form of government bonds or stocks in government corporations, and the new owners were given twenty years to pay off their accumulated debt. As a result of this law, tenancy was reduced to about twenty percent. The new landed proprietors were helped by an admirable Sino-American joint commission for rural reconstruction, which had been created on the mainland before the flight to Formosa. The commission gave free scientific advice about fertilizers, pest and disease controls, and seed improvement; it also gave help in the establishment of cooperatives and the construction of irrigation facilities.

The farmer's life was improved by small hand and power machinery, electric water pumps for the rice fields, locally made bicycles, and rubber tires for the clumsy carts which hauled his produce to the market. Almost every village had teahouses and pool halls for the men, beauty shops with lipsticks and permanent waves for the ladies, and motion picture theaters for all the family. Villages had their own schools and free textbooks. The optimism and obvious good nature of the youngsters in school contributed to the feeling that life was more cheerful in the villages than in the large cities.

Industrial development kept pace with agricultural improvement. By 1952, industrial production recovered prewar levels and it doubled during the decade which followed. Electric power, mining, transportation facilities, and new industries boomed. One American company, the J. G. White Engineering Company, gave the same boost to industry which the joint commission on rural reconstruction gave to agriculture. The landscape was dotted with new power plants, fertilizer factories, petroleum refineries, and mills for the processing of wheat, soy beans, lumber, pulp and paper, aluminum, and assorted metals. The first of a series of four-year plans was introduced in 1952 for planned development toward self-sufficiency, but the plans would have been meaningless without American assistance. Taiwan would not have been able to balance its international income account, nor prevent ruinous inflation, without the steady stream of raw materials, machinery, and vehicles from the United States. Taiwan had practically no automobiles, industrial machinery, or capital goods of any kind except as received from American sources.

Between 1952 and 1962 the real national income doubled, but the gain per capita was limited by the phenomenal rise in population. In 1945 Taiwan had six million people; the outlook was for twelve million in twenty years. The net annual increase was at the distressingly high rate of three and a half to four percent, and the government expressed no interest in birth control. The respectable showing in economic growth and the ten percent annual gain in capital accumulation strained the government's resources. Yet, because of the population expansion, Taiwan was not able to do much more than prevent an actual decline in the level of living. The government set a goal of providing 300,000 new jobs per year, but this could not satisfy the demand for employment on the part of the large number of high school and college graduates. Taiwan had a vocal and increasing supply of unemployed intelligentsia—a class which is always social dynamite.

The state, with its economic planning and monopoly on assistance from the United States, took the lead in economic development. It was deemed unhealthy that there should be so little private enterprise in the Taiwan showcase of democracy. Overseas Chinese and other potential foreign investors were reluctant to entrust their capital to a place which seemed to have such a precarious future. By 1962 the private sector of the economy represented about sixty percent of industrial production, and a campaign was launched to attract further investments. A law which was placed on the books in 1959 was intended to speed the flow of additional funds. Foreigners were permitted to invest in all types of "needed" industries or enterprises which would contribute to Taiwan's economic and social development. Full remittance of profits was promised, together with a capital repatriation privilege of fifteen percent annually. The government gave guarantees that it would not take over foreign shares in joint undertakings for at least twenty years. Other incentives for private investment included a five-year tax holiday on new enterprises, a corporate income tax cut from 32.5 to 18 percent, and tax-exemptions on reinvested earnings. Regulations such as these were standard in most Asian areas. A research team from the United States made an extensive study of opportunities for private investors in Taiwan and reported extensive and reasonable prospects for substantial profits in many lines including lumber, pulp and paper, textiles, electrical apparatus, small machined goods, cement, glass, plastics, chemical fertilizers, and pharmaceuticals.

The state aimed at constant improvement of the lot of the common man but the obstacles were staggering. Per-capita income doubled, but prices tripled. Goods were in short supply and printing-press "money" was abundant—so inflation could not be avoided. Prices of eggs were expressed in terms of a dollar apiece, and chickens sold for fifteen dollars a pound. The government was obliged to turn out one-hundred dollar notes where ten dollar notes had originally proved adequate. Very few people had any opportunity to accumulate wealth, and the masses could barely make ends meet. The ordinary farmer argued that he was no better off than when he worked for a landlord. His debts did not seem like much when the land was redistributed, but the burden seemed to grow heavier with each annual installment. Taxes increased—and so did the argument that it was no use to work harder when added income simply meant added taxes.

The burden of the military was oppressive. In 1963 a population of 11,000,000 was called upon to support an armed establishment of 600,000 combat effectives. The worst feature was that the armed forces were equipped with expensive American material and their ideas of preparation for war were based on expensive American presumptions. The armed forces of the Republic of China could not be sustained for a single month without American support. In addition to American help, they represented eighty percent of all government costs. It was no use to reduce the size of the army because no jobs were available for those who would have been discharged. Strong men without jobs—who had weapons and knew how to use them—would have constituted a grave social menace had they been driven by desperation to disregard the law. The army was expensive —but it was also a boon to the economy. A million people earned their living as soldiers or as civilian employees of the military. Money came out of one pocket as taxes and went back into the other in the form of paychecks. The pay was small, but the commissary was vital for food, clothing, and shelter. It was arguable that without the army there would have been more, rather than less, poverty.

The island of Taiwan was fertile, and it possessed great potential for industrial expansion. Its people were as skillful in agriculture and industry—and as thrifty and hardworking—as the best of the Chinese anywhere. But they were weighted down by the problems of poverty, inflation, population expansion, and a military policy geared to the reconquest of the mainland. Taiwan's prosperity—and possibly its survival—depended upon the goodwill and support of the United States.

Social conditions in Taiwan reflected postwar political and economic changes. At the base of the social pyramid were the Taiwanese themselves—Chinese in origin—working on their farms and edging into the stream of modernization as the Japanese had guided them. Half a million Japanese worked and lived in Taiwan before World War II, and, although they were "imperialists," it was they who brought prosperity to the island. Japanese farming methods and industrial know-how combined with Chinese skills to achieve high production levels in sugar, rice, bananas, and products of the forests and the sea. The Japanese brought with them the unmistakable trade marks of the Japanese homeland: the hotels, inns, public bathhouses, shrines, and love for mountain resorts and natural beauty spots. The Japanese intermarried with Taiwanese and taught them the Japanese language. The young were trained to do some small part of the nation's work. The Japanese increased the assets of Taiwan which were lost to them as part of the price of defeat.

The Taiwanese expected those assets for themselves. They argued that it was their labor which accounted for Japanese wealth. Therefore they were its rightful heirs. The mainlanders replied that they were entitled to Taiwan as the reward of military victory. Admittedly, they had nothing to bring to Taiwan but "blood, sweat and tears." Taiwanese would have to share their poverty. The streets of Taipei became deserted and the buildings deteriorated. The people looked poor. Their clothes were ragged and their homes were dilapidated. Patriotism was called upon to assuage the pains of empty stomachs. The Taiwanese resented the attempted remolding of island life into continental patterns.

The appearance of the Americans added a new dimension to Taiwan's social structure. The cities were affected more than the countryside. Money was forthcoming for physical rehabilitation and new construction. The streets presented a new façade. The Chinese still rode bicycles and pedicabs, but automobiles were made available for Americans and those Chinese who worked for the Americans. Traffic jams occurred when the offices closed and the Americans returned to their homes. The shops stocked expensive Hong Kong–style slit skirts, the best perfumes from New York and Paris, and all manner of luxury items for the Americans and their friends. Bottles of Scotch and Bourbon made their way from the PX to Chinese stores by way of the black market. Kaohsiung in the south, Keelung in the northeast, and the capital city of Taipei added the inevitable accouterments to cater to the whims of servicemen on duty overseas. Hotels, bars, restaurants, dance halls, and night clubs vied for American dollars. Some Chinese aped American ways; other discovered a new and deeper affection for their ancient values. Western ways did not seem to imbed themselves deeply in Formosan society. One could not escape the feeling that with the swing of the political pendulum, the veneer would be destroyed and only the strong core of Chinese character would be preserved.

Foreign Relations

The government of the Republic of China insisted upon its right to continue as the legal representative of the millions of all China in international affairs. Chiang Kai-shek and the Kuomintang did not give up their fight against Mao Tse-tung and the Communists on retiring to Taiwan. Chiang issued orders to close mainland ports and to intercept vessels trading with Communist China. He could not enforce these orders, but they showed how he felt. He sent his air force on reconnaissance flights and continuous propaganda raids. His planes dropped leaflets which were intended to cause dissatisfaction and stir up trouble. He sent guerrilla fighters and espionage agents with such missions as to blow up bridges and railways and set fire to arsenals. His objective was to prepare the way for ultimate liberation.

Chiang ridiculed all suggestions for a "two Chinas" policy which would have the effect of confirming the Communists in power on the mainland and would leave him with sovereignty over Taiwan. He called such a policy "cowardly and selfish, like pacifying the tiger with one's own flesh and inviting the robber to become the master of the house." His government was recognized as the only legal government of China by two out of three nations in the world including the United States, the Latin American republics, the Philippines, Thailand, France, Belgium, and the non-Asian nations of the British Commonwealth, except the United Kingdom itself.

The government of the Republic of China was the legal representative of China in the United Nations. It occupied a seat as a permanent member of the Security Council and represented China in the General Assembly and the specialized agencies. It opposed any suggestion that the Nationalist delegate should represent Formosa only and that an additional delegation should speak for Communist China. In 1949 the Chinese delegation persuaded the General Assembly to pass a resolution calling on all states to respect the political independence of China and to reaffirm the principles of the Nine Power Treaty negotiated in Washington in 1922.

The Formosan problem receded far into the background when the Chinese Communists intervened in force in Korea. A special Communist spokesman in the United Nations was given the privilege of presenting his case in November 1950, and he tried to shunt international attention from Korea to Formosa. In his intemperate diatribe against the United States, he repeated his demands for the ouster of the Kuomintang delegation from the United Nations and restated the Communist demand for the recovery of Taiwan. He won no new converts to his position.

No further discussions about Taiwan were held in the United Nations until 1952. Then the Chinese delegate succeeded in convincing the General Assembly to pass a resolution which asserted that Russia had failed to live up to its obligations under the treaty of August 14, 1945, between Russia and the China of Chiang Kai-shek. In 1955 Ambassador Tsiang Ting-fu, representing China, delivered an impassioned address in which he accused the iron-curtain countries of endangering the peace by their inhuman practices. He said that containment of the threat of massive retaliation were insufficient and that the only free-world tactic which would bring success would be the rollback. He called upon member states to embark upon indirect reprisals against communist states by stirring up revolts and internal uprisings—but his words were unheeded. The Chinese delegation survived the annual effort to substitute a Communist for a Nationalist representation in the General Assembly.

Nationalists and Communists contested for the favor and support of neighboring nations in Asia. Chiang Kai-shek sounded out Korea, Japan, and the Philippines on the possibility of a strong anti-Communist multilateral nonaggression pact for the Pacific area. He wanted a strong military organization and a unified command structure similar to that in Europe. He could not persuade Japan and Korea to cooperate in any joint undertaking, and he was firmly rebuffed by the United States.

Normal foreign relations between Taiwan and its neighbors were unspectacular. Taiwan regularized its diplomatic and commercial relations with Japan. The two nations signed a separate peace pact concurrently with the peace settlement between Japan and the allied nations at San Francisco. Taiwan negotiated annual trade agreements with Japan and permitted some Japanese businessmen and economic advisers to return to Taiwan. The Chinese could not forget entirely their suffering at the hands of the Japanese, and they dreaded the return of Japan to the seats of the mighty in the Pacific area. The Taiwanese objected bitterly to every evidence of a possible tie between Tokyo and Peking. Above all the Republic of China feared the evidence of "neutralism" in Japan, and they warned the Japanese it would have to be one or the other—either Taipei or Peking—it could not be both.

China and the Philippines enjoyed friendly relations. They exchanged goodwill missions and concluded satisfactory arrangements about trade and civil aviation. However, Chiang's government viewed with grave concern the anti-Chinese legislation in the Philippines and objected to the Philippine determination to deport Chinese who ran afoul of technicalities in Philippine immigration laws. Taiwan maintained a fundamental attitude of understanding and sympathy toward Thailand in spite of the latter's nationalistic anti-Chinese legislation. Naturally, Taiwan sympathized with Vietnam in its war against the Communists. To court the goodwill of Burma, Taiwan agreed to repatriate a band of guerillas under Li Mi, a former Kuomintang general who sought refuge in the China-Burma border area. Chiang manifested a deep interest in overseas Chinese and tried to attract their loyalty. He showed little community of interest with India or with those whom Hu Shih called "the very foolish people like Nehru who believe that there is a third force in the world."

Chiang did not develop very friendly relations with the United Kingdom. He resented the British amorality in extending recognition to Peking. He felt a personal insult because of British suggestions that Taiwan should be neutralized, that the offshore islands should be abandoned, and that the Peking regime should be admitted to the United Nations. He objected to British "defeatism" and questioned very seriously whether the British would make a determined stand in the event of a Communist attack against Hong Kong. He disliked British trade with the Chinese Communists. He understood that whatever sympathy he received from the British was most likely out of consideration for the United States. He was aware of an underlying British sentiment that Taiwan was not a vital interest of the free world and that any British support for Chiang's scheme to return to the mainland was "absolute lunacy."

Taipei made an impressive effort to keep up with Peking in Latin America and Africa. It offered diplomatic recognition to new nations as they emerged and entered freely into economic and cultural pacts. In spite of severe limitations in manpower and money, it opened up new embassies and sent delegations to a multitude of international conferences. Taiwan, which received so much assistance from overseas, was generous in extending help to others. In a single year, a hundred experts in fields ranging from agriculture to public health were sent to a dozen underdeveloped countries in Africa and Latin America. Not to be outdone by Peking, Taipei entertained annually in the neighborhood of a thousand distinguished visitors from nonwhite areas. Taiwan was determined that it—and not the People's Republic of Peking—should be accepted as widely as possible as the symbol of China.

RELATIONS WITH THE UNITED STATES

Much of the fate of Taiwan was in the hands of the United States. Taiwan depended upon the United States for moral support and for material assistance. Hopes soared or waned according to American moods. The government on Taiwan wished to return to the mainland; the United States was opposed to such a military adventure. The difference in objectives between Taipei and Washington and the awareness of inequality in relations between the two capitals led to constant misunderstanding and frequent quarrels. It was the Chinese misfortune to have no military or diplomatic initiative except that which was permitted by their American allies.

It was expected after the fall of Shanghai in 1949 that Formosa would be next. In January 1950, President Truman announced that the United States would not pursue a course which would lead to involvement in the civil conflict in China and would not provide military aid or advice to Chinese forces on Formosa. He changed his mind and his policy immediately after the outbreak of the fighting in Korea. On June 27, 1950, the president ordered the Seventh Fleet to prevent any attack on Formosa and called upon the government on Formosa to cease all air and sea operations against the mainland. (In 1953 President Eisenhower canceled the latter half of the Truman directive.)

As Chiang Kai-shek built up his strength, the United States generated a new faith in Formosa as an unsinkable aircraft carrier (as General MacArthur called it) and as the keystone in the defense perimeter in the western Pacific. Americans created a new military advisory group and began a huge program of military, economic, and technical assistance. Formosa was regarded as the first and last line of defense against the Communists. The Americans declared that Formosa's legal status would have to be determined by international action, and in the meantime they expressed hearty approval of a full investigation of the Formosa question by the United Nations.

After the disaster to the French at Dien Bien Phu in Indochina, it seemed logical that the Communists would next turn their guns on Formosa. By this time American opinion was steeled against any further surrenders. On December 2, 1954, the United States and the Republic of China signed a treaty which stated:

> Each party recognizes that an armed attack in the West Pacific area directed against the territories of either of the parties would be dangerous to its own peace and safety and declares that it would act to meet the common danger in accordance with its constitutional processes.

According to the treaty, the territories of China involved were specifically limited to Taiwan and the neighboring Pescadores. The treaty gave the United States the right, but not the obligation, to dispose land, air, and sea forces in and about those territories. When the treaty was ratified, it contained a clarifying satement of the American Senate which effectively barred the government on Taiwan from undertaking military operations against the mainland, except by joint agreement with the United States.

The question of the offshore islands came to a head in 1955. These islands—primarily the Quemoy Islands off the harbor of Amoy and the

Matsu Islands offshore from Foochow—were occupied by the Nationalists. They were shelled by the Communists. The question arose whether
the United States would aid the Nationalists in the event of an armed attack on those tiny bits of land under the shadow of Communist guns. The
nearest point on the islands was less than three miles from mainland
artillery emplacements, but it was more than a hundred miles from Quemoy to the nearest Formosan coastline. On January 25, 1955, the American
Congress passed a resolution "that the President of the United States be
authorized to employ the Armed Forces of the United States as he deems
necessary for the specific purpose of securing and protecting Formosa and
the Pescadores against armed attack." This did not amount to an unconditional American guarantee to fight for the offshore islands. It was a
limited declaration that Americans would take action, or refrain from
taking action, only if making those islands secure seemed necessary, *in
the judgment of the president,* for the defense of Formosa and the Pescadores.

The Communists unleashed a new bombardment of the offshore islands in 1958 which continued for seven weeks. Joint Chinese-American
action in ferrying food and supplies to the beleaguered garrison made it
clear that the Communists could not force the islands to surrender by
any means short of actual invasion. This they were not ready to undertake
—possibly for fear of precipitating a global war. The Communists settled
down to a nonsensical policy of shelling the islands lightly every other
day. This gave Chiang Kai-shek and Secretary of State Dulles opportunity
to reassess their positions and reappraise their policies.

Chiang was unhappy that the Americans were more interested in
restraining him than in unleashing him. He agreed to the issue of a joint
statement on October 23, 1958, which said:

> The Government of the Republic of China considers that the restora-
> tion of freedom to its people on the mainland is its sacred mission.
> It believes that the foundation of this mission resides in the minds
> and hearts of the Chinese people and that the principal means of
> successfully achieving its mission is the implementation of Dr. Sun
> Yat-sen's Three People's Principles (nationalism, democracy and
> social well-being) and not the use of force.

However, he insisted that these words did not imply that he surrendered his right of self-defense or his obligation to give support to any
large-scale uprising which might occur against the Communist regime on
the mainland. He refused to evacuate the offshore islands, for fear it
looked like surrender; and he objected to any relaxation of his right to
call upon the Seventh Fleet or American air power in the face of the
Communist threat. Chiang was against a negotiated cease-fire or a re-

nunciation of force. He was not nearly so much afraid of war—or even use of the atom bomb—as he was afraid of appeasement and coexistence. He did not intend to be a sacrificial victim to the Communists as he had been to the fascists.

The government in Taiwan existed in fear of possible abandonment by its American allies. It faced one crisis of confidence after another because it could not share the American enthusiasm for peace and orderly processes in the settlement of international disputes. Taiwan was obliged to adjust itself to constant reductions in American programs of economic assistance, and conceived of itself as the victim of American hesitation to use military might for the accomplishment of legitimate aims. Although the idea was seldom discussed, Taiwan was also afraid of a basic American penchant for isolation.

In its own judgment, Taiwan was by no means a mere pawn of the United States. In size, wealth, and population it had as favorable prospects for an auspicious future as a good one-third of the members of the United Nations. Few people on Taiwan entertained serious thoughts of retaking the mainland, although it was an article of faith to be ready should opportunity knock. In cold fact there was much doubt that Chiang Kai-shek and the Kuomintang would be chosen to head a new government in China even if the Communist regime in Peking should be overthrown.

Everyone in Taipei and throughout the country realized that some day the temporary arrangement under Chiang Kai-shek and his government would come to an end. What then? Perhaps a plebiscite might be conducted, under the auspices of the United Nations, which would give the local people a voice in the determination of their destiny. Several alternatives appeared possible, although few spirits were sufficiently courageous to discuss any alternative except an indefinite future under the successors of Chiang Kai-shek in the Kuomintang. Practically no one supported the idea of rejoining the body politic of the mainland, although rumors were frequent about the possibility of Kuomintang-Communist deals being consummated in Hong Kong. The daily radio from Peking held out a promise of forgiveness to any one who would desert Taiwan and come back "home." A certain age group among the Taiwanese, with memories of good old days under Japan, advocated reversion to Japan. A few expressed the wishful thought that they might become wards of the United States, or accepted as a trusteeship under the United Nations. A Democratic Independent party of Formosans in exile, under Dr. Thomas Liao, a Ph.D. in Chemical Engineering, campaigned abroad for "Formosa for the Formosans." Whatever the future, Taiwan's main job was to survive under the *status quo*, discharging its international obligations with honor and providing its growing millions with the best possible standard of living.

SUGGESTED READING

American Assembly, *United States and the Far East* (Englewood Cliffs, Prentice, 1962). Article by Allen Whiting and Robert Scalapino on United States and Taiwan.

Ballantine, Joseph, *Formosa, a Problem for United States Foreign Policy* (Washington, Brookings Institution, 1952).

China Year Book (Taipei, China Publishing Co.) Annual.

Government of the Republic of China, *Free China*. Annual.

International Cooperation Administration, *Economic Progress of Free China, 1951–1958* (Taipei, Mutual Security Mission to China, 1958).

Joint Commission on Rural Reconstruction (Taipei). Annual Reports.

Koen, R. Y., *China Lobby and American Politics* (New York, Macmillan, 1960).

Linebarger, Paul M. A., Djang Chu and Burks, Ardath, *Far Eastern Governments and Politics, China and Japan* (second ed.) (Princeton, Van Nostrand, 1956).

Luard, Evan, *Britain and China* (Baltimore, Johns Hopkins U., 1962).

Quigley, Harold, *China's Politics in Perspective* (Minneapolis, U. of Minnesota, 1962).

Raper, Arthur F., and others, *Urban and Industrial Taiwan—Crowded and Resourceful* (Taipei, Foreign Operations Administration, Mutual Security Mission to China & National Taiwan University, 1954).

Riggs, Fred W., *Formosa under Chinese Nationalist Rule* (New York, Macmillan, 1952).

Tang Tsou, *America's Failure in China, 1941–1950* (Chicago, U. of Chicago, 1962).

United Nations Economic Commission for Asia and the Far East, *Economic Survey of Asia and the Far East*. Annual.

Vinacke, Harold, *Far Eastern Politics in the Post-War Period* (New York, Appleton, 1956).

Whitaker, Urban G., (ed.), *Foundations of U.S. China Policy* (Berkeley, Pacifica Foundation, 1959).

Young, Arthur, *China and the Helping Hand* (Cambridge, Harvard U., 1963).

32

India, Pakistan, and Ceylon

The United States has no need to be reminded of the importance of China and Japan in the contemporary world, and it has become indelibly impressed with the vital role of the nations of the subcontinent. Together, India, Pakistan, and Ceylon equal half the size of the United States and contain one-fifth of the people of the world. India alone exceeds the combined population of the United States, the Soviet Union, and the United Kingdom. In 1963 Pakistan—larger than France, Italy, Switzerland, and the Netherlands—approached 100,000,000. Ceylon, which is small by comparison, passed the 10,000,000 mark. It is not size alone which is important, nor the distinctiveness of the culture of South Asia. The historical heritage of India, Pakistan, and Ceylon will exercise a great influence on the shape of things to come in the rest of Asia and in the world at large.

The nations of South Asia developed customs, traditions, and institutions which passed through changes and modifications as they came in contact with foreign influences. The British were the last on a long line of intruders who came from the alien lands of Asia or Europe. The people of India received them all, and took from their visitors or conquerors those ideas which proved useful or advantageous. The vast subcontinent of the twentieth century exhibited all the characteristics of its original self, plus the enrichment of time and experience.

Independence did not bring utopia. Nationalism did little more than increase the tempo and the intensity of the fight against ignorance, poverty, and disease. The men who fought long and successfully for self-government and independence learned that the tasks of nation-building just began with the exodus of the British. In all three countries a constitution had to be drawn up and a workable form of government set in motion. Economic development had to be undertaken on a massive coordinated scale to provide food and jobs for exploding populations. Social changes had to be recognized, encouraged, and kept within the bounds of law and order. The Western-educated elite spoke freely and enthusiastically of the "revolution" which they intended to complete in order to fulfill the requirements of modern, independent nationhood.

The leaders of India, Pakistan, and Ceylon learned their lessons well from their British teachers. They showed they would not be slaves to political labels, and they did not hesitate to try out national-socialistic policies. South Asian statesmen offered stiff resistance to the wiles and blandishments of the Communists. In international affairs, they followed policies of "respectable independence." If anything they were anachronistic in their concern for the rights of absolute sovereignty. They developed a well-known tactic of "neutralism" or "nonalignment" as the best possible means of protecting and promoting their particular interests. In seeking the best possible position for their countries in the contemporary world, they charted a course which was followed to a large degree by neighbors in Southeast Asia who were also newcomers to the community of sovereign and independent nations.

India: Internal Developments

India was fortunate to have a leader with the power and prestige of Jawaharlal Nehru. As president of the Congress Party and prime minister, he was in a unique position to put his ideas into action. It was his responsibility to insure freedom, uphold the rule of law and give the diverse groups in his country a growing sense of national solidarity. He considered his first job to be the completion of India's territorial sovereignty. He came to terms with France on the remaining pinpoints of French imperialism in 1954, and he used military measures to drive the Portuguese out of Goa in 1961. He also had to pay some attention to the organization of the Indian states, many of which were larger than countries of Europe. The process was carried out by a national commission created for the purpose. Sixteen states were created, largely along linguistic lines. Together with some specially designated federal territories, these states became the basic units of government in India's federal union.

Prime Minister Nehru boasted that his country was the world's largest working democracy. The ballot was secret, and every adult was given the right to vote. National elections were held at five-year intervals, beginning in 1952. In the election of 1962 more than 210,000,000 adults were eligible to vote, and nearly two-thirds exercised their right. Voting places were arranged so that no person needed to travel more than three miles to cast his ballot. The Congress Party polled less than sixty percent of the votes but gained more than two-thirds of the seats in the lower house of the national parliament. Of the opposition parties, the Communists returned 29 members to the parliament, the *Swatantra* (Freedom Party, representing free enterprise on the right) 18, the Jan Sangh (also Rightist) 14, the Prajad (People's) Socialist Party 12, other Socialists 6, and Independents 59.

The Congress Party made an equally strong showing in the states, in spite of the obvious complacency and intrigue in the Party's ranks. Its success was due primarily to the maladroitness of its opposition. The Socialists barely managed to hold on. The Communists showed their greatest strength in Andhra, West Bengal (Calcutta city), Uttar Pradesh, and Bihar. In Kerala—the state with the highest literacy rate and the largest percentage of Christians, where for a short period the Communists controlled the government—the Communists polled strong, but they failed to capture many seats. The party was split to the extent that the secretary-

SOUTH ASIA
1963

0 100 200 300 400 500 600
Miles

general and the chairman could not agree on a single line, and the opposition pulled together in order to defeat the Communists.

It was no easy matter to make democracy work in India. A high degree of illiteracy limited the possibilities of electioneering. Castes and subcastes with their rigidities and lingering loyalties determined in large measure a candidate's political acceptability. Disparity in conditions between urban Bombay and the hill country in Assam, for example, made it impossible to fashion a single program with nation-wide appeal. The most meaningful issue was the endorsement of the Congress Party. Although the Indian parliament functioned with dignity and credit, many traditional elements in Indian society remained skeptical of the Western-style democratic process. Democracy worked because of the skill, experience, and training of the Congress' leaders, aided and abetted by such constructive forces as the army and the bureaucrats who were the heirs of the Indian civil service. Indians did not produce new leaders with the genius of Nehru or Gandhi, but they developed a large reservoir of lesser talents which might be expected to rise to power "after Nehru."

The real foundations of Indian democracy lay not in the legislatures, nor in the national election process, but in the operation of representative institutions at the grass roots level. Politicians with nation-wide reputations talked easily about freedom fighters and the national revolution, but they formed a class apart from the average citizens. The ideas and interests of the elite were beyond the grasp or the intellectual range of the masses. National matters seldom commanded the attention of the ordinary villager. The challenge to political leaders was to energize their followers and to stir up interest in the intangible factors which influenced the common welfare. India struggled to "decentralize democracy" and to find the democratic forms and procedures which would be best adapted to the Indian people and their environment.

The lives of the masses centered about their village. Before 1952 the representative of the district officer—who came from the world beyond the village—was the man of greatest prestige in the village. After the adoption of the constitution of 1952, an effort was initiated to shift the prestige—and the responsibility—from the civil servant and the petty bureaucrat to the elected representatives of the people. Village councils and district boards, as well as municipal officials in the urban areas, were elected on the basis of adult franchise. With this shift in emphasis, interest in the success of democratic methods spread beyond the middle classes to the masses, including the untouchables, agricultural laborers, small peasants, and city workers. Democracy in India penetrated as deeply into the grass roots as any alternate communistic program might have done.

In 1957 India decided to liquidate the old district system of local government. In its place was substituted a panchayati raj or a system of rule by councils of villages. A group of several villages replaced the single self-sustaining village as the basic unit of political action. More than 220,000 major community centers were established, each presided over by a panchayat or council, elected by the member villages. More than a million councilors were thus given responsibility and authority for the remolding of community life. It was up to them to take the leadership in every phase of rural rehabilitation and community development.

Nehru was as interested in economic justice as political democracy. He departed from the economic ideas of Gandhi and dedicated himself to the building of a "socialistic" state, without too much concern for the doctrinaire definition of that word. He was preoccupied with the struggle against poverty. The basic fact of life in India was the starvation level of existence. Indian economy was not only backward, but it was incapable of providing a rising standard of living for its zooming population. With the introduction of penicillin, DDT, and purified water, the death rate dipped; the annual increase of new mouths to feed exceeded five millions.

It was clear that if India were to achieve political progress, it would have to subordinate everything to the problems of food and jobs. At the beginning of independence, half the peasants earned less than three hundred dollars per year; a fifth earned less than one hundred fifty dollars per year. The city proletariat was no better off, which accounted for the appalling conditions in the city slums and the hordes of people who had no place to sleep except the pavements. The solution of the food problem required the modernization of agricultural methods, extensive irrigation systems, reclamation of wastelands, and a radical reform in the system of landholding. The average holding of an Indian farming family was less than five acres. At the same time, a veritable social revolution would be required to make economic reforms acceptable. The solution of the job problem depended upon accelerated industrialization.

In 1951 India launched its first five-year plan for economic development. Greatest emphasis was placed upon agriculture, including dams for irrigation and power, flood control and reclamation projects, and coordinated plans for improvement of age-old methods of farming. Schemes in Bihar, the Punjab, Orissa, Madya Pradesh, Rajasthan, and in Andhra added twenty million acres to the fifty millions under irrigation and made possible the increase in annual food production from fifty-four million tons to sixty-four millions. National income was increased by eighteen percent, but because of population growth the per-capita income was increased by approximately half that amount. Transportation systems were improved during that period; a huge fertilizer plant was erected, all in the interest of more food for hungry people.

The first five-year plan also laid the foundation for industrial advance and provided modestly for the expansion of such social services as health, housing, education, technical training, and welfare work for the poorest elements of the population. India's industrial objective was a mixed economy in which basic industries would be owned and developed by the state. Other sectors of the economy were open for development by private initiative. This policy, reminiscent of Japan during the Meiji era, was not based on prejudice or doctrinaire theories. It was accepted as the best hope for quick development of national resources and the best means of avoiding gross inequalities in the accumulation of wealth. State control guaranteed the location of various enterprises in the best strategic areas and made possible a concerted effort to avoid the miseries which had come along with industrialization in the countries of the West. If the masses were to remain unspeakably poor, India wanted as few of the conspicuous rich as possible. Fewer than a million people in India made sufficient money to pay any kind of an income tax.

Steel plants, machine-making industries, heavy chemicals, petroleum, electronics, shipbuilding, airplanes, locomotives, and railway coaches were placed in the public sector. Textiles, cement, automobiles, pharmaceuticals, and engineering works were left in the private sector. India also placed great emphasis on small-scale factories and handicrafts and designed its tax and subsidy policies so that the budding industrial giants could not squeeze the little men out of business. Capitalism was not strong in India, largely because it was so difficult to accumulate savings. The state had to take the lead wherever large initial investments were required. India started practically from scratch in its efforts to industrialize. In spite of its wealth of resources, factories were scarce. In 1947 industry accounted for only six percent of the national income and employed less than two percent of those gainfully employed. India possessed great water-power potential, but on the eve of the first five-year plan the whole country did not generate enough electricity to light up New York City.

The second five-year plan (1956–1961) carried on agricultural projects but placed more stress on development toward a self-sufficient industrial structure. Substantial increases were hoped for in the production of steel, aluminum, and phosphates; great expansion was planned in the output of gas, minerals, and coal. Improvements were undertaken in transportation, communications, and transmission of electric power. Targets included a twenty-five percent increase in national income and a sixty-four percent increase in industrial production. It was expected that the share of industry in the national income would rise to twenty-five percent. It was planned to invest some $20,000,000,000 in the accomplishment of the second five-year plan, but without the forced draft of compulsory savings or slave labor. India planned to raise three-quarters of the money by taxation and to borrow the rest from abroad. It obtained loans from Great Britain, Germany, Russia, and the United States; and from the Colombo Plan, the World Bank, and the United Nations. Because of the strains on the national economy, India drastically curtailed its imports and subjected its people to a life of austerity.

In 1961, the third five-year plan was launched. Further agricultural and industrial progress was anticipated, but problems increased faster than achievements. A military menace complicated the ordinary peacetime procedures, and a large portion of the budget was transferred from development to defense. It became increasingly difficult to find the fifteen percent of the gross national product which had to be reinvested to keep the economy going. Foreign loans were required in amounts beyond India's capacity to pay. The gains which were made seemed distressingly small when measured against the greatness of the national effort. By 1961 only 23,000 villages out of 500,000 had electricity; steel capacity was only three and a half million tons as compared with thirty times that amount in the United States. The encouraging feature of the five-year plans was that India registered substantial improvement in agriculture and made a real beginning in industrialization, no matter how small the actual figures. The discouraging feature was that the take-off point, the point where its economy could sustain itself, receded into the distance. With the population increase, India made very little, if any net gain, in the struggle to raise its overall standard of living. It fell farther and farther behind in its effort to catch up with the level of prosperity in the swiftly moving West.

These large-scale efforts brought no more than slight relief to rural India, which suffered from primitive agricultural methods, rigidity of social conditions, and an uneconomic system of landholding. The national government turned over the program of land reform to the states because it was too big and too complicated to handle on a centralized, nation-wide scale. Some state governments undertook a program of land distribution looking toward a goal of land to the tiller. Rents were controlled, and more rights of tenure were guaranteed for the tenant. These things brought about more social justice, but they alone did not bring about higher rates of production per acre. Nor did they abolish tenantry, because in 1961 tenancy still covered one-fourth of India, and one-seventh of all agricultural families were landless. With the beginning of the third-year plan, the various governments worked harder than ever with the formation of cooperatives, the elimination of fragmented holdings, and the abandonment of out-moded bullock-and-stick methods of cultivation.

As early as 1952 a huge program of community development was inaugurated. This was a scheme for the integrated development of a group of about one hundred villages, and it antedated by six years the much-heralded adoption of the "communes" in China. It was admitted frankly in India that a single village was too small a unit for economic planning and social development. Therefore about a hundred villages were combined into a project area to undertake its own measures for the introduction of new techniques in agriculture, encouragement of cooperative societies, promotion of cottage industries to stop the drain of agricultural workers to the cities, repair or construction of roads and schools, promotion of adult education, and improvement in all the amenities of group living. Village-level workers trained in rural extension work (not party cadres) were brought in to collaborate the conservative peasants. Through discussions, demonstrations, and audio-visual aids, villagers were introduced to practical ways and means to a better life. This community-development movement showed imperfections, but by 1962 it reached three-fifths of rural India. Historian Arnold Toynbee called it one of the most beneficial revolutions in the life of the peasantry in human history.

Another action program peculiar to India was the *Bhoodan* or "voluntary land gift" movement of Vinoba Bhave, a ninety-pound ascetic disciple of Gandhi who walked from village to village preaching that in a just and equitable society land must belong to all. At first he suggested that landowners should give one-sixth of their land to the landless; then he went so far as to urge entire villages to give over all their land to joint community control. He also taught that a man might offer his life in public service if he had no land to give. Such was his prescription for collectivization at the village level by nonviolent means. Some of Bhave's critics argued that landlords only surrendered the worst of their land and that the well-intentioned reformer only confounded confusion by further fragmentation of landholding. However, he attracted thousands of followers and caused the redistribution of hundreds of thousands of acres. With his gentle teaching and selfless life, he hoped to promote a casteless, classless society.

The planned social revolution in India was no less important than India's political and economic changes. The government itself took the leadership in modernization. The government endeavored to reorganize the structure of Hinduism and bring India's social institutions to the level of other modern countries. Substantial modifications were made in the caste system, the joint family, and in traditional concepts of Hindu law. It has already been noted that the constitution abolished untouchability, proclaimed the equality of women, and dedicated the state to equality and social justice. Laws were passed to implement these elusive ideals. The Untouchabilities Offenses Act came into effect in June 1955, forbidding discrimination in the use of wells, for example, or in access to shops, restaurants, hotels, and places of entertainment. The tempo of modern life, factories, schools, public hospitals, and the one-man–one-vote system of politics eliminated some of the worst evils of untouchability and made some progress in India's battle against social discrimination. A new marriage law recognized the marriage relationship as a contractual one, permitted marriages between different castes and sanctioned divorces for women as well as for men. The inheritance law was changed so that daughters were given equal rights with sons in the inheritance of property.

Education played a significant role in social change. Boys and girls went to school together, and became infected with the spirit of progress. In 1961, India reported some fifty million in schools, with another million in colleges and universities. Language barriers were monumental in the struggle to give equal educational opportunities to all students throughout the country. It was also an impossible task to provide suitable jobs for the large numbers of graduates. The intelligentsia, that is, all who attended college or even high school for a short time, demanded white collar jobs and looked down upon manual labor, technical, or engineering positions. Nehru urged young educated Indians to go to the villages, to soil their hands, and to work side by side with the villagers in building roads and digging wells. He wanted them to learn the theory of scientific agriculture, and also to go into the fields and practice it.

In 1961 most of India was illiterate—perhaps seventy-five percent—but the mass of the population was young. Three-quarters of India's people were under thirty-five; half were in the age group five to twenty-four. Their chances for a life span of sixty years were reasonable, and they were neither fatalistic nor pessimistic about their future. The "little men" who previously had had no voice in public affairs were just beginning to feel the effects of social change. Workers joined unions, city crowds listened to political speeches, and peasants made their wishes known to their district councilors. In many ways, India remained socially backward, but it was set in motion toward integration and modernization on such a large scale and with such speed that it was entitled to be called a nation in revolution.

India in World Affairs

In spite of its rapid development, and in spite of its ancient grievances against Great Britain, India placed great value on its place as a member of the Commonwealth of Nations. India derived benefit in security, trade, and friendships because of its freely chosen close ties with its former ruler. India also played a substantial role in the United Nations and came to be identified as the leading peacemaker in a world of brush-fire wars.

As the leading country among the neutralists, or the chief of the

so-called Colombo Powers, India achieved an eminence which would
have been impossible had it linked itself exclusively either with the Communist or the anti-Communist bloc. India was foremost in the struggle
against colonialism and racial inequality; it was strong for national liberation movements, absolute sovereignty and "Asia for the Asians." India
insisted no nation was always good and none absolutely bad in world
affairs; therefore India would choose its course of action on each issue as
it arose. Freedom of choice and action was an essential perquisite of
independence. India's nonalignment did not stem from passivity, coward-
ice, or lack of conviction, but from a realistic appreciation of its national
advantage. India took its stand firmly for what it called the *Panch Sheela,*
or five principles of peaceful coexistence, which were first subscribed
to by Nehru and Chou En-lai in their agreement over Tibetan affairs in
1954. These principles were mutual respect for each other's territorial
integrity and sovereignty, noninterference in the internal affairs of another, nonaggression, equality, and peaceful coexistence. Nehru argued
passionately for disarmament, particularly of nuclear weapons. As an
Asian, he felt a sense of personal grievance that the atomic bomb was
used against the nonwhites of Asia. He wanted peace and the opportunity
to lead his nation as fast and as far as possible on the path of progress.
With regard to the United Nations, Nehru said, "It may yet lead us out
of this fear and strife-ridden age into a more settled future when the full
potentialities of science and technology could be applied to the well-
being of all peoples."

In relations with the United States, India blew hot and cold. India
professed to object to American "militarism," selfishness in aid programs
and ambivalence on questions involving imperialism, such as in West Irian
and Tunisia. India differed from the United States in its attitudes toward
the Japan peace treaty, the recognition of the People's Republic of China,
and the action of the United Nations in Korea. India was offended because
the United States failed to take an unequivocal stand in support of the
Indian position on Kashmir and pursued an active policy of military
assistance to Pakistan. India showed no sympathy for the American
initiative in promoting the Southeast Asia Treaty Organization or for the
American determination to resist the spread of communism in Laos and
Vietnam. Nehru said repeatedly that he believed the United States gave
too much importance to the factor of communism in its cold war against
Russia, China, and the entire Communist bloc.

Relations with the United States took a turn for the better when
the Americans refused to cooperate with the British and the French in the
Suez crisis of 1956. Nehru was heartened with every evidence of peaceful
coexistence between Russia and the United States, and he was pleased
with the warmth and cordiality shown by President Eisenhower in his

goodwill visit to India. The thermometer of friendship rose as Americans seemed to grow more understanding of the Indian policy of nonalignment. American aid to India mounted steadily and reached the staggering sum of four billion dollars by 1963. The Americans increasingly accepted India as the pivotal country in South Asia, as the model for economic development in a democratic, constitutional way. In 1959 the United States Senate's Foreign Relations Committee went on record as saying that "India's experiment in national economic growth is, in and of itself and without reference to Communist China, one of the great, dramatic efforts of planned, democratic development of the twentieth century, and is for this reason alone worthy of support and encouragement." The high point of Indian-American relations came with the prompt and dramatic American response to Nehru's appeal for assistance against the Chinese invasion of his border territories in 1962.

India was careful to foster the goodwill of the Soviet Union at the same time it edged closer to the United States. Nehru found Khrushchev to be a willing collaborator in maintaining ties of friendship. The government of Russia discreetly refrained from interfering in relations between India's Communists and the international Communist party organization. When Nehru put Indian Communists in jail, the Russian papers contented themselves with the observation that the arrests were due to reactionary forces within India (and not the reactionary government of India as the Chinese alleged). At times Khrushchev's attitudes toward India were so cordial that it appeared possible that he was bent on wooing India as a counterweight to China in Asia. When Khrushchev, with Marshal Bulganin, visited India in 1955, he set the pattern of Russian economic assistance. He sent substantial aid for India's economic development and built for India the country's largest steel mill near Calcutta. By the time of the third five-year plan, Russian aid exceeded a billion dollars and Russian trade amounted to a billion dollars per year. Russian officials made frequent goodwill trips to India and conducted a lively program of cultural exchange. In the United Nations, Russia made a particular point of supporting India in its quarrel with Pakistan over Kashmir. In the matter of the border dispute between India and China, Russia shied away from support of China. Officially Russia advocated peaceful settlement of the dispute, and quietly it sent military aid to India rather than to China.

India's greatest problem in world affairs was its unexpected breach in good relations with China. The issue was the frontier between the two countries. In April 1954, India and China reached agreement on their relations in Tibet, without taking up the matter of the frontier. A year later, the two nations joined twenty-seven other countries of Asia and Africa in a meeting at Bandung, Indonesia, where they exhibited complete harmony in their devotion to common Asian purposes. This was the heyday of India-China cooperation, when "Hindi and Chinese are brothers." Chou En-lai visited India in 1956 and declared that, in spite of the difference in the social and political systems, there was no clash of interest between the two peoples.

Until that time, the Indians considered that the border problem was settled in accordance with British-Chinese negotiations of 1914. The Indians would certainly have beeen willing to discuss minor modifications had the Chinese so desired. The Chinese gave no hint of dissatisfaction with existing boundaries, which had been ostensibly accepted by the Manchu dynasty and by the Kuomintang. Later the Chinese declared that in their view, *all* border problems between China and India, including the exact location of the 2500-mile-long mountainous boundary line, should be renegotiated.

In 1959 some Tibetans revolted against harsh features of the Chinese military administration in Tibet. When their rebellion was suppressed, thousands of Tibetans with their spiritual leader, the Dalai Lama, took refuge in India. Peking was indignant because of Delhi's hospitality. The cordiality of peaceful coexistence disappeared as harsh feelings came with border incidents. In India's northwest—where Kashmir touches Tibet and where rugged peaks 20,000 feet high make it impossible to fix any precise geographic marker—the only boundary line was the customary frontier along the passes through the Himalayas. This line was subject to perennial disputes.

Beginning in 1957, Red China improved the old caravan route between Sinkiang and Tibet to make it usable for trucks. The prime object of the repair job was to link together the two distant provinces of China, but an incidental result was the increase of the military menace to India and Pakistan. A part of the improved route passed over the Aksai Chin plateau in the Ladakh section of Kashmir state, a territory to which three nations (India, Pakistan, China) laid claim. This disputed territory was relatively uninhabited. A sign by the side of the road said, "You are now entering the highest road in the world, check your oxygen supply." The Indians did not know of the Chinese activity until the road was practically finished. In 1958 they sent a party to survey the situation, and the Indian party was promptly arrested by the Chinese. Subsequent incidents flared, which both sides minimized. Then the Chinese published official maps which indicated large areas of territory as belonging to China, and the Chinese quietly advanced their military position. India and China initiated diplomatic negotiations in April 1960, to fix a new boundary line.

At the same time, trouble developed more than a thousand miles to the east on the border of the northeast frontier agency. This region is a giant hilly horseshoe at the foot of the Himalayas, controlling the approaches to the Brahmaputra valley in Assam. It touches Burma on the east and Bhutan on the west. Because of the thick tropical jungles, the hill country is inaccessible and relatively unexplored. It is inhabited by various tribes who differ from the Indians, Chinese and from each other in culture, language, dress, and custom. The way of life of the mountain people is a primitive one, and before the border conflicts was of interest only to officers of the Indian government and a few anthropologists.

In this region the MacMahon Line was generally recognized as the boundary. Here also the Chinese built new roads and set up outposts in Indian territory. On October 20, 1962, the Chinese launched major military operations both in Ladakh in the northwest and the northeast frontier agency in the northeast. They pushed ahead as much as eighty miles without effective Indian opposition, and on November 21, 1962, they announced an unexpected pullback and cease-fire. They withdrew twenty kilometers behind the line of their actual control in Ladakh and a like distance behind the MacMahon Line in the northeast frontier agency. The Chinese released their Indian prisoners and returned the food, blankets and military supplies which they had taken. Nehru appealed to the West for help. He declared that he would never bend before Chinese aggression, and he offered to turn the dispute over to an arbitrator or the Permanent Court of International Justice. He made no mention of the United Nations because of possible embarrassment to Mr. Khrushchev. He also indicated his willingness to abide by the findings of a six-nation commission of Asian and African neutrals which recommended that the dis-

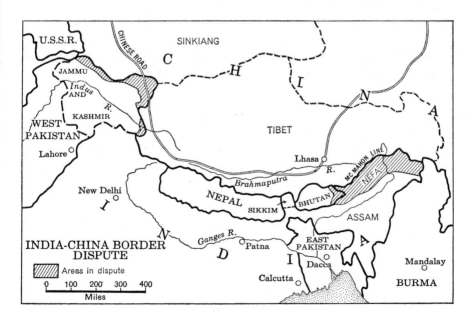

INDIA-CHINA BORDER DISPUTE

Areas in dispute

0 100 200 300 400
Miles

pute be settled by peaceful means. He closed Chinese consulates in India, but he refused to break off diplomatic relations. Immediate danger of war passed, but the atmosphere of tension and distrust remained.

The Chinese insisted that they merely wanted to complete the definition of their national boundaries. They said they had made agreements with everybody from Mongolia all the way around to Burma, with the exception of India. They felt that the time had come to reach an understanding with India. Chou En-lai asserted that Chinese actions represented no fundamental clash between the peoples of India and China. He argued that "Indians and Chinese should not cross swords on this issue and even less should allow United States imperialism to poke in its hand and develop the present unfortunate border conflict into a war in which Asians are made to fight Asians." Papers in Peking showed less concern with India than with the Cuban affair.

Nehru felt differently from Chou En-lai. Nehru appealed for help from the United States, Great Britain, Russia, and everybody else. He was afraid that military necessity might oblige him to divert his assets from economic development. He told his people that "wanton, massive invasion brought incalculable, ominous and explosive new elements into the situation" and "India will not lose this war, no matter how long it lasts." He accused China of premeditated aggression. He declared that India would have to give up its daydreams of peace and adjust itself to the perpetual threat of invasion. He calmed down the war fever but prepared his people for a permanent condition of tension. He caused the passage of emergency rules for the defense of India which provided severe penalties for all who disobeyed orders, abandoned their jobs, or acted against the interest of national defense. Nehru was hard put to restore the morale of the frontier people, but with all his problems he displayed no inclination to abandon his traditional policy of nonalignment.

PAKISTAN'S FOREIGN RELATIONS

One of the worst features of the India-China border conflict was the manner in which it inflamed the long-smoldering quarrels between India and Pakistan over Kashmir. Part of the disputed boundary was in the state of Kashmir, where both India and Pakistan were vitally concerned. After the 1952 agreement between India and Pakistan, India proceeded to integrate Kashmir and to preach that "taking away any part of Kashmir would be like taking away a man's arm or his leg." Statements of this nature infuriated Pakistan. India also stationed three-quarters of its armed forces on the Pakistan border. Defense against each other—because of Kashmir—cost both nations precious funds which might advantageously have been used for national development. Kashmir was the perennial obstacle to better understanding between Pakistan and India; in April 1962, it was placed for the hundredth time on the agenda of the Security Council of the United Nations.

In 1956 Nehru proposed a division of Kashmir along the cease-fire line, without any plebiscite. He subsidized Kashmir's economic development in order to win goodwill, and he cooperated cordially with the government of Kashmir, which stood for close relations with India. Sheik Abdullah, the champion of home rule, was jailed, and the ordinary people of Kashmir showed less interest in annexation to either Pakistan or India than they showed in the lucrative tourist trade. In 1957 the Constituent assembly of Kashmir arranged for the state's formal accession to India. Pakistan brought the matter to the Security Council, which voted 10–0 (Russia abstaining) that this procedure would not accord with the principle of self determination. India did not send troops into Kashmir to make the accession definitive, but contented itself with the announcement that "accession is irrevocable." After that, the dispute smoldered. Suggestions were made for a plebiscite or for division of Kashmir, but neither Pakistan nor India could be persuaded to relax from its extreme position.

At this point, a survey of Pakistan's general international position should be made in order to understand its response to the China-India border conflict which flared up in 1962.

Pakistan, like India, chose to stay within the framework of the Commonwealth of Nations. This brought the advantages of association with the British army and navy, and the profits of preferred British trade relations. Pakistan boasted of its heritage of British political institutions and accepted Britain as the embodiment of "liberalism" in the modern world. Nevertheless, Pakistan did not see eye to eye with Great Britain in world affairs, particularly in the Middle East. Because of common religious interests, Pakistan was sympathetic with Iran, Iraq, Turkey, and Egypt, with whom Great Britain was often at odds. Pakistan was vigorous in the promotion of the pan-Islamic idea, arguing that "Islam is a body, the Moslem states are its limbs—a pain in one is a pain to all." Pakistan accused the British of siding with India in Kashmir, and, with India, it resented the discriminatory policies of some of the dominions in racial matters. Many Pakistanis became convinced that it was better for them to develop close ties with other Asians even at the possible cost of Commonwealth solidarity.

Pakistan was situated deep in the heart of Asia. It shared the psychological sensitivity of most Asians and their passionate devotion to political independence and economic development. Pakistan wanted no Western interference or advice in its problems with other Asians, namely India, Afghanistan, Burma, and China. Pakistan was ambivalent in its attitudes toward China, although it recognized the People's Republic of China at the outset and voted consistently for its admission into the United Nations. Pakistan was pro-Chinese, in wishing China success in its struggle against poverty; it was anti-Chinese in opposing China's communism.

Pakistan differed sharply from India in its attitudes toward the cold war. Pakistan rejected the policies of nonalignment. Because of the nation's Islamic character, it had no affinity for the atheistic aspects of communism. Pakistan disliked Russia's support of India in Kashmir, and objected to Russia's active economic policies in Pakistan's neighbors, first Afghanistan and later India. However, Pakistan was not pathologically anti-Communist or anti-Russian. Pakistan expressed its approval whenever Russia spoke out for the end of colonialism, or endorsed national liberation movements, or extended aid to Asians for purposes of economic development. Pakistan was impressed by the spectacular progress of Russia and felt that it had much to learn from Russia in the scientific and technical fields, especially in agriculture. Pakistan had the feeling that Russia was not guilty of racial discrimination and was to be praised for its treatment of Moslem minorities in Central Asia. Pakistan also gave Russia a sympathetic hearing because Russia was accepted as the champion of the poor and oppressed. A psychological link was established between the war against poverty and disease on the one hand and the policies of the Soviet Union on the other. The word revolution which was appropriated by the Communists had an acceptable as well as an objectionable connotation. When Khrushchev came to power in Russia, he received a good press in Pakistan for his tolerance of Asian nationalism and his active support of peaceful coexistence.

Pakistan's attitudes toward the United States were reflections of its basic attitudes toward the Middle Eastern Islamic countries, India and the Soviet Union. When the United States stood up against Great Britain—for example in the Suez crisis, negotiations for new petroleum agreements in Iran, or in treaty revision in Iraq—Pakistan applauded. Pakistan entered eagerly into CENTO (Central Treaty Organization), which promoted Middle Eastern solidarity against the advance of communism. Pakistan likewise joined SEATO (Southeast Asia Treaty Organization), which was set up to oppose Communist aggression or subversion in that part of the world. Pakistan chose to promote its own national security by accepting large sums in military and economic assistance from the United States. Pakistan "leaned to one side" but that side was the side of the United States. However, Pakistan entertained many reservations in its attitudes toward the United States. It disapproved American race-consciousness, tendency to compromise with imperialism, and willingness to "use Asians to fight Asians." Having been hewers of wood and drawers of water for the British, Pakistanis had no intention of becoming cannon fodder for the Americans. Pakistan received American aid without enthusiasm, convinced as it was that American aid was designed for American security and not for generous purposes of helping the underdeveloped. When the India-China border conflict prompted the United States to step up its assistance programs to India, Pakistan intimated that it would make fundamental reappraisals of existing policies.

Although the international spotlight focused on border clashes between China and India, both Pakistan and India paid closer attention to the malady of the heart in Kashmir than to the blemish on the skin in Ladakh. Some Pakistanis even suggested that the frontier incident was a hoax designed to attract sympathy and military aid to India. Naturally the Americans urged the Pakistanis and the Indians to solve their problems in Kashmir. For years, the Americans had sent arms to Pakistan; in 1962 they began to send arms to India. It was the American assumption that the recipients would use the arms against Communists, and not against each other. The British shared the American view and joined in notifying both Pakistan and India that continuing military support would depend upon a peaceful settlement in Kashmir. Pakistan bristled at American interference and American military aid to India and stated that it might be obliged to pull out of CENTO and out of SEATO. Feeling in Pakistan ran so high against the United States that the government deemed it prudent to post a special guard outside the American embassy. A Pakistan official put the case succinctly when he said, "We might be obliged to shake hands now with those who through no fault of our own have heretofore been our enemies."

On the surface it seemed that India, the nonaligned country, chose to fight China rather than surrender its territory, while Pakistan, the ally of the West, came to terms with Peking. The foreign minister of Pakistan journeyed to Peking and negotiated an agreement demarcating 300 miles of border as between Pakistan and China. The terms were extremely favorable to Pakistan. A clause in the agreement stated "after the settlement of the Kashmir dispute the sovereign authority concerned will reopen negotiations with the Chinese government so that the present agreement may be replaced by a formal treaty." Pakistan pointed to this clause as a clear intention not to prejudice the claims of India to the disputed territory, but the Indian government insisted that the Pakistan-China agreement was a stab in the back, designed to aggravate India-Pakistan differences.

Due largely to pressures from the United States and Great Britain, India and Pakistan continued their marathon talks about Kashmir. In 1963 Nehru took the position that anything upsetting the *status quo* in Kashmir would be harmful. He indicated he might consider a plebiscite provided that it be confined to political and economic issues, omitting the problems of religion. India was contented with the cease-fire line, because the vale of Kashmir was on the India side of the line. India was also satisfied with the government of Kashmir, which was extremely pro-Indian. However, some Indians felt that active steps should be taken for closer reconciliation with Pakistan. A voice in the Indian parliament said: "When Gandhi died, did they not shed as many tears for him in Pakistan as we did in India—we must remind ourselves of those tears." But behind the façade of the conciliatory mood, the feelings of mistrust and suspicion lingered on. India was convinced that it was right in Kashmir, and that more than ever it could not afford to lose Srinagar. The vale of Kashmir became the strategic highway for Indian troops on their way to defend the frontier posts in Ladakh.

Ayub Khan, as president of Pakistan, was equally adamant in his stand. He assured Nehru that he wanted peace with all countries especially India. He said: "If we can settle the Kashmir dispute, and I do not see why we cannot, we can bring solace and happiness to the 540,000,000 people of the subcontinent." However, he clung to his rights in Kashmir. He also accepted Russian overtures for economic assistance to Pakistan, and he negotiated his first trade pacts with Communist China. He arranged for direct air service between Karachi and Peking. He assured China that he would not join with India in any anti-Chinese action because he considered that friendship with the Chinese people was fundamental. He also said that he considered Indian imperialism more dangerous than communism; and that such organizations as SEATO and CENTO had perhaps lost their effectiveness and outlived their usefulness. He made sarcastic remarks about the United States which "deserted old friends for new ones" and suggested that Pakistan would seek new markets and new economic arrangements as a part of Pakistan's decision to follow a positive, independent political line.

PAKISTAN: INTERNAL DEVELOPMENTS

Democratic methods in Pakistan got off to a bad start. They did not produce a satisfactory government nor did they preserve law and order. In 1953 riots in Lahore and neighboring towns obliged the governor-general to call out the troops and to proclaim martial law. He dismissed one prime minister and appointed another. It was the governor-general, rather than the prime minister, who kept his hands on the nation's political steering wheel.

The process of constitution-making by popular debate was interrupted by the provincial elections in East Pakistan in 1954 when the Moslem League met its first defeat at the hands of an opposition united front. The victors demanded improved status for East Pakistan in the federation of East and West, and insisted that the powers of the central government should be limited to foreign affairs, defense, and currency. Within a month East Pakistan was swept by riots, and some West Pakistan officials on duty in East Pakistan were murdered. Again the governor-general acted swiftly. He suspended the constituent assembly, dismissed the cabinet, and ordered his defense minister to serve as governor of Bengal, with full administrative powers.

The governor-general, Major General Iskander Mirza, who was a graduate of Sandhurst, kept the reins of government in his own hands. He made and unmade prime ministers and created a second constituent assembly. In February 1956—after eight and a half years of intermittent discussion—the constitution of the Islamic republic of Pakistan was passed into law. The constitution of 1956 was dedicated to the promotion of Moslem unity and international peace and to the promotion of Islamic principles. The head of the state—no longer a governor-general, but a president—had to be a Moslem, but the state promised to discourage all forms of discrimination against minority groups. The constitution provided for a parliamentary system, defining parliament as the president and the unicameral national assembly. The supremacy of the parliament was supposedly established by the clause "the President shall act in accordance with the advice of the Cabinet." Within three months the new constitution was suspended because of a new ministerial crisis.

No prime minister was able to command an absolute majority in the assembly nor to rise above the personal intrigues of the political leaders. A triangular struggle for power between East Pakistan, West Pakistan, and the central government blocked any kind of progress. Legislatures were weak and the premiership lost its prestige. Power actually rested on the ability of the prime minister to manipulate the machinery of administration so as to gratify or terrify the legislators. Political processes degenerated as bribery and corruption flourished. The moral climate became so rotten, and the political situation so menacing, that the president assumed power to himself in October 1958.

The president declared martial law, dismissed the central and the provincial governments, abolished all political parties, abrogated the constitution and appointed General Ayub Khan as chief administrator. Within a month, President Mirza was requested by a military deputation to leave the country. He boarded a plane for England, and General Ayub Khan took over. His authority was the revolution; he had no sanction in law or the constitution. As an ultraconservative graduate of Sandhurst, he renounced the dogma nurtured by generations of Westernized leaders that the inevitable goal of Asian nationalists should be a Western-style, parliamentary, democratic system.

The first task which faced General Ayub Khan was to clean up the political mess. He gave civilian posts to military men and ordered them to reduce prices and look after the interests of the ordinary people. Former officials were given the choice of retiring (which they usually took) or facing charges. Ayub then turned to the senior civil servants, lawyers, and intellectuals and examined their records for misconduct or inefficiency. Ayub objected to the "smallness" of lawyers who accused him of illegal procedures, and he decided to put an end to the extracurricular political activities of the students. He scorned the urban middle class because he blamed them for many of Pakistan's failures. He turned to the local squirearchy and yeoman farmers (not the big landlords) for support; on October 27, 1959, he created the "Basic Democracies" as Pakistan's institutions of local self-government.

Between October 1959 and February 1960, he set up some 8,000 union councils throughout Pakistan. Each council, representing a union of twenty or so villages, consisted of fifteen members, of whom ten were elected. The councils were charted with the responsibilities of local government, like the panchayati in India. It was expected that these councils would be followed by similar councils at the country, district, division, and provincial level in accordance with the organizational pattern of the army. Ayub's idea was to construct a strong local base for national development, and he looked to the army for his inspiration and his model. He felt that the army was the most honest and progressive force in the country. It had taken the lead in opposing religious obscurantism and in encouraging the officers' wives to participate in the social services. Ayub wanted political leaders, like officers, to be chosen because of their superior training and education and to provide discipline and leadership. He regarded the peasant mass as the ranks in the army, as deserving good leadership but not qualified to make decisions on grave and complicated issues. His problem was to integrate the union councils into a unified nation and to persuade the conservative rural council members that it was to their interest to get behind a dynamic program of social and economic reform.

Ayub first obtained a public mandate for its own assumption of authority. The Basic Democracies were required to give a vote of confidence to the president, after which he took the oath of office and announced the appointment of a new constitutional commission. Martial law continued until March 1, 1962, when the new constitution was proclaimed. According to the preamble, "Sovereignty over the entire Universe belongs to Almighty Allah alone and the authority exercisable by the people is a sacred trust. It is the will of the people of Pakistan that the principles of democracy, freedom, equality, tolerance and social justice as enumerated by Islam should be fully observed in Pakistan." Moslems should be enabled individually and collectively to order their lives in accordance with the teachings and requirements of Islam.

The constitution of 1962 created a strong, stable, "disciplined, democratic" system of government. Power was concentrated in the hands of the president, who was given authority to appoint commanders of the armed forces, governors of provinces, ministers of the national government, and the chief-justice of the supreme court. The president was empowered to issue ordinances with the validity of law for six months and to refer any dispute between himself and the assembly to the Basic Democracies. The president was to be elected by the Basic Democracies and was eligible for two five-year terms. His administrative capital was to be the newly constructed city of Islamabad, West Pakistan.

Legislative authority was vested in a national assembly and two provincial legislatures. Dacca was named as the national capital area and the principal seat of the central legislature. The national assembly was to consist of a single chamber composed of the president, 150 members drawn equally from East Pakistan and West Pakistan, and six special women representatives. Similarly, provincial legislatures were to be made up of 150 members plus five women representatives. The Basic Democracies served as an electoral college. The national assembly was severely curtailed in its tax powers and its control over expenditures, and it had no voice in naming the cabinet or administrative officers. Political parties were abolished, but might be revived in the future. Both Urdu and Bengali were recognized as official languages.

The constitution of 1962 gave a legal cloak to the continuation of the military dictatorship, but it represented an effort to create an acceptable political framework for economic development and social change. Ayub hoped for a powerful, vigorous state which in due course could be reconverted to democracy. The first elections passed without incident and returned a surprising number of the old guard to the national assembly and to the provincial legislatures. Old attitudes reappeared and former quarrels were resumed. The difference was that the president permitted the legislators to talk and to argue about such matters as judicial review of legislation and the guarantee of civil rights, while he looked after the security of the state, conducted foreign policy, and carried forward reform policies as he deemed for the best interests of the state.

Pakistan's problems of economic development were at least as difficult as those of India. After the bottom fell out of the jute market at the end of the Korean War, Pakistan turned its attention to basic requirements of agriculture and industrialization. Reform in methods of landholding was impossible because of the political strength of the landlords, and the abolition of tenantry seemed less compelling than the increase in agricultural output. Attention was focused on irrigation and land reclamation. Agreements were made with India on the distribution of water from rivers which drained both Indian and Pakistan territory, and a half-dozen large dams were constructed with the assistance of foreign loans. Four million acres of desert land were reclaimed in the lower Sind.

Taking a leaf from India's book, Pakistan announced its first Five-Year Plan in 1956. Pakistan allotted portions of its assets to agriculture, transportation, power, industrialization, and the social services; but the sums were modest. In five years, Pakistan planned to spend $2,200,000,000 on economic development, two-thirds of which was to be raised from local sources. It was hoped that all danger of famine could be eliminated, that the level of the national income could be raised by twenty percent and that some progress could be achieved in the building of factories. Pakistan made the same distinction which India made between the public sector and the private sector of the economy and encouraged its own investors to build plants for the manufacture of cement, glass, caustic soda, sulphuric acid, and fertilizers and for the processing of jute and sugar. Progress was slow because of the political situation.

Although Ayub was conservative by nature, he was devoted to the task of bringing Pakistan in step with the modern world. He encouraged moves toward the emancipation of women and discouraged polygamy. He provided school facilities for 6,000,000 children and pointed with pride to 100,000 Pakistanis in colleges and universities. He was as active as Nehru in looking after the welfare of the poorest classes and in improving the standards of public health. He also faced the same problems as Nehru in the figures of increasing population. Ayub was the enemy of poverty, disease, and bigotry; he struggled to lift the burdens of superstition and unhappy tradition from the backs of his people.

Pakistan launched its own variety of community development before the advent of Ayub to power. In 1954 the Village Agricultural and Industrial Development (AID) program was launched to help the peasants improve their own welfare by their own efforts. Some program such as this was undertaken in every country of South and Southeast Asia. District officers worked as guides and friends, rather than as local despots, but their impact was very limited. In five years the AID movement reached only two percent of rural Pakistan. In 1959 AID was renamed the National Development Organization, but the latter also was immobilized by its own preoccupation with statistics, graphs, and charts. The people directing the program too often were the people who stood to lose by its success; hence the gap between theory and practice. The National Development Organization lost its importance with the formation of the Basic Democracies, which thus became the primary instruments for social and economic welfare as well as for political progress. Ayub staked the entire future of his country on his grass roots concepts.

CEYLON

In its own way, Ceylon experienced all the tribulations of India and Pakistan in its search for stable government, economic development, social progress, and security in world affairs.

Politically, Ceylon was governed until 1956 by a United National Party which was slightly right-of-center domestically and pro-West in foreign affairs. In the elections that year, the victors were the Sri Lanka (Ceylon) Freedom Party led by Oxford-educated S. W. R. D. Bandaranaike. The new government was pledged to social and economic reforms and was strongly neutralist in its approach to the cold war. The government was no sooner in power than it passed the Singhalese language law which provided that Singhala should be the one official language. The Tamils were incensed. Vicious riots broke out as communal feelings blazed. Hundreds were killed and the army was called to restore order. As a climax to chaos, the prime minister himself was assassinated, and his widow became the world's first woman prime minister.

Economically, Ceylon discovered that its traditional resources of rice, tea, rubber, and coconuts could not sustain the customary high level of living for its growing population. Like the rest of the subcontinent, Ceylon expanded too rapidly for its own welfare. An acre of land, which had to support four people in 1954, had to support six in 1960. Since Ceylon only produced forty percent of its own food, it was obliged to expand its agricultural production or its export trade. Plans for export gave rise to ideas of industrialization, but Ceylon was small, and it had little iron and no coal or petroleum. The only possible factories seemed to be limited to small enterprises like cement, plywood, paper, ceramics, caustic soda, and food processing.

Nevertheless, Ceylon came up in 1954 with its own six-year plan of investments. It covered the public sector of the economy—and the private sector—and it made provisions for improved social services. It planned development in irrigation and land reclamation projects, agricultural marketing, roads, railways, hydroelectric plants, telecommunications, village enterprises, tourism, improved health and sanitation facilities, technical and teacher-training schools; and expansion of administrative and defense services. Ceylon borrowed heavily from abroad and in 1956 became another recipient of American aid. The plans were ambitious, and their fulfillment was impossible. Ceylon's resources were limited, and its national income was subject to great fluctuations due to variations in the world price of its leading exports. The capitalistic section of Ceylon's society objected to the country's socialistic schemes, and the United States halted its aid program in 1963 due to the nationalization of Ceylon's petroleum activities.

Nothing interfered with Ceylon's economic development more than its political instability and its traditional attitudes toward work. Social status accrued to governmental position or to white collar jobs, not to manual labor or even to commercial occupations. Exchange students on returning to Ceylon looked forward to government jobs, not to establishing businesses of their own. Attitudes toward business careers ranged from distaste to disgust. Acquiring wealth or saving one's money were not considered useful except in anticipation of greater spending. The caste system, as in India, was the enemy of ambition and the assassin of progress. The status-seekers relied upon their knowledge of English, or their English mannerisms (or after 1956 their learning in Singhalese culture and Buddhism) instead of hard work in order to achieve their goals.

Socially, Ceylon was torn by the rift between the Singhalese and the Tamils and by the difference in outlook between the moderns and the traditionalists. The Singhalese would have liked to send the Tamils back to India, but India would not receive them. Superficially, Singhalese and Tamils seemed friendly. Before independence they cooperated well against the common British enemy, but after independence they became more bitter toward one another. Communal hatreds never seemed more than an inch below the surface. Responsible officials urged the use of reason in applying the language law, but demagogues used the cultural issue to stir up the Singhalese peasants against the feudal landlords and the government which they controlled.

The schism between the traditionalists and the moderns also impeded Ceylon's path to progress. Practitioners of old-style medicine resented the money spent on modern medical schools. Buddhist monks objected to the current emphasis on material values. Teachers in the vernacular schools objected to the higher salaries which were paid to teachers in English-speaking schools. Officials at the district level protested against the influence, the size, and the pay of the growing bureaucracy in Colombo. Antagonism increased as the unemployed intellectuals took their grievances to their respective communities.

In world affairs, Ceylon was the prime exhibit of "friendship toward all, alignment with none." Ceylon, like its larger neighbors, chose to remain in the Commonwealth of Nations. In 1950 Colombo gave its name to the Colombo Plan, or the Commonwealth scheme for assistance to underdeveloped countries. In 1954 Colombo was the meeting place for the five powers—India, Pakistan, Ceylon, Indonesia, and Burma—which became known as the Colombo Powers, and the leading exponents of neutralism. Ceylon joined the United Nations in 1955 when Soviet Russia relaxed its veto. Ceylon wears the distinctive marks of previous British imperial domination, and it fostered close relations with the British once the stigma of colonialism was removed. Ceylon negotiated a defense agreement with Great Britain under which its defense forces were coordinated with those of Britain, its officers were trained by Britain, and British personnel were retained in Ceylon by mutual agreement. Ceylon is Buddhist in religion and has built up close religious ties with the other Buddhist countries— Thailand, Burma, Cambodia, and, to a lesser degree, Japan.

Ceylon is the logical place to make the transition from South Asia to Southeast Asia in examining the role of these regions in the contemporary world. All the countries in these regions bear the marks of the West in their evolution. They bear a grudge against the recent past, but they are psychologically confident in their attitudes toward the future. They seek their own solutions to political problems of liberty and authority, and they will find those solutions in accordance with their own genius—not in obedience to the command of a communist dictator or in slavish adoption of the ways of Western democracy. In economics they want to develop and to move forward. They are determined to improve their agriculture and provide jobs for those who cannot be taken care of on the farms. On the international market, they wish to sell as well as to buy, and they wish to liberate themselves from the vagaries of a single crop. On the social plane, they are determined to eliminate that which has been found harmful and stifling. They want a better, more prosperous, way of life, and they will make whatever adjustments they find advisable between the values of their own past and the demands of the living present. They know much of gentleness, simplicity, the oneness of life and the importance of the spirit behind material things. They may not lead the world in automation and luxury living, but they will carry their own weight in scientific and technological achievement. They have much to teach in mankind's understanding of itself and the human art of living.

SUGGESTED READING

Ahmad, Mushtaq, *Government and Politics in Pakistan* (Karachi, Pakistan Publishing House, 1959).

Brown, Joe David, and the Editors of *Life, India* (New York, Time, Inc., 1961).

Berkes, Ross, and Bedi, M. S., *Diplomacy of India* (Standford, Stanford U., 1958).

Fisher, Margaret, Rose, Leo, and Huttenback, Robert, *Himalayan Battleground* (New York, Praeger, 1963).

Griffiths, Sir Percival, *Modern India* (New York, Praeger, 1957).

Grimes, Paul, *India, Fifteen Years of Freedom* (New York, Foreign Policy Association, 1962).

Harrison, Selig, *India, Most Dangerous Decades* (Princeton, Princeton U., 1960).

Overstreet, G. P., and Windmiller, M., *Communism in India* (Berkeley, U. of California, 1959).

Palmer, Norman, *Indian Political System* (Boston, Houghton, 1961).

Panikkar, K. M., *Common Sense about India* (New York, Macmillan, 1960).

Narayan, R. K., *Financial Expert* (New York, Noonday, 1959). A novel.

Philips, C. H., *Politics and Society in India* (New York, Praeger, 1962).

Rose, Saul, (ed.), *Politics in Southern Asia* (New York, Macmillan, 1963).

Smith, Bradford, *Portrait of India* (Philadelphia, Lippincott, 1962).

Tressider, Argus, *Ceylon* (New York, Van Nostrand, 1961).

Weiner, Myron, *Politics of Scarcity* (Chicago, U. of Chicago, 1962).

Weiner, Myron, *Party Politics in India* (Princeton, Princeton U., 1960).

Wilcox, Wayne, Pakistan, *Consolidation of a Nation* (New York, Columbia U., 1963).

Wriggins, V. Howard, *Ceylon, Dilemmas of a New Nation* (Princeton, Princeton U., 1960).

Zinkin, Taya, *India Changes!* (New York, Oxford U., 1958).

33

The Nations of Southeast Asia

The course of history in India, Pakistan, and Ceylon after independence was paralleled by developments in the nations of Southeast Asia. Changes in every realm—psychological, political, economic, social, and international—occurred with the speed and intensity of revolution in spite of the outward appearance of calmness of life in the tropics. World War II constituted a dramatic climax to the surge toward self-government and brought the cherished status of political independence to people who for centuries had been ruled by imperialist powers. The brief but excruciating period of transition from empire to nation ushered the new states into a world with which the seasoned "freedom-fighters" were ill-prepared to cope. Men like U Nu, Sukarno, and Ho Chi Minh won distinction in driving out their alien masters but they found new and baffling challenges in operating wisely and efficiently as heads of states. Furthermore, they were rescued from the expansive menace of Japan with its philosophy of the co-prosperity sphere only to be exposed to the new threat of aggression from the strong, reinvigorated People's Republic of China with its ideology of communism. Southeast Asia became a vital stake in the cold war.

The nations of Southeast Asia faced common problems which conditioned the tempo and direction of their historical development. Psychologically, all were determined to throw aside the stigma of being second-class citizens. As nonwhites they demanded the respect and the recognition of equality on the part of Europeans and Americans. As new states they were exceedingly jealous of their status of respectable independence, and every other issue had to be subordinated to their insistence upon absolute sovereignty. On this fundamental matter, no questions were permitted about ability, wisdom, or the desirability of compromise.

In the political realm, each country struggled to find the type of government and political institutions best adapted to its own people, economic condition, and stage of development. All had internal difficulties ranging from powerful ethnic minorities to lawless dissident groups like the Communists. The preservation of order sometimes permitted the adoption of democratic procedures; at other times it demanded the strong hand of authoritarianism or a military dictatorship. All the countries faced the problem of integrating a well-equipped, knowledgeable, expensive army with a conservative, disciplined, elitist officer corps into the structure of its traditional society. All were obliged to seek out the best means to deal with their own Communists—whether to tolerate them as an ordinary political party or whether to outlaw them as instruments of subversion and agencies of a foreign power. Leadership groups themselves were far from perfect. They quarreled among themselves and contested for the spoils of office. They were often more interested in their own power and privileges than in the welfare of the masses. No Gandhi appeared in Southeast Asia who was able to make ideals meaningful to those humble people who in the imagery of the great Indian were the "children of God."

From the viewpoint of economics, the countries were "rich," but they were also poor. The low standard of living was the most cogent evidence, and the birth rate raced ahead of economic development. In Southeast Asia, as in South Asia, the gap grew continually wider between the underdeveloped and the advanced countries. Land reform was only the beginning of improvement. The reduction or abolition of tenantry did not automatically result in increased production of food or money crops nor in the enhanced welfare of the peasant family. For some, the old feudal relationships had their human compensations. Everybody wanted to diversify his holdings in order to relieve the dependence on the market vagaries of a single crop, but diversification demanded skills and capital, which were lacking. All the countries dreamed of industrialization, but the dreams could not come true because of no money, no personnel, and no experience. Some progress was made, but it was due largely to the stimulus of foreign grants and loans. Attitudes toward work were difficult to change, and local capitalists preferred to put their money in the good earth rather than in factories. A middle class was painfully slow in coming into existence and it often consisted primarily of hard-working Chinese. Economic disparity aggravated the frictions in every country between the alien Chinese and the nationalistic native inhabitants. Economic nationalism retarded foreign investments and prevented the growth of any Asian idea comparable to the European Common Market. Regional cooperation was difficult at best because the economic patterns in all the Southeast Asian countries were competitive rather than complementary.

Socially, none of the countries enjoyed a genuine open society. Those groups which benefited from the traditional social structure fought to retain their privileges; such new groups as the unemployed college graduates and the city workers struggled for greater recognition and increased rewards. The war against poverty, disease, and ignorance was universal. The masses became more aware of their condition and demanded the "rights" to more food and social security than had ever been theirs. Progress was irregular and social goals usually succeeded all possibility of achievement. The lack of synchronization between good intentions and good works contributed to political instability which was at once a promise and a danger. The masses were awakened and restive. The danger was that if the conservative, constructive forces in the community did not satisfy popular demands, the Communists would take advantage of unrest to promote the Marxian conception of revolution.

Internationally, Southeast Asian nations realized their position and none cherished any ideas of isolation or "going it alone." They were all exhilarated by the lifting of the imperialist yoke and they wanted to flex muscles which were toned up by freedom. They entered the game of power politics with zest. They refused to admit that their countries constituted a "power vacuum" and they rejected any idea that they were helpless as pawns in a contest reserved for great powers and their satellites. They learned to play both ends against the middle, or to take advantage of the struggle between Communist powers and anti-Communist powers for their own advantage. One nation, the Democratic Republic of Vietnam, staked its future on the side of the Communists; two nations, Thailand and the Philippines, committed themselves to the anti-Communists. The rest adopted policies of nonalignment as the highway to their national security. Some nations showed feelings of goodwill toward their former masters; others harbored a great deal of resentment. Nothing approaching a "normal situation" could come into existence in Southeast Asia as long as the region was swept by brush-fire wars and guerrilla fighting. Furthermore, the existence of antagonisms and bitter feelings in Southeast Asia kept the whole world on the brink of global conflict.

In spite of common problems, and parallel courses of historical development, each nation in Southeast Asia possessed a distinct personality. Particularism, or pride in one's own self, was far more pronounced than any inclination to get together in a regional organization. Each country had its own language, literature, religion, territory, government, and historical heritage, and each was more than a little jealous of its neighbor. All showed more willingness to look abroad, especially to their own former mentors, than to one another in seeking to carve out for themselves their own particular niches in the modern world. The concept of "one Asia," or even of "one Southeast Asia," was completely exploded when Asians tried to formulate cooperative policies or find' an acceptable basis for common action.

BURMA

The Socialist Party, dominated by U Nu and his friends in the Anti-Fascist People's Freedom League (AFPFL) ran Burma as they pleased until new elections were held in 1956. The AFPFL got 48 percent of the votes and 170 seats in the parliament; the opposition National Unity Front (NUF) got 30 percent of the votes but only 50 seats. Since the Communists were outlawed as a party in 1953, the extremists worked through the Burma Workers and Peasants Party, which formed the core of the NUF.

U Nu continued as prime minister until 1958. He was apparently a good man, a gentle Buddhist, but he was an inefficient administrator. During his tenure of office, crime and insurgency flourished. Burma became notorious as the most unsafe country in Southeast Asia, with the possible exception of Indonesia. U Nu tried to make Burma a Buddhist state, and he refused to deal harshly with guerillas, bandits, and other lawless elements. He also tolerated the idea of "federalism" with the minority elements, which antagonized the nationalistic Burman elements around Rangoon beyond their endurance. In 1958 U Nu stepped aside and turned over his government to a caretaker regime under General Ne Win.

From 1958 to 1962 the army junta concentrated on wiping out corruption and cleaning up the physical appearance of the capital city. Long-range plans were shelved temporarily. Ne Win's responsibility was to improve the government, put the government enterprises on a paying basis, and revitalize the social services. Army officers branched out into every phase of political life. The military regime was tough on crooked politicians and Communist fellow-travelers. It closed down newspapers for criticizing the government, jailed actors for hidden meanings in apparently innocent lines, and exiled hundreds of students to Coco Island for their irresponsible behavior. Old-style neighborhood associations or National Solidarity Associations as they were called were reorganized for purposes of safeguarding internal security. The army retained the framework of constitutional government and abided by the spirit of the constitution. When it felt that its cleanup job was finished, it permitted new elections and returned to the background from which it had emerged.

The eclipse was only temporary. U Nu was re-elected in 1960 and returned to power as prime minister. In a brief time Burma showed the signs of deterioration which seemed to come along with the experiment in democracy. Politicians and party leaders wrangled, while the country split at the seams. On March 2, 1962, General Ne Win, after the manner of Ayub Khan or Nasser, took over power. He jailed U Nu, five of his cabinet ministers, and some fifty local tribal chieftains or political leaders. His was no longer a caretaker government, but a new revolutionary creation. With a clique of generals and colonels, he set up a revolutionary council to run the government. He abolished the constitution and disbanded the parliament. Political parties, including U Nu's reorganized Union Party, were permitted to function provided that they engage in no hostile activity against the new regime. Ne Win was hypersensitive to political criticism. He blew up the student union on the campus of the University of Rangoon as a symbol of his determination to stamp out student dissatisfaction. He assumed full executive, legal, and judicial powers and made unsuccessful attempts to deal with chronic insurgents.

General Ne Win announced the creation of a single party to be called the "Burma Socialist Programme Party" and he proclaimed a policy statement which he called "the Burmese Way to Socialism." He put an end to the ineffective Four-Year Plans and launched Burma on the way to total socialism. In rapid succession, he seized the oil industry and nationalized all trade except that which was conducted by small retail shops. He took over the rice trade and made it a government monopoly. Peasants were ordered to sell their crops to the state marketing organization and they were paid only about one-quarter of the current selling price for their rice. This differential represented a tremendous tax burden on the peasantry. The private sector of the economy was practically forced out of business—not only foreigners but the Burmese as well. Private industry was permitted to exist only if it contributed to the welfare of the state. Import and export trade was monopolized by the government, and in February 1963 all banks were nationalized and renamed as "People Banks."

Ne Win's regime was not a popular one, partially because the general himself was not particularly personable. No strong man could occupy the same place in Burmese esteem as a "good man" and the father image of U Nu loomed brighter than the success image of Ne Win. The general was not too strong physically, nor did he have the masculine handsomeness of either Nasser or Ayub Khan. He was not gregarious nor was he the extrovert with the qualities of Marshal Sarit in Thailand or President Sukarno in Indonesia. His regime took on the aspects of "uncomfortable puritanism"—as a correspondent for the *New York Times* phrased it— when he decreed the banning of beauty contests, the gradual elimination of horse racing, and the closing down of the dance halls. He made people get to work on time, but he was not able to generate the marching, shouting, singing enthusiasm which Communist China, for example, displayed in its early days of victory. The public was indifferent to his revolution and his own bureaucrats did not seem to throw off their customary lethargy in the performance of their duties. Fundamentally, the economy failed to register any spectacular advances and the political situation in the countryside showed continuing evidences of banditry and terror.

In foreign affairs, Ne Win made only cautious changes in the policies of U Nu. At times, Ne Win showed evidences of closer understanding with the United States and its allies, because of their obvious ability to assist him in keeping order and developing his economy. As an army man, he could not be indifferent to American military power. However, he objected to American capitalism and he was suspicious of American aid. He wanted nothing from the Americans except the improvement of the road from Rangoon to Mandalay. He ousted American foundations from Burma and even hesitated to permit scholars and journalists to carry on their ordinary peacetime pursuits in his country. On the other hand, he seemed warmer rather than cooler in his relations with the Soviet Union and Communist China. He continued to receive their aid and he seemed to enjoy his visits to their countries more than he enjoyed his trips to the United States. He did not go out of his way to condemn Chinese aggressive action on the Indian frontier and in 1963 he signed a treaty with Communist China to settle their mutual border problems. General Ne Win, like U Nu, kept Burma in the camp of the neutralists. A distinguished Burmese, U Thant, served as Secretary General of the United Nations and the Burmese occupied front rank among the powers which were most vitally concerned with Buddhism, socialism, Asianism, or world peace.

New Federation of Malaysia

While Burma remained in the throes of political disorder, trusted its economic future to total socialism and adopted a foreign policy of neutralism with slight favoritism toward the Communist bloc, Malaya achieved more favorable results by using more orthodox methods. Malaya became genuinely peaceful after the termination of the emergency in 1960. It relied upon as much private enterprise as possible for economic development and welcomed foreign investments. Malaya also followed an official policy of nonalignment, but its sympathies were with Great Britain and the United States. In September 1957 Malaya was admitted to the United Nations and in the following month Malaya and Great Britain signed an agreement on external defense and mutual assistance. British investments expanded as Malaya prospered, and British troops remained to give Malaya protection, not as a ruling army but as invited allies.

With independence the government of Malaya was challenged to maintain the high standards of the civil service and to carry forward the excellent economic and social program which it had inherited. It was called upon to preserve racial harmony and to make a success of its unique democratic constitution. The first elections to the Malaya house of representatives was held in 1959. The Malay-Chinese-Indian Alliance won seventy of the hundred seats, as against thirteen which were obtained by its one and only significant rival, the Pan-Malayan Islamic Party. Tengku Abdul Rahman was chosen as prime minister and his bosom friend, the extremely competent Tun Abdul Razak, was continued in his position as minister for rural development.

After its beginning as a self-governing state, Singapore functioned smoothly as a political entity but faltered because of its economic difficulties. Prime Minister Lee Kuan-yew, with his substantial majority in the legislative assembly, coped successfully with the job of guaranteeing the personal, civil rights of the Chinese without sacrificing the security interests of Singapore State. He worked harmoniously, as prescribed by the constitution, with representatives of Malaya and the resident officials of the British government in Singapore. Economically, his great problem was to keep commerce and industry at a sufficiently high level to take care of the almost four percent annual increase of the population. Singapore was separate from Malaya, economically as well as politically, and was therefore forced to look outward instead of inward for ways and means to enrich itself. Industries were invited to Singapore but they were handicapped by the growing demands of trade union leaders. Rising labor costs and expensive programs of social services, as demanded by the trade unions, made it difficult for Singapore to hold its own against its great commercial rival, Hong Kong. It was next to impossible for the government to be sufficiently conservative to guarantee financial stability and reasonable prosperity and at the same time to satisfy the strident demands of socialist leaders and to prevent Communist subversion.

In 1961 the two prime ministers worked out a plan for the formation of a new federation of Malaysia. Malaya and Singapore would join with the crown colonies of North Borneo and Sarawak and the British-protected, oil-rich sultanate of Brunei in a single state which would thus extend over 1600 miles from the borders of Thailand to the Philippine archipelago. The difficulties were enormous—racial, linguistic, and religious diversity, economic disparity, political dissimilarities, and foreign opposition from Indonesia and the Philippines. But with the blessing of the British, the Tengku pressed forward with his ambitious scheme. He declared that we wanted a state which would "provide our people with food instead of bullets, clothing instead of uniforms and houses instead of barracks." He saw in unity the possibility of harmonious economic development, the best possible utilization of resources, and the promise of a common market. The most important dividend from the creation of a greater Malaysia was the solution of the desirable but difficult merger between Singapore and Malaya. The addition of the Borneo territories would prevent the Chinese of Singapore from becoming the dominant factor in Malayan politics. Kuala Lumpur would be the Washington of the new federation, Singapore would be its New York City and the Borneo territories would serve as the great hinterland. Furthermore, it could reasonably be expected that the new state would be prosperous, and as such would constitute a bulwark against Communist expansion, and incidentally against all Chinese from the mainland.

The government of Malaya accepted the idea of greater Malaysia; so did the voting populace of Singapore in a state-wide referendum. The sultan of Brunei was apparently converted to the project, and the British crown colonies of North Borneo and Sarawak gave their consent after a royal commission reported that federation would serve the best interests of all Borneo people. In December 1962 an abortive revolt in Brunei almost wrecked the proceedings. Brunei was the place where revolt was least expected because of the tremendous wealth of the sultanate. Thanks to petroleum royalties, Brunei had unrivaled possibilities for economic development. However an opposition party in Brunei's first legislative assembly engineered a revolt which led to the suspension of the constitution, the hasty importation of thousands of British security troops, and the creation of an emergency government. At the moment of forming the federation of Malaysia, the sultan of Brunei refused to join.

Sarawak also showed signs of local opposition. One out of three persons in Sarawak's population of 750,000 is Chinese. Many Chinese seemed to prefer the continuation of the British rule to the new federation, because the British would be better for business and would be less likely to be guilty of political discrimination against the Chinese. These ideas were incorporated into the Sarawak United People's Party, which was apparently infiltrated by Communist-inclined elements. A local uprising was feared, with the possibility of a new jungle campaign reminiscent of the emergency in Malaya. Furthermore, the possibility existed that Sarawak guerillas might be organized into a Borneo liberation army which would receive the active support of the Indonesian government. President Sukarno said that Indonesians were sympathetic to all liberation movements, especially the one in Borneo. Perhaps he was less deeply troubled by the "liberation" than by the extension of Malayan—and British—influence into his own territorial domain.

The creation of the federation of Malaysia on September 16, 1963 practically brought to an end the era of imperialism in Southeast Asia. The only exception were the British-protected state of Brunei, Portuguese Timor in Indonesia, Macao off the southern coast of China, and Hong Kong. The fate of Timor and Macao was only a question of time. With Hong Kong the future was less certain. The British strengthened their security position and expanded the colony's commercial and industrial importance. It became a haven for refugees from the People's Republic and played a go-between role which was exceedingly valuable both for Great Britain and for China. It would be difficult to imagine a more efficient administration and a better government than that which the British gave to Hong Kong. Yet the population was Chinese and it showed a nascent interest in the privilege of taking care of itself. The ominous fact remained that the lease on part of Kowloon was scheduled for re-negotiation in 1997, and Hong Kong was the greatest of the offshore islands.

REPUBLIC OF THE PHILIPPINES

The Philippines was closer to Malaya than to Burma in its manner of solving its domestic and foreign problems. The Philippines clung to its American-style democracy and placed itself categorically in the ranks of the anti-Communist powers. The election of President Ramon Magsaysay and his running mate on the Nacionalista ticket, Carlos Garcia, in 1953 inaugurated a new and promising era in Philippine politics. The campaign of 1953 introduced the most sophisticated Madison Avenue techniques to Southeast Asia. A committee for free elections worked for honesty at the ballot box. A Magsaysay-for-President movement helped to create mass enthusiasm for the "guy." Magsaysay endeared himself to the common man. With an unfailing human touch, he won the hearts of the *barrio,* or village, people from one end of the islands to the other. He broke the grip which the traditional combination of landlords and politicians had held on the electorate.

In office, Magsaysay invited "people in barefeet to the palace." He demanded an honest day's work and integrity from his appointees. He went to work immediately for the welfare of the tenants and poor farmers, and initiated a community-development movement which was similar to that in India. He interpreted his economic program in terms of jobs and prices which the people could understand. His critics said that he leaned too much on religion and the church, not enough on education and the public schools. They accused him of spending too much on the army and of having no foreign policy except dependence on the United

States. On March 17, 1957, when his plane crashed on a mountainside on the island of Cebu, the Philippines lost its most exciting political leader. He was well on his way to enduring greatness. Farmers, fishermen, and taxi-drivers felt that they had been robbed of one to whom they could talk—one who really cared.

In 1957 the Nacionalistas gained control of the presidency and the congress in the person of Carlos Garcia. The opposition Liberal Party succeeded in electing their candidate, Diosdado Macapagal to the vice-presidency. The Nacionalista administration pledged itself to good government, better living, and peace, but its performance was disappointing. The habits of inefficiency, extravagance, and corruption clung to politicians; these were relentlessly exposed by a vigorous free press. Law and order presented no particular problems after the dispersal of the Huks, but too many people lived too close to the level of merest subsistence. The Garcia formula for more prosperity was the obvious one: increase agricultural production and provide more jobs by industrialization. It was urgent to find jobs for nearly two million unemployed and for the annual surplus of the college graduates. Resources existed for significant industrial expansion, but the Philippines lacked managerial talent, a pool of skilled labor, adequate electric power, and a good transportation network. Foreign governments, especially the United States, made grants and loans, but private investors held back pending an acceptable compromise between their requirements for profit and nationalistic demands for self-sufficiency.

The national economic council urged a policy of economic nationalism or "Filipino First." This discouraged private American capital and caused the overseas Chinese to divert their own investments from the Philippines to Hong Kong. New factories were built in Manila, hundreds of them, but they were packaging rather than manufacturing industries. More raw materials were required from abroad, and strict import and exchange controls were relied upon to keep imports reasonably in balance with exports. Trade tended to dwindle and the government reserves dipped to dangerously low levels at the time of the election in 1961.

Former Vice-President Macapagal was elected to the presidency in 1961 and his Liberal Party also gained control of the senate. Macapagal, using the barnstorming tactics perfected by Magsaysay, promised decency and honesty in government and more prosperity. He was a sincere advocate of American-style democracy, without its abuses, and a staunch defender of private enterprise, with all its shortcomings. He abolished the system of economic controls which had given rise to many abuses and irregularities and permitted the peso to seek its own level in foreign exchange. He used taxes and the tariff schedule to curtail the import of luxuries or nonessential items and to encourage the development of local industries. He changed the atmosphere of private investment with the hope of attracting foreign dollars, and he soft-pedaled the philosophy of "Filipino First."

In foreign affairs, the Philippines always stood for "frank, whole-hearted and open cooperation with the United States." Close political and economic ties were drawn even closer after the Communist victory in China, because both the United States and the Philippines were whole-heartedly and unreservedly dedicated to the containment of Chinese power and Communist ideology. Manila played host to the eight nations (United States, United Kingdom, France, Australia, New Zealand, Thailand, Pakistan, and the Philippines) which in 1954 created the Southeast Treaty Organization for the defense of the entire region. Manila wanted more, not less, American military activity on behalf of its friends and allies in Southeast Asia. A curious similarity of outlook on military affairs developed between Korea, Formosa-China, Vietnam, the Philippines, and to a lesser extent, Thailand. However, the Philippines insisted on the courtesy and respect to full-fledged allies; they refused to be treated as the tail on an American military kite.

Outside of relations with the United States, the Philippines continued to play an active role in the United Nations. The Philippines wanted nothing to do with Russia or mainland China or with what it called the "nonsense of neutralism." In an effort to strengthen the posture of respectable independence, and to reduce its one-sided reliance on the United States, it renewed economic relations with Japan. Filipinos also broadened the search for trade and investments among the nations of western Europe. Progressively, they took a more active role in the affairs of Asia. They sent observers and workers to Laos and Vietnam, and their officials exchanged frequent visits with heads of state among their friendly neighbors. In 1961 the Philippines took the lead in creating an Association of Southeast Asia, which was intended to link the Philippines, Thailand, and Malaya (all anti-Communist) in a closer economic and cultural organization.

Indonesia was the only country in Southeast Asia which kept the Philippines on guard. President Macapagal liked the idea of a Pan-Malayan confederation. He visualized some kind of an "Maphilindo" understanding between the Philippines, Malaya, and Indonesia. However, he disliked the apparent threat of Communism in Indonesia and he distrusted Sukarno's policy of nonalignment. He found a basis for *rapprochement* with his southern neighbor in common fear of China and the Chinese and in common opposition to the project for greater Malaysia. The Philippines had claims to territory in north Borneo which the government felt should be settled by the British before completion of the merger. Representatives of the Philippines, Indonesia, and Malaya met in 1963 to discuss their differences over greater Malaysia and they agreed to form a consultative council of the three nations ostensibly to "consider common measures to restrain Chinese expansionism." Dissatisfaction with SEATO, fear of disaster in either Laos or Vietnam, and apprehension about subversive Chinese activities in their respective countries prompted the various non-Communist leaders to weigh possibilities for such things as a large common market, mutual defense plans, and an organization of local states only for security purposes.

THAILAND

Thailand's regional commitments were as deep and sincere as those of the Philippines, but Thailand seemed more disposed to concentrate on its internal affairs. It was as stable, peaceful, and prosperous as any country in Southeast Asia. Its people were described as "friendly, tolerant, contented, indolent, carefree and charming, full of bubbling laughter and passionately devoted to gambling." The peasants did not have much money, but they had food, shelter, their king and queen, their Buddhist religion, and a way of life which pleased them tremendously. They were quite happy to let the politicians worry about the affairs of state. Only the few who attended a university, or traveled abroad began to speculate about social justice and the rights of man. Man's contentment with his lot was the ally of the authoritarian regime and the foe of modernization in Thailand.

Phibun Songgram was prime minister for ten years, 1948–1957, and during his tenure, political power gravitated toward three men—Phibun himself; Phao Sriyanond, the chief of police; and Sarit Thannarat, field marshal of the 85,000-man army. Each tried to out-jockey the other and in 1957, after informing the king of his plans, Sarit moved. Without bloodshed, without firing a shot, he took over police headquarters, bridges, highways, and vital communications centers. This was the art of the *coup d'etat*. The people clanging to work in the early morning hours were not even aware that anything had happened. Sarit published his charges of corruption and inefficiency against the Phibun government (of which he himself had been one of the strongest members). He alleged that the government was unable to keep order, was guilty of inefficient financial administration, followed an inept foreign policy, provided insufficient education for the people, permitted high prices and unnecessarily low living standards, pursued a poor economic policy, promoted corrupt practices, honored cabinet officers who did not keep their promises, and in general conducted an irresponsible, antidemocratic administration.

Phibun and Phao were hustled out of the country. Phibun's journeys took him to Cambodia, to Berkeley, California, to Japan, and eventually to India. Phao went to Switzerland, where he died. Sarit had no precise political program and his main interests were economic. He established a board of investment on which his friends took complete charge of industrialization and economic development. He was no more "democratic" or concerned about civil rights than his predecessor. Sarit was made commander-in-chief of the navy and air force as well as the army, and he eliminated all political opposition. An interim constitution was adopted which conferred strong powers upon the prime minister. Empowered to appoint a constituent assembly which would also act as a legislature, he abolished all political parties except his own—the Revolutionary Party —and did away with sham elections. Government was placed in the hands of friends, mostly army officers, who occupied the key positions in the armed services, the bureaucracy, and state economic enterprises. Sarit exercised supreme power until his death in 1963.

Sarit, expressing exasperation with irresponsible politicians, the left-wing press, and the deteriorating economic situation, arrested some of his own former cronies for "irregularities." He took harsh measures against Communists and suspected Communists, closed publishing houses which he said were communistic, and put a stop to communistic movies. He arrested editors, writers, minor politicians, leaders of Chinese associations, Vietnamese refugees, labor agitators, and businessmen (usually Chinese) who were accused of Communist leanings. He exercised particular vigilance in the areas bordering on Laos in the northeast and on the Malayan states in the south because of the dangers of Communist infiltration. Sarit expressed his hatred of communism because of its menace to "king, religion and the Constitution" and he feared the identification of Communist ideology with China more than Russia. His policies and ideas were continued by his successor, Thanom Kittikachorn.

Thailand's internal political moves were not without diplomatic significance. As long as Phibun was prime minister, Thailand was extensively, exclusively, and perhaps helplessly in the American camp. American economic and military assistance were indispensable to Thailand's national life. The replacement of Phibun by Sarit did not indicate a change of attitude, but it gave Thailand the strength which comes with freedom of action. Sarit was very friendly to Americans in Thailand—particularly the American military—and he welcomed the aid which supplied his armed forces, built his highways, and stimulated his economy. However, he had to be extremely careful toward China because of his own minority group and the geographic nearness of the Chinese state. Roads which the Chinese built into Laos continued naturally across the plains of Thailand to Bangkok. He wanted to be prepared in the event that the United States should give up the ghost in Laos.

Sarit made no open offers to compromise in any way with China, but he relaxed his personal boycott against Russian diplomatic officials in Bangkok. He made it clear that he would not tolerate Communists in Thailand, but he suggested that as a matter of principle he would consider aid from Russia should it be offered without strings. He taunted SEATO for indecisive action and extracted from the United States a unilateral commitment to come to the aid of Thailand in case of danger. He welcomed the American marines, and the token forces from the Commonwealth of Nations, which took up their stations on the Thailand side of the Mekong River when the flames of Laos threatened to spread into Thailand. Both Sarit and Thanom felt sympathetic to South Vietnam, but they turned their backs on Indonesia. They expressed a lively interest in the affairs of the Buddhist bloc of Cambodia, Laos and Burma. They went out of their way to show friendship to Laos and Burma, but they engaged in constant quarrels with Cambodia. Contemporary Thai diplomats measured up to the traditionally high standards of skill and adroitness associated with their race.

Indonesia, the "Guided Democracy"

The problems of Thailand, internal and external, were simple and uncomplicated as compared with those of Indonesia. The huge, sprawling, former paradise of the Dutch in the tropical seas experienced great difficulties in its struggle for good government and better living. The first national elections in Indonesia in 1955 gave the Nationalists and the Masjumi about 20 percent each of the 38,000,000 votes cast and of the seats in the 263-member national assembly. The *Nahdatul Ulama* (NU), or conservative Moslem Scholars, received about 18 percent of the votes while the Communists polled slightly less. Elections for a constituent assembly returned approximately the same proportions. No party won a majority. The political machine was without a chauffeur, so President Sukarno took the wheel in his own hands. On February 21, 1957, he announced a new concept of government which he called Democracy with Leadership, or the Guided Democracy. He proclaimed martial law. He placed the government under a national advisory council, made up of Nationalists, Moslem religious groups, and Communists. A new cabinet was sworn in whose job was to stamp out rebellion, shore up the national economy, break the last ties with the Dutch, and establish a strong, central government.

In spite of hopeful words, the crisis persisted. The economic situation showed no signs of improvement and the Communists registered significant gains in local elections. Disorder swept the country. In February

1958 an ill-timed and ineptly managed rebellion broke out in Sumatra and the Celebes. Army officers and high-ranking civilian officials were involved, but the government forces stamped out the opposition after long, drawn-out campaigns and negotiations. In 1959 Sukarno restored the constitution of 1945, which provided for strong, presidential authority. He "retooled" the nation by dissolving the elected parliament and replacing it with an appointed "mutual-help" legislative authority made up of political parties and functional groups. The new legislature was called the People's Consultative Congress and in 1960 it conferred upon Sukarno the title of "Great Leader of the Revolution."

Armed with his new prestige, he directed Indonesian politics according to his personal whims. He found his chief support in the Nationalists, the Moslem Conservatives, the Communists, and the army. He prevented any one group from obtaining too much power and played each one against the other for his own benefit. He permitted only eight political parties to exist, not including the Masjumi and the Socialist party, which he banned previously because of their connection with the rebellion. He organized a national front which he used as a means of manipulating the masses. He supervised the press and he prohibited such organizations as the Rotary Club and the Boy Scouts, which he declared were foreign-controlled. In May 1963 he decreed the end of martial law; and he was made president of the Indonesian Republic for life by the People's Consultative Congress.

He made no pronouncements about his political intentions, whether he proposed to continue the Guided Democracy indefinitely or whether he might allow new elections. His leadership was not likely to be challenged successfully because of his glamour as a great revolutionary hero. Nationalists were solidly behind him. Moslem religious groups were too divided to unite in opposition to him. Likewise the cliques in the army prevented the repetition in Indonesia of the developments which occurred in Pakistan and Burma. Nor was Sukarno in immediate danger from a Communist revolution. The Communists in Indonesia claimed more than two million members by 1962, which was the largest party outside of China and the Soviet Union. An additional ten million fellow-travelers were enrolled in such organizations as the Peasants' Front, the Federation of Trade Unions, the Women's Organization, and the Youth Corps. The Communists were split on the question of the parliamentary road to power—Russian style—or active revolution China-style. The number-one Communist, D. N. Aidit, favored the former; the number-two Communist, M. H. Lukman, inclined toward the latter. As Sukarno himself said, "They have tried to topple Sukarno by political means and gossip. They call Sukarno a terrible man. They say Sukarno is a love hunter. But Sukarno cannot be toppled." By 1963 five attempts were made to assassinate him, but as he said, "With God's protection, I am still safe."

The Guided Democracy did not uncover any way out of an endemic condition of near-bankruptcy. In what should have been a rich country, undernourishment was prevalent. Agricultural production failed to keep pace with the growth in population. Economic development lagged in every category in spite of huge sums in foreign assistance. Industry seldom operated at more than twenty percent capacity. The excellent prewar railway system deteriorated and inter-island shipping services practically disappeared with the departure of the Dutch. About the only reliable support for the economy was the petroleum industry, which was in the hands of foreigners. In the impending shadow of nationalization, an understanding was reached in 1963 making possible the production, refining, and marketing operations on a 60-40 basis for as much as 20 years (60 percent of the profits to Indonesia; 40 percent to the foreign companies). Prices skyrocketed as inflation multiplied the miseries and discontent of salaried employees and urban wage earners. Exports from "wealthy" Indonesia failed by $300,000,000 to pay for needed imports in 1963.

Many of Indonesia's economic woes resulted from Sukarno's emphasis on the army and his own military convictions. Eighty percent of the budget was spent on the armed services. More than a billion dollars was borrowed from the Soviet Union to pay for cruisers, tanks, guns, and ammunition. Sukarno's only foreign foe was the Dutch, who retained control over the western portion of New Guinea. In May 1963 the Dutch withdrew in a peaceful and orderly way. Sukarno was left with an army but without a fight. Would he be tempted to use the army to drive the Portuguese out of Timor, to attack the Australian position in the eastern portion of New Guinea, or perhaps to support local resistance movements against greater Malaysia in North Borneo, Brunei, or Sarawak? Sukarno showed a new and friendly interest in President Macapagal's ideas of Pan-Malaya and he made outward shows of cordiality toward Prime Minister Tengku Abdul Rahman. But he insisted that a plebiscite should be held in the British possessions in Indonesia before proceeding with the federation. He made no secret of his conviction that the whole idea of greater Malaysia was an unpleasant type of new imperialism. He expressed his opposition by a determined policy of "confrontation." His government looked the other way while young Indonesians sacked and burned the British embassy in Djakarta and gave aid and encouragement to dissident elements in all parts of British Borneo.

Threatened with the possibility of complete chaos within his country, Sukarno followed a foreign policy which was anticolonial, actively independent, and based on the moral principles of peace and faith in God. Sukarno believed that communism and democracy could coexist, but colonialism and peace could not. He forgot all the good things in centuries of relationships between Dutch and Indonesians and treated the Netherlands as the incarnation of a bitter memory. He dissolved the union with the Dutch and dismissed the Dutch military mission. He denounced unilaterally all economic and financial agreements and for a time broke off formal diplomatic relations.

He used western New Guinea (or Irian Barat as it was known to the Indonesians) as a battle cry. Legal arguments between the Dutch and the Indonesians were of little consequence, and they were eventually resolved by a diplomatic understanding reached largely through the good offices of the United States. The territory involved was not of critical strategic, economic, or human importance. It was primarily a jungle area about the size of California inhabited by some 700,000 of the most primitive people on earth. The anger and resentment which was stirred up over Irian Barat defied reason. On occasions Indonesian mobs spattered paint on foreign cars and buildings and daubed trees and walls with "kill the Dutch" or "Dutch get out" signs. Indonesians boycotted Dutch places of business and ordered the 50,000 Dutch passport holders to leave the country. No improvement in Dutch-Indonesian relations was possible until after the Dutch gave up in New Guinea then relations improved.

"Active independence" was the phrase which Sukarno applied to his concepts of nonalignment. He was cool toward the United States and he accepted American aid—a billion dollars' worth of it—with caution. He was more responsive to Russia. He, like Castro, relied upon the Russians for military advice and equipment. He visited Russia repeatedly and welcomed a stream of distinguished Russian visitors to Indonesian. Next to India, he was favored by Russia's most generous program of technical assistance in Asia. He was ambivalent toward China, distinguishing carefully between the interests of the Chinese element in his own population and the value of sympathetic understanding with the Chinese nation. He did not hesitate to apply discriminatory measures against Chinese traders within Indonesia, but he was circumspect in his attitudes toward the Peking government. He extended diplomatic recognition to Peking—not to Taipei—and he exchanged visits and cultural missions with the Communist Chinese. He was impressed with the unity and improved level of living in China and in 1956 he called China a "happier, freer country than the U.S.S.R." He was not modest in his relations with the other nonaligned nations. He believed neutralists should work together as a third force in the world. He sponsored the Bandung meeting of the Afro-Asian nations in 1955 and with Nasser and Tito he engineered a conference of the uncommitted in Belgrade in 1961. One of his most novel ideas was for a games for the emerging nations which he offered as a substitute for the "imperialistic" Olympic games. His fertile brain worked incessantly to get the maximum advantage from the Afro-Asian bloc.

Each passing year seemed like a year of crisis or a year of decision in the history of Indonesia. Sukarno's position was safe as long as wrangling continued within the ranks of the religious leaders, the army, and the Communists. Sukarno was valuable as the symbol of unity and the only alternative to anarchy. The danger was that he would purchase prestige at the cost of national destitution. He had a large military establishment and the temptation to use it was strong. On the other hand he was faced with an empty treasury and a sputtering economic machine. It was up to him to decide whether to concentrate on such vital things as increased agricultural production and the rehabilitation of a transport system that was in such shambles that in a country of 3,000 islands rice lay rotting at the docks while people were hungry; or whether he would squander public funds on projects of questionable value such as a sports stadium, a luxury hotel, a monumental column, and a fleet of jets for Indonesia's international air service. In spite of work to be done at home, Sukarno decided it was more important for him and his country to indulge in frequent junkets abroad, which he disguised as tours of inspection or visits of state.

THE INDOCHINESE PENINSULA: CAMBODIA, LAOS, AND VIETNAM

While Indonesia lived in the dread prospect of anarchy, the Indochinese peninsula experienced an interminable tragedy of blood and revolution. The Conference of Geneva in 1954 did not put an end to civil war. It merely caused a regrouping of the participants and produced changes in the conditions of fighting.

Cambodia was the most favored of the four political entities which emerged from the former French empire. This small country of four millions, the heirs of the ancient Khmers, nestled in the hands of Prince Sihanouk, of the royal Norodom family, who proved himself to be an enlightened head of state. He tried to lead his people toward more effective participation in government. He devoted his basic economic attention to rice and fish and used the army in a far-reaching civic-action program. He invited foreign aid from all sources to help him in economic development. He was restrained in his anti-imperialism and he retained large numbers of French advisers. He treated both the United States and Russia with dignified diffidence and weighed carefully his policies toward China. As a member of the royal family, a devout Buddhist, and a person accustomed to splendid living he had no sympathy for communism. However, he refused to outlaw the Communist Party in his own country on the theory that it was better to observe the Communists than to drive them underground. He resembled Nehru in his refusal to commit himself to either side in the cold war. An expression attributed to him was that "the ant must beware when the elephants fight." He sent some of his sons to school in Paris, others to Peking. He was more perturbed about his neighbors than about Russia or the United States. He distrusted Thailand and South Vietnam and tried desperately to keep his country from becoming another Laos. He was a keen student of international affairs and an uncommonly dignified and observing traveler when he went abroad. His repeated hope was that his country might be neutralized like Switzerland and protected by international agreement.

Cambodia's neighbor, Laos, was the smallest in population of the countries which gained independence by the Geneva agreements in 1954. Laos, because of its geography, was the most strategic piece of real estate in Southeast Asia. It was a buffer zone blocking Communist access to Thailand, Cambodia, and much of Vietnam. Because of its isolation, it was centuries behind the tempo of modern times. Due to traditional cleavages between the feudal houses of Champassac in the south and Luang Prabang in the north, it lacked a consciousness of nationalism. From the point of view of stark poverty, education, public health, linguistic diversity, and persistence of tribal organization of the people, Laos was primitive. The tiny elite was composed of the king and his household, landholding barons, the Buddhist priesthood, and a small assortment of newly rich who were favored by the French. After Geneva, France and the United States engaged in a serious effort—first, to prevent local Communists, known as the Pathet Lao, from taking over the government, and second, to thwart the penetration of non-Laos Communists into Lao from China or North Vietnam.

Political progress was very, very slow. It required two and a half years for two royal half-brothers, the Princes Souvanna Phouma and Souphanouvong, to reach agreement on terms for a coalition government. Representatives of the right were not even included in the negotiations. Souvanna Phouma was neutralist in his philosophy. Souphanouvong was communistic, Paris-educated, and extremely partial to his friend and neighbor, Ho Chi Minh. In 1957 it was agreed that the neutralist should be prime minister and the Communist should take over two cabinet posts. The Communist base in the two northeastern provinces was to be incorporated into the regular state administrative system in the same manner that Yenan was integrated into Nationalist China during the years of the united front. The rebel Pathet Lao army was to be nationalized and the Communist-inclined politicians were to be allowed to operate as a legalized party known as the *Neo Lao Hak Sat,* or Laos Patriotic Front. American aid in large quantities was to be given to the coalition government, known as the royal Laotian government, and some portion of that aid was to be prorated to the Pathet Laos within the coalition. Elections were decreed from 1958 and it was assumed that Laos was on the way to democracy and economic improvement.

The assumptions were false. Right-wing elements gained ascendancy in the government and followed closely the assorted ideas of American representatives in Laos. Rebellious elements precipitated one crisis after another. The three main lines in the power struggle were constant—right, center, and left—and the respective leaders were identifiable. General Phoumi Nosovan, with his patron Prince Boun Oum from the south and the officer corps of the royal Laotian army, was the leader of the right; Souvanna Phouma of the center; and Souphanouvong of the left. The king stayed above the rivals. The followers of the three leaders changed sides with ease and it was never clear who was fighting whom. In 1962 the center was with the left against the right; in 1963 the center was with the right against the left. Neutralists in the center quarreled among themselves. They were without firm convictions or strong principles, and they were always open to persuasion and offers of compromise from both sides. If they proved to be stubborn or too expensive, their leaders were assassinated and their troops were attacked. No amount of juggling of foreign aid was sufficient to clarify the situation and to bring all factions together in a program of peace and progress.

The international implications of the continuing crisis in Laos kept the world on the brink of war. The anti-Communists (Americans) backed the right and the Communists (North Vietnamese, Russians, and Chinese) backed the left. Neither side placed any confidence in Prince Souvanna Phouma in the center but he was accepted as the only hope of peace. In 1961 President Kennedy and Prime Minister Khrushchev agreed to a formula of "independence, neutrality and peace" for Laos which was embodied in a declaration of fourteen nations at Geneva in July 1962. In accordance with this declaration, foreign military missions were to pull out of Laos. An International Control Commission (ICC) composed of an Indian, a Canadian, and a Pole, was set up in Laos to see that the declaration was enforced. A new coalition government was inaugurated with the perennial prime minister, Souvanna Phouma, at the helm. His rival of the right, General Phoumi Nosovan, was made minister of finance and his half-brother on the left, Souphanouvong, was given the portfolio of economic affairs.

The *troika*, or three-pronged administrative structure, was doomed from the start. A three-way agreement on any major decision was impossible. Besides which, each faction kept control of its own military forces although all were incorporated into the national army. The former Pathet Lao troops were stationed in the north and northeast, on the strategic borders of China and Vietnam; the troops of General Phoumi were kept in the south and in the area of Vientiane. The troops who professed allegiance primarily to Souvanna Phouma (especially those of Kong Le) were assigned to the so-called Plain des Jarres in central Laos, where their positions could be whittled away either by the right or the left.

All foreign aid, military and economic, was delivered to the central government and each leader struggled to channel as much as possible to his own contingents. This foreign aid, supplied by the United States and Russia, was vital. Without it there would have been no arms and equipment, and possibly no war. Fighting seemed to come to a halt whenever any faction reached the point where its opponents would rather fight than grant further concessions.

In 1963 the situation in Laos looked like frustration without end. Neither Russia nor the United States wanted any expansion in the area of conflict. Russia, confident in the growing strength of the left, terminated its air lift and withdrew its technicians. Americans kept their aid operations within the letter of the law, but maintained a strong military posture in neighboring Thailand and in the South China Sea. However, the Chinese and the North Vietnamese were unrestrained. The Chinese were "closer, hungrier and more numerous" than the Russians and they wanted the "revolution" in Laos to continue whatever the cost, whatever the means. The North Vietnamese were of the same mind. They gave the Pathet Lao advice and assistance because they felt that every Communist advance in Laos was a further step toward the conquest of their own country, Vietnam.

Vietnam, too, was in a state of chronic civil war after the Geneva settlement in 1954. The country was divided after the manner of Germany and Korea, half to the Communists and half to the anti-Communists. The northern half of Vietnam took the name of the Democratic Republic of Vietnam (DRV), continued with Ho Chi Minh as its leader, and selected Hanoi as its capital. The southern half took the name of the Republic of Vietnam, chose Ngo Dinh Diem instead of Bao Dai, the former emperor of Annam, as its leader and established its capital in Saigon. Provision was made at Geneva for nationwide elections to be held in 1956 to put "Humpty Dumpty together again," but by that time peaceful reunion was out of the question.

Ho Chi Minh and his men of the DRV came away from Geneva with a feeling of victory. They were glad for the armistice which sealed the fate of the French and recognized the independence of Vietnam. Ho was confident that with time he would come into control of his entire country. In 1955, before the twentieth congress of the Communist Party of the Soviet Union, Ho announced a fatherland front (or united front, Vietnamese style) for all his people. Its policies were mild toward everyone except the "American imperialists." Its platform promised unification of Vietnam, prosperity, high wages, shorter working hours, and better conditions for farmers. The DRV insisted upon the implementation of the Geneva agreements and called for national elections as prescribed. It called "foul" when South Vietnam refused to participate in a plebiscite under the terms and conditions which the Communists wanted.

Politically, the DRV was a typical totalitarian regime, organized with Communists in key party and government positions, and it operated according to the principles of democratic centralism. The party controlled the army and the government, while a small group of leaders, headed by Ho Chi Minh, controlled the party.

Economically, the DRV faced a new set of conditions. Instead of destroying roads and bridges, it had to repair them. Instead of rousing peasants against landlords, it had to produce more food. Instead of encouraging strikes and preaching the rights of the proletariat, it had to provide more jobs, mine more coal, and make its factories hum. The Communist leadership faced the endemic problems of East Asia: a low level of living, a meager income and a hopeless future. Starvation threatened in North Vietnam when partition cut off the customary import of rice from the rich Bekong Delta. A million refugees left the north for the south. Those who remained behind had to be given better living conditions. The government inaugurated its own version of land reform, which amounted to confiscation of lands from the rich and the introduction of collectivization. In the north, the rapid socialization of industry was considered more promising of economic relief. Technical and economic assistance was welcomed from China, the Soviet Union, and every member of the satellite bloc. Substantial progress was possible because of North Vietnam's abundance of raw materials. To implement its program of socialization further, the DRV issued regulations for its own national bank and currency and for the control of foreign trade. In domestic commerce, local Chinese as well as private Vietnamese traders were subordinated to the needs of the state.

In foreign affairs, the DRV regarded itself as a brother socialist nation and not as a satellite. Ho proved to be a genius in keeping the goodwill and active support of both China and Russia. He managed to remain friends with Mao and Tito, and he was one of the most popular Communist leaders in the neutralist world. He sought to preserve his cultural contacts with France and with the 40,000 Vietnamese in France. After the rift between Russia and China, he favored the Russian peaceful coexistence line in order to build up his own economy, but he expressed an undeniable interest in all liberation movements, particularly in Southeast Asia. Most of all he worked for the reunification of Vietnam—his country —under the Communist banner. He was not merely a sentimentalist nor a revolutionary; he understood the value to North Vietnam of the rice which grew in the south.

Ho Chi Minh, the leader of the Democratic Republic of Vietnam, met his match in Ngo Dinh Diem who rose to power in South Vietnam. President Ngo resented the term "South Vietnam." In his view he was the rightful president of all Vietnam and in due course he would extend his dominion over that part of *his country* temporarily in the control of a traitorous foreign agent who happened to be his fellow citizen.

After the Geneva settlement, South Vietnam faced a dubious future. Its former guardian, France, was helpless in Asia; its new mentor, the United States, was untested. The political system was destroyed, the administrative services disrupted, the economy shattered, and the treasury empty. The country was plagued with politico-religious sects which had their own independent armies. Ngo Dinh Diem was the man of the hour. He installed himself as premier and maneuvered the politicians to make him their president. He facilitated the election of a national assembly which passed his own constitution. The constitution of October 26, 1956, delegated unusually strong powers to the executive, and guaranteed the rights of a citizen only in the absence of a state of crisis.

Encouraged and assisted by the United States, President Diem set to work to restore law and order. A Roman Catholic, and a bachelor, he surrounded himself with individuals (particularly his own relatives) whom he could trust. Individual loyalty was the first test of administrative responsibility. He created a political machine which would carry out his will. He fed, clothed, housed, and resettled nearly one million refugees, a tenth of the entire population. He rebuilt the army, and he dispersed the forces of the dissident sects. Although aristocratic and diffident by nature, he sought to win the loyalty of the common people from Uncle Ho, the symbol of independence throughout all Vietnam.

His basic problems were those of the common people. Their age-old way of life—bounded by the rice fields, the village, and the emperor—had been upset. The dependence of the poor upon the rich had been destroyed. No training in individual responsibility and self-government had been given by the French. Independence had brought nothing but hatred and arson, the misery and murder of civil war. In the West there was talk of democracy in South Vietnam; in South Vietnam there was no basis upon which democracy could be built. Ngo Dinh Diem believed in the theories of democracy. He believed the sole legitimate end and object of the state was to protect the fundamental rights of the human person to existence and the free development of his intellectual, moral, and spiritual life. In his estimation, important things were evil or good. Communism was evil—it was atheistic materialism and he knew at first-hand its tyranny and its terror. Democracy was good—it was the permanent effort to find the right political means for all citizens to develop their maximum potentialities.

In his view, Vietnam—perhaps most of Asia—was not ready for the application of these good theories. Fundamental work was necessary to fill empty stomachs, to clothe ragged people, and to abolish filthy shacks and crowded slums. His economic program called for the completion of economic independence and the renovation of the national economy. He tried to replace foreigners—French, Indians, and primarily the Chinese—by Vietnamese in the economic development of the country. He ended the treaties which accorded economic privileges to the Chinese and decreed assimilation or abandonment of their chief commercial and professional activities. He pushed agrarian reform. He wanted to ease the burdens of rural indebtedness and to find land for the landless. He understood the importance of modernizing the methods of agriculture. In the matter of industrialization, President Ngo was nationalistic and ambitious, but he was helpless. He had very few natural resources and practically no factories. He lacked capital and industrial know-how, and he looked with reserve upon the American aid program and the local Chinese. He sponsored laws and projects which "would reconcile the interests of the state and the legitimate requirements of foreign investors."

In foreign policy, the president insisted that Vietnam must be "independent, Asian, free, peace-loving and progressive." The Vietnamese elite were bitter in their memories of French policy, but grateful for the French culture which they inherited. They appreciated American aid— which paid as high as eighty-five percent of their budget commitments —but they needed time to adjust to Americans and their ways. In all Southeast Asia, their hatred of Communism was the deepest. It was based on suffering and unforgettable memories. But it was not sufficiently strong to plunge them unreservedly into the camp of the Americans. They would not sacrifice their independence of judgment or freedom of action in fighting the civil war.

Civil war flared with the failure to reunite Vietnam in the summer of 1956. Its first evidences were ambushes on country roads and bombs hurled into the heart of crowds in Saigon. Teachers and government officials were murdered at the rate of four or five per day. These incidents occurred in spite of American aid and advice to the government, and in spite of President Ngo's ostensible devotion to democracy.

Two explanations were offered for the trouble. The president explained that incidents were caused by Communists who remained loyal to the Viet Minh or by infiltrators from the DRV, Laos, or Cambodia. Opponents of the president discounted the role of neighboring countries. The opponents declared that the incidents were the results and not the cause of repressive measures resorted to in the name of anti-Communism. Tens of thousands of non-Communists—democrats, socialists, liberals, and adherents of the sects—were arrested and sent to re-education centers. By 1958 the roundup of dissidents became more frequent and more brutal. Suspects took to the forests and the marshes to escape the police. They became guerillas, and in 1959 President Ngo Dinh Diem announced "Vietnam is a nation at war." Within two years, the government lost control over eighty percent of its own territory, and in Diem's hour of crisis Americans sent troops to help him.

Resistance to Diem's "fascist dictatorship" (as his opponents called it) crystallized into a National Liberation Front with a people's liberation army. The titles were the same as those used by the Communists in China and Malaya. The rebel forces (called the *Viet Cong*, or simply Vietnamese Communists by the government) consisted of fully trained, well-disciplined hard-core soldiers who were backed by local guerillas who were farmers by day and fighters by night. Their tactics were the same as those developed by Mao Tse-tung and his North Vietnamese disciple, Vo Nguyen Giap. They succeeded in winning the people and confining the government troops to the main centers of population and arterial lines of communication. The question of the nature of the National Liberation Front was open to dispute. In its own propaganda it was a melange of all parties whose first objective was the overthrow of Ngo Dinh Diem. Its philosophy was that the fighting must stop, a liberal government must be installed in Saigon, and peaceful steps must be taken toward reunification. In the view of Secretary of State Dean Rusk the Front was an agency of Communist aggression. He said, "The aggression against South Vietnam from the north is a major Communist enterprise, carefully and elaborately prepared, heavily staffed and relentlessly pursued."

The United States was involved in the civil war in Vietnam because of its determination that the Communists should not spread below the seventeenth parallel. Americans sent supplies and equipment for a regular South Vietnamese army of 210,000, civil guards numbering 72,000 and a self-defense corps of local militia of 80,000. The Americans also sent thousands of "Matadors" (Military Assistance Training Advisors) to Vietnam, of whom one in ten was assigned to combat zones with Vietnamese troops. Americans helped Vietnamese build thousands of "strategic hamlets." American initiative improved the Vietnamese military effort, but it failed to win the war. By the end of 1963 casualties still ran at the rate of 1,000 per week on both sides. As Senator Mansfield reported, after seven years and two and a half billion dollars of American effort, the government was further removed from, rather than closer to, the people.

The Americans, with all their effort, made little progress in persuading President Ngo Dinh Diem to liberalize his ideas. For a time he agreed to offer an amnesty to his enemies. His officers erected "welcome booths" for all guerrillas who would lay down their arms. But he refused to bring about any fundamental relaxation of his policies in spite of ominous signs of unrest and public dissatisfaction. Twice his palace was attacked by officers of his own air force; and his police were sometimes stoned by reckless, angered demonstrators. In 1963 some Buddhist priests publicly burned themselves to death as a protest against alleged discriminatory measures taken against the followers of their religion. Students joined in political demonstrations. Diem was stubborn. His conviction was that the Communists and their sympathizers must be stamped out—then his country could join the rest of Asia in carrying forward its needed revolution.

Diem's stubbornness led to his death. During a *coup d'état*, on the second day of November, 1963, President Diem and his brother Ngo Dinh Nhu were senselessly killed. The military junta which succeeded to power promised to continue the war against the Vietcong with renewed vigor. The new and essential element in its program was that in the process it would devote great effort to winning the support of its own long-suffering people.

In a way the position of Asia in the contemporary world was reflected in the ordeal of Vietnam. The adjustment between the past and the present was soaked in "blood, sweat and tears." Bitter, costly, and tragic as it was, it could offer no assurance of a better future. The return of peace could only bring another chance to work for more food and more happiness. Victory for the Viet Cong would mean working under rules prescribed by them; victory for the government forces would mean working in accordance with conditions and looking toward ideals of freedom. And it was to the latter which the United States was obligated.

When the late President Kennedy was senator from Massachusetts he said: "What we must offer them (the people of Asia) is a revolution, a political, economic and social revolution, far superior to anything the Communists can offer, (and) far more democratic." We can offer them our way as a choice which they will consider along with the way of others. Much of our way they will accept, but not all. Nor is it likely that they will reject everything which Communists have made a part of their ideology and their practise. The great truth of modern times is that all mankind has become aware of its right to freedom of choice. In Asia, as in Europe and America, free minds will subject all human experience to critical analysis. They will seek to build a future which in their judgment preserves the best of the past and holds out a further hope of progress.

SUGGESTED READING

Butwell, Richard, *Southeast Asia, Today and Tomorrow* (New York, Praeger, 1961).

Fall, Bernard B., *Two Viet-Nams* (New York, Praeger, 1963).

Feith, Herbert, *Decline of Constitutional Democracy in Indonesia* (Ithaca, Cornell U., 1962).

Fishel, Wesley, (ed.), *Problems of Freedom, South Vietnam since Independence* (New York, Free Press, 1962).

Honey, P. J., (ed.), *North Vietnam Today* (New York, Praeger, 1962).

Jordan, Colonel Amos A., Jr., *Foreign Aid and Defense of Southeast Asia* (New York, Praeger, 1962). (P)

Johnstone, William C., *Burma's Foreign Policy* (Cambridge, Harvard, 1963).

Kahin, George McT., *Asian-African Conference, Bandung, Indonesia, April, 1955* (Ithaca, Cornell U. 1956).

Kaye, Barrington, *Upper Nankin Street, Singapore* (Singapore, U. of Malaya, 1960).

Montogomery, John D., *Politics of Foreign Aid* (New York, Praeger, 1962). (P)

Modelski, George, (ed.), *SEATO—Six Studies* (Melbourne, Cheshire [for the Australian National University], 1962).

Mossman, James, *Rebels in Paradise; Indonesia's Civil War* (London, Cape, 1961).

Ravenholt, Albert, *Philippines* (Princeton, Van Nostrand, 1962).

Selosoemardjan, *Social Changes in Jogjakarta* (Ithaca, Cornell U. 1962).

Walinsky, Louis J., *Economic Development in Burma, 1951–1960* (New York, Twentieth-Century Fund, 1961).

Wertheim, W. F., *Indonesian Society in Transition* (The Hague & Bandung, W. van Hoeve, 1956).

Wilson, David A., *Politics in Thailand* (Ithaca, Cornell U., 1962).

A General Bibliographic Note

A mass of material in Western languages is readily available in the rapidly growing field of Asian Studies. The selected list of titles which follows is offered as a help to teachers who wish to build up a useful working library and to students who may do further reading. The symbol (P) after a title means that it appears as a paperback.

BIBLIOGRAPHIC AIDS

American Bibliographic Service, Quarterly Check-list of Oriental Studies (Darien, Conn., 1960).

American Historical Association, Guide to Historical Literature (New York, Macmillan, 1961).

American Historical Association, Service Center for Teachers of History:
> Cole, Allan B., *Forty Years of Chinese Communism* (1962).
> Crane, Robert I., *The History of India* (1958).
> Hall, John W., *Japanese History* (1961).
> Hucker, Charles O., *Chinese History* (1958).

American Universities Field Staff, *Select Bibliography: Asia, Africa, Eastern Europe, Latin America* (New York, 1960).

The Asia Society, *An Introductory Reading Guide to Asia* (second rev. ed.) (New York, 1962).

Borton, Hugh, and others, *A Selected List of Books and Articles on Japan in English, French, and German* (revised and enlarged) (Cambridge, Harvard U., 1954).

Embree, John F., and Dotson, Lillian, *Bibliography of the Peoples and Cultures of Mainland Southeast Asia* (New Haven, Yale U., 1950).

Fairbank, John K., *Bibliographical Guide to Modern China: Works in Western Languages* (Cambridge, Harvard U., 1948).

Hay, Stephen N., and Case, Margaret H., *Southeast Asian History: A Bibliographic Guide* (New York, Praeger, 1962).

Hobbs, Cecil, *Southeast Asia, An Annotated Bibliography of Selected Reference Sources* (Washington, Library of Congress, 1952).

Hucker, Charles O., *China, A Critical Bibliography* (Tucson, U. of Arizona, 1962).

Kerner, R. J., *Northeastern Asia: A Selected Bibliography* (two vols.) (Berkeley, U. of California, 1939).

Patterson, Maureen L. P., and Inden, Ronald B., (eds.), *South Asia: Introductory Bibliography* (Chicago, U. of Chicago, 1962).

Pritchard, Earl, and others, *Bulletin of Far Eastern Bibliography* (five vols.) (Washington, American Council of Learned Societies, 1936–1940). Continued in *Far Eastern Quarterly* and *Journal of Asian Studies*.

Quan, L. King, *Introduction to Asia, A Selective Guide to Background Reading* (Washington, Reference Department, Library of Congress, 1955). 214 pages.

School of Oriental and African Studies, *Monthly List of Periodical Articles on the Far East and South East Asia* (London, London U.).

Silberman, Bernard S., *Japan and Korea, A Critical Bibliography* (Tucson, U. of Arizona, 1962).

Sorich, Richard, (ed.), *Contemporary China*. Bibliography of Reports on China Published by the United States Joint Publications Research Service (New York, 1961).

Yuan, Tung-li, *China in Western Literature* (New Haven, Yale U. Far Eastern Publications, 1958).

DOCUMENTS AND SOURCE MATERIALS

Beasley, W. G., *Select Documents on Japanese Foreign Policy, 1853–1868* (New York, Oxford, 1955).

Brandt, Conrad, Schwartz, Benjamin, and Fairbank, John K., *Documentary History of Chinese Communism* (Cambridge, Harvard U., 1952).

Dutt, V. P., *Select Documents on Asian Affairs: East Asia, 1947–1950* (New York, Oxford, 1958).

East Asian Research Center, *Communist China 1955–1959. Policy Documents with Analysis* (Cambridge, Harvard U., 1962).

Hart, Donn V., "Southeast Asia: A Bibliographical Introduction" in *Social Education* (New York, Asia Society, October, 1962).

Hsüeh, Chün-tu, *Chinese Communist Movement, 1921–1937* (Stanford, Hoover Institution, 1960).

Isaacs, Harold R., *New Cycle in Asia, Selected Documents, 1943–1947* (New York, Macmillan, 1947).

MacNair, Harley Farnsworth, *Modern Chinese History Selected Readings* (Shanghai, Commercial Press, 1927).

Maki, John M., *Conflict and Tension in the Far East, Key Documents, 1894–1940* (Seattle, U. of Washington, 1961).

Philips, C. H., *Evolution of India and Pakistan, 1858–1947* (volume four) (New York, Oxford, 1962). Select Documents on the history of India and Pakistan. (Earlier volumes to appear later.)

Tewksbury, Donald G., *Sourcebook on Far Eastern Ideologies* (two vols.) (New York, Columbia U., 1949 and 1952).

PERIODICAL LITERATURE

Asian Recorder, New Delhi (since 1955).
Asian Survey, Berkeley, U. of California Institute of International Studies.
China Quarterly, London W.1, 133 Oxford Street.
Contemporary Japan, Tokyo, Foreign Affairs Association of Japan.
Eastern World, London W.1, 58 Paddington Street.
Far East Economic Review, Hong Kong.
India Press Digest, Berkeley, U. of California.
Japan Quarterly, Tokyo, Asahi Shimbunsha.

Journal of Asian Studies, Ann Arbor, Association for Asian Studies, U. of Michigan.
Journal of Southeast Asian History, Singapore, U. of Singapore.
Pacific Affairs, Vancouver, U. of British Columbia.

USEFUL CATALOGS

Asia Society/Japan Society, 112 E. 64 Street, New York 21, New York.
The East and West Book Gallery, 140 E. 59 Street, New York 21, New York.
Orientalia, Inc., 11 E. 12 Street, New York 3, New York.
Paperbound Book Guide for Colleges—Annual, R. R. Bowker Company, 1180 Avenue of the Americas, New York 36, New York.
The Paragon Book Gallery, 140 E. 59 Street, New York 22, New York.
Talbott, Nathan M., *Selected List of Paperbound Books on Asia* (Tucson, U. of Arizona, 1962).

TEXTBOOKS

Beckmann, George, *Modernization of China and Japan* (New York, Harper, 1962).
Cameron, Meribeth E., and others, *China, Japan and the Powers* (second ed.) (New York, Ronald, 1960).
Clyde, Paul H., *Far East* (third ed.) (Englewood Cliffs, Prentice-Hall, 1958).
Crofts, Alfred, and Buchanan, Percy, *History of the Far East* (New York, Longmans, 1958).
Greene, Fred, *Far East* (New York, Rinehart, 1957).
Latourette, Kenneth Scott, *Short History of the Far East* (New York, Macmillan, 1957).
Michael, Franz H., and Taylor, George, *Far East in the Modern World* (New York, Holt, 1956).
Peffer, Nathaniel, *Far East* (Ann Arbor, U. of Michigan, 1958).
Vinacke, Harold M., *History of the Far East in Modern Times* (sixth ed.) (New York, Appleton, 1956).

ASIAN GEOGRAPHY

Cressey, George B., *Asia's Lands and Peoples; A Geography of One-Third the Earth and Two-Thirds of Its People* (third ed.) (New York, McGraw-Hill, 1963).
Furman, Dorothy W., *Asia* (New York, Golden, 1960). Book four of *Golden Book Picture Atlas of the World.*
Ginsburg, Norton, *Pattern of Asia* (Englewood Cliffs, Prentice-Hall, 1958).
Murphey, Rhoads, *Introduction to Geography* (Chicago, Rand-McNally, 1961).
Spencer, Joseph E., *Asia East by South* (New York, Wiley, 1954).
Stamp, A. D., *Asia: A Regional and Economic Geography* (eighth ed.) (London, Dutton, 1950).
Thompson, Warren S., *Population and Progress in the Far East* (Chicago, U. of Chicago, 1959).

ASIA AND THE FAR EAST

Dean, Vera M., *Nature of the Non-Western World* (New York, Mentor, 1961). (P)

DeBary, William Theodore, (ed.), *Introduction to Oriental Civilizations* (New York, Columbia University, 1958 and 1960):
Volume   I. *Sources of the Japanese Tradition.*
Volume II. *Sources of Indian Tradition.*
Volume III. *Sources of Chinese Tradition.*

Dhingra, Baldoon, *Asia Through Asian Eyes* (Rutland, Tuttle, 1959).

Edwardes, Michael, *Asia in the European Age* (London, Thames & Hudson, 1961).

Edwardes, Michael, *Asia in the Balance* (Baltimore, Penguin, 1962). (P)

Fairservis, Walter A., Jr., *Origins of Oriental Civilization* (New York, Mentor, 1959).

Isaacs, Harold R., *Images of Asia* (New York, Capricorn, 1962). (P)

Jackson, Barbara Ward, *Interplay of East and West: Elements of Conflict and Cooperation,* (New York, Norton, 1957).

Matthew, Helen G., (ed.), *Asia in the Modern World* (New York, Mentor, 1963). (P)

Northrop, F. S. C., *Meeting of East and West* (New York, Macmillan, 1946).

Panikkar, K. M., *Asia and Western Dominance* (New York, Day, 1954).

Radhakrishnan, S., *Eastern Religions and Western Thought* (New York, Oxford, 1940). (P)

Reischauer, Edwin O., and Fairbank, John K., *East Asia, The Great Tradition* (Boston, Houghton, 1960).

Romein, Jan, *Asian Century* (Berkeley, U. of California, 1962).

Smith, Huston, *Religions of Man* (New York, Mentor, 1958).

Yohannan, John D., (ed.), *Treasury of Asian Literature* (New York, Day, 1956).

Zinkin, Maurice, *Asia and the West* (London, Clarke, Irwin, 1951).

CHINA

Barnett, A. Doak, *Communist China and Asia* (New York, Random, 1960). (P)

Buss, Claude A., *People's Republic of China* (Princeton, Van Nostrand, 1962). (P)

Clubb, O. Edmund, *Twentieth Century China* (New York, Columbia U., 1964).

Creel, H. G., *Confucius and the Chinese Way* (New York, Torchbooks, 1960). (P)

Eberhard, Wolfram, *History of China* (rev. ed.) (Berkeley, U. of California, 1960).

Fairbank, John K., *United States and China* (rev. ed.) (Cambridge, Harvard U., 1958).

Fitzgerald, Charles P., *Revolution in China* (New York, Praeger, 1952).

Goodrich, L. Carrington, *Short History of the Chinese People* (New York, Torchbooks, 1962). (P)

Grousset, Rene, *Chinese Art and Literature* (New York, Grove, 1961). (P)

Grousset, Rene, *Rise and Splendour of the Chinese Empire* (Berkeley, U. of California, 1958). (P)

Hu, Chang-tu, and others, *China: Its People, Its Society, Its Culture* (New Haven, HRAF Press, 1960).

Hudson, G. F., *Europe and China* (Boston, Beacon, 1961). (P)

Latham, R. E., (trans.), *Travels of Marco Polo* (Baltimore, Penguin, 1958).

North, Robert, *Moscow and Chinese Communists* (second ed.) (Stanford, Stanford U., 1963).

Payne, Robert, (ed.), *White Pony* (New York, Mentor, 1960).

Schwartz, Benjamin I., *Chinese Communism and the Rise of Mao,* (Cambridge, Harvard U., 1961).

Sickman, Laurence, and Soper, Alexander, *Art and Architecture of China* (Baltimore, Penguin, 1956).

Snow, Edgar, *Other Side of the River, Red China Today* (New York, Random, 1962).

Waley, Arthur, *Three Ways of Thought in Ancient China* (New York, Anchor, 1956).

White, Theodore, and Jacoby, Annalee, *Thunder Out of China* (New York, Sloane, 1961).

Yule, Henry, (ed.), *Cathay and the Way Thither* (new ed., revised by Henri Cordier) (London, The Hakluyt Society, 1913).

JAPAN

Butow, R. J. C., *Tojo and the Coming of War* (Princeton, Princeton U., 1962).

Dening, Sir Esler, *Japan* (New York, Praeger, 1961).

Japan, Ministry of Education, Japan UNESCO Committee, *Japan: Its Land, People, and Culture* (Tokyo, Ministry of Education, Japanese National Commission for UNESCO, 1958).

Kase, Toshikazu, *Journey to the "Missouri"* (New Haven, Yale U., 1950).

Kawai, Kazuo, *Japan's American Interlude* (Chicago, U. of Chicago, 1960). (P)

Keene, Donald, (ed.), *Anthology of Japanese Literature: From the Earliest Era to the Mid-Nineteenth Century* (New York, Grove, 1955). (P)

Keene, Donald, *Living Japan* (New York, Doubleday, 1959).

Keene, Donald, (ed.), *Modern Japanese Literature, an Anthology,* (New York, Grove, 1957).

Kiyooka, Eiichi, (trans.), *Autobiography of Fukuzawa Yukichi* (Tokyo, Hokuseido, 1949).

Reischauer, Edwin O., *Japan, Past and Present* (Tokyo, Tuttle, 1962). (P)

Reischauer, Edwin O., *United States and Japan* (rev. ed.) (Cambridge, Harvard U., 1957).

Sansom, George B., *Japan: A Short Cultural History* (rev. ed.) (New York, Appleton, 1962).

Sansom, George B., *Western World and Japan* (New York, Knopf, 1950).

Silberman, Bernard S., (ed.), *Japanese Character and Culture, Selected Readings* (Tucson, U. of Arizona, 1962).

Smith, Robert J., and Beardsley, Richard K., *Japanese Culture: Its Development and Characteristics* (Viking Fund Publication 34, 1963). (P)

Storry, Richard, *History of Modern Japan* (Baltimore, Penguin, 1961). (P)

Tiedemann, Arthur, *Modern Japan* (rev. ed.) (Princeton, Van Nostrand, 1963).
(P)
Waley, Arthur, (trans.), *Tale of the Genji: A Novel in Six Parts* by Lady Mura-
saki (Boston, Houghton, 1935). (P)
Yashiro Yukio, and Swann, Peter C., *2000 Years of Japanese Art* (New York,
Abrams, 1958).

INDIA

Basham, A. L., *Wonder That Was India* (New York, Grove, 1954). (P)
Brecher, Michael, *Nehru, A Political Biography* (Boston, Beacon, 1962). (P)
Brown, W. Norman, *The United States and India and Pakistan* (revised and
enlarged) (Cambridge, Harvard U., 1963).
Dean, Vera M., *New Patterns of Democracy in India* (Cambridge, Harvard U.,
1959).
Dodwell, H. H., (ed.), *Cambridge Shorter History of India* (New York, Cam-
bridge U., 1943).
Edwardes, Michael, *History of India* (London, Thames & Hudson, 1961).
Gandhi, M. K., *Autobiography, Story of My Experiments with Truth* (trans.
by Mahadev Desai) (Washington, Public Affairs Press, 1954).
Gandhi, M. K., *Non-Violent Resistance* (New York, Schocken, 1961). (P)
Lamb, Beatrice Pitney, *India—A World in Transition* (New York, Praeger,
1963). (P)
Majumdar, R. C., and others, *Advanced History of India* (London, George Allen
& Unwin, 1950).
Moreland, W. H., and Chatterjee, A. C., *Short History of India* (fourth ed.)
(New York, Longmans, 1957).
Nehru, Jawaharlal, *Discovery of India* (New York, Anchor, 1959). (P)
Prabhavananda, Swami, and Manchester, Frederick, *Upanishads: Breath of
the Eternal* (New York, Mentor, 1957). (P)
Rawlinson, H. G., *India: A Short Cultural History* (New York, Praeger, 1952).
Rowland, Benjamin, *Art and Architecture of India: Buddhist, Hindu, Jain*
(Baltimore, Penguin, 1953).
Sen, Gertrude Emerson, *Pageant of Indian History* (New York, Harper, 1959).
(P)
Singer, Milton, (ed.), *Introducing India in Liberal Education* (Chicago, U.
of Chicago, 1957).
Smith, Vincent, *Oxford History of India* (third ed., edited by Percival Spear)
(New York, Oxford, 1958).
Spear, Percival, *India* (Ann Arbor, U. of Michigan, 1961).
Tinker, Hugh, *India and Pakistan* (New York, Praeger, 1962). (P)
Wallbank, T. Walter, *Short History of India and Pakistan* (New York, Mentor,
1958). (P)

SOUTHEAST ASIA

Ball, W. MacMahon, *Nationalism and Communism in East Asia* (second rev.
ed.) (New York, Cambridge U., 1956).

Bone, Robert C., Jr., *Contemporary Southeast Asia* (New York, Random, 1962). (P)

Brimmell, J. H., *Communism in South East Asia* (New York, Oxford, 1959).

Buss, Claude A., *Southeast Asia and the World Today* (Princeton, Van Nostrand, 1958). (P)

Cady, John F., *Southeast Asia, Its Historical Development* (New York, McGraw-Hill, 1964).

Clubb, Oliver E., Jr., *United States and the Sino-Soviet Bloc in Southeast Asia* (Washington, Brookings Institution, 1962). (P)

Dobby, Ernest H. G., *Southeast Asia* (seventh ed.) (London, U. of London, 1960).

DuBois, Cora, *Social Forces in Southeast Asia* (Minneapolis, U. of Minnesota, 1949).

Elsbree, Willard H., *Japan's Role in Southeast Asian Nationalist Movements, 1940–1945* (Cambridge, Harvard U., 1953).

Emerson, Rupert, *From Empire to Nation* (Boston, Beacon, 1962). (P)

Fisher, C. A., *Southeast Asia* (New York, Dutton, 1963).

Furnivall, J. S., *Colonial Policy and Practice* (New York, New York U., 1956).

Hall, D. G. E., *History of South-East Asia* (New York, St. Martin's, 1955).

Harrison, Brian, *South-East Asia: A Short History* (rev. ed.) (New York, St. Martin's, 1963).

Kahin, George McT., (ed.), *Governments and Politics of Southeast Asia* (rev. ed.) (Ithaca, Cornell U., 1963).

Landon, Kenneth P., *Southeast Asia, Crossroads of Religion* (Chicago, U. of Chicago, 1949).

LeMay, Reginald, *Culture of Southeast Asia* (London, George Allen & Unwin, 1954).

Maude, Angus, *Southeast Asia Today* (announced for 1963).

Rose, Saul, *Britain and South-East Asia* (Baltimore, Johns Hopkins U., 1962).

Rose, Saul, *Socialism in Southern Asia* (New York, Oxford, 1960).

Trager, Frank N., (ed.), *Marxism in Southeast Asia* (Stanford, Stanford U., 1959).

INDEX

753